'Madrusan's Cocktail Companion *is truly comprehensive, forward-looking but historically informed, clearly organized, generous with its credit and full of common sense (a thing that is not common at all). In that, it is a perfect monument to the best of what the 21st-century cocktail revolution has achieved.'*

DAVID WONDRICH, AUTHOR, *IMBIBE!*

'If you could stock only one bartender's guide as a recipe reference behind your bar, this is it. Michael and Zara have compiled the definitive ark of our generation: a glamorous time capsule of mixology from the east and west that shows readers not only how to expertly mix drinks confidently; but who created them, what family they belong to, when they were developed, and where they hail from. An instant classic.'

JIM MEEHAN, AUTHOR, *MEEHAN'S BARTENDER MANUAL*

'Michael sees bartending clearly: not as theater, but as a discipline rooted in humility and service. The Madrusan Cocktail Companion *is sharp, structured, and deeply grounded in the realities of the job. More than a manual – it's a manifesto. After years in this industry, I can say without hesitation: if you plan to take this work seriously, start here.'*

JEFFREY MORGENTHALER, AUTHOR, *THE BAR BOOK: ELEMENTS OF COCKTAIL TECHNIQUE*

'Michael Madrusan is one of the world's foremost experts on classic and forgotten cocktails. This book details perfectly how to teach any bartender the complete spectrum of cocktails in very few formulas. A must for every level of cocktail enthusiast.'

SAM ROSS, OWNER/OPERATOR, ATTABOY NYC & NASHVILLE

To Sasha Petraske, Milk & Honey, Little Branch, and the great city of New York where it all started.

And to The Everleigh – and all who sailed in her – for proudly holding the torch in Melbourne with such integrity for the last 14 years.

THE MADRUSAN COCKTAIL *COMPANION*

We acknowledge the traditional owners of the lands on which this book was written and made – the Wurundjeri, Bunurong, Ngunnawal, Gadigal and Cammeraygal people.

We acknowledge that stories and recipes have been shared on these lands for over 60,000 years.

We encourage those who sell and drink alcohol to do so considerately and responsibly. The drinks in this book can bring much joy when consumed in moderation.

THE MADRUSAN COCKTAIL *COMPANION*

EVERY DRINK WORTH DRINKING IN THE HISTORY *OF MODERN + CLASSIC COCKTAILS*

MICHAEL AND ZARA MADRUSAN

edited by
Matty Hirsch

murdoch books
Sydney | London

CONTENTS

THE BRANCHES 60

BY POPULAR REQUEST 408

FOREWORD

By Alex Day

Co-Author, *Death & Co: Modern Classic Cocktails; Cocktail Codex;* and *Death & Co Welcome Home*

Partner, Death & Co, Gin & Luck, and various other distractions

Many years ago, I found myself perched on a stool in an impossibly dark Manhattan bar. The room was lit, if you could call it that, by a few carefully placed candles and a solitary pendant, casting the faintest glow onto a bartender. He built a round of cocktails before me; he was impeccably dressed in a suit vest, a broad tie with a perfect Double Windsor knot, secured by a shiny brass clip that flickered in the dim light. His technique was deliberate, his voice warm as he spoke to another guest – an entire aura that exuded both confidence and sincerity.

I had been to Milk & Honey once or twice before, but I hadn't yet met Michael Madrusan. At the time, the mystique surrounding this tiny bar on the Lower East Side was intense – reverence from the press and the city's intelligentsia that verged on comical. But it was, to a twenty-something me, what made my heart flutter and mind race. The place was otherworldly, its staff magicians of precision and knowledge, the curators of a room that transported you to a place that was somehow both modest and over-the-top. Even now, I sometimes wonder if it was all real: the always-changing phone number, waiting patiently in the cold while pressing a discreet doorbell, the incense subtly hitting your nose after the buzzer unlatched a lock, the curtains parting, and a shift from one universe to another – the smells and chaos of New York City outside, a serene temple to the cocktail within.

Your eyes would adjust to the dim light, and you couldn't help but fixate on the garnish box piled high with fresh fruit, resting atop a white mountain of crushed ice. The *thunk-thunk* of block ice shaking perfect Daiquiris mingled with the subtle din of Dave Brubeck in the background. And then there was the breathtaking sight of a cocktail tray lit by a candle, dainty glasses with amber liquid surrounding it, moving through the room glowing until it was deftly lowered in front of the elated faces of guests. I'm convinced it was the best bar room the world has ever seen, and in those early days, Milk & Honey was my church.

I don't recall the drinks Michael made for me that first time or even whether we talked much, but I do remember the way he made me feel: inspired, curious, compelled to learn more. Like the other bartenders at Milk & Honey, he seemed to possess a knowledge of recipes that I couldn't access, drinks that weren't available in any book I could find or eGullet forum I consumed like the geek I am. More than that, they were curators of not just drinks, but an *experience*. I always left feeling like I had gone on a journey that had a definitive start, middle and finish.

Through persistence (or perhaps an act of charity), I was eventually asked if I wanted to help out: to cut ice, work the floor, maybe even take a shift behind the bar if I could cut it. I was terrified and I said yes, promptly quitting a job at a hyped new restaurant (sorry, Brian and Lynette!). As an unspoken rule, you didn't turn down an offer to work at Milk & Honey.

It was there that I worked most often with Michael, filling in for Richie Boccato as he opened Dutch Kills in Queens, Michael McIlroy as he set down the roots of The Raines Law Room, or Sam Ross as he flew off to LA to revolutionise how *that* city drank. Over the course of a year or so, I got to know Michael better, and the secrets of his approach to bartending began to reveal themselves. We often talked late into the night about cocktails, and I discovered his scholarly soul. For guests, he was the consummate bartender, and as a colleague, an open book. He was a student of tenacious curiosity, with the kind of mind that couldn't stop at the assumed facts. It was, I found, a potent combination of humility, empathy and unquenchable desire to learn more, to dive deeper into the history books and refine recipes – not for ego, but to find more ways to connect with guests and live up to the promise that was Milk & Honey.

Working together, nights turned desperately late as we debated and challenged each other on the 'right' approach to specs and techniques. My mind bended avant-garde, his classicist, but there was always a shared excitement about where these tensions converge. It was exhilarating and so, so nerdy. From those conversations and my off-and-on time working at Milk & Honey, much of the foundation of my career was formed: how I think about cocktails (a significant influence on the ideas within my book *Cocktail Codex*), how to build a relationship with a guest that's far deeper than a transaction, the importance of a life lived learning, and most of all, how I want people to feel after spending time at my bar.

Over the years, Michael has quietly contributed to the larger cocktail world in profound ways – many you probably don't realise even if, like me, you are a fan of his first book and his fantastic bars. What you hold now started first as a document passed around secretly among bartenders, the 'branches' – a brilliant collection of an entire world of cocktails, assembled and organised by Michael in an intuitive and interconnected way. We coveted it, and when Michael shared updates that added more recipes, it was like Christmas. As it has grown and now expanded into this book, the power of that original idea is fully realised. Yes, it contains cocktail recipes – excellent ones, both classic and modern, from the world's best bartenders – but the true power of Michael and Zara's opus lies in the white space between these recipes: the ideas, people and stories that explain the *why* behind the tiny cups of cold booze we call cocktails and how they're all connected.

Over the course of a year or so, I got to know Michael better, and the secrets of his approach to bartending began to reveal themselves. We often talked late into the night about cocktails, and I discovered his scholarly soul. For guests, he was the consummate bartender, and as a colleague, an open book.

Many years later, a world away in Melbourne, I found myself again on a stool in front of Michael. He was back behind the stick, and as we caught up, shared stories of lives lived so far apart, he told me about this book. I was so excited for it to exist in the world, to be a resource for those of us who love cocktails, and I nearly fell off the bar stool when he asked me to pen this foreword. You may not be as lucky as I was to work with Michael and absorb his knowledge firsthand, but I'm confident that studying this book in detail is the next best thing. I hope you dig in, reader, not only looking at the recipes, but also immersing yourself in everything around them – Michael and Zara's vast wisdom in ink and image. Most importantly, I hope from there you share these cocktails with others – to find that perfect cocktail for a friend or guest and to give them, much like I had all those years ago in New York City, a life-changing experience.

Cheers!

Alex

PREFACE

Michael's Story
By Michael Madrusan

The Land of Milk & Honey

It wasn't until my 25th birthday that I knew exactly what I wanted to be: a Milk & Honey bartender. I was a competent bartender at a restaurant in downtown New York City at the time, with a huge passion for bartending and cocktails. I had a lot of discipline and a great work ethic. I thrived being knee-deep with my comrades as people hailed for drinks. I came alive behind the bar; it was where I felt most comfortable.

My mum and dad owned restaurants in Newcastle, Australia, where I grew up. I was a shy kid, and while I preferred to work in the kitchen with Dad, my mother, Gina, pushed me to get on the bar. She was a bartender, and so was my stepfather, Stu. I began learning drink specs as soon as I could read. Mum would make me test her as she studied recipes for work; by age 15, I could make B-52 shots, blended Margaritas, Midori Illusions and most of the other fashionable '90s cocktails.

I left Newcastle at 21 to join the growing flock of Aussies working in London for five pounds an hour. It was in London that I fell in love with being a bartender. I worked in pubs and nightclubs, made some great friends and picked up critical skills like speed and multitasking.

Two years later, when I started work in New York City, I began to hear about these expertly trained bartenders with encyclopaedic knowledge of classic cocktails. They were considered the cream of the bartending crop. They were the Milk & Honey bartenders.

At a focus group one evening, I remember spotting two of them arriving late. They had long hair and beards. They wore flannel shirts and leather jackets. They looked like rock stars. The music may have even stopped as they entered the room. Everything seemed to move in slow motion until they reached our table. Needless to say, I thought they were pretty cool.

As luck would have it, a friend of mine was going out with somebody who worked there – his name was Michael (Micky) McIlroy. I'd asked my friend to bring him to my bar so we could meet. A week before my birthday, he came in. He seemed somewhat uninterested but was still polite. Stupidly, I gave him one of my cocktails; I wasn't upset that he didn't finish it.

'What is this?' I asked, as I wandered in. Then, I walked through the second curtain and was instantly transported to another place – far, far away from Eldridge Street. It was beautiful. On second thought, it wasn't beautiful, but I wish I could feel like I did in that moment forever.

For my 26th birthday, I'd arranged a reservation at Milk & Honey after dinner. It was really tough to land a booking, so I'd called a few weeks earlier to nab a Wednesday night spot. We got out of the taxi on the corner of Delancey and Eldridge streets and walked down Eldridge to number 134. The street smelled like trash and rotten fish. Like all first-timers, we walked right past it, then doubled back slowly and pressed the buzzer (which didn't work). The door was unlocked, and we entered through a thick black curtain, only to be greeted by another thick black curtain.

'What is this?' I asked, as I wandered in. Then, I walked through the second curtain and was instantly transported to another place – far, far away from Eldridge

Street. It was beautiful. On second thought, it wasn't beautiful, but I wish I could feel like I did in that moment forever. The room was tiny, dark and candlelit. Six booths and four seats at the bar. Soft, soothing jazz on the speakers. I was in love with everything.

Right then and there, I knew I wanted in, no matter the pain I would have to endure. It just felt right, though I was so incredibly intimidated. Our waiter was the great Sam Ross, another illegal Australian bartender in New York City. Micky was behind the bar, but I was so nervous that I didn't dare say hello. They were both so cool and collected. Their confidence – and lack of arrogance – was truly remarkable. As I sat, I took in the room piece by piece. My senses came alive and every detail proved that bit more intoxicating. My drink arrived with a massive block of ice in it, and each sip tasted like heaven. I needed to make this place my home.

> *Sitting there at table five, I begged him to let me barback or mop the floors and he promised me I'd have a job there soon enough. I'll always be grateful that he fulfilled his promise.*

I started visiting these boys as often as I could. I got to know them, and I tipped really well so they'd care to get to know me. I'd still not met the elusive owner, Sasha Petraske, though I was dying to get a glimpse of this visionary known for his militant training style. One evening, over drinks at Little Branch, Milk & Honey's sister bar, I asked Micky if Sasha even really existed. I remember him laughing as a man in gym clothes descended the stairs. That was the first time I met Sasha. We met about four times more before he remembered who I was. He was, as he would have told you himself, 'like a goldfish – every time around the bowl is like the first'.

As the months passed, Micky and I got to know each other. He would come by my restaurant, Adrienne's Pizzabar, for the best old-fashioned square pie you could find and a lemon-and-chilli oil for the crusts I made especially for him. After service one night, he invited me back to Milk & Honey for a couple of drinks. He still had to call ahead to make sure we could get a table; I loved that even the staff always respected the rules. Sitting there at table five, I begged him to let me barback or mop the floors and he promised me I'd have a job there soon enough. I'll always be grateful that he fulfilled his promise.

Micky arranged for me to meet Joseph Schwartz, Sasha's business partner in Little Branch. Before opening their joint venture, Joseph had been Sasha's head bartender at Milk & Honey, and now he was the boss. A few weeks after that encounter, I got a call from Micky asking if I wanted to learn how to cut ice at Little Branch. I didn't even flinch. And so, for three months over the course of a New York City winter, I'd set out for Little Branch on Tuesday afternoons after my day shift at Adrienne's. Hand-cutting ice took three hours. Back then, we used a mallet and a five-prong prick to sculpt blocks and Collins spears. By the end of the shift, all feeling in your hands was lost.

One Sunday at brunch, I got the call I'd been waiting for. Joseph asked if I was interested in hosting at Little Branch on Sundays, and if I could start that evening. I dropped my knife and fork and went searching for an outfit straight away. For a last-minute scramble, I think I did pretty well – I still have the Cartier vest today.

Then, at long last, it began. In secret, I'd already asked Micky for the Milk & Honey service manual, and I'd been studying it like crazy for the previous three months. Each day, I'd read it over and make changes at Adrienne's, implementing and rehearsing Milk & Honey methods until my next shift at Little Branch. Soon, I quit the pizzabar and took a massive pay cut, but quickly realised that two shifts a week did not provide enough to live on. So, I set up a meeting with a guy named Jim Meehan who was consulting on a new project on St. Marks Place. It was a bar you entered through a phone booth inside Crif Dogs, a divey joint serving hot dogs with names like the Spicy Redneck. (You haven't lived until you've had a Spicy Redneck, wrapped in bacon and stacked with chilli, coleslaw and jalapeños – the perfect fuel for a few games of pool at Lucy's around the corner.) The bar, of course, was going to be called Please Don't Tell. I'm still not sure who was watching over me, but I knew I was very lucky to be working in such places with such people.

Two and a half years later, I was on the bar at Milk & Honey and Sasha walked in. By that stage, I'd stopped sweating bullets every time he entered the room. He was talking about how he'd procured finances to fund a bar for Sam Ross and he said that my own bar would come next. I remember the moment vividly. He asked me how I felt about the Upper West Side.

'It's great,' I said, 'but how about we take this thing further?'

'Sure. Anywhere,' he replied.

'How about Australia?' I asked.

'Done!' he answered back. 'I love Melbourne.' Then, in true Sasha fashion, he walked straight out of the bar without saying goodbye. My co-worker Richard Boccato turned to me and said, 'Dude, you just got your bar!'. I smiled and went back to work. I felt like I was walking on sunshine.

Three years later, in 2011, The Everleigh was born. While The Everleigh had a unique identity and reputation, there was a lot of Milk & Honey flowing through her. Milk & Honey captured my heart and changed my life, and it will live on in me and my bars forever.

By the time this book is released, The Everleigh will have closed after fourteen incredible years.

INTRODUCTION

How it started

By Michael Madrusan

The very first seeds for this book were planted in 2008. I was with Micky and Death & Co's Alex Day at Clover Club in Brooklyn, just after its opening. We were standing at the end of this long bar, looking across it and chatting about drinks. Even on our nights off, cocktails were all we cared to talk about. The conversation turned into a bit of a contest over who knew the most drinks, and Alex commented that the Milk & Honey team wasn't as knowledgeable as he'd expected for a bar of its calibre. That hit me like a tonne of bricks and proved to be a real light-bulb moment. I was very studious at the time and cared deeply about being a knowledgeable bartender. Yet, even though I'd memorised the Milk & Honey spec sheet months before my first shift and practically inhaled all the cocktail manuals I could get my hands on, I got the feeling Alex was right. This was the height of the renaissance of classic cocktails, after all. Suddenly, it dawned on me that we had so much more to learn if we wanted to deliver on the service style that we'd built the bar upon. At Milk & Honey we never had a menu; instead, we asked each guest to describe what they felt like and used our knowledge of approximately 50 classic cocktails to fit the bill. Our style of service was unique, and everybody loved it. While all the other competing bars in town relied on a printed menu, operating without one made it seem as though the possibilities were endless.

Only, they weren't. I knew that for us to succeed in the long haul, we had to build up our repertoire – and fast.

Back then, I worked mostly with Micky and Sammy. Whereas Sammy was really interested in creating drinks, my passion lay in digging up the great forgotten drinks that nobody was making. I had already started collecting classic cocktail books a few years earlier, my first being Ted Haigh's *Vintage Spirits and Forgotten Cocktails*, followed by *The Gentleman's Companion* by Charles H. Baker Jr. and *Trader Vic's Bartender's Guide*. I devoured these books, cover to cover, numerous times. Securing a job at Milk & Honey made me decide that bartending was the career for me, and I was determined to make my mark. With an insatiable thirst, I started hunting for as many vintage books, guides and manuals as possible. It quickly became about much more than just the drinks; I got lost in the worlds of the bars and bartenders who came before me, their personalities and stories. These books became my companions and, outside of the long shifts, I spent more time with them than anything or anybody else.

Alex's comment whirled around my mind regularly and studying soon became an obsession. I had about a 30-minute subway ride to work from my place in Brooklyn each day, and I started using the time to jot down drinks from the book I was reading to take to the team for use in service. On November 29th of 2008, I sent my first email to the Milk & Honey team containing what I then described as my 'Approved Cocktails' – the best recipes from the books I was reviewing, which I'd tested and absorbed. One week later, that email grew to encompass a summary of the corresponding book, and I began adding relevant references, dates and notes I could find to all the Approved Cocktails. This knowledge-seeking wasn't about me being the best bartender I could be, it was about the need to prove myself to my team, each of whom I looked up to so much. The team loved what I was doing, and my Approved Cocktails started flying over the bar.

Unlike other young bartenders putting forward their own cocktails, I wasn't coming up with new recipes that needed to be tested and signed-off on before serving. These were all classic drinks that aligned with our house style, and I recalibrated them ever so slightly to reflect the formulas and methods that we used at Milk & Honey. Often, these original recipes featured spirits and liqueurs that were no longer being produced, or were made with ingredients or production methods that varied substantially from their 21st century counterparts. They also weren't always reflective of current trends and modern tastes, which had evolved substantially over the previous hundred or so years. Sasha and Joseph had always reformulated the classics with this in mind, and I followed those same rules with my variations. As the months passed, I continued sending my weekly emails, gathered pace in my studies and became more sophisticated in my data capture.

Before long, word had got out that I was the go-to guy if you were serious about drinks and wanted to expand your repertoire. Joseph had my Approved Cocktails permanently added to the Little Branch spec sheet, and stars of the New York City and LA scenes, such as Giuseppe Gonzalez, David Meyers, Greg Boehm and Eric Alperin, began asking to be added to the email list, which filled me with such pride. As I mentioned, this was never intended as a selfish endeavour, and I didn't hesitate in being generous with my discoveries. The list soon grew to include some of the Milk & Honey regulars, along with a handful of journalists and liquor reps, and eventually made it across the pond to peers in London and Australia, too. The recognition and appreciation of my hard work propelled me forward. There really was no stopping me now. I continued sending these emails for five years, long after I left New York City, eventually calling it quits two years after I opened The Everleigh.

> *With an insatiable thirst I started hunting for as many vintage books, guides and manuals as possible. It quickly became about much more than just the drinks; I got lost in the worlds of the bars and the bartenders who came before me, their personalities and stories.*

After opening my first bar, I had less time for research, though I continued to collect books – and still do to this day, combing through them for any notable variations worth adding. My focus became more about maintaining the collection, keeping specs up to date and ensuring the organisation and categorisation of the document allowed for maximum efficiency and speedy use in service. By then, all the Approved Cocktails had been grouped together into a master list called 'Madrusan's Cocktail Branches' for The Everleigh team. The list, now in the neighbourhood of 1500 drinks, was grouped by 'mother' cocktail or 'branch' – a category that referred either to the original or most influential version of that particular drink, or the style of that drink more broadly.

Madrusan's Cocktail Branches was essentially an expansive reference guide designed for bartenders. At the bar, we referred to it as 'The Bible', and for us it was sacred – a laminated thing of beauty that sat underneath the bar top and was used constantly throughout the night by every member of the team as they set about recommending drinks based on each individual's preferences. If, for example, a guest requested something along the lines of a classic gin Martini but more complex and vegetal, we'd tell them to leave it with us, dig through the Martini family tree and return with a drink tailored to their request, such as the Poet's Dream (p 321).

We called this approach 'The Bartender's Choice' (p 22), and we listed those very words as an item on our menu, encouraging our guests to engage in a conversation with their bartender in order to identify a drink that suited their desires. Madrusan's Cocktail Branches was the tool that allowed us to get there quickly, by navigating an extensive compilation of high-quality contenders. At The Everleigh, we'd talk to our guests about how we'd built up our knowledge, pointing them to a glass bookcase in the entryway, which housed many of the seminal volumes on classic cocktails. It didn't take long for Australian drinkers to take notice, and we quickly became known for our collection of resources and the impressive bible of drinks we kept under the bar.

In those days, the compendium was in shorthand and only detailed specs in ounces, as that was our preferred unit of measurement. Some dates and historical references still needed finalising; some drinks sat in multiple categories. Still, I always intended to lay claim to that body of work and finish the job that I had started all those years ago.

The Cocktail Companion

This book is the next phase in the evolution of that journey that began in 2008. To take that industrious compendium from behind the bar and transform it into a sophisticated reference guide for industry professionals, home bartenders and cocktail enthusiasts alike. This compilation includes input from more than 100 books and upwards of 200 of our most respected colleagues and peers from around the world.

Every recipe that follows has been tried, tested, balanced and designed with today's ingredients and the modern drinker in mind – and to allow for universal use, all recipes feature both metric and imperial measurements. Most of these drinks are quite simple, which was a big part of the brief to our contributors; there are, however, certainly some that require more advanced techniques than others and reflect the handiwork of some of the trailblazers on the scene today. In addition to the recipes, there's a full guide to ingredients at the back of the book, as well as a chapter of syrups, infusions and tinctures that can be used for the drinks in this book as well as many others.

Where possible, each cocktail is accompanied by the details of its origin – who created it, where and when, or what book, pamphlet, periodical or website the recipe was lifted from. There's some storytelling, too, which offers you an insight into some of the people and places behind these wonderful creations. When it came to getting our facts straight, we deferred mostly to heavyweight historians such as David Wondrich, Simon Difford, Greg Boehm, Jeff "Beachbum" Berry and Martin Doudoroff, to whom we are deeply indebted, as well as to reliable online resources such as Difford's Guide, Punch, Imbibe, DrinkBoy, Martin's Index of Cocktails, Doc Cocktail and the EUVS Digital Collection, which we thank for their generosity in uploading every guide (some scarce) for all to read, for free.

While every effort has been made to be as all-encompassing as possible, not every drink style has been covered here. Some of the more antiquated types of drinks remain very obscure and are largely irrelevant to today's landscape and palate. Other niche styles, which only offer a small handful of variations, have also been sidelined. What's more, these pages are not intended to be a facsimile or the last word in cocktail genealogy. Almost every single one of these recipes has been modified – in some cases, that difference might be a few dashes of bitters; in others, it can mean the inclusion or exclusion of ingredients altogether, or notably different ratios to the original.

Ultimately, the hope is that our thorough research and discerning editing enhance your understanding of the breadth and depth of the cocktail craft. As a drinker, consider this book an invitation to embark on an incredible journey of discovery; as a bartender or host, think of it as a means to help you play the role of a most experienced tour guide. Every drink has been included for a reason, and there's every chance you'll find one that deserves to be as ubiquitous as the Negroni. By shining a light on these lesser-known classics and unsung heroes, you, too, can enrich conversations and exchanges across the bar around the world for years to come.

This project has been the most remarkable trip down memory lane. Not only have we met some incredibly passionate people, but Michael has also reconnected with his favourite bartenders and industry folk who've endlessly inspired him over the last 25 years, from the original Milk & Honey crew to the individuals responsible for most of the best practices in today's best bars. The reward has been rekindling these ties and building new relationships with the most exceptional humans. It has been a reminder, as though we needed it, that the world of drinks and those who inhabit it are really unlike any other.

HOW TO USE THIS BOOK

This book is your go-to guide for making a multitude of great cocktails. First up, drinks are split into categories ('the branches') based on style – think Collins, Old Fashioned and Sour, as well as other popular categories, including Cream, Tropical, Beer and Non-alcoholic. Within each branch, drinks are listed under their focal spirit, so if you're looking for a drink with gin or whisk(e)y, you'll find a bunch of ideas grouped together. Most recipes in each branch follow the same method (found at the bottom of the page), but if a drink needs a different approach, there's a bolded method under the recipe to guide you through.

ANATOMY OF A RECIPE

Below is a helpful guide to the different components of each recipe.

① ········ **Whizbang Cooler**
② ········ (Gin-Gin Mule with peppermint)
③ ········ 100 Cocktails: How to Mix Them,
④ ········ *"Bernard", 1958*
⑤ ········ 2 oz (60 ml) gin
⑥ ········ 1 oz (30 ml) lime juice
½ oz (15 ml) ginger syrup (p 496)
½ oz (15 ml) simple syrup
6–8 mint leaves
1 drop peppermint oil
⑦ ········ Soda, to top
⑧ ········ **Add all ingredients except soda to a shaker, shake briefly, then strain into a frozen Collins glass with ice and top with soda.**
⑨ ········ Garnish: mint sprig and candied ginger
⑩ ········ ▼ Originally made with ginger ale.

① RECIPE NAME

② AKA

③ ATTRIBUTION/SOURCE

④ BARTENDER/BAR/YEAR

⑤ ALCOHOLIC INGREDIENTS

⑥ SYRUPS, JUICES AND OTHER MODIFIERS

⑦ MIXER OR TOPPER

⑧ METHOD

⑨ GARNISH

⑩ NOTE

A GUIDE TO BARTENDING

What Makes a Great Bartender?

In *The Official Mixer's Manual* (1934), Patrick Gavin Duffy asserted that bartending was not a profession, but an 'old and honourable trade'. The notion of calling a bartender a 'professor or mixologist', he added, 'is nonsense'. Frank Meier, head bartender at the Ritz Paris and author of *The Artistry of Mixing Drinks* (1936), meanwhile, famously claimed that 'to be a bartender is to be a chemist and a psychologist'. Meier believed that the head bartender's role was to work the floor while the lesser experienced bartender would make the drinks, ensuring that the head bartender's focus remained fixed on the guest's experience from beginning to end.

While we are the first to acknowledge that bartending is a bona fide craft, we are of the opinion that a great bartender is much more than someone who can make a drink. In fact, we'd go so far as to say that's the easy bit. Anyone can be a good bartender by learning to mix drinks with the right training and degree of discipline. A great bartender, however, will possess exemplary communication skills, a willingness to learn and keep challenging themselves, as well as the ability to work cooperatively as part of a team. Great bartenders never cut corners, always pay close attention to the finer details and constantly interrogate their own thought process and technique to ensure that they're delivering the best drink they can without slowing or impeding service.

Perhaps most importantly, great bartenders truly care about people and delivering a memorable experience. They light up a room with infectious energy and enthusiasm, and they leave a lasting impression that makes you want to come back for more.

In our decades of experience both as bartenders and owner-operators, we've learned the value and power of the connections forged behind and across the bar – and that they should never be taken for granted.

Basic Principles of Bartending

1. MISE EN PLACE – '*EVERYTHING IN ITS RIGHT PLACE*'

Mise en place, a French term that translates to 'put in place', is a familiar concept to most people who've worked in hospitality. But what does it really mean? Beyond simply having an organised workstation, the phrase highlights the significance of a thought-through design and arrangement of space for everyone who uses it.

When it comes to setting up a bar, it is absolutely essential that everything is in its right place, and that the system is structured to prioritise speed in service. The most frequently used items should be always within arm's reach. If you need to take an extra step to access that tool or ingredient, consider how regularly you'll need to do that during a service. What may seem inconsequential at 5pm will likely feel pretty different when you're slammed at 1am. When everything has a place, a well-trained bartender will be able to move using muscle memory during service – doing 'the dance', as we say, multitasking and flowing seamlessly with focus. This means there's less thinking time and energy required, fewer calls to colleagues to check where they left things, less of a strain on your body by the end of the shift and, above all, a shorter wait time on drinks for your guests. If there are tools or products you only use once a week, get them out of your station so there are no unnecessary distractions.

Of course, muscle memory develops with time, but you should always set up your space so that someone can locate everything they need quickly enough on their first shift. Labelling everything that isn't easily identifiable certainly helps. In theory, any other bartender should be able to step into your station and make a drink efficiently at any stage during service. Above all, maintaining a clean and orderly space shows both your team and your guests that you take pride in your work and take no short cuts when it comes to organisation, presentation and good hygiene.

2. ATTENTION TO DETAIL – *'ALL THE SMALL THINGS'*

When the time comes, there's every chance the phrase 'It's all in the details' will be etched into Michael's headstone. It is a human superpower to notice all the small things, and a skill every hospitality professional should hone. Not only is it vital to listen to exactly what your guests are saying, but you should also pay close attention to their body language throughout their visit. By engaging with all of your senses during service, you have the opportunity to observe and gather the information that lets you stay one step ahead.

In the bar: *Did I hear a small crack in the glass as I added that ice block?* Let me check and replace it if so.

On the floor: *Did I spot those guests shivering ever so slightly?* I'll raise the temperature a notch or two.

Outside the venue: *Did it just start raining?* I'll lay the mat by the door, move the umbrella holder and stay vigilant about making sure the entrance floor doesn't get slippery.

The world's finest venues are detail-orientated to the nth degree, offering an invitation to another world and a break from everyday life. When every aspect of the interior design, furnishings, music, product offering and service style is considered, they all come together to write a narrative and put on a show like no other. But while a venue can be as flash and fancy as all get-out, the story simply won't come to life if the cushions aren't fluffed, the light bulbs aren't changed, the shelves aren't dusted, the streaks on the mirrors aren't wiped and the hand soap and toilet paper aren't topped up. When all these gears click into place, they add up to create much more than just a paint-by-numbers experience; they make people feel well and truly taken care of. And, most importantly, our golden rule of a great bar? Turn the lights down and the music up!

3. DISCIPLINE EQUALS CONSISTENCY – *'THE RIGHT WAY EVERY DAY'*

Consistency is paramount in all aspects of hospitality, from the language we use to our style of service, as well as the preparation of drinks and food. This, of course, also applies to other controllable parts of the guest experience – the playlist, the lighting, the way that tables are set, how the bill is folded and presented. In the end, consistency breeds trust, and people will keep returning if they know they can rely on you to deliver time and time again. That sense of trust is what builds a loyal community of regulars, which anyone will tell you is integral to long-term success.

In truth, consistency is as much about attitude as it is about execution. That means arriving to work with the energy to care, avoiding the easy way out and taking that extra second to make each drink that little bit better, every time. At the loftiest level, cocktail bartending dictates that drinks and service should be of the highest quality, consistently, without compromise. Of course, getting it right every time is impossible, but striving to do so with the same degree of care and effort will get you very close.

That same sense of discipline should be applied not just to the bar itself, but to the venue as a whole. The professional working in the upper echelon never fails to take that extra step – restocking the business cards at the end of each shift, replacing the register roll the moment the red lines appear on the side, sweeping the floor even when it looks 'good enough'. With practise, discipline like this becomes contagious, creating an aligned culture of consistency within a venue that makes shifts seamless and successful far more often than not.

4. PEOPLE BEFORE DRINKS – '*WHAT IS HOSPITALITY, ANYWAY?*'

The word 'hospitality' is derived from the Latin word 'hospes', which means both guest and host, visitor and stranger. As a concept, hospitality has its roots in 'hospitium', the ancient Greco-Roman custom of providing food, shelter and protection to visitors, perceived as both a divine duty of the host and a divine right of the guest. In essence, hospitality professionals are relied upon to provide sustenance, but more than that, they also provide inspiration, a sense of escape or – at the very least – a bit of entertainment and good company. As hospitality professionals, it is our privilege to embark on a journey with each guest and to be responsible for catering to their individual tastes.

Ultimately, the lifespan of a cocktail is short, but people will always remember the way you make them feel. This requires us to put the guest first, and to act with empathy, curiosity and with a lack of ego in doing so. Being proactive, showing generosity and going the extra mile builds relationships that have the potential to last a lifetime. Asking whether a drink is to the guest's liking is a good start, but asking *why* will demonstrate you care to engage in a more profound way. Similarly, remembering a guest's face or name is of great value, but recounting what they liked (or didn't) on their last visit and recommending something new takes it to another level.

It goes without saying that not every guest is the same; some prefer to be left alone, while others want all the bells, whistles and more. Our job is to interpret those cues to the best of our ability in order to provide personalised service. In general, a good rule of thumb is that service should always be attentive, but never obtrusive. Taking initiative seldom goes unnoticed, nor does a desire to connect more deeply with each guest or exceed their expectations. It really can mean the world to someone.

A NOTE TO MICHAEL'S YOUNGER SELF (AS IF HE'D LISTEN ...)

Key learnings from the last 25 years behind the bar and over half a million drinks served ...

1. ***Do pilates.***
   We'd go so far as to say pilates should be mandatory for everyone working in hospitality. Understanding your body and strengthening all those tiny muscles you never knew existed to protect the big ones doing all the work is essential to prevent wear, tear and injury as your career progresses.

2. ***Stay hydrated and eat healthy food on shift.***
   You really do only get out what you put in. The body requires the right input to feel good and stay strong. If you can, prepare healthy home-cooked meals for your shift rather than resorting to carb-heavy fast food. Supplement the things you know aren't easy to get enough of, such as vitamin D in the winter. Always drink more water than you think you need and go easy on the caffeine.

3. ***Stretch.***
   Before and after each shift. Particularly your back, arms, shoulders and chest. The amount of lifting and twisting and bending that happens on shift should not be underestimated. Michael's early barbacking days had his lower back in bits the next day. Again, pilates. Or see below.

4. ***Strengthen your body.***
   Weight training under the guidance of someone who understands how you move your body in service will make meeting the physical demands of your job much easier. Full stop.

5. ***Get good shoes and insoles.***
   A supportive pair of shoes or boots is more important than you'd imagine and will save your lower back and knees. Arrange a quick visit to a podiatrist, and you'll be set up with a custom pair of insoles that will soon become your best friend.

THE BARTENDER'S CHOICE

The Bartender's Choice service style involves asking a series of questions designed to engage the guest and provide a clear picture of their preferences to help choose the right drink for them at the given moment. The approach is systematic – a navigation tool if you will, and a process of elimination. With practice, the exchange becomes more and more seamless and efficient. The guest always feels that you have a genuine interest in their tastes and, furthermore, in getting to know them. You can even use this method on yourself, whether you're trying to identify what you'd like to make at home or simply wanting a better understanding of how different drinks relate to one another.

Spirit

Do you prefer light or dark spirits?
Light spirits typically refer to gin, vodka, tequila or light rum and cane spirits. Dark spirits include whisk(e)y, Cognac and aged dark rums. This is a good place to start, as most people can quickly identify their preference.

It's just as important that we pay equal attention to the flavours or ingredients they are averse to, particularly if it is the first time you are serving a particular guest. Get it right the first time, and there may be an opportunity to explore uncharted territory in the next round.

Style

Do you feel like something refreshing with citrus or something smooth and serious?
This marks the fork in the road where the guest must decide whether they're looking for a fresher, lighter drink shaken with citrus or a spirit-driven cocktail stirred and served up or on the rocks. While there are many drinks that don't fit comfortably into either of these two categories, the response to this question helps us decipher what style or mood of drink is preferable. Language is powerful, and the precise words we use create images in the minds of our guests. Note the difference between the description 'smooth and serious' versus 'stiff and strong'. Both are apt descriptors, but there's every chance the latter might be off-putting to some.

'REFRESHING WITH CITRUS'
Are you after something tall with ice, or short and sharp?
Tall drinks with ice, such as a Collins (p 62), Rickey (p 78), Buck (p 90) or Highball (p 108), are generally lengthened with carbonated mixers, like soda or occasionally sparkling wine.

Shorter, punchier-style drinks, such as Sours (p 152), Sidecars (p 184), Daisies (p 184), Gimlets (p 206) and Daiquiris (p 224) are shaken with ice and served in a coupe or Sour glass (or occasionally on the rocks). Other citrusy styles include Batidas (p 236), Cobblers (p 264), Fixes (p 244) and Smashes (p 274), all served over crushed ice.

'SMOOTH & SERIOUS'
On the rocks or stirred and served up?
On the rocks refers to drinks that are built in the glass and served on ice, such as a Negroni (p 288) or Old Fashioned (p 362).

Stirred drinks include Martinis (p 304) and Manhattans (p 334), which are spirit forward, made without citrus and often combined with vermouth, liqueurs and/or bitters.

If the guest is looking for a more specific category, such as a creamy drink, dessert-style cocktail, a hot Toddy (p 400), or a non-alcoholic option (p 480), they may have given us some clues by this point. If they mention that they've come from dinner but skipped dessert, you might suggest a dessert-style cocktail instead. Similarly, if they indicate that dinner was filling, you might propose a digestif-style cocktail, such as those featuring fresh ginger or bitter herbal liqueurs like Fernet-Branca or Cynar.

Flavour

'REFRESHING WITH CITRUS'
Do you feel like something clean and crisp? On the sweeter side? Tart, spicy, savoury or bitter?
Taste your fresh produce during set-up to determine the impact each ingredient is going to have on your drinks that evening, as citrus and other fruits can vary depending on whether they're ripe, in season, locally sourced and so on. Syrups can also differ from batch to batch as a result. Our house-made grenadine (p 496) offers a distinctly tart flavour compared to bottled brands, and our cold-pressed ginger syrup (p 496) is quite fiery. Understanding the role each of these ingredients plays and how to balance the ingredients is essential to delivering the drink that's best suited to your guest's request.

'SMOOTH & SERIOUS'
Something on the sweeter or drier side?
Spirit-driven drinks without citrus often comprise of more complex, sometimes unfamiliar flavours. Smooth and serious drinks on the sweeter side often feature sweet vermouth and/or other fruit-driven liqueurs. Drier-style cocktails might include dry vermouth or Sherry. Ingredients such as Campari, bitters or herbal liqueurs can be used to create a bittersweet balance.

While absinthe might startle a guest if you suggest it without context, it is an incredibly effective, even approachable, ingredient offering gentle spice or a drier finish to an otherwise sweeter cocktail when used sparingly.

Off Limits

Any flavours or ingredients to avoid?
It is the bartender's responsibility to do a final flick through some divisive and potentially disruptive ingredients, and to ensure that they're across any allergies, intolerances or aversions. If you have a recommendation in mind that contains any of the following ingredients, be sure to run them by your guest first:

- honey
- pomegranate
- ginger
- absinthe/anise
- eggs
- cream/dairy
- nuts
- chilli
- mint
- mushroom (if they weren't paying attention, they are now).

Michael's mother's recipe book from 1987, alongside Michael's own

TOOLS

Bartending Tools and their Purpose

We like to keep things pretty simple behind the bar and believe that most things can be done with a set of shaking tins, a pint glass and a chopstick. That being said, a good set of tools will certainly help you, but they don't need to be flashy – they just need to be effective.

MUST HAVE

- **Stirring spoon:** A smooth spoon with a defined angle on the dish makes stirring easy, especially when stirring two drinks at the same time. Make sure it has a ball on the end for crushing sugar cubes. Or you can use a plastic chopstick.
- **Muddler:** We like food-grade plastic muddlers as we find them the easiest to clean and they last much longer than those made of wood.
- **Hand-press juicer:** A simple juice extractor that catches pips and pulp.
- **Hawthorne strainer:** We use these for shaken drinks and look for heavy-duty strainers with extra-tight coils and a wide frame that extends beyond the rim of your glass. This makes pouring much easier and keeps more unwanted mint and bits of fruit out of the final drink. (These are also good to use upside down if you're without an egg separator.)
- **Julep strainer:** We use these for stirred drinks as they fit neatly into a mixing glass. They can also be used to scoop excess mint and other unwanted bits from a drink in a coupe.
- **Jiggers:** We use a variety of jiggers, and much of it comes down to aesthetic preference. The tall, slim, Japanese jiggers are handsome, no doubt, but for us, the perfect option for both home and professional use is the graduated, conically shaped, 2½ oz (75 ml) jigger that features engraved increments of measurement along the outside.
- **Knife:** One that is small and serrated is best, with a rounded tip. Make sure it's always sharp.
- **Y-Peeler (aka Swiss peeler):** This is the quickest and deadliest tool in the kit, and definitely requires safety training. Zara took the top off her fingers with one twice in a night. Most of us learn the hard way.
- **Microplane:** Essential for not only zesting citrus and fresh ginger, but also grating garnishes such as coffee beans and whole spices like nutmeg and cinnamon. Freshly grated is always best.
- **28 oz (828 ml) weighted shaker:** Your big shaker sits over your little one. 'Weighted' refers to the reinforced base, which not only makes for a sturdier shake but also holds up against wear and tear much longer.
- **18 oz (532 ml) weighted shaker:** You build your drink in the little one, add ice to the bigger one, then they come together for the 'show'.
- **Mixing glass:** Simple, tempered American pint glasses are ideal for a single stirred drink and store quite easily in the freezer. Double mixing glasses live next to these, also in the freezer.

NICE TO HAVE

- **Bitters bottles and atomisers:** Handy for adding bitters, tinctures and ingredients like absinthe in small measures.
- **Fork-tipped bar spoon:** When it comes to cracking ice, the inexpensive fork-tipped bar spoon is a favourite of ours. Hold it by the fork end when you crack – you'll find the weight of the spoon works well against the ice and doesn't require much force.
- **Swizzle spoon:** Bonzer makes the consummate spoon for Swizzles and Mojitos. The twisted stem works a treat when swizzling drinks, and the flat top is great for crushing sugar cubes and pressing the likes of mint leaves, lime and cucumbers.
- **Egg separator:** Thanks to Joseph Schwartz, one of our indispensable tools is the wired egg separator. Hang it on the side of the tin, crack your egg, then crack on with the rest of your round while the yolk separates from the white.
- **Ice pick:** We use a three-prong pick, which does a bang-up job of taking the ends and corners off ice blocks.
- **Juicer:** We love Ra Chand juicers. They get the job done super fast, and you completely control the squeeze. Our friends at New York City's Attaboy prefer the slower Hamilton Beach juicer. Be warned: some juicers and presses go so hard that you end up tasting the bitterness in the pith. No thanks.
- **Garnish tongs:** We like tweezer-like stainless-steel tongs for plucking olives and cherries from the jar and picking up more delicate garnishes, and sugar tongs for handling sugar cubes and fresh berries.
- **Squeeze bottle:** We make our house cream (p 506) in these bottles. For hand-whipped cream, we shake the bottles to aerate the cream. We also use these bottles to float cream onto drinks.

TOOLS IN THE RAIL

In your tool cup, found in the speed rail behind the bar, you should only need these items:

- **Stirring spoons** – 2–3
- **Fork-tipped bar spoon** – 1
- **Swizzle spoon** – 1
- **Muddler** – 1

Best practice tips

- *To prevent accidents, never keep a knife, ice pick or peeler in your tool cup.*
- *Strainers and egg separators should be stored separately to avoid cross-contamination.*

Rheingold
EXTRA DRY
Lager Beer

ICE

The Role & Importance of Ice

Ice is one of the most fundamental yet misused ingredients in cocktails. It's actually the only ingredient with a job to do: it chills a drink and adds dilution. Its role is so vital that it can make or break the final product. Every cocktail requires a certain amount of dilution, but a drink should never be over-diluted or under-diluted, in the same way that a dish should never be undercooked or overcooked. Knowing how to differentiate between an under-diluted, over-diluted and perfect drink is of utmost importance, and the washline is a great indicator.

Clear, high-quality ice matters as much to a cocktail as well-made spirits and ultra-fresh produce. It is an ingredient that's as essential to a drink as any other, and an inferior ingredient will result in an inferior drink, plain and simple.

Ice of the highest quality is produced using large, industrial block makers that freeze roughly 330 lb (150 kg) of ice over three to four days, circulating purified water to ensure that all impurities are extracted. These giant blocks of ice are then cut down with saws to produce a variety of shapes to suit cocktail glassware. In other words, that pristine block you see in your glass has had quite a journey. Hand-cut ice is extremely labour intensive, and ice manufacturers doing the hard yards around the world deserve a lot more love.

When we opened Navy Strength Ice Co. in 2015, we were the first to market in Australia, having learned our trade from trailblazers such as Penny Pound Ice in LA and New York City's Hundredweight Ice. Today, we're all the more fortunate to have several specialist cocktail ice companies operating in most major cities, available to cater to both venues and home bars.

Common Examples of Misuse of Ice

1. Drinks being shaken too long. This results in over-dilution and the drink being too large for the glassware, throwing out the washline (p 36). See Shaking (p 33) for more guidance.
2. Drinks being left in the shaker with ice and not strained immediately after shaking. This also results in over-dilution.
3. Drinks served over ice waiting to be delivered on the bar top. These drinks must be served promptly to ensure that they don't over-dilute.
4. Ice stored in a freezer unsealed, along with other items. Ice can absorb aromas and flavours and must always be stored in sealed containers, never with food.
5. Drinks with block ice being served too soon. These blocks are harder and denser, so be vigilant in monitoring them so they reach the guest at the appropriate moment.
6. Cracked ice in drinks served on the rocks, like a Negroni (p 288) or Old Fashioned (p 362), mean that the ice wasn't tempered properly – i.e. it was allowed to rise in temperature and melt (or 'sweat') a little before the liquid was added. A cracked block is less attractive and compromises the slow dilution process desired in these cocktails.

Types of Ice

We use five types of ice:

1. **Rocks/blocks** – Large, dense, crystal-clear blocks used for shaking drinks and drinks served on the rocks.
2. **Spears** – Long crystal-clear spears of ice used for drinks like Highballs (p 108), Collins (p 62), Buck (p 90) and Rickey (p 78), and spirits with mixers.
3. **Cracked** – Usually offcuts of blocks, used for stirring drinks.
4. **Crushed** – Small pebbles or pellets of machine ice used for crushed ice drinks like the Fix (p 244), Cobbler (p 264) or Swizzle (p 244).
5. **Hoshizaki/kold-draft cubes** – Large 1 in (2.5 cm) cubes of machine ice.

Before you ask, ice from the service station has no place in your drink, ever.

Handling Ice

Ice is very temperamental, so it's important to be mindful of how you handle it and consider how you use it. If it's too cold, it will crack when you add it to your drink and must then be discarded. If it's too warm, it will add too much dilution to the shake or the drink. In order to produce the perfect drink, the ice must be just right.

We 'sweat' our ice blocks and spears by sitting them outside the freezer for a minute or two until they lose their frost and start to shine prior to adding them to liquid. By raising the block's temperature slightly, the ice is less likely to crack from shock when it comes into contact with room-temperature liquids in the glass or shaker. Of course, ice must always be handled with clean hands.

Shaking with Block Ice

We believe it's a necessary expense to shake cocktails with block ice given its superior ability to control the temperature and dilution of our drinks. Shaking with block ice is harder, heavier and longer, but it delivers lighter, fluffier, colder drinks. That foamy lid on your Daiquiri? That's all thanks to the ice – if tempered properly, of course.

METHODOLOGY, TECHNIQUE & TERMINOLOGY

Naturally, there is much method to all of the madness in cocktail bartending, and in our eyes, a right way to make drinks. Through all our years of practice and experience – including constant knowledge-seeking, striving and questioning within our tight-knit community of industry peers, all united in the opinion that if there's a better way, we're ready to implement it – we have sought to design the most efficient steps to achieve quality cocktails, consistently. Take what you will from the following in-depth descriptions of each process. There is some entry-level information to set beginners on the right track, and some more heavy-duty detail for those further along in their bartending journey. In short, if you want to make a great drink, forget cutting corners. With practice and precision these methods and techniques can become second nature to anyone.

Jiggering & Measuring – '*Work Fast, Jigger Slow*'

Jiggering, which is to say using a jigger to measure your liquids, is the only way to guarantee consistency when making drinks. If you take the time to measure properly and precisely, your drinks will be exactly the same at primetime on a Friday night as they are on a quiet Tuesday.

When you're pouring, always be sure to handle branded products with the label facing outwards. And likewise, if you're placing the bottle on the bar top for display, ensure that the label is facing is the guest.

What is Jigger Tipping?

It's one thing to use a jigger, and another to use it properly. 'Tipping' happens when you hold your jigger on an angle to speed up pouring, instead of keeping it upright in the hand. This is all too common, and it actually short-changes the drink by skewing the smaller and sometimes more vital measures of ingredients. (It's particularly true if you're using a graduated jigger without any overhead light.)

Tipping is an easy habit to fall into when you're busy, in a rush or trying to multitask. When you're jiggering, consider your posture: stand up straight, and relax your hand and fingers. Be sure that the jigger is balanced between your fingers, and always pour to the line.

Can I Use the Same Jigger when Making a Round?

- You can use the same jigger for lemon juice, lime juice and simple syrup when you're making a round of shaken drinks. Stop and rinse once you start drastically changing the flavours for cocktails.
- Jiggers used for vodka do not need to be rinsed before using other spirits.
- Light rum can be used before dark rum. Either can be used before cachaça.
- Neat whisk(e)y must be measured and poured using a clean jigger, but for mixed drinks with citrus and whisk(e)y there's no need to rinse the jigger between ingredients.

Muddle or Press?

Distinguishing between these two is important.

Muddling is used when you want to extract maximum flavour, aroma and texture from an ingredient, the way you do with limes in a Caipirinha (p 242), for instance. You're pushing down hard, in order to draw out the juice, the oils and the peel. Note that most drinks do not need to be muddled for more than 6–8 seconds.

Pressing is a gentler method, used when you want to obtain a more nuanced character without pulverising an ingredient, such as the mint leaves in a Mojito (p 253).

Controlling Dilution

Control is the name of the game. Every cocktail needs dilution; the key is knowing just how much is required for each drink.

When adding ingredients to a glass, mixing glass or shaker, ALWAYS ADD ICE LAST. This allows you to control the dilution, so that the drink finds perfect balance right as it reaches the guest. In drinks on the rocks, we call this 'undercooking'. In truth, the first sip of a cocktail on ice shouldn't be the best one; a cocktail with ice should be served with the intention of longevity, to be enjoyed as the dilution process unfolds rather than as soon as it is served.

When building a cocktail on the rocks (we call this a 'durable' drink), add your ingredients first, then your ice so that the drink does not become too diluted too quickly. If you're serving a guest seated at the bar, where the cocktail will be delivered more promptly, give the ice a few spins in the glass to speed up the dilution slightly.

When building a cocktail on crushed ice (we call this a 'fragile' drink), add your ingredients to the glass first, then add your crushed ice. Shimmy the glass to settle the ice then top up with more crushed ice to form a generous mound before serving.

Order of Ingredients

Building your drink the same way each and every time is best practice. The rule of thumb is to always add ingredients in order of cost, from least to most expensive. (This is mostly true unless you're deep in an Australian summer and forced to take out a loan for a case of limes.) It may seem counterintuitive – and you've probably watched countless bartenders do it in reverse – but this way, if a mistake is made early on (we all make them, especially when in conversation with a guest), discarding and remaking the drink is not costly.

1. First, add your bitters, sugar cube and/or any ingredients that require pressing or muddling. If the recipe requires egg, this is also the point at which you should crack it into a separate tin.
2. The next ingredient is freshly squeezed citrus.
3. Then we add any modifiers, such as syrups or liqueurs.
4. Finally, add the spirits.

Shaking vs Stirring

This is pretty easy to resolve. Generally speaking, if it's a translucent drink, stir it; if it's a cloudy drink with freshly squeezed juice and/or a drink textured with the likes of eggs and cream, shake it. Shaking creates a lighter, livelier and more aerated drink while stirring delivers a weightier style that's perfect for sipping.

There are, of course, exceptions to the rule, and a few are in this book. And, at the end of the day, remember that this is ultimately dictated by the guest – if someone prefers a shaken Martini, they get a shaken Martini, no questions asked.

Shaking

To shake is to shake with block ice, or a shaker packed with considerably sized cubes.

These are the dos and don'ts of shaking a cocktail:

- If you're using block ice that's extra cold, begin by 'rolling' the ice in the shaker for a little bit to bring it up to temperature so it doesn't shatter when it comes into contact with room-temperature ingredients. Once ingredients have been added to your shaker, first taste to ensure that you haven't missed anything, then it's time to start shaking. If the ice does shatter, you'll have to finish your shake sooner, strain tightly and use your Julep strainer to catch any shards.
- To seal your tins properly, ensure that both shakers are flush with each other along one side. Don't seal your tins using the bar top, or other tins if you're shaking two drinks at once – it may look cool, but you'll dent the shakers and bend them out of shape. Use the heel of your hand to seal them, and they will lock together as you start to shake.

- Hold your tins by each end in case they come apart during the shake. It happens to the best of us – Michael will never forget Table 3 on that Saturday night at Little Branch back in 2008. No one needed that dry- cleaning bill!
- With block ice, you must shake hard, and you must shake longer than you would with machine-cubed ice.
- Drinks served straight up should be shaken vigorously for about 10 seconds. Drinks with egg require twice as much time – warm egg drinks are particularly unpleasant, and lower temperatures help to mask any undesirable odour.
- If you don't shake for long enough, your drink will be warm and lack proper dilution. If you shake for too long, your drink will be overly diluted, watery and flat.
- When shaking, make sure you're aware of your posture to avoid strain or injury over time. Keep your feet a good distance apart so you're balanced, bend your knees slightly so you're not locked up, and try to activate your core to save your back.
- Everyone will have a different shake. That's a good thing. You must choose the shake that feels natural for you as it's hard on the body.
- Strain your drink as soon as you've finished shaking it. Don't let it sit on the ice, dying!

TYPES OF SHAKING

Shaking with ice

For us, 'shake with ice' means to shake with a large block of ice (about the size of a kiwi fruit), preferably, or a shaker full of ice cubes that are large in size (about 1¼ in/3 cm). Drinks shaken with ice are predominantly citrus cocktails such as Gimlets (p 206), Daiquiris (p 224) and both Non-traditional and Traditional Sours (p 152), but also include other drinks with egg white, egg yolk, a whole egg or cream, such Fizzes (p 134), Flips (p 388) and dessert-style drinks. Shaking hard with a large piece of ice brings the ingredients together and gets the drink very cold while adding the requisite degree of dilution. Block ice undeniably gives you the most control over your drink.

Dry shaking

Coined by Milk & Honey alumna Christy Pope, 'dry shaking' is the term we use to describe shaking without ice. It's the method typically employed to emulsify the ingredients in drinks with eggs prior to shaking with ice. Once a drink has been dry shaken, it must be shaken with ice immediately.

Tossing

To 'toss' is to shake very briefly with ice (for about 5 seconds), when we know we need to chill a drink and add foam, but don't want too much dilution – think Champagne cocktails (p 420) and the Caipirinha (p 242).

Whipping

This is a term invented by another Milk & Honey alumnus, Michael McIlroy. We 'whip' when we need to incorporate the ingredients and create a bit of air for tall drinks like a Buck (p 90) or a Collins (p 62) without adding too much dilution. There are a few ways to do this, but we prefer to use a single 1 in (2.5 cm) ice cube and shake until it dissolves into the drink. This creates quite a frothy head on the drink when it is topped with soda.

- **Pebble whipping**
  Shaking with four or five small ice pebbles to mix and aerate before pouring into a glass to be topped with crushed ice. Often used for crushed ice drinks such as Cobblers (p 264) and a range of tropical drinks.
- **Cube whip**
  Shaking hard with a cube of ice about 1 in (2.5 cm) long until it dissolves to create a very foamy, slightly chilled drink to be served tall and topped with soda, like Bucks (p 90), Collins (p 62) and Rickeys (p 78).

Rinse

The 'rinse' – a method where a spirit is added to a glass before straining the drink into it – is seen in many old books. We don't believe a rinse is suitable in shaken drinks as it kills the head and won't be incorporated into the drink. Instead, add the dashes to the shaker. If an aroma is desired on top of the cocktail, a spritz from an atomiser is recommended.

The Sazerac (p 366) has the absinthe added to the crushed ice during the chill; the absinthe is strained off into a shot glass and can be served on the side.

Stirring

Here are the dos and don'ts of stirring a cocktail:

- Stirring is almost like a smooth and elegant dance, in that there should be a seamless flow to your technique. Unlike in shaken drinks, there is no need to agitate the ingredients or create aeration.
- Before stirring, add your spirits to an ice-cold mixing glass straight from the freezer, cheapest ingredients first in case of error.
- Once all ingredients have been added to the mixing glass, add your ice for stirring. To prevent splashes when adding your ice, hold your spoon against the edge of your glass, place your ice onto the spoon and lower the ice down to the bottom.
- Try to hold your spoon near the top of the stem, in between your thumb, forefinger and middle finger, almost like a pencil grip. Place the spoon down the bottom of the mixing glass with the back rubbing against the glass, and start stirring.
- You taste a stirred drink three times: (1) when you've added all your ingredients; (2) when the ingredients have been stirred to produce a rise in washline and the glass is cold; and (3) when the washline has risen to a familiar level and you believe the drink is ready. By the final taste (some time around 25–30 seconds), the initial sting of the liquor should be gone, but the drink should not carry the weight of over-dilution due to water. At this point, the drink will be ice cold. That is perfection.

Swizzle vs Shimmy

If you want to incorporate your ingredients in a drink with crushed ice, you swizzle. To swizzle, place your swizzle spoon or stick in the drink and swizzle briefly by rolling the swizzle stick back and forth between your palms, just enough to mix the ingredients. Remember to top up with more crushed ice when you're finished.

If you just need to settle the crushed ice with an already incorporated drink, you shimmy, as there is less risk of over-dilution with this method. To shimmy is to press your palms against the sides of the lower part of the glass and roll the glass back and forth with your hands a few times to aid gravity in settling the crushed ice.

Straining, Pouring & Emptying

The dos and don'ts of straining, pouring and emptying:

- When straining cocktails, there are two strainers we use: a Julep strainer for stirred drinks and a Hawthorne strainer for shaken drinks.
- When using the Julep strainer, place the strainer inside the mixing glass and pour slowly into the chilled glass.
- When using the Hawthorne strainer, make sure the strainer covers the mouth of the shaker and have your index finger pressed down firmly enough so that the coils and lid are flush with the lip of the shaker. We call this 'closing the gate'. This ensures that the strainer and its springs are as tight as can be to stop any unwanted ice chips, mint or fruit coming through and compromising your head. The goal here is to strain only from the two holes at the bottom. We call these 'fangs' because that's what the liquid looks like when it's strained out properly. Keep the tin close to the top of the glass and strain slowly. Be gentle when straining a drink that you've shaken with block ice; the block will want to slide forward, which will cause the drink to splash. And don't bounce or shake your tin to get the liquid out – that looks sloppy. Once the main tin has been emptied, ALWAYS pour what's left from the little tin as there's always some left in there. This shows the guest that they are getting every last drop.
- When straining or pouring into a glass with ice, aim for the side of the glass rather than straight on top of the ice, and pour slowly so the liquid doesn't splash.
- When 'dumping' the contents of a drink like a Caipirinha (p 242), pour some of the shaken mix into your little tin first (this is your top-up tin), then empty the big tin slowly and top up with the little one. This gives you some wiggle room if you've used too much ice and don't need it all in the glass, saving you from overfilling or having to take the ice chunks out.

Floating

When layering drinks with a squeeze bottle like a La Dominicana (p 465) or White Russian (p 464), pause, steady your hand and layer with grace. Begin by shaking the bottle vigorously to achieve an even consistency and allow the cream to settle. Then, pick a spot on the drink's surface and squeeze onto that spot – not too slow or too fast. The cream needs to float perfectly on top without getting mixed into the drink. Ideally, the cream should look smooth and consistent. If it has found its way into the drink, the cream hasn't been hand-whipped enough.

Straining More than One of the Same Drink

WHEN MAKING TWO OF THE SAME DRINK ...
If you have just shaken two drinks in the one shaker, pour them simultaneously into two glasses, one in front of the other. If you're straining correctly, each 'fang' should pour into a separate glass. If one glass is filling faster, rock the shaker to the side. Alternatively, fill each glass halfway first before topping them both up. Never fill one glass to the top then start the other. They must be identical.
Note: Drinks with ice must have the ice added after the liquid is poured.

WHEN MAKING FOUR OF THE SAME DRINK ...
Fill each glass at the same time from both shakers. Again, so they are all the same, i.e. two shakers filling four glasses.

Washlines & Dilution

A shaken cocktail must have a foamy head. This is non-negotiable. The space formed between the foam and the top of the glass is called the washline. For example, in a regular coupe measuring 5½ oz (150 ml) total capacity, most shaken cocktails, once strained into the glass, should allow for a washline – a gap between the surface of the drink and the rim of the glass – that is approximately 5 mm (¼ inch).

Washlines are not used nearly enough. Too many bartenders strain their drinks to the top of the glass, which not only leads to messy spillage, but also makes the drink suffer aesthetically as a result because it has no head. We consider a perfect washline to be the ideal garnish.

Every time you shake a drink, think about your washline. To create tidy washlines, think specifically about the type of glassware you're using and plan accordingly. Every drink must fit the glass, but drinks with ice must also adhere to washlines. A bigger glass doesn't necessarily mean a bigger drink, and if there's a large block of ice in it, it doesn't mean the drink is any smaller.

If your glass is approximately 6 oz (180 ml) and your liquid should equate to about 4 oz (120 ml), the liquid shouldn't reach the rim of the glass. If it does, it might have been shaken too long or not jiggered properly. On the flipside, a washline that is well under the rim of the glass will look short, and has likely been under-diluted or measured incorrectly.

Fragile vs Durable Drinks

These are terms used to describe the fragility of a drink and how quickly it can break down. As Sasha used to say: 'A cocktail waits for no man.' In other words: 'Get that drink to the guest, ASAP!'

Harry Craddock, author of *The Savoy Cocktail Book* (1930), was once asked how quickly you should drink a cocktail. His response? 'Quickly, while it's laughing at you!' He was referring to the ice chips moving and disappearing in the glass as they melted and diluted into the drink.

So, while all drinks are fragile to a certain extent, we like to think of them as follows:

FRAGILE DRINKS

These drinks are best consumed ice cold and can easily become over-diluted.

- Stirred drinks served 'up' (in a coupe without ice), like Martinis (p 304) and Manhattans (p 334)
- Shaken drinks served 'up' (in a coupe without ice), like Daiquiris (p 224) and Gimlets (p 206)
- Crushed ice drinks are *very* fragile

DURABLE DRINKS

These drinks remain intact for longer periods of time and can withstand dilution.

- Stirred 'down' drinks (built on the rocks), like Old Fashioneds (p 362) and Negronis (p 288)
- Shaken 'down' drinks (built on the rocks), like a Gold Rush (p 175) and Penicillin (p 177)
- Whisk(e)y neat is *highly* durable

BUILDING DRINKS BY THE ROUND

Building drinks by the round is one of the greatest lessons developed by Sasha Petraske and his original team for the Milk & Honey method. It is the most efficient way to make all the drinks on the same ticket simultaneously, with the fewest number of steps.

A GUIDE TO ROUND BUILDING

Stage 1 – Preparation & Building

1. Before you begin, ensure that everything you need for the drinks on your ticket is either at your station or within arm's reach.
2. Wine. The most durable alcoholic drink behind the bar. White wine is usually slightly too cold in the refrigerator, so giving it a little time to 'come up' a degree or two is a good thing. When possible, a member of the floor team can take care of pouring wines while the bartender is on step three.
3. Citrus. This is the ingredient with the highest margin of error. An extra ¼ oz (7 ml) of lime juice can ruin a cocktail, whereas a splash more rum will certainly not. What's more, if a mistake is made at this point, it can be corrected without wasting alcohol.
4. Non-alcoholic modifiers, such as syrups and cream.
5. Muddle/press.
6. Alcoholic modifiers, such as maraschino liqueur, triple sec, Bénédictine, etc.
7. Base alcohol. (See rules about using the same jigger listed on p 32.)
8. Rinse jiggers, or toss them into a plunge sink full of HOT, clear water (no soap) and clean them after the round along with the shakers.
9. At this point, prepare any garnish that is cut to order. Check that a member of the floor staff is ready to run the round, and if possible, check that the table the round is heading to is set with napkins/coasters and that all the guests are there. (If a guest has gone to the restroom, set their cocktail aside, deliver the rest of the round, and then finish the drink as you see them return.)
10. If any hand-cracked ice is necessary, crack it, and leave it in the empty end of the shaker set. Before cracking ice, rinse off hands in HOT water without soap, and slightly turn away from any customers seated at the bar so you don't hit them with ice shards. Keeping the flattest part of the ice block face-side up, use a fork-tipped bar spoon and strike the face. Hold the spoon by the fork end and use the weight of the spoon.
11. Take a moment to assess the drinks in front of you and determine the order in which you'll be adding the ice – ice the most durable cocktails first and the most fragile last.

Stage 2 – Adding Ice

1. Begin with two-ingredient Highballs (p 108) and spirits on the rocks.
2. Start your built rocks glass cocktails, such as Negronis (p 288) and Old Fashioneds (p 362). If there are a substantial number of these cocktails on the ticket, you can just let them sit and give them a quick stir at the end of the round. When shaping your ice block to fit the glass, use the side of the spoon on your fork-tipped bar spoon to lightly chip at the corners.
3. Start your stirred straight up cocktails. Always use a chilled mixing glass. Once you add the ice, start stirring, keeping an eye on the water content. If possible, immerse the mixing glass in crushed ice.
4. Shaken down drinks, such as a Tom Collins (p 72) or Penicillin (p 177). Remove rocks and Collins/Highball glasses from the freezer. Place on the work area, or directly on the clean, candlelit serving tray.
5. Shaken straight up cocktails, such as Gimlets (p 206) and Daiquiris (p 224). Remove straight up serving glassware from the freezer. Place on the work area, or directly on the clean, candlelit serving tray.
6. Remove glassware from the freezer for your stirred straight up cocktails, then strain them off.
7. Finish with your crushed ice drinks, such as Fixes and Swizzles (p 244), Cobblers (p 264) and Juleps (p 274). There should be a nice, ample washline on any crushed ice drink when it arrives at the table. If the glass is full to the brim, you've either over-poured, over-shaken, or let the drink sit for too long.

Stage 3 – Floats, Top-ups & Finishing Touches

1. Float the cream on top of drinks, such as the Irish Coffee (p 467).
2. Pour sparkling wines by the glass or top sparkling wine cocktails like the Air Mail (p 426) or French 75 (p 425).
3. Finish topping off soda in Highballs (p 108), Collins (p 62), Rickeys (p 78), etc. Foam should be just over the rim of the glass when it arrives at the table.
4. Add garnishes and straws.

Note: If a drink is topped with soda or sparkling wine, such as in categories like Collins (p 62) and Rickey (p 78), add a splash of soda to the shaker before straining the cocktail to further incorporate the bubbles into the drink.

Lifespan of a Cocktail – '*A Cocktail Waits For No One*'

A cocktail begins expiring from the moment it is made, and therefore should never be seen sitting on the bar top. As soon as a bartender receives the order, they should start planning the round and signal the server to pick it up at the appropriate time. The server should strive to get the drinks to the guests as soon as the round is ready.

Serve

When putting drinks forward for garnishing or pick-up, and when serving drinks, be sure to hold the glass by the lowest point, with no exception. Place drinks in order on the tray according to the guests' position at the table working clockwise to ensure that everyone is effortlessly delivered the correct drink and no one needs to ask, 'Who's getting the Margarita?'

Then step away, and listen for expressions of wonder and elation.

QUICK NOTES ON SERVING THE DRINK

- Never serve an empty seat.
- Always use fresh napkins.
- Try to serve the table at once so no one misses out.
- If someone leaves the table, take the drink and put it in the freezer until they return.

Reset

Clean the work area. Clean all equipment. Change water in the plunge sink if necessary. Clean the bar and check if any customer needs attention.

Take a deep breath.
Start the next round.

EXAMPLE ROUND

Cocktails:

- Old Fashioned (p 366)
- Honeysuckle (p 231)
- Sweet Manhattan (p 342)
- Tom Collins (p 72)
- Caipirinha (p 242)
- Mai Tai (p 449)

Stage 1 – Preparation & Building

- Build Old Fashioned
- Using the same jigger, build Sweet Manhattan, ice up and set to the side (stirring where possible), then toss the jigger in hot water.
- Build Honeysuckle, Tom Collins, Caipirinha, Mai Tai, with a new jigger.
  - i. Place lime chunks and sugar cube in the Caipirinha tin.
  - ii. Add lime juice to both the Honeysuckle and Mai Tai.
  - iii. Using the same jigger, add lemon juice to the Tom Collins.
  - iv. Using the same jigger, add simple syrup to the Tom Collins.
  - v. Using the same jigger, add honey syrup to the Honeysuckle.
  - vi. Muddle the lime chunks and sugar in the Caipirinha.
  - vii. Add orgeat and orange curaçao to the Mai Tai.
  - viii. Add light rum to the Honeysuckle.
  - ix. Add Jamaican dark rum to the Mai Tai.
  - x. Using the same jigger, add cachaça to the Caipirinha.
  - xi. Using a new jigger, add gin to the Tom Collins.

Stage 2 – Adding Ice

- Crack ice for the Caipirinha.
- Toss and strain the Tom Collins.
- Shake and dump the Caipirinha.
- Shake and strain the Honeysuckle.
- Strain the Sweet Manhattan.
- Pebble whip the Mai Tai.
- Add crushed ice to Mai Tai.

Stage 3 – Floats, Top-ups & Finishing Touches

- Float the overproof rum on the Mai Tai.
- Top up Tom Collins with soda.
- Add garnishes and straws.

METHODS AT A GLANCE

These default methods can be used to make most of the drinks in their respective chapters. If a drink requires a different method to the one listed here, it'll be listed within the relevant recipe.

COLLINS
Add all ingredients except soda to a shaker and cube whip. Pour into a frozen Collins glass with ice and top with soda.

RICKEY
Add all ingredients except soda to a shaker and cube whip. Pour into a frozen Collins glass with ice and top with soda.

BUCK & MULE
Add all ingredients except soda to a shaker and cube whip. Pour into a frozen Collins glass with ice and top with soda.

HIGHBALL & MIXED DRINK
Build all ingredients in a frozen Highball glass and stir briefly.

CUP
Muddle all ingredients, except carbonated, in a shaker, then shake briefly with ice and strain into a frozen Spritz glass with ice. Top with a mixer, beer or sparkling wine and stir briefly to combine.

PUNCH
Chill all ingredients, then combine in a punchbowl with large blocks of ice and stir briefly to combine. To serve, ladle into rocks glasses or Punch cups with ice.

FIZZ
Add all ingredients except soda to a shaker and dry shake. Add ice, shake again, then strain into a frozen footed Delmonico glass and top with soda simultaneously.

SOUR (TRADITIONAL)
Add all ingredients to a shaker and dry shake vigorously to emulsify. Add ice, then shake and strain into a frozen Sour glass.

SOUR (NON-TRADITIONAL)
Add all ingredients to a shaker, then shake with ice and strain into a frozen coupe.

CRUSTA
Add all ingredients to a shaker, then shake with ice and strain into a frozen footed cocktail glass.

DAISY & SIDECAR
Add all ingredients to a shaker, then shake with ice and strain into a frozen coupe.

GIMLET & SHAKE
Add all ingredients to a shaker, then shake with ice and strain into a frozen coupe.

DAIQUIRI
Add all ingredients to a shaker, then shake with ice and strain into a frozen coupe.

BATIDA
Muddle fruit and sugar in a shaker, then add remaining ingredients and cracked ice. Shake briefly and empty into a frozen double rocks glass.

FIX
Build all ingredients in a shaker, then pour into a frozen double rocks glass with crushed ice. Shimmy and top with more crushed ice.

SWIZZLE
Build all ingredients in a shaker, then pour into a frozen Collins glass with crushed ice. Swizzle and top with more crushed ice.

COBBLER
Muddle citrus and sugar in a shaker, then add remaining ingredients. Toss and strain into a frozen Spritz glass, then top with crushed ice. Shimmy, then top with more crushed ice.

JULEP
Press mint with sugar and/or syrup and/or liqueur in a frozen Julep cup, then add remaining ingredients. Fill the cup with crushed ice, then swizzle and top with more crushed ice.

SMASH
Muddle mint (plus other fruits in modern variations) in a shaker. Add spirit, then shake with ice and strain into a frozen double rocks glass with cracked ice.

STINGER
Build all ingredients in a frozen double rocks glass, then fill the glass with crushed ice.

NEGRONI
Build all ingredients in an Old Fashioned glass, then add ice.

MARTINI
Add all ingredients to a mixing glass, then stir with ice and strain into a frozen coupe.

MANHATTAN
Add all ingredients to a mixing glass, then stir with ice and strain into a frozen coupe.

OLD FASHIONED
Build all ingredients in an Old Fashioned glass, then add ice.

SAZERAC
Fill a small Old Fashioned glass with crushed ice, add four dashes of absinthe and set aside to chill. Add the sugar cube, bitters and soda to a frozen mixing glass and crush the sugar. Add spirit and ice, then stir until ice cold, ensuring that sugar granules are well mixed but take care not to over-dilute. Strain the absinthe into a chilled shot glass, discard the ice and strain the cocktail into the small Old Fashioned glass. Express a lemon twist over the cocktail, then lay the peel across the rim and serve the cocktail along with the absinthe shot as a sidecar.

FLIP
Add all ingredients to a shaker and dry shake to emulsify. Add ice, then shake again and strain into a frozen footed cocktail glass.

TODDY
Warm a Toddy glass by filling with boiling water. Empty water, then build ingredients in the glass and top with fresh boiling water. Alternatively, add room-temperature filtered water and use a milk frother or steamer to steam all ingredients until hot. Stir to combine.

SPIRITS, LIQUEURS & MODIFIERS

There is every chance that you're going to stumble upon a few ingredients you've never heard of in this book. In the case of classic cocktails, those may be archaic liqueurs, some of which might still be lurking in your grandmother's cupboard. Seriously – Michael recently found a bottle of Cynar from the '60s in his. Talk about striking gold! Ultimately, these are simple drinks that rely on the strength and character of each component. If you want to build a great drink, you need a great foundation, so it's worth investing in high-quality key ingredients. Micro-distillers and other small-scale makers are also coming out with new products all the time, so it's just as important to stay up to date and experiment, too. Opposite are the essential spirits needed for the drinks in this book, a simple shopping list that makes no mention about which monks added how many obscure herbs to closely guarded recipes 500 years ago.

BARE NECESSITIES

The absolute essentials to get you started making some of the best known classics.

Spirits

COGNAC
Mix with VS. VSOP and XO for slow-sipping drinks, but you can shake with a VS. Explore options in Sour (p 152), Manhattan (p 334) and Old Fashioned (p 362).

GIN
We opt for London Dry styles mostly. Navy Strength (high proof) styles are great, as is Old Tom. Easily the hardest-working spirit in this book, dominating categories such as Martini (p 304), Collins (p 62), Gimlet (p 206) and Negroni (p 288).

RUM
AGED DARK RUM
You can go a little wild here and, depending on your budget, get some great mixing rums. Try Plantation Original Dark, Havana 7yr Rum. Features heavily in the Buck (p 90), Daiquiri (p 224) and Tropical (p 442) categories.

JAMAICAN DARK RUM
Smith and Cross is by far our favourite, but mostly unavailable in Australia. Both Appleton Estate and Plantation produce great rums. Wray & Nephew satisfies all your overproof needs at 63% ABV. Jamaican Dark Rum is an incredibly aromatic spirit that lends itself to floats in crushed ice drinks. Find it in the Daiquiri (p 224) and Tropical (p 442).

LIGHT (WHITE) RUM
We have long loved Flor de Cana 4yr Old and Havana 3yr Old. There's no Daiquiri (p 224) or Swizzle (p 244) without it.

TEQUILA
This is where you can really get in a twist. Many tequilas that have held the main stage for years are, in fact, really poor-quality products that simply sabotage great drinks. It's been a long road, but quality tequila is finally widely available. Proof makes a lot of difference here in cocktails; we suggest choosing something over 40% (80 proof). Tequila spreads the love throughout the categories, with standout recipes in Gimlet (p 206), Daisy (p 184) and Old Fashioned (p 362).

VODKA
Take your pick here, ensuring that it's smooth and good quality. Popular vodka cocktails include the Vesper (p 322) and Espresso Martini (p 464).

WHISK(E)Y
BLENDED SCOTCH WHISKY
A robust spirit that gives citrus and stirred cocktails a strong backbone. Blended Scotch is most versatile in mixed drinks, featuring across the board in Sour (p 152), Manhattan (p 334), Old Fashioned (p 362) and Highball (p 108).

BOURBON WHISKEY
American whiskey that tends to be softer and sweeter than other styles. There are plenty of great quality products here; it's a great segment to explore to find your specific preference. The definitive spirit in Old Fashioned (p 362) with plenty of appearances in Sour (p 152).

RYE WHISKEY
A spicy and robust style of American whiskey. We enjoy this spirit most when it's stirred and served up in one of the many recipes in Manhattan (p 334).

Liqueurs

AMARETTO
This fragrant, slightly bitter almond liqueur is incredibly distinct in flavour. We say be playful with it, like Jeffrey Morgenthaler did with his Amaretto Sour (Morgenthaler version) (p 169), splitting the base with bourbon, which we agree improved the cocktail immensely; it is now a commonly used recipe around the world.

APEROL
The Spritz, sure, but we also discovered a long time ago that it was really delicious blended with Campari in our Americano (House Recipe) (p 112). We use it for Negroni (p 288) style variations to balance the bitter sweetness of Campari with a bright, tart pop. See Aperitivo & Spritz (p 410) for a selection of light and lively options.

BÉNÉDICTINE
One of the great modifiers of classic cocktail culture. This herbal liqueur shakes and stirs very well with all spirits. Our tip would be don't overcrowd it, as it's complex enough without any additional help from other modifiers. Explore age-old recipes in the Martini (p 304) category like the Poet's Dream (p 321) and Manhattan riffs such as the Preakness (p 345).

CAMPARI
Bold red and bittersweet, dominating Negroni (p 288) and Aperitivo & Spritz (p 410) cocktails, it needs little introduction. While the taste has definitely changed over the years, its flavour is still unique. There are many other great Italian bitters out there that we encourage you to experiment with, such as Cappelletti Aperitivo Americano Rosso, Contratto Bitter, or even Gran Classico Bitter for a slight sideways option.

COFFEE LIQUEUR
Coffee liqueurs should absolutely contain quality coffee. We blend Mr. Black Coffee Liqueur with Kahlua and steep coffee beans for a short period, which works well.

There's a whole coffee category to explore that shows just how well coffee can play with other flavours and ingredients such as whisk(e)y, tequila, pineapple, ginger and cream. Explore categories like Buck (p 90), Flip (p 388), Cream (p 470) and Aperitivo & Spritz (p 410).

GRAND MARNIER
We use this to make our house orange curaçao (p 498) by blending it with simple syrup. It's rich and decadent, but also really citrusy, which makes it very versatile in cocktails, especially as a modifier in Sours (p 152), Daisies (p 184) and Crustas (p 184) with drinks like the Bronco Buster (p 174) and Brandy Crusta (p 194).

MARASCHINO LIQUEUR
Another staple of classic cocktail culture, this product is big and can scare away first-timers if it's not balanced correctly.

Maraschino makes an appearance in a number of prolific cocktails such as the Aviation (p 195) and Hemingway Daiquiri (p 228) and stirs down well in Old Fashioned (p 362) style drinks like the Fancy Free (p 376).

TRIPLE SEC
While Cointreau has established itself as the more notable triple sec, we open the floor to the other great brands like Combier and Merlet.

This ingredient is prominent in the Daisy (p 184) category, with the Sidecar (p 184) setting a fine example.

Fortified

DRY VERMOUTH
We find vermouth styles are often a personal choice and there are a number from many different regions. We look for a really light and delicate dry vermouth for cocktails, favouring both Dolin and Carpano Dry. Find your favourite by mixing in Dry Martini (p 314) variations. It also lends itself to highballs and tall drinks like the Rome with a View (p 84). Store this in the fridge once opened.

SWEET VERMOUTH
This is definitely a personal choice and one many discerning drinkers are quite passionate about. You've got big hitters like Carpano Antica Formula, which is rich with lots of vanilla, raisin and chocolate, or the softer and lighter Cocchi Vermouth di Torino, a moscato-based sweet vermouth that has to be our preference for the way it dances with both light and dark spirits. Carpano also makes a great product called Punt e Mes, which dials up the bitter in its vermouth.

Try blending it with a favourite sweet vermouth or use it straight in a Red Hook (p 345). We must note that Lustau Vermut Rojo from Jerez, Spain, is an exceptional sweet vermouth that we love. This on the rocks or neat is sheer pleasure.

The options are endless here. Look at Highball (p 108) Aperitivo & Spritz (p 410) Manhattan (p 334) and Martini (p 304). Store this in the fridge once opened.

Syrups

There are so many, and we list a large number in this book. Though the ones we keep within reach at all times are:

AGAVE (P 494)
Essential in categories such as Gimlet (p 206) and Old Fashioned (p 362)

GINGER (P 496)
Essential in categories such as Buck (p 90), Tropical (p 442) and Sour (p 152)

GRENADINE/POMEGRANATE (P 496)
Essential in categories such as Sour (p 152), Gimlet (p 206) and Daiquiri (p 224)

HONEY (P 496)
Essential in categories such as Cream (p 470), Sour (p 152), Toddy (p 400), Flip (p 388) and Old Fashioned (p 362)

ORGEAT (P 499)
Essential in categories such as Daisy (p 184), Sour (p 152) and Tropical (p 442)

SIMPLE (P 493)
Essential in the majority of cocktails shaken with citrus.

Bitters

ANGOSTURA BITTERS
These bitters are still the most popular product on the market, spanning a vast number of cocktail recipes. Keep them on hand to decorate your Whiskey Sour (p 156) and liven your Old Fashioned (p 362). See also how it transforms simple shaken drinks such as Gimlet (p 206) variation the Bennett (p 214) with just a few dashes, or as a more dominant ingredient in a cocktail like the Trinidad Sour (p 183).

ORANGE BITTERS
We blend two types of orange bitters to make ours, and it's essential for our preferred style of Martini (p 304), the Hoffman House Cocktail (p 318).

PEYCHAUD'S AROMATIC COCKTAIL BITTERS
This product is also unlikely to gather dust. Integral to the Sazerac (p 362) and other stirred classics.

Other Ingredients

CHERRIES
Morello cherries in Kirsch are our preferred style, with the Fabbri and Luxardo cherries in syrup in at a close second. Essential for categories such as Manhattan (p 334)

CREAM
We make our house cream by blending double cream with full-cream milk for useability. Essential for categories such as Cream (p 470) and Flip (p 388)

EGGS
Free range only. Essential for categories such as Traditional Sour (p 160), Fizz (p 134) and Flip (p 388)

LEMON JUICE
Ripe, freshly squeezed and strained. Essential for categories such as Collins (p 62) and Non-traditional Sour (p 169)

LIME JUICE
Ripe, freshly squeezed and strained. Essential for categories such as Daiquiri (p 224) and Rickey (p 78)

MINT
Freshly picked leaves. Essential for categories such as Julep (p 274), Stinger (p 274), Smash (p 274) and Swizzle (p 244)

OLIVES
We love Cerignola olives for their size and meaty flesh. Essential for categories such as Martini (p 304) and Aperitivo & Spritz (p 410)

FULLY STOCKED

This list does not include every product featured in this book, but it is a comprehensive capture of some of the most frequently used ingredients to upgrade your essential collection.

Spirits

BONDED APPLE BRANDY
Apple brandy/Apple Jack vs Calvados. It's really up to you. We like bonded apple brandy. It's more like a whisk(e)y than a brandy – bold and robust, which suits us well when mixing drinks. A split base of equal parts apple brandy and Calvados makes for an interesting take on the Jack Rose (p 221).

CACHAÇA
A distinct cane product that lies at the heart of most drinks in the Batida (p 236) category, featuring heroes like the Caipirinha (p 242).

Try sweetening it with a different sugar such as Demerara and adding fresh mint in the El Draque (p 234). It also shows up in the Negroni (p 288) category in a fine drink called the Shadow Boxer (p 301).

GOSLINGS BLACK SEAL RUM
The Dark 'n' Stormy (p 94) cocktail is Goslings' claim to fame, though the product has plenty more to give. This wonderful export from Bermuda delivers distinct flavours of butterscotch, vanilla and caramel, which pair well with whisk(e)y in stirred drinks and can be used in instances that call for 'blackstrap rum'. They also make a 151 proof which adds another dimension to any drink as a tiny float on top.

IRISH WHISKEY
Applicable to more than just the Irish Coffee (p 467), although this is a great place to start or, should we say, finish. Try it also in a Weeski (p 352).

ISLAY SCOTCH WHISKY
Islay or Peated Scotch whisky is used a lot in contemporary cocktails to increase a drink's complexity, similar to how we use ingredients like absinthe and mezcal. We keep these items in small cruets, making it easy to add small measures.

Islay Scotch can be used in various cocktail styles, with undoubtedly the most recognisable being the modern classic Penicillin (p 177) which elevates a simple Scotch and ginger Sour with an Islay float.

MEZCAL
This is truly a spirit like no other. Sip it, stir and shake with it. Its versatility never fails to astound us. Blend it with blanco tequila to add more depth and smoke in any tequila-based cocktail. We're suckers for citrus styles, such as the Medicina Mexicana (p 219) and experimental agave-driven Old Fashioned (p 362) variations.

PISCO
A South American unaged brandy deriving from both Peru and Chile. We use both Quebranta, which is less aromatic, and Acholado, which is blended and more floral, perfect for drinks like the Frantic Atlantic (p 255).

SINGLE MALT SCOTCH WHISKY
We use this in slower drinks like Old Fashioned (p 362) and Manhattan (p 334) variations that don't include citrus, although we suggest sampling the Porridge Colada (p 457) to see how Scotch whisky lends itself to tropical drinks, too.

Liqueurs

ABSINTHE
There are too many great options out there to name any one in particular. We tend to avoid the bright green ones and opt for the more delicate products like Jade, which a regular introduced me to and is beautiful. Negroni (p 288) lovers should see how a few dashes transform the Quill (p 298). We also love how this ingredient gives a drier finish to citrus drinks like the Admiral (p 223).

AMARO MONTENEGRO & OTHER AMARI
A light, floral amaro for sipping and mixing. This product works well alongside other liqueurs like amaretto in cocktails like the 5am Club (p 249). We tend to mix it with light spirits, both shaken and stirred, based on this profile, though it also shines in Rob Roy (p 351) riff, the Monte Burns (p 351). Other pre-dinner picks appear in the Aperitivo & Spritz (p 410) chapter.

If you're curious about other amari, we recommend: Nonino Amaro Quintessentia, Rucolino alla Rucola, Ramazzotti Amaro and Bràulio Amaro Alpino.

APRICOT BRANDY
We use Giffard Abricot du Roussillon and Merlet Lune d'Abricot Liqueur. If you can get your hands on it in Australia, also try Luxardo Apricot Liqueur.

Stir it with rye whiskey in The Slope (p 345), or shake it in a Pisco Bell-Ringer (p 180) or Pisco-Apricot Tropicáls (p 255) on crushed ice.

BANANA LIQUEUR
We like to use two different products. Tempus Fugit makes an amazing version called Crème de Banane that we use for stirred drinks for its rich banana bread flavour. You can also enjoy it on its own – yes, really!

It's memorable in Old Fashioned (p 362) style recipes like the King Kong (p 377). For a more tropical nose, try Giffard Banane du Brésil, which lends itself to shaken drinks like The Chunky Dunk (p 235) or the Breakfast Mai Tai (p 447).

CRÈME DE CACAO
We use two: Tempus Fugit dark cacao, mostly for stirred and Old Fashioned (p 362) style drinks without citrus, and white crème de cacao for shaking.

The dark cacao is thick, luscious and mixes elegantly in slow sippers like the Hand in Glove (p 354). In contrast, we prefer a white cacao like Giffard White Crème de Cacao or Joseph Cartron White Crème de Cacao for lighter-style, citrus cocktails.

CYNAR
This bittersweet amaro made from artichokes is undoubtedly one of our favourite products behind the bar. Exemplary in slow-sippers like the Berlioni (p 299) and Cynarita (p 294), or alongside citrus in Sour (p 152) variation the Too Soon? (p 174).

DRAMBUIE
Made famous in the Rusty Nail (p 382), this Scotch-based liqueur works really well with other spirits, such as gin, and shakes well with citrus.

Find it in Martini (p 304) riff, the Bonnie Prince (p 315), or shaken with citrus and served on the rocks in the Silver Nail (p 177).

ELDERFLOWER LIQUEUR
The most famous elderflower liqueur is St Germain, which is a great product we make good use of. Try it in Traditional Sour (p 160) variation, the Saint-Germain-des-Prés (p 162).

FERNET-BRANCA & BRANCA MENTA
There are more and more Fernet-style products on the shelves these days. We love both of these in cocktails, especially Branca Menta, which is often overlooked.

Our go-to has to be stirred up in the Toronto (p 347) or Apotheke (p 286) cocktails, or alongside spicy ginger in Buck (p 90) variation the Late Night Reviver (p 99).

GALLIANO
Like Strega Liquore, Galliano L'Autentico brings a lot to the table in terms of vegetal Italian liqueurs.

This product is a welcome addition to a really interesting drink called the Yellow Submarine (p 370) with celery bitters and cucumber, and the St. Rose Sour (p 166).

GREEN CHARTREUSE
A true powerhouse of a spirit with so much life and complexity. Shake it up in a Last Word (p 188) or a Champs Élysées (p 179).

Tame it with rye whiskey and bonded apple brandy in a Diamondback Cocktail (p 342) or scan Martini (p 304) variations for the Warday's No. 2 (p 327).

HEERING CHERRY LIQUEUR
There are also many other great cherry liqueurs on the market now. While the Singapore Sling (p 446) made this product famous, we recommend trying it in the Remember the Maine (p 345) cocktail, an outstanding Manhattan (p 334) variation.

ORANGE CURAÇAO & DRY CURAÇAO
We use two: a lighter and drier one called Pierre Ferrand Dry Curaçao, and a slightly sweeter one that we blend ourselves with Grand Marnier.

The house Orange Curaçao (p 498) features mostly in shaken drinks like the Appendicitis De Luxe (p 160), whereas we reserve Pierre Ferrand Dry Curaçao for stirred drinks like the Guatemalan Square (p 358) when we want to control the sweetness.

PEACH LIQUEUR
We use Giffard Crème de Pêche de Vigne, which is light and delicate. It stirs and shakes really well, which is important for such a flavour when making simple drinks like the Peach Bamboo (p 386) or The Real Georgia Mint Julep (p 285).

We love this product in a Perfect Lady (p 162), a vibrant Traditional Sour (p 160) variation.

PICON AMER
You can't make one of our favourite Manhattan (p 334) riffs, the Brooklyn Cocktail (p 340) without it, though we did replace it with the fantastic Amaro CioCiaro for many years due to its unavailability in the United States.

SLOE GIN
The Sloe Gin Fizz (p 150) is the most popular option. We also admire the Ocean Shore Cocktail (p 162) where sloe gin is combined with gin and pomegranate for a little extra punch.

SUZE & OTHER GENTIAN LIQUEURS
We also suggest exploring Avèze (the softest of the gentian liqueurs) and Salers. This French gentian apéritif is the most bitter of the three and offers personality and depth to cocktails.

There's bitterness, but also honey and chamomile. You'll find this character prominent in Negroni (p 288) riffs, such as the White Negroni (p 292), and Beer (p 432) cocktails like the Haymarket (p 437).

VANILLA LIQUEUR
We've flipped between Galliano Vanilla, Giffard Vanille de Madagascar and Licor 43, and have all three behind the bar. They each have a unique profile. Again, quality should be the only consideration when it comes to liqueurs.

Explore The Expedition (p 452) or the Golden Cadillac (p 478) which is one of our most sought-after recipes of all time.

VIOLET LIQUEUR
A common complaint with violet drinks is that they can have a soapy taste. We counter this by blending our own violet using violet liqueur, violet syrup and gin.

While most popular in the Aviation Cocktail (p 195), we enjoy it in the Act of Violets (p 160).

WHITE CRÈME DE MENTHE
We opt not to use the bright green crème de menthe, and instead our Grasshopper (p 478) gets its green tint from fresh mint.

YELLOW CHARTREUSE
Very unlike its green counterpart, it offers a softer, sweeter profile. Yellow can ride beside Bénédictine in many cases and makes for a great riff on the Puritan Cocktail (p 321). Explore drinks like the Greenpoint (p 343) and the Yellow (p 197) cocktail also.

Fortified

AMONTILLADO SHERRY
Sits between Fino and Oloroso sherries in weight. It's an essential ingredient in many recipes in the Cobbler (p 264) category. You'll also find it shaken down with reposado tequila and apricot brandy in the Repossession (p 198) and stirred up in the Haberdasher (p 331), or served tall in a Collins (p 62) with the Cádiz Collins (p 70).

Store this in the fridge once opened.

BIANCO & BLANC VERMOUTH
These styles are sweet and aromatic, with a spot in the fridge next to your Cocchi Americano. You've got French or Italian. We like both, though tend to lean more towards the French and our love of Chambery vermouths like Dolin.

It's Martini (p 304) heaven here with the variations. Try the Atlas Martini (p 315), Quick Step (p 330) and the Salt & Pepper Martini (p 321).

Store this in the fridge once opened.

COCCHI AMERICANO
This is one of our favourite products. A worthy replacement for Kina Lillet in drinks such as the Corpse Reviver No. 2 (p 195), the Vesper (p 322) and The Richmond No. 1 (p 312).

Store this in the fridge once opened.

COCCHI ROSA
Sister to the Americano but utilising Bracchetti and Malvasia grapes, resulting in a bright berry fruit- and floral-driven apéritif. Find it in Whole Lotta Rosa (p 149) and Milady's Martini (p 326).

Store this in the fridge once opened.

EAST INDIA CREAM SHERRY
A blend of Oloroso and Pedro Ximénez wines. Find it in the Manhattan (p 334) category with drinks like La Viña (p 343) and Night Owl (p 356), and in the Martini (p 304) category in the Prima Donna (p 332).

Store this in the fridge once opened.

FINO SHERRY
More full-bodied than Manzanilla Sherry, Fino has a slightly more savoury character that works great in the London Calling (p 172), served tall with Amaro Montenegro in the Second Serve (p 89) or stirred up in the Bamboo (p 331) and the Tuxedo (p 310).

Store this in the fridge once opened.

MANZANILLA SHERRY
A lighter, dry sherry and our most used, Manzanilla is brighter and fresher than Fino. We're big fans of Non-traditional Sour (p 169) variation the Sherry Lady (p 204), and stirred-up style, the Woolworth (p 352). Explore also the Aperitivo & Spritz (p 410) category.

Store this in the fridge once opened.

OLOROSO SHERRY
Darker than Amontillado, this sherry is dry, woody and nutty. You'll find it in Cobblers (p 264) but it loves to play with funk, too, like in the Olive Oil Sour (p 167) or Negroni (p 288) riff with Jamaican dark rum, Tropicale (p 301), or stirred up with bourbon in the Up to Date Cocktail (p 349).

Store this in the fridge once opened.

PEDRO XIMÉNEZ (PX) SHERRY
Rich dessert-style sherry made from grapes left out in the sun to dry. Think dates, raisins and toffee. Perfect on its own as a digestif or in slow-sipping cocktails.

Favourite Manhattan (p 334) variations include the William Wallace (p 352), Linchpin (p 358) or enjoy Old Fashioned (p 362) variations such as the Haitian Divorce (p 371) and Second Marriage (p 385).

PINEAU DES CHARENTES
A combination of grape juice and Cognac, which is bottled at around 17% ABV.

A great apéritif to play with, shining in drinks such as Martinelle (p 319) and Simon Difford's Sidecar (p 205) variation.

Store this in the fridge once opened.

PORT
Tawny, ruby and white all get used behind the bar, but Tawny is mixed most frequently. A rich and generous ingredient that lends itself to a number of recipes in the Flip (p 388) category. Favourites include warming nightcap the New York Flip (p 397) or stirred up-style, the Chancellor No. 2 (p 350).

POMMEAU DE NORMANDIE
This product is a blend of apple juice and Calvados, and a fun ingredient to work with.

Try it stirred up in the Black Mamba (p 342) and the Serpent's Kiss (p 356), or in an Apple Sour (p 165).

Store this in the fridge once opened.

Syrups

RASPBERRY (P 500)
Essential for categories such as Non-traditional Sour (p 169) and Daisy (p 152).

PASSIONFRUIT (P 499)
Essential for categories such as Tropical (p 442), Sour (p 152) and Collins (p 62).

PINEAPPLE (P 499)
Essential for categories such as Tropical (p 442) and Cobbler (p 264).

Bitters

CHOCOLATE BITTERS
We like Bittermens Xocolatl. Essential for categories such as Manhattan (p 334) and Old Fashioned (p 362).

CHUNCHO BITTERS
Essential in the Pisco Sour (p 166).

PIMENTO BITTERS
Essential for categories such as Tropical (p 442) and Old Fashioned (p 362).

Other Ingredients

BLACKBERRIES
Ripe and whole. Essential for categories such as Fix (p 244) and Cobbler (p 264).

BLACK PEPPER
Essential for drinks that need a savoury finish, such as the Hot Ticket (p 183).

BLUEBERRIES
Ripe and whole. Essential for categories such as Fix (p 244) and Cobbler (p 264).

CAYENNE PEPPER
Essential for cocktails, such as Devil's Cocktail (p 282).

CINNAMON
Essential for categories such as Toddy (p 400), Flip (p 388) and Tropical (p 442).

COCO LÓPEZ
Essential for categories such as Tropical (p 442).

CUCUMBER
Ripe and sliced. Essential for categories such as Cup (p 122) and Batida (p 236).

GRAPEFRUIT
Ripe, freshly squeezed and strained. Essential for categories such as Rickey (p 78) and Gimlet (p 206).

HOT SAUCE
Essential for drinks like the Michelada (p 438.

MAPLE SYRUP
Essential for categories such as Old Fashioned (p 362) and Sour (p 152).

NUTMEG
Essential for categories such as Toddy (p 400) and Flip (p 388).

ORANGE
Ripe, freshly squeezed and strained. Essential for categories such as Buck (p 90), Highball (p 108) and Tropical (p 442).

ORANGE BLOSSOM WATER
Essential for categories such as Fizz (p 134) and Traditional Sour (p 160).

PINEAPPLE
Ripe, freshly juiced and strained. Essential for categories such as Tropical (p 442) and Buck (p 90).

RASPBERRIES
Ripe and whole. Essential for categories such as Fix (p 244) and Cobbler (p 264).

ROSE WATER
Essential for categories such as Fizz (p 134) and Traditional Sour (p 160).

SALT FLAKES
Essential for drinks like the Chelada (p 437).

SMOKED PAPRIKA
Essential in cocktails like Red Grasshopper (p 220).

SUGAR CUBES
Essential for categories such as Old Fashioned (p 362).

WONDER FOAM
A vegan foaming agent that acts as an alternative to egg white. Essential for vegan variations in categories such as Traditional Sour (p 160) and Fizz (p 134).

WORCESTERSHIRE SAUCE
Essential for categories such as Highball (p 108).

GLASSWARE & GARNISHING

Glassware

There are specific glasses out there for every drink, so it's imperative that you use the right glass for the right drink. Our ice is also shaped and cut around the drink and the glass, meaning the ice is cut to proportions that give the perfect washline once the drink is poured. Not exactly science, but we take this, and our washlines, very seriously.

CHILLED VS ROOM-TEMPERATURE GLASSWARE
Temperature plays a critical role in drink service. More often than not, the goal is to deliver the coldest drink to the guest that we can. As a result, we like to freeze or chill as much glassware as possible.

All glasses marked with an asterisk (*) in the list to the right should live in the freezer. Be sure to restock the freezer properly, putting warm glassware in the back and bringing cold glasses to the front. Unless the recipe calls for the glass to be warmed, a warm glass is never an acceptable vessel for a drink.

Collins *
For tall shaken drinks like a Buck, Rickey and Collins, of course. *12 oz (350 ml)*

Highball *
For Highball and Mixed Drinks.
10 oz (300 ml)

Punch cup *
For Punches ladled from a punch bowl.
6 oz (180 ml)

Footed Delmonico *
For Fizzes. *8 oz (240 ml)*

Sour *
Slightly larger than a regular coupe to hold drinks with egg white.
8⅔ oz (260 ml)

Coupe *
For shaken up drinks like Non-Traditional Sours and stirred drinks like Martinis.
5½–6 oz (170–185 ml)

Double Rocks *
For your Fixes, Penicillin and Gold Rush. *13¼–14 oz (370–400 ml)*

Julep *
For Juleps. *12 oz (350 ml)*

Old Fashioned
For drinks on the rocks, like Negronis and Old Fashioneds. *9–10 oz (270–300 ml)*

Footed cocktail *
For Flips. *5½ oz (170 ml)*

Toddy
For hot drinks/Toddies. *8 oz (250 ml)*

Spritz (short-stemmed) *
For Aperitivo, Spritz and Tropical cocktails.
14–16 oz (400–455 ml)

Flute
For Champagne cocktails – and Champagne, too, obviously. *6–7 oz (180–210 ml)*

Beer *
For Beer cocktails. *12–14 oz (350–400 ml)*

Tiki mug *
For Tropical/Tiki-style drinks.
16 oz (455 ml)

A Guide to Garnishes

Cocktail garnishes are both aesthetic and aromatic. They have the opportunity to make your cocktail look incredibly appealing or, in contrast, put someone off the drink before their first sip. Garnishes should always be intentional and exact. Before selecting a garnish for your cocktail, first consider its role in terms of what it adds to the drink. A garnish for garnish's sake that has no relationship to the cocktail is superfluous. However, a garnish that enhances the drink's appearance, offers an indication of the drink's ingredients, or provides a fragrant aroma, is incredibly enticing, building further anticipation and excitement about the flavour of the cocktail itself. All garnishes must be ripe, fresh and prepared with precision. Regarding citrus, be mindful to avoid gathering too much pith as this carries unwanted bitterness.

BERRIES
Most often blueberries, raspberries or blackberries. One berry spiked on two cocktail skewers and placed vertically on the rim of the glass.

For Cobblers (p 264) that specify multiple berries, arrange these neatly on top of the drink.

BITTERS CROWN
Used in crushed ice drinks. Finish the drink by topping up crushed ice, then add 5–6 dashes on top evenly.

BITTERS DROP & SWIRL
Using a dasher bottle, drop the bitters onto the drink's surface and swirl using a cocktail skewer.

BITTERS FLOAT
To float bitters is to dash before topping up with soda on tall drinks or topping up with ice for crushed ice drinks.

BITTERS STRIPE
Most often Angostura or Peychaud's Aromatic Cocktail Bitters. Swiftly drawn across the top of the drink, slightly to one side, using a flick of the wrist with a bitters bottle.

CITRUS DISC
A small circle of citrus peel made using a Y or Swiss peeler and/or small knife, spritzed over the drink, then laid on top of the cocktail.

CITRUS FLAG
Two small triangles of citrus made using a small knife. First cut a citrus half-wheel (see below) then cut again so you have two quarters. Place on top of one another and use two cocktail skewers to spike before placing on the rim of the glass.

CITRUS HALF-WHEEL
Fresh, thin slices of citrus cut in half and laid on top of the cocktail to one side.

CITRUS PIGTAIL
A long, continuous strip of citrus peel that has been tightly wrapped around a barspoon to create a spiral before being laid on the rim of the glass.

CITRUS TWIST
Most often lemon and orange, made using a Y or Swiss peeler around the diameter of the fruit, creating a peel approximately 2¾ in (7 cm) in length for stirred up drinks and a little longer at 4 in (10 cm) for drinks on the rocks.

CITRUS TWIST (DISCARD)
Most often lemon, made using a Y or Swiss peeler around the diameter of the fruit, creating a peel approximately 2–2¾ in (5–7 cm) in length. Oils are expressed from the citrus skin over the top of the cocktail by placing the twist lengthways and pinching it three or four times between forefinger and thumb before discarding the skin.

CITRUS WEDGE
Freshly cut wedges of citrus (approximately 6–8 per whole citrus fruit) made with a small incision just off-centre in order to position the wedge on the rim of the glass with the larger portion facing out from the drink. Note: remove all seeds, remove the white pith at the fruit's core, and avoid skin with any blemishes or discoloration.

CITRUS WHEEL
Fresh, thin slices of citrus laid on top of the cocktail to one side.

CUCUMBER FAN
Made using three freshly sliced cucumber wheels (see below), spiked with two cocktail skewers and splayed into a fan pattern then placed on the rim of the glass.

CUCUMBER RIBBON
Made using a Y or Swiss peeler along the length of a fresh, ripe cucumber. Most often placed around the inside of the glass prior to straining your cocktail into it. Alternatively, you can fold the slice over a long cocktail skewer and lay it horizontally across the top of the cocktail.

CUCUMBER WHEEL
Fresh slices made with a small incision in order to position the wheel vertically on the rim of the glass.

FRUIT FAN
Most often fresh apple half-slices. Approximately three thin slices spiked with two cocktail skewers, layered and splayed so as to create a fan that is positioned vertically on the rim of the glass.

GINGER CANDY
Spiked on two cocktail skewers and placed vertically on the rim of the glass. Sometimes you will combine this garnish with cucumber or a mint sprig, as seen in the Gin-Gin Mule (p 94).

GRATED GARNISHES
Most often nutmeg and cinnamon, grated using a microplane. Citrus peels grated over crushed ice drinks are also aromatic and look elegant.

HORSE'S NECK
Made with a whole, fresh, ripe fruit, using a Y or Swiss peeler to circle the diameter of the fruit multiple times until you have a continuous peel approximately 4½–5½ in (12–14 cm) in length. Most often placed around the inside of the glass prior to straining your cocktail into it. A defining characteristic of the Crusta (p 184).

MINT BOUQUET
A preferred mint garnish for its incredible fragrance. A generous 3–4 mint sprigs are slapped on the back of the hand to awaken, then pinched together and drilled into the centre of the drink for crushed ice drinks like the Swizzle (p 244), or carefully positioned into one side of the glass for cocktails like the Rickey (p 78).

MINT LEAF
Take a healthy mint leaf, fold it gently and cut a diagonal incision then place it on the edge of the glass.

MINT SPRIG
Referring to a single mint sprig of approximately 6–8 leaves. Appropriate for small drinks often in stemmed cocktail glasses, but we recommend a bouquet (see above) in tall drinks or those with crushed ice.

OLIVE, MORELLO CHERRY, PICKLED ONION
Place gently inside the glass, ensuring that they are not so large they significantly raise the drink's washline (see p 36). Additional serves may also be delivered in a sidecar on request for the Martini (p 304).

PINEAPPLE FRONDS
Two fronds placed neatly together in the drink.

PINEAPPLE WEDGE
Cut a small wedge with an incision to be placed on the edge of the glass.

SALT RIM
We only rim half the glass with salt as a rule. Swipe the outer rim of the glass with a citrus wedge (most often lime) then roll this edge on a bed of salt. Clean the rim with a napkin to create a straight line.

SPRINKLED/DUSTED GARNISHES
Most often salt flakes, black pepper or cayenne pepper, pinched and sprinkled evenly over the top of the drink.

SPRITZ
Most often rosewater or orange blossom water. One spray over the glass using an atomiser.

We also use this method for absinthe, Islay Scotch and mezcal.

SUGAR RIM
Swipe the whole glass rim with a citrus wedge (most often lime) and dip the glass edge into a sugar bowl.

THE BRANCHES

COLLINS

Tom Collins p 72

Collins

A simple citrus cocktail served over ice in a Collins glass and lengthened with soda.

spirit + lemon juice + sugar + soda

Add all ingredients except soda to a shaker and cube whip. Pour into a frozen Collins glass with ice and top with soda.

John Collin, head waiter and bar manager of the Limmer's Hotel, London, is credited with creating the Collins in the early 19th century. Collin was known to serve a popular Gin Punch by the tankard, back in 1834. In the 1860s, some 20 years after his death in 1843, the drink started popping up around the world in a similar form to the one we see today, featuring sweeter-style Old Tom gin or genever.

As Old Tom gin became more readily available in the United States, American drinkers began differentiating between the genever version, dubbed John Collins (p 71), and the gin version, naturally called Tom Collins (p 72). By the late 1940s, dry gin had replaced Old Tom as the preferred style, and a dip in genever's popularity also saw the John Collins made with American whiskey instead.

The evolution didn't stop there. Over time, the Collins family has grown to encompass variations of the drink with several headline spirits, including: Scotch (Sandy Collins, p 75), Irish whiskey (Mike Collins, p 77), bourbon (Colonel Collins, p 75), light rum (Pedro Collins, p 73), applejack (Jack Collins, p 75) and brandy (Pierre Collins, p 75).

Tom Collins – essentially a Non-traditional gin Sour served tall with soda – remains the most popular of the bunch. The progression of the Collins category has been profound, due largely to the drink's approachability, versatility and near-universal appeal. The tall, refreshing format also lends itself to experimentation with a multitude of fruits, such as oranges, pineapples, grapefruits and berries.

Grapefruit Collins

Sam Ross, Little Branch, NYC, 2005
2 oz (60 ml) gin
1½ oz (45 ml) pink grapefruit juice
½ oz (15 ml) lemon juice
½ oz (15 ml) simple syrup
3 dashes Peychaud's Aromatic Cocktail Bitters, to float
Soda, to top

Add all ingredients except soda to a shaker and cube whip. Pour into a frozen Collins glass with ice and top with soda.
Garnish: grapefruit half-wheel

Bartender, bar owner and cocktail consultant Sam Ross has been a prolific contributor to the modern cocktail canon, and the Grapefruit Collins is merely one of the many contemporary classics he has put his name to. Like Michael, Ross grew up in Australia and began his hospitality career at the age of 15, working at a high-volume Melbourne café. In 2001, once he'd finished school, he helped his sister and mother open their first bar, Ginger, on Melbourne's bustling Brunswick Street in Fitzroy. The bar was ahead of its time, responsible for kickstarting a revival of classic cocktails in the Melbourne scene.

Ross moved to New York City in 2004 and trained under the late Sasha Petraske, who brought the classic cocktail renaissance to global attention at his first bar, Milk & Honey. Michael had the pleasure of working with Ross during their time both at Little Branch and Milk & Honey in the early 2000s, and they remain close friends.

Created at Little Branch in 2005, the Grapefruit Collins is a Milk & Honey family favourite, a simple and sessionable cocktail that really quenches the thirst. Pink grapefruit juice brings a tart dimension to the traditional Tom Collins (p 72), while a few dashes of Peychaud's Aromatic Cocktail Bitters add hints of cherry, cloves and anise that round out the drink perfectly and accentuate its striking sunset colour.

Although grapefruit can be divisive, those who like it tend to embrace it with gusto, and its distinctive bittersweetness works particularly well in apéritif-style refreshers. Some favourites of ours include the Paloma (p 88) and Hemingway Daiquiri (p 228).

Stay Up Late

Veronica Harrold
The Stork Club Bar Book, *Lucius Beebe, 1946*
1½ oz (45 ml) gin
½ oz (15 ml) Cognac
¾ oz (22 ml) lemon juice
¾ oz (22 ml) simple syrup
Soda, to top

Add all ingredients except soda to a shaker and cube whip. Pour into a frozen Collins glass with ice and top with soda.
Garnish: lemon wedge

The Stay Up Late is an easy and elegant take on the Tom Collins (p 72) that cuts the original gin base with a bit of Cognac and comes from *The Stork Club Bar Book*, written by Lucius Beebe in 1946. Beebe was a noted American journalist, gourmand and raconteur, famous for his coverage of café society and nightlife throughout the 1930s and '40s. He was also a regular at New York City's Stork Club, a legendary gathering spot for celebrities, socialites, politicians and gangsters, described by gossip columnist Walter Winchell as 'New York's New Yorkiest place'.

For an appendix to the bulk of the cocktail recipes in his book, Beebe collected submissions from staff members, such as Veronica Harrold from the 'hat checking department'. Her Stay Up Late is an absolute cracker, proving that gin and Cognac make a blessed union when balanced correctly, with the Cognac lending gentle warmth and depth. The Stay Up Very Late (p 72), a riff devised by Michael in 2008, takes it one step further by incorporating a dash of absinthe.

If the combination of Cognac and gin ticks your boxes, we suggest you try the Loudspeaker Cocktail (p 203) and Chinatown Cocktail (p 324) – both by Trader Vic.

Stay Up Late (left), Grapefruit Collins (right)

Highlander Highball

(Sandy Collins with pineapple)
Hoffman House Bartender's Guide,
Charles S. Mahoney, 1905
2 oz (60 ml) Scotch
1½ oz (45 ml) pineapple juice
½ oz (15 ml) lemon juice
½ oz (15 ml) simple syrup
Soda, to top

Add all ingredients except soda to a shaker and cube whip. Pour into a frozen Collins glass with ice and top with soda.
Garnish: 2 pineapple fronds

The Highlander Highball was first published in the *Hoffman House Bartender's Guide* by Charles S. Mahoney in 1905. Mahoney was the head bartender at New York City's lavish Hoffman House, a hotel renowned for its 'grand salon' (bar), which attracted high-society types and big-name politicians of the day. The hotel also gave birth to several notable bartenders, including Harry Craddock (1876–1963) prior to his time at The Savoy in London.

In addition to mapping out cocktails, Mahoney's work served as a guidebook for bartenders and bar owners on all aspects of how to run a successful business and potential pitfalls to be aware of. In the book's preface, Mahoney asserts: 'No one man knows it all, and we can all learn, no matter how old or experienced we are.'

The Highlander Highball is a Sandy (Scotch) Collins with the addition of pineapple juice and an absolute unsung hero of the classic cocktail world. A lighter-style drink that sees the bold profile of Scotch softened by complementary tropical fruit and soda, it makes both a great introduction to Scotch for those less familiar and a playful diversion for whisky lovers curious to see what else Scotch can play with in the sand.

Fans of pineapple, meanwhile, can – and should – look further than the tropical paradise of the Piña Colada (p 450), as magnificent as it is. This highly nutritious South American fruit lends a bright sweetness to a variety of cocktails and is well suited to so many spirits. See for yourself in drinks like the Invisible Gin Highball (p 99), another winner from Mahoney, as well as the Pineapple Blossom Cocktail (p 175), the Los Altos (p 87) and the Chelsea Cobbler (p 270).

North Side Special

Myrtle Bank Hotel, Kingston
Trader Vic's Book of Food & Drink,
Trader Vic, 1947
2 oz (60 ml) Jamaican dark rum
1½ oz (45 ml) orange juice
½ oz (15 ml) lemon juice
½ oz (15 ml) simple syrup
Soda, to top

Add all ingredients except soda to a shaker and cube whip. Pour into a frozen Collins glass with ice and top with soda.
Garnish: orange wedge

Restaurateur and author Victor Jules Bergeron Jr. – better known as "Trader Vic" – is perhaps best remembered for his eponymous chain of Polynesian-themed restaurants, which originated in California and spread across the world as 'tiki culture' flourished throughout the 1950s and '60s. Bergeron penned 10 food and drink books during his lifetime and is one of two people who claimed to have invented the Mai Tai (p 449), the second being his contemporary and rival, Donn Beach (better known as "Don the Beachcomber").

The North Side Special first appeared in *Trader Vic's Book of Food & Drink* in 1946. Bergeron notes that the cocktail was made famous at the Myrtle Bank Hotel in Kingston, Jamaica, in the 1920s. The Myrtle Bank was one of the largest Jamaican hotels at the time, owned by the United Fruit Company and designed to attract the affluent passengers travelling to and from the West Indies in 'banana boats' – refrigerated ships originally designed to transport bananas to North America and Europe without spoiling.

Jamaican dark rum brings its signature funk and complex fruit notes, attributed to traditional production methods, such as a longer fermentation process, together with the use of dunder, an acidic mix of leftover yeast and cultures from previous distillations, unique to each distillery. Notes of tropical fruits, molasses, berries and spice from this rich spirit combine with freshly squeezed (and strained) orange juice to create a vibrant citrus cocktail that's something special indeed. You can easily give the drink a different palate weight and mouthfeel by switching up the style of rum, or even adding a splash of coconut cream or grenadine.

Northside Special (left), Highlander Highball (right)

Collins

VODKA

Asta Collins
Toby Maloney, The Violet Hour, 2007
2 oz (60 ml) vodka
¼ oz (7 ml) Campari
1 oz (30 ml) pink grapefruit juice
¾ oz (22 ml) lime juice
¾ oz (22 ml) simple syrup
Soda, to top
Garnish: lime wheel

Cider with Rosie
Pete Kendall, The Player, London, 2005
¾ oz (22 ml) vodka
½ oz (15 ml) dry vermouth
½ oz (15 ml) sweet vermouth
1 oz (30 ml) Red Gala apple juice
½ oz (15 ml) lemon juice
½ oz (15 ml) simple syrup
Soda, to top
Garnish: apple fan

Dear Prudence
Joaquín Simó, Pouring Ribbons, NYC
2 oz (60 ml) vodka
1 oz (30 ml) pink grapefruit juice
¾ oz (22 ml) raspberry syrup (p 500)
½ oz (15 ml) lemon juice
1 dash Peychaud's Aromatic Cocktail Bitters
Soda, to top

Harvey Wallbanger Collins
Michael Madrusan, The Everleigh, Melbourne, 2025
2 oz (60 ml) vodka
1½ oz (45 ml) orange juice
½ oz (15 ml) lemon juice
¼ oz (7 ml) simple syrup
2 drops saline solution (p 493)
½ oz (15 ml) Galliano L'Autentico, to float
Soda, to top
Add all ingredients to a shaker, then cube whip, pour into a frozen Collins glass with ice, float Galliano L'Autentico and top with soda.
Garnish: orange half-wheel

Park Side Fizz
Jim Meehan, Gramercy Tavern, NYC, 2005
2 oz (60 ml) vodka
¾ oz (22 ml) lemon juice
½ oz (15 ml) orgeat
6–8 mint leaves
Soda, to top
Add all ingredients except soda to a shaker and shake briefly. Strain into a frozen Collins glass with ice and top with soda.
Garnish: mint sprig

White Lie
Kimberly Lamb, The Everleigh, Melbourne, 2022
1¼ oz (37 ml) vodka
¾ oz (22 ml) Italicus Rosolio di Bergamotto
1 oz (30 ml) pink grapefruit juice
½ oz (15 ml) lemon juice
¼ oz (7 ml) simple syrup
2 cucumber wheels
Soda, to top
Press cucumber with simple syrup, add remaining ingredients, then shake briefly with ice, strain into a frozen Collins glass with ice and top with soda.
Garnish: cucumber fan

GIN & GENEVER

Abrikoos Collins
Karin Stanley, Dutch Kills, NYC
1½ oz (45 ml) genever
¾ oz (22 ml) lemon juice
½ oz (15 ml) apricot liqueur
½ oz (15 ml) simple syrup
Soda, to top

Bicycle Thief
Zachary Gelnaw-Rubin and Abraham Hawkins, Dutch Kills, NYC, 2012
1 oz (30 ml) gin
1 oz (30 ml) Campari
1½ oz (45 ml) pink grapefruit juice
½ oz (15 ml) lemon juice
½ oz (15 ml) simple syrup
Soda, to top
Garnish: grapefruit half-wheel

Bitter Collins
Vincenzo Errico, Forio d'Ischia, 2009
2 oz (60 ml) gin
½ oz (15 ml) Campari
1 oz (30 ml) pink grapefruit juice
1 oz (30 ml) lemon juice
¾ oz (22 ml) simple syrup
Soda, to top
Garnish: grapefruit half-wheel

Cádiz Collins
Alex Day, Death & Co, NYC, 2008
2 oz (60 ml) gin
¾ oz (22 ml) Amontillado Sherry
½ oz (15 ml) lemon juice
½ oz (15 ml) Demerara syrup (p 495)
3 dashes Fee Brothers Gin Barrel-Aged Orange Bitters
1 orange half-wheel
Soda, to top
Muddle orange with Demerara syrup, add remaining ingredients, then shake briefly with ice, strain into a frozen Collins glass with ice and top with soda.
Garnish: orange wedge

Carlsbad Cooler
Anthony Schmidt, Noble Experiment, San Diego, 2012
1 oz (30 ml) gin
1 oz (30 ml) Cocchi Americano
¾ oz (22 ml) lemon juice
¾ oz (22 ml) simple syrup
2 strawberries
Soda, to top
Muddle strawberries with simple syrup, add remaining ingredients, then shake briefly with ice, strain into a frozen Collins glass with ice and top with soda.
Garnish: strawberry

Collect Call
Rob Libecans, Melbourne, 2018
1½ oz (45 ml) gin
½ oz (15 ml) Fino Sherry
¾ oz (22 ml) lemon juice
¼ oz (7 ml) simple syrup
2 dashes orange bitters
Soda, to top
Garnish: grapefruit twist

Add all ingredients except soda to a shaker and cube whip. Pour into a frozen Collins glass with ice and top with soda.

Daydreaming
Bianca Wendt, Bar Que Sera, Sawtell, 2024
1½ oz (45 ml) gin
¾ oz (22 ml) Lillet Blanc
¾ oz (22 ml) lemon juice
½ oz (15 ml) simple syrup
3 raspberries
Soda, to top
Muddle raspberries with simple syrup, add remaining ingredients, then shake briefly with ice, strain into a frozen Collins glass with ice and top with soda.
Garnish: raspberry

Dr. Fink
(aka **Hays Collins** or Tom Collins with absinthe)
Trader Vic's Bartender's Guide, *Trader Vic, 1947*
2 oz (60 ml) gin
¾ oz (22 ml) lemon juice
¾ oz (22 ml) simple syrup
3 dashes absinthe
Soda, to top
Garnish: lemon wedge

Eagle Eye Collins
Oscar Shaw, The Everleigh, Melbourne, 2022
1½ oz (45 ml) gin
½ oz (15 ml) Fino Sherry
¾ oz (22 ml) lemon juice
⅜ oz (11 ml) passionfruit syrup (p 499)
⅜ oz (11 ml) simple syrup
Soda, to top
Garnish: lemon wedge

From *The Gentleman's Companion* (1939):

May you live as long as you want and never want as long as you live.

Easy Street
Anthony Schmidt, Noble Experiment, San Diego, 2010
1½ oz (45 ml) gin
¾ oz (22 ml) St Germain Elderflower Liqueur
¾ oz (22 ml) lemon juice
¼ oz (7 ml) simple syrup
2 cucumber wheels
Soda, to top
Press cucumber with simple syrup, add remaining ingredients, then shake briefly with ice, strain into a frozen Collins glass with ice and top with soda.
Garnish: cucumber fan

First Rodeo
Kathryn "Pepper" Stashek, Attaboy, NYC, 2017
1 oz (30 ml) gin
1 oz (30 ml) Cocchi Americano
1½ oz (45 ml) pink grapefruit juice
½ oz (15 ml) lemon juice
½ oz (15 ml) simple syrup
Soda, to top
Garnish: orange half-wheel

Fort Tilden Cooler
Andrew Rice, Attaboy, NYC, 2017
1 oz (30 ml) gin
1 oz (30 ml) Fino Sherry
¾ oz (22 ml) lemon juice
¾ oz (22 ml) simple syrup
2 dashes absinthe
Soda, to top
Garnish: orange twist

Hawksmoor Collins
Hawksmoor, London
1½ oz (45 ml) gin
½ oz (15 ml) Campari
¾ oz (22 ml) lemon juice
½ oz (15 ml) simple syrup
2 dashes orange bitters
Soda, to top
Garnish: grapefruit half-wheel

Jasmine's Cooler
(aka **Jasmine Collins**)
Michael Madrusan, The Everleigh, Melbourne, 2016
¾ oz (22 ml) gin
¾ oz (22 ml) Campari
½ oz (15 ml) triple sec
¾ oz (22 ml) lemon juice
1 teaspoon (5 ml) simple syrup
Soda, to top
Garnish: lemon half-wheel
▼ A 2016 adaptation of Paul Harrington's beloved cocktail, the Jasmine (p 192).

John Collins
(aka **Genever Collins**)
New and Improved Bartender's Manual, *Harry Johnson, 1882*
2 oz (60 ml) genever
¾ oz (22 ml) lemon juice
¾ oz (22 ml) simple syrup
Soda, to top
Garnish: orange half-wheel and cherry

Kinsale Cooler
Eryn Reece, Death & Co, NYC, 2014
1 oz (30 ml) Tanqueray No. 10 Gin
1 oz (30 ml) Manzanilla Sherry
½ oz (15 ml) Suze
½ oz (15 ml) St Germain Elderflower Liqueur
¾ oz (22 ml) lemon juice
½ oz (15 ml) simple syrup
1 dash celery bitters
Soda, to top
Garnish: lemon half-wheel

New Wave
Alicia Perry and Leigh Lacap, Starlite, San Diego, 2024
1½ oz (45 ml) navy strength gin (preferably Plymouth Navy Strength Gin)
¼ oz (7 ml) Giffard Crème do Pamplemousse Rose
1¼ oz (37 ml) fruit cup syrup (p 496)
¾ oz (22 ml) lemon juice
Soda, to top
Garnish: grapefruit twist

Add all ingredients except soda to a shaker and cube whip. Pour into a frozen Collins glass with ice and top with soda.

Noon & Night
Felix Woods, Black Pearl, Melbourne, 2022
1 oz (30 ml) gin
½ oz (15 ml) Cognac
¼ oz (7 ml) Giffard Crème de Pêche de Vigne
¾ oz (22 ml) lemon juice
½ oz (15 ml) simple syrup
Tonic water, to top
Garnish: grapefruit half-wheel

Piedmont Fizz
Leo Robitschek, The NoMad Bar, NYC
1 oz (30 ml) gin
1 oz (30 ml) Cocchi Americano
¾ oz (22 ml) lemon juice
¾ oz (22 ml) simple syrup
¼ oz (7 ml) absinthe, to float
Soda, to top
Add all ingredients to a shaker, then cube whip and pour into a frozen Collins glass with ice, float absinthe and top with soda.
Garnish: lemon half-wheel

Polka Dot Collins
(Tom Collins with blueberries and orange bitters)
David Molyneux, The Everleigh, Melbourne, 2015
2 oz (60 ml) gin
¾ oz (22 ml) lemon juice
¾ oz (22 ml) simple syrup
2 dashes orange bitters
6 blueberries
Soda, to top
Muddle blueberries with simple syrup, add remaining ingredients, then shake briefly with ice, strain into a frozen Collins glass with ice and top with soda.
Garnish: blueberry and lemon half-wheel

Roman Cooler
Jones' Complete Barguide, *Stan Jones, 1977*
1 oz (30 ml) gin
1 oz (30 ml) sweet vermouth
¾ oz (22 ml) lemon juice
½ oz (15 ml) simple syrup
Soda, to top
Garnish: lemon horse's neck

Saint Helena
Felix Woods, Black Pearl, Melbourne, 2022
1 oz (30 ml) gin
½ oz (15 ml) Islay Scotch
¾ oz (22 ml) lemon juice
¾ oz (22 ml) simple syrup
1 teaspoon (5 ml) Poire Williams
2 dashes absinthe
Soda, to top
Garnish: lemon wedge and a pinch of salt flakes

Shifting Sands
Sasha Petraske, Milk & Honey, NYC, 2009
1½ oz (45 ml) gin
¼ oz (7 ml) maraschino liqueur
1½ oz (45 ml) pink grapefruit juice
½ oz (15 ml) lemon juice
¼ oz (7 ml) simple syrup
Soda, to top
Garnish: grapefruit half-wheel and cherry

Special for Widows
What'll You Have?, *Julien J. Proskauer, 1933*
1½ oz (45 ml) gin
½ oz (15 ml) Bénédictine
¾ oz (22 ml) lemon juice
¾ oz (22 ml) simple syrup
Soda, to top
Garnish: orange half-wheel and cherry

Stay Up Very Late
(Stay Up Late with absinthe)
Michael Madrusan, Little Branch, NYC, 2008
1½ oz (45 ml) gin
½ oz (15 ml) Cognac
¾ oz (22 ml) lemon juice
¾ oz (22 ml) simple syrup
3 dashes absinthe
Soda, to top
Garnish: lemon wedge

Tarzan
Zachary Gelnaw-Rubin, Attaboy, NYC, 2012
1 oz (30 ml) gin
1 oz (30 ml) Campari
1½ oz (45 ml) pineapple juice
½ oz (15 ml) lemon juice
½ oz (15 ml) simple syrup
Soda, to top
Garnish: orange wedge

Texas Fizz
(Tom Collins with orange juice)
The Art of Mixing, *James A. Wiley and Helene M. Griffith, 1932*
2 oz (60 ml) gin
1½ oz (45 ml) orange juice
½ oz (15 ml) lemon juice
½ oz (15 ml) simple syrup
Soda, to top
Garnish: orange half-wheel garnish

Tiffany Collins
Zachary Pease, Attaboy, NYC, 2016
1 oz (30 ml) gin
½ oz (15 ml) Suze
½ oz (15 ml) triple sec
¾ oz (22 ml) lemon juice
¾ oz (22 ml) simple syrup
Soda, to top
Garnish: lemon wedge

Tom Collins
(aka **Gin Twist** in *The Gentleman's Table Guide*, E. Ricket and C. Thomas, 1871)
The Bar-Tender's Guide, *Jerry Thomas, 1876*
2 oz (60 ml) gin
¾ oz (22 ml) lemon juice
¾ oz (22 ml) simple syrup
Soda, to top
Garnish: orange wedge and cherry

Add all ingredients except soda to a shaker and cube whip. Pour into a frozen Collins glass with ice and top with soda.

Trouble Man
Oliver Churcher, Double Deuce Lounge, Sydney, 2021
1 oz (30 ml) gin
1 oz (30 ml) bianco vermouth
¾ oz (22 ml) lemon juice
¾ oz (22 ml) simple syrup
3 cucumber wheels
3 raspberries
Soda, to top
Press cucumber and raspberries with simple syrup, add remaining ingredients, then shake briefly with ice, strain into a frozen Collins glass with ice and top with soda.
Garnish: 2 cucumber wheels and a raspberry

Troublemaker
Danny Gil, Attaboy, NYC, 2012
1 oz (30 ml) gin
1 oz (30 ml) sweet vermouth
¾ oz (22 ml) lemon juice
¾ oz (22 ml) simple syrup
2 cucumber wheels
1 strawberry, halved
Soda, to top
Press cucumber and strawberry with simple syrup, add remaining ingredients, then shake briefly with ice, strain into a frozen Collins glass with ice and top with soda.
Garnish: cucumber wheel and strawberry half

Unicorn Tears
Sam Ross, Electra Cocktail Club, Las Vegas, 2018
1 oz (30 ml) gin
1 oz (30 ml) Fino Sherry
1 oz (30 ml) pineapple juice
½ oz (15 ml) lemon juice
½ oz (15 ml) simple syrup
1 dash absinthe
2 cucumber wheels
Soda, to top
Press cucumber with simple syrup, add remaining ingredients, then shake briefly with ice, strain into a frozen Collins glass with ice and top with soda.
Garnish: cucumber fan

Yarra Valley Cooler
Sam Ross, Attaboy, NYC, 2019
1 oz (30 ml) gin
1 oz (30 ml) Cocchi Americano
¾ oz (22 ml) lemon juice
¾ oz (22 ml) simple syrup
3 dashes absinthe
2 cucumber wheels
Soda, top
Press cucumber with simple syrup, add remaining ingredients, then shake briefly with ice, strain into a frozen Collins glass with ice and top with soda.
Garnish: lemon wedge

RUM & CANE SPIRIT

Durkee
The World's Drinks and How to Mix Them, *Wm. T. Boothby, 1908*
2 oz (60 ml) Jamaican dark rum
¾ oz (22 ml) orange curaçao (p 498)
¾ oz (22 ml) lemon juice
Soda, to top
Garnish: orange half-wheel and cherry

Fisherman's Prayer
(Light Rum Collins with raspberry)
Bariana, *Louis Fouquet, 1896*
2 oz (60 ml) light rum
¾ oz (22 ml) lemon juice
¾ oz (22 ml) simple syrup
3 raspberries
Soda, to top
Muddle raspberries with simple syrup, add remaining ingredients, then shake briefly with ice, strain into a frozen Collins glass with ice and top with soda.
Garnish: lemon half-wheel and raspberry

FLD Fizz
Sam Ross, Milk & Honey, NYC, 2005
2 oz (60 ml) aged dark rum
1½ oz (45 ml) pineapple juice
½ oz (15 ml) lemon juice
½ oz (15 ml) simple syrup
2 dashes Angostura Bitters
Soda, to top
Garnish: pineapple fronds

Midnight Cooler
Benjamin Baxter, Bar Margaux, Melbourne, 2021
1¾ oz (52 ml) light rum
¾ oz (22 ml) lemon juice
¾ oz (22 ml) simple syrup
3 dashes absinthe
2 blackberries
Soda, to top
Muddle blackberries with simple syrup, add the remaining ingredients, then shake briefly with ice, strain into a frozen Collins glass with ice and top with soda.
Garnish: blackberry

Morning Cooler
American Bar, *Frank P. Newman, 1900*
2 oz (60 ml) light rum
¾ oz (22 ml) orange curaçao (p 498)
¾ oz (22 ml) lemon juice
Soda, to top
Garnish: orange half-wheel and cherry

Pedro Collins
(aka **Light Rum Collins**)
The Fine Art of Mixing Drinks, *David A. Embury, 1948*
2 oz (60 ml) light rum
¾ oz (22 ml) lemon juice
¾ oz (22 ml) simple syrup
Soda, to top
Garnish: orange wedge and cherry

Razzmatazz
Elijah Harriss, The Everleigh, Melbourne, 2023
1 oz (30 ml) Jamaican dark rum
1 oz (30 ml Amaro Ramazzotti
¾ oz (22 ml) lemon juice
½ oz (15 ml) simple syrup
1 teaspoon (5 ml) passionfruit syrup (p 499)
2 dashes Angostura Bitters
Soda, to top
Garnish: lemon wedge

Add all ingredients except soda to a shaker and cube whip. Pour into a frozen Collins glass with ice and top with soda.

South Side Special
(aka **Jamaican Dark Rum Collins**)
The Fine Art of Mixing Drinks,
David A. Embury, 1948
2 oz (60 ml) Jamaican dark rum
¾ oz (22 ml) lemon juice
¾ oz (22 ml) simple syrup
Soda, to top
Garnish: orange wedge and cherry

Warwick Cooler
Michael McCollum, Attaboy, Nashville, 2018
1½ oz (45 ml) Goslings Black Seal Rum
½ oz (15 ml) Amaro di Angostura
¾ oz (22 ml) lemon juice
¾ oz (22 ml) simple syrup
1 orange wedge
Press orange wedge with simple syrup, add remaining ingredients, then shake briefly with ice, strain into a frozen Collins glass with ice and top with soda.
Soda, to top
Garnish: orange wedge

AGAVE

Freddy Fudpucker Collins
Michael Madrusan, Heartbreaker, Melbourne, 2024
2 oz (60 ml) blanco tequila
½ oz (15 ml) Galliano L'Autentico
1½ oz (45 ml) orange juice
½ oz (15 ml) lemon juice
¼ oz (7 ml) simple syrup
2 drops saline solution (p 493)
Soda, to top
Garnish: orange wedge
▼ Adapted from the original mixed drink of the same name by Donato "Duke" Antone from the 1960s.

Paris, Texas
Kathryn "Pepper" Stashek, Attaboy, NYC, 2017
1 oz (30 ml) blanco tequila
1 oz (30 ml) Cocchi Americano
1 oz (30 ml) pink grapefruit juice
½ oz (15 ml) lemon juice
½ oz (15 ml) simple syrup
3 dashes Peychaud's Aromatic Cocktail Bitters, to float
Soda, to top
Add all ingredients to a shaker, then shake with ice, strain into a frozen Collins glass with ice, float bitters and top with soda.
Garnish: orange half-wheel

Rodeo Queen
Luke Kelly, The Everleigh, Melbourne, 2023
1 oz (30 ml) mezcal
1 oz (30 ml) Aperol
1 oz (30 ml) pink grapefruit juice
½ oz (15 ml) lemon juice
½ oz (15 ml) simple syrup
Soda, to top
Garnish: orange half-wheel

The Long Shot
Julian de Féral, Milk & Honey, London, 2007
1½ oz (45 ml) reposado tequila
½ oz (15 ml) orange curaçao (p 498)
¾ oz (22 ml) lemon juice
¼ oz (7 ml) simple syrup
2 dashes Angostura Bitters
Soda, to top
Garnish: orange and lemon half-wheel

BRANDY

Alabazam
American & Other Drinks,
Leo Engel, 1878
1½ oz (45 ml) Cognac
¾ oz (22 ml) Pierre Ferrand Dry Curaçao
¾ oz (22 ml) lemon juice
½ oz (15 ml) simple syrup
3 dashes Angostura Bitters
Soda, to float
Garnish: orange half-wheel and cherry

Black-Eyed Susan
Jayne's Bartender's Guide, *1934*
2 oz (60 ml) Cognac
½ oz (15 ml) Jamaican dark rum
¾ oz (22 ml) orange curaçao (p 498)
¾ oz (22 ml) lemon juice
Soda, to top
Garnish: lemon wedge

Charlie Collins
John Hallet, The Everleigh, Melbourne, 2023
1 oz (30 ml) bonded apple brandy
1 oz (30 ml) Amaro Meletti
¾ oz (22 ml) lemon juice
½ oz (15 ml) simple syrup
Soda, to top
Garnish: orange half-wheel and cherry

Golden Harvest
Paul Hammond and Priscilla Leong
¾ oz (22 ml) bonded apple brandy
¾ oz (22 ml) rye whiskey
¼ oz (7 ml) apricot brandy
1½ oz (45 ml) pineapple juice
½ oz (15 ml) lemon juice
⅜ oz (11 ml) honey syrup (p 496)
2 dashes Angostura Bitters
Soda, to top
Garnish: lemon half-wheel

Grand Prix
Elijah Harriss, The Everleigh, Melbourne, 2023
1½ oz (45 ml) Cognac
½ oz (15 ml) Tempus Fugit Gran Classico Bitter
¾ oz (22 ml) lemon juice
¾ oz (22 ml) simple syrup
2 dashes orange bitters
3 red grapes
Soda, to top
Press grapes with simple syrup, add remaining ingredients, then shake briefly with ice, strain into a frozen Collins glass with ice and top with soda.
Garnish: orange half-wheel and cherry

Add all ingredients except soda to a shaker and cube whip. Pour into a frozen Collins glass with ice and top with soda.

Jack Collins
(aka **Moonlight** or **Applejack Collins**)
The Fine Art of Mixing Drinks, *David A. Embury, 1948*
2 oz (60 ml) bonded apple brandy
¾ oz (22 ml) lemon juice
¾ oz (22 ml) simple syrup
Soda, to top
Garnish: orange half-wheel and cherry

Old Chum's Reviver
(Pierre Collins with strawberry)
Recipes of American and Other Iced Drinks, *Charlie Paul, 1902*
2 oz (60 ml) Cognac
¾ oz (22 ml) lemon juice
¾ oz (22 ml) simple syrup
1 strawberry, halved
Soda, to top
Muddle strawberries with simple syrup, add remaining ingredients, then shake briefly with ice, strain into a frozen Collins glass with ice and top with soda.
Garnish: lemon half-wheel and strawberry

Pierre Collins
(aka **Cognac Collins**)
The Fine Art of Mixing Drinks, *David A. Embury, 1948*
2 oz (60 ml) Cognac
¾ oz (22 ml) lemon juice
¾ oz (22 ml) simple syrup
Soda, to top
Garnish: lemon half-wheel and cherry

Pisces Rising
Spirits of Latin America, *Ivy Mix, 2020*
1½ oz (45 ml) pisco
½ oz (15 ml) Manzanilla Sherry
½ oz (15 ml) lemon juice
½ oz (15 ml) pink grapefruit juice
½ oz (15 ml) simple syrup
½ teaspoon (2.5 ml) Giffard Crème de Pêche de Vigne
2 dashes celery bitters
Soda, to top
Garnish: grapefruit half-wheel garnish

AMERICAN WHISKEY

Bizzy Izzy Highball
The Ideal Bartender, *Tom Bullock, 1917*
1 oz (30 ml) rye whiskey
1 oz (30 ml) Amontillado Sherry
1 oz (30 ml) pineapple juice
½ oz (15 ml) lemon juice
½ oz (15 ml) simple syrup
Soda, to top
Garnish: orange half-wheel and cherry

California Lemonade
Old Mr. Boston Deluxe Official Bartender's Guide, *Leo Cotton, 1935*
2 oz (60 ml) bourbon
¾ oz (22 ml) grenadine (p 496)
⅜ oz (11 ml) lemon juice
⅜ oz (11 ml) lime juice
Soda, to top
Garnish: lemon wedge

Colonel Collins
(aka **Bourbon Collins**)
The Fine Art of Mixing Drinks, *David A. Embury, 1948*
2 oz (60 ml) bourbon
¾ oz (22 ml) lemon juice
¾ oz (22 ml) simple syrup
Soda, to top
Garnish: orange half-wheel and cherry

Evening Cooler
Jakob Etzold, The Everleigh, Melbourne, 2015
1½ oz (45 ml) bourbon
½ oz (15 ml) tawny Port
¾ oz (22 ml) lemon juice
¾ oz (22 ml) simple syrup
Soda, to top
Garnish: orange half-wheel and freshly grated nutmeg

Hunting Party
Paul Hammond
1¼ oz (37 ml) Jack Daniel's Old No. 7 Tennessee Whiskey
¼ oz (7 ml) Giffard Banane du Brésil et des Caraïbes
1½ oz (45 ml) pineapple juice
½ oz (15 ml) lemon juice
⅜ oz (11 ml) falernum
2 dashes Angostura Bitters
Soda, to top
Garnish: 2 pineapple fronds

Kentucky Cooler
Abraham Holder, The Everleigh, Melbourne, 2019
1 oz (30 ml) bourbon
1 oz (30 ml) Fino Sherry
1½ oz (45 ml) white grapefruit juice
½ oz (15 ml) lemon juice
½ oz (15 ml) simple syrup
Soda, to top
Garnish: white grapefruit half-wheel and cherry

Lynchburg Lemonade
Tony Mason, 1980
1⅜ oz (41 ml) Jack Daniel's Old No. 7 Tennessee Whiskey
¾ oz (22 ml) triple sec
⅜ oz (11 ml) lemon juice
⅜ oz (11 ml) lime juice
Soda, to top
Garnish: lemon wedge

Lynchburg Lemonade
Daly's Bartenders' Encyclopedia, *Tim Daly, 1903*
2 oz (60 ml) bourbon
¾ oz (22 ml) lemon juice
¾ oz (22 ml) simple syrup
2 dashes Angostura Bitters
2 dashes absinthe
Soda, to top
Garnish: lemon wedge

Add all ingredients except soda to a shaker and cube whip. Pour into a frozen Collins glass with ice and top with soda.

Razzle Dazzle
Felix Woods, Romeo Lane, Melbourne, 2019
1½ oz (45 ml) rye whiskey
¾ oz (22 ml) lemon juice
¾ oz (22 ml) simple syrup
1 teaspoon (5 ml) pastis
3 raspberries
Soda, to top
Muddle raspberries with simple syrup, add remaining ingredients, then shake briefly with ice, strain into a frozen Collins glass with ice and top with soda.
Garnish: mint sprig

Ross Collins
Sam Ross, Milk & Honey, NYC, 2007
2 oz (60 ml) rye whiskey
¾ oz (22 ml) lemon juice
¾ oz (22 ml) simple syrup
1 orange wedge
Soda, to top
5 dashes Angostura Bitters, to float
Press orange wedge with simple syrup, add remaining ingredients, then shake briefly with ice, strain into a frozen Collins glass with ice, float bitters and top with soda.
Garnish: orange half-wheel

Steady Hand
Andrew Cordero, Seneca, San Diego, 2022
1 oz (30 ml) bourbon
½ oz (15 ml) Campari
½ oz (15 ml) sweet vermouth
¾ oz (22 ml) lemon juice
¾ oz (22 ml) simple syrup
1 dash chocolate bitters
Soda, to top
Garnish: orange twist

Tongue & Cheek
Toby Maloney, The Violet Hour, Chicago, 2009
1½ oz (45 ml) bourbon
¾ oz (22 ml) sweet vermouth
¾ oz (22 ml) lemon juice
¾ oz (22 ml) simple syrup
1 strawberry, halved
Soda, to top
Muddle strawberry with simple syrup, add remaining ingredients, then shake briefly with ice, strain into a frozen Collins glass with ice and top with soda.
Garnish: mint sprig

SCOTCH

Morning Reviver
(Sandy Collins with absinthe and Angostura Bitters)
Daly's Bartenders' Encyclopedia, *Tim Daly, 1903*
2 oz (60 ml) Scotch
¾ oz (22 ml) lemon juice
¾ oz (22 ml) simple syrup
2 dashes absinthe
2 dashes Angostura Bitters
Soda, to top
Garnish: lemon wedge

Napoleon's Own
Bariana, *Louis Fouquet, 1896*
1 oz (30 ml) Scotch
1 oz (30 ml) gin
¾ oz (22 ml) lemon juice
¾ oz (22 ml) simple syrup
Soda, to top
Garnish: lemon wedge

Sandy Collins
(aka **Scotch Collins**)
Here's How: Mixed Drinks, *W. C. Whitfield, 1941*
2 oz (60 ml) Scotch
¾ oz (22 ml) lemon juice
¾ oz (22 ml) simple syrup
Soda, to top
Garnish: orange wedge and cherry

Tall, Dark & Then Some
Michael Madrusan, Bar Margaux, Melbourne, 2019
1½ oz (45 ml) Scotch
¾ oz (22 ml) Pommeau de Normandie
¾ oz (22 ml) lemon juice
½ oz (15 ml) simple syrup
3 dashes absinthe
Soda, to top
Garnish: lemon wedge and cherry

The Braver
Good Things to Drink with Mr. Lyan & Friends, *Ryan Chetiyawardana, 2015*
1½ oz (45 ml) Scotch
⅓ oz (10 ml) triple sec
½ oz (15 ml) simple syrup
½ oz (15 ml) lemon juice
⅓ oz (10 ml) lime juice
4 dashes absinthe
1 dash Angostura Bitters
3 mint leaves
Soda, to top
Garnish: lemon twist

Ultimatum
Will Shearman, The Everleigh, Melbourne, 2023
1 oz (30 ml) Scotch
1 oz (30 ml) Amaro Braulio
1 oz (30 ml) lemon juice
¾ oz (22 ml) simple syrup
3 raspberries
Soda, to top
Muddle raspberries with simple syrup, add remaining ingredients, then shake briefly with ice, strain into a frozen Collins glass with ice and top with soda.
Garnish: orange half-wheel and raspberry

Add all ingredients except soda to a shaker and cube whip. Pour into a frozen Collins glass with ice and top with soda.

WORLD WHISK(E)Y

Mike Collins
(aka **Irish Whiskey Collins**)
The Fine Art of Mixing Drinks,
David A. Embury, 1948
2 oz (60 ml) Irish whiskey
¾ oz (22 ml) lemon juice
¾ oz (22 ml) simple syrup
Soda, to top
Garnish: orange wedge and cherry

FORTIFIED & LIQUEUR

Artful Dodger
Angus Payne, The Everleigh, Melbourne, 2021
2 oz (60 ml) Amontillado Sherry
1½ oz (45 ml) pineapple juice
½ oz (15 ml) lemon juice
½ oz (15 ml) falernum
2 dashes orange bitters
Soda, to top
Garnish: 2 pineapple fronds

Bambino
Greg Keesee, Attaboy, Nashville
1½ oz (45 ml) Fino Sherry
1 oz (30 ml) pineapple juice
½ oz (15 ml) Giffard Banane du Brésil et des Caraïbes
½ oz (15 ml) lemon juice
½ oz (15 ml) simple syrup
Soda, to top
Garnish: orange wedge

Rebujito
Andalusia, Spain
2 oz (60 ml) Fino Sherry
¾ oz (22 ml) lemon juice
¾ oz (22 ml) simple syrup
Soda, to top
Garnish: orange wedge and cherry

Blackbriar
Will Shearman, The Everleigh, Melbourne, 2022
1½ oz (45 ml) Cynar
⅜ oz (11 ml) apricot brandy
¾ oz (22 ml) lemon juice
⅜ oz (11 ml) simple syrup
2 dashes orange bitters
2 blackberries
Soda, to top
Muddle blackberries with simple syrup, add remaining ingredients, then shake briefly with ice, strain into a frozen Collins glass with ice and top with soda.
Garnish: orange half-wheel and blackberry

Late Check Out
Luke Kelly, The Everleigh, Melbourne, 2023
2 oz (60 ml) dry vermouth
¾ oz (22 ml) lemon juice
¾ oz (22 ml) simple syrup
3 dashes absinthe
Soda, to top
Garnish: lemon wedge and Cerignola olive

Mendoza Line
Sam Ross, Attaboy, NYC, 2017
1½ oz (45 ml) Amontillado Sherry
½ oz (15 ml) apricot brandy
¾ oz (22 ml) lemon juice
¾ oz (22 ml) simple syrup
Soda, to top
Garnish: orange wedge

Seven Hills
(See p 418)

Tomasu Collins
Liana Oster, Side Hustle, London, 2022
2 oz (60 ml) yuzushu
1 oz (30 ml) blanco tequila
½ oz (15 ml) honey syrup (p 496)
¼ oz (7 ml) lemon juice
Soda, to top

OTHER

Naive Melody
Ewan Bennie, Part Time Lover, San Diego, 2022
1 oz (30 ml) shochu
¾ oz (22 ml) pear brandy
¼ oz (7 ml) blanc vermouth
¾ oz (22 ml) lemon juice
¾ oz (22 ml) simple syrup
Soda, to top
Garnish: pear fan

From *The Gentleman's Companion* (1939):

There are two kinds of people: those who drink good cocktails and those who wish they did.

Add all ingredients except soda to a shaker and cube whip. Pour into a frozen Collins glass with ice and top with soda.

RICKEY

Rickey

Rickey

A long, cooling cocktail characterised by fresh lime, served tall and lengthened with soda.

spirit + lime + sugar + soda

Add all ingredients to a shaker and cube whip. Pour into a frozen Collins glass with ice and top with soda.

Traditionally a Whiskey or Gin Highball invigorated with a squeeze of fresh lime, the Rickey originated in Washington D.C. in the 1880s at a bar called Shoomaker's. The story goes that a lobbyist from Missouri, Colonel Joseph Rickey, came up with the idea for the simple, spirited drink when chatting to a friend in the carbonated water business. Rickey then took the idea to George Williamson – the head bartender at "Shoo's", as it was known – who assisted in showcasing the new drink to the bar's loyal patrons. It is said that Rickey preferred his whiskey-based cocktail with lemon rather than lime, but ultimately Williamson was the one cutting the fruit. The lime version, referred to by the locals as a Joe Rickey, became very popular at Shoo's, and by 1889 the nation's capital was awash with Rickeys. It wasn't long before the rest of the country followed suit.

Initially, whiskey was the Rickey's most popular base spirit, but the Gin Rickey had firmly taken over by the turn of the 20th century, enjoying many summers of success as an unrivalled refresher across the United States. Only a handful of years later, however, the Rickey became obsolete, besides perhaps in D.C., where it was declared the official native cocktail in 2011 by the city council.

The Rickey is a close relative of the Collins (p 62), which follows the same formula but uses lemon instead of lime. Like other cocktail branches that specify lime, such as Gimlet (p 206), this chapter includes a generous collection of agave-based options, a Rickey subcategory that is fast evolving thanks to the growing popularity of tequila and mezcal in the 21st century. Don't look past fruit-forward, mezcal cocktail, the Cantaloupe Paloma (p 87), or aperitivo-style tequila cocktail, the Fancy Paloma (p 87).

Whiskey Freezer

(aka **Bourbon Mint Rickey**)
The Standard Cocktail Guide, *Crosby Gaige, 1944*
2 oz (60 ml) bourbon
1 oz (30 ml) lime juice
¾ oz (22 ml) simple syrup
6–8 mint leaves
Soda, to top

Add all ingredients except soda to a shaker, shake briefly with ice, then strain into a frozen Collins glass with ice and top with soda.
Garnish: mint bouquet

The Whisky Freezer, a bourbon-based Rickey with fresh mint, made its first appearance in *The Standard Cocktail Guide* by Crosby Gaige, published in 1944. Gaige – a prominent theatre producer, author and socialite – was born in Nelson, New York, in 1882 and received an Ivy League education at Columbia University. Throughout his career, he served as chairman of New York City's Wine and Food Society, wrote for *The New York Times* and produced several Broadway shows, making him central to New York City's media scene in the mid-20th century. Celebrated writer and bon vivant Lucius Beebe once wrote of Gaige, his friend and contemporary: 'He is the high priest of spice and seasoning and flavour to these entire United States and their naval bases ... I sometimes think of him as Aristotle or the *Encyclopedia Britannica* or William Lyon Phelps, who have taken all knowledge as their province, or sometimes as just a friend with whom it is pleasant to lunch or dine.'

The Standard Cocktail Guide was Gaige's second book on cocktail culture, preceded by 1941's *Cocktail Guide and Ladies' Companion*. Both these post-Prohibition publications raised the bar for American cocktails substantially, reviving a culture that had been forcibly buried for over a decade. Gaige's guide not only documented the bar basics of the Waldorf Astoria's famous glass service but also commented on the philosophy of drinking and the art of sociability in the day and age of World War II.

Like many of the greats, the Whiskey Freezer succeeds for its spellbinding succinctness, with the bourbon and mint combining beautifully to create a warm, soft finish. Our updated recipe, balanced with simple syrup, is reminiscent of Jerry Thomas's classic Whiskey Julep (p 285), spritzed with lime juice and lengthened with soda. Those chasing something similar – albeit shorter, sharper, more citrusy and without ice – should try the Expat (p 222), a minty Shake with bourbon and Angostura Bitters. Scotch fans, meanwhile, might prefer the Smoke & Mirrors (p 223) by Death & Co legend Alex Day: a Shake with Islay Scotch, fresh mint and absinthe served on the rocks.

Rome with a View

Michael McIlroy, Milk & Honey, NYC, 2008
1 oz (30 ml) Campari
1 oz (30 ml) dry vermouth
1 oz (30 ml) lime juice
¾ oz (22 ml) simple syrup
Soda, to top

Add all ingredients to a shaker and cube whip. Pour into a frozen Collins glass with ice and top with soda.
Garnish: orange wedge

One of the true titans of the low-ABV cocktail category, the Rome with a View is the love child of the Rickey and the immortal Italian aperitivo, the Americano, created by our dear friend Michael McIlroy. Born in Belfast in 1982, McIlroy was bartending at The Apartment when he got wind of the incredible influence Sasha Petraske's New York City bar, Milk & Honey, was having on the cocktail world. Ambitious and inspired, McIlroy wrote Petraske a letter asking for a job and, to his surprise, it was returned with an invitation to join the team. McIlroy left home for New York City in 2005 to board and work at Milk & Honey, and remained there for eight years. Following the bar's relocation in 2013, McIlroy and his best friend Sam Ross, with whom he'd worked alongside at Milk & Honey, had the opportunity to reimagine the intimate and iconic Eldridge Street space, transforming it into Attaboy, one of the most celebrated bars in New York City's modern cocktail age.

Like other Milk & Honey alumni, McIlroy was enthused by reinvigorating pre-Prohibition classics with subtle riffs that honoured their simplicity. McIlroy came up with this cocktail in 2008, long before the Euro-inspired Spritz craze of the late 2010s. Customers, he says, would often tell him that they hated bitterness, and he challenged himself to defend the flavour profile, ditching the Americano's sweet vermouth in favour of an equal-parts base of Campari, dry vermouth and lime for a long, bittersweet afternoon drink inspired by the bel paese's pre-dinner ritual.

The Rome with a View feels timeless in its formula, which has no doubt contributed to a degree of global success that shows no sign of slowing down thanks to the growing low- and no-alcohol drinks movement. Similar concoctions include the North Beach Cooler (p 88), a boozier tequila-based riff by Paul Hammond and Priscilla Leong.

Rickey

GIN

Bootstrap Rickey
Cameron Parish, The Everleigh, Melbourne, 2018
1½ oz (45 ml) gin
½ oz (15 ml) Fino Sherry
1 oz (30 ml) lime juice
¾ oz (22 ml) simple syrup
2 dashes absinthe
Soda, to top
Garnish: mint sprig and lime wedge

Brass Hammer
Dan Greenbaum and Sam Ross, Diamond Reef, NYC, 2017
1½ oz (45 ml) gin
½ oz (15 ml) Cynar
1 oz (30 ml) lime juice
¾ oz (22 ml) simple syrup
2 orange wedges
Soda, to top
Press orange wedges with simple syrup, add remaining ingredients, then shake briefly with ice, strain into a frozen Collins glass with ice and top with soda.
Garnish: orange wedge

Chinatown Rickey
Sam Ross, Attaboy, NYC, 2017
1½ oz (45 ml) gin
½ oz (15 ml) Fino Sherry
1 oz (30 ml) lime juice
¾ oz (22 ml) simple syrup
6–8 mint leaves
Soda, to top
Shake all ingredients briefly with ice and strain into a frozen Collins glass with ice, then top with soda.
Garnish: mint bouquet

Circus Rickey
(aka **Pomegranate Rickey**)
The Cocktail Book: A Sideboard Manual for Gentlemen, *Frederic, Lawrence Knowles, 1913*
2 oz (60 ml) gin
¾ oz (22 ml) lime juice
¾ oz (22 ml) grenadine (p 496)
Soda, to top
Garnish: lime wedge

East Side Rickey
Milk & Honey, NYC, 2005
2 oz (60 ml) gin
¾ oz (22 ml) lime juice
¾ oz (22 ml) simple syrup
6–8 mint leaves
2 cucumber wheels
Soda, to top
Press cucumber with simple syrup, add remaining ingredients, then shake briefly with ice and strain into a frozen Collins glass with ice and top with soda.
Garnish: mint sprig and cucumber fan

First Post
Alastair Walker, The Everleigh, Melbourne, 2012
1½ oz (45 ml) gin
½ oz (15 ml) Suze
1 oz (30 ml) lime juice
¾ oz (22 ml) simple syrup
3 dashes absinthe
Soda, to top
Garnish: lime wedge

Gin Rickey
Harry Johnson's New and Improved Illustrated Bartenders' Manual, *1900*
2 oz (60 ml) gin
1 oz (30 ml) lime juice
¾ oz (22 ml) sugar syrup
Soda, to top
Garnish: lime wedge

South Side Rickey
(aka **Mint Rickey**)
2 oz (60 ml) gin
¾ oz (22 ml) lime juice
¾ oz (22 ml) simple syrup
6–8 mint leaves
Soda, to top
Garnish: mint bouquet

Triple Black Diamond
Zachary Gelnaw-Rubin, Lion Lion, NYC, 2019
1 oz (30 ml) gin
1 oz (30 ml) Amaro Braulio
1 oz (30 ml) lime juice
¾ oz (22 ml) simple syrup
Soda, to top
Garnish: lime wedge

Tritter Rickey
(aka **Tritter Fizz**)
Milk & Honey, NYC
2 oz (60 ml) gin
1 oz (30 ml) lime juice
¾ oz (22 ml) simple syrup
6–8 mint leaves
3 dashes absinthe
Soda, to top
Shake all ingredients briefly with ice and strain into a frozen Collins glass with ice, then top with soda.
Garnish: mint bouquet

RUM & CANE SPIRIT

Bird of Paradise
Mitchell Taylor and Brandon Bramhall, Attaboy, Nashville, 2018
1½ oz (45 ml) Jamaican dark rum
½ oz (15 ml) Tempus Fugit Gran Classico Bitter
1½ oz (45 ml) pineapple juice
½ oz (15 ml) lime juice
½ oz (15 ml) simple syrup
Soda, to top
Garnish: 2 pineapple fronds and pinch of salt flakes

Callaloo Cooler
Melissa Garcia
Smuggler's Cove: Exotic Cocktails, Rum and the Cult of Tiki, *Martin and Rebecca Cate, 2016*
2 oz (60 ml) aged dark rum
½ oz (15 ml) Heering Cherry Liqueur
¾ oz (22 ml) lime juice
½ oz (15 ml) cinnamon syrup (p 495)
2 dashes Angostura Bitters
Soda, to top
Garnish: mint bouquet and freshly grated cinnamon

Add all ingredients to a shaker and cube whip. Pour into a frozen Collins glass with ice and top with soda.

Coco de Água
The South American Gentleman's Companion, *Charles H. Baker Jr., 1951*
2 oz (60 ml) light rum
1 oz (30 ml) coconut water
1 oz (30 ml) lime juice
¾ oz (22 ml) simple syrup
Soda, to top
Garnish: 2 pineapple fronds and cherry

Dr. Funk
Trader Vic's Book of Food and Drink, *Trader Vic, 1946*
2 oz (60 ml) aged dark rum
¾ oz (22 ml) lime juice
¾ oz (22 ml) grenadine (p 496)
3 dashes absinthe
Soda, to top
Garnish: lime wedge

Long Weekend
Zachary Gelnaw-Rubin, Lion Lion, NYC, 2017
2 oz (60 ml) aged dark rum
¾ oz (22 ml) lime juice
½ oz (15 ml) orgeat
6–8 mint leaves
Soda, to top
Shake all ingredients briefly with ice and strain into a frozen Collins glass with ice, then top with soda.
Garnish: mint bouquet

Rum Ramsey
Albert Martin
Trader Vic's Book of Food and Drink, *Trader Vic, 1946*
1½ oz (45 ml) aged dark rum
½ oz (15 ml) bourbon
1 oz (30 ml) lime juice
¾ oz (22 ml) simple syrup
2 dashes Peychaud's Aromatic Cocktail Bitters
Garnish: lime wedge

AGAVE

Cantaloupe Paloma
Leo Robitschek, The NoMad Bar, NYC
1 oz (30 ml) mezcal
1½ oz (45 ml) rockmelon (cantaloupe) juice
¾ oz (22 ml) lime juice
¾ oz (22 ml) jasmine-infused agave syrup (p 496)
Soda, to top
Garnish: salt-and-pink-peppercorn rim and grapefruit twist

Casa Montaña
Sam Ross, Attaboy, NYC, 2023
2 oz (60 ml) mezcal
1 oz (30 ml) watermelon juice
½ oz (15 ml) lime juice
½ oz (15 ml) agave syrup (p 494)
2 drops saline solution (p 493)
Soda, to top
Garnish: lime wedge and cherry

El Tucan
Leo Robitschek, The NoMad Bar, NYC
1 oz (30 ml) mezcal
1 oz (30 ml) Dolin Génépi des Alpes
¾ oz (22 ml) lime juice
½ oz (15 ml) pink grapefruit juice
½ oz (15 ml) celery juice
½ oz (15 ml) agave syrup (p 494)
4 dashes Peychaud's Bitters, to float
Soda, to top
Shake all ingredients briefly with ice and strain into a frozen Collins glass with ice, then float bitters and top with soda.
Garnish: salt rim and lime wedge

Fancy Paloma
Naren Young, Sweet Liberty, Miami
1½ oz (45 ml) blanco tequila
¼ oz (7 ml) Select Aperitivo
1 oz (30 ml) pink grapefruit juice
½ oz (15 ml) lime juice
¼ oz (7 ml) triple sec
½ oz (15 ml) pink-peppercorn-infused agave syrup (p 500)
5 drops pink peppercorn bitters
3 drops saline solution (p 493)
Pink grapefruit soda, to top
Garnish: grapefruit half-wheel topped with smoked salt

Gift Horse
Angus Payne, The Everleigh, Melbourne, 2021
1 oz (30 ml) blanco tequila
1 oz (30 ml) sweet vermouth
1 oz (30 ml) lime juice
½ oz (15 ml) simple syrup
2 dashes orange bitters
Soda, to top
Garnish: lime wedge

Los Altos
David Molyneux, The Everleigh, Melbourne, 2016
1½ oz (45 ml) blanco tequila
½ oz (15 ml) mezcal
1½ oz (45 ml) pineapple juice
½ oz (15 ml) lime juice
½ oz (15 ml) simple syrup
Soda, to top
Garnish: 2 pineapple fronds

Margarita Soda
Tony Milici and Ben Howell, Hellbender, NYC
2 oz (60 ml) blanco tequila
1 oz (30 ml) lime juice
¾ oz (22 ml) agave syrup (p 494)
Soda, to top
Garnish: salt rim and lime wedge

Mexican "Firing Squad" Special
(Tequila Rickey with grenadine and Angostura Bitters)
The Gentleman's Companion, *Charles H. Baker Jr., 1939*
2 oz (60 ml) blanco tequila
¾ oz (22 ml) lime juice
¾ oz (22 ml) grenadine (p 496)
3 dashes Angostura Bitters
Soda, to top
Garnish: orange half-wheel and cherry

Mezcal Cider Rickey
Chris Bostick, Half Step, Austin
2 oz (60 ml) mezcal
¾ oz (22 ml) lime juice
¾ oz (22 ml) honey syrup (p 496)
2½ oz (75 ml) dry apple cider, to top
Garnish: lime wedge

Add all ingredients to a shaker and cube whip. Pour into a frozen Collins glass with ice and top with soda.

Nautilus
Trader Vic's Bartender's Guide, Revised, *Trader Vic, 1972*
2 oz (60 ml) blanco tequila
2 oz (60 ml) cranberry juice
½ oz (15 ml) lime juice
½ oz (15 ml) simple syrup
Soda, to top
Garnish: lime wedge

North Beach Cooler
Priscilla Leong and Paul Hammond, Singapore, 2020
¾ oz (22 ml) blanco tequila
¾ oz (22 ml) dry vermouth
½ oz (15 ml) Campari
1 oz (30 ml) lime juice
¾ oz (22 ml) simple syrup
Soda, to top
Garnish: lime wedge

Paloma
Mexico, 1950s
2 oz (60 ml) blanco tequila
1½ oz (45 ml) pink grapefruit juice
½ oz (15 ml) lime juice
½ oz (15 ml) simple syrup
Soda, to top
Garnish: lime wedge and pinch of salt

Palomita
Michael and Zara Madrusan, The Everleigh Bottling Company, 2020
¾ oz (22 ml) blanco tequila
1½ oz (45 ml) pink grapefruit juice
¼ oz (7 ml) lime juice
¼ oz (7 ml) agave syrup (p 494)
2 drops saline solution (p 493)
1 oz (30 ml) Champagne, to top
Soda, to top
Garnish: grapefruit half-wheel and pinch of salt

Pemberton Fizz
Vincenzo Errico, L'Artefatto, Forio d'Ischia, 2023
1½ oz (45 ml) blanco tequila
1 oz (30 ml) pink grapefruit juice
½ oz (15 ml) lime juice
½ oz (15 ml) vanilla syrup (p 502)
½ oz (15 ml) cinnamon syrup (p 495)
Soda, to top
Garnish: lime wedge

Pep Talk
David Molyneux, The Everleigh, Melbourne, 2018
1 oz (30 ml) blanco tequila
1 oz (30 ml) Cynar
1 oz (30 ml) lime juice
½ oz (15 ml) simple syrup
1 cucumber wheel
Soda, to top
Press cucumber with simple syrup, add remaining ingredients, then shake with ice and strain into a frozen Collins glass with ice and top with soda.
Garnish: mint sprig and cucumber fan

Rio Star Paloma
Chad Solomon, Midnight Rambler, Dallas, 2018
2 oz (60 ml) blanco tequila
1 oz (30 ml) enhanced grapefruit juice (p 495)
½ oz (15 ml) grapefruit oleo-saccharum (p 496)
1 teaspoon (5 ml) Giffard Crème de Pamplemousse Rose
½ teaspoon (2.5 ml) maraschino liqueur
2 dashes The Bitter Truth Grapefruit Bitters
2 drops saline solution (p 493)
Soda, to top
Garnish: salt rim and grapefruit twist

Rio Verde
Ingrid Archer, The Everleigh, Melbourne, 2018
1 oz (30 ml) blanco tequila
1 oz (30 ml) Manzanilla Sherry
1 oz (30 ml) lime juice
¾ oz (22 ml) simple syrup
1 teaspoon (5 ml) Poire Williams
Soda, to top
Garnish: lime wedge and freshly grated cinnamon

Tequila Special à la Bertita
(Tequila Rickey with orange bitters)
The Gentleman's Companion, *Charles H. Baker Jr., 1939*
2 oz (60 ml) blanco tequila
1 oz (30 ml) lime juice
¾ oz (22 ml) simple syrup
2 dashes orange bitters
Soda, to top
Garnish: lime wedge

The Ernesto
Smuggler's Cove: Exotic Cocktails, Rum and the Cult of Tiki, *Martin and Rebecca Cate, 2016*
2 oz (60 ml) blanco tequila
¼ oz (7 ml) apricot brandy
1½ oz (45 ml) pink grapefruit juice
½ oz (15 ml) lime juice
½ oz (15 ml) honey syrup (p 496)
1 dash absinthe
1 dash Angostura Bitters
Soda, to top
Garnish: lime wheel

Vibras
Alicia Perry and Anthony Schmidt, Quixote, San Diego, 2023
1½ oz (45 ml) mezcal
¼ oz (7 ml) Angeleno Amaro (or Aperol)
¼ oz (7 ml) Giffard Crème de Pamplemousse Rose
1 oz (30 ml) guava nectar
1 oz (30 ml) pink grapefruit juice
¾ oz (22 ml) lime juice
Soda, to top
Garnish: salt rim and grapefruit twist

Zebra
Felix Woods, The Everleigh, Melbourne, 2015
1½ oz (45 ml) blanco tequila
½ oz (15 ml) Campari
1 oz (30 ml) lime juice
¾ oz (22 ml) simple syrup
2 dashes orange bitters
Soda, to top
Garnish: lime wedge

Add all ingredients to a shaker and cube whip. Pour into a frozen Collins glass with ice and top with soda.

BRANDY

Oh Rickey
Otis Florence, Attaboy, NYC, 2016
1 oz (30 ml) pisco
1 oz (30 ml) Suze
1 oz (30 ml) lime juice
¾ oz (22 ml) simple syrup
2 cucumber wheels
6–8 mint leaves
Soda, to top
Press cucumber wheel with simple syrup, add remaining ingredients, then shake briefly with ice and strain into a frozen Collins glass with ice and top with soda.
Garnish: mint sprig and cucumber wheel

Steeplejack
Jones' Complete Barguide, *Stan Jones, 1977*
2 oz (60 ml) bonded apple brandy
1½ oz (45 ml) Red Gala apple juice
½ oz (15 ml) lime juice
½ oz (15 ml) simple syrup
Soda, to top
Garnish: apple fan

AMERICAN WHISKEY

California Lemonade
Old Mr. Boston Deluxe Official Bartender's Guide, *Leo Cotton, 1935*
2 oz (60 ml) bourbon
¾ oz (22 ml) lime juice
¾ oz (22 ml) grenadine (p 496)
Soda, to top
Garnish: lemon wedge

Double Standard
(aka **New York Sazerac Rickey**)
Priscilla Leong and Paul Hammond, 2022
1 oz (30 ml) rye whiskey
¾ oz (22 ml) Cognac
1 oz (30 ml) lime juice
¾ oz (22 ml) simple syrup
5 dashes Peychaud's Aromatic Cocktail Bitters
4 dashes absinthe
Soda, to top
Garnish: lime wedge

Mint Cocktail
(Bourbon Mint Rickey with absinthe)
"Harry" of Ciro's ABC of Mixing Cocktails, *Harry MacElhone, 1923*
2 oz (60 ml) bourbon
1 oz (30 ml) lime juice
¾ oz (22 ml) simple syrup
3 dashes absinthe
1 dash Angostura Bitters
1 dash orange bitters
6–8 mint leaves
Soda, to top
Shake all ingredients with ice and strain into a frozen Collins glass with ice, then top with soda.
Garnish: lime wedge

Single Standard
(aka **Bourbon Rickey**)
Straub's Manual of Mixed Drinks, *Jacques Straub, 1913*
2 oz (60 ml) bourbon
¾ oz (22 ml) lime juice
¾ oz (22 ml) simple syrup
Soda, to top
Garnish: lime wedge

FORTIFIED & LIQUEUR

Mojito aux Fleurs
Mori Toshiki, Bar Tram, Tokyo, 2024
1 oz (30 ml) St Germain Elderflower Liqueur
⅓ oz (10 ml) absinthe
½ oz (15 ml) lime juice
8–10 mint leaves
1½ oz (45 ml) soda, to top
Toss and strain into a frozen Collins glass with crushed ice, then add soda, swizzle and top with more crushed ice.
Garnish: mint sprig and 3 drops of peppermint bitters

Kingston Club
The Bar Book: Elements of Cocktail Technique, *Jeffrey Morgenthaler, 2014*
1½ oz (45 ml) Drambuie
1½ oz (45 ml) pineapple juice
¾ oz (22 ml) lime juice
1 teaspoon (5 ml) Fernet-Branca
3 dashes Angostura Bitters
Soda, to top
Garnish: orange twist

Porto Rico
(Sloe Gin Rickey with pomegranate)
The Old Waldorf-Astoria Bar Book, *Albert Stevens Crockett, 1935*
2 oz (60 ml) sloe gin
¾ oz (22 ml) lime juice
½ oz (15 ml) simple syrup
¼ oz (7 ml) grenadine (p 496)
Soda, to top
Garnish: lime wedge

Second Serve
Dan Greenbaum, Attaboy, NYC, 2016
1 oz (30 ml) Fino Sherry
1 oz (30 ml) Amaro Montenegro
1 oz (30 ml) lime juice
¾ oz (22 ml) simple syrup
Soda, to top
Garnish: orange wedge

Wayfarer's Cocktail
Burke's Complete Cocktail & Drinking Recipes, *Harman Burney Burke, 1934*
2 oz (60 ml) dry vermouth
¾ oz (22 ml) lime juice
¾ oz (22 ml) grenadine (p 496)
Soda, to top
Garnish: lime wedge

OTHER

Kaiju
Ewan Bennie, Part Time Lover, San Diego, 2022
1 oz (30 ml) aquavit
½ oz (15 ml) Dolin Génépi des Alpes
½ oz (15 ml) Midori
1 oz (30 ml) lime juice
¾ oz (22 ml) simple syrup
Soda, to top
Garnish: long cucumber ribbon

Add all ingredients to a shaker and cube whip. Pour into a frozen Collins glass with ice and top with soda.

BUCK & MULE

Moscow Mule p 98

Buck & Mule

A tall, spiced cocktail combining ginger beer and citrus, served over ice.

spirit + citrus + ginger syrup + soda

Add all ingredients except soda to a shaker and cube whip. Pour into a frozen Collins glass with ice and top with soda.

Ginger beer, as we know it today, was first popularised in England in the 18th century – a brewed, fermented beverage made from ginger, sugar and water. Although ginger had long been utilised in China as a natural remedy for digestive discomfort and the common cold, it wasn't until trade routes expanded to Europe that ginger beer became a staple.

The fermentation process gave birth to a fiery, fizzy, low-alcohol drink that could be enjoyed as a stand-alone beverage or given extra kick with a splash of spirit. By the early 1900s, American bars were serving the Horse's Neck, a tall drink with ginger beer, sometimes bitters and – most significantly – an exceptionally long lemon rind garnish that wound around the inside of the glass. The Horse's Neck soon spawned variations made with gin, Cognac or bourbon, such as the Horse's Neck with a Kick or Stiff Horse's Neck, which was eventually shortened to a Buck. Huzzah!

It wasn't until the early 1940s that the Mule stepped onto the scene, supposedly at the Cock 'n Bull, an English-style tavern on the Sunset Strip in Los Angeles. The Moscow Mule (p 98) – a combination of vodka, ginger beer and lime – is said to have been designed by the bar's proprietor, Jack Morgan, keen to increase sales of his branded ginger beer, together with John Martin, a representative of Smirnoff vodka. An effective marketing strategy ensued, pitching the drink consistently in striking copper mugs that stood out among standard glassware and which have since become as integral to the drink's identity as the ingredients themselves.

Technically, the Mule is a Buck variation, although the term Buck dropped out of common parlance midway through the 20th century. And while both drinks refer to tall, spirited cocktails featuring citrus (generally lime) and ginger beer, Bucks often feature darker spirits, such as aged dark rum, Cognac or whisk(e)y, while Mules are more commonly associated with lighter spirits like vodka and gin. Our house ginger beer (see Gunner, p 485) comprises of ginger syrup (p 496), fresh lime and soda.

Dark 'n' Stormy

(aka **Goslings Buck**)
2 oz (60 ml) Goslings Black Seal Rum
½ oz (15 ml) lime juice
¾ oz (22 ml) ginger syrup (p 496)
Soda, to top

Add all ingredients except soda to a shaker and cube whip. Pour into a frozen Collins glass with ice and top with soda.
Garnish: candied ginger

Unofficially dubbed the national drink of Bermuda, the Dark 'n' Stormy is a foolproof Buck that calls for Goslings Black Seal Rum, the flagship spirit from Gosling Brothers Limited, which has been in production since the early 1860s. Gosling Brothers claims that the Dark 'n' Stormy was born in Bermuda at the close of World War I and that the drink's name originated when an unknown fisherman declared the combination of dark rum and fiery ginger beer was the 'colour of a cloud only a fool or a dead man would sail under.'

The Dark 'n' Stormy is one of a handful of cocktails that has a successful trademark against its name (the version with a single apostrophe), a decisive step that was taken by Gosling Brothers in 1991 when competing rum companies also began promoting the cocktail around the world. It's worth noting that this cocktail is also the unofficial cocktail of Milk & Honey NYC alumni, a drink we all agree suits every occasion. We simply can't get enough.

While beer cocktails can be polarising, India Pale Ale also works particularly well in Bucks and Mules, which Zara proves in both her Dark 'n' Hoppy No. 1 (p 437) and Dark 'n' Hoppy No. 2 (p 437).

Gin-Gin Mule

Audrey Saunders, Beacon, NYC, 2000
2 oz (60 ml) gin
1 oz (30 ml) lime juice
½ oz (15 ml) ginger syrup (p 496)
½ oz (15 ml) simple syrup
6–8 mint leaves
Soda, to top

Add all the ingredients except soda to a shaker with ice, shake briefly then strain into a frozen Collins glass with ice and top with soda.
Garnish: mint bouquet and candied ginger

This fragrant and zesty gin-based Buck livened with fresh mint was made famous by Audrey Saunders in New York City at Beacon restaurant in 2000. Saunders has since cemented herself as one of the world's most distinguished bartenders, thanks largely to her work at Pegu Club, the now-closed downtown Manhattan cocktail bar she co-founded in 2005.

Saunders' influence cannot be understated. Not only is she responsible for a number of modern classics, including the Old Cuban (p 426), but she also oversaw the development of leading lights in the international bartending scene, such as Phil Ward and Jim Meehan. The widespread revival of the Nick & Nora glass for drinks like the Martini is another one of her significant contributions.

When Michael went down his rabbit hole of research in 2007, he discovered a drink of a similar style, the Favorite Cocktail (p 98), published almost seventy years prior, followed by a further appearance under a new name in 1958.

The Favorite Cocktail – a tall combination of gin, lime, mint and ginger ale – appears in the 1933 edition of *Jack's Manual* by J.A. Grohusko. With several editions published, beginning in 1908, *Jack's Manual* is arguably one of the most comprehensive cocktail collections written before World War II, featuring over 1000 cocktails, each detailed with specifications for glass, bowl or barrel-sized serves.

Twenty-five years on, we find a variation of the Favorite Cocktail called the Whizbang Cooler (p 99) in *100 Cocktails: How to Mix Them* by "Bernard", which calls for a 'dash of Peppermint and the sprigs of mint on top'. Notably, this drink also calls for ginger ale – which was typically rather sweet and non-alcoholic – but we much prefer it with Saunders' house-made ginger beer and can attest to why her recipe has become the global benchmark.

Dark 'n' Stormy (left), Gin-Gin Mule (right)

Kitty

(aka **Red Wine Buck**)
The World's Drinks and How to Mix Them, *Wm. T. Boothby, 1908*
2 oz (60 ml) dry red wine
½ oz (15 ml) lime juice
¾ oz (22 ml) ginger syrup (p 496)
Soda, to top

Add all ingredients except soda to a shaker and cube whip. Pour into a frozen Collins glass with ice and top with soda.
Garnish: candied ginger

The Kitty, a simple Buck that uses red wine instead of spirit, was first mentioned by William T. "Cocktail" Boothby in his 1908 volume, *The World's Drinks and How to Mix Them*. In Boothby's era, the bartender was considered a pillar of society, and it would be no leap to suggest that Boothby regarded himself as something of a skyscraper. Boothby, born in San Francisco in 1862, had various careers in comedy, the arts and insurance sales before becoming a bartender.

He was introduced to hospitality at 12 years old, when his parents purchased Frank Johnson's Chop House and Oyster Saloon. A decade later, he opened his own venue, Boothby's Coffee Saloon, and in 1891 he published his first book, *Cocktail Boothby's American Bartender*, which went on to sell an outstanding 50,000 copies across three editions. In the introduction to *The World's Drinks and How to Mix Them* – his second book, which he describes as his 'little encyclopedia' – Boothby tells how he shared the manuscript with connoisseurs and experts around the globe, 'all of whom have unhesitatingly declared it to be 'The Dope''. Notably, Boothby organised his cocktails by style, or 'branch' in our terms, rather than simply by their alcoholic base. His book has a fantastic flair and personality, detailing not only cocktail recipes but also poetic and playful recommendations for 19th-century American life.

The Kitty is a classic low-ABV cocktail that is bold in both body and flavour, and excellent as an apéritif. While Boothby's recipe called for claret, most full-bodied reds fit the bill. Another of Boothby's fortified low-ABV cocktails that has stood the test of time is the Klondyke (p 106), a Buck with a split base of sweet and dry vermouth. For other drinks featuring wine and spirits side by side, check out the New York Sour (p 167) and Falling Leaves (p 333).

Floradora Cooler

(London Buck Cocktail with raspberry)
Straub's Manual of Mixed Drinks, *Jacques Straub, 1913*
¾ oz (22 ml) lime juice
½ oz (15 ml) ginger syrup (p 496)
½ oz (15 ml) raspberry syrup (p 500)
Soda, to top

Add all ingredients except soda to a shaker and cube whip. Pour into a frozen Collins glass with ice and top with soda.
Garnish: raspberry and candied ginger

The Floradora Cooler, now more commonly known as the Floradora, debuted in *Straub's Manual of Mixed Drinks* by Jacques Straub, self-published in 1913. This book is an incredibly rare find and, as a result, became overshadowed by Straub's better-known book, *Drinks*, published the following year. *Drinks* is acknowledged as a seminal reference point for early 20th-century bartenders and remains a key inspiration behind our work as well. Straub's practical and comprehensive cocktail guides are regarded for their utilitarian tone and dense collection of recipes.

Straub, born to a distiller in Switzerland, was one of the world's most famous wine and spirits experts of his time. He made his name at the Pendennis Club in Louisville, where he worked for 21 years before taking a role at The Blackstone in Chicago until Prohibition hit. Despite his vast knowledge of wine and areas of beverage management, Straub was not in fact ever a bartender, nor did he drink any alcohol. Unfortunately, this means we can't blame too many Floradoras for Straub's spelling of 'Daiguiri' and 'Cafe de Paree', among others.

Like many fruit-forward Bucks, the Floradora is bright and charismatic, with ginger beer and raspberries creating a punchy pink-lemonade-like fizz that's well suited to any occasion. If raspberries are your thing, get your paws around Sasha Petraske's Cosmonaut (p 170) and the Pink Lady Cocktail (p 162), a glorious Gin Sour variation also found in *Straub's Manual of Mixed Drinks*.

Floradora Cooler (left), Kitty (right)

Buck & Mule

VODKA

Headless Horseman
(Moscow Mule with Angostura Bitters)
Jones' Complete Barguide, *Stan Jones, 1977*
2 oz (60 ml) vodka
¾ oz (22 ml) ginger syrup (p 496)
½ oz (15 ml) lime juice
3 dashes Angostura Bitters
Soda, to top
Garnish: candied ginger

Moscow Mule
Wes Price, Cock'n Bull, Los Angeles, 1940s
The Stork Club Bar Book, *Lucius Beebe, 1946*
2 oz (60 ml) vodka
¾ oz (22 ml) ginger syrup (p 496)
½ oz (15 ml) lime juice
Soda, to top
Garnish: candied ginger
▼ Traditionally served in a copper mug.

Palma Fizz
(Moscow Mule with rosewater)
Sasha Petraske, Milk & Honey, NYC
2 oz (60 ml) vodka
¾ oz (22 ml) ginger syrup (p 496)
½ oz (15 ml) lime juice
Soda, to top
Garnish: candied ginger and spritz of rosewater

Prancing Horse
John Parra and Kyle Hankin, Fox Liquor Bar, Raleigh
1½ oz (45 ml) vodka
¼ oz (7 ml) Fernet-Branca
¼ oz (7 ml) Campari
¾ oz (22 ml) ginger syrup (p 496)
½ oz (15 ml) lime juice
1 dash Angostura Bitters
Soda, to top
Garnish: candied ginger

GIN

Andalusian Buck
Jeffrey Morgenthaler, Clyde Common, Portland, 2010
1 oz (30 ml) gin
1 oz (30 ml) Amontillado Sherry
¾ oz (22 ml) ginger syrup (p 496)
½ oz (15 ml) lime juice
Soda, to top
Garnish: lime wedge

Ardsley Cooler
(aka **Old Tom Gin-Gin Mule**)
Jack's Manual, *J.A. Grohusko, 1908*
2 oz (60 ml) Old Tom gin
1 oz (30 ml) lime juice
½ oz (15 ml) ginger syrup (p 496)
½ oz (15 ml) simple syrup
6–8 mint leaves
Soda, to top
Add all ingredients except soda to a shaker, shake briefly, then strain into a frozen Collins glass with ice and top with soda.
Garnish: mint sprig and candied ginger

Buck Buck Mule
Josh Pape, The Diamond, Vancouver, 2009
1 oz (30 ml) gin
1 oz (30 ml) Fino Sherry
¾ oz (22 ml) ginger syrup (p 496)
½ oz (15 ml) lime juice
4 cucumber wheels
Soda, to top
Press cucumber with ginger syrup, add remaining ingredients, shake briefly, then strain into a frozen Collins glass with ice and top with soda.
Garnish: cucumber wheel and candied ginger

Bull-Dog
(New Orleans Buck with gin and no bitters)
"Harry" of Ciro's ABC of Mixing Cocktails, *Harry MacElhone, 1923*
2 oz (60 ml) gin
1 oz (30 ml) orange juice
½ oz (15 ml) lemon juice
½ oz (15 ml) ginger syrup (p 496)
Soda, to top
Garnish: candied ginger

Colombo Buck
Ryan Chetiyawardana
2 oz (60 ml) Colombo No. 7 London Dry Gin
2 oz (60 ml) coconut water
½ oz (15 ml) lime juice
¾ oz (22 ml) ginger syrup (p 496)
Soda, to top
Garnish: candied ginger

Favorite Cocktail
(Gin-Gin Mule with ginger ale)
Jack's Manual, *J.A. Grohusko, 1933*
2 oz (60 ml) gin
1 oz (30 ml) lime juice
6–8 mint leaves
Ginger ale, to top
Add all ingredients except ginger ale to a shaker, shake briefly, then strain into a frozen Collins glass with ice and top with ginger ale.
Garnish: mint sprig and candied ginger

500 Days of Summer
Kevin Peters, Hotel Esplanade, Melbourne, 2019
1 oz (30 ml) navy strength gin
1 oz (30 ml) St Germain Elderflower Liqueur
¾ oz (22 ml) lime juice
½ oz (15 ml) ginger syrup (p 496)
2 strawberries
5–8 mint leaves
Soda, to top
Muddle strawberries with ginger syrup, add remaining ingredients, shake briefly, then strain into a frozen Collins glass and top with soda.
Garnish: mint sprig and half a strawberry

Flower Shop
Mitchell Taylor, Attaboy, Nashville, 2018
1½ oz (45 ml) gin
½ oz (15 ml) St Germain Elderflower Liqueur
¾ oz (22 ml) ginger syrup (p 496)
½ oz (15 ml) lime juice
Soda, to top
Garnish: candied ginger

Add all ingredients except soda to a shaker and cube whip. Pour into a frozen Collins glass with ice and top with soda.

Go-To
Rob Krueger, Extra Fancy, NYC
1½ oz (45 ml) gin
½ oz (15 ml) St Germain Elderflower Liqueur
1 oz (30 ml) lime juice
½ oz (15 ml) ginger syrup (p 496)
½ oz (15 ml) simple syrup
3 cucumber wheels
8–10 mint leaves
Soda, to top
Press cucumber, add remaining ingredients, shake briefly, then strain into a frozen Collins glass with ice and top with soda.
Garnish: cucumber wheel and mint sprig

Hilly Croft Cooler
(aka **Old Tom Buck** or **Marguerite**)
Old Waldorf Bar Days, *Albert Stevens Crockett, 1931*
2 oz (60 ml) Old Tom gin
¾ oz (22 ml) ginger syrup (p 496)
½ oz (15 ml) lime juice
Soda, to top
Garnish: candied ginger

Horse & Cart
Michael McIlroy, Attaboy, NYC
1½ oz (45 ml) gin
½ oz (15 ml) Aperol
¾ oz (22 ml) ginger syrup (p 496)
½ oz (15 ml) lime juice
Soda, to top
Garnish: candied ginger

Invisible Gin Highball
Hoffman House Bartender's Guide, *Charles S. Mahoney, 1905*
1½ oz (45 ml) gin
½ oz (15 ml) apricot brandy
1 oz (30 ml) pineapple juice
½ oz (15 ml) lemon juice
½ oz (15 ml) ginger syrup (p 496)
Soda, to top
Garnish: 2 pineapple fronds and candied ginger

Invisible London Fog
Daniel Zacharczuk, The Varnish, Los Angeles, 2024
2 oz (60 ml) gin
1 oz (30 ml) pineapple juice
½ oz (15 ml) lime juice
½ oz (15 ml) ginger syrup (p 496)
2 dashes absinthe
Soda, to top
Garnish: candied ginger and 2 pineapple fronds

Late Night Reviver
Michael McIlroy, Milk & Honey, NYC, 2008
1½ oz (45 ml) gin
½ oz (15 ml) Fernet-Branca
¾ oz (22 ml) ginger syrup (p 496)
½ oz (15 ml) lime juice
Soda, to top
Garnish: candied ginger

Light Horseman
David Molyneux, The Everleigh, Melbourne, 2014
2 oz (60 ml) gin
¾ oz (22 ml) lime juice
½ oz (15 ml) ginger syrup (p 496)
½ oz (15 ml) passionfruit syrup (p 499)
Soda, to top
Garnish: candied ginger

London Buck Cocktail
(aka **Gin Buck, Mamie Taylor's Sister** or **Foghorn**)
The Savoy Cocktail Book, *Harry Craddock, 1930*
2 oz (60 ml) gin
¾ oz (22 ml) ginger syrup (p 496)
½ oz (15 ml) lime juice
Soda, to top
Garnish: candied ginger

Peach Buck
1½ oz (45 ml) gin
½ oz (15 ml) Giffard Crème de Pêche de Vigne
¾ oz (22 ml) lime juice
½ oz (15 ml) ginger syrup (p 496)
Soda, to top
Garnish: candied ginger

Robert E. Lee Cooler
(Gin Buck with absinthe)
Jones' Complete Barguide, *Stan Jones, 1977*
2 oz (60 ml) gin
¾ oz (22 ml) ginger syrup (p 496)
½ oz (15 ml) lime juice
2 dashes absinthe
Soda, to top
Garnish: candied ginger

Shaky Pete's Ginger Brew
(See p 439)

Suffering Bastard
(See p 103)

Very Late Night Reviver
Oscar Shaw, The Everleigh, Melbourne, 2022
1½ oz (45 ml) gin
½ oz (15 ml) coffee liqueur
¾ oz (22 ml) ginger syrup (p 496)
½ oz (15 ml) lime juice
Soda, to top
Garnish: candied ginger

Whizbang Cooler
(Gin-Gin Mule with peppermint)
100 Cocktails: How to Mix Them, *"Bernard", 1958*
2 oz (60 ml) gin
1 oz (30 ml) lime juice
½ oz (15 ml) ginger syrup (p 496)
½ oz (15 ml) simple syrup
6–8 mint leaves
1 drop peppermint oil
Soda, to top
Add all ingredients except soda to a shaker, shake briefly, then strain into a frozen Collins glass with ice and top with soda.
Garnish: mint sprig and candied ginger
▼ Originally made with ginger ale.

Add all ingredients except soda to a shaker and cube whip. Pour into a frozen Collins glass with ice and top with soda.

Young Buck

David Molyneux, The Everleigh, Melbourne, 2015

1 oz (30 ml) gin
1 oz (30 ml) sloe gin
¾ oz (22 ml) ginger syrup (p 496)
½ oz (15 ml) lime juice
2 dashes absinthe
Soda, to top
Garnish: candied ginger

RUM & CANE SPIRIT

Añejo Highball

Dale DeGroff, Rainbow Room, NYC, 1990s

1½ oz (45 ml) aged dark rum
¾ oz (22 ml) ginger syrup (p 496)
½ oz (15 ml) orange curaçao (p 498)
½ oz (15 ml) lime juice
4 dashes Angostura Bitters
Soda, to top
Garnish: orange half-wheel and candied ginger

Apple's Eye Buck

Andrew Rice, Attaboy, NYC, 2017

1 oz (30 ml) aged dark rum
1 oz (30 ml) bonded apple brandy
¾ oz (22 ml) ginger syrup (p 496)
½ oz (15 ml) lime juice
3 dashes Angostura Bitters
Soda, to top
Garnish: candied ginger

Brooklyn Burro

Ivy Mix, Leyenda, NYC

2 oz (60 ml) light rum
½ oz (15 ml) pineapple juice
½ oz (15 ml) lime juice
½ oz (15 ml) ginger syrup (p 496)
1 dash Angostura Bitters
Soda, to top
Garnish: lime wheel and candied ginger

Café Dark 'n' Stormy

Michael McCollum, Attaboy, Nashville

2 oz (60 ml) Goslings Black Seal Rum
¾ oz (22 ml) ginger syrup (p 496)
½ oz (15 ml) coffee liqueur
½ oz (15 ml) lime juice
Soda, to top
Garnish: candied ginger

Colonel Beach's Plantation Punch

Ernest "Don the Beachcomber" Gantt

¾ oz (22 ml) Jamaican dark rum
½ oz (15 ml) aged dark rum
¼ oz (7 ml) light rum
1 oz (30 ml) pineapple juice
½ oz (15 ml) lime juice
¼ oz (7 ml) ginger syrup (p 496)
¼ oz (7 ml) falernum
2 dashes absinthe
2 dashes Angostura Bitters
Soda, to top
Garnish: mint sprig bouquet and candied ginger

Company Buck

Phil Ward, Death & Co, NYC, 2007

2 oz (60 ml) Goslings Black Seal Rum
1 oz (30 ml) pineapple juice
¾ oz (22 ml) ginger syrup (p 496)
½ oz (15 ml) lime juice
3 dashes Angostura Bitters
Soda, to top
Garnish: candied ginger

Dark 'n' Hoppy No. 1

(See p 437)

Diablo

The How and When, *Hyman Gale and Gerald F. Marco, 1940*

2 oz (60 ml) light rum
½ oz (15 ml) lime juice
¾ oz (22 ml) ginger syrup (p 496)
¼ oz (7 ml) crème de cassis, to float
Soda, to top
Cube whip and pour into a frozen Collins glass with ice, then top with soda and float crème de cassis.
Garnish: candied ginger

Georgetown Buck

Zachary Pease, My Friend Duke, NYC, 2018

1½ oz (45 ml) aged dark rum
½ oz (15 ml) Tempus Fugit Gran Classico Bitter
1 oz (30 ml) pineapple juice
¾ oz (22 ml) ginger syrup (p 496)
½ oz (15 ml) lime juice
3 dashes Angostura Bitters
Soda, to top
Garnish: candied ginger

Ginger Rogers

(See p 103)

Imperial Buck

2 oz (60 ml) Cruzan Black Strap Rum
1 oz (30 ml) pineapple juice
¾ oz (22 ml) ginger syrup (p 496)
½ oz (15 ml) lime juice
Soda, to top
Garnish: 2 pineapple fronds and candied ginger

Joe Buck

Chris Bostick, The Varnish, Los Angeles

2 oz (60 ml) Jamaican dark rum
¾ oz (22 ml) lime juice
½ oz (15 ml) ginger syrup (p 496)
½ oz (15 ml) honey syrup (p 496)
2 dashes Angostura Bitters
2 dashes Peychaud's Aromatic Cocktail Bitters
Soda, to top
Garnish: candied ginger

La Guidive

Smuggler's Cove: Exotic Cocktails, Rum and the Cult of Tiki, *Martin and Rebecca Cate, 2016*

1½ oz (45 ml) aged dark rum
⅓ oz (10 ml) Licor 43
⅓ oz (10 ml) Giffard Crème de Pêche de Vigne
¾ oz (22 ml) ginger syrup (p 496)
½ oz (15 ml) lime juice
Soda, to top
Garnish: lime wheel

New Orleans Buck

2 oz (60 ml) aged dark rum
1 oz (30 ml) orange juice
½ oz (15 ml) lemon juice
½ oz (15 ml) ginger syrup (p 496)
3 dashes Angostura Bitters
Soda, to top
Garnish: orange half-wheel and candied ginger
▼ Pineapple can also be used instead of orange.

Add all ingredients except soda to a shaker and cube whip. Pour into a frozen Collins glass with ice and top with soda.

Perfect Storm
Alastair Burgess, Happiness Forgets, London
2 oz (60 ml) Demerara dark rum
¾ oz (22 ml) lemon juice
⅓ oz (10 ml) ginger syrup (p 496)
⅓ oz (10 ml) honey syrup (p 496)
1 teaspoon (5 ml) plum brandy
Soda, to top
Garnish: candied ginger

Port in a Storm
Tim Philips-Johansson, Dead Ringer, Sydney, 2017
1 oz (30 ml) Goslings Black Seal Rum
¾ oz (22 ml) tawny Port
¾ oz (22 ml) lime juice
¾ oz (22 ml) ginger syrup (p 496)
Soda, to top
Garnish: candied ginger

Q.B. Cooler
Ernest "Don the Beachcomber" Gantt, 1937
¾ oz (22 ml) Jamaican dark rum
½ oz (15 ml) light rum
¼ oz (7 ml) Demerara dark rum
1 oz (30 ml) orange juice
½ oz (15 ml) lime juice
⅜ oz (11 ml) ginger syrup (p 496)
1 teaspoon (5 ml) falernum
1 teaspoon (5 ml) honey syrup (p 496)
2 dashes Angostura Bitters
Soda, to top
Garnish: orange half-wheel and mint sprig
▼ 'Q.B.' is an acronym for 'quiet birdmen' – the fraternity of male aviators during WWI.

Rum Buck
(Aged Dark Rum Buck with Angostura Bitters)
2 oz (60 ml) aged dark rum
¾ oz (22 ml) ginger syrup (p 496)
½ oz (15 ml) lime juice
3 dashes Angostura Bitters
Soda, to top
Garnish: candied ginger

Sailor's Sunset
Punch
1½ oz (45 ml) Jamaican dark rum
½ oz (15 ml) Campari
½ oz (15 ml) pink grapefruit juice
½ oz (15 ml) lime juice
½ oz (15 ml) ginger syrup (p 496)
½ oz (15 ml) simple syrup
Soda, to top
Garnish: candied ginger

Street & Flynn Special
Joseph Schwartz, Little Branch, NYC
2 oz (60 ml) Jamaican dark rum
½ oz (15 ml) pimento (allspice) dram
½ oz (15 ml) lime juice
½ oz (15 ml) ginger syrup (p 496)
Soda, to top
Garnish: candied ginger

Susie Taylor
(aka **Jamaican Rum Buck**)
Jack's Manual, *J.A. Grohusko, 1916*
2 oz (60 ml) Jamaican dark rum
¾ oz (22 ml) ginger syrup (p 496)
½ oz (15 ml) lime juice
Soda, to top
Garnish: candied ginger

The Famous Shanghai Buck
(aka **Aged Dark Rum Floradora**)
The Gentleman's Companion, *Charles H. Baker Jr., 1939*
2 oz (60 ml) aged dark rum
¾ oz (22 ml) lime juice
½ oz (15 ml) ginger syrup (p 496)
½ oz (15 ml) grenadine (p 496)
Soda, to top
Garnish: raspberry and candied ginger

Thunderbird
Joey Durana, Caretaker, Auckland
1½ oz (45 ml) spiced dark rum
½ oz (15 ml) Pedro Ximénez
½ oz (15 ml) lime juice
½ oz (15 ml) ginger syrup (p 496)
Soda, to top
Garnish: candied ginger

Winter
(Jamaican Buck with pimento bitters)
The Old Waldorf-Astoria Bar Book, *Albert Stevens Crockett, 1935*
2 oz (60 ml) Jamaican dark rum
¾ oz (22 ml) ginger syrup (p 496)
½ oz (15 ml) lime juice
2 dashes Dale DeGroff's Pimento Aromatic Bitters
2 dashes Angostura Bitters
Soda, to top
Garnish: candied ginger
▼ Originally served up.

AGAVE

Border Crossing
David Molyneux, The Everleigh, Melbourne, 2014
2 oz (60 ml) blanco tequila
1 oz (30 ml) orange juice
½ oz (15 ml) lime juice
½ oz (15 ml) ginger syrup (p 496)
3 dashes Angostura Bitters
Soda, to top
Garnish: orange half-wheel and candied ginger

Breakfast Buck
Matt Clark, Attaboy, NYC, 2017
1½ oz (45 ml) mezcal
½ oz (15 ml) Cruzan Black Strap Rum
1 oz (30 ml) pineapple juice
¾ oz (22 ml) ginger syrup (p 496)
½ oz (15 ml) lime juice
Soda, to top
Garnish: 2 pineapple fronds and candied ginger

Buck Wild
Conor Johns, Red Hook Tavern, NYC, 2023
1 oz (30 ml) mezcal
¾ oz (22 ml) Amaro Braulio
½ oz (15 ml) Ancho Reyes Verde
1 oz (30 ml) lime juice
½ oz (15 ml) ginger syrup (p 496)
¼ oz (7 ml) passionfruit syrup (p 499)
2 dashes orange bitters
Garnish: orange wheel and candied ginger

Add all ingredients except soda to a shaker and cube whip. Pour into a frozen Collins glass with ice and top with soda.

Caballo Blanco
Michael McIlroy, Attaboy, NYC, 2013
1½ oz (45 ml) blanco tequila
½ oz (15 ml) mezcal
1 oz (30 ml) pineapple juice
½ oz (15 ml) lime juice
½ oz (15 ml) ginger syrup (p 496)
3 dashes Angostura Bitters
Soda, to top
Garnish: 2 pineapple fronds and candied ginger

Ginger Paloma
Chris Bostick, Half Step, Austin
1½ oz (45 ml) blanco tequila
¾ oz (22 ml) pink grapefruit juice
½ oz (15 ml) lime juice
½ oz (15 ml) ginger syrup (p 496)
2½ oz (75 ml) grapefruit soda, to top
Garnish: grapefruit half-wheel and pinch of salt

Hollow Man
Michael McCollum, Attaboy, Nashville, 2018
1½ oz (45 ml) mezcal
½ oz (15 ml) apricot brandy
1 oz (30 ml) pineapple juice
½ oz (15 ml) ginger syrup (p 496)
½ oz (15 ml) lemon juice
3 dashes Angostura Bitters
Soda, to top
Garnish: orange half-wheel and candied ginger

Hot Tin Roof
Paul Hammond and Priscilla Leong, 2019
¾ oz (22 ml) mezcal
½ oz (15 ml) dry vermouth
½ oz (15 ml) Campari
1 oz (30 ml) lime juice
¾ oz (22 ml) ginger syrup (p 496)
Soda, to top

Huarache Nights
Chris Bostick and Steven Robbins, Half Step, Austin, 2016
2 oz (60 ml) blanco tequila
½ oz (15 ml) lime juice
½ oz (15 ml) ginger syrup (p 496)
½ oz (15 ml) grenadine (p 496)
Soda, to top
Garnish: candied ginger

Mexican El Diablo
(aka **El Diablo**)
Trader Vic's Book of Food and Drink, *Trader Vic, 1946*
2 oz (60 ml) blanco tequila
½ oz (15 ml) lime juice
¾ oz (22 ml) ginger syrup (p 496)
¼ oz (7 ml) crème de cassis, to float
Soda, to top
Cube whip and pour into a frozen Collins glass with ice, then top with soda and float crème de cassis.
Garnish: candied ginger
▼ Also great with raspberry syrup in place of the cassis.

Mezcal Mule
Jim Meehan, PDT, NYC, 2009
1½ oz (45 ml) mezcal
¾ oz (22 ml) lime juice
½ oz (15 ml) ginger syrup (p 496)
½ oz (15 ml) passionfruit syrup (p 499)
¼ oz (7 ml) agave syrup (p 494)
3 cucumber wheels
Soda, to top
Press cucumber with ginger syrup, add remaining ingredients, shake briefly with ice, then strain into a frozen Collins glass with ice and top with soda.
Garnish: cucumber wheel, candied ginger and pinch of chilli powder

Oaxacan Buck
2 oz (60 ml) mezcal
½ oz (15 ml) lime juice
¾ oz (22 ml) ginger syrup (p 496)
2 dashes Angostura Bitters
Soda, to top
Garnish: candied ginger

Reposado Buck
Good Things to Drink with Mr. Lyan & Friends, *Ryan Chetiyawardana, 2015*
1½ oz (45 ml) reposado tequila
½ oz (15 ml) Lillet Blanc
¾ oz (22 ml) ginger syrup (p 496)
½ oz (15 ml) lemon juice
1 dash Angostura Bitters
Soda, to top
Garnish: mint spring and candied ginger

BRANDY

Biarritz "Monk-Buck"
The Gentleman's Companion, *Charles H. Baker Jr., 1939*
1¾ oz (52 ml) Cognac
¼ oz (7 ml) Yellow Chartreuse
¾ oz (22 ml) ginger syrup (p 496)
½ oz (15 ml) lime juice
Soda, to top
Garnish: lemon horse's neck

Chilcano
Spirits of Latin America, *Ivy Mix, 2020*
2 oz (60 ml) pisco
¾ oz (22 ml) ginger syrup (p 496)
½ oz (15 ml) lime juice
½ strawberry
Soda, to top
Muddle strawberry with ginger syrup, add remaining ingredients, shake briefly with ice, then strain into a frozen Collins glass with ice and top with soda.
Garnish: candied ginger

Flash of Lightning
(aka **Cognac Floradora**)
American & Other Drinks, *Leo Engel, 1878*
2 oz (60 ml) Cognac
¾ oz (22 ml) lime juice
½ oz (15 ml) ginger syrup (p 496)
½ oz (15 ml) raspberry syrup (p 500)
Soda, to top
Garnish: raspberry and candied ginger

French Maid
Jim Meehan, PDT, NYC, 2008
1½ oz (45 ml) Cognac
¾ oz (22 ml) lime juice
½ oz (15 ml) ginger syrup (p 496)
½ oz (15 ml) simple syrup
¼ oz (7 ml) falernum
3 cucumber wheels
6–8 mint leaves
Soda, to top
Press cucumber with simple syrup, add remaining ingredients, shake briefly with ice, then strain into a frozen Collins glass with ice and top with soda.
Garnish: mint sprig and cucumber wheel

Add all ingredients except soda to a shaker and cube whip. Pour into a frozen Collins glass with ice and top with soda.

Ginger Rogers
Brian Miller, Death & Co, NYC
1 oz (30 ml) Cognac
1 oz (30 ml) Goslings Black Seal Rum
½ oz (15 ml) lemon juice
½ oz (15 ml) ginger syrup (p 496)
½ oz (15 ml) simple syrup
1 dash Peychaud's Aromatic Cocktail Bitters
Soda, to top
Garnish: candied ginger

Grenadier
The South American Gentleman's Companion, *Charles H. Baker Jr., 1951*
1½ oz (45 ml) Cognac
½ oz (15 ml) Goslings 151 Proof Black Seal Rum
¾ oz (22 ml) ginger syrup (p 496)
½ oz (15 ml) lime juice
Soda, to top
Garnish: candied ginger

Jungle Buck
(Inspired by Matthias Soberon)
Michael Madrusan, The Everleigh, Melbourne, 2024
1½ oz (45 ml) Cognac
½ oz (15 ml) Campari
1 oz (30 ml) pineapple juice
½ oz (15 ml) lime juice
½ oz (15 ml) ginger syrup (p 496)
Soda, to top
Garnish: mint sprig and candied ginger

Kits Buck
Daniel Zacharczuk, The Varnish, Los Angeles, 2024
1½ oz (45 ml) pisco
½ oz (15 ml) St Germain Elderflower Liqueur
½ oz (15 ml) lime juice
½ oz (15 ml) ginger syrup (p 496)
½ oz (15 ml) raspberry syrup (p 500)
Soda, to top
Garnish: raspberry and candied ginger

None But the Brave
(Cognac Buck with pimento bitters)
Crosby Gaige's Cocktail Guide and Ladies' Companion, *Crosby Gaige, 1941*
2 oz (60 ml) Cognac
¾ oz (22 ml) ginger syrup (p 496)
½ oz (15 ml) lime juice
2 dashes Dale DeGroff's Pimento Aromatic Bitters
Soda, to top
Garnish: candied ginger

Roland-Garros
Tom Lasher-Walker, Brasserie Laurel, Miami, 2023
1 oz (30 ml) Cognac
1 oz (30 ml) sweet vermouth
¾ oz (22 ml) lemon juice
½ oz (15 ml) ginger syrup (p 496)
½ oz (15 ml) simple syrup
3 cucumber wheels
6–8 mint leaves
Soda, to top
Press cucumber with simple syrup, add remaining ingredients, shake briefly with ice, then strain into a frozen Collins glass with ice and top with soda.
Garnish: mint sprig, cucumber wheel and strawberry

Sleepy Head Cocktail
(Gin-Gin Mule with Cognac)
The Official Mixer's Manual, *Patrick Gavin Duffy, 1934*
2 oz (60 ml) Cognac
1 oz (30 ml) lime juice
½ oz (15 ml) ginger syrup (p 496)
½ oz (15 ml) simple syrup
6–8 mint leaves
Soda, to top
Add all ingredients to shaker, shake briefly with ice, then strain into a frozen Collins glass with ice and top with soda.
Garnish: mint sprig and candied ginger

Southern as Buck
Michael Madrusan, Bar Margaux, Melbourne, 2021
1½ oz (45 ml) Cognac
½ oz (15 ml) Giffard Crème de Pêche de Vigne
¾ oz (22 ml) lemon juice
½ oz (15 ml) ginger syrup (p 496)
6–8 mint leaves
3 dashes Angostura Bitters
Soda, to top
Add all ingredients to shaker, shake briefly with ice, then strain into a frozen Collins glass with ice and top with soda.
Garnish: mint sprig and candied ginger

Suffering Bastard
Joe Scialom, circa 1942
1 oz (30 ml) Cognac
1 oz (30 ml) gin
¾ oz (22 ml) ginger syrup (p 496)
½ oz (15 ml) lime juice
Soda, to top
Garnish: candied ginger

AMERICAN WHISKEY

Banjo Hitter
Jon Nutter, Attaboy, NYC
1 oz (30 ml) bourbon
1 oz (30 ml) Amaro Nardini
1 oz (30 ml) cloudy apple juice
¾ oz (22 ml) ginger syrup (p 496)
½ oz (15 ml) lime juice
Soda, to top
Garnish: apple fan and candied ginger

Bodega Buck
Brandon Bramhall, Attaboy, NYC, 2016
1½ oz (45 ml) bourbon
½ oz (15 ml) Amontillado Sherry
¾ oz (22 ml) ginger syrup (p 496)
½ oz (15 ml) lime juice
3 dashes Angostura Bitters
Soda, to top
Garnish: candied ginger

Add all ingredients except soda to a shaker and cube whip. Pour into a frozen Collins glass with ice and top with soda.

Bourbon Ginger Highball
(aka **Bourbon Buck**)
2 oz (60 ml) bourbon
1 oz (30 ml) lime juice
½ oz (15 ml) ginger syrup (p 496)
½ oz (15 ml) simple syrup
Soda, to top
Garnish: candied ginger

Bourbon Special
Kon-Tiki restaurants, North America, 1950s
2 oz (60 ml) bourbon
¾ oz (22 ml) lime juice
½ oz (15 ml) ginger syrup (p 496)
¼ oz (7ml) falernum
2 dashes Angostura Bitters
Soda, to top
Garnish: candied ginger

Buck Rogers
Michael Madrusan, Heartbreaker, Melbourne, 2023
2 oz (60 ml) bourbon
1 oz (30 ml) white grapefruit Juice
½ oz (15 ml) lemon juice
½ oz (15 ml) ginger syrup (p 496)
2 dashes The Bitter Truth Grapefruit Bitters
Soda, to top
Garnish: mint sprig and candied ginger

Cablegram
(aka **Rye Buck**)
The World's Drinks and How to Mix Them, *Wm. T. Boothby, 1908*
2 oz (60 ml) rye whiskey
¾ oz (22 ml) ginger syrup (p 496)
½ oz (15 ml) lime juice
Soda, to top
Garnish: candied ginger

Dark 'n' Hoppy No. 2
(See p 104)

Flu Cocktail
The Art of Mixing, *James A. Wiley and Helene M. Griffith, 1932*
1 oz (30 ml) rye whiskey
1 oz (30 ml) Cognac
¾ oz (22 ml) ginger syrup (p 496)
½ oz (15 ml) lime juice
Soda, to top
Garnish: candied ginger

Gentleman's Buck
(New Orleans Buck with bourbon)
Michael Madrusan, Little Branch, NYC, 2009
2 oz (60 ml) bourbon
1 oz (30 ml) orange juice
½ oz (15 ml) lemon juice
½ oz (15 ml) ginger syrup (p 496)
3 dashes Angostura Bitters
Soda, to top
Garnish: orange half-wheel and candied ginger

Gentleman's Buck No. 2
(Gentleman's Buck with pineapple)
Michael Madrusan, Little Branch, NYC, 2009
2 oz (60 ml) bourbon
1 oz (30 ml) pineapple juice
½ oz (15 ml) lemon juice
½ oz (15 ml) ginger syrup (p 496)
3 dashes Angostura Bitters
Soda, to top
Garnish: mint sprig and candied ginger

Kentucky Buck
Erick Castro, Bourbon & Branch, San Francisco, 2009
2 oz (60 ml) bourbon
¾ oz (22 ml) lemon juice
½ oz (15 ml) ginger syrup (p 496)
½ oz (15 ml) simple syrup
1 strawberry, halved
Soda, to top
Muddle strawberry with simple syrup, add remaining ingredients, shake briefly with ice, then pour into a frozen Collins glass with ice and top with soda.
Garnish: strawberry and candied ginger

Kickback
Angus Payne, The Everleigh, Melbourne, 2021
1½ oz (45 ml) bourbon
½ oz (15 ml) Giffard Crème de Pêche de Vigne
1 oz (30 ml) lime juice
½ oz (15 ml) ginger syrup (p 496)
Soda, to top
Garnish: candied ginger

Manhattan Buck
Michael Madrusan, Connie's Italian Diner, Melbourne, 2022
1 oz (30 ml) rye whiskey
¾ oz (22 ml) sweet vermouth
¾ oz (22 ml) lemon juice
¾ oz (22 ml) ginger syrup (p 496)
2 dashes Angostura Bitters
Soda, to top
Garnish: candied ginger and cherry

Monongahela Mule
Phil Ward, Death & Co, NYC, 2007
2 oz (60 ml) rye whiskey
¾ oz (22 ml) lemon juice
¾ oz (22 ml) ginger syrup (p 496)
4 raspberries
6–8 mint leaves
Soda, to top
Muddle raspberries with ginger syrup, add remaining ingredients, shake briefly with ice, then pour into a frozen Collins glass with ice and top with soda.
Garnish: mint sprig and candied ginger

New Orleans Mule
Difford's Guide
1½ oz (45 ml) bourbon
½ oz (15 ml) coffee liqueur
1 oz (30 ml) pineapple juice
¾ oz (22 ml) ginger syrup (p 496)
½ oz (15 ml) lime juice
Soda, to top
Garnish: candied ginger

Newport Buck
Brandon Bramhall, Last Saint, Charlotte, 2022
1 oz (30 ml) bourbon
1 oz (30 ml) Branca Menta
1 oz (30 ml) pineapple juice
½ oz (15 ml) lime juice
¾ oz (22 ml) ginger syrup (p 496)
Soda, to top
Garnish: 2 pineapple fronds and candied ginger

Add all ingredients except soda to a shaker and cube whip. Pour into a frozen Collins glass with ice and top with soda.

Oh, Henry! Cocktail
The Savoy Cocktail Book,
Harry Craddock, 1930
1½ oz (45 ml) bourbon
½ oz (15 ml) Bénédictine
¾ oz (22 ml) ginger syrup (p 496)
½ oz (15 ml) lime juice
Soda, to top
Garnish: candied ginger

Poppa's Pride
Jay Zimmerman, Ba'sik, NYC
2 oz (60 ml) bourbon
¾ oz (22 ml) lemon juice
½ oz (15 ml) ginger syrup (p 496)
½ oz (15 ml) simple syrup
5 dashes Angostura Bitters
5 mint leaves
Soda, to top
Add all ingredients to shaker, shake briefly with ice, then strain into a frozen Collins glass with ice and top with soda.
Garnish: mint bouquet

Small Branch Mule
Oliver Churcher, Double Deuce Lounge, Sydney, 2021
1 oz (30 ml) bourbon
1 oz (30 ml) Aperol
¾ oz (22 ml) lemon juice
¾ oz (22 ml) ginger syrup (p 496)
6–8 mint leaves
Soda, to top
Add all ingredients to shaker, shake briefly with ice, then strain into a frozen Collins glass with ice and top with soda.
Garnish: mint sprig and candied ginger

Southern Buck
Sam Ross, Attaboy, NYC
2 oz (60 ml) bourbon
1 oz (30 ml) lime juice
½ oz (15 ml) ginger syrup (p 496)
½ oz (15 ml) simple syrup
1 cucumber wheel
Soda, to top
Press cucumber with simple syrup, add all remaining ingredients, shake briefly with ice, then strain into a frozen Collins glass and top with soda.
Garnish: cucumber wheel and candied ginger

Twentieth Century
Straub's Manual of Mixed Drinks,
Jacques Straub, 1913
1½ oz (45 ml) bourbon
½ oz (15 ml) Jamaican dark rum
¾ oz (22 ml) ginger syrup (p 496)
⅜ oz (11 ml) lemon juice
⅜ oz (11 ml) lime juice
Soda, to top
Garnish: candied ginger

SCOTCH

Cupid Deluxe
José Cardenas, Dutch Kills, NYC, 2019
1½ oz (45 ml) Scotch
¾ oz (22 ml) Giffard Banane du Brésil et des Caraïbes
¾ oz (22 ml) pineapple juice
¾ oz (22 ml) lemon juice
½ oz (15 ml) ginger syrup (p 496)
2 dashes chocolate bitters
Soda, to top
Garnish: cucumber wheel and candied ginger

Fast Canoe
Paul McGee, Lost Lake, Chicago
1 oz (30 ml) single malt Scotch
¾ oz (22 ml) ginger syrup (p 496)
½ oz (15 ml) lemon juice
½ oz (15 ml) pandan syrup (p 499)
Soda, to top
Garnish: pandan leaf

Glasgow Mule
Damon Boelte, Grand Army, NYC
1½ oz (45 ml) Scotch
½ oz (15 ml) St Germain Elderflower Liqueur
¾ oz (22 ml) lemon juice
¾ oz (22 ml) ginger syrup (p 499)
1 dash Angostura Bitters
Soda, to top
Garnish: lemon half-wheel and candied ginger

Mamie Taylor
(aka **Scotch Buck** or **Presbyterian**)
Daly's Bartenders' Encyclopedia,
Tim Daly, 1903
2 oz (60 ml) Scotch
½ oz (15 ml) lime juice
¾ oz (22 ml) ginger syrup (p 496)
Soda, to top
Garnish: candied ginger

Tenderloin Reviver
(Scotch Buck with a lemon horse's neck garnish)
The New and Improved Illustrated Bartenders' Manual, *Harry Johnson, 1900*
2 oz (60 ml) Scotch
¾ oz (22 ml) ginger syrup (p 496)
½ oz (15 ml) lime juice
Soda, to top
Garnish: lemon horse's neck

Viceroy Buck
Julian Goglia, The Mercury, Atlanta
2 oz (60 ml) Scotch
¾ oz (22 ml) ginger syrup (p 496)
½ oz (15 ml) falernum
½ oz (15 ml) lime juice
Soda, to top
Garnish: candied ginger

White Horse
(New Orleans Buck with Scotch)
Straub's Manual of Mixed Drinks,
Jacques Straub, 1913
2 oz (60 ml) Scotch
1 oz (30 ml) orange juice
½ oz (15 ml) lemon juice
½ oz (15 ml) ginger syrup (p 496)
3 dashes Angostura Bitters
Soda, to top
Garnish: candied ginger

WORLD WHISK(E)Y

Accidental Guru
(See p 436)

Add all ingredients except soda to a shaker and cube whip. Pour into a frozen Collins glass with ice and top with soda.

Irish Buck
(Irish Whiskey Buck with Angostura Bitters)
2 oz (60 ml) Irish whiskey
¾ oz (22 ml) ginger syrup (p 496)
½ oz (15 ml) lime juice
3 dashes Angostura Bitters
Soda, to top
Garnish: candied ginger

FORTIFIED & LIQUEUR

Andalusian Buck
(See p 98)

Aperitivo Buck
(See p 436)

Bliz's Royal Rickey
The Ideal Bartender, *Tom Bullock, 1917*
1½ oz (45 ml) sweet vermouth
1 oz (30 ml) gin
½ oz (15 ml) lime juice
½ oz (15 ml) raspberry syrup (p 500)
½ oz (15 ml) ginger syrup (p 496)
Soda, to top
Garnish: raspberry and candied ginger

Broken Spanish
Yao Wong, The Elysian Whisky Bar, Melbourne, 2021
1 oz (30 ml) dry vermouth
1 oz (30 ml) Fino Sherry
¾ oz (22 ml) ginger syrup (p 496)
½ oz (15 ml) lemon juice
1 dash Peychaud's Aromatic Cocktail Bitters
Soda, to top
Garnish: lemon wedge

Buck Buck Mule
(See p 98)

Clip Joint Cup
Leo Robitschek, The NoMad Bar, NYC
1 oz (30 ml) Amaro Averna
1 oz (30 ml) Punt e Mes
¾ oz (22 ml) lime juice
½ oz (15 ml) ginger syrup (p 496)
½ oz (15 ml) Demerara syrup (p 495)
¾ oz (22 ml) soda, to top
¾ oz (22 ml) tonic water, to top
1 grapefruit twist
2 cucumber wheels
Press cucumber and grapefruit, add remaining ingredients, then shake briefly and strain into a frozen Collins glass with ice and top with soda and tonic water.
Garnish: mint sprig, grapefruit twist (discard) and cucumber wheel

Cloudy Sky
(aka **Sloe Gin Buck** or **Sloe Gin Bump**)
Cocktails: How to Mix Them, *Robert Vermeire, 1922*
2 oz (60 ml) sloe gin
¾ oz (22 ml) lime juice
½ oz (15 ml) ginger syrup (p 496)
½ oz (15 ml) simple syrup
Soda, to top
Garnish: candied ginger

Cosa Nostra No. 2
Dane Barca
Smuggler's Cove: Exotic Cocktails, Rum and the Cult of Tiki, *Martin and Rebecca Cate, 2016*
1½ oz (45 ml) Amaro Averna
1 oz (30 ml) light rum
¾ oz (22 ml) lemon juice
¾ oz (22 ml) ginger syrup (p 496)
1 dash Angostura Bitters
Soda, to top
Garnish: lemon horse's neck

Embassy Buck
Brandon Bramhall, Attaboy, Nashville
1 oz (30 ml) Fino Sherry
1 oz (30 ml) Cynar
1 oz (30 ml) pineapple juice
1 oz (30 ml) lime juice
½ oz (15 ml) ginger syrup (p 496)
½ oz (15 ml) falernum
Soda, to top
Garnish: 2 pineapple fronds and candied ginger

Ginger Snap
2 oz (60 ml) Fino Sherry
¾ oz (22 ml) ginger syrup (p 496)
½ oz (15 ml) lemon juice
Soda, to top
Garnish: candied ginger
▼ Based on a 17th-century Pennsylvania Dutch drink, which originates from a medieval recipe from 13th-century German monks.

Guernsey Cocktail
American Bar, *Frank P. Newman, 1900*
1½ oz (45 ml) Pierre Ferrand Dry Curaçao
¾ oz (22 ml) ginger syrup (p 496)
½ oz (15 ml) lime juice
Soda, to top
Garnish: candied ginger

Infernal Collins
Zac Overman, L'Oursin, Seattle
1 oz (30 ml) Maurin Quina
½ oz (15 ml) Campari
½ oz (15 ml) lime juice
½ oz (15 ml) ginger syrup (p 496)
Soda, to top
Garnish: candied ginger

Italian Buck
Jamie Boudreau, Canon, Seattle, 2015
1½ oz (45 ml) Cynar
1½ oz (45 ml) Amaro Montenegro
¾ oz (22 ml) ginger syrup (p 496)
½ oz (15 ml) lime juice
Soda, to top
Garnish: lime wheel and candied ginger

Klondyke
The World's Drinks and How to Mix Them, *Wm. T. Boothby, 1908*
1 oz (30 ml) sweet vermouth
1 oz (30 ml) dry vermouth
¾ oz (22 ml) ginger syrup (p 496)
½ oz (15 ml) lemon juice
Soda, to top
Garnish: candied ginger

Add all ingredients except soda to a shaker and cube whip. Pour into a frozen Collins glass with ice and top with soda.

Monkey Grip
Cameron Parish, The Everleigh, Melbourne, 2018
1½ oz (45 ml) Fino Sherry
½ oz (15 ml) Campari
¾ oz (22 ml) lemon juice
½ oz (15 ml) ginger syrup (p 496)
½ oz (15 ml) simple syrup
2 dashes Peychaud's Aromatic Cocktail Bitters
Soda, to top
Garnish: orange half-wheel and candied ginger

Paid in Pleasure
Alicia Perry and Anthony Schmidt, The Gutter, San Diego, 2023
1 oz (30 ml) dry red wine
½ oz (15 ml) Campari
½ oz (15 ml) raspberry eau de vie
¾ oz (22 ml) ginger syrup (p 496)
½ oz (15 ml) lime juice
Soda, to top
Garnish: raspberry

Pentecost
Brandon Bramhall and Andrew Rice, Attaboy, NYC, 2016
1 oz (30 ml) Fernet-Branca
1 oz (30 ml) sweet vermouth
1 oz (30 ml) lime juice
½ oz (15 ml) ginger syrup (p 496)
½ oz (15 ml) simple syrup
1 orange wedge
Soda, to top
Add all ingredients to shaker, shake briefly, then strain into a frozen Collins glass with ice and top with soda.
Garnish: orange wedge and candied ginger

Roman Highball
Michael Madrusan, Little Branch, NYC, 2008
1½ oz (45 ml) Amaro CioCiaro
¾ oz (22 ml) ginger syrup (p 496)
½ oz (15 ml) lime juice
Soda, to top
Garnish: candied ginger

Roof Garden Cooler
Old Waldorf Bar Days, *Albert Stevens Crockett, 1931*
2 oz (60 ml) dry vermouth
¾ oz (22 ml) ginger syrup (p 496)
½ oz (15 ml) lime juice
Soda, to top
5 dashes Angostura Bitters, to float
Add all ingredients to a shaker and cube whip, strain into a frozen Collins glass, then top with soda and float bitters.
Garnish: candied ginger

Session Dark 'n' Stormy
Session Cocktails, *Drew Lazor, 2018*
1 oz (30 ml) Amaro Montenegro
¾ oz (22 ml) Cruzan Black Strap Rum
½ oz (15 ml) lime juice
¾ oz (22 ml) ginger syrup (p 496)
Soda, to top
Garnish: candied ginger

Sippy Cup
Leo Robitschek, The NoMad Bar, NYC
1½ oz (45 ml) Amaro Averna
1 oz (30 ml) sweet vermouth
1 oz (30 ml) lime juice
½ oz (15 ml) ginger syrup (p 496)
½ oz (15 ml) simple syrup
3 dashes Angostura Bitters
Soda, to top
Garnish: mint sprig and orange wedge

The Waterfront
Damon Boelte, Prime Meats, NYC
1½ oz (45 ml) Fernet-Branca
¾ oz (22 ml) Branca Menta
¾ oz (22 ml) ginger syrup (p 496)
½ oz (15 ml) lime juice
Soda, to top
Garnish: mint sprig and candied ginger

Topside Buck
Felix Woods, The Everleigh, Melbourne, 2018
1 oz (30 ml) Amaro Braulio
1 oz (30 ml) sweet vermouth
¾ oz (22 ml) lemon juice
½ oz (15 ml) ginger syrup (p 496)
¼ oz (7 ml) simple syrup
Soda, to top
Garnish: candied ginger

Tuscan Mule
Sammy Berry, Brighton, 2003
2 oz (60 ml) Tuaca Liqueur
¾ oz (22 ml) lime juice
¾ oz (22 ml) ginger syrup (p 496)
Soda, to top
Garnish: candied ginger

Venenciador
Brandon Bramhall, Attaboy, Nashville, 2017
1 oz (30 ml) Amontillado Sherry
½ oz (15 ml) Fino Sherry
½ oz (15 ml) Pedro Ximénez
¾ oz (22 ml) ginger syrup (p 496)
½ oz (15 ml) lime juice
Soda, to top
Garnish: candied ginger

OTHER

Bohemian Mule
Giovanni Burdi, 1990s
1 oz (30 ml) absinthe
¾ oz (22 ml) ginger syrup (p 496)
½ oz (15 ml) lime juice
Soda, to top
Garnish: candied ginger

Dead Bastard
Joe Scialom, circa 1942
½ oz (15 ml) gin
½ oz (15 ml) Cognac
½ oz (15 ml) bourbon
½ oz (15 ml) aged dark rum
¾ oz (22 ml) ginger syrup (p 496)
½ oz (15 ml) lime juice
Soda, to top
Garnish: candied ginger

Dying Bastard
Joe Scialom, circa 1942
¾ oz (22 ml) gin
¾ oz (22 ml) Cognac
¾ oz (22 ml) bourbon
¾ oz (22 ml) ginger syrup (p 496)
½ oz (15 ml) lime juice
Soda, to top
Garnish: candied ginger

Suffering Bastard
(see p 103)

Add all ingredients except soda to a shaker and cube whip. Pour into a frozen Collins glass with ice and top with soda.

HIGHBALL & MIXED DRINK

Chrysantonic p 119 (left), Gin & Tonic Al Fresco p 117 (right)

Highball & Mixed Drink

Simple drinks with few base ingredients, topped with a carbonated mixer and/or juice, served tall with ice.

spirit/wine + soda/carbonated mixer/ juice

Build all ingredients in a frozen Highball glass and stir briefly.

The name 'highball' most likely originates from the term 'ball': a common name for a glass of whiskey in Ireland and in English golf club bars in the late-19th century. It may also have come from early American railroad signs, where the depiction of a raised ball – or 'highball' – indicated a clear path ahead. A highball is a simple mix of spirits and soda served tall over ice, a smart way to savour the flavour and quality of a drink's ingredients in a long, refreshing format. Carbonation, however, was discovered in 1767 when Joseph Priestley first infused water with carbon dioxide, eventually leading to the use of soda to lengthen spirits (first brandy, then whisky as its quality improved) becoming customary in the United Kingdom by the mid-19th century.

The narrow, chimney-like style of both Highball and Collins glasses has a practical purpose: it keeps ice cubes stacked vertically, which reduces surface area, and makes the ice melt more slowly. The Collins glass is intended to hold multiple ingredients topped with a sparkling component, whereas the Highball glass was originally intended for a spirit and a mixer only.

Across the pond, Americans were quite satisfied with their Rickeys and Coolers until the 1870s, when Britain's Tom Collins (p 72), featuring Old Tom gin, began to make a stir. By the 1880s, New York City bars were serving what they dubbed a Scotch Highball, and it wasn't long before American whiskey found its way into the fold. By the 1950s, the Highball had become the most popular way to enjoy spirits the world over and countless variations emerged in the leading markets, steered by changing trends and prominent liquor brands.

Unlike the Collins, the classic Highball often forfeits citrus juice allowing the base ingredient to shine, making it a popular choice for fans of premium spirits. In Japan, for example, the Highball has long been a symbol of minimalist sophistication and precision, showcasing high-quality ingredients along with clear, largely hand-cut ice. In the 21st century, the Highball's understated elegance has found favour with the modern drinker, and bartenders continue to creatively reshape the genre by incorporating house-made sodas and mixers, adding bitters and spotlighting wine-based products that cater to the growing demand for low-ABV options.

Other 'splits' (drinks with two ingredients: a base and a lengthener) and easily built drinks with few ingredients have also been included here as 'Mixed Drinks'. Often a foray into cocktails, Mixed Drinks have far-reaching appeal due to their fuss-free formulation and approachable ingredients, commonly centred around fresh juices and flavoured sodas. For best results, we strongly suggest chilling your base alcoholic ingredient(s) prior to preparation.

ESSENTIAL VARIATIONS

Americano (House Recipe)
1½ oz (45 ml) sweet vermouth
½ oz (15 ml) Campari
½ oz (15 ml) Aperol
1 oz (30 ml) soda, to top

Build in a frozen footed Delmonico glass and stir briefly.
Garnish: orange half-wheel and Cerignola olive

Americano (Gaspare Campari Recipe)
Gaspare Campari, Caffè Campari, 1860s
1¼ oz (37 ml) sweet vermouth
1¼ oz (37 ml) Campari
1 oz (30 ml) soda, to top

Build in a frozen footed Delmonico glass and stir briefly.
Garnish: orange half-wheel

Italian for 'American style', the Americano is a distinctly Italian cocktail combining sweet vermouth with digestive bitters and soda. The name references the American preference for enjoying bitters in Italian vermouth during the latter half of the 18th century, when Italy's bartenders would make drinks in the 'American' way, by lengthening vermouth with bitters, soda and ice. It is thought that the Americano and its shorter sibling, the Milano-Torino (p 417) – a merger of Milano's Campari with Torino's vermouth – surfaced in the 1860s at bars such as Caffè Camparino in Milan, owned by legendary Italian beverage manufacturer Gaspare Campari.

Campari had been selling a bitter aperitivo under the name 'Bitter all'uso d'Holanda', inspired by a cordial he'd experienced in Holland since the 1840s, but it wasn't until 1860 that the product we now know as Campari was born. While the recipe is still somewhat confidential, we know the bitters contained more than 60 natural ingredients, from herbs and spices to fruit peels. By 1930, Campari dominated the Italian bitters market, but the Americano had been eclipsed by a bolder cocktail: the almighty Negroni (p 292).

In our humble opinion, there are few finer things in life than a well-made Americano before dinner. The key to its beauty is the right amount of soda, so be mindful to measure precisely. Other worthy low-alcohol aperitivi in the American style include the Bicicletta Spritz (p 414, aka the Veneziano Spritz) with dry Italian white wine instead of sweet; the Negroni Sbagliato (p 417), with sparkling wine in place of soda; and the Americano Perfecto (p 436), which is topped with a crisp pilsner.

Batanga

Don Javier Delgado Corona, La Capilla, Tequila, 1961
2 oz (60 ml) blanco tequila
½ oz (15 ml) lime juice
4 oz (120 ml) Coca-Cola, to top

Build ingredients in a frozen Highball glass with ice, then stir with the knife used to cut the limes.
Garnish: salt rim and lime wedge

The Batanga was created in 1961 by Don Javier Delgado Corona, the owner of La Capilla ('The Chapel'), a cantina located in the town of Tequila, Mexico. This simple and sweet tequila Highball is best understood both as a Mexican riff on the Cuba Libre (p 117) – a combo of light rum, lime and cola – and an evolution of the Changuirongo (p 118), a mixture of tequila and sweet soda (most commonly ginger ale) popularised in the 1940s. The Batanga is just one of many vintage drinks that has experienced a resurgence thanks to increased interest in tequila and mezcal in the 21st century.

Fresh lime and a salt rim certainly contribute to the drink's charm, but it's Don Javier's distinct touch that really makes the drink special. Prior to his death in 2020, Don Javier would famously stir the ingredients using a long knife with a wooden handle, the same knife he had used to chop the limes and maybe even avocados or chillies for guacamole and salsa moments prior.

Though they don't include remnants of Don Javier's guacamole, there are other tall, sweet and fresh tequila-based cocktails deserving of your attention, such as the Mexican El Diablo (p 102), a Buck with a splash of crème de cassis by Trader Vic, and the Palomita (p 426) – a riff on the iconic Paloma topped with Champagne that we created for The Everleigh Bottling Co. in 2020.

JARRIT
Mexican
NEW YORK WORLD'S FAIR

Highball & Mixed Drink

VODKA

Bloody Mary (Jeffrey Morgenthaler 'All-Day' Recipe)
Fernand "Pete" Petiot, Harry's New York Bar, Paris, circa 1921
1½ oz (45 ml) vodka
2 oz (60 ml) All-Day Bloody Mary Mix (p 494)
2 oz (60 ml) tomato juice
Add ingredients to a shaker with ice, roll back and forth to chill but not aerate, then strain into a frozen 16 oz (455 ml) pint glass with ice.
Garnish: salt-and-pepper rim, lemon wedge and dill pickle spear

There are plenty of recipes for this classic, but we've chosen Morgenthaler's because it's easy to execute and makes a great-tasting drink.

For a more complex drink, try the Maison Premiere Bloody Mary Mix (p 494) instead, which is also fantastic.

Notable Variations
- **Red Snapper**: Bloody Mary with gin
- **Bloody Maria**: Bloody Mary with blanco tequila
- **Bloody Caesar**: Bloody Mary with Clamato juice instead of tomato juice

Bloody Mary (Maison Premiere Recipe)
The Maison Premiere Almanac, *Joshua Boissy, Krystof Zizka and Jordan Mackay with William Elliott, 2023*
1½ oz (45 ml) vodka
½ oz (15 ml) oyster stout
½ oz (15 ml) lemon juice
5 oz (150 ml) Maison Premiere Bloody Mary mix (p 494)
3 dashes Tabasco
freshly ground black pepper, to taste
Add the vodka, stout, lemon juice, Tabasco and pepper to a poco grande glass with ice and stir. Add the Bloody Mary mix and stir again. Garnish with a celery stalk, lemon wedge and pickled vegetables. Finish with a little more pepper.
Garnish: celery stalk, lemon wedge, skewer of pickled vegetables

Bloody Mary Verde
Devon Tarby, 2013
Cocktail Codex, *Alex Day, David Kaplan and Nick Fauchald, 2018*
1½ oz (45 ml) jalapeño-infused vodka (p 503)
5 oz (150 ml) verde mix (p 507)
1 oz (30 ml) lime juice
Kosher salt, chilli powder and lime wedge, to rim
Garnish: chilli-salt rim, cherry tomato and lemon wedge on a cocktail skewer

Greyhound
The Savoy Cocktail Book, *Harry Craddock, 1930*
2 oz (60 ml) vodka
4 oz (120 ml) pink grapefruit juice
¼ oz (7 ml) lemon juice
2 dashes grapefruit bitters, to float
Garnish: grapefruit wedge

Madras
1970s
2 oz (60 ml) vodka
3 oz (90 ml) cranberry juice
2 oz (60 ml) orange juice
Garnish: lime wedge

Rangoon Ruby
(Cape Codder with soda)
Trader Vic's Bartender's Guide, Revised, *Trader Vic, 1972*
2 oz (60 ml) vodka
1½ oz (45 ml) cranberry juice
½ oz (15 ml) lime juice
Soda, to top
Garnish: spent lime shell and mint sprig
Notable Variations
- **Cape Cod**: Rangoon Ruby without soda or lime
- **Cape Codder**: Rangoon Ruby without soda
- **Cape Cod Cooler**: Rangoon Ruby without lime
- **Harpoon**: Cape Codder with light rum

Screwdriver
Iran, 1940s
2 oz (60 ml) vodka
1 teaspoon (5 ml) lemon juice
2 dashes orange bitters
4 oz (120 ml) orange juice, to top
Garnish: orange half-wheel
Add all ingredients to a shaker and pebble whip. Pour into a frozen Highball glass with ice and top with orange juice.

Supposedly come from American oil engineers who'd add vodka to their orange juice and stir it with a screwdriver.

Testarossa
1 oz (30 ml) vodka
1½ oz (45 ml) Campari
Soda, to top
Garnish: orange wedge

Yuzu Flame of Love
Paul Hammond, Connie's Italian Diner, Melbourne, 2022
2 oz (60 ml) vodka
1 teaspoon (5 ml) Fino Sherry
2 dashes orange bitters
2 oz (60 ml) yuzu soda, to top
Add all ingredients to a shaker and pebble whip. Pour into a frozen double rocks glass with ice and top with yuzu soda.
Garnish: 2 flamed orange twists

Build all ingredients in a frozen Highball glass and stir briefly.

GIN

Bitter Corpse
Michael Madrusan, The Everleigh, Melbourne, 2023
1¼ oz (37 ml) gin
¾ oz (22 ml) Cocchi Americano
2 dashes absinthe
Bitter lemon soda, to top
Add all ingredients to a shaker and pebble whip. Pour into a frozen Highball glass with ice and top with bitter lemon soda.
Garnish: lemon wedge

Dirty Martini Highball
Fanny Chu
1½ oz (45 ml) gin
¾ oz (22 ml) bianco vermouth
¾ oz (22 ml) Manzanilla Sherry
¼ oz (7 ml) olive brine
Tonic water, to top
Add all ingredients to a shaker and pebble whip. Pour into a frozen Highball glass with ice and top with tonic water.
Garnish: Cerignola olive and lemon twist

G.P.T (Gin, Peperoncini, Tonic)
Sean O'Connor-Combee, J & Tony's Discount Cured Meats and Negroni Warehouse, San Diego, 2022
1 oz (30 ml) gin
½ oz (15 ml) Manzanilla Sherry
¾ oz (22 ml) peperoncini brine
Tonic water, to top
Add all ingredients to a shaker and pebble whip. Pour into a frozen Highball glass with ice and top with tonic water.
Garnish: lime wedge (squeezed and dropped into the drink) and salami slice (optional)

Gin & Tonic Al Fresco
Dale DeGroff, Jovia, NYC, 2007
1½ oz (45 ml) gin
½ oz (15 ml) Cynar
1 dash orange bitters
Tonic water, to top
Garnish: long cucumber slice

Gin Sonic
Tokyo, 1990s
1½ oz (45 ml) gin
⅓ oz (10 ml) lime juice
2 oz (60 ml) soda, to top
2 oz (60 ml) tonic water, to top
Garnish: lime wedge

Grapefruit White Negroni
Paul Hammond, Connie's Italian Diner, Melbourne, 2022
¾ oz (22 ml) gin
½ oz (15 ml) Cocchi Americano
½ oz (15 ml) Suze
2 oz (60 ml) pink grapefruit soda, to top
Serve in a frozen double rocks glass with ice.
Garnish: grapefruit wedge

Messenger's Tonic
Hawksmoor, London
1 oz (30 ml) gin
½ oz (15 ml) Cocchi Americano
½ oz (15 ml) Manzanilla Sherry
Tonic water, to top
Garnish: lemon wedge

Salmoncito
Khristian de la Torre, Mexico City, 2013
1½ oz (45 ml) gin
⅓ oz (10 ml) Campari
⅓ oz (10 ml) pink grapefruit juice
4 oz (120 ml) tonic water, to top
Garnish: grapefruit twist (discard) and grapefruit wedge

Salty Dog
(Gin Greyhound with a salt rim)
Late 1950s or early 1960s
2 oz (60 ml) gin
¼ oz (7 ml) lemon juice
2 drops saline solution (p 493)
4 oz (120 ml) pink grapefruit juice, to top
Garnish: salt rim

Shiso Gin & Tonic
Masahiro Urushido, Katana Kitten, NYC
1½ oz (45 ml) gin (preferably Fords Gin)
¾ oz (22 ml) shiso-quinine cordial (p 500)
¼ oz (7 ml) lime juice
Soda, to top
Garnish: shiso leaf

Vesper Highball
Simon Difford, Dmytro Grypachevskyy and Lucian Obreja, L'Ortolan, Reading, 2018
1 oz (30 ml) gin
½ oz (15 ml) vodka
½ oz (15 ml) Cocchi Americano
2 drops saline solution (p 493)
Tonic water, to top (preferably Schweppes Salty Lemon Tonic Water)
Add all ingredients to a shaker and pebble whip. Pour into a frozen Highball glass with ice and top with tonic water.
Garnish: lemon twist

White Negroni Highball
Orlando Franklin McCray
1½ oz (45 ml) gin
1 oz (30 ml) bianco vermouth
¾ oz (22 ml) Suze
Tonic water, to top (preferably Fever-Tree Mediterranean Tonic Water)
Garnish: lemon wedge

RUM

Cuba Libre
Havana, early 1900s
2 oz (60 ml) light rum
½ oz (15 ml) lime juice
4 oz (120 ml) Coca-Cola, to top
1 dash Angostura Bitters
Garnish: lime wedge

Build all ingredients in a frozen Highball glass and stir briefly.

AGAVE

Changuirongo
Mexico, 1940s
2 oz (60 ml) blanco tequila
½ oz (15 ml) lime juice
4 oz (120 ml) ginger ale, to top
Garnish: lime wedge

Freddy Fudpucker
(Harvey Wallbanger with tequila)
Donato "Duke" Antone, circa 1960s
2 oz (60 ml) blanco tequila
5 oz (150 ml) orange juice
1 teaspoon (5 ml) lemon juice
½ oz (15 ml) Galliano L'Autentico, to float
Garnish: orange half-wheel

Ranch Water
West Texas, 1960s
2 oz (60 ml) blanco tequila
1 oz (30 ml) lime juice
sparkling water, to top (preferably Topo Chico)
Garnish: lime wedge

Ranch Water (Eight Row Flint Recipe)
Morgan Weber, Eight Row Flint, Houston
2 oz (60 ml) sotol, chilled in freezer until very cold
1 oz (30 ml) lime juice
1 oz (30 ml) lime oleo-saccharum (p 497)
pinch of salt
sparkling water, to top (preferably Topo Chico)
Garnish: 3 grapefruit peels

Reposado Highball
Good Things to Drink with Mr. Lyan & Friends, *Ryan Chetiyawardana, 2015*
1½ oz (45 ml) reposado tequila
½ oz (15 ml) Lillet Blanc
1 dash Angostura Bitters
4 oz (120 ml) ginger ale, to top
Garnish: mint sprig

Siete
Sid Chi, Holy Ghost, Portland
2 oz (60 ml) coconut-washed tequila (p 503)
½ oz (15 ml) pineapple juice
½ oz (15 ml) lime juice
Soda water, to top
Garnish: salt rim and lime wheel

Tequila Sunrise (Andrew Rice Recipe)
Bobby Lozoff and Billy Rice, The Trident, Sausalito, 1970
2 oz (60 ml) blanco tequila
¼ oz (7 ml) crème de cassis
5 oz (150 ml) orange juice
½ oz (15 ml) lime juice
½ oz (15 ml) grenadine (p 496)
1 dash orange bitters
2 drops saline solution (p 493)
Pour grenadine and crème de cassis into a frozen Collins glass with ice, then cube whip remaining ingredients and slowly pour into the glass.
Garnish: orange wedge

AMERICAN WHISKEY

Four-Way Split
Felix Woods, Romeo Lane, Melbourne, 2019
¾ oz (22 ml) bourbon
¾ oz (22 ml) sweet vermouth
¾ oz (22 ml) dry vermouth
¾ oz (22 ml) Campari
2 oz (60 ml) soda, to top
Add all ingredients to a shaker and pebble whip. Pour into a frozen Highball glass with ice and top with soda.
Garnish: orange wedge

Honolulu Cocktail
(Bourbon and soda with bitters)
Straub's Manual of Mixed Drinks, *Jacques Straub, 1913*
2 oz (60 ml) bourbon
2 dashes Angostura Bitters
4 oz (120 ml) soda, to top
Garnish: lime wedge

Manhattan Highball
Alexis Simonidis, Theory Bar, Athens
1 oz (30 ml) rye whiskey
1 oz (30 ml) sweet vermouth
Tonic water, to top
Garnish: orange twist and cherry

SCOTCH

Blood Orange Backwards Point
Paul Hammond, Connie's Italian Diner, Melbourne, 2022
1 oz (30 ml) Scotch
⅓ oz (10 ml) Cynar
¼ oz (7 ml) sweet vermouth
2 oz (60 ml) blood orange soda, to top
Add all ingredients to a shaker and pebble whip. Pour into a frozen double rocks glass with ice and top with blood orange soda.
Garnish: orange wedge

Half-Time Highball
Felix Woods, Black Pearl, Melbourne, 2020
¾ oz (22 ml) Scotch
¾ oz (22 ml) sweet vermouth
⅜ oz (11 ml) Campari
⅜ oz (11 ml) Aperol
3 dashes Angostura Bitters
Soda, to top
Add all ingredients to a shaker and pebble whip. Pour into a frozen Collins glass with ice, then top with soda.
Garnish: orange wedge

WORLD WHISK(E)Y

Tropical Popsicle
Tony Roehr, Noble Experiment, San Diego
1½ oz (45 ml) Japanese whisky
½ oz (15 ml) Aperol
¾ oz (22 ml) lime juice
¾ oz (22 ml) passionfruit syrup (p 499)
Soda, to top
Add all ingredients to a shaker and pebble whip. Pour into a frozen Collins glass with ice, then top with soda.
Garnish: lime wedge

Build all ingredients in a frozen Highball glass and stir briefly.

FORTIFIED & LIQUEUR

Americano Chinato
(See p 414)

Apple Garibaldi
Punch
¾ oz (22 ml) Manzanilla Sherry
¾ oz (22 ml) bianco vermouth
½ oz (15 ml) gin
¼ oz (7 ml) lemon juice
5 oz (180 ml) Granny Smith apple juice, to top
Pebble whip the apple juice until fluffy, then add remaining ingredients to a frozen Collins glass with ice and top with apple juice.
Garnish: apple wedge

Bamboo Highball
Stacey Swenson, Dante, NYC
1¼ oz (37 ml) Manzanilla Sherry
1¼ oz (37 ml) dry vermouth
2 dashes The Bitter Truth Olive Bitters
2 dashes The Bitter Truth Lemon Bitters
Tonic water, to top
Garnish: rosemary sprig and Cerignola olive

Belafonte
Cas Oh, London, 2014
1 oz (30 ml) Campari
1 oz (30 ml) white Port
3 oz (90 ml) tonic water, to top
Garnish: orange wedge

Bonanza
The How and When, Hyman Gale and Gerald F. Marco, 1938
1½ oz (45 ml) Cognac
¾ oz (22 ml) Manzanilla Sherry
Riesling, to top
Garnish: lemon wedge

Braulio-Cano
I'm Just Here for the Drinks, *Sother Teague, 2018*
1½ oz (45 ml) Amaro Braulio
1½ oz (45 ml) Cocchi Rosa
2 drops Bittermens Orange Cream Citrate
Soda, to top
Add all ingredients to a shaker and pebble whip. Pour into a frozen Highball glass with ice and top with soda.
Garnish: orange half-wheel

Chrysantonic
1 oz (30 ml) dry vermouth
½ oz (15 ml) Bénédictine
3 dashes absinthe
Tonic water, to top
Garnish: long lemon twist

Excelsior Special
(See p 415)

Fumata Bianca
Tim Miner, NYC, 2016
1 oz (30 ml) bianco vermouth (preferably Carpano Bianco)
1 oz (30 ml) Suze
½ oz (15 ml) mezcal
Soda, to top
Garnish: grapefruit twist

Garibaldi
(See p 416)

J & Tony's Kold Brew Americano
Anthony Schmidt, J & Tony's Discount Cured Meats and Negroni Warehouse, San Diego
1 oz (30 ml) sweet vermouth
1 oz (30 ml) Campari
1 oz (30 ml) cold-brew coffee
¼ oz (7 ml) lemon juice
2 oz (60 ml) soda, to top
Add all ingredients to a shaker and pebble whip. Pour into a frozen Collins glass with ice and top with soda.
Garnish: orange wedge

Jai-Alai
Floridita Cock-tails, *Constante Ribalaigua Vert, 1939*
1½ oz (45 ml) Picon Amer
¾ oz (22 ml) gin
¾ oz (22 ml) sweet vermouth
Soda, to top
Add all ingredients to a shaker and pebble whip. Pour into a frozen Collins glass with ice and top with soda.
Garnish: orange half-wheel

Ladybird
(See p 416)

Mid-Morning Americano
(See p 417)

No Hands
(See p 417)

Overspin
Tom Opie, The Waratah, Sydney, 2024
1 oz (30 ml) Campari
¾ oz (22 ml) blanco tequila
2½ oz (75 ml) tangelo juice
1 teaspoon (5 ml) white crème de cacao
Mandarin soda, to top (preferably StrangeLove Very Mandarin Lo-Cal Soda)
Add all ingredients to a shaker and pebble whip. Pour into a frozen Collins glass with ice and top with mandarin soda.
Garnish: tangelo wedge

Pineapple Garibaldi
Punch
1½ oz (45 ml) génépy
¼ oz (7 ml) lemon juice
6 oz (180 ml) pineapple juice, to top
Whip the pineapple juice until fluffy, then add remaining ingredients to a frozen Collins glass with ice and top with pineapple juice.
Garnish: pineapple wedge

Build all ingredients in a frozen Highball glass and stir briefly.

Pompière
Rob Libecans, Melbourne, 2013
1½ oz (45 ml) dry vermouth
½ oz (15 ml) crème de cassis
1 dash absinthe
Soda, to top
Add all ingredients to a shaker and pebble whip. Pour into a frozen Highball glass and top with soda.
Garnish: lemon wedge

Spumoni
1 oz (30 ml) Campari
1½ oz (45 ml) pink grapefruit juice
3 oz (90 ml) tonic water, to top
Add all ingredients to a shaker and pebble whip. Pour into a frozen Highball glass and top with tonic water.
Garnish: grapefruit wedge

Spumoni (Lorenzo Antinori Recipe)
Lorenzo Antinori, Bar Leone, Hong Kong, 2023
1 oz (30 ml) Campari
¾ oz (22 ml) yuzushu
½ oz (15 ml) pink grapefruit juice
⅜ oz (11 ml) lime juice
1½ oz (45 ml) tonic water, to top
Pebble whip, then pour into a frozen Highball glass and top with tonic water.
Garnish: grapefruit wedge

Suzie Americano
Tristan Willey, The Long Island Bar, NYC
1½ oz (45 ml) Suze
1½ oz (45 ml) bianco vermouth
Soda, to top
Garnish: grapefruit half-wheel

Teqtonic
Felix Woods, Black Pearl, Melbourne, 2022
1¼ oz (37 ml) Cocchi Americano
¾ oz (22 ml) reposado tequila
¾ oz (22 ml) Fino Sherry
1 dash Angostura Bitters
1 dash orange bitters
Tonic water, to top
Add all ingredients to a shaker and pebble whip. Pour into a frozen double rocks glass with ice and top with tonic water.
Garnish: orange wedge and a pinch of salt flakes

Venetian Blinds
Brandon Bramhall, Attaboy, Nashville, 2021
1¼ oz (37 ml) Amontillado Sherry
1¼ oz (37 ml) Select Aperitivo
3 dashes absinthe
Soda, to top
Add all ingredients to a shaker and pebble whip. Pour into a frozen Highball glass and top with soda.
Garnish: long orange twist

From *The Savoy Cocktail Book* (1930):

Here's to alcohol—because no great story ever started with someone eating a salad.

OTHER

Absinthe Sonic
Takuya Itoh, Bar Tram, Tokyo, 2005
1 oz (30 ml) absinthe (preferably Mansinthe)
3 oz (90 ml) tonic water, to top
1 oz (30 ml) soda, to top
Garnish: lime wedge

Brain-Duster
Modern American Drinks, *George J. Kappeler, 1895*
1 oz (30 ml) absinthe
½ oz (15 ml) bourbon
½ oz (15 ml) sweet vermouth
1 teaspoon (5 ml) simple syrup
Soda, to top
Add all ingredients to a shaker and pebble whip. Pour into a frozen Highball glass with ice and top with soda.
Garnish: orange half-wheel and cherry

Normandie Club Bloody Mary
Devon Tarby, 2015
Cocktail Codex, Alex Day, David Kaplan and Nick Fauchald, 2018
1½ oz (45 ml) Krogstad aquavit (can use gin, vodka, amontillado)
5 oz (150 ml) Normandie Club Bloody Mary mix (p 498)
¼ oz (7 ml) fresh lemon juice
¼ oz (7 ml) fresh lime juice
lemon wedge
Lemon pepper salt (p 507)
Rub the lemon wedge along the upper 1 cm (½ in) of a Collins glass, halfway around its circumference, then roll the wet portion in the lemon pepper salt. Fill the glass with ice, add the remaining ingredients and stir.
Garnish: 1 cherry tomato and 1 lemon wedge on a skewer

Build all ingredients in a frozen Highball glass and stir briefly.

CUP & PUNCH

Mint Punch p 132 (left), Fruit Cup Italiano p 130 (right)

Cup & Punch

Festive, often fruit-forward, cocktails combining citrus, spices and an abundance of ingredients.

CUP

spirit/s + wine, liqueur/s + citrus + sugar + spices

Muddle all ingredients, except carbonated, in a shaker, then shake with ice and strain into a chilled Spritz glass with ice. Top with a mixer, beer or sparkling wine and stir briefly to combine.

PUNCH

spirit/s + citrus + sugar + spices + filtered water/mixer

Chill all ingredients, then combine in a punchbowl with large blocks of ice and stir briefly to combine. To serve, ladle into rocks glasses or Punch cups with ice.

The Cup, dating back to the 1800s, was traditionally a wine-based cocktail mixed with citrus, liqueurs and spices (and sometimes gin or brandy), distinguished by a large-format serving vessel, such as a jug or a punchbowl. Today, however, the style is famously associated with Pimm's, the quintessential gin-based English liqueur, or 'Fruit Cup'.

In order to aid digestion, James Pimm – a fishmonger and son of a farmer from Kent, England – designed a mysterious gin-based tonic somewhere between 1823 and 1840, which he served in a small tankard at his London oyster bar. That drink was called the No.1 Cup, the name we now associate with the unmistakable label of the most successful product in the Pimm's range. Pimm's expanded into large-scale production in 1851 and went on to develop Pimm's Cup variations for every spirit. Though Pimm's (owned by Diageo since 1997) remains very successful worldwide, many contemporary bars now produce their own proprietary Fruit Cups – see p 126 for ours.

Predating the Cup by almost 200 years – and similar in style and form – is the drink that started it all, long before modern American mixology took off: the Punch. First recorded in the papers of the East India Company in 1632, the Punch was concocted by the English in India using various local ingredients and alleged to have taken its name from the Hindi word for 'five' (due to the number of essential components), or the barrels, or puncheons, from which it was served. This hearty combination of spirit, citrus, sugar, water and spices was enjoyed as a group ritual, served cold in the summer and hot in the winter. The Punch reigned supreme as a drink of choice around the world until the 1840s, when the faster pace of Victorian life allowed for less time to gather around a communal bowl, making single-serve cocktails a more fashionable option.

→

For tradition's sake, we've chosen to focus on large-format punch recipes here, despite the fact that they're now more often reserved for special occasions or English tennis tournaments. Of course, single-serve Cups and Punches are just as attractive to today's drinker, and you'll find plenty of those recipes elsewhere, such as the chapter devoted to Tropical drinks (p 442). No matter the size, these are fragrant, fresh and abundantly garnished drinks that offer almost limitless opportunities for interpretation depending on whether you lengthen with carbonated soft drinks, beer or sparkling wine.

ESSENTIAL VARIATIONS

Fruit Cup (House Recipe)

(aka **Pimm's Cup**, James Pimm, London, 1800s)
2 oz (60 ml) fruit cup syrup (see p 496), or Pimm's No.1 for Pimm's Cup
2 cucumber wheels
1 lime wedge
1 lemon wedge
1 orange wedge
1 strawberry
6–8 mint leaves
Lemonade, to top

Add all ingredients, except lemonade, to a shaker and press. Add ice then shake briefly and strain into a frozen Spritz glass with ice. Top with lemonade and stir briefly.
Garnish: mint bouquet, cucumber wheels and a strawberry half

Our interpretation of the classic Pimm's Cup calls for a house-made blend of gin, sweet vermouth, Grand Marnier and Heering Cherry Liqueur. The combination of Heering and sweet vermouth gives it a cola-like quality, and the slightly higher alcohol content than Pimms No. 1 makes for a punchier yet equally fruity and refreshing cocktail. Muddled fruits play a big role in this drink, so sourcing the ripest and freshest is key.

True to its design, the Fruit Cup cocktail encapsulates afternoon picnics in the park under the English sun, although it's worth noting the drink also has a strong following in New Orleans, where it is enjoyed during the sweltering summers, especially at Napoleon House, supposedly the first bar in the United States to serve it. Of course, the drink's strongest affiliation is with Wimbledon, the iconic Grand Slam tennis tournament, where a Pimm's bar has been stationed since 1971 and reportedly serves upwards of 280,000 drinks each year.

Add ginger syrup (p 496) and swap lemonade for soda and you get the Fruit Cup Rangoon (p 130), the most ordered variation during Michael's time in New York City. For a glitzier riff, you can lengthen it with Champagne, and you'll wind up with a Fruit Cup Spritz (p 130).

Philadelphia Fish House Punch

Serves 10–12
(aka **Fish House Punch**)
Schuylkill Fishing Company of Pennsylvania, Philadelphia, 1795
17 oz (500 ml) Jamaican dark rum
8½ oz (255 ml) Cognac
6 oz (175 ml) Giffard Crème de Pêche de Vigne
8½ oz (255 ml) lemon juice
2½ oz (75 ml) simple syrup
8½ oz (255 ml) filtered water (or to taste)

Chill all ingredients, then combine in a punchbowl with large blocks of ice and stir gently to combine. To serve, ladle into rocks glasses or Punch cups with ice.
Garnish: 6 lemon half-wheels, 6 peach slices and freshly grated nutmeg

There's a little place just out of town,
Where, if you go to lunch,
They'll make you forget your mother-in-law,
With a drink called Fish House Punch.

By the end of the 17th century, Punch's reputation had successfully evolved from sailors' grog and scurvy preventative to a cocktail for all classes. Different spirits came at vastly varying price tags, of course, with gin being the affordable option in England, and rum in the colonies. It is thought that the diminished popularity of Punch by the beginning of the 1800s was partially due to improved methods of distillation and liquor production, which made spirits more palatable on their own and less prone to modification.

The Philadelphia Fish House Punch is perhaps the most famous American Punch recipe in history, thanks to its origin as one of America's earliest mixed drinks and, in drink historian David Wondrich's words, it 'deserves to be protected by law, taught in the schools, and made a mandatory part of every Fourth of July celebration.' Born at a Philadelphia fishing club nicknamed the "State in Schuylkill" and founded in 1732 by colonial Americans prior to the Revolution, and popular among America's Founding Fathers, it combines a boozy base of Cognac, Jamaican dark rum and peach liqueur with citrus, water and ice in a large bowl.

For similar brandy-based options that are equally peachy, try The Real Georgia Mint Julep (p 285), a Cognac and peach Julep from Jerry Thomas in 1887, or the more contemporary Last One Standing (p 285) by Natasha David from 2014 – a combination of Cognac, Jamaican gold rum, Amaro CioCiaro and peach liqueur.

Cup

Muddle all ingredients, except carbonated, in a shaker, then shake briefly with ice and strain into a frozen Spritz glass with ice. Top with a mixer, beer or sparkling wine and stir briefly to combine.

#3 Cup
(aka **Cognac Fruit Cup Rangoon**)
1 oz (30 ml) Cognac
¾ oz (22 ml) sweet vermouth
½ oz (15 ml) orange curaçao (p 498)
½ oz (15 ml) Heering Cherry Liqueur
½ oz (15 ml) ginger syrup (p 496)
3 cucumber wheels
1 lemon wedge
1 lime wedge
1 orange half-wheel
1 strawberry, halved
6–8 mint leaves
Soda, to top
Garnish: mint bouquet, cucumber wheel and strawberry

B*A*P*S
Devin Kennedy, Pouring Ribbons, NYC
1½ oz (45 ml) fruit cup syrup (p 496)
½ oz (15 ml) Cognac
¼ oz (7 ml) Amaro CioCiaro
2 cucumber wheels
1 lemon wedge
1 lime wedge
1 orange wedge
1 strawberry, halved
Soda, to top
Garnish: mint bouquet, cucumber wheel and strawberry

Champagne Cup
(See p 415)

Fruit Cup Italiano
The New Craft of the Cocktail, *Dale DeGroff, 2020*
1½ oz (45 ml) fruit cup syrup (p 496)
½ oz (15 ml) Cynar
2 cucumber wheels
1 lemon wedge
1 lime wedge
1 orange wedge
1 strawberry, halved
Tonic water, to top
Garnish: mint bouquet, cucumber wheel and strawberry

Fruit Cup Rangoon
2 oz (60 ml) fruit cup syrup (p 496)
½ oz (15 ml) ginger syrup (p 496)
3 cucumber wheels
1 lemon wedge
1 lime wedge
1 orange half-wheel
1 strawberry, halved
6–8 mint leaves
Soda, to top
Garnish: mint bouquet, cucumber wheel and strawberry

Fruit Cup Spritz
2 oz (60 ml) fruit cup syrup (p 496)
3 cucumber wheels
1 lemon wedge
1 lime wedge
1 orange half-wheel
1 strawberry, halved
6–8 mint leaves
Champagne, to top
Garnish: mint bouquet, cucumber wheel and strawberry

Kola Cup
Michael Madrusan, The Everleigh, 2024
2 oz (60 ml) fruit cup syrup (p 496)
¾ oz (22 ml) kola tonic
2 cucumber wheels
1 lemon wedge
1 lime wedge
1 orange wedge
1 strawberry, halved
6–8 mint leaves
Soda, to top
Garnish: mint bouquet, cucumber wheel and strawberry

Maison Summer Fruit Cup #16
Will Elliott, Maison Premiere, NYC
1 oz (30 ml) fruit cup syrup (p 496)
¾ oz (22 ml) Aperol
½ oz (15 ml) cachaça
4 dashes Angostura Bitters
2 drops saline solution (p 493)
1 lemon wedge
1 grapefruit wedge
Soda, to top
Garnish: 5 bruised tarragon leaves

Noval Cup
Jim Meehan, PDT, NYC, 2010
2 oz (60 ml) Quinta do Noval Black Reserve Port
½ oz (15 ml) lemon juice
½ oz (15 ml) simple syrup
1 strawberry, halved
Soda, to top
Garnish: cucumber wheel

Rustic Fruit Cup
(See p 439)

The Mulberry Cup
The Manor House Hotel, Moreton-in-Marsh, 2006
2 oz (60 ml) fruit cup syrup (p 496)
½ oz (15 ml) St Germain Elderflower Liqueur
½ oz (15 ml) lemon juice
½ oz (15 ml) simple syrup
1 teaspoon mulberry jam
6–8 mint leaves
Soda, to top
Add all ingredients to a shaker and stir to dissolve the jam. Add ice, then shake and strain into a frozen Spritz glass with ice. Top with soda and stir briefly.
Garnish: mint bouquet

Muddle all ingredients, except carbonated, in a shaker, then shake briefly with ice and strain into a frozen Spritz glass with ice. Top with a mixer, beer or sparkling wine and stir briefly to combine.

Wimbledon

Sam Ross, Hearts, Nashville, 2020
1 oz (30 ml) fruit cup syrup (p 496)
¼ oz (7 ml) lemon juice
¼ oz (7 ml) agave syrup (p 494)
3 oz (90 ml) Prosecco, to top
Add all ingredients, except for Prosecco, to a shaker with ice and shake briefly, then strain and top with Prosecco.
Garnish: 2 cucumber wheels and half a strawberry

Winter Fruit Cup

(See p 439)

Winter Fruit Cup (Kevin Diedrich Recipe)

Kevin Diedrich, Pacific Cocktail Haven, San Francisco
2 oz (60 ml) fruit cup syrup (p 496)
1 oz (30 ml) Royal Gala apple juice
½ oz (15 ml) lemon juice
½ oz (15 ml) white grapefruit juice
½ oz (15 ml) ginger syrup (p 496)
¼ oz (7 ml) cinnamon syrup (p 495)
2 dashes Angostura Bitters
Soda, to top
Add all ingredients except soda to a shaker with ice and toss. Strain into a frozen Spritz glass with ice, then top with soda and stir briefly.
Garnish: mint sprig, cucumber ribbon and apple fan

From *Harry Johnson's Bartenders' Manual* (1900):

Alcohol may be man's worst enemy, but the Bible says love your enemy.

Punch

Chill all ingredients, then combine in a punchbowl with large blocks of ice and stir briefly to combine. To serve, ladle into rocks glasses or Punch cups with ice.

Café Brûlot

Serves 12
Michael Madrusan, 2025
(aka **Cafe Diabolique** and **Devil's Coffee**)
Antoine's, New Orleans, 1880s
12 oz (350 ml) Cognac
6 oz (180 ml) Grand Marnier
1 oz (30 ml) Tempus Fugit Crème de Cacao
½ oz (15 ml) 151 overproof rum
10 whole cloves
peels of 2 oranges
2 cinnamon sticks, broken
17 oz (500 ml) hot, strong black coffee
6 oz (180 ml) Demerara syrup (p 495)
2 oz (60 ml) house cream, to float (p 506; optional)
Combine all ingredients except coffee and house cream in a small saucepan over low heat, stirring for 1 minute. Turn off heat, stand back a bit and carefully light mixture on fire. Let it burn for 30 seconds to 1 minute to singe the orange peel and cinnamon, then pour the hot coffee into the pan to douse the flames. Stir well. Fine-strain into warmed toddy glasses and float house cream. Garnish with orange zest.
Garnish: finely grated orange zest

Champagne Punch

Serves 10
The Bar-Tender's Guide, *Jerry Thomas, 1862*
6 oz (180 ml) lemon juice
6 oz (180 ml) raspberry syrup (p 500)
50 oz (1.5 litres) Champagne, to top
Garnish: 10–12 raspberries, 3 orange wheels, 3 lemon wheels and 2 pineapple rings

Dear Prudence

Serves 20
Joaquín Simó
33 oz (975 ml) vodka
12 oz (350 ml) Lillet Rosé
25 oz (740 ml) raspberry syrup (p 500)
18 oz (530 ml) lemon juice,
18 oz (530 ml) pink grapefruit juice
20 oz (590 ml) soda, to top
10 dashes Peychaud's Aromatic Cocktail Bitters

Fruit Cup Punch

Serves 10–12
6 oz (180 ml) gin
6 oz (180 ml) Cocchi Storico Vermouth di Torino
3 oz (90 ml) Grand Marnier
2 oz (60 ml) Heering Cherry Liqueur
24–33 oz (700 ml–1 litre) Sprite lemon soda, to top (adjust to taste)
Garnish: 10–12 seasonal berries, 8 cucumber wheels, 6 orange half-wheels, 6 lemon half-wheels, 6 lime half-wheels and a handful of mint leaves

Invisible Gin Punch

Serves 10–12
Hoffman House Bartender's Guide, *Charles S. Mahoney, 1905*
24 oz (700 ml) gin
15 oz (450 ml) pineapple juice
8 oz (240 ml) lemon juice
17–24 oz (500–700 ml) ginger beer, to top (adjust to taste)
Garnish: 6 pineapple half-rings and 6 lemon half-wheels
▼ Originally a single-serve drink, the **Invisible Gin Highball**.

Chill all ingredients, then combine in a punchbowl with large blocks of ice and stir briefly to combine. To serve, ladle into rocks glasses or Punch cups with ice.

Mint Punch

Serves 10–12

"Harry" of Ciro's ABC of Mixing Cocktails, *Harry MacElhone, 1923*

24 oz (700 ml) bourbon
12 oz (350 ml) lime juice
9 oz (265 ml) mint sugar syrup (p 498)
17 oz (500 ml) soda, to top
20–24 dashes absinthe (adjust to taste)

Stir all ingredients except soda and absinthe to a punch bowl with large blocks of ice and stir. Add absinthe to taste – not enough to overpower the other flavours, but just enough for a subtle refreshing spice.

Garnish: 10 lime half-wheels and a handful of mint leaves

▼ Originally a single-serve drink, the **Mint Cocktail**.

Paris Hall Punch

Serves 8

Damon Boelte

Sherry, *Talia Baiocchi, 2014*

4 oz (120 ml) gin (preferably Greenhook Ginsmiths' Old Tom Gin or Hayman's Old Tom)
4 oz (120 ml) Amontillado Sherry
4 oz (120 ml) Basque cider (preferably Isastegi or Sarasola)
¼ cup (55 g) caster (superfine) sugar
peel of 2 grapefruits
4 oz (120 ml) ginger beer (preferably Fever-Tree)
2 oz (60 ml) sparkling water

Muddle the sugar and grapefruit peels in a large bowl, then leave to sit for 20 minutes. Add the gin, sherry, cider, ginger beer and sparkling water and stir. Garnish with ginger and grapefruit peels. Serve in punch cups over ice.

Garnish: 3 in (7.5 cm) piece fresh ginger, peeled and cut into coins, grapefruit peel

Pisco Punch

Serves 10–12

Duncan Hill, Bank Exchange, San Francisco, 1850s

24 oz (700 ml) pisco
17 fl oz (500 ml) filtered water
10½ fl oz (300 ml) lemon juice
10½ fl oz (300 ml) pineapple syrup (p 499)

Garnish: 10 pineapple half-rings

Tiramisù Milk Punch

Serves 10

Darren Leaney, Capitano, Melbourne 2018

17½ oz (520 ml) savoiardi milk (p 507)
6 oz (180 ml) fortified muscat
3 oz (90 ml) cacao nib rum (p 502)
1½ oz (45 ml) coffee liqueur (preferably Mr Black Cold Brew Coffee Liqueur)
4 oz (120 ml) chilled filter coffee (preferably a light roast with bright citrus notes)
1½ oz (45 ml) simple syrup
1 oz (30 ml) lactic acid

Combine all ingredients except savoiardi milk in a large 70 oz (2 litre) jug and stir to combine. Add the savoiardi milk, stirring gently to incorporate. As the mixture starts to curdle, use a spoon to gently move the curds around. Leave to rest for 10 minutes. Next, line a chinois with a paper coffee filter and slowly pour the mixture through the chinois into a separate 70 oz (2 litre) jug. Allow to filter through for about 10 minutes before passing the filtered mixture through the chinois and a fresh coffee filter once more. Leave the remaining mixture to filter through slowly in the fridge overnight. Serve in rocks glasses with ice.

▼ The clarified punch can be stored in a glass bottle in the fridge for up to 12 months.

Tom and Jerry

Serves 25

The Bar-Tender's Guide, *Jerry Thomas, 1862*

25 oz (750 ml) Cognac
25 oz (750 ml) aged dark rum
12 whole eggs
4 oz (110 g) unsalted butter (room temperature)
1 cup (220 g) caster (superfine) sugar
1 teaspoon vanilla extract
1 teaspoon ground allspice
1 teaspoon freshly ground cinnamon
1 teaspoon ground cloves
38 oz (1.125 litres) whole (full cream) milk, to top

Make a 'light batter' by separating the egg whites and egg yolks into two separate large bowls. Add the butter and sugar to the egg yolks and whisk to combine. Beat the egg whites vigorously until they form stiff peaks and gently fold them into the yolk mixture along with the spices and vanilla extract until the mixture attains the consistency of a light batter.

To build the drink, warm the milk in a saucepan over low heat until hot but not boiling. Add 1 tablespoon of the 'light batter' to a mug, then slowly add 1 oz (30 ml) each of Cognac and rum while stirring gently to combine. Top with milk and stir briefly.

Garnish: freshly grated nutmeg

Chill all ingredients, then combine in a punchbowl with large blocks of ice and stir briefly to combine. To serve, ladle into rocks glasses or Punch cups with ice.

LONDON

FIZZ

Silver Fizz p 138

Fizz

A light and fluffy citrus cocktail shaken with egg, topped with soda and intended for swift enjoyment.

spirit + lemon + sugar + egg white + soda

Add all ingredients except soda to a shaker and dry shake. Add ice, shake again, then strain into a frozen footed Delmonico glass and top with soda simultaneously.

First recorded by Jerry Thomas in 1876, the Gin Fiz (initially spelled with only one 'z') was basically a shorter Tom Collins (p 72) (spirit, citrus, sugar and sparkling water) shaken up and served without ice. Thought to have originated in New York City, like its close relative the Daisy, the Fizz was enjoyed as a short, simple reviver that conveniently doubled as a successful hangover cure. As bartenders of the time suggested, the Fizz is designed to be knocked back at pace, while the drink's aerated head is still alive and the glass is ice cold.

Many creative and popular Fizz recipes emerged during the 1870s, and in 1882 Harry Johnson – one of the key players in 19th-century cocktail culture – published recipes for Fizzes incorporating egg white (Silver Fizz, p 138) and egg yolk (Golden Fizz, p 138), as well as inventions of his own, such as the Morning Glory Fizz (p 149), a Scotch-based Silver Fizz with a few dashes of absinthe.

While the original Fiz by Jerry Thomas was superseded by the Collins, the Silver Fizz was embraced in all its frothy glory and remains the Fizz template we see most often in contemporary cocktails. We believe the foamy texture is a defining characteristic of the Fizz family in the modern age and, as a result, some of the early Fizz recipes featured in this chapter have been amended to include eggs where they were otherwise absent.

When a whole egg is incorporated, we call it a Royal Fizz (p 138), and if a Silver Fizz gets topped with Champagne instead of soda, it becomes a Diamond Fizz (p 138). Regardless of which part of the egg is used, an expressed and discarded citrus twist is a compulsory final flourish, so that any unwanted eggy aromas are done away with.

CORE STYLES:

Silver Fizz

(Fizz with an egg white)
The Modern Bartenders' Guide, *O.H. Byron, 1884*
2 oz (60 ml) gin
¾ oz (22 ml) lemon juice
¾ oz (22 ml) simple syrup
1 egg white
1 oz (30 ml) soda, to top
Garnish: lemon twist (discard) and lemon wedge
▾ Add 2 dashes of orange bitters to make a **Silver King Fizz.**

Golden Fizz

(Fizz with an egg yolk)
New and Improved Bartender's Manual, *Harry Johnson, 1882*
2 oz (60 ml) gin
¾ oz (22 ml) lemon juice
¾ oz (22 ml) simple syrup
1 egg yolk
1 oz (30 ml) soda, to top
Garnish: lemon twist (discard) and lemon wedge

Royal Fizz

(Fizz with a whole egg)
Jack's Manual, *J.A. Grohusko, 1908*
2 oz (60 ml) gin
¾ oz (22 ml) lemon juice
¾ oz (22 ml) simple syrup
1 whole egg
1 oz (30 ml) soda, to top
Garnish: lemon twist (discard) and lemon wedge

Diamond Fizz

(Silver Fizz with Champagne)
Straub's Manual of Mixed Drinks, *Jacques Straub, 1913*
2 oz (60 ml) gin
¾ oz (22 ml) lemon juice
¾ oz (22 ml) simple syrup
1 egg white
1 oz (30 ml) Champagne, to top
Garnish: lemon twist (discard) and lemon wedge
▾ Originally without egg.

Add all ingredients, except soda or Champagne, to a shaker and dry shake. Add ice, shake again, then strain into a frozen footed Delmonico glass and top with soda simultaneously.

ESSENTIAL VARIATIONS

Ramos Gin Fizz

(aka **New Orleans Fizz**)
Henry Charles Ramos, Imperial Cabinet Saloon, New Orleans, 1888
2 oz (60 ml) gin
⅜ oz (11 ml) lemon juice
⅜ oz (11 ml) lime juice
¾ oz (22 ml) simple syrup
½ oz (15 ml) house cream (p 506)
2 dashes orange blossom water
1 egg white
1 oz (30 ml) soda, to top

Add all ingredients, except soda, to a shaker and dry shake. Add ice, shake again, then strain into a frozen footed Delmonico glass and top with soda simultaneously.
Garnish: lemon twist (discard)

While Harry Johnson's Morning Glory Fizz (p 149) was undoubtedly a widely popular morning-after remedy in 19th-century America, it's the Ramos Gin Fizz – a New Orleans classic – that most people associate with this particular cocktail style. The famously laborious – yet glorious – Silver Fizz variation is one of a handful of cocktails with a reputation that truly precedes it.

The drink's inventor, Henry Charles Ramos, was born in 1856 to Prussian immigrants in Indiana. When Ramos turned 18, he began his career as a bartender in New Orleans, and in 1880 he opened the Capitol Saloon, which he ran for seven years. In 1887, Ramos took over the Imperial Cabinet Saloon, and by this point he was widely regarded as one of the most trusted bar owners and operators in the Big Easy. Some time in the early 1890s, Ramos jazzed up a non-alcoholic Cream Lemonade that he became known for with gin and orange blossom water. To pull off its famously fluffy texture, Ramos called for a line of 'shakermen', who, together, shook the drink, sparkling water already added, one-by-one for a total of 12 minutes until the ice completely dissolved. Today's methods are less laborious, but we still recommend an initial dry shake (without ice), followed by a second hard shake using one large dense ice block to do the Ramos justice.

One of the greatest gifts the contemporary cocktail renaissance has given us is the popularisation of the dry shake – the technique used to emulsify egg whites by shaking all ingredients without ice prior to a second (or wet) shake with ice. This extra step agitates the drink, creating a lighter, foamier texture.

Ramos enthusiasts should also seek out the curiously named Peach Blow Fizz (p 144), a creamy, strawberry-filled concoction invented by Hugo R. Ensslin in 1916 that's more like an English Eaton Mess in a glass.

Electric Current Fizz

(Silver Fizz with a seasoned egg yolk on the side)
Modern American Drinks, *George J. Kappeler, 1895*
2 oz (60 ml) gin
¾ oz (22 ml) lemon juice
¾ oz (22 ml) simple syrup
1 egg white
1 oz (30 ml) soda, to top
1 egg yolk
salt
freshly ground black pepper
2–3 dashes malt vinegar

Add all ingredients, except soda, egg yolk, salt, pepper and vinegar, to a shaker and dry shake. Add ice, shake again, then strain into a frozen footed Delmonico glass and top with soda simultaneously. Serve the egg yolk in a small glass on the side with pinches of salt and pepper, plus two or three dashes of malt vinegar.
Garnish: lemon twist (discard) and lemon wedge

In 1895, some years after O.H. Byron's first mention of the Silver Fizz, New York City bartender George J. Kappeler gave us *Modern American Drinks* – a volume widely praised for clearly articulated and well-balanced recipes that proved to be a leading resource in its era. By then, the Silver Fizz was a well-known cocktail, and variations were popping up on menus across the United States. Kappeler published 15 or so of these, including a truly unique recipe for the Electric Current Fizz. The method, in Kappeler's words, is simple: 'Make a Silver Fizz; save the yolk of the egg and serve it in the half-shell, with a little pepper, salt, and vinegar, with the fizz.'

While it's an entirely uncomplicated drink – or perhaps even more of a meal – it stands tall as a signature serve that delivers in more ways than one. Both the novelty of the presentation and the two-part drinking ritual (we suggest shooting the yolk first, then sipping the drink) never fail to entertain guests or spark conversation over the bar. Admittedly, knocking back raw egg isn't for everyone, but much like Harry Johnson's Morning Glory Fizz (p 149), the Electric Current Fizz is a worthy recommendation for those suffering from the previous night's antics. (Plus, it's a sustainable way to make use of the whole egg.)

Cracking eggs can get messy, so we suggest serving the yolk in a shot glass or small whisk(e)y glass rather than in the shell as Kappeler prescribed. When we discovered this drink, we had no vinegar behind the bar and opted for both Worcestershire sauce and hot sauce instead. The combination works wonderfully, and it was the house style at The Everleigh. If you're on the hunt for other cure-all-evils cocktails, we suggest our personal favourite, the Dark 'n' Stormy (p 94) or Bloody Mary–inspired Beer cocktail, the Red-Eye (p 438), which uses a whole egg.

Fizz

GIN

Anniversary Fizz
J. Cowley, 2007
1½ oz (45 ml) gin
½ oz (15 ml) Aperol
½ oz (15 ml) lemon juice
½ oz (15 ml) simple syrup
¼ oz (7 ml) passionfruit syrup (p 499)
1 egg white
1 oz (30 ml) soda, to top
Garnish: lemon twist (discard)

Bayard Fizz
Straub's Manual of Mixed Drinks, *Jacques Straub, 1913*
1½ oz (45 ml) gin
½ oz (15 ml) maraschino liqueur
½ oz (15 ml) lemon juice
½ oz (15 ml) raspberry syrup (p 500)
½ oz (15 ml) house cream (p 506)
1 egg white
1 oz (30 ml) soda, to top
Garnish: lemon twist (discard)

Bird of Paradise Fizz
(aka **Albemarle Fizz** in *Recipes for Mixed Drinks*, Hugo R. Ensslin, 1917 or Silver Fizz with raspberry)
Straub's Manual of Mixed Drinks, *Jacques Straub, 1913*
1½ oz (45 ml) gin
¾ oz (22 ml) lemon juice
¾ oz (22 ml) raspberry syrup (p 500)
1 egg white
1 oz (30 ml) soda, to top
Garnish: lemon twist (discard) and raspberry

Caliente Cocktail
(Silver Fizz with cream)
The How and When, *Hyman Gale and Gerald F. Marco, 1937*
2 oz (60 ml) gin
¾ oz (22 ml) lemon juice
¾ oz (22 ml) simple syrup
¾ oz (22 ml) house cream (p 506)
1 egg white
1 oz (30 ml) soda, to top
Garnish: lemon twist (discard)

Celine Fizz
(Silver Fizz with elderflower liqueur)
Phil Ward, Death & Co, NYC, 2008
1½ oz (45 ml) gin
¾ oz (22 ml) St Germain Elderflower Liqueur
¾ oz (22 ml) lemon juice
½ oz (15 ml) simple syrup
1 egg white
1 oz (30 ml) soda, to top
Garnish: lemon twist (discard)

Creole Fizz
The Gentleman's Companion, *Charles H. Baker Jr., 1939*
¾ oz (22 ml) gin
¾ oz (22 ml) sloe gin
¾ oz (22 ml) lemon juice
¾ oz (22 ml) house cream (p 506)
¾ oz (15 ml) simple syrup
2 dashes orange blossom water
1 egg white
1 oz (30 ml) soda, to top
Garnish: lemon twist (discard) and mint leaf

Crimson Fizz
(Silver Fizz with strawberries)
The Fine Art of Mixing Drinks, *David A. Embury, 1948*
2 oz (60 ml) gin
¾ oz (22 ml) lemon juice
¾ oz (22 ml) simple syrup
2 strawberries, halved
1 egg white
1 oz (30 ml) soda, to top
Add strawberries and simple syrup to a shaker and muddle, then add remaining ingredients, except soda, and dry shake. Add ice, shake again, then strain into a frozen footed Delmonico glass and top with soda simultaneously.
Garnish: lemon twist (discard) and strawberry half

Eagle Fizz
Hoffman House Bartender's Guide, *Charles S. Mahoney, 1905*
1½ oz (45 ml) gin
¾ oz (22 ml) Giffard Vanille de Madagascar
¾ oz (22 ml) lemon juice
¾ oz (22 ml) house cream (p 506)
2 dashes orange blossom water
1 egg white
1 oz (30 ml) soda, to top
Garnish: lemon twist (discard) and orange wedge

Elsie Ferguson Fizz
Straub's Manual of Mixed Drinks, *Jacques Straub, 1913*
2 oz (60 ml) gin
¾ oz (22 ml) lemon juice
¾ oz (22 ml) grenadine (p 496)
½ oz (15 ml) house cream (p 506)
1 strawberry, halved
1 egg white
1 oz (30 ml) soda, to top
Muddle strawberry with grenadine, then add remaining ingredients and dry shake. Add ice, shake again, then strain into a frozen footed Delmonico glass and top with soda simultaneously.
Garnish: lemon twist (discard) and strawberry

First Bloom
Brandon Bramhall, Attaboy, NYC, 2018
1½ oz (45 ml) gin
½ oz (15 ml) crème de violette
¼ oz (7 ml) maraschino liqueur
¾ oz (22 ml) lemon juice
¼ oz (7 ml) simple syrup
1 orange half-wheel
1 egg white
1 oz (30 ml) soda, to top
Press orange with simple syrup in a shaker, add remaining ingredients, except soda, and dry shake. Add ice, shake again, then strain into a frozen footed Delmonico glass and top with soda simultaneously.
Garnish: lemon twist (discard)

Add all ingredients except soda to a shaker and dry shake. Add ice, shake again, then strain into a frozen footed Delmonico glass and top with soda simultaneously.

Silver Fox

Richard Boccato, Little Branch, NYC, 2007

1½ oz (45 ml) gin
½ oz (15 ml) amaretto
¾ oz (22 ml) lemon juice
½ oz (15 ml) orgeat
1 egg white
1 oz (30 ml) soda, to top
Garnish: lemon twist (discard)

Silver Stallion

The How and When, *Hyman Gale and Gerald F. Marco, 1937*

2 oz (60 ml) gin
¾ oz (22 ml) lemon juice
¾ oz (22 ml) simple syrup
1 small scoop (about 1 tablespoon) vanilla ice cream
1 egg white
1 oz (30 ml) soda, to top
Mix ice cream with gin, lemon juice and simple syrup until combined, then add egg white and dry shake. Add ice, shake again, then strain into a frozen footed Delmonico glass and top with soda simultaneously.
Garnish: lemon twist (discard) and lemon wedge

South Side Fizz

(Silver Fizz with mint)
Recipes for Mixed Drinks, *Hugo R. Ensslin, 1916*

2 oz (60 ml) gin
¾ oz (22 ml) lemon juice
¾ oz (22 ml) simple syrup
6–8 mint leaves
1 egg white
1 oz (30 ml) soda, to top
Garnish: lemon twist (discard) and mint leaf

Summer's Day

(Silver Fizz shaken with orange)
Michael McIlroy, Milk & Honey, NYC, 2010

2 oz (60 ml) gin
¾ oz (22 ml) lemon juice
¾ oz (22 ml) simple syrup
1 orange half-wheel
1 egg white
1 oz (30 ml) soda, to top
Press orange with simple syrup, add remaining ingredients and dry shake. Add ice, shake again, then strain into a frozen footed Delmonico glass and top with soda simultaneously.
Garnish: orange twist (discard) and orange wedge

The Fitzcarraldo

Travis Dutton, Bar 355, Oakland

2 oz (60 ml) gin
¾ oz (22 ml) chamomile syrup (p 494)
⅜ oz (11 ml) lemon juice
⅜ oz (11 ml) lime juice
3 drops Bittermens Elemakule Tiki Bitters
1 oz (30 ml) soda, to top
Garnish: lemon twist (discard)

Violet Fizz

Straub's Manual of Mixed Drinks, *Jacques Straub, 1913*

1½ oz (45 ml) gin
½ oz (15 ml) crème de violette
¾ oz (22 ml) lemon juice
½ oz (15 ml) simple syrup
1 egg white
1 oz (30 ml) soda, to top
Garnish: lemon twist (discard)

RUM & CANE SPIRIT

Caribbean Parachute

Nick Kokonas, Avondale Bowl, Chicago

1½ oz (45 ml) light rum
½ oz (15 ml) Amaro Montenegro
¾ oz (22 ml) lime juice
½ oz (15 ml) simple syrup
1 egg white
2 oz (60 ml) tonic water, to top
Garnish: lemon twist (discard)

Chicago Fizz

Straub's Manual of Mixed Drinks, *Jacques Straub, 1913*

1 oz (30 ml) Jamaican dark rum
1 oz (30 ml) tawny Port
¾ oz (22 ml) lemon juice
½ oz (15 ml) simple syrup
1 egg white
1 oz (30 ml) soda, to top
Garnish: orange twist (discard)

Imperial Fizz No. 2

1 oz (30 ml) Jamaican dark rum
1 oz (30 ml) rye whiskey
¾ oz (22 ml) lemon juice
¾ oz (22 ml) simple syrup
1 egg white
1 oz (30 ml) soda, to top
Garnish: lemon twist (discard) and lemon wedge

Inhaler

Paul Hammond, Bulletin Place, Sydney, 2017

1 oz (30 ml) light rum
½ oz (15 ml) Manzanilla Sherry
¼ oz (7 ml) white crème de menthe
1 oz (30 ml) pineapple juice
½ oz (15 ml) lemon juice
⅜ oz (11 ml) orgeat
3 dashes absinthe
1 egg white
1 oz (30 ml) soda, to top
Garnish: lemon twist (discard) and mint leaf

Add all ingredients except soda to a shaker and dry shake. Add ice, shake again, then strain into a frozen footed Delmonico glass and top with soda simultaneously.

King's Fizz
(Light Rum Fizz with orange bitters)
2 oz (60 ml) light rum
¾ oz (22 ml) lemon juice
¾ oz (22 ml) simple syrup
2 dashes orange bitters
1 egg white
1 oz (30 ml) soda, to top
Garnish: lemon twist (discard) and orange wedge

Lalla Rookh Fizz
Drinks, *Jacques Straub, 1914*
¾ oz (22 ml) Jamaican dark rum
¾ oz (22 ml) Cognac
½ oz (15 ml) Giffard Vanille de Madagascar
¾ oz (22 ml) lemon juice
½ oz (15 ml) house cream (p 506)
1 egg white
1 oz (30 ml) soda, to top
Garnish: lemon twist (discard)

Racquet Club Fizz
Trader Vic's Book of Food and Drink, *Trader Vic, 1946*
1½ oz (45 ml) light rum
1 oz (30 ml) pineapple juice
¾ oz (22 ml) simple syrup
½ oz (15 ml) lemon juice
1 egg white
1 oz (30 ml) soda, to top
Garnish: lemon twist (discard) and pineapple wedge
▾ Named after the Racquet Club in Kailua, Hawaii.

Rosita Cocktail No. V
Hotel Riviera, Mar del Plata
The South American Gentleman's Companion, *Charles H. Baker Jr., 1951*
1½ oz (45 ml) light rum
¾ oz (22 ml) lemon juice
¾ oz (22 ml) grenadine (p 496)
½ oz (15 ml) house cream (p 506)
1 egg white
1 oz (30 ml) soda, to top
Garnish: spritz of rosewater

Silverback Fizz
Sarah Ellis, Sycamore Den, San Diego
1½ oz (45 ml) light rum
½ oz (15 ml) Giffard Vanille de Madagascar
¾ oz (22 ml) lemon juice
½ oz (15 ml) house cream (p 506)
1 egg white
1 strawberry, halved
1 oz (30 ml) soda, to top
Muddle strawberry, then add remaining ingredients and dry shake. Add ice, shake again, then strain into a frozen footed Delmonico glass and top with soda simultaneously.
Garnish: lemon twist (discard) and half a strawberry

Snowball
Jack's Manual, *J.A. Grohusko, 1916*
2 oz (60 ml) aged dark rum
¾ oz (22 ml) ginger syrup (p 496)
½ oz (15 ml) lemon juice
1 egg white
1 oz (30 ml) soda, to top
Garnish: lemon twist (discard) and candied ginger
▾ Grohusko also recommends swapping rum for Cognac.

Tropical Fizz
Michael Madrusan, The Everleigh, Melbourne, 2015
1½ oz (45 ml) light rum
1 oz (30 ml) pineapple juice
¾ oz (22 ml) house cream (p 506)
½ oz (15 ml) lime juice
½ oz (15 ml) passionfruit syrup (p 499)
1 egg white
1 oz (30 ml) soda, to top
Garnish: lemon twist (discard) and 2 pineapple fronds

Wonka Fizz
Karin Stanley, Dutch Kills, NYC
1½ oz (45 ml) aged dark rum
¾ oz (22 ml) lemon juice
¾ oz (22 ml) simple syrup
2 drops Bittermens Xocolatl Mole Bitters
1 whole egg
1 oz (30 ml) soda, to top
Garnish: orange twist (discard)

AGAVE

Almond
Davide Segat, Side Hustle at NoMad London, London
1⅓ oz (40 ml) mezcal
½ oz (15 ml) Poire Williams
1 oz (30 ml) orgeat
¾ oz (22 ml) lime juice
2 drops saline solution (p 493)
1 egg white
1 oz (30 ml) soda, to top
Garnish: freshly grated lime zest

Empire Fizz
Michael Madrusan, Bar Margaux, Melbourne, 2019
2 oz (60 ml) blanco tequila
¾ oz (22 ml) lemon juice
¾ oz (22 ml) hibiscus syrup (p 496)
1 cucumber wheel
1 egg white
1 oz (30 ml) soda, to top
Press cucumber, then add remaining ingredients and dry shake. Add ice, shake again, then strain into a frozen footed Delmonico glass and top with soda simultaneously.
Garnish: lemon twist (discard) and cucumber fan

Formosa Fizz
Jeffrey Morgenthaler, Clyde Common, Portland
1½ oz (45 ml) blanco tequila
¾ oz (22 ml) lemon juice
½ oz (15 ml) raspberry syrup (p 500)
¼ oz (7 ml) simple syrup
1 egg white
1½ oz (45 ml) soda, to top
Garnish: lemon twist (discard) and raspberry

Add all ingredients except soda to a shaker and dry shake. Add ice, shake again, then strain into a frozen footed Delmonico glass and top with soda simultaneously.

White Dragon Fizz
Jim Meehan, Portland
2 oz (60 ml) blanco tequila
½ oz (15 ml) triple sec
¾ oz (22 ml) lemon juice
¼ oz (7 ml) agave syrup (p 494)
3 drops saline solution (p 493)
1 egg white
1 oz (30 ml) soda, to top
Garnish: lemon twist (discard) and orange wedge
▾ Originally a Traditional Sour.

Young Man's Delight (Texas or Mexico)
My New Cocktail Book, *G.F. Steele, 1934*
2 oz (60 ml) blanco tequila
½ oz (15 ml) orange juice
½ oz (15 ml) ginger syrup (p 496)
¼ oz (7 ml) lemon juice
1 egg white
1 oz (30 ml) soda, to top
Garnish: lemon twist (discard) and candied ginger

BRANDY

Apple Blow Fizz
Recipes for Mixed Drinks, *Hugo R. Ensslin, 1917*
1½ oz (45 ml) bonded apple brandy
¾ oz (22 ml) lemon juice
¾ oz (22 ml) simple syrup
1 egg white
1 oz (30 ml) soda, to top
Garnish: lemon twist (discard) and apple fan

Cuzco
Julie Reiner, NYC, 2007
2 oz (60 ml) pisco
¾ oz (22 ml) Aperol
¾ oz (22 ml) simple syrup
½ oz (15 ml) pink grapefruit juice
½ oz (15 ml) lemon juice
½ teaspoon (2.5 ml) kirsch
Garnish: grapefruit twist (discard)

Cuzco Fizz
Lynnette Marrero, NYC, 2007
2 oz (60 ml) pisco
1 oz (30 ml) St Germain Elderflower Liqueur
¾ oz (22 ml) lime juice
5 green grapes
1 egg white
1 oz (30 ml) soda, to top
Muddle grapes with lime juice, add remaining ingredients and dry shake. Add ice, shake again, then strain into a frozen footed Delmonico glass and top with soda simultaneously.
Garnish: lemon twist (discard) and green grape

41 Jane Does
Toby Maloney, Milk & Honey, NYC, 2003
1 oz (30 ml) bonded apple brandy
1 oz (30 ml) Poire Williams
¾ oz (22 ml) lemon juice
¾ oz (22 ml) simple syrup
1 egg white
1 oz (30 ml) soda, to top
Garnish: lemon twist (discard) and apple fan

Gazette Fizz
(aka **Golden Cognac Fizz**)
Hoffman House Bartender's Guide, *Charles S. Mahoney, 1905*
2 oz (60 ml) Cognac
¾ oz (22 ml) lemon juice
¾ oz (22 ml) simple syrup
1 egg yolk
1 oz (30 ml) soda, to top
Garnish: lemon twist (discard) and lemon wedge

Kilroy's Bracer
The Gentleman's Companion, *Charles H. Baker Jr., 1939*
2 oz (60 ml) Cognac
¾ oz (22 ml) lemon juice
¾ oz (22 ml) simple syrup
2 dashes absinthe
2 dashes Angostura Bitters
1 whole egg
1 oz (30 ml) soda, to top
Garnish: lemon twist (discard) and whole star anise

Magnolia Highball
The How and When, *Hyman Gale and Gerald F. Marco, 1937*
1½ oz (45 ml) Cognac
¾ oz (22 ml) orange curaçao (p 498)
¾ oz (22 ml) lemon juice
1 egg yolk
1 oz (30 ml) Champagne, to top
Garnish: lemon twist (discard)
▾ Based on the Magnolia (à la Simmons) in *American & Other Drinks*, Leo Engel, 1878 (see p 396).

Pisco Aperol Fizz
1 oz (30 ml) pisco
¾ oz (22 ml) Aperol
¾ oz (22 ml) lemon juice
½ oz (15 ml) simple syrup
1 strawberry, halved
1 egg white
1 oz (30 ml) soda, to top
Muddle strawberry with simple syrup, add remaining ingredients and dry shake. Add ice, shake again, then strain into a frozen footed Delmonico glass and top with soda simultaneously.
Garnish: lemon twist (discard) and strawberry half

Rosita No. I
The South American Gentleman's Companion, *Charles H. Baker Jr., 1951*
2 oz (60 ml) bonded apple brandy
¾ oz (22 ml) lemon juice
¾ oz (22 ml) grenadine (p 496)
½ oz (15 ml) house cream (p 506)
1 egg white
1 oz (30 ml) soda, to top
Garnish: spritz of rosewater

Rosita No. IV
Jorge E. Meiss, Hotel O'Higgins, Viña del Mar
The South American Gentleman's Companion, *Charles H. Baker Jr., 1951*
1 oz (30 ml) Cognac
1 oz (30 ml) gin
¾ oz (22 ml) lemon juice
¾ oz (22 ml) grenadine (p 496)
½ oz (15 ml) house cream (p 506)
1 egg white
1 oz (30 ml) soda, to top
Garnish: spritz of rosewater

Add all ingredients except soda to a shaker and dry shake. Add ice, shake again, then strain into a frozen footed Delmonico glass and top with soda simultaneously.

Southern Whiskey Fizz
What'll You Have?, *Julien J. Proskauer, 1933*
2 oz (60 ml) bonded apple brandy
⅜ oz (11 ml) lemon juice
⅜ oz (11 ml) lime juice
¾ oz (22 ml) simple syrup
½ oz (15 ml) house cream (p 506)
1 whole egg
1 oz (30 ml) soda, to top
Garnish: lemon twist (discard) and apple fan

St. Mark's Reviver
The South American Gentleman's Companion, *Charles H. Baker Jr., 1951*
1½ oz (45 ml) Cognac
¼ oz (7 ml) maraschino liqueur
¼ oz (7 ml) Heering Cherry Liqueur
¾ oz (22 ml) lemon juice
¼ oz (7 ml) simple syrup
2 dashes Angostura Bitters
2 dashes orange bitters
1 egg white
1 oz (30 ml) soda, to top
Garnish: lemon twist (discard) and cherry

Telephone Fizz
Hoffman House Bartender's Guide, *Charles S. Mahoney, 1905*
2 oz (60 ml) Cognac
⅜ oz (11 ml) maraschino liqueur
¾ oz (22 ml) lemon juice
⅜ oz (11 ml) simple syrup
1 whole egg
1 oz (30 ml) soda, to top
Garnish: lemon twist (discard) and lemon wedge

The Astor Hotel Special
The Gentleman's Companion, *Charles H. Baker Jr., 1939*
2 oz (60 ml) Cognac
¼ oz (7 ml) maraschino liqueur
¾ oz (22 ml) lemon juice
¼ oz (7 ml) simple syrup
2 dashes absinthe
1 egg white
1 oz (30 ml) soda, to top
Garnish: lemon twist (discard) and lemon wedge

Yankee Clipper
The South American Gentleman's Companion, *Charles H. Baker Jr., 1951*
1½ oz (45 ml) Cognac
¾ oz (22 ml) tawny Port
1 oz (30 ml) espresso
¾ oz (22 ml) house cream (p 506)
1 egg white
1 oz (30 ml) soda, to top
Garnish: freshly grated nutmeg

AMERICAN WHISKEY

Bourbon Lift
Erik Adkins, Hard Water, San Francisco
1½ oz (45 ml) bourbon
½ oz (15 ml) coffee liqueur
½ oz (15 ml) orgeat
¾ oz (22 ml) house cream (p 506)
1 oz (30 ml) soda, to top

Brown Derby Fizz
(Morning Glory Fizz with bourbon)
Jayne's Bartender's Guide, *1934*
1½ oz (45 ml) bourbon
¾ oz (22 ml) lemon juice
¾ oz (22 ml) simple syrup
2 dashes absinthe
1 egg white
1 oz (30 ml) soda, to top
Garnish: lemon twist (discard) and lemon wedge

Buffalo Fizz
Hoffman House Bartender's Guide, *Charles S. Mahoney, 1905*
1½ oz (45 ml) rye whiskey
½ oz (15 ml) Pedro Ximénez
¾ oz (22 ml) lemon juice
½ oz (15 ml) simple syrup
1 egg white
1 oz (30 ml) soda, to top
Garnish: orange twist (discard) and orange wedge

Double Standard Sour
Straub's Manual of Mixed Drinks, *Jacques Straub, 1913*
1 oz (30 ml) rye whiskey
1 oz (30 ml) gin
⅜ oz (11 ml) lemon juice
⅜ oz (11 ml) lime juice
¾ oz (22 ml) raspberry syrup (p 500)
1 egg white
1 oz (30 ml) soda, to top
Garnish: lemon twist (discard) and raspberry

Eggnog Fizz
Ricky Gomez, Palomar, Portland
1½ oz (45 ml) bourbon
½ oz (15 ml) Amontillado Sherry
½ oz (15 ml) Giffard Caribbean Pineapple
¾ oz (22 ml) lemon juice
½ oz (15 ml) Demerara syrup (p 495)
2 drops Bittermens Elemakule Tiki Bitters
1 whole egg
1 oz (30 ml) soda, to top
Garnish: lemon twist (discard)

Elk's Fizz
(aka **Elk's Own Fizz, Elk's Club Fizz** or **Japanese Fizz** in *Straub's Manual of Mixed Drinks*, Jacques Straub, 1913)
Peter F. Sindar, St. Paul
Hoffman House Bartender's Guide, *Charles S. Mahoney, 1905*
1½ oz (45 ml) rye whiskey
½ oz (15 ml) tawny Port
¾ oz (22 ml) lemon juice
½ oz (15 ml) simple syrup
1 egg white
1 oz (30 ml) soda, to top
Garnish: lemon twist (discard)
▾ Won the Police Gazette bartenders' medal in 1901.

Rye Maple Fizz
Erick Castro, Eveleigh, Los Angeles
2 oz (60 ml) rye whiskey
¾ oz (22 ml) lemon juice
½ oz (15 ml) maple syrup
2 dashes Angostura Bitters
1 egg white
1 oz (30 ml) soda, to top
Garnish: freshly grated cinnamon

Add all ingredients except soda to a shaker and dry shake. Add ice, shake again, then strain into a frozen footed Delmonico glass and top with soda simultaneously.

Silver Lining
Joseph Schwartz, Milk & Honey, NYC, 2001
1½ oz (45 ml) rye whiskey
¾ oz (22 ml) Licor 43
¾ oz (22 ml) lemon juice
¼ oz (7 ml) simple syrup
1 egg white
1 oz (30 ml) soda, to top
Garnish: lemon twist (discard) and lemon wedge

Sitting Bull Fizz
What'll You Have?, *Julien J. Proskauer, 1933*
1½ oz (45 ml) bourbon
½ oz (15 ml) aged dark rum
¾ oz (22 ml) lemon juice
¾ oz (22 ml) simple syrup
1 egg white
1 oz (30 ml) soda, to top
Garnish: lemon twist (discard)

SCOTCH

Derby Fizz
Old Mr. Boston Deluxe Official Bartender's Guide, *Leo Cotton, 1935*
1½ oz (45 ml) Scotch
¾ oz (22 ml) orange curaçao (p 498)
¾ oz (22 ml) lemon juice
1 whole egg
1 oz (30 ml) soda, to top
Garnish: lemon twist (discard) and lemon wedge

Golden Thistle
(Golden Scotch Fizz with orange bitters)
The New and Improved Illustrated Bartenders' Manual, *Harry Johnson, 1900*
2 oz (60 ml) Scotch
¾ oz (22 ml) lemon juice
¾ oz (22 ml) simple syrup
2 dashes orange bitters
1 egg yolk
1 oz (30 ml) soda, to top
Garnish: lemon twist (discard) and lemon wedge

Morning Glory Fizz
New and Improved Bartender's Manual, *Harry Johnson, 1882*
2 oz (60 ml) Scotch
¾ oz (22 ml) lemon juice
¾ oz (22 ml) simple syrup
2 dashes absinthe
1 egg white
1 oz (30 ml) soda, to top
Garnish: lemon twist (discard) and whole star anise

Morning Star Fizz
Jack's Manual, *J.A. Grohusko, 1916*
1½ oz (45 ml) Scotch
¾ oz (22 ml) tawny Port
¾ oz (22 ml) house cream (p 506)
1 egg yolk
1 oz (30 ml) soda, to top
Garnish: lemon twist (discard) and lemon wedge

FORTIFIED & LIQUEUR

Beyond the Infinite
Turk Dietrich
Cure: New Orleans Drinks and How to Mix 'Em, *Neal Bodenheimer and Emily Timberlake, 2022*
1 oz (30 ml) Bonal Gentiane-Quina
½ oz (15 ml) bourbon
½ oz (15 ml) triple sec
½ oz (15 ml) lemon juice
½ oz (15 ml) simple syrup
1 egg white
½ oz (15 ml) soda, to top
Garnish: lemon twist (discard) and Angostura Bitters stripe

5am Club
Michael Madrusan, The Everleigh, Melbourne, 2024
1½ oz (45 ml) Amaro Montenegro
½ oz (15 ml) amaretto
¾ oz (22 ml) lemon juice
½ oz (15 ml) simple syrup
1 egg white
1 oz (30 ml) soda, to top
Garnish: lemon twist (discard) and lemon wedge

Kohinoor
American & Other Drinks, *Leo Engel, 1878*
1 oz (30 ml) Bénédictine
¾ oz (22 ml) lemon juice
¾ oz (22 ml) raspberry syrup (p 500)
1 whole egg
1½ oz (45 ml) Champagne, to top
Garnish: lemon twist (discard) and raspberry

Merry Widow Fizz
Jones' Complete Barguide, *Stan Jones, 1977*
1½ oz (45 ml) sloe gin
1 oz (30 ml) orange juice
½ oz (15 ml) lemon juice
½ oz (15 ml) simple syrup
1 egg white
1 oz (30 ml) soda, to top
Garnish: orange twist (discard) and orange wedge

Milano Fizz
Michael Madrusan, The Everleigh, Melbourne, 2019
1½ oz (45 ml) Campari
¾ oz (22 ml) lemon juice
½ oz (15 ml) simple syrup
1 egg white
1 oz (30 ml) Prosecco, to top
Garnish: orange twist (discard) and orange wedge

Whole Lotta Rosa
Michael Madrusan, The Everleigh, Melbourne, 2019
1½ oz (45 ml) Cocchi Rosa
½ oz (15 ml) gin
¾ oz (22 ml) lemon juice
½ oz (15 ml) simple syrup
2 orange half-wheels
1 egg white
1 oz (30 ml) soda, to top
Press orange wheels with simple syrup, add remaining ingredients and dry shake. Add ice, shake again, then strain into a frozen footed Delmonico glass and top with soda simulatenously.
Garnish: orange twist (discard) and orange wedge
▾ Named for the AC/DC song.

Add all ingredients except soda to a shaker and dry shake. Add ice, shake again, then strain into a frozen footed Delmonico glass and top with soda simultaneously.

Morning Bracer No. 2
A Life-Time Collection of 688 Recipes for Drinks, *1934*
1 oz (30 ml) white crème de cacao
1 oz (30 ml) orange juice
½ oz (15 ml) lemon juice
½ oz (15 ml) lime juice
½ oz (15 ml) simple syrup
1 egg white
1 oz (30 ml) soda, to top
Garnish: orange twist (discard) and orange wedge

Sloe Gin Fizz
(aka **Bismarck Fizz** in *Straub's Manual of Mixed Drinks*, Jacques Straub, 1913)
Jack's Manual, *J.A. Grohusko, 1910*
1½ oz (45 ml) sloe gin
½ oz (15 ml) gin
¾ oz (22 ml) lemon juice
¾ oz (22 ml) simple syrup
1 egg white
1 oz (30 ml) soda, to top
Garnish: lemon twist (discard)
▾ Swap soda for Champagne to make the **Sloe Gin Fizz Royale**.

Suissesse
Famous New Orleans Drinks and How to Mix 'Em, *Stanley Clisby Arthur, 1937*
1 oz (30 ml) pastis
¾ oz (22 ml) dry vermouth
¼ oz (7 ml) white crème de menthe
¾ oz (22 ml) lemon juice
½ oz (15 ml) orgeat
1 egg white
1 oz (30 ml) soda, to top
Garnish: lemon twist (discard) and cherry

The Royale We
Brandon Bramhall, Attaboy, Nashville
1½ oz (45 ml) Select Aperitivo
¾ oz (22 ml) lemon juice
½ oz (15 ml) simple syrup
2 orange half-wheels
1 egg white
1 oz (30 ml) Champagne, to top
Press orange wheels with simple syrup, then add remaining ingredients and dry shake. Add ice, shake again, then strain into a frozen footed Delmonico glass and top with Champagne.
Garnish: orange twist (discard) and orange wedge

OTHER

Absinthe Cream Fizz
Will "Oxy" Oxenham
1 oz (30 ml) absinthe (preferably Lemercier Absinthe 45%)
⅓ oz (10 ml) Plymouth Gin
½ oz (15 ml) lemon juice
⅓ oz (10 ml) simple syrup
⅓ oz (10 ml) house cream (p 506)
1 egg white
1 oz (30 ml) soda, to top
Garnish: lemon twist (discard)

Angostura Fizz
Straub's Manual of Mixed Drinks, *Jacques Straub, 1913*
1 oz (30 ml) Angostura Bitters
⅜ oz (11 ml) lemon juice
⅜ oz (11 ml) lime juice
½ oz (15 ml) pineapple juice
½ oz (15 ml) simple syrup
½ oz (15 ml) house cream (p 506)
1 egg white
1 oz (30 ml) soda, to top
Garnish: lemon twist (discard) and 2 pineapple fronds

Claret Fizz
Straub's Manual of Mixed Drinks, *Jacques Straub, 1913*
1½ oz (45 ml) dry red wine
¾ oz (22 ml) lemon juice
¾ oz (22 ml) simple syrup
1 egg white
1 oz (30 ml) soda, to top
Garnish: lemon twist (discard)

Equator
1½ oz (45 ml) aquavit
½ oz (15 ml) St Germain Elderflower Liqueur
¾ oz (22 ml) lemon juice
½ oz (15 ml) simple syrup
1 egg white
1 oz (30 ml) soda, to top
Garnish: lemon twist (discard) and lemon wedge

Sea Fizz
The Fine Art of Mixing Drinks, *David A. Embury, 1948*
1¼ oz (37 ml) absinthe
¾ oz (22 ml) lemon juice
¾ oz (22 ml) simple syrup
1 egg white
1 oz (30 ml) soda, to top
Garnish: lemon twist (discard) and whole star anise

Seapea "C.P."
The Artistry of Mixing Drinks, *Frank Meier, 1936*
¾ oz (22 ml) absinthe
¾ oz (22 ml) lemon juice
¾ oz (22 ml) simple syrup
1 egg white
1 oz (30 ml) soda, to top
Garnish: lemon twist (discard) and whole star anise

Add all ingredients except soda to a shaker and dry shake. Add ice, shake again, then strain into a frozen footed Delmonico glass and top with soda simultaneously.

SOUR

Non-Traditional Sour (left), Traditional Sour (right)

Sour

A short and sharp citrus cocktail, shaken with or without egg white, and served in a frozen stemmed cocktail glass.

TRADITIONAL SOUR

spirit + citrus (predominantly lemon) + sugar + egg white

Add all ingredients to a shaker and dry shake vigorously to emulsify. Add ice, then shake and strain into a frozen Sour glass.

NON-TRADITIONAL SOUR

spirit + citrus (predominantly lemon) + sugar

Add all ingredients to a shaker, then shake with ice and strain into a frozen coupe.

Sour is, in fact, a gargantuan category of short drinks defined by the use of citrus. An evolution of the early Punch (p 122) – a drink with multiple ingredients, citrus and often spices – and mother to many cocktail subcategories, a Sour broadly describes spirited drinks shaken with citrus and a sweetener, served up. Surfacing in the United States sometime in the 1850s, Sour recipes modified the longer, more alcoholic cocktails of the time into shorter, colder variations served in stemmed glasses slightly larger than the classic coupes used for Martinis (p 304) and Manhattans (p 334).

Today, the biggest differentiation is between Traditional Sours (shaken with an egg white) and Non-Traditional Sours (without egg white), but the nuanced terminology doesn't stop there. If a Traditional Sour is topped with soda, for instance, it becomes a Fizz (p 134). And if a Non-Traditional Sour is served with crushed ice, it's considered a Fix (p 244). In essence, the uncomplicated combination of spirit, citrus and sweetener is responsible for most of the modern cocktail recipes on menus today.

So many interpretations of the Sour, including the Gimlet (p 206) and Sidecar (p 184), have become iconic subcategories in their own right and have given rise to innumerable variations. For the purposes of this book, we have listed some of these smaller subcategories independently where warranted. We've done this in a bid to drill down into each drink's specific components (the use of lime rather than lemon, say) as well as the precise method and presentation attributed to that style. We hope this makes for both speedier referencing and a more comprehensive understanding of the category as a whole.

CORE STYLE (TRADITIONAL):

Whiskey Sour

The Bar-Tender's Guide, *Jerry Thomas, 1862*
2 oz (60 ml) bourbon
¾ oz (22 ml) lemon juice
¾ oz (22 ml) simple syrup
1 egg white

Add all ingredients to a shaker and dry shake vigorously to emulsify. Add ice, then shake and strain into a frozen Sour glass.
Garnish: Angostura stripe

ESSENTIAL VARIATIONS

Little Rebel

(aka **Littlest Rebel**, *The Official Mixer's Manual*, Patrick Gavin Duffy, *1934)*
Recipes for Mixed Drinks, *Hugo R. Ensslin, 1916*
1 oz (30 ml) Scotch
1 oz (30 ml) bonded apple brandy
¾ oz (22 ml) lemon juice
¾ oz (22 ml) grenadine (p 496)
1 egg white

Add all ingredients to a shaker and dry shake vigorously to emulsify. Add ice, then shake and strain into a frozen Sour glass.

Born in Germany in 1880, Hugo Richard Ensslin is one of the unsung heroes in the development of classic cocktails, responsible for the last bartender's guide published prior to the American Prohibition. A talented and trained photographer and painter in his youth, Ensslin decided to travel to the United States alone at age 16, where he moved between New York and Ohio picking up work in retail and hospitality. In 1907, he married New York native Margaret Quigley, with whom he had a son.

Ensslin began working at Hotel Wallick in Times Square, where he honed his bartending skills and developed a small following. His book, *Recipes for Mixed Drinks*, was published in 1916, with an expanded second edition released the following year. When the United States entered World War I, Ensslin – by then an American citizen – willingly joined the fight against Germany, his country of birth. In 1925, his wife Margaret died and, in his grief, Ensslin followed Hotel Wallick's manager to Pennsylvania, taking the restaurant manager role at Hotel Sterling. Ensslin tragically took his own life four years later, at just 49 years old.

Although it received little acclaim at the time, Ensslin's book is a significant work that documents some of the earliest recipes for legendary, era-defining drinks such as the original Aviation Cocktail (p 195). Interestingly enough, many of these cocktails have been incorrectly credited to Harry Craddock's *The Savoy Cocktail Book* in recent years, which was published 14 years later in 1930. In addition to chronicling the cocktails of the time, *Recipes for Mixed Drinks* also explores the popular spirits and prevalent bartending methods of the 1910s.

The Little Rebel is one of several cocktails in the book featuring somewhat obscure ingredients for the time: bonded apple brandy (also known as applejack) and grenadine (pomegranate syrup). Those who appreciate bonded apple brandy used this way should also try The Delicious Sour (p 166) by William Schmidt – a Traditional Sour with lime and peach from 1891 – or Ensslin's Apple Blow Fizz (p 147).

Non-traditional
Bees' Knees [*sic*]
(aka **Bee's Knees** or Non-traditional Gin Sour with honey)
Frank Meier, Bar du 'Ritz'
Cocktails de Paris, *Georges Gabriel Thenon, 1929*
2 oz (60 ml) gin
¾ oz (22 ml) lemon juice
¾ oz (22 ml) honey syrup (p 496)

Add all ingredients to a shaker, then shake with ice and strain into a frozen coupe.

The Bee's Knees – a simple and soothing combination of gin, lemon and honey – is easily the most famous cocktail by Frank Meier, one of the world's most industrious bartenders. Meier was born in Austria in 1884 and grew up in hospitality, starting out at his parents' hotel. After a short time in hotel school, Meier pursued bar work around the globe, with stints in Paris, London, Cairo and New York City, notably at the celebrated Hoffman House. In 1908, Meier returned to Paris, bartending there until World War I broke out in 1914. After four years of fighting, Meier resumed his career in the City of Light and had the honour of opening a bar inside the prestigious Ritz Paris, where he achieved celebrity status. His repertoire quickly became the talk of the Parisian elite and included groundbreaking drinks such as the first-ever vintage cocktail: a Sidecar featuring Cognac from 1865.

The Bee's Knees made its first print appearance in 1929's *Cocktails de Paris*, a collection of the city's leading cocktails throughout the 1920s, compiled by French bon vivant and singer Georges Gabriel Thenon (known better to some by his stage name, Rip), and beautifully illustrated by French artist Paul Colin. Meier also published a recipe in his own 1936 volume, *The Artistry of Mixing Drinks*, another stunningly designed collection that captures the recipes of the legendary French hotel bar in its prime. Meier remained at the helm of the Ritz Paris throughout World War II and is rumoured to have secretly assisted the French Resistance against the Germans.

While this foolproof, three-ingredient cold elixir is hard to trump, honey enthusiasts should definitely explore both the Honeysuckle (p 231) and Honey Bee (p 234), which feature light and dark rum, respectively, along with the bourbon-based Gold Rush (p 174). The Bebbo (p 170), Stan Jones's variation with a splash of orange juice, is also worth a look.

Traditional Sour

Add all ingredients to a shaker and dry shake vigorously to emulsify. Add ice, then shake and strain into a frozen sour glass.

GIN

Ace Cocktail
Trader Vic's Bartender's Guide, *Trader Vic, 1947*
2 oz (60 ml) gin
¾ oz (22 ml) lemon juice
¾ oz (22 ml) grenadine (p 496)
¾ oz (22 ml) house cream (p 506)
1 egg white
Garnish: freshly grated nutmeg

Act of Violets
Ryan Chetiyawardana, Bramble, Edinburgh, 2009
2 oz (60 ml) gin
½ oz (15 ml) crème de violette
⅓ oz (10 ml) dry vermouth
¾ oz (22 ml) lemon juice
¼ oz (7 ml) simple syrup
2 dashes Angostura Bitters
1 egg white
Garnish: freshly grated nutmeg

Appendicitis De Luxe
The Fine Art of Mixing Drinks, *David A. Embury, 1948*
2 oz (60 ml) gin
¾ oz (22 ml) orange curaçao (p 498)
¾ oz (22 ml) lime juice
1 egg white

Bahia Busy Bee Cocktail
Dom Manoel Condé, Salvador
The South American Gentleman's Companion, *Charles H. Baker Jr., 1951*
2 oz (60 ml) gin
¼ oz (7 ml) triple sec
¾ oz (22 ml) lime juice
½ oz (15 ml) honey syrup (p 496)
6–8 mint leaves
1 egg white

Beekeeper
Lacy Hawkins, The NoMad Bar, NYC
1½ oz (45 ml) Plymouth Gin
¼ oz (7 ml) St Germain Elderflower Liqueur
¼ oz (7 ml) Islay Scotch
¾ oz (22 ml) lemon juice
½ oz (15 ml) honey syrup (p 496)
2 dashes orange bitters
1 egg white

Bidú Cocktail
The South American Gentleman's Companion, *Charles H. Baker Jr., 1951*
1½ oz (45 ml) gin
½ oz (15 ml) dry vermouth
½ oz (15 ml) Giffard Crème de Pêche de Vigne
½ oz (15 ml) lemon juice
1 teaspoon (5 ml) orgeat
1 egg white

Chanticleer
(Traditional Gin Sour with raspberries)
Trader Vic's Bartender's Guide, *Trader Vic, 1947*
2 oz (60 ml) gin
¾ oz (22 ml) lemon juice
¾ oz (22 ml) simple syrup
3 raspberries
1 egg white
Add raspberries and simple syrup to a shaker and muddle. Add remaining ingredients and dry shake. Add ice, shake again, then strain into a frozen Sour glass.
Garnish: raspberry

Clover Club Cocktail
(Traditional Gin Sour with grenadine)
The World's Drinks and How to Mix Them, *Wm. T. Boothby, 1908*
2 oz (60 ml) gin
¾ oz (22 ml) lemon juice
¾ oz (22 ml) grenadine (p 496)
1 egg white

Clover Club Cocktail (Robert Vermeire Recipe)
Cocktails: How to Mix Them, *Robert Vermeire, 1922*
1½ oz (45 ml) gin
½ oz (15 ml) dry vermouth
¾ oz (22 ml) lime juice
¾ oz (22 ml) raspberry syrup (p 500)
1 egg white

Clover Leaf
(Clover Club Cocktail with mint leaf garnish)
Jack's Manual, *J.A. Grohusko, 1910*
2 oz (60 ml) gin
¾ oz (22 ml) lemon juice
¾ oz (22 ml) raspberry syrup (p 500)
1 egg white
Garnish: mint leaf

Disco Sour
Felix Woods, Black Pearl, Melbourne, 2021
1 oz (30 ml) gin
½ oz (15 ml) pisco
¼ oz (7 ml) Giffard Crème de Pêche de Vigne
¾ oz (22 ml) lemon juice
½ oz (15 ml) simple syrup
2 dashes orange bitters
1 egg white
Serve in a frozen double rocks glass with ice.
Garnish: mint sprig

Douglas Fairbanks
Sloppy Joe's Cocktails Manual, *1932*
1½ oz (45 ml) gin
½ oz (15 ml) apricot brandy
¾ oz (22 ml) lemon juice
¼ oz (7 ml) simple syrup
1 egg white

Add all ingredients to a shaker and dry shake vigorously to emulsify. Add ice, then shake and strain into a frozen Sour glass.

Eagle's Dream
Hoffman House Bartender's Guide, *Charles S. Mahoney, 1905*
1½ oz (45 ml) gin
½ oz (15 ml) rose liqueur
¾ oz (22 ml) lemon juice
½ oz (15 ml) simple syrup
½ oz (15 ml) red wine, to float
1 egg white
Add all ingredients, except red wine, to a shaker and shake vigorously without ice to emulsify. Add ice, shake again, then strain into a frozen Sour glass and float red wine.

Eagle's Dream Cocktail
(aka **Violet Sour**)
"Harry" of Ciro's ABC of Mixing Cocktails, *Harry MacElhone, 1923*
1½ oz (45 ml) gin
½ oz (15 ml) crème de violette
¾ oz (22 ml) lemon juice
¾ oz (22 ml) simple syrup
1 egg white
Garnish: cherry

Edith Day Cocktail
The Stork Club Bar Book, *Lucius Beebe, 1946*
2 oz (60 ml) gin
1 oz (30 ml) pink grapefruit juice
¾ oz (22 ml) simple syrup
1 teaspoon (5 ml) lemon juice
1 egg white
Garnish: pink grapefruit twist (discard)

Everything But The Flowers
Liber & Co., Austin
2 oz (60 ml) gin
½ oz (15 ml) white crème de cacao
¾ oz (22 ml) lemon juice
¾ oz (22 ml) simple syrup
2 strawberries, halved
1 egg white
Add strawberry and simple syrup to a shaker and muddle. Add remaining ingredients and dry shake. Add ice, shake again, then strain into a frozen Sour glass.
Garnish: dried rose petal

Gin Side Car Cocktail
The How and When, *Hyman Gale and Gerald F. Marco, 1937*
1½ oz (45 ml) gin
½ oz (15 ml) triple sec
¼ oz (7 ml) Bénédictine
¾ oz (22 ml) lime juice
1 egg white
Garnish: lemon twist (discard)

Grande Bretagne Cocktail No. 1
The Gentleman's Companion, *Charles H. Baker Jr., 1939*
2 oz (60 ml) gin
½ oz (15 ml) apricot brandy
⅜ oz (11 ml) lemon juice
⅜ oz (11 ml) lime juice
¼ oz (7 ml) simple syrup
2 dashes orange bitters
1 egg white
Garnish: orange twist (discard)

Green Eyes
Andrew Volk, Portland Hunt + Alpine Club, Portland
1½ oz (45 ml) gin
¾ oz (22 ml) Green Chartreuse
¾ oz (22 ml) lime juice
½ oz (15 ml) simple syrup
1 egg white
Serve in a frozen double rocks glass with ice.
Garnish: lime wheel and cherry

Green Park
Erik Lorincz, American Bar, The Savoy, London, 2011
2 oz (60 ml) gin
¾ oz (22 ml) lemon juice
¾ oz (22 ml) simple syrup
3 dashes celery bitters
5 basil leaves
1 egg white

Hotel Georgia
The Canon Cocktail Book, *Jamie Boudreau and James O. Fraioli, 2016*
2 oz (60 ml) gin
¾ oz (22 ml) lemon juice
½ oz (15 ml) orgeat
6 drops orange blossom water
1 egg white

Le Coq d'Or Special
(Traditional Gin Sour with crème de cassis)
"Jack" of Le Coq d'Or
An Anthology of Cocktails, *1930s*
2 oz (60 ml) gin
½ oz (15 ml) crème de cassis
¾ oz (22 ml) lemon juice
¼ oz (7 ml) simple syrup
1 egg white

Marqueray Cocktail
Straub's Manual of Mixed Drinks, *Jacques Straub, 1913*
2 oz (60 ml) gin
¾ oz (22 ml) lime juice
¾ oz (22 ml) grenadine (p 496)
2 dashes absinthe
1 egg white

Mr. Pickles
Jason Williams
1½ oz (45 ml) gin
¾ oz (22 ml) lemon juice
⅓ oz (10 ml) raspberry liqueur
⅓ oz (10 ml) strawberry vinegar
1 egg white
Garnish: lemon twist (discard)

Montreal Gin Sour
(aka **Traditional Gin Sour**)
The Fine Art of Mixing Drinks, *David A. Embury, 1948*
2 oz (60 ml) gin
¾ oz (22 ml) lemon juice
¾ oz (22 ml) simple syrup
1 egg white
Garnish: Angostura Bitters stripe

Neptune's Wrath
Toby Maloney, Violet Hour, Chicago, 2007
1½ oz (45 ml) gin
¼ oz (7 ml) absinthe
¾ oz (22 ml) lemon juice
½ oz (15 ml) simple syrup
1 egg white
¼ oz (7 ml) Green Chartreuse, to top
Make the Sour, then set the Green Chartreuse aflame in a Blazer cup and slowly pour the liquid into the centre of the cocktail.

Add all ingredients to a shaker and dry shake vigorously to emulsify. Add ice, then shake and strain into a frozen Sour glass.

Ocean Shore Cocktail
The World's Drinks and How to Mix Them, *Wm. T. Boothby, 1908*
1 oz (30 ml) gin
1 oz (30 ml) sloe gin
¾ oz (22 ml) lime juice
¾ oz (22 ml) grenadine (p 496)
1 egg white

Orange Paradise Cocktail
The South American Gentleman's Companion, *Charles H. Baker Jr., 1951*
1½ oz (45 ml) gin
¾ oz (22 ml) orange curaçao (p 498)
½ oz (15 ml) lemon juice
½ oz (15 ml) orange juice
1 egg white

Perfect Lady
(Traditional Gin Sour with peach liqueur)
Sidney Cox, Grosvenor House, London, 1936
2 oz (60 ml) gin
¾ oz (22 ml) Giffard Crème de Pêche de Vigne
¾ oz (22 ml) lemon juice
1 egg white
▼ First prize winner at the 1936 British Empire Cocktail Competition.

Petruchio Cocktail
The Canon Cocktail Book, *Jamie Boudreau and James O. Fraioli, 2016*
1 oz (30 ml) gin
1 oz (30 ml) Aperol
¾ oz (22 ml) lemon juice
½ oz (15 ml) simple syrup
1 egg white
Garnish: edible orchid

Pink Lady Cocktail
Straub's Manual of Mixed Drinks, *Jacques Straub, 1913*
1 oz (30 ml) gin
1 oz (30 ml) bonded apple brandy
¾ oz (22 ml) lemon juice
¾ oz (22 ml) grenadine (p 496)
1 egg white
Garnish: apple fan
▼ Originally published as equal parts gin, applejack and lime juice, with a few dashes of grenadine. Egg white appears later in recipes by Harry Craddock and W.J. Tarling, which do not feature applejack or citrus. This modern variation is a hybrid of both.

Pink Rose Cocktail
The Savoy Cocktail Book, *Harry Craddock, 1930*
2 oz (60 ml) gin
½ oz (15 ml) lemon juice
½ oz (15 ml) grenadine (p 496)
½ oz (15 ml) house cream (p 506)
1 egg white

Prince of Wales Special Cocktail
The South American Gentleman's Companion, *Charles H. Baker Jr., 1951*
1½ oz (45 ml) gin
½ oz (15 ml) Cognac
1 oz (30 ml) pineapple juice
¾ oz (22 ml) simple syrup
¼ oz (7 ml) lemon juice
1 egg white

Rizzo Sour
Gregor de Gruyther, Ronnie Scott's, London, 2006
1 oz (30 ml) gin
1 oz (30 ml) bonded apple brandy
¾ oz (22 ml) pink grapefruit juice
½ oz (15 ml) lime juice
¼ oz (7 ml) grenadine (p 496)
¼ oz (7 ml) passionfruit syrup (p 499)
1 egg white
Garnish: apple fan

Rose Petal
(Royal Clover Club Cocktail with rosewater)
Ernesto Jara, Hosteria Providencia, Santiago
The South American Gentleman's Companion, *Charles H. Baker Jr., 1951*
2 oz (60 ml) gin
¾ oz (22 ml) lemon juice
¾ oz (22 ml) grenadine (p 496)
1 whole egg
Garnish: spritz of rosewater

Rubi Silver Cocktail
Bar La Florida Cocktails, *1935*
1½ oz (45 ml) gin
½ oz (15 ml) Heering Cherry Liqueur
¾ oz (22 ml) lemon juice
¼ oz (7 ml) simple syrup
1 egg white
Garnish: cherry

Saint-Germain-des-Prés
Nico de Soto, Mama Shelter, Paris, 2008
1½ oz (45 ml) gin (preferably Hendrick's Gin)
¾ oz (22 ml) St Germain Elderflower Liqueur
¾ oz (22 ml) lime juice
½ oz (15 ml) simple syrup
1 teaspoon (5 ml) cucumber juice
5 dashes Thai chilli tincture (p 505)
1 egg white
Garnish: cucumber wheel

Savannah
Old Waldorf Bar Days, *Albert Stevens Crockett, 1931*
1½ oz (45 ml) gin
¾ oz (22 ml) white crème de cacao
1 oz (30 ml) orange juice
¼ oz (7 ml) lemon juice
¼ oz (7 ml) simple syrup
2 dashes orange bitters
1 egg white

Add all ingredients to a shaker and dry shake vigorously to emulsify. Add ice, then shake and strain into a frozen Sour glass.

Silver King Cocktail
(Traditional Gin Sour with orange bitters)
The Savoy Cocktail Book, *Harry Craddock, 1930*
2 oz (60 ml) gin
¾ oz (22 ml) lemon juice
¾ oz (22 ml) simple syrup
2 dashes orange bitters
1 egg white

Spanish Monk Cocktail
Don Eduardo Lopéz, Guayaquil
The South American Gentleman's Companion, *Charles H. Baker Jr., 1951*
1½ oz (45 ml) gin
½ oz (15 ml) Green Chartreuse
¾ oz (22 ml) lemon juice
½ oz (15 ml) simple syrup
1 egg white

State Street Cocktail
Famous New Orleans Drinks and How to Mix 'Em, *Stanley Clisby Arthur, 1937*
2 oz (60 ml) gin
¾ oz (22 ml) unsweetened pineapple juice
⅜ oz (11 ml) lemon juice
⅜ oz (11 ml) lime juice
½ oz (15 ml) simple syrup
1 egg white
▼ Arthur's wife "brought the recipe back from Mexico under the name *'Franco'*".

The Riviera
Toby Maloney, 2007
2 oz (60 ml) Riviera mix (p 507)
¾ oz (22 ml) lemon juice
¾ oz (22 ml) simple syrup
1 egg white
Garnish: mint leaf and 3 drops of orange bitters

White Lady Cocktail
(Traditional Gin Sour with triple sec)
Victor Cabrin, Grosvenor House Hotel, London, late 1920s
2 oz (60 ml) gin
½ oz (15 ml) triple sec
¾ oz (22 ml) lemon juice
1 teaspoon (5 ml) simple syrup
1 egg white

White Rose Cocktail
Recipes for Mixed Drinks, *Hugo R. Ensslin, 1917*
2 oz (60 ml) gin
⅜ oz (11 ml) maraschino liqueur
½ oz (15 ml) lime juice
½ oz (15 ml) orange juice
⅜ oz (11 ml) simple syrup
1 egg white

RUM & CANE SPIRIT

Bermuda Sour
Sam Ross, Milk & Honey, NYC, 2006
2 oz (60 ml) Goslings Black Seal Rum
¾ oz (22 ml) lemon juice
¾ oz (22 ml) simple syrup
1 orange wedge
1 egg white
Press orange and simple syrup in a shaker. Add remaining ingredients, then shake vigorously without ice to emulsify. Add ice, shake again, then strain into a frozen double rocks glass with ice.
Garnish: Angostura Bitters stripe and orange wedge

Bumble-Bee Cocktail
J.K.L. Ponsonby-Foulcques
The South American Gentleman's Companion, *Charles H. Baker Jr., 1951*
2 oz (60 ml) aged dark rum
1 oz (30 ml) lime juice
¾ oz (22 ml) honey syrup (p 496)
1 egg white
Garnish: orange twist (discard) and Angostura Bitters stripe

Conquistador
Sam Ross, Little Branch, NYC, 2007
1 oz (30 ml) aged dark rum
1 oz (30 ml) blanco tequila
¾ oz (22 ml) simple syrup
½ oz (15 ml) lemon juice
½ oz (15 ml) lime juice
2 dashes orange bitters
1 egg white

Cora Middleton
(Clover Club Cocktail with Jamaican dark rum)
Old Waldorf Bar Days, *Albert Stevens Crockett, 1931*
2 oz (60 ml) Jamaican dark rum
¾ oz (22 ml) lemon juice
¾ oz (22 ml) grenadine (p 496)
1 teaspoon (5 ml) simple syrup
1 egg white

Demerara Red Lion Cocktail
The South American Gentleman's Companion, *Charles H. Baker Jr., 1951*
1½ oz (45 ml) Demerara dark rum (preferably El Dorado 12yr Rum)
¼ oz (7 ml) orange curaçao (p 498)
¾ oz (22 ml) lime juice
½ oz (15 ml) grenadine (p 496)
1 dash Angostura Bitters
1 egg white
Garnish: pineapple wedge

Marikoriko
(Daiquiri with egg white, raspberry and chocolate bitters)
Matthias Soberon
2 oz (60 ml) light rum
¾ oz (22 ml) lime juice
¾ oz (22 ml) simple syrup
1 dash Bittermens Xocolatl Mole Bitters
3 raspberries
1 egg white
Add raspberries and simple syrup to a shaker and muddle. Add remaining ingredients and dry shake. Add ice, shake again, then strain into a frozen Sour glass.
Garnish: raspberry

Peligroso
La Factoría, San Juan
1½ oz (45 ml) light rum
½ oz (15 ml) Campari
½ oz (15 ml) Amaro Averna
¾ oz (22 ml) lime juice
¼ oz (7 ml) simple syrup
2 dashes Angostura Bitters
2 dashes Dale DeGroff's Pimento Aromatic Bitters
2 drops saline solution (p 493)
1 egg white
Garnish: lime wedge

Add all ingredients to a shaker and dry shake vigorously to emulsify. Add ice, then shake and strain into a frozen Sour glass.

Ramoncita Lopez Special

(Daiquiri with egg white)
The Fine Art of Mixing Drinks, *David A. Embury, 1948*
2 oz (60 ml) light rum
1 oz (30 ml) lime juice
¾ oz (22 ml) simple syrup
1 egg white
Garnish: lime wedge
▼ Swap the lime wedge garnish for an Angostura Bitters stripe to make The Wedding March from *Crosby Gaige's Cocktail Guide and Ladies' Companion*, Crosby Gaige, 1941.

September Morn

(Daiquiri with egg white and grenadine)
Recipes for Mixed Drinks, *Hugo R. Ensslin, 1916*
2 oz (60 ml) light rum
¾ oz (22 ml) lime juice
¾ oz (22 ml) grenadine (p 496)
1 egg white
Garnish: lime wedge

Sleeper

The Bar-Tender's Guide, *Jerry Thomas, 1862*
2 oz (60 ml) aged dark rum
¾ oz (22 ml) lemon juice
¾ oz (22 ml) simple syrup
3 whole cloves
3 whole coriander seeds
1 whole egg
Press cloves and coriander seeds in a shaker. Add remaining ingredients and dry shake. Add ice, shake again, then strain into a frozen Sour glass.
▼ Originally served hot; be sure to fine strain this cocktail so the spices don't end up in the glass.

Smiling Ivy

Sidney Cox, 1953
1½ oz (45 ml) Jamaican dark rum
¾ oz (22 ml) Giffard Crème de Pêche de Vigne
1 oz (30 ml) pineapple juice
1 teaspoon (5 ml) lemon juice
1 egg white

Snow White

The Fine Art of Mixing Drinks, *David A. Embury, 1948*
2 oz (60 ml) light rum
1 oz (30 ml) pineapple juice
¼ oz (7 ml) lime juice
1 egg white
Garnish: lime wedge

AGAVE

Baby Turtle

Morgan Schick, Trick Dog, San Francisco
2 oz (60 ml) reposado tequila
¼ oz (7 ml) Campari
¾ oz (22 ml) lime juice
½ oz (15 ml) pink grapefruit juice
½ oz (15 ml) cinnamon syrup (p 495)
2 drops saline solution (p 493)
1 egg white
Serve in a frozen double rocks glass with ice.
Garnish: freshly grated cinnamon

Love Bug

Sam Penton, Death & Co, Denver, 2019
1½ oz (45 ml) blanco tequila
½ oz (15 ml) mezcal
½ oz (15 ml) pineapple juice
½ oz (15 ml) lime juice
½ oz (15 ml) raspberry syrup (p 500)
1 egg white
Garnish: Peychaud's Aromatic Cocktail Bitters stripe

Mezcal Sour

2 oz (60 ml) mezcal
¾ oz (22 ml) lemon juice
¾ oz (22 ml) simple syrup
1 egg white
Garnish: lemon twist (discard)

Pepino

(Traditional Tequila Sour with cucumber)
Michael Madrusan, Little Branch, NYC, 2009
2 oz (60 ml) blanco tequila
¾ oz (22 ml) lemon juice
¾ oz (22 ml) simple syrup
2 cucumber wheels
1 egg white
Press cucumber and simple syrup in a shaker. Add remaining ingredients, then shake vigorously without ice to emulsify. Add ice, shake again, then strain into a frozen Sour glass.
Garnish: cucumber wheel

Prado Cocktail

Hotel del Prado, Mexico City
Esquire Drink Book, *1956*
2 oz (60 ml) blanco tequila
¾ oz (22 ml) lemon juice
⅜ oz (11 ml) maraschino liqueur
⅜ oz (11 ml) grenadine (p 496)
1 egg white
Garnish: lemon twist (discard)

Sandilla

Riley Perrin Ellis, Attaboy, Nashville, 2018
1 oz (30 ml) blanco tequila
1 oz (30 ml) Fino Sherry
¾ oz (22 ml) lemon juice
¾ oz (22 ml) simple syrup
2 cucumber wheels
1 egg white
Press cucumber and simple syrup in a shaker. Add remaining ingredients, then shake vigorously without ice to emulsify. Add ice, shake again, then strain into a frozen Sour glass.
Garnish: cucumber wheel

The Hummingbird

Toby Maloney, 2008
1¾ oz (52 ml) blanco tequila
¾ oz (22 ml) Heering Cherry Liqueur
¾ oz (22 ml) lemon juice
½ oz (15 ml) simple syrup
3 dashes cherry bitters
1 egg white
Garnish: lemon twist (discard)

Add all ingredients to a shaker and dry shake vigorously to emulsify. Add ice, then shake and strain into a frozen Sour glass.

BRANDY

Amendment Cocktail
(Traditional Cognac Sour with orange blossom water and rosewater)
Michael Madrusan, Milk & Honey, NYC, 2008
2 oz (60 ml) Cognac
¾ oz (22 ml) lemon juice
¾ oz (22 ml) simple syrup
1 dash orange blossom water
1 egg white
Garnish: spritz of rosewater
▼ Created by Michael upon passing his American citizenship test.

Apple Sour
Michael Madrusan, The Everleigh, Melbourne, 2020
1 oz (30 ml) bonded apple brandy
1 oz (30 ml) Pommeau de Normandie
¾ oz (22 ml) lemon juice
½ oz (15 ml) simple syrup
1 egg white
Garnish: freshly grated cinnamon

Autumn Sweater
Michael Madrusan, The Everleigh, 2024
1½ oz (45 ml) bonded apple brandy
½ oz (15 ml) amaretto
¾ oz (22 ml) lemon juice
¼ oz (7 ml) simple syrup
1 egg white
Garnish: Angostura Bitters stripe

Basque Sour
David Molyneux, Mr. West, Melbourne, 2023
1½ oz (45 ml) Calvados
¾ oz (22 ml) lemon juice
¾ oz (22 ml) honey syrup (p 496)
¼ oz (7 ml) guindilla chilli brine
1 teaspoon (5 ml) pear eau de vie, to float
Add all ingredients to a shaker and shake vigorously without ice to emulsify. Add ice, shake again, then strain into a frozen double rocks glass with ice and float eau de vie.
Garnish: caperberry and lemon wedge

Brewster Sour
1½ oz (45 ml) pisco
¾ oz (22 ml) St Germain Elderflower Liqueur
¾ oz (22 ml) lemon juice
1 teaspoon (5 ml) simple syrup
1 egg white
Garnish: Angostura Bitters stripe

Brooklyn Sour
(New York Sour with Cognac)
Milk & Honey, NYC
2 oz (60 ml) Cognac
¾ oz (22 ml) lemon juice
¾ oz (22 ml) simple syrup
1 egg white
½ oz (15 ml) dry red wine, to float
Add all ingredients to a shaker and shake vigorously without ice to emulsify. Add ice, shake again, then strain into a frozen double rocks glass with ice, and float red wine.

Eiffel Sour
Darren Leaney, Caretaker's Cottage, Melbourne, 2024
1 oz (30 ml) Calvados
1 oz (30 ml) St Germain Elderflower Liqueur
¾ oz (22 ml) lime juice
⅓ oz (10 ml) honey syrup (p 496)
2 dashes Peychaud's Aromatic Cocktail Bitters
1 egg white
Garnish: mint sprig and lime wheel

Flip Off the Devil
The Canon Cocktail Book, *Jamie Boudreau and James O. Fraioli, 2016*
1½ oz (45 ml) bonded apple brandy
½ oz (15 ml) apricot brandy
¾ oz (22 ml) lemon juice
1 teaspoon (5 ml) simple syrup
2 dashes Angostura Bitters
1 egg white

Forget-Me-Not
The Flowing Bowl, *William Schmidt, 1891*
2 oz (60 ml) Cognac
¾ oz (22 ml) lime juice
½ oz (15 ml) simple syrup
1 teaspoon (5 ml) maraschino liqueur
1 egg white

Golden Gate Sour
Jason Crawley, Sydney
1½ oz (45 ml) pisco
1 oz (30 ml) pineapple juice
¾ oz (22 ml) lemon juice
¾ oz (22 ml) pineapple syrup (p 499)
1 teaspoon (5 ml) Golden State Yellow Chili Brine
2 dashes habanero bitters
1 egg white
Garnish: pinch of black pepper

Iron Cross
Toby Maloney, 2007
2 oz (60 ml) pisco
1 oz (30 ml) simple syrup
¾ oz (22 ml) lemon juice
3 drops orange blossom water
1 dash Bittermens Hopped Grapefruit Bitters
1 egg white
Garnish: 5 drops of Angostura Bitters, swirled

Judgment Day
Charles Vexenat, PDT, NYC, 2008
1½ oz (45 ml) pisco
½ oz (15 ml) St Germain Elderflower Liqueur
½ oz (15 ml) lemon juice
½ oz (15 ml) lime juice
½ oz (15 ml) simple syrup
2 dashes absinthe
1 egg white
Garnish: spritz of pimento (allspice) dram

Kiss the Boys Goodbye
Esquire Drink Book, *1956*
1 oz (30 ml) Cognac
1 oz (30 ml) sloe gin
¾ oz (22 ml) lemon juice
½ oz (15 ml) simple syrup
1 egg white

Pink Pearl
1700 Cocktails for the Man Behind the Bar, *R. de Fleury, 1934*
1½ oz (45 ml) bonded apple brandy
½ oz (15 ml) lemon juice
½ oz (15 ml) pink grapefruit juice
½ oz (15 ml) grenadine (p 496)
1 egg white

Add all ingredients to a shaker and dry shake vigorously to emulsify. Add ice, then shake and strain into a frozen Sour glass.

Pisco Sour
Nuevo Manual de Cocina a la Criolla, *S.E. Ledesma, 1903*
2 oz (60 ml) pisco
¾ oz (22 ml) lemon juice
¾ oz (22 ml) simple syrup
1 egg white
Garnish: freshly grated cinnamon and Amargo Chuncho (or Angostura Bitters) stripe

Rose Sour
Sam Ross, Attaboy, NYC, 2016
1½ oz (45 ml) pisco
½ oz (15 ml) blanc vermouth
¾ oz (22 ml) simple syrup
⅜ oz (11 ml) lemon juice
⅜ oz (11 ml) lime juice
1 strawberry, halved
1 egg white
Add strawberry and simple syrup to a shaker and muddle. Add remaining ingredients, then shake vigorously without ice to emulsify. Add ice, shake again, then strain into a frozen Sour glass.
Garnish: half a strawberry

Rosy-John
The South American Gentleman's Companion, *Charles H. Baker Jr., 1951*
1 oz (30 ml) pisco
1 oz (30 ml) gin
¾ oz (22 ml) lemon juice
¾ oz (22 ml) grenadine (p 496)
1 egg white
Garnish: Angostura Bitters stripe

St. Rose Sour
Ryan Gannon
Cure: New Orleans Drinks and How to Mix 'Em, *Neal Bodenheimer and Emily Timberlake, 2022*
¾ oz (22 ml) pisco
¾ oz (22 ml) Fino Sherry
½ oz (15 ml) Galliano L'Autentico
¾ oz (22 ml) pink grapefruit juice
¼ oz (7 ml) simple syrup
1 egg white
Garnish: lemon twist (discard)

Sourise
David Wondrich, 2010
2 oz (60 ml) Cognac
½ oz (15 ml) lemon juice
¼ oz (7 ml) orgeat
¼ oz (7 ml) simple syrup
5 raspberries
1 egg white
Add raspberry and simple syrup to a shaker and muddle. Add remaining ingredients and shake. Add ice, shake again, then strain into a frozen Sour glass.
Garnish: raspberry

Spicy Llama
Spirits of Latin America, *Ivy Mix, 2020*
1½ oz (45 ml) pisco
½ oz (15 ml) blanco tequila
¾ oz (22 ml) lime juice
¾ oz (22 ml) pineapple juice
½ oz (15 ml) simple syrup
2 dashes The Bitter Truth Celery Bitters
1 egg white
Garnish: edible orchid

The Delicious Sour
(aka **Immortal Sour**)
The Flowing Bowl, *William Schmidt, 1891*
2 oz (60 ml) bonded apple brandy
½ oz (15 ml) Giffard Crème de Pêche de Vigne
¾ oz (22 ml) lime juice
¼ oz (7 ml) simple syrup
1 egg white
Garnish: apple fan

"The Evening Sun"
The Flowing Bowl, *William Schmidt, 1891*
1½ oz (45 ml) Cognac
½ oz (15 ml) Green Chartreuse
¾ oz (22 ml) lemon juice
½ oz (15 ml) simple syrup
1 egg white
1 oz (30 ml) Champagne, to top
Make the Sour, then strain into a frozen Sour glass, topping with Champagne simultaneously.
Garnish: spritz of rosewater

The Ranelagh
F. Woodward
Café Royal Cocktail Book, *W.J. Tarling, 1937*
2 oz (60 ml) Cognac
½ oz (15 ml) Tempus Fugit Crème de Banane
¼ oz (7 ml) orange curaçao (p 498)
¾ oz (22 ml) lemon juice
1 egg white
Garnish: cherry

Turkish Brandy Sour
What'll You Have?, *Julien J. Proskauer, 1933*
1½ oz (45 ml) Cognac
½ oz (15 ml) Giffard Crème de Pêche de Vigne
¾ oz (22 ml) lemon juice
1 teaspoon (5 ml) simple syrup
1 dash orange blossom water
1 egg white

AMERICAN WHISKEY

Boston Sour
(aka **Dry Bourbon Sour**)
2 oz (60 ml) bourbon
1 oz (30 ml) lemon juice
½ oz (15 ml) simple syrup
1 egg white

Club Rose
1 oz (30 ml) rye whiskey
1 oz (30 ml) bonded apple brandy
¾ oz (22 ml) lemon juice
¾ oz (22 ml) grenadine (p 496)
1 egg white

Add all ingredients to a shaker and dry shake vigorously to emulsify. Add ice, then shake and strain into a frozen Sour glass.

Covington
Just Cocktails, *W.C. Whitfield, 1939*
1½ oz (45 ml) bourbon
½ oz (15 ml) tawny Port
¾ oz (22 ml) lemon juice
¾ oz (22 ml) simple syrup
1 egg white
Garnish: cherry

Dizzy Sour
Hoffman House Bartender's Guide, *Charles S. Mahoney, 1905*
1½ oz (45 ml) rye whiskey
½ oz (15 ml) Jamaican dark rum
½ oz (15 ml) Bénédictine
¾ oz (22 ml) lemon juice
¼ oz (7 ml) simple syrup
1 egg white
Garnish: lemon twist (discard)

Double Standard Sour
Old Waldorf Bar Days, *Albert Stevens Crockett, 1931*
1 oz (30 ml) rye whiskey
1 oz (30 ml) gin
¾ oz (22 ml) lime juice
¾ oz (22 ml) raspberry syrup (p 500)
1 egg white
Serve in a frozen double rocks glass with ice.
Garnish: raspberry
▼ Originally without egg white.

Elk's Own Cocktail
Barflies and Cocktails, *Harry MacElhone, 1927*
1½ oz (45 ml) rye whiskey
½ oz (15 ml) tawny Port
¾ oz (22 ml) lemon juice
½ oz (15 ml) simple syrup
1 egg white
▼ Top with 1 oz (30 ml) soda to make an **Elk's Fizz** from *Hoffman House Bartender's Guide*, Charles S. Mahoney, 1905.

Harvest Sour
Sam Ross, Attaboy, NYC, 2017
1 oz (30 ml) rye whiskey
1 oz (30 ml) bonded apple brandy
¾ oz (22 ml) lemon juice
¾ oz (22 ml) simple syrup
1 egg white
Garnish: Angostura Bitters stripe
▼ We refer to a rye whiskey and bonded apple brandy split as a Harvest.

Lamb's Club Sour
(Traditional Bourbon Sour with pastis)
Lamb's Club, NYC
2 oz (60 ml) bourbon
¼ oz (7 ml) pastis
1 oz (30 ml) lemon juice
¾ oz (22 ml) simple syrup
1 egg white
Garnish: whole star anise

Mama Tried
Alicia Perry and Anthony Schmidt, The Gutter, San Diego, 2023
1½ oz (45 ml) bourbon
½ oz (15 ml) sweet vermouth
¾ oz (22 ml) lemon juice
¾ oz (22 ml) simple syrup
½ oz (15 ml) orange juice
1 egg white
¾ oz (22 ml) dry red wine, to float
Add all ingredients, except red wine, to a shaker and shake vigorously without ice to emulsify. Add ice, shake again, then strain into a frozen double rocks glass with ice and float red wine.

Mountain
(Perfect Manhattan shaken with lemon and egg white)
Irvin S. Cobb's Own Recipe Book, *Irvin S. Cobb, 1936*
2 oz (60 ml) rye whiskey
½ oz (15 ml) sweet vermouth
½ oz (15 ml) dry vermouth
½ oz (15 ml) lemon juice
3 dashes Angostura Bitters
1 egg white
Garnish: cherry

Mountain Cocktail
(Sweet Manhattan shaken with lemon and egg white)
Hoffman House Bartender's Guide, *Charles S. Mahoney, 1905*
2 oz (60 ml) rye whiskey
½ oz (15 ml) sweet vermouth
½ oz (15 ml) lemon juice
½ oz (15 ml) simple syrup
1 egg white
Garnish: Angostura Bitters stripe and cherry

Mr. & Mrs.
(New Yorker with an egg white)
Walter Kiernan, Radio Commentator
Ted Saucier's Bottoms Up, *Ted Saucier, 1951*
2 oz (60 ml) rye whiskey
¾ oz (22 ml) lime juice
¾ oz (22 ml) grenadine (p 496)
1 egg white

New York Sour
(Traditional Bourbon Sour on the rocks with red wine)
The Cocktail Book: A Sideboard Manual for Gentlemen, *Repeal Edition, 1933*
2 oz (60 ml) bourbon
¾ oz (22 ml) lemon juice
¾ oz (22 ml) simple syrup
1 egg white
¾ oz (22 ml) red wine, to float
Add all ingredients, except red wine, to a shaker and shake vigorously without ice to emulsify. Add ice, shake again, then strain into a frozen double rocks glass with ice and float red wine.

Olive Oil Sour
Lorenzo Antinori, Bar Leone, Hong Kong
1 oz (30 ml) bourbon
¾ oz (22 ml) brandy (preferably Italian brandy)
⅓ oz (10 ml) Oloroso Sherry
½ oz (15 ml) lemon juice
½ oz (15 ml) honey syrup (p 496)
1 teaspoon (5 ml) extra virgin olive oil
1 egg white
Garnish: freshly grated nutmeg

Add all ingredients to a shaker and dry shake vigorously to emulsify. Add ice, then shake and strain into a frozen Sour glass.

Pink Puff
1700 Cocktails for the Man Behind the Bar, *R. de Fleury, 1934*
2 oz (60 ml) bourbon
½ oz (15 ml) apricot brandy
¾ oz (22 ml) lemon juice
1 teaspoon (5 ml) simple syrup
1 egg white

Port Light
Trader Vic's Bartender's Guide, *Trader Vic, Revised 1972*
2 oz (60 ml) bourbon
¾ oz (22 ml) lemon juice
½ oz (15 ml) honey syrup (p 496)
¼ oz (7 ml) passionfruit syrup (p 499)
1 egg white
Garnish: cherry and freshly grated cinnamon

Rattlesnake Cocktail
(Traditional Rye Whiskey Sour with absinthe)
The Savoy Cocktail Book, *Harry Craddock, 1930*
2 oz (60 ml) rye whiskey
¾ oz (22 ml) lemon juice
¾ oz (22 ml) simple syrup
3 dashes absinthe
1 egg white
▼ "So called because it will either cure Rattlesnake bite, or kill Rattlesnakes, or make you see them."

Stone Sour (Difford's Recipe)
Difford's Guide
1½ oz (45 ml) bourbon
½ oz (15 ml) apricot brandy
¾ oz (22 ml) lemon juice
½ oz (15 ml) orange juice
1 teaspoon (5 ml) simple syrup
2 drops saline solution (p 493)
1 egg white
Garnish: cherry
▼ The name Stone Sour is typically used to denote the addition of orange juice.

SCOTCH

Coaxer
(Traditional Scotch Sour without bitters)
Bariana, *Louis Fouquet, 1896*
2 oz (60 ml) Scotch
¾ oz (22 ml) lemon juice
¾ oz (22 ml) simple syrup
1 egg white
Garnish: lemon twist (discard)

Gloom Daisy
The Connaught Bar, *Agostino Perrone, Giorgio Bargiani & Maura Milia, 2024*
1¾ oz (52 ml) Islay Scotch
¾ oz (22 ml) lemon juice
¾ oz (22 ml) grenadine (p 496)
½ oz (15 ml) raspberry purée
1 egg white
Garnish: raspberry

Los Angeles
Café Royal Cocktail Book, *W.J. Tarling, 1937*
1½ oz (45 ml) Scotch
½ oz (15 ml) sweet vermouth
¾ oz (22 ml) lemon juice
¾ oz (22 ml) simple syrup
1 egg white
Garnish: cherry

Morning Glory Daisy
Cocktails: How to Mix Them, *Robert Vermeire, 1922*
2 oz (60 ml) Scotch
¾ oz (22 ml) lemon juice
¾ oz (22 ml) simple syrup
3 dashes absinthe
1 egg white
▼ Based on the Morning Glory Fizz, *New and Improved Bartender's Manual*, Harry Johnson, 1882.

Scotch Bracer
(Traditional Scotch Sour with absinthe and Peychaud's Aromatic Cocktail Bitters)
Alex Collins
Hoffman House Bartender's Guide, *Charles S. Mahoney, 1905*
2 oz (60 ml) Scotch
¾ oz (22 ml) lemon juice
¾ oz (22 ml) simple syrup
2 dashes absinthe
2 dashes Peychaud's Aromatic Cocktail Bitters
1 egg white
▼ Originally without egg white, stirred with ice and served up, garnished with an olive. The drink "won the fourth prize in the Police Gazette contest for 1903".

Scotch Lady
Phil Ward, Death & Co, NYC, 2008
1½ oz (45 ml) Scotch
½ oz (15 ml) bonded apple brandy
¾ oz (22 ml) lemon juice
¾ oz (22 ml) grenadine (p 496)
1 egg white

WORLD WHISK(E)Y

Evening Daisy
Daly's Bartenders' Encyclopedia, *Tim Daly, 1903*
2 oz (60 ml) Irish whiskey
1 oz (30 ml) lime juice
¾ oz (22 ml) simple syrup
2 dashes absinthe
1 egg white
Garnish: whole star anise

From *The Ideal Bartender* (1917):

Drink to the past for all that was good, drink to the present for all that is great, and drink to the future, for who knows what's next?

Add all ingredients to a shaker and dry shake vigorously to emulsify. Add ice, then shake and strain into a frozen Sour glass.

Gloom Lifter
Old Waldorf Bar Days, *Albert Stevens Crockett, 1931*
1½ oz (45 ml) Irish whiskey
½ oz (15 ml) Cognac
¾ oz (22 ml) lemon juice
¾ oz (22 ml) simple syrup
3 raspberries
1 egg white
Add raspberries and simple syrup to a shaker and muddle. Add remaining ingredients and shake. Add ice, shake again, then strain into a frozen Sour glass.
Garnish: raspberry

Lavender Honey Sour
Dre Masso, The Lonsdale, London, 2006
1½ oz (45 ml) Irish whiskey
½ oz (15 ml) Bénédictine
¾ oz (22 ml) lemon juice
½ oz (15 ml) honey syrup (p 496)
3 dashes Peychaud's Aromatic Cocktail Bitters
1 egg white
Garnish: dried lavender flowers

FORTIFIED & LIQUEUR

Amaretto Sour (Jeffrey Morgenthaler Recipe)
Jeffrey Morgenthaler, Portland, 2012
1½ oz (45 ml) amaretto
1 oz (30 ml) bourbon
¾ oz (22 ml) lemon juice
1 teaspoon (5 ml) Demerara syrup (p 495)
1 egg white
Garnish: Angostura Bitters stripe

Amaretto Sour (Patty Dennison and Ally Marrone Recipe)
Patty Dennison and Ally Marrone, Grand Army Bar, NYC
2 oz (60 ml) amaretto
¼ oz (7 ml) Campari
1 oz (30 ml) lemon juice
1 egg white
Serve in a frozen double rocks glass with ice.
Garnish: orange twist (discard)

Aperol Sour
2 oz (60 ml) Aperol
¾ oz (22 ml) lemon juice
¼ oz (7 ml) simple syrup
1 egg white

Colour in Your Cheeks
Hayley Wilson, Hunt + Alpine Club, Portland
1¼ oz (37 ml) Fernet-Branca
½ oz (15 ml) bonded apple brandy
¾ oz (22 ml) lemon juice
¾ oz (22 ml) maple syrup
1 egg white
Garnish: apple fan

Milan-Torino Sour
Dan Sabo, Los Angeles
1 oz (30 ml) Campari
1 oz (30 ml) dry vermouth
¾ oz (22 ml) pink grapefruit juice
½ oz (15 ml) lime juice
½ oz (15 ml) simple syrup
2 dashes orange bitters
1 egg white

St Germaine Cocktail
(aka **Green Elevator** in *Crosby Gaige's Cocktail Guide and Ladies' Companion*, Crosby Gaige, 1941)
The Savoy Cocktail Book, *Harry Craddock, 1930*
1½ oz (45 ml) Green Chartreuse
1 oz (30 ml) pink grapefruit juice
½ oz (15 ml) lemon juice
½ oz (15 ml) simple syrup
1 egg white

Sloe Gin Sour
Hains & Co, Adelaide
1½ oz (45 ml) sloe gin
½ oz (15 ml) overproof bourbon
¾ oz (22 ml) lemon juice
¾ oz (22 ml) simple syrup
1 drop saline solution (p 493)
1 egg white

The Imposter
Hayden Lambert, Above Board, Melbourne
¾ oz (22 ml) Amaro Montenegro
¾ oz (22 ml) amaretto
¾ oz (22 ml) lemon juice
¼ oz (7 ml) orange juice
¼ oz (7 ml) simple syrup
1 egg white

Non-Traditional Sour

Add all ingredients to a shaker, then shake with ice and strain into a frozen coupe.

VODKA

Lemon Drop (Lorenzo Antinori Recipe)
Lorenzo Antinori, Bar Leone, Hong Kong, 2024
¾ oz (22 ml) vodka
¾ oz (22 ml) Cocchi Americano
¾ oz (22 ml) Pierre Ferrand Dry Curaçao
¼ oz (7 ml) limoncello
¾ oz (22 ml) lemon juice
Garnish: salt rim

Monella Sour
Vincenzo Errico, L'Artefatto, Forio d'Ischia, 2022
1½ oz (45 ml) vodka
1 oz (30 ml) orange juice
¾ oz (22 ml) cinnamon syrup (p 495)
½ oz (15 ml) lime juice

New York Minute
Toby Maloney, 2015
1½ oz (45 ml) vodka
½ oz (15 ml) bonded apple brandy
¾ oz (22 ml) lemon juice
¾ oz (22 ml) grenadine (p 496)
1 dash absinthe

Add all ingredients to a shaker and dry shake vigorously to emulsify. Add ice, then shake and strain into a frozen Sour glass.

Violet 38
2 oz (60 ml) vodka
⅜ oz (11 ml) crème de violette
¾ oz (22 ml) lemon juice
⅜ oz (11 ml) simple syrup
Garnish: cherry and lemon twist (discard)

GIN & GENEVER

Army & Navy
The Fine Art of Mixing Drinks, *David A. Embury, 1948*
2 oz (60 ml) gin
¾ oz (22 ml) lemon juice
¾ oz (22 ml) orgeat
2 dashes Angostura Bitters
▼ Swap Angostura Bitters for absinthe, and garnish with a whole star anise to make the **Coo-ee Special** by T. D. Nagle in *Approved Cocktails*, United Kingdom Bartenders' Guild, 1937.

Aviation Cocktail
(See p 195)

Aviation Cocktail (Harry Craddock Recipe)
(aka Non-Traditional Gin Sour with maraschino liqueur or **Aviation No. 2**)
The Savoy Cocktail Book, *Harry Craddock, 1930*
2 oz (60 ml) gin
⅜ oz (11 ml) maraschino liqueur
¾ oz (22 ml) lemon juice
⅜ oz (11 ml) simple syrup
Garnish: cherry
▼ Add 2 dashes of Angostura Bitters to make the **Betty James** from *Jones' Complete Barguide*, Stan Jones, 1977.

Banana Calling
Cameron Attfield, Dandelyan, London, 2018
1¾ oz (52 ml) gin
½ oz (15 ml) Giffard Banane du Brésil et des Caraïbes
⅜ oz (11 ml) Fino Sherry
¾ oz (22 ml) lemon juice
¼ oz (7 ml) simple syrup
Garnish: pink grapefruit twist (discard)

Bebbo
Jones' Complete Barguide, *Stan Jones, 1977*
2 oz (60 ml) gin
½ oz (15 ml) lemon juice
½ oz (15 ml) orange juice
½ oz (15 ml) honey syrup (p 496)
Garnish: Angostura Bitters stripe

Blue Devil
(Aviation No. 2 with butterfly pea flower extract)
The Savoy Cocktail Book, *Harry Craddock, 1930*
2 oz (60 ml) gin
⅜ oz (11 ml) maraschino liqueur
¾ oz (22 ml) lemon juice
⅜ oz (11 ml) simple syrup
2 drops Wild Hibiscus b'Lure Butterfly Pea Flower Extract
Garnish: cherry

Braham
D. Cavaliere
Approved Cocktails, *United Kingdom Bartenders' Guild, 1937*
1 oz (30 ml) gin
1 oz (30 ml) vodka
¾ oz (22 ml) lemon juice
¾ oz (22 ml) simple syrup
Garnish: lemon twist (discard)

Brixton Fix
Jessica Gonzalez, The NoMad Bar, NYC
1½ oz (45 ml) gin
¾ oz (22 ml) dry vermouth
¼ oz (7 ml) apricot brandy
¾ oz (22 ml) lemon juice
½ oz (15 ml) cane syrup (p 494)
3 dashes absinthe

Casino Cocktail
(Aviation No. 2 with orange bitters)
The Reminder, *J.A. Didier, 1909*
2 oz (60 ml) gin
⅜ oz (11 ml) maraschino liqueur
¾ oz (22 ml) lemon juice
⅜ oz (11 ml) simple syrup
2 dashes orange bitters
Garnish: cherry

Casino (David A. Embury Recipe)
The Fine Art of Mixing Drinks, *David A. Embury, 1948*
2 oz (60 ml) gin
⅜ oz (11 ml) maraschino liqueur
½ oz (15 ml) lemon juice
½ oz (15 ml) orange juice
⅜ oz (11 ml) simple syrup
Garnish: cherry

Chelsea Smile
(Non-Traditional Gin Sour with cayenne pepper)
Michael Madrusan, The Everleigh, Melbourne, 2012
2 oz (60 ml) gin
¾ oz (22 ml) lemon juice
¾ oz (22 ml) simple syrup
Garnish: dusting of cayenne pepper

Cherry Pop
Jane Danger, PDT, NYC, 2009
2 oz (60 ml) gin
⅜ oz (11 ml) maraschino liqueur
¾ oz (22 ml) lemon juice
⅜ oz (11 ml) simple syrup
3 fresh cherries
Add cherries and simple syrup to a shaker and muddle. Add remaining ingredients, then shake with ice and strain into a frozen coupe.
Garnish: fresh cherry

Communist
Cocktail Parade, *1933*
1½ oz (45 ml) gin
½ oz (15 ml) Heering Cherry Liqueur
1 oz (30 ml) orange juice
½ oz (15 ml) lemon juice
¼ oz (7 ml) simple syrup
Garnish: cherry

Cosmonaut
Sasha Petraske, Milk & Honey, NYC, 2004
2 oz (60 ml) gin
¾ oz (22 ml) lemon juice
1 tablespoon (18 g) raspberry jam
Add raspberry jam and lemon juice to a shaker and stir to combine, then add gin, shake with ice and strain into a frozen coupe.
Garnish: raspberry

Add all ingredients to a shaker, then shake with ice and strain into a frozen coupe.

Cucumber-Mint Creole
Audrey Saunders, NYC, 2007
1½ oz (45 ml) Sipsmith London Dry Gin
½ oz (15 ml) Dry Sack Sherry
½ oz (15 ml) aquavit
½ oz (15 ml) lemon juice
½ oz (15 ml) simple syrup
3 cucumber wheels
1 mint sprig
Muddle cucumber, mint and simple syrup in a shaker. Add remaining ingredients, then stir with ice and strain into a frozen coupe.
Garnish: cucumber wheel and mint sprig

English Marmalade
(aka **Hawksmoor Marmalade Martini**)
Hawksmoor, London
2 oz (60 ml) gin
¾ oz (22 ml) lemon juice
¼ oz (7 ml) simple syrup
1 teaspoon (5 ml) Campari
4 teaspoons (24 g) orange marmalade
Stir marmalade, lemon juice and simple syrup in a shaker, then add remaining ingredients, shake with ice and strain into a frozen coupe.

Enzoni
Vincenzo Errico, Milk & Honey, NYC, 2003
¾ oz (22 ml) gin
¾ oz (22 ml) Campari
¾ oz (22 ml) lemon juice
¾ oz (22 ml) simple syrup
3 green grapes
Press grapes and simple syrup in a shaker. Add remaining ingredients, then shake with ice and strain into a frozen double rocks glass with ice.
Garnish: orange half-wheel and green grape

Fitzgerald
(Non-Traditional Gin Sour with Angostura Bitters)
Dale DeGroff, Rainbow Room, NYC, 1990s
2 oz (60 ml) gin
¾ oz (22 ml) lemon juice
¾ oz (22 ml) simple syrup
Garnish: Angostura Bitters stripe

Gershwin
Becky McFalls-Schwartz, Little Branch, NYC, 2007
2 oz (60 ml) gin
¾ oz (22 ml) lemon juice
½ oz (15 ml) ginger syrup (p 496)
½ oz (15 ml) simple syrup
Garnish: candied ginger and spritz of rosewater

Gin Basil Smash
Joerg Meyer, Le Lion Bar de Paris, Hamburg, 2008
2 oz (60 ml) gin
¾ oz (22 ml) lemon juice
½ oz (15 ml) simple syrup
4 basil sprigs
Shake with ice and fine strain into a frozen double rocks glass with ice.
Garnish: basil sprig

Grand Passion
(Non-Traditional Gin Sour with passionfruit and Angostura Bitters)
The Fine Art of Mixing Drinks, *David A. Embury, 1948*
2 oz (60 ml) gin
¾ oz (22 ml) lemon juice
¾ oz (22 ml) passionfruit syrup (p 499)
2 dashes Angostura Bitters

Grapevine Cocktail
(Non-Traditional Gin Sour with grapes)
Trader Vic's Bartender's Guide, *Trader Vic, 1947*
2 oz (60 ml) gin
¾ oz (22 ml) lemon juice
¾ oz (22 ml) simple syrup
3 red grapes
Press grapes and simple syrup in a shaker. Add remaining ingredients, then shake with ice and strain into a frozen coupe.
Garnish: red grape

Havana (Stan Jones Recipe)
Jones' Complete Barguide, *Stan Jones, 1977*
1½ oz (45 ml) gin
½ oz (15 ml) apricot brandy
½ oz (15 ml) Cocchi Americano
¾ oz (22 ml) lemon juice

Holland Razor Blade
The Gentleman's Companion, *Charles H. Baker Jr., 1939*
2 oz (60 ml) genever
¾ oz (22 ml) lemon juice
¾ oz (22 ml) simple syrup
Garnish: dusting of cayenne pepper

Hummingbird
Felix Woods, Black Pearl, Melbourne, 2021
1½ oz (45 ml) gin
½ oz (15 ml) pink grapefruit juice
½ oz (15 ml) lemon juice
½ oz (15 ml) lavender honey syrup (p 497)
2 dashes orange bitters
Garnish: grapefruit twist (discard)

Inimitable Cocktail
Modern American Drinks, *George J. Kappeler, 1895*
2 oz (60 ml) Old Tom gin
¾ oz (22 ml) lemon juice
¾ oz (22 ml) simple syrup
2 dashes Peychaud's Aromatic Cocktail Bitters
Serve in a frozen double rocks glass with ice.
Garnish: lemon wedge

Iris Cocktail
(Non-Traditional Gin Sour with mint)
A Life-Time Collection of 688 Recipes for Drinks, *Herbert Jenkins Ltd, 1934*
2 oz (60 ml) gin
¾ oz (22 ml) lemon juice
¾ oz (22 ml) simple syrup
6–8 mint leaves
Garnish: mint leaf

Jockey Club
Just Cocktails, *W.C. Whitfield, 1939*
1½ oz (45 ml) gin
½ oz (15 ml) white crème de cacao
¾ oz (22 ml) lemon juice
¼ oz (7 ml) simple syrup
2 dashes Angostura Bitters
Garnish: lemon twist (discard)

Add all ingredients to a shaker, then shake with ice and strain into a frozen coupe.

Jockey Club Cocktail
"Harry" of Ciro's ABC of Mixing Cocktails, *Harry MacElhone, 1923*
1½ oz (45 ml) gin
½ oz (15 ml) crème de noyaux
¾ oz (22 ml) lemon juice
¼ oz (7 ml) simple syrup
1 dash orange bitters
1 dash Angostura Bitters
Garnish: lemon twist (discard)

Kind of Blueberry
The Bartender's Pantry, *Jim Meehan, Bart Sasso with Emma Janzen, 2024*
2 oz (60 ml) gin
⅜ oz (11 ml) maraschino liqueur
¾ oz (22 ml) lemon juice
⅜ oz (11 ml) simple syrup
3 blueberries
Muddle blueberries with simple syrup, add remaining ingredients and shake briefly with ice. Strain into a frozen coupe.
Garnish: blueberry

London Calling
Chris Jepson, Milk & Honey, London, 2002
1½ oz (45 ml) gin
½ oz (15 ml) Fino Sherry
½ oz (15 ml) lemon juice
½ oz (15 ml) simple syrup
2 dashes orange bitters
Garnish: grapefruit twist (discard)

London to Italy
Travis Hernandez, Half Step, Austin
2 oz (60 ml) gin
½ oz (15 ml) Amaro Montenegro
¾ oz (22 ml) lemon juice
¼ oz (7 ml) honey syrup (p 496)
Serve in a frozen double rocks glass with ice.
Garnish: orange half-wheel

Maiden's Blush
Bariana, *Louis Fouquet, 1896*
2 oz (60 ml) gin
¾ oz (22 ml) lemon juice
¾ oz (22 ml) simple syrup
2 dashes absinthe
2 raspberries
Muddle raspberries and simple syrup in a shaker. Add remaining ingredients, then shake with ice and strain into a frozen coupe.
Garnish: raspberry

Maiden's Blush (Madrusan Recipe)
1¾ oz (52 ml) gin
1 oz (30 ml) pink grapefruit juice
½ oz (15 ml) lemon juice
½ oz (15 ml) grenadine (p 496)

Marmalade Cocktail
The Savoy Cocktail Book, *Harry Craddock, 1930*
2 oz (60 ml) gin
¾ oz (22 ml) lemon juice
¼ oz (7 ml) simple syrup
2 teaspoons (12 g) orange marmalade
Stir marmalade, lemon juice and simple syrup in a shaker, then add gin, shake with ice and strain into a frozen coupe.
Garnish: orange twist (discard)

Monkey's Gland Cocktail
(aka **Monkey Gland**)
"Harry" of Ciro's ABC of Mixing Cocktails, *Harry MacElhone, 1923*
2 oz (60 ml) gin
1 oz (30 ml) orange juice
½ oz (15 ml) grenadine (p 496)
¼ oz (7 ml) lemon juice
2 dashes absinthe

Nervous Light of Sunday
Michael Yusko, Cure, New Orleans
1½ oz (45 ml) gin
¾ oz (22 ml) Luxardo Bitter Rosso
¾ oz (22 ml) lemon juice
½ oz (15 ml) simple syrup
14 drops Bittermens Hopped Grapefruit Bitters
2 dashes orange bitters
Serve in a frozen double rocks glass with ice.
Garnish: grapefruit twist (discard)

Old Vermont
(Bebbo with maple syrup)
"Cocktail Bill" Boothby's World Drinks and How to Mix Them, *Wm. T. Boothby, 1934*
2 oz (60 ml) gin
½ oz (15 ml) lemon juice
½ oz (15 ml) orange juice
½ oz (15 ml) maple syrup
2 dashes Angostura Bitters

Prince's Smile Cocktail
(aka **Tender and True** in *Crosby Gaige's Cocktail Guide and Ladies' Companion*, Crosby Gaige, 1941)
The Official Mixer's Manual, *Patrick Gavin Duffy, 1934*
1 oz (30 ml) gin
1 oz (30 ml) bonded apple brandy
½ oz (15 ml) apricot brandy
¾ oz (22 ml) lemon juice
¼ oz (7 ml) simple syrup

Royal Hawaiian
(aka **Princess Kaiulani**)
Honolulu, 1920s
2 oz (60 ml) gin
1 oz (30 ml) pineapple juice
½ oz (15 ml) orgeat
¼ oz (7 ml) lemon juice
Garnish: pineapple wedge and cherry

Royal Smile
Jack's Manual, *J.A. Grohusko, 1910*
1 oz (30 ml) gin
1 oz (30 ml) Calvados
¾ oz (22 ml) lemon juice
¾ oz (22 ml) grenadine (p 496)
▼ A close relative of the Jack Rose Cocktail.

Sensation
(Aviation No. 2 with mint)
Cocktails: How to Mix Them, *Robert Vermeire, 1922*
2 oz (60 ml) gin
⅜ oz (11 ml) maraschino liqueur
¾ oz (22 ml) lemon juice
⅜ oz (11 ml) simple syrup
6–8 mint leaves
Garnish: mint leaf

Add all ingredients to a shaker, then shake with ice and strain into a frozen coupe.

Silver Bullet Cocktail
The Savoy Cocktail Book, *Harry Craddock, 1930*
2 oz (60 ml) gin
½ oz (15 ml) kummel
¾ oz (22 ml) lemon juice
¼ oz (7 ml) simple syrup

Sleepy Hollow
Jones' Complete Barguide, *Stan Jones, 1977*
1½ oz (45 ml) gin
½ oz (15 ml) apricot brandy
¾ oz (22 ml) lemon juice
¼ oz (7 ml) simple syrup
6–8 mint leaves
Garnish: mint leaf

Smile
(Non-Traditional Gin Sour with grenadine)
Just Cocktails, *W.C. Whitfield, 1939*
2 oz (60 ml) gin
¾ oz (22 ml) lemon juice
¾ oz (22 ml) grenadine (p 496)

Son of a Bee Sting
Michael Madrusan, Milk & Honey, NYC, 2009
2 oz (60 ml) gin
¾ oz (22 ml) lemon juice
⅜ oz (11 ml) ginger syrup (p 496)
⅜ oz (11 ml) honey syrup (p 496)
Serve in a frozen double rocks glass with ice.
Garnish: candied ginger and spritz of rosewater

Spring Feeling Cocktail
The Savoy Cocktail Book, *Harry Craddock, 1930*
1½ oz (45 ml) gin
½ oz (15 ml) Green Chartreuse
¾ oz (22 ml) lemon juice
½ oz (15 ml) simple syrup
Garnish: lemon twist (discard)
▼ Add 2 dashes of absinthe to make the **Biter Cocktail** also from *The Savoy Cocktail Book*, Harry Craddock, 1930.

Stone Sour
The Ideal Bartender, *Tom Bullock, 1917*
2 oz (60 ml) gin
1 oz (30 ml) orange juice
½ oz (15 ml) simple syrup
½ oz (15 ml) lemon juice
Serve in a frozen double rocks glass with ice.

Tango (Bellagio Recipe)
Bellagio, Las Vegas
2 oz (60 ml) gin
1 oz (30 ml) pink grapefruit juice
½ oz (15 ml) passionfruit syrup (p 499)
¼ oz (7 ml) lemon juice
Garnish: orange twist (discard)

The Black Widow
Crosby Gaige's Cocktail Guide and Ladies' Companion, *Crosby Gaige, 1941*
1½ oz (45 ml) gin
½ oz (15 ml) apricot brandy
¾ oz (22 ml) orange juice
½ oz (15 ml) lemon juice
1 teaspoon (5 ml) simple syrup

The Cornell Special
Here's How!, *Judge Jr., 1927*
1½ oz (45 ml) gin
½ oz (15 ml) Bénédictine
¾ oz (22 ml) lemon juice
¼ oz (7 ml) simple syrup
Garnish: lemon twist (discard)

The 1508
(aka **Rose Cocktail** in *A Life-Time Collection of 688 Recipes for Drinks*, 1934 or Monkey Gland without absinthe)
The Saloon in the Home or A Garland of Rumblossoms, *Ridgley Hunt and George S. Chappell, 1930*
2 oz (60 ml) gin
1 oz (30 ml) orange juice
½ oz (15 ml) grenadine (p 496)
¼ oz (7 ml) lemon juice

The Southern Bride
Crosby Gaige's Cocktail Guide and Ladies' Companion, *Crosby Gaige, 1941*
2 oz (60 ml) gin
¼ oz (7 ml) maraschino liqueur
1 oz (30 ml) pink grapefruit juice
¼ oz (7 ml) lemon juice
¼ oz (7 ml) simple syrup
Garnish: cherry

Too Soon?
Sam Ross, Milk & Honey, NYC, 2011
1 oz (30 ml) gin
1 oz (30 ml) Cynar
¾ oz (22 ml) lemon juice
½ oz (15 ml) simple syrup
2 orange wedges
Press orange and simple syrup in a shaker. Add remaining ingredients, then shake with ice and strain into a frozen coupe.

AMERICAN WHISKEY

Adderley
(Casino Cocktail with rye whiskey)
Sam Ross, Milk & Honey, NYC, 2005
2 oz (60 ml) rye whiskey
⅜ oz (11 ml) maraschino liqueur
¾ oz (22 ml) lemon juice
⅜ oz (11 ml) simple syrup
2 dashes orange bitters

After the Gold Rush
Joshua Perez, Bar Trench, Tokyo, 2022
1½ oz (45 ml) bourbon
½ oz (15 ml) Giffard Crème de Pêche de Vigne
½ oz (15 ml) lemon juice
¼ oz (7 ml) honey syrup (p 496)
3 dashes Scrappy's Bitters Fire Tincture
Serve in a frozen double rocks glass with ice.
Garnish: lemon half-wheel and pinch of cayenne pepper

Add all ingredients to a shaker, then shake with ice and strain into a frozen coupe.

Big Red Machine
Jon Nutter, Attaboy, NYC
1 oz (30 ml) bourbon
1 oz (30 ml) Campari
¾ oz (22 ml) lemon juice
¾ oz (22 ml) Red Gala apple juice
¾ oz (22 ml) ginger syrup (p 496)
1 strawberry, halved
Muddle strawberry and ginger syrup in a shaker. Add remaining ingredients, then shake with ice and strain into a frozen double rocks glass with ice.
Garnish: candied ginger and half a strawberry

Bittersweet
The Fine Art of Mixing Drinks, *David A. Embury, 1948*
2 oz (60 ml) rye whiskey
1 oz (30 ml) orange juice
¼ oz (7 ml) lemon juice
½ oz (15 ml) simple syrup

Blinker
The Official Mixer's Manual, *Patrick Gavin Duffy, 1934*
2 oz (60 ml) rye whiskey
¾ oz (22 ml) grenadine (p 496)
¾ oz (22 ml) pink grapefruit juice
¼ oz (7 ml) lemon juice

Bourbon Renewal
Jeffrey Morgenthaler, Clyde Common, Portland, 2003
1½ oz (45 ml) bourbon
½ oz (15 ml) crème de cassis
¾ oz (22 ml) lemon juice
½ oz (15 ml) simple syrup
1 dash Angostura Bitters
Serve in a frozen double rocks glass with ice.

Bourbon Stone Sour
Sardi's Bar Guide, *Vincent Sardi and George Shea, 1988*
2 oz (60 ml) bourbon
1 oz (30 ml) orange juice
¾ oz (22 ml) simple syrup
½ oz (15 ml) lemon juice
Serve in a frozen double rocks glass with ice.
Garnish: orange half-wheel and cherry

Bronco Buster
Arizona Biltmore, Phoenix
Ted Saucier's Bottoms Up, *Ted Saucier, 1951*
1 oz (30 ml) rye whiskey
1 oz (30 ml) bonded apple brandy
¾ oz (22 ml) orange curaçao (p 498)
¾ oz (22 ml) lemon juice
Serve in a frozen double rocks glass with ice.
Garnish: orange twist

Bumpy Hayride
Chris Hughes, Attaboy, NYC
1½ oz (45 ml) rye whiskey
½ oz (15 ml) Pedro Ximénez
1 oz (30 ml) Gala apple juice
½ oz (15 ml) lemon juice
½ oz (15 ml) simple syrup
2 dashes Angostura Bitters
Serve in a frozen double rocks glass with ice.

Buster Brown
(Non-Traditional Bourbon Sour with orange bitters)
The Fine Art of Mixing Drinks, *David A. Embury, 1948*
2 oz (60 ml) bourbon
¾ oz (22 ml) lemon juice
¾ oz (22 ml) simple syrup
2 dashes orange bitters

Continental Sour
(aka **Brunswick Sour** or **Saratoga Sour** in *A Life-Time Collection of 688 Recipes for Drinks*, 1934 or Non-Traditional New York Sour with rye whiskey)
The Ideal Bartender, *Tom Bullock, 1917*
2 oz (60 ml) rye whiskey
¾ oz (22 ml) lemon juice
¾ oz (22 ml) simple syrup
¾ oz (22 ml) red wine, to float
Serve in a frozen double rocks glass with ice.
▼ Shake with an egg white to make the **Continental Sour** recipe from the *Esquire Drink Book*, 1956.

Deadpan Fix
Jessica Gonzalez, Death & Co, NYC, 2011
1½ oz (45 ml) rye whiskey
¼ oz (7 ml) Campari
¼ oz (7 ml) Grand Marnier
¾ oz (22 ml) pink grapefruit juice
¼ oz (7 ml) lemon juice
¼ oz (7 ml) ginger syrup (p 496)
Garnish: orange twist (discard) and candied ginger

Devil's Share
Pete Kendall, Match Bar, London, 2006
2 oz (60 ml) bourbon
¾ oz (22 ml) lemon juice
½ oz (15 ml) ginger syrup (p 496)
½ oz (15 ml) orange juice
¼ oz (7 ml) maple syrup
2 dashes Angostura Bitters
Serve in a frozen double rocks glass with ice.
Garnish: orange half-wheel and candied ginger

Frisco
The Fine Art of Mixing Drinks, *David A. Embury, 1948*
2 oz (45 ml) bourbon
½ oz (22 ml) Bénédictine
¾ oz (22 ml) lemon juice
¼ oz (7 ml) simple syrup
Garnish: lemon twist (discard)

Gold Rush
(Bee's Knees with bourbon on the rocks)
T.J. Siegal, Milk & Honey, NYC, 2001
2 oz (60 ml) bourbon
¾ oz (22 ml) lemon juice
¾ oz (22 ml) honey syrup (p 496)
Serve in a frozen double rocks glass with ice.
Garnish: lemon wedge
▼ Serve this straight up in a frozen coupe to make the **Honey Sour** from *Ted Saucier's Bottoms Up*, Ted Saucer, 1951.

Add all ingredients to a shaker, then shake with ice and strain into a frozen coupe.

Habitant (No. 2)
Larry Denis, The Log Chateau, Quebec
Ted Saucier's Bottoms Up, *Ted Saucier, 1951*
2 oz (60 ml) rye whiskey
¾ oz (22 ml) lemon juice
½ oz (15 ml) maple syrup
2 dashes Angostura Bitters
Garnish: lemon twist (discard)

Hawaiian Stone Sour
Dale DeGroff, Rainbow Room, NYC, 2000
2 oz (60 ml) bourbon
1 oz (30 ml) pineapple juice
¾ oz (22 ml) simple syrup
½ oz (15 ml) lemon juice
1 dash Dale DeGroff's Pimento Aromatic Bitters
Serve in a frozen double rocks glass with ice.

High Hat
The Fine Art of Mixing Drinks, *David A. Embury, 1948*
1½ oz (45 ml) rye whiskey (or bourbon)
½ oz (15 ml) Heering Cherry Liqueur
¾ oz (22 ml) lemon juice
¼ oz (7 ml) simple syrup
Garnish: lemon twist (discard)

Honeycomb
Joe Schofield, Schofield's Bar, Manchester, 2024
1½ oz (45 ml) bourbon
¾ oz (22 ml) honey syrup (p 496)
½ oz (15 ml) yuzu juice
1 teaspoon (5 ml) lemon juice
Serve in a frozen double rocks glass with ice.
Garnish: orange twist (discard)

Kentucky Cantina
(Gold Rush with rye whiskey and smoked paprika)
Chris Bostick, Half Step, Austin, 2018
2 oz (60 ml) rye whiskey
¾ oz (22 ml) lemon juice
¾ oz (22 ml) honey syrup (p 496)
Serve in a frozen double rocks glass with ice.
Garnish: dusting of smoked paprika

Lemon Cocktail
Hoffman House Bartender's Guide, *Charles S. Mahoney, 1905*
2 oz (60 ml) bourbon
¾ oz (22 ml) lemon juice
¾ oz (22 ml) simple syrup
2 dashes Peychaud's Aromatic Cocktail Bitters
2 dashes orange bitters
Garnish: lemon twist (discard)

Mad Hatter
Ted Saucier's Bottoms Up, *Ted Saucier, 1951*
2 oz (60 ml) rye whiskey
¾ oz (22 ml) simple syrup
⅜ oz (11 ml) lemon juice
⅜ oz (11 ml) lime juice
2 dashes absinthe
Garnish: lemon twist (discard)
▼ Swap rye whiskey for Scotch to make the **Wonderland** by Tom Lasher-Walker, NYC, 2018.

Maple Leaf
The Artistry of Mixing Drinks, *Frank Meier, 1936*
2 oz (60 ml) bourbon
¾ oz (22 ml) lemon juice
½ oz (15 ml) maple syrup
Garnish: lemon twist (discard)

Mountain Man
Natasha David, Nitecap, NYC
2 oz (60 ml) bourbon
¼ oz (7 ml) Giffard Crème de Pêche de Vigne
¾ oz (22 ml) lemon juice
¼ oz (7 ml) maple syrup
¼ oz (7 ml) ginger syrup (p 496)
Serve in a frozen double rocks glass with ice.
Garnish: candied ginger

Pall Mall Cocktail
Shake 'Em Up!, *Virginia Elliott and Phil D. Strong, 1930*
1 oz (30 ml) rye whiskey
1 oz (30 ml) bonded apple brandy
½ oz (15 ml) lemon juice
½ oz (15 ml) orange juice
½ oz (15 ml) grenadine (p 496)

Pan Am Sour
Spirits of Latin America, *Ivy Mix, 2020*
1¼ oz (37 ml) bourbon
¾ oz (22 ml) cachaça
¾ oz (22 ml) simple syrup
¾ oz (22 ml) lemon juice
½ oz (15 ml) orange juice
½ oz (15 ml) dry red wine (preferably malbec), to float
Add all ingredients, except red wine, to a shaker with ice. Shake and strain into a frozen double rocks glass with ice then float red wine.

Pineapple Blossom Cocktail
The Cocktail Book: A Sideboard Manual for Gentlemen, Repeal Edition, *1933*
2 oz (60 ml) bourbon
1 oz (30 ml) pineapple juice
½ oz (15 ml) simple syrup
¼ oz (7 ml) lemon juice
Garnish: candied pineapple

From *The Gentleman's Companion* (1939):

Here's to our livers—may they live as long as we do!

Add all ingredients to a shaker, then shake with ice and strain into a frozen coupe.

Scofflaw
Maxim's, Paris, 1920s
1½ oz (45 ml) rye whiskey
¾ oz (22 ml) dry vermouth
½ oz (15 ml) lemon juice
½ oz (15 ml) grenadine (p 496)
1 dash orange bitters
▼ Reported in the *Chicago Tribune* on 21 January 1924, but also often attributed to a bartender named Jock from Harry's New York Bar in Paris around the same time.

Strawberry Blonde
(Gold Rush with strawberries)
Michael Madrusan, The Everleigh, Melbourne, 2022
2 oz (60 ml) bourbon
¾ oz (22 ml) lemon juice
¾ oz (22 ml) honey syrup (p 496)
1 strawberry, halved
Muddle strawberry and honey syrup in a shaker. Add remaining ingredients, shake with ice and strain into a frozen double rocks glass with ice.
Garnish: half a strawberry

Tennessee
The Fine Art of Mixing Drinks, *David A. Embury, 1948*
2 oz (60 ml) rye whiskey
⅜ oz (11 ml) maraschino liqueur
¾ oz (22 ml) lemon juice
⅜ oz (11 ml) simple syrup
Garnish: lemon twist (discard)

T.N.T.
Tay Garnett
Ted Saucier's Bottoms Up, *Ted Saucier, 1951*
1 oz (30 ml) rye whiskey
½ oz (15 ml) Cognac
½ oz (15 ml) apricot brandy
¾ oz (22 ml) lemon juice
¼ oz (7 ml) simple syrup
Serve in a frozen double rocks glass with ice.

Tough Cookie
Ally Marrone, NYC
1½ oz (45 ml) bourbon
½ oz (15 ml) tawny Port
1 oz (30 ml) guava purée
½ oz (15 ml) lemon juice
½ oz (15 ml) simple syrup
2 drops saline solution (p 493)
2 dashes Angostura Bitters
1 dash Dale DeGroff's Pimento Aromatic Bitters

Turnpike
Joseph Schwartz, Little Branch, NYC
1 oz (30 ml) rye whiskey
1 oz (30 ml) bonded apple brandy
¾ oz (22 ml) lemon juice
¾ oz (22 ml) simple syrup

Ward Eight
The Cocktail Book: A Sideboard Manual for Gentlemen, *1913*
2 oz (60 ml) rye whiskey
¾ oz (22 ml) lemon juice
¾ oz (22 ml) grenadine (p 496)

Ward Eight Cocktail
Cocktails: How to Mix Them, *Robert Vermeire, 1922*
2 oz (60 ml) rye whiskey
½ oz (15 ml) lemon juice
½ oz (15 ml) orange juice
½ oz (15 ml) grenadine (p 496)
▼ Swap rye whiskey for bourbon to make the **Shady Cocktail** from *The Art of Mixing*, James A. Wiley and Helene M. Griffith, 1932.

Western Sour
Kon-Tiki restaurants, North America
Beachbum Berry Remixed, *Jeff Berry, 2010*
2 oz (60 ml) bourbon
1 oz (30 ml) white grapefruit juice
½ oz (15 ml) lime juice
½ oz (15 ml) falernum
¼ oz (7 ml) cane syrup (p 494)
Serve in a frozen double rocks glass with ice.
Garnish: grapefruit half-wheel and cherry

Westpoint
Daniel Zacharczuk, Salt's Cure, Los Angeles, 2015
1½ oz (45 ml) rye whiskey
½ oz (15 ml) Jamaican dark rum
¾ oz (22 ml) lemon juice
¾ oz (22 ml) honey syrup (p 496)
2 dashes Angostura Bitters
Serve in a frozen double rocks glass with ice.
Garnish: lemon wedge

Whiskey Business
Meaghan Dorman, Dear Irving, NYC, 2014
1 oz (30 ml) rye whiskey
1 oz (30 ml) Ancho Reyes Original
½ oz (15 ml) lemon juice
½ oz (15 ml) cinnamon syrup (p 495)
1 dash Angostura Bitters
Garnish: lemon wedge and dusting of ancho chilli powder

SCOTCH

Appetizer
(aka **Scotch Sour**)
American and Other Iced Drinks, *Charlie Paul, 1902*
2 oz (60 ml) Scotch
¾ oz (22 ml) lemon juice
¾ oz (22 ml) simple syrup
Garnish: lemon twist (discard)

Calling Card
Paul Hammond and Priscilla Leong
1½ oz (45 ml) Scotch
½ oz (15 ml) Manzanilla Sherry
½ oz (15 ml) lemon juice
½ oz (15 ml) simple syrup
2 dashes peach bitters
Garnish: orange twist (discard)

Cameron's Kick Cocktail
"Harry" of Ciro's ABC of Mixing Cocktails, *Harry MacElhone, 1923*
1 oz (30 ml) Scotch
1 oz (30 ml) Irish whiskey
¾ oz (22 ml) lemon juice
¾ oz (22 ml) orgeat
Garnish: lemon twist (discard)

Add all ingredients to a shaker, then shake with ice and strain into a frozen coupe.

Cicada
Brandon Bramhall, Attaboy, Nashville, 2021
1 oz (30 ml) Islay Scotch
1 oz (30 ml) Amaro Braulio
¾ oz (22 ml) lemon juice
¾ oz (22 ml) ginger syrup (p 496)
Garnish: candied ginger

Glasgow Razor Blade
(Holland Razor Blade with Scotch on the rocks)
Tom Lasher-Walker, Fresh Kills, NYC, 2017
1½ oz (45 ml) Scotch
½ oz (15 ml) Islay Scotch
¾ oz (22 ml) lemon juice
¾ oz (22 ml) simple syrup
Serve in a frozen double rocks glass with ice.
Garnish: dusting of cayenne pepper

Lauder's Daisy
Here's How: Mixed Drinks, *W.C. Whitfield, 1941*
2 oz (60 ml) Scotch
¾ oz (22 ml) simple syrup
⅜ oz (11 ml) lemon juice
⅜ oz (11 ml) lime juice
Garnish: lemon twist (discard)

Pantheon
Daisuke Ito, Land Bar Artisan, Tokyo
2 oz (60 ml) Scotch
½ oz (15 ml) Bénédictine
¾ oz (22 ml) lemon juice
¼ oz (7 ml) simple syrup
Garnish: lemon twist (discard)

Penicillin
Sam Ross, Milk & Honey, NYC, 2005
2 oz (60 ml) Scotch (originally Compass Box Aslya)
¾ oz (22 ml) lemon juice
⅜ oz (11 ml) ginger syrup (p 496)
⅜ oz (11 ml) honey syrup (p 496)
¼ oz (7 ml) Islay Scotch, to float (originally Compass Box The Peat Monster)
Add all ingredients, except Islay Scotch, to a shaker with ice. Shake and strain into a frozen double rocks glass with ice, then float Islay Scotch.
Garnish: candied ginger

Sand Fly
Zac Pease, Attaboy, NYC, 2017
¾ oz (22 ml) Islay Scotch
¾ oz (22 ml) Campari
¾ oz (22 ml) lemon juice
¾ oz (22 ml) ginger syrup (p 496)

Serious Kick
(Cameron's Kick with Islay Scotch split on the rocks)
Sarah Ellis, Noble Experiment, San Diego, 2012
1 oz (30 ml) Islay Scotch
1 oz (30 ml) Irish whiskey
¾ oz (22 ml) lemon juice
¾ oz (22 ml) orgeat
Serve in a frozen double rocks glass with ice.
Garnish: lemon twist (discard)

Silver Nail
¾ oz (22 ml) Scotch
¾ oz (22 ml) gin
½ oz (15 ml) Drambuie
¾ oz (22 ml) lemon juice
½ oz (15 ml) simple syrup
Serve in a frozen double rocks glass with ice.
Garnish: lemon twist

Smoke Signal
Oska Whitehart, The Everleigh, Melbourne, 2017
1½ oz (45 ml) Scotch
½ oz (15 ml) Islay Scotch
1 oz (30 ml) pineapple juice
½ oz (15 ml) lemon juice
½ oz (15 ml) simple syrup
2 dashes orange bitters
Serve in a frozen double rocks glass with ice.
Garnish: 3 pineapple fronds

"The Bellamy Scotch Sour"
The Stork Club Bar Book, *Lucius Beebe, 1946*
2 oz (60 ml) Scotch
½ oz (15 ml) lemon juice
½ oz (15 ml) orange juice
½ oz (15 ml) honey syrup (p 496)
Garnish: Angostura Bitters stripe

The Crow
Here's How!, *Judge Jr., 1927*
2 oz (60 ml) Scotch
¾ oz (22 ml) lemon juice
¾ oz (22 ml) grenadine (p 496)
▼ Swap Scotch for bourbon to make the **Crow Cocktail** from *The Official Mixer's Manual*, Patrick Gavin Duffy, 1934.

Whisky Flash
(Non-Traditional Scotch Sour with pineapple)
Bariana, *Louis Fouquet, 1896*
2 oz (60 ml) Scotch
1 oz (30 ml) pineapple juice
½ oz (15 ml) simple syrup
¼ oz (7 ml) lemon juice
Garnish: candied pineapple

Yuzu Peni-chillin'
Joshua Perez, Bar Trench, Tokyo, 2023
1 oz (30 ml) Scotch
½ oz (15 ml) Islay Scotch
½ oz (15 ml) lemon juice
⅓ oz (10 ml) ginger syrup (p 496)
1 teaspoon (5 ml) honey syrup (p 496)
1 dash Angostura Bitters
1½ oz (40 g) yuzu sorbet
2¾ oz (80 g) crushed ice
Add all ingredients to a *blender*, then blend until smooth and pour into a frozen double rocks glass.
Garnish: lemon wheel and Angostura Bitters stripe

Add all ingredients to a shaker, then shake with ice and strain into a frozen coupe.

WORLD WHISK(E)Y

Cameron
(Cameron's Kick with Irish Whiskey)
2 oz (60 ml) Irish whiskey
¾ oz (22 ml) lemon juice
¾ oz (22 ml) orgeat
Garnish: lemon twist (discard)

Suntory Time Machine
Jeff Bell, PDT, NYC
1½ oz (45 ml) Suntory Toki Whisky
¾ oz (22 ml) kimoto sake (preferably Tamagawa Time Machine 1712)
¾ oz (22 ml) lemon juice
¼ oz (7 ml) maple syrup
1 dash Miracle Mile Bitters Co. Toasted Pecan Bitters
1 teaspoon (6 g) fig jam
Stir jam, lemon juice and maple syrup in a shaker, then add remaining ingredients, shake with ice and strain into a frozen coupe.

BRANDY

After All
Harry's American Bar, Paris
1½ oz (45 ml) bonded apple brandy
½ oz (15 ml) Giffard Crème de Pêche de Vigne
¾ oz (22 ml) lemon juice
¼ oz (7 ml) simple syrup

Autumn in Jersey
Anthony Schmidt, Noble Experiment, San Diego, 2010
2 oz (60 ml) bonded apple brandy
¾ oz (22 ml) lemon juice
¾ oz (22 ml) orgeat
2 dashes Angostura Bitters
Serve in a frozen double rocks glass with ice.
Garnish: mint sprig

B&B Sour
Michael Butt, London
1½ oz (45 ml) Cognac
¾ oz (22 ml) Bénédictine
¾ oz (22 ml) lemon juice
¼ oz (7 ml) simple syrup
2 dashes Angostura Bitters
Serve in a frozen double rocks glass with ice.
Garnish: orange half-wheel

Bayana
1700 Cocktails for the Man Behind the Bar, *R. de Fleury, 1934*
2 oz (60 ml) Cognac
¾ oz (22 ml) lemon juice
¾ oz (22 ml) simple syrup
2 dashes absinthe
2 dashes orange bitters
Garnish: lemon twist (discard)

Brandy Gump Cocktail
(Ward Eight with Cognac)
The Savoy Cocktail Book, *Harry Craddock, 1930*
2 oz (60 ml) Cognac
¾ oz (22 ml) lemon juice
¾ oz (22 ml) grenadine (p 496)

Butterflies Cocktail
Fred Armour
The Stork Club Bar Book, *Lucius Beebe, 1946*
1½ oz (45 ml) bonded apple brandy
½ oz (15 ml) gin
¾ oz (22 ml) lemon juice
¾ oz (22 ml) grenadine (p 496)

Calvados Sour
American Bar, *Frank P. Newman, 1900*
1½ oz (45 ml) Calvados
¾ oz (22 ml) orange curaçao (p 498)
¾ oz (22 ml) lemon juice
2 dashes orange bitters
Garnish: lemon twist (discard)

Champs Élysées
Drinks – Long & Short, *Nina Toye and A. H. Adair, 1925*
1½ oz (45 ml) Cognac
½ oz (15 ml) Green Chartreuse
¾ oz (22 ml) lemon juice
½ oz (15 ml) simple syrup
2 dashes Angostura Bitters
Garnish: lemon twist (discard)

Crop Duster
(Aviation No. 2 with bonded apple brandy)
2 oz (60 ml) bonded apple brandy
⅜ oz (11 ml) maraschino liqueur
¾ oz (22 ml) lemon juice
⅜ oz (11 ml) simple syrup
Garnish: cherry

Cuban Cocktail #1
1½ oz (45 ml) Cognac
½ oz (15 ml) apricot brandy
¾ oz (22 ml) lemon juice
1 teaspoon (5 ml) simple syrup

Depth Bomb Cocktail
(aka **The Deadly Amonita** in The Saloon in the Home, *Ridgley Hunt and George S. Chappell, 1930*)
Cocktails: How to Mix Them, *Robert Vermeire, 1922*
1 oz (30 ml) Cognac
1 oz (30 ml) bonded apple brandy
¾ oz (22 ml) lemon juice
¾ oz (22 ml) grenadine (p 496)

Filmograph Cocktail
(aka **Pickfair Cocktail** in *Trader Vic's Bartender's Guide*, Trader Vic, 1947)
The Savoy Cocktail Book, *Harry Craddock, 1930*
2 oz (60 ml) Cognac
¾ oz (22 ml) kola tonic
½ oz (15 ml) lemon juice
¼ oz (7 ml) simple syrup
Garnish: lemon twist (discard)

Finding Rose
Lucinda Sterling, Seaborne, NYC, 2019
2 oz (60 ml) Cognac
¾ oz (22 ml) lemon juice
½ oz (15 ml) honey syrup (p 496)
½ oz (15 ml) passionfruit syrup (p 499)

Add all ingredients to a shaker, then shake with ice and strain into a frozen coupe.

Fish House Punch (Kappeler Recipe)
Modern American Drinks, *George J. Kappeler, 1895*
1 oz (30 ml) Cognac
½ oz (15 ml) Jamaican dark rum
½ oz (15 ml) Giffard Crème de Pêche de Vigne
¾ oz (22 ml) lemon juice
¼ oz (7 ml) simple syrup
Serve in a frozen double rocks glass with ice.
Garnish: mint sprig, 2–3 berries and freshly grated nutmeg

Golden Delicious
(Bee's Knees with bonded apple brandy on the rocks)
Jim Kearns, NYC
2 oz (60 ml) bonded apple brandy
¾ oz (22 ml) lemon juice
¾ oz (22 ml) honey syrup (p 496)
Serve in a frozen double rocks glass with ice.
Garnish: apple fan

Harmony Cocktail
The How and When, *Hyman Gale and Gerald F. Marco, 1937*
2 oz (60 ml) Cognac
⅜ oz (11 ml) maraschino liqueur
¾ oz (22 ml) lemon juice
⅜ oz (11 ml) simple syrup
2 dashes orange bitters
1 strawberry, halved
Muddle strawberry and simple syrup in a shaker. Add remaining ingredients, then shake with ice and strain into a frozen double rocks glass with ice.
Garnish: half a strawberry

"Hoop La!" Cocktail
(aka **Frank Sullivan** or **Odd McIntyre**)
The Savoy Cocktail Book, *Harry Craddock, 1930*
¾ oz (22 ml) Cognac
¾ oz (22 ml) Cocchi Americano
½ oz (15 ml) triple sec
¾ oz (22 ml) lemon juice
1 teaspoon (5 ml) simple syrup
Garnish: lemon twist (discard)

Jack in the Box
The Fine Art of Mixing Drinks, *David A. Embury, 1948*
2 oz (60 ml) bonded apple brandy
1 oz (30 ml) pineapple juice
½ oz (15 ml) simple syrup
¼ oz (7 ml) lemon juice
2 dashes Angostura Bitters

Louisiana Purchase
(Bee's Knees with Cognac on the rocks)
Michael Madrusan, Milk & Honey, NYC, 2008
2 oz (60 ml) Cognac
¾ oz (22 ml) lemon juice
¾ oz (22 ml) honey syrup (p 496)
Serve in a frozen double rocks glass with ice.
Garnish: lemon wedge

Madame Banane
ms. franky marshall, NYC, 2023
1½ oz (45 ml) Cognac
¾ oz (22 ml) Tempus Fugit Crème de Banane
½ oz (15 ml) lemon juice
Serve in a frozen double rocks glass with ice.
Garnish: long plantain chip

Munich Sour
Trader Vic, Trader Vic's, Munich, 1970s
2 oz (60 ml) Cognac
1 oz (30 ml) orange juice
½ oz (15 ml) lemon juice
¼ oz (7 ml) orgeat
¼ oz (7 ml) simple syrup
Serve in a frozen double rocks glass with ice.
Garnish: cherry, orange wedge and lemon wedge

NY Snap
Good Things to Drink with Mr Lyan & Friends, *Ryan Chetiyawardana, 2015*
1 oz (30 ml) Cognac
½ oz (15 ml) aged dark rum
1½ oz (45 ml) pineapple juice
½ oz (15 ml) lemon juice
½ oz (15 ml) simple syrup
½ oz (15 ml) dry red wine, to float
2 dashes Angostura Bitters, to float
Shake all ingredients, except red wine and bitters, with ice, then strain into a frozen double rocks glass with ice and float red wine and bitters.

Pisco Bell-Ringer
How to Mix Drinks, *James C. Maloney, 1903*
2 oz (60 ml) pisco
½ oz (15 ml) lemon juice
¼ oz (7 ml) simple syrup
2 dashes Peychaud's Aromatic Cocktail Bitters
1 dash orange bitters
1 teaspoon (5 ml) apricot brandy, to coat
Coat the inside of a frozen coupe with apricot brandy and place back in freezer. Add remaining ingredients to a shaker, then shake with ice and strain into the coupe.
▼ The term 'Bell-Ringers' was patented by Maloney to describe drinks served in glasses rinsed with apricot brandy.

Pobre Isabel
Toby Maloney
1½ oz (45 ml) pisco (preferably Italia)
½ oz (15 ml) unaged pear brandy
½ oz (15 ml) Green Chartreuse
¾ oz (22 ml) lemon juice
¼ oz (7 ml) simple syrup
3 dashes Peychaud's Aromatic Cocktail Bitters
Garnish: flamed pink grapefruit twist (discard)

Add all ingredients to a shaker, then shake with ice and strain into a frozen coupe.

Poor Liza
Toby Maloney, 2007
2 oz (60 ml) unaged pear brandy
¼ oz (7 ml) Green Chartreuse
¾ oz (22 ml) lemon juice
½ oz (15 ml) simple syrup
3 dashes Peychaud's Aromatic Cocktail Bitters
Garnish: flamed orange twist (discard)

Port of Call
Sam Ross, Attaboy, NYC, 2016
1½ oz (45 ml) bonded apple brandy
¾ oz (22 ml) tawny Port
¾ oz (22 ml) lemon juice
½ oz (15 ml) honey syrup (p 496)
Serve in a frozen double rocks glass with ice.
Garnish: freshly grated cinnamon

Quaker's Cocktail
"Harry" of Ciro's ABC of Mixing Cocktails, *Harry MacElhone, 1923*
1 oz (30 ml) Cognac
1 oz (30 ml) aged dark rum
¾ oz (22 ml) lemon juice
¾ oz (22 ml) simple syrup
2 raspberries
Muddle raspberries with simple syrup, add remaining ingredients, then shake with ice and strain into a frozen coupe.
Garnish: raspberry
▼ Swap aged dark rum for rye whiskey to make the **Quaker** from *The Artistry of Mixing Drinks*, Frank Meier, 1936.

The Applejack Rabbit Cocktail
The Official Mixer's Manual, *Patrick Gavin Duffy, 1934*
2 oz (60 ml) bonded apple brandy
½ oz (15 ml) lemon juice
½ oz (15 ml) orange juice
½ oz (15 ml) maple syrup
Garnish: apple fan

The Philly Sling
Derek Brown, Columbia Room, Washington D.C.
1½ oz (45 ml) Calvados
1 oz (30 ml) sloe gin
½ oz (15 ml) lemon juice
¼ oz (7 ml) simple syrup
1 dash Fee Brothers Whiskey Barrel-Aged Bitters
Garnish: apple fan

Truly Scrumptious
Trevor Easter, The Snug, Sacramento
1 oz (30 ml) pisco
½ oz (15 ml) Poire Williams
¾ oz (22 ml) lime juice
¾ oz (22 ml) pineapple syrup (p 499)
Serve in a frozen double rocks glass with ice.
Garnish: freshly grated cinnamon

Voorhees
D. Skinner
1 oz (30 ml) bonded apple brandy
1 oz (30 ml) genever
¾ oz (22 ml) lemon juice
½ oz (15 ml) cinnamon syrup (p 495)
¼ oz (7 ml) simple syrup
Garnish: dusting of cayenne pepper

Willie Smith Cocktail
(Aviation No. 2 with Cognac)
Trader Vic's Bartender's Guide, *Trader Vic, 1947*
2 oz (60 ml) Cognac
⅜ oz (11 ml) maraschino liqueur
¾ oz (22 ml) lemon juice
⅜ oz (11 ml) simple syrup
Garnish: cherry

RUM & CANE SPIRIT

Adam
Approved Cocktails, *United Kingdom Bartenders' Guild, 1937*
2 oz (60 ml) Jamaican dark rum
¾ oz (22 ml) lemon juice
¾ oz (22 ml) grenadine (p 496)

Beehive Sour
2 oz (60 ml) aged dark rum
½ oz (15 ml) lemon juice
½ oz (15 ml) orange juice
⅓ oz (10 ml) honey syrup (p 496)
⅓ oz (10 ml) ginger syrup (p 496)
Garnish: dusting of cayenne pepper

Century Club Punch
The Bar-Tender's Guide, *Jerry Thomas, 1887*
1 oz (30 ml) aged dark rum
1 oz (30 ml) Jamaican dark rum
¾ oz (22 ml) lemon juice
¾ oz (22 ml) simple syrup
Serve in a frozen double rocks glass with ice.
Garnish: lemon wedge

Columbia Cocktail
Crosby Gaige's Cocktail Guide and Ladies' Companion, *Crosby Gaige, 1941*
2 oz (60 ml) light rum
¾ oz (22 ml) lemon juice
¾ oz (22 ml) simple syrup
2 raspberries
Muddle raspberries and simple syrup in a shaker. Add remaining ingredients, then shake with ice and strain into a frozen double rocks glass with ice.
Garnish: raspberry

Coral
Jones' Complete Barguide, *Stan Jones, 1977*
1½ oz (45 ml) light rum
½ oz (15 ml) apricot brandy
1 oz (30 ml) pink grapefruit juice
½ oz (15 ml) lemon juice
1 teaspoon (5 ml) simple syrup

Cubaine
The Fine Art of Mixing Drinks, *David A. Embury, 1948*
2 oz (60 ml) light rum
½ oz (15 ml) lemon juice
½ oz (15 ml) orange juice
½ oz (15 ml) simple syrup

Add all ingredients to a shaker, then shake with ice and strain into a frozen coupe.

Eclipse No. 2
1700 Cocktails for the Man Behind the Bar, *R. de Fleury, 1934*
1½ oz (45 ml) light rum
½ oz (15 ml) Green Chartreuse
½ oz (15 ml) lemon juice
½ oz (15 ml) simple syrup
Garnish: cherry

JuJu Man
(Penicillin with dark rum)
Zachary Gelnaw-Rubin, Lion Lion, NYC, 2017
1 oz (30 ml) Cruzan Black Strap Rum
1 oz (30 ml) pot still Jamaican dark rum (preferably Smith & Cross Traditional Jamaica Rum)
¾ oz (22 ml) lemon juice
⅜ oz (11 ml) honey syrup (p 496)
⅜ oz (11 ml) ginger syrup (p 496)
Serve in a frozen double rocks glass with ice.
Garnish: candied ginger

King's Jubilee
(Aviation No. 2 with light rum)
Harry Craddock, The Savoy, London, 1935
2 oz (60 ml) light rum
⅜ oz (11 ml) maraschino liqueur
¾ oz (22 ml) lemon juice
⅜ oz (11 ml) simple syrup
Garnish: cherry
▼ Created for the Silver Jubilee of King George V.

La Japonaise
Toby Cecchini, The Long Island Bar, NYC, 2018
1 oz (30 ml) Cognac
1 oz (30 ml) El Dorado 12yr Rum
½ oz (15 ml) lemon juice
½ oz (15 ml) lime juice
½ oz (15 ml) Calpico concentrate
½ oz (15 ml) orgeat
Garnish: orange twist (discard)

Philadelphia Fish House Punch
(aka **Fish House Punch**)
Schuylkill Fishing Company of Pennsylvania, Philadelphia, 1795
1½ oz (45 ml) Jamaican dark rum
¾ oz (22 ml) Cognac
½ oz (15 ml) Giffard Crème de Pêche de Vigne
¾ oz (22 ml) lemon juice
¼ oz (7 ml) simple syrup
Toss and strain into a frozen Spritz glass with crushed ice, shimmy and top with more crushed ice.
Garnish: mint sprig, 2–3 berries and freshly grated nutmeg
▼ Add 1 oz (30 ml) cold black tea for a variation.

Rabbit's Foot
Jones' Complete Barguide, *Stan Jones, 1977*
1 oz (30 ml) aged dark rum
1 oz (30 ml) bonded apple brandy
½ oz (15 ml) orange juice
½ oz (15 ml) lemon juice
½ oz (15 ml) grenadine (p 496)

Rhubarb
Sebastian Tollius, Eleven Madison Park, NYC, 2022
1½ oz (45 ml) white chocolate-washed aged cachaça (p 505)
½ oz (15 ml) lemon verbena–infused gin (p 503)
¼ oz (7 ml) dry vermouth
¾ oz (22 ml) pink peppercorn shrub (p 500)
½ oz (15 ml) lemon juice
2 dashes absinthe
Serve in a frozen double rocks glass with ice.
Garnish: hibiscus-pickled rhubarb

Sea B3
(Ward Eight Cocktail with Goslings Black Seal Rum)
Phil Ward, Death & Co, NYC, 2008
2 oz (60 ml) Goslings Black Seal Rum
½ oz (15 ml) lemon juice
½ oz (15 ml) orange juice
½ oz (15 ml) grenadine (p 496)

Shanghai Cocktail
The Savoy Cocktail Book, *Harry Craddock, 1930*
2 oz (60 ml) Jamaican dark rum
¾ oz (22 ml) lemon juice
¾ oz (22 ml) grenadine (p 496)
2 dashes absinthe

Stanley Cocktail
Barflies and Cocktails, *Harry MacElhone, 1927*
1 oz (30 ml) light rum
1 oz (30 ml) gin
¾ oz (22 ml) lemon juice
¾ oz (22 ml) grenadine (p 496)

The Million
(aka **Non-Traditional Jamaican Dark Rum Sour**)
2 oz (60 ml) Jamaican dark rum
¾ oz (22 ml) lemon juice
¾ oz (22 ml) simple syrup
2 dashes Angostura Bitters
Garnish: lemon twist (discard)
▼ Split the Jamaican dark rum with 151 Rum for a **Royal Million**.

Twelve Mile Limit
Thomas Franklin Fairfax Millard
Vintage Spirits and Forgotten Cocktails, *Ted Haigh, 2009*
1 oz (30 ml) light rum
½ oz (15 ml) rye whiskey
½ oz (15 ml) Cognac
¾ oz (22 ml) lemon juice
¾ oz (22 ml) grenadine (p 496)
Garnish: lemon twist (discard)

Add all ingredients to a shaker, then shake with ice and strain into a frozen coupe.

AGAVE

Bombardier
Andrew Cordero, The Reading Club, San Diego, 2022
1 oz (30 ml) reposado tequila
1 oz (30 ml) mezcal
¾ oz (22 ml) lemon juice
¾ oz (22 ml) orgeat
Serve in a frozen double rocks glass with ice.
Garnish: Cerignola olive

Camarón
Robert Simonson, 2019
1 oz (30 ml) blanco tequila
1 oz (30 ml) mezcal
¾ oz (22 ml) lemon juice
¼ oz (15 ml) orgeat
Garnish: lemon twist (discard)

Charo's Kick
Anthony Schmidt, Noble Experiment, San Diego, 2012
1½ oz (45 ml) blanco tequila
½ oz (15 ml) mezcal
¾ oz (22 ml) lemon juice
¾ oz (22 ml) orgeat
Garnish: lemon twist (discard)

Corpse Reviver #5
Rickhouse, San Francisco, 2011
¾ oz (22 ml) blanco tequila
¾ oz (22 ml) Cocchi Americano
¾ oz (22 ml) lemon juice
¾ oz (22 ml) pineapple syrup (p 499)
2 dashes absinthe
Garnish: lemon twist (discard)

Crystal Lake
Matt Clark, Dutch Kills, NYC
1 oz (30 ml) mezcal
1 oz (30 ml) pear brandy
¾ oz (22 ml) lemon juice
¾ oz (22 ml) cinnamon syrup (p 495)
Garnish: dusting of cayenne pepper

Dahlia's Revenge
(Bee's Knees with mezcal)
Mikka Kristola, The Varnish, Los Angeles
2 oz (60 ml) mezcal
¾ oz (22 ml) lemon juice
¾ oz (22 ml) honey syrup (p 496)
Garnish: dusting of cayenne pepper

Dragonfly
Brandon Bramhall, Attaboy, Nashville
¾ oz (22 ml) mezcal
¾ oz (22 ml) Amaro Braulio
¾ oz (22 ml) lemon juice
¾ oz (22 ml) ginger syrup (p 496)
Garnish: candied ginger

Flor de Jalisco
Joaquín Simó, Death & Co, NYC, 2009
2 oz (60 ml) blanco tequila
¾ oz (22 ml) lemon juice
¼ oz (7 ml) agave syrup (p 494)
1 teaspoon (6 g) orange marmalade
Add the marmalade, lemon juice and agave syrup to a shaker and stir to combine, then add tequila, shake with ice and strain into a frozen coupe.
Garnish: lemon twist (discard)

Glandula del Mono
Phil Ward, Death & Co, NYC, 2008
1½ oz (45 ml) blanco tequila
½ oz (15 ml) lemon juice
½ oz (15 ml) orange juice
½ oz (15 ml) grenadine (p 496)
2 dashes absinthe

Hot Lips
Jessica Gonzalez, Death & Co, NYC, 2009
¾ oz (22 ml) jalapeño-infused blanco tequila (p 503)
¾ oz (22 ml) mezcal
½ oz (15 ml) lemon juice
½ oz (15 ml) pineapple juice
½ oz (15 ml) vanilla syrup (p 502)
1 teaspoon (5 ml) cane syrup (p 494)
Serve in a frozen double rocks glass with ice.
Garnish: salt rim and 3 pineapple fronds

Hot Ticket
(Non-Traditional Tequila Sour with hot sauce)
Felix Woods and Zara Madrusan, The Everleigh, Melbourne, 2014
2 oz (60 ml) blanco tequila
¾ oz (22 ml) lemon juice
¾ oz (22 ml) simple syrup
2 dashes Cholula Original Hot Sauce
Garnish: pinch of black pepper

Jalisco
(Tequila Monkey Gland without absinthe)
Café Royal Cocktail Book, *W.J. Tarling, 1937*
2 oz (60 ml) blanco tequila
1 oz (30 ml) orange juice
½ oz (15 ml) grenadine (p 496)
¼ oz (7 ml) lemon juice

Loisaida Avenue
Leo Robitschek, The NoMad Bar, NYC
¾ oz (22 ml) jalapeño-infused blanco tequila (p 503)
¾ oz (22 ml) mezcal
½ oz (15 ml) Green Chartreuse
¾ oz (22 ml) lemon juice
½ oz (15 ml) simple syrup
Garnish: Angostura Bitters stripe

Maximilian Affair
Misty Kalkofen, Green Street Grill, Boston, 2008
1 oz (30 ml) mezcal
1 oz (30 ml) St Germain Elderflower Liqueur
½ oz (15 ml) sweet vermouth
¾ oz (22 ml) lemon juice
Garnish: lemon twist (discard)

Mosquito
Sam Ross, Attaboy, NYC, 2017
¾ oz (22 ml) mezcal
¾ oz (22 ml) Campari
¾ oz (22 ml) lemon juice
¾ oz (22 ml) ginger syrup (p 496)
Garnish: candied ginger

Add all ingredients to a shaker, then shake with ice and strain into a frozen coupe.

New Mexico
Felix Woods, The Everleigh, Melbourne
1 oz (30 ml) blanco tequila
½ oz (15 ml) mezcal
⅜ oz (11 ml) maraschino liqueur
¾ oz (22 ml) lemon juice
⅜ oz (11 ml) simple syrup
2 dashes orange bitters
Garnish: cherry

Paris is Burning
Leo Robitschek, The NoMad Bar, NYC
1 oz (30 ml) mezcal
1 oz (30 ml) gin
½ oz (15 ml) St Germain Elderflower Liqueur
1 oz (30 ml) pineapple juice
½ oz (15 ml) lemon juice
¼ oz (7 ml) cane syrup (p 494)
Garnish: Angostura Bitters stripe

Queen River West
Daniel Zacharczuk, The Varnish, Los Angeles, 2024
1 oz (30 ml) añejo tequila
1 oz (30 ml) Cognac
¾ oz (22 ml) pineapple juice
½ oz (15 ml) lemon juice
½ oz (15 ml) simple syrup
2 dashes absinthe
2 cucumber wheels
Press cucumber and simple syrup in a shaker. Add remaining ingredients, then shake with ice and strain into a frozen double rocks glass with ice.
Garnish: cucumber fan

Reforma
Dan Greenbaum, The Beagle, NYC, 2012
1 oz (30 ml) blanco tequila
1 oz (30 ml) Poire Williams
¾ oz (22 ml) lemon juice
¾ oz (22 ml) ginger syrup (p 496)
Garnish: candied ginger

Seaport
Brandon Bramhall, Attaboy, Nashville, 2018
1½ oz (45 ml) mezcal
½ oz (15 ml) Green Chartreuse
1 oz (30 ml) pineapple juice
½ oz (15 ml) lemon juice
1 teaspoon (5 ml) cane syrup (p 494)
1 dash orange bitters

Sister Mary
Evan Harrison, Deep Ellum, Boston
1 oz (30 ml) blanco tequila
1 oz (30 ml) St Germain Elderflower Liqueur
¼ oz (7 ml) Aperol
1 oz (30 ml) grapefruit juice
¼ oz (7 ml) lemon juice

White Dahlia
Lea Madda, Brick & Mortar, Boston
1½ oz (45 ml) mezcal
½ oz (15 ml) Giffard Crème de Pamplemousse Rose
½ oz (15 ml) Cocchi Americano
⅜ oz (11 ml) lemon juice
⅜ oz (11 ml) lime juice
1 dash Angostura Bitters

21st Century
Jim Meehan, Pegu Club, NYC, 2007
2 oz (60 ml) blanco tequila
¾ oz (22 ml) white crème de cacao
¾ oz (22 ml) lemon juice
2 dashes absinthe
Garnish: lemon twist (discard)

FORTIFIED & LIQUEUR

Intro to Aperol
Audrey Saunders, Pegu Club, NYC, 2006
2 oz (60 ml) Aperol
1 oz (30 ml) gin
¾ oz (22 ml) lemon juice
2 dashes Angostura Bitters
Garnish: orange twist (discard)

OTHER

Far East Side
Kenta Goto, Bar Goto, NYC
2 oz (60 ml) sake
¾ oz (22 ml) elderflower liqueur
½ oz (15 ml) blanco tequila
¼ oz (7 ml) lemon juice
2 shiso leaves
Garnish: shiso leaf

Susudara
Kirk Estopinal, Cure, New Orleans
1½ oz (45 ml) pear eau de vie
½ oz (15 ml) elderflower liqueur
¾ oz (22 ml) lemon juice
½ oz (15 ml) simple syrup
3 dashes Angostura Bitters
Garnish: Angostura Bitters stripe

Trinidad Sour
Giuseppe Gonzalez, Clover Club, NYC, 2009
1½ oz (45 ml) Angostura Bitters
½ oz (15 ml) rye whiskey
¾ oz (22 ml) lemon juice
¾ oz (22 ml) orgeat

From *Crosby Gaige's Cocktail Guide and Ladies' Companion* (1941):

A cocktail should be like a gentle nudge from a friend—not a shove down the stairs.

Add all ingredients to a shaker, then shake with ice and strain into a frozen coupe.

CRUSTA, DAISY & SIDECAR

Aviation Cocktail p 195 (left), Side-Car Cocktail p 205 (middle), Whiskey Crusta p 194 (right)

Crusta, Daisy & Sidecar

A short citrus cocktail sweetened with liqueur(s) and/or syrup(s), served in a frozen footed cocktail glass.

spirit + citrus + liqueur(s) + and/or syrup(s)

Add all ingredients to a shaker, then shake with ice and strain into a frozen coupe or footed cocktail glass.

A collective of short, shaken drinks that are subcategories of the overarching Sour family (p 152), Crustas, Daisies and Sidecars are all cocktails that take the simple Sour formula of spirit, citrus and sugar and add liqueurs and/or syrups.

The first of these to emerge was the Crusta – a descendant of the Sour comprising spirit, citrus, either curaçao or maraschino, and bitters – created by Italian bartender Joseph Santini, who worked in New Orleans in the 1850s. In its day, the Crusta was perceived as an improved short citrus cocktail, distinguished by a sugared rim, or crust, on the cocktail glass and long citrus peel wrapped around the inside. Early recipes can also be linked to the 'Fancy Cocktails' that evolved from the original Whiskey Cocktail (p 387). Many of these Crusta recipes featured smaller measures of citrus and were most commonly stirred over cracked ice.

The Daisy, a sweeter and fruitier cousin of the Sour, defined by its inclusion of multiple liqueurs and/or syrups, was popular in the United States in the 1870s and first published in the second edition of *The Bar-Tender's Guide* by Jerry Thomas in 1876. The earliest versions of this cocktail combined spirits and citrus with at least one liqueur – often curaçao or Yellow Chartreuse – as well as a splash of soda. Over time, other variations have cropped up on cracked ice, and lime and lemon have been used interchangeably depending on tastes, trends and availability. Ever heard of a little cocktail called the Margarita? That's right, that heroic cocktail is a simple Daisy made with tequila.

The Sidecar, meanwhile, is an icon in its own right, born in the Roaring Twenties and emblematic of the new era of fine drinking and luxury that followed World War I. This effortlessly glamorous cocktail originated

→

in France and was first published in *Cocktails: How to Mix Them* by Robert Vermeire in 1922. Vermeire was a Belgian bartender working in London, most notably as the head bartender at the Embassy Club. *Cocktails: How to Mix Them* featured both classic American cocktails and newer European drinks, such as the Sidecar, and is thought to be one of the most commercially successful classic cocktail guides, with more than 100,000 copies printed.

The Sidecar, too, found global success and remained a symbol of opulence and elegance well into the 21st century. A clear derivative of the Sour cocktail family with close ties to the Crusta, the rich combination of Cognac, triple sec (a drier orange liqueur compared to curaçao) and lemon juice is often served with a sugar-crusted rim in American bars. While the initial recipes called for all ingredients in equal proportions (which no doubt kept the high price of Cognac in check), we prefer a more spirit-forward formula that lets high-quality Cognac shine in all its golden glory. Although Cognac is still considered key to the Sidecar, several alternatives featuring rum, gin and whisk(e)y have also found footing. When it comes to the sugar rim, we say each to their own, but a spritz of oil from a lemon twist is non-negotiable, providing the perfect aromatic finish.

While the 1850s Crusta disappeared almost entirely, likely due to its elaborate garnishes, the Daisy (sans soda) and its elegant European cousin, the Sidecar, continue to hold court in contemporary cocktail culture. However, it remains relevant to understand how these categories have intertwined and influenced each other throughout the course of history – take the Margarita 'crusted' with a salt rim as a defining feature, for example. This chapter brings together the fanciful sweetened Sours of old with new and interesting recipes incorporating inventive liqueurs, syrups and juices à la mode.

ESSENTIAL VARIATIONS

Last Word

Detroit Athletic Club, Detroit, 1916
¾ oz (22 ml) gin
¾ oz (22 ml) Green Chartreuse
⅜ oz (11 ml) maraschino liqueur
¾ oz (22 ml) lime juice
⅜ oz (11 ml) simple syrup

Add all ingredients to a shaker, then shake with ice and strain into a frozen cocktail glass.
Garnish: cherry

First found on the menu at the Detroit Athletic Club in 1916, the Last Word is a Daisy made up of a tidy, equal-parts combination of gin, maraschino liqueur, Green Chartreuse and lime juice. Originally located on Detroit's Woodward Avenue, the DAC was established by a group of young athletes in 1887. In 1913, the venue was relocated and renovated under new ownership, reopening in 1915 as a majestic multistorey private social club designed by architect Albert Kahn; it still stands in the heart of the Motor City's sports and theatre district.

The Last Word was circulated in a newsletter to members following the club's reopening, listed at a bold 35 cents – twice the price of the DAC's other menu items at the time. Fast-forward 35 years and we see the recipe detailed in full for the first time in Ted Saucier's splendidly suggestive 1951 cocktail book, *Ted Saucier's Bottoms Up*. While the combination of ingredients appears somewhat unusual, this distinctive cocktail is a real party on the palate, bouncing between sweet, sour, bitter and herbaceous.

Although the drink faded into obscurity towards the end of the 20th century, it reappeared on the menu at Seattle's Zig Zag Café in 2003, after bartender Murray Stenson rediscovered it in Saucier's book. With the classic cocktail renaissance in full swing, news of the Last Word caught the attention of bartenders across the United States, paving the way for a wave of drinks that celebrated Green Chartreuse and other herbal liqueurs.

There are now several memorable Last Word variations in circulation, including the Final Ward (p 201) by Phil Ward of New York City's Death & Co, which switches gin for whiskey and lime for lemon, as well as the Other Word (p 198) by our friends at The Varnish in Los Angeles – a combo of Yellow Chartreuse, maraschino liqueur, lime juice, agave and salt, served on the rocks.

Margarita

2 oz (60 ml) blanco tequila
⅜ oz (11 ml) triple sec
¾ oz (22 ml) lime juice
⅜ oz (11 ml) agave syrup (p 494)

Add all ingredients to a shaker, then shake with ice and strain into a frozen coupe.
Garnish: salt half-rim (optional) and lime wedge

The written origins of the Margarita (perhaps not coincidentally the Spanish word for 'daisy') can be traced back to a 1937 cocktail book by William J. Tarling, head bartender of London's popular Café Royal. The cocktail appeared under the name 'Picador' (p 204), and called for a simple combination of tequila, Cointreau and lemon or lime juice. Two years later, a 'Tequila Sour' with the same ingredients was printed in a book of mixed drinks by Charlie Connolly for New York City's famed Cotton Club, this time calling for a salt-rimmed glass and a lime-wedge garnish.

Most people safely assume that the cocktail had originated further south, closer to the home of its lead spirit, and many more tales - some highly plausible but hardly documented - stem back to the bars of Mexico and Los Angeles in the 1930s. The name 'Margarita', however, didn't emerge in print until 1953, when it showed up in a piece about Mexico in *The Press Democrat*, a California newspaper. If the drink's identity was once disputed, it was laid to rest when José Cuervo launched the first national advertising campaign for tequila in 1956, calling out the Margarita as the perfect way to enjoy the spirit.

It is no stretch to say that the Margarita has become the most famous tequila cocktail on Earth, with a constellation of contemporary variations that tip their garnishes to the original formula. Perhaps the most influential contribution to come out of the classic cocktail renaissance belongs to Julio Bermejo of Tommy's Mexican Restaurant in San Francisco. Around 1987, Bermejo devised the Tommy's Margarita (p 220), a breezy, ingredient-driven blend of 100% agave tequila, fresh lime juice (goodbye, sour mix!) and agave syrup, served on the rocks. While the drink is quite a deviation from the prototype - and technically more of a Shake (p 206) than a Daisy - the role it has played in putting classic, high-quality tequila cocktails on menus worldwide is undeniable.

Classic Margarita devotees, meanwhile, would do well to explore other tequila-based Shakes such as the Viva Villa (p 221) finished with a sprinkle of salt, or Michael's Red Grasshopper (p 219) with honey and a dusting of smoked paprika.

Jasmine

Paul Harrington, Townhouse, Emeryville, 1993
Cocktail: The Drinks Bible for the 21st Century,
Paul Harrington and Laura Moorhead, 1998
¾ oz (22 ml) gin
¾ oz (22 ml) Campari
½ oz (15 ml) triple sec
¾ oz (22 ml) lemon juice
1 teaspoon (5 ml) simple syrup

Add all ingredients to a shaker, then shake with ice and strain into a frozen coupe.
Garnish: lemon twist (discard)

The Jasmine is a modern classic by Paul Harrington, included in his 1998 book with Laura Moorhead, *Cocktail: The Drinks Bible for the 21st Century*. Harrington created the drink in 1993 for a friend, Matt Jasmin, during his time working at Townhouse in Emeryville, California. At the time, Harrington was a big fan of the Pegu Club Cocktail (p 196), a punchy Daisy consisting of gin, lime, orange curaçao and bitters, which he would regularly recommend to patrons. When challenged to come up with an original drink for his pal, Harrington thought fast and used Campari instead of bitters, and lemon in place of lime. Jasmin was reportedly impressed by the cocktail's bright blush-like hue and bittersweet flavour, which closely resembled fresh grapefruit juice.

Arriving on the scene a couple of years after the Cosmopolitan, the Jasmine caught the attention of the industry's movers and shakers in the early 2000s due to its clever incorporation of Campari, rarely seen at the time. Harrington's refreshingly bitter cocktail also gave way to a cohort of short, sharp creations utilising bittersweet liqueurs and amari, which have since become icons of the modern era. Must-try cocktails from this generation include Sam Ross's Paper Plane (p 201) from 2008, spiked with Aperol and Amaro Nonino, as well as Joaquín Simó's Naked & Famous (p 198) from 2011, which combines mezcal, lime, Aperol and Yellow Chartreuse.

Crusta

Add all ingredients to a shaker, then shake with ice and strain into a frozen footed cocktail glass.

Almond Blossom Crusta
Hotel Crillón, Santiago
The South American Gentleman's Companion, *Charles H. Baker Jr., 1951*
1½ oz (45 ml) Cognac
½ oz (15 ml) gin
¾ oz (22 ml) lemon juice
¾ oz (22 ml) orgeat
Garnish: sugar rim and a long lemon peel curled inside the glass

Brandy Crusta (Harry Johnson Recipe)
New and Improved Bartender's Manual, *Harry Johnson, 1882*
1½ oz (45 ml) Cognac
⅜ oz (11 ml) maraschino liqueur
¾ oz (22 ml) lemon juice
⅜ oz (11 ml) simple syrup
3 dashes Angostura Bitters
Garnish: sugar rim and a long lemon peel curled inside the glass

Brandy Crusta (House Recipe)
1½ oz (45 ml) Cognac
⅜ oz (11 ml) orange curaçao (p 498)
⅜ oz (11 ml) maraschino liqueur
¾ oz (22 ml) lemon juice
2 dashes Angostura Bitters
Garnish: sugar rim and a long lemon peel curled inside the glass

Brandy Crusta (Jerry Thomas Recipe)
The Bar-Tender's Guide, *Jerry Thomas, 1862*
1½ oz (45 ml) Cognac
¾ oz (22 ml) orange curaçao (p 498)
¾ oz (22 ml) lemon juice
2 dashes Angostura Bitters
Garnish: sugar rim and a long lemon peel curled inside the glass

Daiquiri Crusta Especiál
The South American Gentleman's Companion, *Charles H. Baker Jr., 1951*
1½ oz (45 ml) light rum
¼ oz (7 ml) maraschino liqueur
1 oz (30 ml) pink grapefruit juice
½ oz (15 ml) lime juice
½ oz (15 ml) grenadine (p 496)
2 dashes Angostura Bitters
Garnish: sugar rim

Dama de la Noche Crusta Cocktail
The South American Gentleman's Companion, *Charles H. Baker Jr., 1951*
1½ oz (45 ml) Cognac
¾ oz (22 ml) orange curaçao (p 498)
1 oz (30 ml) pineapple juice
¼ oz (7 ml) lime juice
1 dash Angostura Bitters
Garnish: sugar rim and a spritz of orange blossom water

Feather Duster Crusta
Gregor de Gruyther, Ronnie Scott's, London, 2006
1½ oz (45 ml) bonded apple brandy
½ oz (15 ml) maraschino liqueur
¾ oz (22 ml) pink grapefruit juice
½ oz (15 ml) lemon juice
¼ oz (7 ml) passionfruit syrup (p 499)
¼ oz (7 ml) grenadine (p 496)
2 dashes Peychaud's Aromatic Cocktail Bitters

Kingston Crusta
The Gentleman's Companion, *Charles H. Baker Jr., 1939*
2 oz (60 ml) Jamaican dark rum
¾ oz (22 ml) lime juice
½ oz (15 ml) ginger syrup (p 496)
1 teaspoon (5 ml) maraschino liqueur
1 dash Bittermens Hellfire Habanero Shrub
3 dashes Angostura Bitters
Garnish: sugar rim, a long lime peel curled inside the glass and a pinch of cayenne pepper

Whiskey Crusta
New and Improved Bartender's Manual, *Harry Johnson, 1882*
1½ oz (45 ml) bourbon
½ oz (15 ml) maraschino liqueur
¾ oz (22 ml) lemon juice
¼ oz (7 ml) simple syrup
3 dashes Angostura Bitters
Garnish: sugar rim and a long lemon peel curled inside the glass

Daisy

Add all ingredients to a shaker, then shake with ice and strain into a frozen coupe.

VODKA

Aqueduct
1½ oz (45 ml) vodka
½ oz (15 ml) triple sec
¼ oz (7 ml) apricot brandy
¾ oz (22 ml) lime juice
1 teaspoon (5 ml) simple syrup

Calabrian Cosmo
Nathan McCarley-O'Neill, Torrisi, NYC, 2024
2 oz (60 ml) vodka (preferably Grey Goose vodka)
½ oz (15 ml) Aperol
½ oz (15 ml) triple sec
1 oz (30 ml) lime juice
⅓ oz (10 ml) simple syrup
1 teaspoon (5 ml) red capsicum (red pepper) juice
1 teaspoon (5 ml) cranberry juice

Cosmo #2
Conor Johns, Red Hook Tavern, Brooklyn, 2022
¾ oz (22 ml) vodka
¾ oz (22 ml) Calvados
½ oz (15 ml) apricot brandy
1 oz (30 ml) lime juice
½ oz (15 ml) cranberry cordial (p 495)
2 dashes Angostura Bitters
Garnish: cranberry

Add all ingredients to a shaker, then shake with ice and strain into a frozen footed cocktail glass.

Cosmopolita
Bianca Wendt, Bar Que Sera, Sawtell, 2024
1 oz (30 ml) vodka
½ oz (15 ml) triple sec
⅓ oz (10 ml) Fino Sherry
¾ oz (22 ml) lime juice
¾ oz (22 ml) grenadine (p 496)

Cosmopolitan
Toby Cecchini, The Odeon, NYC, 1988
1½ oz (45 ml) vodka (preferably Absolut Citron)
½ oz (15 ml) triple sec
½ oz (15 ml) unsweetened cranberry juice
½ oz (15 ml) lime juice
½ oz (15 ml) simple syrup
3 dashes orange bitters
Garnish: lemon twist (discard) and lime wheel

Jalisco
Café Royal Cocktail Book, *W.J. Tarling, 1937*
2 oz (60 ml) blanco tequila
1 oz (30 ml) orange juice
½ oz (15 ml) grenadine (p 496)
¼ oz (7 ml) lime juice
▼ This was likely a precursor to the **Tequila Sunrise** (p 118).

Trick Pony
Toby Maloney, 2011
1 oz (30 ml) vodka
1 oz (30 ml) Cocchi Americano
¾ oz (22 ml) pink grapefruit juice
½ oz (15 ml) lemon juice
½ oz (15 ml) simple syrup
1 teaspoon (5 ml) apricot brandy

GIN & GENEVER

Aviation Cocktail
Recipes for Mixed Drinks, *Hugo R. Ensslin, 1916*
2 oz (60 ml) gin
¼ oz (7 ml) maraschino liqueur
¼ oz (7 ml) crème de violette
¾ oz (22 ml) lemon juice
¼ oz (7 ml) simple syrup
Garnish: cherry

Corpse Reviver No. 2 (Difford's Recipe)
Difford's Guide
¾ oz (22 ml) gin
¾ oz (22 ml) Yellow Chartreuse
¾ oz (22 ml) Cocchi Americano
¾ oz (22 ml) lemon juice
2 dashes absinthe
Garnish: lemon twist (discard)

Crop Top
Devon Tarby, Death & Co, NYC
¾ oz (22 ml) gin
¾ oz (22 ml) Amaro Montenegro
¾ oz (22 ml) Giffard Crème de Pamplemousse Rose
¾ oz (22 ml) lemon juice
2 dashes absinthe
Garnish: lemon twist (discard)

Dahlia
Michael McCollum, Attaboy, Nashville
¾ oz (22 ml) gin
¾ oz (22 ml) Suze
¾ oz (22 ml) St Germain Elderflower Liqueur
¾ oz (22 ml) lemon juice
2 dashes absinthe
Garnish: lemon twist (discard)

Daily Mail
E.C. Chisnall
Approved Cocktails, *United Kingdom Bartenders' Guild, 1937*
1½ oz (45 ml) gin
¾ oz (22 ml) Bénédictine
¾ oz (22 ml) lemon juice
1 teaspoon (5 ml) orange curaçao (p 498)
2 dashes Angostura Bitters

Dead Flowers
Trevor Shores, Death & Co, Denver, 2023
¾ oz (22 ml) barrel-aged gin
¾ oz (22 ml) Amaro Nonino
¾ oz (22 ml) Liquore Strega
¾ oz (22 ml) lemon juice
2 dashes absinthe

Gilded Lily
Brandon Bramhall, Attaboy, Nashville
1½ oz (45 ml) gin
½ oz (15 ml) crème de violette
¾ oz (22 ml) lemon juice
½ oz (15 ml) honey syrup (p 496)

Gin Daisy (Charlie Paul Recipe)
American and Other Iced Drinks, *Charlie Paul, 1902*
1½ oz (45 ml) genever
½ oz (15 ml) maraschino liqueur
¾ oz (22 ml) lemon juice
½ oz (15 ml) orgeat
Garnish: lemon twist (discard)

Gin Daisy (Harry Johnson Recipe)
The New and Improved Illustrated Bartenders' Manual, *Harry Johnson, 1900*
1½ oz (45 ml) gin
½ oz (15 ml) Yellow Chartreuse
¾ oz (22 ml) lemon juice
¼ oz (7 ml) simple syrup
Garnish: lemon twist (discard)

Gin Daisy (Jerry Thomas Recipe)
The Bar-Tender's Guide, *Jerry Thomas, 1887*
1½ oz (45 ml) genever
⅜ oz (11 ml) maraschino liqueur
¾ oz (22 ml) lemon juice
⅜ oz (11 ml) simple syrup
Garnish: lemon twist (discard)

Godfrey's Corpse Reviver
Godfrey Baldini
Café Royal Cocktail Book, *W.J. Tarling, 1937*
1½ oz (45 ml) gin
¾ oz (22 ml) vodka
¾ oz (22 ml) lemon juice
¾ oz (22 ml) grenadine (p 496)
2 dashes Angostura Bitters

Good Word
Michael McCollum, Attaboy, Nashville, 2022
¾ oz (22 ml) gin
¾ oz (22 ml) génépy
¾ oz (22 ml) lime juice
¾ oz (22 ml) falernum
Garnish: cherry

Add all ingredients to a shaker, then shake with ice and strain into a frozen coupe.

Light as a Feather

Katie Rose, Goodkind, Milwaukee, 2014
The Bartender's Pantry, *Jim Meehan and Bart Sasso with Emma Janzen, 2024*
1 oz (30 ml) gin
½ oz (15 ml) sloe gin
½ oz (15 ml) Cocchi Americano
1 oz (30 ml) lime juice
½ oz (15 ml) simple syrup
6–8 mint leaves
Garnish: mint leaf

L'Ultima Parola

David Wondrich, 2018
1¼ oz (37 ml) gin
½ oz (15 ml) Liquore Strega
¼ oz (7 ml) maraschino liqueur
¾ oz (22 ml) lime juice
¼ oz (7 ml) simple syrup
Garnish: lime twist (discard) and cherry

Monk's Daisy

(Gin Daisy with Green Chartreuse)
1½ oz (45 ml) gin
¾ oz (22 ml) orange curaçao (p 498)
¾ oz (22 ml) lemon juice
1 teaspoon (5 ml) Green Chartreuse
Garnish: lemon twist (discard)

Novara

The Canon Cocktail Book, *Jamie Boudreau and James O. Fraioli, 2016*
1½ oz (45 ml) gin
½ oz (15 ml) Campari
¾ oz (22 ml) lemon juice
½ oz (15 ml) passionfruit syrup (p 499)

Old Friend

Jim Meehan, Chefs Club, Aspen, 2012
1½ oz (45 ml) gin
½ oz (15 ml) Campari
¼ oz (7 ml) St Germain Elderflower Liqueur
¾ oz (22 ml) pink grapefruit juice
1 teaspoon (5 ml) lemon juice
Garnish: lemon twist (discard)

Pegu Club Cocktail

"Harry" of Ciro's ABC of Mixing Cocktails, *Harry MacElhone, 1923*
2 oz (60 ml) gin
¾ oz (22 ml) orange curaçao (p 498)
¾ oz (22 ml) lime juice
1 dash orange bitters
2 dashes Angostura Bitters
Garnish: lime wedge

Red Lion

A. Tarling
Café Royal Cocktail Book, *W.J. Tarling, 1937*
2 oz (60 ml) gin
½ oz (15 ml) orange curaçao (p 498)
½ oz (15 ml) orange juice
½ oz (15 ml) lemon juice
Garnish: lemon twist (discard)

South Slope

Michael Madrusan, PDT, NYC, 2007
1 oz (30 ml) gin
¾ oz (22 ml) Cocchi Americano
½ oz (15 ml) Aperol
½ oz (15 ml) Pierre Ferrand Dry Curaçao
¾ oz (22 ml) lemon juice
Garnish: lemon twist (discard)

Star Daisy

Esquire Drink Book, *1956*
¾ oz (22 ml) gin
¾ oz (22 ml) bonded apple brandy
¾ oz (22 ml) orange curaçao (p 498)
¾ oz (22 ml) lemon juice
Garnish: lemon twist (discard)

Stranger Things

Liana Oster, NoMad London, London, 2021
1 oz (30 ml) gin
½ oz (15 ml) St Germain Elderflower Liqueur
½ oz (15 ml) Granny Smith apple juice
½ oz (15 ml) lime juice
½ oz (15 ml) orgeat
1 teaspoon (5 ml) aquavit
1 drop yuzu juice

Thumbs Up!

Michael McIlroy, Milk & Honey, NYC, 2009
1 oz (30 ml) gin
½ oz (15 ml) Aperol
½ oz (15 ml) Green Chartreuse
½ oz (15 ml) maraschino liqueur
¾ oz (22 ml) lime juice
Garnish: cherry

Tokyo Joe

Mari Kamata, The Peninsula Tokyo, Tokyo
1 oz (30 ml) gin
¾ oz (22 ml) umeshu
⅓ oz (10 ml) Drambuie
1 oz (30 ml) unsweetened cranberry juice
⅓ oz (10 ml) lemon juice

Tom & Jerez

Tim McCarthy, Hawksmoor, London
¾ oz (22 ml) gin
¾ oz (22 ml) Manzanilla Sherry
¾ oz (22 ml) pear liqueur
¾ oz (22 ml) lemon juice
½ teaspoon (2.5 ml) orgeat

Twentieth Century

C.A. Tuck
Café Royal Cocktail Book, *W.J. Tarling, 1937*
1½ oz (45 ml) gin
¾ oz (22 ml) Cocchi Americano
¾ oz (22 ml) white crème de cacao
¾ oz (22 ml) lemon juice
Garnish: lemon twist (discard)

Volare

Paul Hammond and Priscilla Leong
¾ oz (22 ml) gin
¾ oz (22 ml) Cocchi Americano
¾ oz (22 ml) Manzanilla Sherry
¼ oz (7 ml) white crème de cacao
⅓ oz (10 ml) lemon juice
¼ oz (7 ml) maple syrup
2 dashes chocolate bitters
1 dash Angostura Bitters
Garnish: lemon twist (discard)

Add all ingredients to a shaker, then shake with ice and strain into a frozen coupe.

Wibble
Dick Bradsell, The Player, London, 1999
1 oz (30 ml) gin
1 oz (30 ml) sloe gin
¼ oz (7 ml) crème de mûre
1 oz (30 ml) pink grapefruit juice
1 teaspoon (5 ml) lemon juice
1 teaspoon (5 ml) simple syrup
Garnish: lemon twist (discard)

Yellow
Franck Audoux, Cravan, Paris, 2018
¾ oz (20 ml) gin
¾ oz (20 ml) Suze
¾ oz (20 ml) Yellow Chartreuse
¾ oz (20 ml) lemon juice
Garnish: 2 lemon twists (discard)

RUM & CANE SPIRIT

Canadian
(Daisy with Jamaican dark rum)
Just Cocktails, *W. C. Whitfield, 1939*
1½ oz (45 ml) Jamaican dark rum
¾ oz (22 ml) orange curaçao (p 498)
¾ oz (22 ml) lemon juice
Garnish: lemon twist (discard)

Daisy de Santiago
The Gentleman's Companion, *Charles H. Baker Jr., 1939*
2 oz (60 ml) light rum
1 oz (30 ml) lime juice
½ oz (15 ml) simple syrup
¼ oz (7 ml) Yellow Chartreuse, to float
Shake and strain into a small wine glass with cracked ice, then float the Chartreuse.
Garnish: mint sprig

Gloom Chaser Cocktail
Barflies and Cocktails, *Harry MacElhone, 1927*
1½ oz (45 ml) light rum
¾ oz (22 ml) orange curaçao (p 498)
¾ oz (22 ml) lemon juice
1 teaspoon (5 ml) grenadine (p 496)
Garnish: lemon twist (discard)

Good Cocktail
Turk Dietrich
1½ oz (45 ml) gold rum
½ oz (15 ml) Tempus Fugit Gran Classico Bitter
¾ oz (22 ml) lemon juice
½ oz (15 ml) orgeat
Garnish: lemon twist (discard)

Maestro's Breakfast
Yao Wong, The Elysian, Melbourne
1½ oz (45 ml) aged dark rum
½ oz (15 ml) orange curaçao (p 498)
¾ oz (22 ml) lemon juice
2 dashes Angostura Bitters
1 teaspoon (6 g) orange marmalade
Stir all ingredients in a shaker to combine, then shake with ice and strain into a frozen coupe.
Garnish: lemon twist (discard)

Mañana
The Fine Art of Mixing Drinks, *David A. Embury, 1948*
2 oz (60 ml) light rum
½ oz (15 ml) apricot brandy
¾ oz (22 ml) lemon juice
½ oz (15 ml) grenadine (p 496)
Garnish: lemon twist (discard)

Morning Rose
The Fine Art of Mixing Drinks, *David A. Embury, 1948*
1½ oz (45 ml) light rum
½ oz (15 ml) triple sec
¾ oz (22 ml) lemon juice
½ oz (15 ml) grenadine (p 496)
Garnish: lemon twist (discard)

Santa Cruz Rum Daisy
The Bar-Tender's Guide, *Jerry Thomas, 1887*
1½ oz (45 ml) Barbados dark rum
⅜ oz (11 ml) maraschino liqueur
¾ oz (22 ml) lemon juice
⅜ oz (11 ml) simple syrup

The Culross Cocktail
The Savoy Cocktail Book, *Harry Craddock, 1930*
1 oz (30 ml) light rum
1 oz (30 ml) Cocchi Americano
½ oz (15 ml) apricot brandy
¾ oz (22 ml) lemon juice
Garnish: lemon twist (discard)

The Southern Cross
The Flowing Bowl, *William Schmidt, 1891*
¾ oz (22 ml) aged dark rum
¾ oz (22 ml) Cognac
½ oz (15 ml) Pierre Ferrand Dry Curaçao
¾ oz (22 ml) lemon juice
¼ oz (7 ml) simple syrup
Garnish: lemon twist (discard)

21st Century
Brandon Bramhall, Attaboy, Nashville
1½ oz (45 ml) Jamaican dark rum
¾ oz (22 ml) blanc vermouth
½ oz (15 ml) white crème de cacao
¾ oz (22 ml) lemon juice
Garnish: lemon twist (discard)

AGAVE

Barracuda (Alicia Perry and Anthony Schmidt Recipe)
Alicia Perry and Anthony Schmidt, The Lafayette Hotel and Club, San Diego, 2023
1½ oz (45 ml) mezcal
½ oz (15 ml) Pierre Ferrand Dry Curaçao
¼ oz (7 ml) unaged rhum agricole
¾ oz (22 ml) lime juice
½ oz (15 ml) orgeat
Serve in a frozen double rocks glass with ice.
Garnish: lime wedge

Butterfly Knife
Michael McCollum, Attaboy, Nashville
1½ oz (45 ml) blanco tequila
½ oz (15 ml) white crème de cacao
1 oz (30 ml) lime juice
¾ oz (22 ml) grenadine (p 496)
2 dashes Scrappy's Bitters Fire Tincture

Add all ingredients to a shaker, then shake with ice and strain into a frozen coupe.

Cadillac Margarita
(aka **Grand Margarita**)
El Torito restaurants, California, 1980s
1½ oz (45 ml) blanco tequila
½ oz (15 ml) Grand Marnier
¾ oz (22 ml) lime juice
1 teaspoon (5 ml) simple syrup
Garnish: salt half-rim (optional) and lime wedge

Chingón
Brian Miller, Death & Co, NYC, 2009
1¾ oz (52 ml) reposado tequila
¼ oz (7 ml) Bénédictine
½ oz (15 ml) orange juice
½ oz (15 ml) lime juice
½ oz (15 ml) orgeat
Garnish: orange twist (discard)

Division Bell
Phil Ward, Mayahuel, NYC, 2009
1 oz (30 ml) mezcal
¾ oz (22 ml) Aperol
½ oz (15 ml) maraschino liqueur
¾ oz (22 ml) lime juice
Garnish: grapefruit twist (discard)

Escape Plan
Conor Johns, Red Hook Tavern, NYC, 2021
1 oz (30 ml) blanco tequila
½ oz (15 ml) Suze
½ oz (15 ml) St Germain Elderflower Liqueur
1 oz (30 ml) lime juice
¾ oz (22 ml) cucumber syrup (p 495)
3 dashes absinthe
Serve in a frozen double rocks glass with ice.
Garnish: bachelor's button flower on a cucumber wheel

Margaux-rita
Michael Madrusan, Bar Margaux, Melbourne, 2019
1 oz (30 ml) blanco tequila
½ oz (15 ml) Suze
½ oz (15 ml) Pierre Ferrand Dry Curaçao
¾ oz (22 ml) lime juice
¼ oz (7 ml) simple syrup
2 dashes orange bitters
2 dashes absinthe
Garnish: salt half-rim (optional) and lime wedge

Naked & Famous
Joaquín Simó, Death & Co, NYC, 2011
¾ oz (22 ml) mezcal
¾ oz (22 ml) Yellow Chartreuse
¾ oz (22 ml) Aperol
¾ oz (22 ml) lime juice

Ninth Wonder
Erick Castro
¾ oz (22 ml) blanco tequila
¾ oz (22 ml) Ancho Reyes Original
¾ oz (22 ml) white crème de cacao
¾ oz (22 ml) lime juice
Garnish: lime wheel garnish

Other Word
The Varnish, Los Angeles
1½ oz (45 ml) mezcal
½ oz (15 ml) Yellow Chartreuse
¾ oz (22 ml) lime juice
1 teaspoon (5 ml) maraschino liqueur
1 teaspoon (5 ml) agave syrup (p 494)
2 drops saline solution (p 493)
Serve in a frozen double rocks glass with ice.
Garnish: lime twist

Pinky Gonzales
Trader Vic's Bartender's Guide, *Trader Vic, 1972*
2 oz (60 ml) blanco tequila
⅜ oz (11 ml) orange curaçao (p 498)
¾ oz (22 ml) lime juice
⅜ oz (11 ml) orgeat
2 dashes Angostura Bitters
Serve in a frozen double rocks glass with ice.
Garnish: orange half-wheel and mint sprig

Repossession
Leo Robitschek, The NoMad Bar, NYC
1 oz (30 ml) reposado tequila
¾ oz (22 ml) Amontillado Sherry
½ oz (15 ml) apricot brandy
½ oz (15 ml) lemon juice
¼ oz (7 ml) cane syrup (p 494)
½ teaspoon (2.5 ml) mezcal, to float
Shake with ice and strain into a double rocks glass with ice, then float mezcal.

Shakedown Street
Rhiannon Enlil, New Orleans
1½ oz (45 ml) blanco tequila
½ oz (15 ml) Aperol
¾ oz (22 ml) lemon juice
¼ oz (7 ml) agave syrup (p 494)
1 cucumber wheel
Press cucumber with agave syrup, add remaining ingredients and shake with ice, then strain into a double rocks glass with ice.
Garnish: cucumber wheel

Smoked Margarita
Nathan McCarley-O'Neill, Torrisi, NYC, 2024
2 oz (60 ml) mezcal
½ oz (15 m) Naranja Orange Liqueur (or triple sec)
¼ oz (7 ml) Nixta Licor de Elote
¾ oz (22 ml) lime juice
½ oz (15 ml) cane syrup (p 494)
2 dashes orange bitters
Serve in a frozen double rocks glass with ice.
Garnish: smoked and torched baby corn

Add all ingredients to a shaker, then shake with ice and strain into a frozen coupe.

Spanish Margarita

Toby Maloney, 2007

2 oz (60 ml) blanco tequila
¾ oz (22 ml) Pierre Ferrand Dry Curaçao
¼ oz (7 ml) Licor 43
¾ oz (22 ml) lime juice
¼ oz (7 ml) simple syrup
7 drops Bittermens Hellfire Habanero Shrub

Serve in a frozen double rocks glass with ice.

Garnish: lime wedge and 5 drops of Bittermens Hellfire Habanero Shrub

Spicy Margarita (Nathan McCarley-O'Neill Recipe)

Nathan McCarley-O'Neill, Torrisi, NYC, 2024

1¾ oz (52 ml) Volcán de mi Tierra Blanco Tequila
¾ oz (22 ml) Naranja Orange Liqueur (or triple sec)
¼ oz (7 ml) Pueblo Viejo Blanco Tequila
½ oz (15 ml) red capsicum (red pepper) juice
¼ oz (7 ml) cane syrup (p 494)
6 dashes MFG spicy bitters (p 505)
4 dashes Oaxacan bitters (p 505)

Serve in a frozen double rocks glass with ice.

Garnish: half a red jalapeño

Sudden Death

Alicia Perry and Anthony Schmidt, Quixote, San Diego, 2023

1½ oz (45 ml) sotol
¾ oz (22 ml) Cappelletti Pasubio Vino Amaro
¾ oz (22 ml) St Germain Elderflower Liqueur
¾ oz (22 ml) lemon juice
¼ oz (7 ml) simple syrup
1 dash absinthe

Serve in a frozen double rocks glass with ice.

Garnish: dahlia flower

Tequila Daisy

A Book of Appetizers, *Helen Evans Brown, 1958*

2 oz (60 ml) blanco tequila
¾ oz (22 ml) lemon juice
¾ oz (22 ml) grenadine (p 496)

▼ The drink's first written mention appeared in *The Moville Mail*, an Iowa newspaper, in 1936.

Tía Mia

Ivy Mix, Lani Kai, NYC, 2010

1 oz (30 ml) mezcal
1 oz (30 ml) Jamaican dark rum
¼ oz (7 ml) Pierre Ferrand Dry Curaçao
½ oz (15 ml) orgeat
¾ oz (22 ml) lime juice

Serve in a frozen double rocks glass with ice.

Garnish: lime wheel, pineapple frond and edible orchid

Ultima Palabra

Simone De Luca, High Road House, London

¾ oz (22 ml) mezcal
¾ oz (22 ml) Green Chartreuse
⅜ oz (11 ml) maraschino liqueur
¾ oz (22 ml) pineapple juice
¾ oz (22 ml) lime juice
⅜ oz (11 ml) simple syrup
Garnish: cherry

Yuzu Serrano Margarita

Nathan McCarley-O'Neill, Torrisi, NYC, 2024

2 oz (60 ml) blanco tequila (preferably Pueblo Viejo Blanco Tequila)
½ oz (15 ml) Pierre Ferrand Dry Curaçao Yuzu Late Harvest
1 oz (30 ml) pineapple juice
1 oz (30 ml) lime juice
½ oz (15 ml) cane syrup (p 494)
4 dashes MFG spicy bitters (p 505)
2 cucumber wheels

Press cucumber with cane syrup, add remaining ingredients and shake with ice, then strain into a frozen double rocks glass with ice.

Garnish: pineapple ring and thinly sliced cucumber ribbon wrapped around a cocktail skewer

BRANDY

Biarritz

(aka **Cognac Daisy**)
The Fine Art of Mixing Drinks, *David A. Embury, 1948*

1½ oz (45 ml) Cognac
¾ oz (22 ml) orange curaçao (p 498)
¾ oz (22 ml) lemon juice
Garnish: lemon twist (discard)

▼ Add 2 dashes of Angostura Bitters to make the **Alabazam** from *American & Other Drinks*, Leo Engel, 1878.

Brandy Daisy

The Bar-Tender's Guide, *Jerry Thomas, 1887*

1½ oz (45 ml) Cognac
¾ oz (22 ml) orange curaçao (p 498)
½ oz (15 ml) Jamaican dark rum
¾ oz (22 ml) lemon juice
Garnish: lemon twist (discard)

Brandy Daisy (Bar La Florida Recipe)

Bar La Florida Cocktails, *1939*

1½ oz (45 ml) Spanish brandy (preferably Cardenal Mendoza Solera Gran Reserva Brandy de Jerez)
½ oz (15 ml) Yellow Chartreuse
¾ oz (22 ml) lemon juice
¼ oz (7 ml) simple syrup
2 dashes Angostura Bitters
6–8 mint leaves

Serve in a frozen double rocks glass with ice.

Garnish: mint sprig

Brandy Daisy (Harry Johnson Recipe)

New and Improved Illustrated Bartender's Manual, *Harry Johnson, 1888*

1½ oz (45 ml) Cognac
½ oz (15 ml) Yellow Chartreuse
¾ oz (22 ml) lemon juice
¼ oz (7 ml) simple syrup
Garnish: lemon twist (discard) and raspberry

Add all ingredients to a shaker, then shake with ice and strain into a frozen coupe.

Calvados Sour
(Calvados Daisy with orange bitters)
American Bar, *Frank P. Newman, 1904*
1½ oz (45 ml) Calvados
¾ oz (22 ml) orange curaçao (p 498)
¾ oz (22 ml) lemon juice
2 dashes orange bitters
Garnish: lemon twist (discard)

Charlie Chaplin
Old Waldorf Bar Days, *Albert Stevens Crockett, 1931*
1½ oz (45 ml) Cognac
½ oz (15 ml) sloe gin
½ oz (15 ml) apricot brandy
¾ oz (22 ml) lime juice
Garnish: lime wedge

Classic Cocktail
The Savoy Cocktail Book, *Harry Craddock, 1930*
1½ oz (45 ml) Cognac
⅜ oz (11 ml) orange curaçao (p 498)
⅜ oz (11 ml) maraschino liqueur
¾ oz (22 ml) lemon juice
Garnish: lemon twist (discard)

Country Gentleman
(Daisy with bonded apple brandy)
The Fine Art of Mixing Drinks, *David A. Embury, 1948*
1½ oz (45 ml) bonded apple brandy
¾ oz (22 ml) orange curaçao (p 498)
¾ oz (22 ml) lemon juice
Garnish: lemon twist (discard)

Forget Me Not
Rob Libecans, Caretaker's Cottage
1½ oz (45 ml) Cognac
½ oz (15 ml) Giffard Crème de Pêche de Vigne
¾ oz (22 ml) lemon juice
⅜ oz (11 ml) honey syrup (p 496)
Garnish: lemon twist (discard)

Honey Moon Cocktail
Recipes for Mixed Drinks, *Hugo R. Ensslin, 1917*
1½ oz (45 ml) bonded apple brandy
½ oz (15 ml) Bénédictine
½ oz (15 ml) orange curaçao (p 498)
¾ oz (22 ml) lemon juice
Garnish: lemon twist (discard)

Marigny
Jason E. Clapham, St. Edward's MCR, Oxford, 2021
¾ oz (22 ml) Cognac
¾ oz (22 ml) bonded apple brandy
½ oz (15 ml) Green Chartreuse
¾ oz (22 ml) lemon juice
½ oz (15 ml) simple syrup
2 dashes Angostura Bitters
Garnish: lemon twist (discard)

Novel Daisy
Daniel Zacharczuk, The Varnish, Los Angeles, 2024
¾ oz (22 ml) pisco
¾ oz (22 ml) añejo tequila
¾ oz (22 ml) orange curaçao (p 498)
¾ oz (22 ml) lemon juice
Garnish: orange twist (discard)

Peaches en Regalia
Joshua Perez, Bar Trench, Tokyo, 2024
1 oz (30 ml) VSOP Armagnac (or Cognac)
¾ oz (22 ml) Lillet Blanc
½ oz (15 ml) Giffard Crème de Pêche de Vigne
¾ oz (22 ml) lemon juice
4 dashes absinthe
Garnish: lemon twist
▼ "Named after the epic Frank Zappa song."

Queen Bee Cocktail
The South American Gentleman's Companion, *Charles H. Baker Jr., 1951*
1½ oz (45 ml) bonded apple brandy
⅜ oz (11 ml) orange curaçao (p 498)
¾ oz (22 ml) lemon juice
⅜ oz (11 ml) honey syrup (p 496)

Soother
Straub's Manual of Mixed Drinks, *Jacques Straub, 1913*
¾ oz (22 ml) Cognac
¾ oz (22 ml) bonded apple brandy
¾ oz (22 ml) orange curaçao (p 498)
¾ oz (22 ml) lemon juice
Garnish: lemon twist (discard)

Southern
A Life-Time Collection of 688 Recipes for Drinks, *1934*
¾ oz (22 ml) Cognac
¾ oz (22 ml) bonded apple brandy
¾ oz (22 ml) orange curaçao (p 498)
¾ oz (22 ml) lemon juice
Pebble whip, pour into a frozen double rocks glass with crushed ice, then shimmy and top with more crushed ice.
Garnish: lemon twist (discard)

Sweet and Lovely
The Fine Art of Mixing Drinks, *David A. Embury, 1948*
1¼ oz (37 ml) bonded apple brandy
1 oz (30 ml) gin
⅜ oz (11 ml) maraschino liqueur
¾ oz (22 ml) lime juice
⅜ oz (11 ml) grenadine (p 496)
Garnish: lime wedge

The Elder Jack
Toby Maloney, 2008
1½ oz (45 ml) bonded apple brandy
½ oz (15 ml) St Germain Elderflower Liqueur
¾ oz (22 ml) lime juice
¾ oz (22 ml) grenadine (p 496)
2 dashes orange bitters
Garnish: orange twist (discard)

Troika
Andy Chu, One or Two, Melbourne, 2024
1¼ oz (37 ml) Cognac
½ oz (15 ml) Calvados
½ oz (15 ml) orange curaçao (p 498)
¾ oz (22 ml) lemon juice
¼ oz (7 ml) simple syrup
2 dashes orange bitters
Garnish: lemon twist (discard)

Willard Hotel
The Willard, Washington DC
Ted Saucier's Bottoms Up, *Ted Saucier, 1951*
2 oz (60 ml) Cognac
½ oz (15 ml) apricot brandy
¼ oz (7 ml) Giffard Crème de Pêche de Vigne
¾ oz (22 ml) lime juice
Garnish: lime wedge

Add all ingredients to a shaker, then shake with ice and strain into a frozen coupe.

AMERICAN WHISKEY

Barracuda
Lynnette Marrero and Jessica Gonzalez, 2015
¾ oz (22 ml) bourbon
¾ oz (22 ml) Oloroso Sherry
¾ oz (22 ml) Aperol
¾ oz (22 ml) lemon juice
½ oz (15 ml) simple syrup
Garnish: lemon twist (discard)

Better Than Ever
Tom Lasher-Walker, Miami, 2020
¾ oz (22 ml) rye whiskey (100% proof)
¾ oz (22 ml) Aperol
¾ oz (22 ml) Giffard Banane du Brésil et des Caraïbes
¾ oz (22 ml) lime juice
2 dashes Angostura Bitters
Garnish: lime wedge

Bird on a Wire
Toby Maloney, 2011
1 oz (60 ml) bourbon
½ oz (15 ml) pear liqueur
¾ oz (22 ml) lemon juice
½ oz (15 ml) cinnamon syrup (p 495)
2 dashes Fee Brothers Old Fashion Aromatic Bitters
Garnish: lemon twist (discard)

Bluegrass Cocktail
Jayne's Bartender's Guide, *1934*
1½ oz (45 ml) rye whiskey
½ oz (15 ml) Bénédictine
¾ oz (22 ml) lemon juice
½ oz (15 ml) grenadine (p 496)
Garnish: lemon twist (discard)

Commodore No. 2
Old Waldorf Bar Days, *Albert Stevens Crockett, 1931*
1½ oz (45 ml) bourbon
½ oz (15 ml) white crème de cacao
½ oz (15 ml) lemon juice
½ oz (15 ml) grenadine (p 496)
Pebble whip, pour into a frozen double rocks glass with crushed ice, then shimmy and top with more crushed ice.
Garnish: cherry and lemon wedge

Final Ward
Phil Ward, Death & Co, NYC, 2007
¾ oz (22 ml) rye whiskey
¾ oz (22 ml) Green Chartreuse
⅜ oz (11 ml) maraschino liqueur
¾ oz (22 ml) lemon juice
⅜ oz (11 ml) simple syrup
Garnish: cherry

Honky-Tonk
Angus Payne, The Everleigh, Melbourne, 2021
¾ oz (22 ml) bourbon
¾ oz (22 ml) Amaro Montenegro
¾ oz (22 ml) lime juice
½ oz (15 ml) grenadine (p 496)
Garnish: lime wedge

Morning Glory Cocktail
The Bar-Tender's Guide, *Jerry Thomas, 1887*
¾ oz (22 ml) rye whiskey
¾ oz (22 ml) Cognac
¾ oz (22 ml) orange curaçao (p 498)
¾ oz (22 ml) lemon juice
2 dashes absinthe
2 dashes Angostura Bitters
Garnish: lemon twist (discard)

19th Century
Brian Miller, Death & Co, NYC, 2009
1½ oz (45 ml) bourbon
¾ oz (22 ml) Lillet Rouge
¾ oz (22 ml) white crème de cacao
¾ oz (22 ml) lemon juice

Paper Plane
Sam Ross, Milk & Honey, NYC, 2008
¾ oz (22 ml) bourbon
¾ oz (22 ml) Aperol
¾ oz (22 ml) Amaro Nonino
¾ oz (22 ml) lemon juice

Southern Cocktail
Shake 'Em Up!, *Virginia Elliott and Phil D. Strong, 1930*
2 oz (60 ml) rye whiskey (or bourbon)
¼ oz (7 ml) Bénédictine
¾ oz (22 ml) lemon juice
½ oz (15 ml) grenadine (p 496)
Garnish: cherry

Whiskey Daisy
The Bar-Tender's Guide, *Jerry Thomas, 1887*
2 oz (60 ml) rye whiskey (or bourbon)
¾ oz (22 ml) lemon juice
½ oz (15 ml) orgeat
¼ oz (7 ml) simple syrup
Garnish: lemon twist (discard)

From *The Ideal Bartender* (Tom Bullock, 1917):

Here's to love and laughter, and a drink now and after!

Whiskey Daisy (Harry Johnson Recipe)
New and Improved Illustrated Bartender's Manual, *Harry Johnson, 1888*
1½ oz (45 ml) rye whiskey
½ oz (15 ml) Yellow Chartreuse
⅜ oz (11 ml) lemon juice
⅜ oz (11 ml) lime juice
¼ oz (7 ml) simple syrup
Garnish: lemon twist (discard) and raspberry on a cocktail skewer

You and I
The Fine Art of Mixing Drinks, *David A. Embury, 1948*
2 oz (60 ml) bourbon
¾ oz (22 ml) orange curaçao (p 498)
¾ oz (22 ml) lemon juice
Garnish: lemon twist (discard)

Add all ingredients to a shaker, then shake with ice and strain into a frozen coupe.

SCOTCH

Artist's Special
Artists Bar, Paris
Barflies and Cocktails,
Harry MacElhone, 1927
¾ oz (22 ml) Scotch
¾ oz (22 ml) Oloroso Sherry
¾ oz (22 ml) lemon juice
¾ oz (22 ml) groseille (redcurrant) syrup or grenadine (p 496)
Garnish: lemon twist (discard)

Blood and Sand Cocktail
The Savoy Cocktail Book,
Harry Craddock, 1930
1 oz (30 ml) Scotch
¾ oz (22 ml) sweet vermouth
¾ oz (22 ml) Heering Cherry Liqueur
¾ oz (22 ml) orange juice
¼ oz (7 ml) lemon juice

Brigadier
Tom Lasher-Walker, The Savoy, London, 2014
1½ oz (45 ml) Scotch
¾ oz (22 ml) white crème de cacao
¾ oz (22 ml) lemon juice
1 teaspoon (5 ml) grenadine (p 496)
Garnish: lemon twist (discard)

Cutter's Daisy
(Scotch Daisy with a spritz of Islay Scotch)
1½ oz (45 ml) Scotch
¾ oz (22 ml) orange curaçao (p 498)
¾ oz (22 ml) lemon juice
Garnish: lemon twist (discard) and a spritz of Islay Scotch

Dundee Special
Tom Lasher-Walker, Fresh Kills, NYC, 2018
¾ oz (22 ml) Islay Whisky
¾ oz (22 ml) Drambuie
¾ oz (22 ml) white crème de cacao
¾ oz (22 ml) lemon juice
Garnish: lemon twist (discard)
▾ Inspired by the Dundee from *Jones' Complete Barguide*, Stan Jones, 1977.

18th Century
Brandon Bramhall, Attaboy, Nashville
1½ oz (45 ml) Scotch
¾ oz (22 ml) sweet vermouth
½ oz (15 ml) white crème de cacao
¾ oz (22 ml) lemon juice
2 orange half-wheels

Flannel Shirt
Jeffrey Morgenthaler, Pacific Standard, Portland, 2012
1¾ oz (52 ml) Scotch
½ oz (15 ml) Amaro Averna
1½ oz (45 ml) non-alcoholic still apple cider (or cloudy apple juice)
¼ oz (7 ml) lemon juice
1 teaspoon (5 ml) Demerara syrup (p 495)
½ teaspoon (2.5 ml) pimento (allspice) dram
2 dashes Angostura Bitters
Serve in a frozen double rocks glass with ice.
Garnish: orange twist

Pete's Word
(Last Word with Islay Scotch)
Phil Ward, Death & Co, NYC, 2008
¾ oz (22 ml) Islay Scotch
¾ oz (22 ml) Green Chartreuse
⅜ oz (11 ml) maraschino liqueur
¾ oz (22 ml) lemon juice
⅜ oz (11 ml) simple syrup
Garnish: cherry

Smoked Cocktail
(Scotch Daisy with mint)
Bar La Florida Cocktails, *1935*
1½ oz (45 ml) Scotch
¾ oz (22 ml) orange curaçao (p 498)
¾ oz (22 ml) lemon juice
6–8 mint leaves
Garnish: lemon twist (discard)

Wildest Redhead
Meaghan Dorman, Lantern's Keep, NYC, 2011
1½ oz (45 ml) Scotch
¾ oz (22 ml) lemon juice
½ oz (15 ml) honey syrup (p 496)
¼ oz (7 ml) pimento (allspice) dram
¼ oz (7 ml) Heering Cherry Liqueur, to coat
Drizzle Heering Cherry Liqueur over ice in a frozen double rocks glass, then shake remaining ingredients with ice and strain into the double rocks glass.

WORLD WHISK(E)Y

Canadian Glory
Max Müller
Café Royal Cocktail Book,
W.J. Tarling, 1937
2 oz (60 ml) Canadian whisky
⅜ oz (11 ml) orange curaçao (p 498)
⅜ oz (11 ml) apricot brandy
¾ oz (22 ml) lemon juice
Garnish: lemon twist (discard)

FORTIFIED & LIQUEUR

Discreet Charm of the Sherry Daisy
Chad Solomon, Midnight Rambler, Dallas, 2018
1¼ oz (37 ml) Fino Sherry
⅜ oz (11 ml) triple sec
¼ oz (7 ml) absinthe
½ oz (15 ml) lime juice
⅜ oz (11 ml) simple syrup
2 drops saline solution (p 493)
Garnish: orange twist (discard), prior to straining the cocktail into the glass
▾ A nod to Luis Buñuel's film *The Discreet Charm of the Bourgeoisie.*

Add all ingredients to a shaker, then shake with ice and strain into a frozen coupe.

Soother (**Michael Madrusan Recipe**)
Michael Madrusan, Milk & Honey, NYC, 2009
¾ oz (22 ml) orange curaçao (p 498)
½ oz (15 ml) Cognac
½ oz (15 ml) bonded apple brandy
½ oz (15 ml) Jamaican dark rum
¾ oz (22 ml) lemon juice
Garnish: lemon twist (discard)

Sidecar

Add all ingredients to a shaker, then shake with ice and strain into a frozen coupe.

GIN

Blue Train Cocktail
(Chelsea Sidecar with blue pea flower extract)
The Savoy Cocktail Book, *Harry Craddock, 1930*
1½ oz (45 ml) gin
½ oz (15 ml) triple sec
¾ oz (22 ml) lemon juice
1 teaspoon (5 ml) simple syrup
2 drops Wild Hibiscus B'Lure Butterfly Pea Flower Extract
Garnish: lemon twist (discard)

Blue Train Cocktail (**Hyman Gale and Gerald F. Marco Recipe**)
(Chelsea Sidecar with crème de violette)
The How and When, *Hyman Gale and Gerald F. Marco, 1937*
1½ oz (45 ml) gin
½ oz (15 ml) triple sec
¾ oz (22 ml) lemon juice
1 teaspoon (5 ml) simple syrup
1 teaspoon (5 ml) crème de violette
Garnish: lemon twist (discard)

Chelsea Sidecar
(aka **White Lady** or White Lady without egg white)
The Savoy Cocktail Book, *Harry Craddock, 1930*
Old Mr. Boston Deluxe Official Bartender's Guide, *Leo Cotton, 1935*
1½ oz (45 ml) gin
½ oz (15 ml) triple sec
¾ oz (22 ml) lemon juice
1 teaspoon (5 ml) simple syrup
Garnish: lemon twist (discard)
▼ Add 2 dashes of Angostura Bitters to make the **Fine and Dandy Cocktail** from *The Savoy Cocktail Book*, Harry Craddock, 1930.

Corpse Reviver No. Blue
Jacob Briars, 2007
¾ oz (22 ml) gin
¾ oz (22 ml) blue curaçao
¾ oz (22 ml) Cocchi Americano
¾ oz (22 ml) lemon juice
2 dashes absinthe
Garnish: lemon twist (discard)

Corpse Reviver No. 2
The Savoy Cocktail Book, *Harry Craddock, 1930*
¾ oz (22 ml) gin
¾ oz (22 ml) Cocchi Americano
¾ oz (22 ml) lemon juice
½ oz (15 ml) triple sec
1 teaspoon (5 ml) simple syrup
2 dashes absinthe
Garnish: lemon twist (discard)

Corpse Reviver No. 4
Will "Oxy" Oxenham
⅔ oz (20 ml) gin
⅔ oz (20 ml) Cocchi Americano
⅔ oz (20 ml) triple sec
⅔ oz (20 ml) lemon juice
⅔ oz (20 ml) fennel juice
1 teaspoon (5 ml) simple syrup
Garnish: lemon twist (discard)

Cosmopolitan (**Charles Christopher Mueller Recipe**)
Pioneers of Mixing at Elite Bars: 1903–1933, *Charles Christopher Mueller, 1936*
2 oz (60 ml) gin
¼ oz (7 ml) triple sec
¾ oz (22 ml) lemon juice
½ oz (15 ml) raspberry syrup (p 500)
Garnish: raspberry

Little Devil Cocktail
Fitz, Ciro's, London
Barflies and Cocktails, *Harry MacElhone, 1927*
¾ oz (22 ml) gin
¾ oz (22 ml) light rum
½ oz (15 ml) triple sec
¾ oz (22 ml) lemon juice
1 teaspoon (5 ml) simple syrup
Garnish: lemon twist (discard)

Loudspeaker Cocktail
(aka **Announcer** or **Winchell**)
Trader Vic's Bartender's Guide, *Trader Vic, 1947*
¾ oz (22 ml) gin
¾ oz (22 ml) Cognac
¾ oz (22 ml) lemon juice
½ oz (15 ml) triple sec
¼ oz (7 ml) simple syrup
Garnish: lemon twist (discard)

Maiden's Prayer Cocktail (No. 1)
The Savoy Cocktail Book, *Harry Craddock, 1930*
1½ oz (45 ml) gin
½ oz (15 ml) triple sec
1 oz (30 ml) orange juice
½ oz (15 ml) lemon juice
1 teaspoon (5 ml) simple syrup

Queen Elizabeth No. 1
(Chelsea Sidecar with absinthe)
1700 Cocktails for the Man Behind the Bar, *R. de Fleury, 1934*
1½ oz (45 ml) gin
½ oz (15 ml) triple sec
¾ oz (22 ml) lemon juice
1 teaspoon (5 ml) simple syrup
2 dashes absinthe
Garnish: lemon twist (discard)

Add all ingredients to a shaker, then shake with ice and strain into a frozen coupe.

Royal York Special
Royal York Hotel, Toronto
Ted Saucier's Bottoms Up, *Ted Saucier, 1951*
1½ oz (45 ml) gin
½ oz (15 ml) triple sec
1 oz (30 ml) pink grapefruit juice
½ oz (15 ml) lemon juice
1 teaspoon (5 ml) simple syrup
Garnish: lemon twist (discard)

Sherry Lady
Frank Korhumel
Approved Cocktails, *United Kingdom Bartenders' Guild, 1937*
¾ oz (22 ml) gin
¾ oz (22 ml) Manzanilla Sherry
½ oz (15 ml) triple sec
¾ oz (22 ml) lemon juice
¼ oz (7 ml) simple syrup
Garnish: lemon twist (discard)

Sunflower
Sam Ross, Milk & Honey, NYC, 2008
¾ oz (22 ml) gin
¾ oz (22 ml) triple sec
¾ oz (22 ml) St Germain Elderflower Liqueur
¾ oz (22 ml) lemon juice
2 dashes absinthe
Garnish: lemon twist (discard)

Veritas Cocktail
Trader Vic's Bartender's Guide, *Trader Vic, 1947*
1½ oz (45 ml) gin
½ oz (15 ml) triple sec
¾ oz (22 ml) lime juice
1 teaspoon (5 ml) crème de cassis
1 teaspoon (5 ml) simple syrup
Garnish: lemon twist (discard)

Water Lily
Richard Boccato, Little Branch, NYC, 2007
1½ oz (45 ml) gin
½ oz (15 ml) triple sec
½ oz (15 ml) crème de violette
¾ oz (22 ml) lemon juice
1 teaspoon (5 ml) simple syrup
Garnish: orange twist (discard)

Windy City
Nate Gross
Ted Saucier's Bottoms Up, *Ted Saucier, 1951*
1½ oz (45 ml) gin
½ oz (15 ml) triple sec
½ oz (15 ml) lemon juice
½ oz (15 ml) orange juice
1 teaspoon (5 ml) simple syrup
Serve in a frozen double rocks glass with ice.

RUM & CANE SPIRIT

Barbaresque Cocktail
(Sidecar with light rum)
Trader Vic's Bartender's Guide, *Victor Bergeron, 1947*
1½ oz (45 ml) light rum
½ oz (15 ml) triple sec
¾ oz (22 ml) lemon juice
1 teaspoon (5 ml) simple syrup
Garnish: lemon twist (discard)
▼ Add 2 dashes of absinthe to make the **New Life** from *Jones' Complete Barguide*, Stan Jones, 1977.

Dachshund
David Molyneux, The Everleigh, Melbourne, 2018
¾ oz (22 ml) Jamaican dark rum
¾ oz (22 ml) Manzanilla Sherry
½ oz (15 ml) triple sec
¾ oz (22 ml) lemon juice
1 teaspoon (5 ml) simple syrup
Garnish: grapefruit twist

Morning Rose
The Fine Art of Mixing Drinks, *David A. Embury, 1948*
1½ oz (45 ml) light rum
½ oz (15 ml) triple sec
¾ oz (22 ml) lemon juice
½ oz (15 ml) grenadine (p 496)
Garnish: lemon twist (discard)

Palmetto Cocktail
The Stork Club Bar Book, *Lucius Beebe, 1946*
1½ oz (45 ml) light rum
½ oz (15 ml) triple sec
½ oz (15 ml) apricot brandy
¾ oz (22 ml) lemon juice
Garnish: lemon twist (discard)

Rum-Hound Cocktail
(Sidecar with Jamaican dark rum)
The Home Bartender's Guide and Song Book, *Charlie Roe and Jim Schwenck, 1930*
1½ oz (45 ml) Jamaican dark rum
½ oz (15 ml) triple sec
¾ oz (22 ml) lemon juice
1 teaspoon (5 ml) simple syrup
Garnish: lemon twist (discard)

X.Y.Z. Cocktail
(Sidecar with aged dark rum)
The Savoy Cocktail Book, *Harry Craddock, 1930*
1½ oz (45 ml) aged dark rum
¾ oz (22 ml) lemon juice
½ oz (15 ml) triple sec
1 teaspoon (5 ml) simple syrup
Garnish: lemon twist (discard)

AGAVE

Picador
(aka **Tequila Daisy** or **Margarita**)
Café Royal Cocktail Book, *W.J. Tarling, 1937*
2 oz (60 ml) blanco tequila
½ oz (15 ml) triple sec
¾ oz (22 ml) lime juice
1 teaspoon (5 ml) simple syrup
Garnish: lime wedge

Sidewinder (Felix Woods Recipe)
Felix Woods, The Everleigh, Melbourne
¾ oz (22 ml) blanco tequila
¾ oz (22 ml) Yellow Chartreuse
½ oz (15 ml) triple sec
¾ oz (22 ml) lime juice
1 teaspoon (5 ml) simple syrup
Garnish: lime wedge

BRANDY

Between-the-Sheets Cocktail
The Savoy Cocktail Book, *Harry Craddock, 1930*
¾ oz (22 ml) Cognac
¾ oz (22 ml) light rum
½ oz (15 ml) triple sec
¾ oz (22 ml) lemon juice
1 teaspoon (5 ml) simple syrup
Garnish: lemon twist (discard)

Add all ingredients to a shaker, then shake with ice and strain into a frozen coupe.

Deauville Cocktail
The Savoy Cocktail Book,
Harry Craddock, 1930
¾ oz (22 ml) Cognac
¾ oz (22 ml) Calvados
½ oz (15 ml) triple sec
¾ oz (22 ml) lemon juice
1 teaspoon (5 ml) simple syrup
Garnish: lemon twist (discard)

"Hoop La!" Cocktail
(aka **Odd McIntyre** in *1700 Cocktails for the Man Behind the Bar*, R. de Fleury, 1934)
The Savoy Cocktail Book,
Harry Craddock, 1930
¾ oz (22 ml) Cognac
¾ oz (22 ml) Cocchi Americano
½ oz (15 ml) triple sec
¾ oz (22 ml) lemon juice
1 teaspoon (5 ml) simple syrup
Garnish: lemon twist (discard)

Knight
The Fine Art of Mixing Drinks,
David A. Embury, 1948
1½ oz (45 ml) Cognac
⅜ oz (11 ml) Green Chartreuse
⅜ oz (11 ml) triple sec
¾ oz (22 ml) lemon juice
1 teaspoon (5 ml) simple syrup
Garnish: cherry

Mangareva
The Fine Art of Mixing Drinks,
David A. Embury, 1948
1½ oz (45 ml) bonded apple brandy
⅜ oz (11 ml) triple sec
¾ oz (22 ml) lime juice
⅜ oz (11 ml) honey syrup (p 496)
Pebble whip, pour into a frozen double rocks glass with crushed ice, then shimmy and top with more crushed ice.
Garnish: pineapple wedge

Royal Jubilee
(Sidecar with bonded apple brandy)
Harry Craddock
Approved Cocktails, *United Kingdom Bartenders' Guild, 1937*
1½ oz (45 ml) bonded apple brandy
½ oz (15 ml) triple sec
¾ oz (22 ml) lemon juice
1 teaspoon (5 ml) simple syrup
Garnish: lemon twist (discard)

Side-Car Cocktail
(aka **Sidecar**)
Pat MacGarry, Buck's Club, London
Harry's ABC of Mixing Cocktails,
Harry MacElhone, 1923
1½ oz (45 ml) Cognac
½ oz (15 ml) triple sec
¾ oz (22 ml) lemon juice
1 teaspoon (5 ml) simple syrup
Garnish: lemon twist (discard)
▼ Add 2 dashes of Angostura Bitters to make the **Chevalier Cocktail** from *The How and When*, Hyman Gale and Gerald F. Marco, 1937.

Sidecar (Difford's Recipe)
Difford's Guide
1½ oz (45 ml) Cognac
½ oz (15 ml) triple sec
½ oz (15 ml) Pineau des Charentes
¾ oz (22 ml) lemon juice
Garnish: lemon twist (discard)

Solera Sidecar
Joaquín Simó, Death & Co, NYC, 2009
1½ oz (45 ml) Cognac
½ oz (15 ml) Lustau East India Solera Sherry
¼ oz (7 ml) Grand Marnier
¼ oz (7 ml) amaretto
¾ oz (22 ml) lemon juice
¼ oz (7 ml) simple syrup
Garnish: lemon twist (discard)

Tantris Sidecar
Audrey Saunders, Beacon, NYC, 2000
1 oz (30 ml) Cognac
½ oz (15 ml) Calvados
½ oz (15 ml) triple sec
¼ oz (7 ml) Green Chartreuse
¼ oz (7 ml) pineapple juice
½ oz (15 ml) lemon juice
1 teaspoon (5 ml) simple syrup
Garnish: lemon twist (discard)

AMERICAN WHISKEY

Cavendish Corpse Reviver
Michael Madrusan, The Everleigh, Melbourne, 2023
¾ oz (22 ml) bourbon
¾ oz (22 ml) Cocchi Americano
¾ oz (22 ml) Giffard Banane du Brésil et des Caraïbes
¾ oz (22 ml) lemon juice
2 dashes absinthe
Garnish: lemon twist (discard)

Commando Cocktail
(Bourbon Sidecar with absinthe)
Cocktail and Wine Digest,
Oscar Haimo, 1943
1½ oz (45 ml) bourbon
½ oz (15 ml) triple sec
¾ oz (22 ml) lemon juice
1 teaspoon (5 ml) simple syrup
2 dashes absinthe
Garnish: lemon twist (discard)

SCOTCH

Silent Third
(aka **Scotch Sidecar**)
Approved Cocktails, *United Kingdom Bartenders' Guild, 1937*
1½ oz (45 ml) Scotch
½ oz (15 ml) triple sec
¾ oz (22 ml) lemon juice
1 teaspoon (5 ml) simple syrup
Garnish: lemon twist (discard)
▼ Add 2 dashes of orange bitters to make the **Prosperity** from *1700 Cocktails for the Man Behind the Bar*, R. de Fleury, 1934.

Add all ingredients to a shaker, then shake with ice and strain into a frozen coupe.

GIMLET & SHAKE

Gimlet (Fresh Lime Recipe) p 215 (left), Chirulín p 221 (right)

Gimlet & Shake

A short, zesty cocktail shaken with fresh lime and sugar, served in a frozen coupe.

spirit + lime + sugar

Add all ingredients to a shaker, then shake with ice and strain into a frozen coupe.

The earliest references to the Gimlet, such as the mention in *"Harry" of Ciro's ABC of Mixing Cocktails* by Harry MacElhone in 1923, call for gin and Rose's Lime Juice Cordial, stirred down in equal measure. The cocktail is believed to have been created some decades prior by Surgeon Rear-Admiral Sir Thomas Gimlette KCB (1857–1943), who worked up the mix for the Royal Navy to help combat scurvy on long voyages. By the 1860s, British ships were required to carry lime juice for their crews, with the understanding that vitamin C helped prevent the disease. Soon after, sugar was added as a preservative, resulting in packaged and bottled lime cordial.

In 1930, Harry Craddock included two variations of the cocktail in *The Savoy Cocktail Book* – the Gimlet Cocktail, comprising equal parts Plymouth Gin and Rose's Lime Juice Cordial, stirred; and the Gimblet Cocktail, a shaken drink made up of three parts gin and one part fresh lime juice, topped up with soda. The Gimblet Cocktail – or Fresh Gimlet (p 215) as it's known today – is best understood as a Non-traditional Gin Sour (p 155) that uses lime instead of lemon, or a Gin Rickey (p 86) if served tall with soda.

While stirred Gimlets still pop up on contemporary cocktail menus, shaken versions with fresh juice and ice are more prevalent. These shaken Gimlets are either served up in a cocktail glass or in a frozen double rocks glass with ice. Sometimes the latter is preferred to lengthen the drinking experience and allow for more refreshment thanks to the additional dilution. For some, the decision is made based on their preferred glassware. This really is a personal preference, and any of these drinks can be served according to your taste.

In most circles, the Gimlet will be made with gin, or sometimes with vodka, but the formula can apply to variations made with other spirits. When tequila, brandy or whisk(e)y get involved, we often see the cocktail referred to as a Shake. And, of course, if rum is at the heart, we're in the world of the Daiquiri Cocktail (p 230). Whatever you like to call it, when balanced correctly, this crisp cocktail dances between sweet and sour on the palate and has inspired many memorable zesty variations.

The Long Island Bar Gimlet

Toby Cecchini, The Long Island Bar, NYC, 2013
2 oz (60 ml) gin
¾ oz (22 ml) lime juice
1 oz (30 ml) lime cordial (p 497)

Add all ingredients to a shaker, then shake with ice and strain into a frozen coupe. Serve in a double rocks glass with ice.
Garnish: 2 lime wheels

The legendary Toby Cecchini – a native Midwesterner and creator of the modern Cosmopolitan (p 195) – earned his stripes in the 1980s, tending bar across New York City. He is the current owner of The Long Island Bar in Brooklyn, which opened in 2013, as well as the author of *Cosmopolitan: A Bartender's Life* and a regular contributor to major food and beverage publications.

While researching bygone lime cordials for a *New York Times* piece in 2011, Cecchini became something of a purist on the matter of the Gimlet. Although he admits Gimlets with fresh lime were his default recipe for years, he ultimately believes – like many of his contemporaries – that the fresh lime Gimlet is more of a Non-Traditional Sour (a combination of spirit, fresh citrus and sugar, see p 152). Cecchini's research generated a new-found appreciation for the original Gimlet and inspired him to develop his own lime cordial that paid homage to the drink's early days.

On sharing the formula and process behind making that cordial for inclusion in this book, Cecchini said: 'I'm very proud of this one, in that while researching the history of lime cordial for the *Times*, I literally had to reverse-engineer it, because I could find no real recipes out there for lime cordial proper. It took me quite some while to come upon the breakthrough of allowing the acid and sugar to do the requisite curing, without heating it at all, allowing it to retain a freshness not otherwise possible.'

The Long Island Bar Gimlet has become a true modern classic, thanks to Cecchini's appreciation for what Rose's Lime Cordial circa 1920 (prior to its acquisition by a multinational conglomerate) contributed to the cocktail and his success in reinvigorating the traditional recipe.

Infante

Giuseppe González, Dutch Kills, NYC, 2009
2 oz (60 ml) blanco tequila
1 oz (30 ml) lime juice
¾ oz (22 ml) orgeat

Add all ingredients to a shaker, then shake with ice and strain into a frozen coupe. Serve in a double rocks glass with ice.
Garnish: lime wedge and freshly grated nutmeg

The Infante is a warming Margarita riff by veteran bartender Giuseppe González, created during his tenure at Dutch Kills in Queens, New York City in 2009. González was raised in the Bronx until the age of nine, before moving to Puerto Rico and returning to New York City to attend the prestigious Cornell University. Although both his father and grandfather were bartenders, González embarked on his career in the industry later in life, following a transformative stint at Sasha Petraske's Milk & Honey in 2005. Before settling in Las Vegas – where he's currently based – he went on to hold court at New York City institutions such as the Clover Club and Pegu Club, and owned and operated the Suffolk Arms, a cocktail bar on the Lower East Side from 2016 until its closure in 2018.

González's cocktail is named after singer and actor Pedro Infante Cruz, a star from the golden age of Mexican cinema who tragically died in a 1957 plane crash en route to Mexico City. A supreme example of a simple and utterly effective twist on an icon, the Infante replaces the Margarita's orange liqueur with orgeat, an almond syrup infused with a dash of fragrant orange blossom water. The orgeat gives the drink a rounded finish, perfectly suited to the cooler end of summer.

For more drinks on the nutty side, try Non-Traditional Sour, Army & Navy (p 170), or the eternal tiki favourite, the Mai Tai (p 449).

Gimlet

Add all ingredients to a shaker, then shake with ice and strain into a frozen coupe.

VODKA

East 8 Hold-Up
Kevin Armstrong, Milk & Honey, London, 2010
1½ oz (45 ml) vodka
½ oz (15 ml) Aperol
½ oz (15 ml) lime juice
½ oz (15 ml) pineapple juice
½ oz (15 ml) simple syrup
¼ oz (7 ml) passionfruit syrup (p 499)
Serve in a frozen double rocks glass with ice.
Garnish: lime wedge

Italian Job
The Connaught Bar, *Agostino Perrone, Giorgio Bargiani & Maura Milia, 2024*
1½ oz (45 ml) vodka
⅜ oz (11 ml) Campari
1 oz (30 ml) pineapple juice
½ oz (15 ml) lime juice
½ oz (15 ml) passionfruit syrup (p 499)
1 teaspoon (5 g) passionfruit pulp
Garnish: passionfruit half-shell

New Maid
(aka **Russian Maid** or **Vodka Maid**)
Sam Ross, East Side Company Bar, NYC, 2004
2 oz (60 ml) vodka
1 oz (30 ml) lime juice
¾ oz (22 ml) simple syrup
2 cucumber wheels
6–8 mint leaves
Press cucumber with simple syrup, add remaining ingredients and shake with ice, then strain into a frozen coupe.
Garnish: 3 cucumber wheels

Part & Parcel
Toby Maloney, The Violet Hour, Chicago, 2008
1½ oz (45 ml) vodka
½ oz (15 ml) St Germain Elderflower Liqueur
¾ oz (22 ml) pink grapefruit juice
½ oz (15 ml) simple syrup
¼ oz (7 ml) lime juice

The Ivy Gimlet
(aka **Vodka South Side** or **Maisonette** in *Ted Saucier's Bottoms Up*, Ted Saucier, 1951)
The Ivy, Los Angeles
2 oz (60 ml) vodka
1 oz (30 ml) lime juice
¾ oz (22 ml) simple syrup
6–8 mint leaves

West Coast Gimlet
1½ oz (45 ml) vodka
½ oz (15 ml) triple sec
¾ oz (22 ml) lime juice
1 teaspoon (5 ml) simple syrup
Garnish: lime wedge

GIN

Awkwardly Tongue Tied
Jarred Weigand, Death & Co, NYC, 2015
2 oz (60 ml) gin (preferably Fords Gin)
½ oz (15 ml) lime juice
½ oz (15 ml) pineapple juice
¼ oz (7 ml) cinnamon syrup (p 495)
¼ oz (7 ml) orgeat
1 teaspoon (5 ml) Fernet-Branca
Garnish: lime wheel

Baltic Gimlet
Felix Woods, The Everleigh, Melbourne
2 oz (60 ml) gin
¾ oz (22 ml) lime juice
½ oz (15 ml) simple syrup
3 blueberries
2 dashes orange bitters
2 drops saline solution (p 493)
Muddle blueberries and simple syrup, add remaining ingredients and shake with ice, then strain into a frozen coupe.
Garnish: blueberry

Barnum was Right
Crosby Gaige's Cocktail Guide and Ladies' Companion, *Crosby Gaige, 1941*
1½ oz (45 ml) gin
½ oz (15 ml) apricot brandy
¾ oz (22 ml) lime juice
1 teaspoon (5 ml) simple syrup
2 dashes Angostura Bitters
Garnish: lime wedge

Bennett
(Gimlet with fresh lime and Angostura Bitters)
Cocktails by "Jimmy" Late of Ciro's London, *1930*
2 oz (60 ml) gin
¾ oz (22 ml) lime juice
¾ oz (22 ml) simple syrup
2 dashes Angostura Bitters
Garnish: lime wedge

Blackout
(aka **Blackberry Gimlet** or **Blackberry Beauty** in *The Fine Art of Mixing Drinks*, David A. Embury, 1948)
The Stork Club Bar Book, *Lucius Beebe, 1946*
2 oz (60 ml) gin
1 oz (30 ml) lime juice
¾ oz (22 ml) simple syrup
2 blackberries
Muddle blackberries with simple syrup, add remaining ingredients and shake with ice, then strain into a frozen coupe.
Garnish: blackberry

Buko Gimlet
Matthew Belanger, Death & Co, Los Angeles, 2019
1 oz (30 ml) navy strength gin (originally Four Pillars Navy Strength Gin)
¾ oz (22 ml) cachaça (preferably Novo Fogo Silver Cachaça)
¼ oz (7 ml) coconut liqueur
¾ oz (22 ml) lime juice
½ oz (15 ml) pandan syrup (p 499)
½ oz (15 ml) coconut water
Serve in a frozen double rocks glass with ice.
Garnish: freshly grated lime zest

Add all ingredients to a shaker, then shake with ice and strain into a frozen coupe.

Business
(Gimlet with honey)
Sasha Petraske, Milk & Honey, NYC, 2002
2 oz (60 ml) gin
1 oz (30 ml) lime juice
¾ oz (22 ml) honey syrup (p 496)
Garnish: lime wedge

Business with Pleasure
Zachary Gelnaw-Rubin, Lion Lion, NYC, 2016
1¾ oz (52 ml) gin
¾ oz (22 ml) lime juice
¾ oz (22 ml) pineapple juice
½ oz (15 ml) honey syrup (p 496)
Garnish: lime wedge

Chilean Cherry Blossom Cocktail
Hosteria Providencia, Santiago
The South American Gentleman's Companion, *Charles H. Baker Jr., 1951*
1½ oz (45 ml) gin
¼ oz (7 ml) Heering Cherry Liqueur
¾ oz (22 ml) lime juice
½ oz (15 ml) simple syrup
2 cherries
Press cherries with simple syrup, add remaining ingredients and shake with ice, then strain into a frozen coupe.
Garnish: cherry

Clarabell
Vincenzo Errico, L'Artefatto, Forio d'Ischia, 2022
1½ oz (45 ml) gin
½ oz (15 ml) Fernet-Branca
1 oz (30 ml) lime juice
¾ oz (22 ml) pineapple dill syrup (p 499)

Debutante
(Pomegranate Gimlet with orange bitters)
Jayne's Bartender's Guide, *1934*
2 oz (60 ml) gin
¾ oz (22 ml) lime juice
¾ oz (22 ml) grenadine (p 496)
2 dashes orange bitters
Garnish: lime wedge
▼ Great Cosmopolitan alternative.

East Side
(Gimlet with cucumber and mint)
Milk & Honey, NYC, 2006
2 oz (60 ml) gin
1 oz (30 ml) lime juice
¾ oz (22 ml) simple syrup
2 cucumber wheels
6–8 mint leaves
Press cucumber with simple syrup, add remaining ingredients and shake with ice, then strain into a frozen coupe.
Garnish: cucumber wheel

Fallen Angel Cocktail
The Savoy Cocktail Book, *Harry Craddock, 1930*
2 oz (60 ml) gin
1 oz (30 ml) lime juice
½ oz (15 ml) simple syrup
1 teaspoon (5 ml) white crème de menthe
2 dashes Angostura Bitters
Garnish: mint leaf

Fave Dilla
Charles Arias, Mechanics' Institute, Perth, 2023
1½ oz (45 ml) gin
⅓ oz (10 ml) St Germain Elderflower Liqueur
1 oz (30 ml) lime juice
½ oz (15 ml) simple syrup
3 dill sprigs
4 cucumber wheels
Press cucumber with simple syrup, add remaining ingredients and shake with ice, then strain into a frozen coupe.
Garnish: 3 drops of extra virgin olive oil

French Pearl
(South Side with pastis)
Audrey Saunders, Pegu Club, NYC, 2006
2 oz (60 ml) gin
1 oz (30 ml) lime juice
½ oz (15 ml) simple syrup
1 teaspoon (5 ml) pastis
6–8 mint leaves
Garnish: mint leaf

Gimlet (Fresh Lime Recipe)
2 oz (60 ml) gin
1 oz (30 ml) lime juice
¾ oz (22 ml) simple syrup
Garnish: lime wedge

Ginger Cocktail
Sasha Petraske, Milk & Honey, NYC, 2002
2 oz (60 ml) gin
1 oz (30 ml) lime juice
¾ oz (22 ml) ginger syrup (p 496)
Garnish: candied ginger

Ginger Cocktail #2
Sam Ross, Milk & Honey, NYC, 2011
2 oz (60 ml) gin
1 oz (30 ml) ginger syrup (p 496)
½ oz (15 ml) pink grapefruit juice
½ oz (15 ml) lime juice
Garnish: candied ginger

Grand Stand
1700 Cocktails for the Man Behind the Bar, *R. de Fleury, 1934*
1 oz (30 ml) gin
1 oz (30 ml) Cognac
⅜ oz (11 ml) maraschino liqueur
¾ oz (22 ml) lime juice
⅜ oz (11 ml) simple syrup
Garnish: cherry

High Five
Alex Day, Death & Co, NYC, 2010
1½ oz (45 ml) gin
½ oz (15 ml) Aperol
1 oz (30 ml) pink grapefruit juice
½ oz (15 ml) lime juice
¼ oz (7 ml) simple syrup

Old Maid
(aka **London Maid** or **East Side** on the rocks)
Sam Ross, East Side Company Bar, NYC, 2005
2 oz (60 ml) gin
1 oz (30 ml) lime juice
¾ oz (22 ml) simple syrup
2 cucumber wheels
6–8 mint leaves
Press cucumber, add remaining ingredients and shake with ice, then strain into a frozen coupe.
Garnish: cucumber fan

Add all ingredients to a shaker, then shake with ice and strain into a frozen coupe.

Pineapple-Gin Cocktail
Hotel El Prado, Barranquilla
The South American Gentleman's Companion, *Charles H. Baker Jr.,1951*
2 oz (60 ml) gin
1 oz (30 ml) pineapple juice
½ oz (15 ml) grenadine (p 496)
¼ oz (7 ml) lime juice
Garnish: cherry

Professor
(aka **Montserrat Cocktail** in *100 Cocktails: How to Mix Them,* "Bernard", 1958)
1700 Cocktails for the Man Behind the Bar, *R. de Fleury, 1934*
2 oz (60 ml) gin
¾ oz (22 ml) lime juice
¾ oz (22 ml) grenadine (p 496)
2 dashes absinthe
Garnish: cherry and lime wedge

Ramona Cocktail
(South Side with Old Tom gin)
Libro de Cocktail, *Juan A. Lasa, 1929*
2 oz (60 ml) Old Tom gin
1 oz (30 ml) lime juice
¾ oz (22 ml) simple syrup
6–8 mint leaves
Garnish: mint leaf

Red Pocket
Andy Chu, One or Two, Melbourne, 2024
1 oz (30 ml) gin
½ oz (15 ml) Pierre Ferrand Dry Curaçao
½ oz (15 ml) Cocchi Americano Rosa
1 oz (30 ml) lime juice
½ oz (15 ml) simple syrup
1 strawberry, halved
Muddle strawberry with simple syrup, add remaining ingredients and shake with ice, then strain into a frozen coupe.
Garnish: strawberry half

Revigorator
1700 Cocktails for the Man Behind the Bar, *R. de Fleury, 1934*
2 oz (60 ml) gin
¾ oz (22 ml) lime juice
¾ oz (22 ml) kola tonic
1 teaspoon (5 ml) simple syrup
Garnish: lime wedge

Sawyer
Don Lee, NYC, 2010
2 oz (60 ml) gin
½ oz (15 ml) lime juice
½ oz (15 ml) simple syrup
14 dashes Angostura Bitters
7 dashes Peychaud's Aromatic Cocktail Bitters
7 dashes orange bitters
Serve in a frozen double rocks glass with ice.

South Side
(Gimlet with mint)
Recipes for Mixed Drinks, *Hugo R. Ensslin, 1917*
2 oz (60 ml) gin
1 oz (30 ml) lime juice
¾ oz (22 ml) simple syrup
6–8 mint leaves
Garnish: mint leaf
▼ Originally published as **South Side Fizz** (p 145).

Suburban Gimlet
David Molyneux, Mr. West, Melbourne, 2023
1½ oz (45 ml) gin
¾ oz (22 ml) lime juice
¾ oz (22 ml) verjus syrup (p 502)
1 drop saline solution (p 493)
Garnish: orange twist (discard)

Summer Rain
I'm Just Here for the Drinks, *Sother Teague, 2018*
1½ oz (45 ml) Plymouth Gin
½ oz (15 ml) Amaro Montenegro
¾ oz (22 ml) lime juice
½ oz (15 ml) ginger syrup (p 496)
¼ oz (7 ml) simple syrup
1 dash Bittermens Orchard Street Celery Shrub
3 cucumber wheels
Press cucumber with simple syrup, add remaining ingredients, shake with ice then strain into a frozen coupe.
Garnish: cucumber wheel

(The Improved) Pendennis Club
Toby Cecchini, The Long Island Bar, NYC, 2013
2 oz (60 ml) gin
½ oz (15 ml) apricot eau de vie (preferably Blume Marillen)
¾ oz (22 ml) apricot brandy
1 oz (30 ml) lime juice
¼ oz (7 ml) simple syrup
5 dashes Peychaud's Aromatic Cocktail Bitters
Garnish: lime wedge

The Pendennis Club's Famous Special
(aka **Pendennis Club**)
The Gentleman's Companion, *Charles H. Baker Jr., 1939*
1½ oz (45 ml) gin
½ oz (15 ml) apricot brandy
¾ oz (22 ml) lime juice
1 teaspoon (5 ml) simple syrup
2 dashes Peychaud's Aromatic Cocktail Bitters
Garnish: lime wedge

Trampoline
Al Sotack, Death & Co, NYC, 2014
1½ oz (45 ml) gin
¾ oz (22 ml) Cocchi Americano
1 oz (30 ml) pineapple juice
¾ oz (22 ml) strawberry basil syrup (p 501)
¾ oz (22 ml) lime juice
2 dashes absinthe
2 dashes Peychaud's Aromatic Cocktail Bitters
Serve in a frozen double rocks glass with ice.
Garnish: lime wheel and strawberry half

White Baby
The Fine Art of Mixing Drinks, *David A. Embury, 1948*
1½ oz (45 ml) gin
½ oz (15 ml) triple sec
¾ oz (22 ml) lime juice
1 teaspoon (5 ml) simple syrup
Garnish: lime wedge
▼ Add 1 teaspoon (5 ml) crème de cassis to make the **Veritas Cocktail** from *Trader Vic's Bartender's Guide,* Trader Vic, 1947.

Add all ingredients to a shaker, then shake with ice and strain into a frozen coupe.

Shake

Add all ingredients to a shaker, then shake with ice and strain into a frozen coupe.

AGAVE

Ancho Problem
Ezra Star, Boston
1 oz (30 ml) blanco tequila
1 oz (30 ml) Ancho Reyes Original
¾ oz (22 ml) lime juice
½ oz (15 ml) Demerara syrup (p 495)
Garnish: lime wedge

Bait 'n' Switch
Jeremy Ortel, Death & Co, NYC, 2014
1½ oz (45 ml) mezcal
½ oz (15 ml) Ancho Reyes Original
¾ oz (22 ml) pineapple juice
½ oz (15 ml) lime juice
½ oz (15 ml) cinnamon syrup (p 495)

Beach House
Felix Woods, Black Pearl, Melbourne, 2020
1 oz (30 ml) blanco tequila
½ oz (15 ml) mezcal
½ oz (15 ml) Aperol
½ oz (15 ml) pineapple juice
½ oz (15 ml) lime juice
¼ oz (7 ml) simple syrup
1 teaspoon (5 ml) passionfruit syrup (p 499)
Serve in a frozen double rocks glass with ice.
Garnish: lime wedge

Bidi Bidi Bom Bom
Tony Roehr, Raised by Wolves, San Diego, 2021
1½ oz (45 ml) blanco tequila
1 oz (30 ml) Aperol
¾ oz (22 ml) lime juice
½ oz (15 ml) simple syrup
1 dash Scrappy's Bitters Fire Tincture
1 strawberry, halved
Muddle strawberry and simple syrup in a shaker. Add remaining ingredients, then shake with ice and strain into a frozen double rocks glass with ice.
Garnish: strawberry half

Boogie Nights
Lorenzo Antinori, Bar Leone, Hong Kong, 2023
1½ oz (45 ml) mezcal
½ oz (15 ml) Aperol
¾ oz (22 ml) lime juice
½ oz (15 ml) pineapple juice
½ oz (15 ml) simple syrup
¼ oz (7 ml) passionfruit syrup (p 499)
3 dashes hot sauce
Serve in a frozen double rocks glass with ice.
Garnish: lime wedge

Bow & Arrow
Scott Teague, Dutch Kills, NYC, 2015
1 oz (30 ml) mezcal
1 oz (30 ml) bourbon
1 oz (30 ml) pineapple juice
½ oz (15 ml) lime juice
½ oz (15 ml) cinnamon syrup (p 495)

Crimes of Passion
Hunter Orahood, Attaboy, NYC, 2018
1½ oz (45 ml) blanco tequila
½ oz (15 ml) mezcal
¾ oz (22 ml) lime juice
¾ oz (22 ml) passionfruit syrup (p 499)
¼ oz (7 ml) honey syrup (p 496)
Garnish: dusting of cayenne pepper

Crown Prince
Nat Yao, Bar Margaux, Melbourne, 2022
1 oz (30 ml) blanco tequila
½ oz (15 ml) white Port
1 oz (30 ml) lime juice
¾ oz (22 ml) orgeat
3 dashes absinthe
Serve in a frozen double rocks glass with ice.
Garnish: lime wedge

Doctor Mindbender
Matthew Belanger, Death & Co, Los Angeles, 2019
2 oz (60 ml) blanco tequila
¾ oz (22 ml) lime juice
¾ oz (22 ml) guava purée
¼ oz (7 ml) simple syrup
3 dashes Scrappy's Bitters Fire Tincture
2 dashes Angostura Bitters
Serve in a frozen double rocks glass with ice.
Garnish: lime wheel

Dovetail
(Hemingway Daiquiri with tequila and bitters)
Andy Chu, The Everleigh, Melbourne, 2015
1½ oz (45 ml) blanco tequila
¼ oz (7 ml) maraschino liqueur
1 oz (30 ml) pink grapefruit juice
½ oz (15 ml) lime juice
¼ oz (7 ml) simple syrup
1 dash Peychaud's Aromatic Cocktail Bitters
Garnish: cherry

Firebird
Greg Keesee, Attaboy, Nashville
1½ oz (45 ml) blanco tequila
½ oz (15 ml) Select Aperitivo
1 oz (30 ml) lime juice
¾ oz (22 ml) simple syrup
2 cucumber wheels
2 dashes Scrappy's Bitters Fire Tincture
Press cucumber with simple syrup, add remaining ingredients and shake with ice, then strain into a frozen coupe.
Garnish: cucumber wheel and dusting of cayenne pepper

Flaming Heart
Toby Maloney, 2010
2 oz (60 ml) blanco tequila
½ oz (15 ml) Licor 43
¾ oz (22 ml) lime juice
½ oz (15 ml) pineapple juice
3 dashes Fee Brothers Old Fashion Aromatic Bitters
3 dashes Tabasco Green Pepper Sauce
Serve in a frozen double rocks glass with ice.
Garnish: lime wheel

Add all ingredients to a shaker, then shake with ice and strain into a frozen coupe.

Fresca Platino
(aka **Victor Tango** or **Tequila East Side** on the rocks)
Christy Pope, Milk & Honey, NYC, 2004
2 oz (60 ml) blanco tequila
1 oz (30 ml) lime juice
¾ oz (22 ml) simple syrup
2 drops saline solution (p 493)
2 cucumber wheels
6–8 mint leaves
Press cucumber with simple syrup, add remaining ingredients and shake with ice, then strain into a frozen coupe.
Garnish: cucumber wheel and mint sprig

Gilda
Brian Miller, Death & Co, NYC, 2009
2 oz (60 ml) blanco tequila
½ oz (15 ml) pineapple juice
½ oz (15 ml) lime juice
½ oz (15 ml) cinnamon syrup (p 495)
Garnish: lime wedge

Ginger #3
Zac Pease, Attaboy, NYC, 2018
1¾ oz (52 ml) mezcal
1 oz (30 ml) ginger syrup (p 496)
½ oz (15 ml) lime juice
½ oz (15 ml) pineapple juice
Garnish: dusting of cayenne pepper

Gringo Peligroso
Lewis Caputa, Rosina Cocktail Lounge, Las Vegas
1 oz (30 ml) mezcal
1 oz (30 ml) Amaro Montenegro
¾ oz (22 ml) lime juice
¾ oz (22 ml) ginger syrup (p 496)
Serve in a frozen double rocks glass with ice.
Garnish: candied ginger

Hole in the Cup
Lauren McLaughlin, Milk & Honey, NYC
2 oz (60 ml) blanco tequila
1 oz (30 ml) pineapple juice
½ oz (15 ml) lime juice
½ oz (15 ml) simple syrup
2 dashes absinthe
2 cucumber wheels
Press cucumber with simple syrup, add remaining ingredients and serve in a double rocks glass with ice.
Garnish: cucumber fan

Jaguar Nap
Matt Clark, Dutch Kills, NYC, 2017
2 oz (60 ml) mezcal
1 oz (30 ml) lime juice
¾ oz (22 ml) simple syrup
3 cucumber wheels
2 dashes Angostura Bitters
Press cucumber with simple syrup, add remaining ingredients and shake with ice, then strain into a frozen coupe.
Garnish: cucumber wheel and dusting of cayenne pepper

Jani (Midsummer)
Rob Libecans, 2019
¾ oz (22 ml) mezcal
¾ oz (22 ml) St Germain Elderflower Liqueur
¾ oz (22 ml) dry vermouth
¾ oz (22 ml) lime juice
1 dash orange bitters
Garnish: lime wedge

Juschu Cocktail
(Tequila Honeysuckle with Angostura Bitters)
The How and When, *Hyman Gale and Gerald F. Marco, 1937*
2 oz (60 ml) blanco tequila
1 oz (30 ml) lime juice
¾ oz (22 ml) honey syrup (p 496)
2 dashes Angostura Bitters
Garnish: lime wedge

La Cigua
Tomer Blechman, Theodora, NYC
1 oz (30 ml) blanco tequila
1 oz (30 ml) mezcal
¾ oz (22 ml) cucumber juice
¾ oz (22 ml) lime juice
½ oz (15 ml) simple syrup
5 dashes Scrappy's Bitters Fire Tincture
Serve in a frozen double rocks glass with ice.
Garnish: salt rim

Matador (Mucho Group Recipe)
Jeremy Blackmore, Mucho Group, Sydney, 2019
2 oz (60 ml) blanco tequila
1 oz (30 ml) pineapple juice
¾ oz (22 ml) lime juice
⅓ oz (10 ml) chamomile syrup (p 494)
▼ Freshly pressed pineapple juice is essential to this recipe.

Medicina Mexicana
1½ oz (45 ml) blanco tequila
½ oz (15 ml) mezcal
1 oz (30 ml) lime juice
½ oz (15 ml) ginger syrup (p 496)
¼ oz (7 ml) agave syrup (p 494)
Serve in a frozen double rocks glass with ice.
Garnish: candied ginger

Mexican Razor Blade
Dan Greenbaum, Diamond Reef, NYC
2 oz (60 ml) blanco tequila
1 oz (30 ml) lime juice
¾ oz (22 ml) simple syrup
1 cucumber wheel
Press cucumber with simple syrup, add remaining ingredients and shake with ice, then strain into a frozen coupe.
Garnish: dusting of cayenne pepper

Add all ingredients to a shaker, then shake with ice and strain into a frozen coupe.

Mexican Standoff
Joe Schofield, Schofield's Bar, Manchester, 2024
1⅓ oz (40 ml) blanco tequila
½ oz (15 ml) Aperol
¾ oz (22 ml) pineapple juice
½ oz (15 ml) lime juice
¼ oz (7 ml) simple syrup
3–5 slices bird's eye chilli
Serve in a frozen double rocks glass with ice.
Garnish: Tajín Clásico half-rim and lime wedge

Oaxaca-Melon
Ben Sprouse, Half Step, Austin
1 oz (30 ml) mezcal
1 oz (30 ml) dry vermouth
1 oz (30 ml) watermelon juice
¾ oz (22 ml) lime juice
½ oz (15 ml) honey syrup (p 496)
Serve in a frozen double rocks glass with ice.
Garnish: watermelon wedge and dusting of cayenne pepper

Oaxacanite
(Brooklynite with tequila and mezcal)
Ben Long, John Dory Oyster Bar, NYC
1 oz (30 ml) mezcal
1 oz (30 ml) blanco tequila
¾ oz (22 ml) lime juice
¾ oz (22 ml) honey syrup (p 496)
3 dashes Angostura Bitters
Garnish: grapefruit twist (discard)

Obvious Choice
Matty Clark, Dutch Kills, NYC
1 oz (30 ml) mezcal
1 oz (30 ml) Amontillado Sherry
¾ oz (22 ml) lime juice
½ oz (15 ml) cinnamon syrup (p 495)
⅜ oz (11 ml) passionfruit syrup (p 499)
Garnish: lime wedge

Overtime
Anthony Jayasekera, Bar Tobalá, Melbourne, 2023
¾ oz (22 ml) mezcal
¾ oz (22 ml) Amaro Ramazzotti
¾ oz (22 ml) lime juice
¾ oz (22 ml) ginger syrup (p 496)
Garnish: lime wedge

Peach
Sebastian Tollius, Eleven Madison Park, NYC, 2022
1 oz (30 ml) blanco tequila (preferably Mijenta Tequila Blanco)
½ oz (15 ml) mezcal (preferably Los Siete Misterios Doba-Yej)
¼ oz (7 ml) aquavit (preferably Linie Original)
¼ oz (7 ml) Rhum Clément Créole Shrubb
¾ oz (22 ml) lime juice
½ oz (15 ml) lacto-fermented peach and lemon verbena syrup (p 497)
1 teaspoon (5 ml) Suze
1 teaspoon (5 ml) Giffard Crème de Pêche de Vigne
Serve in a frozen double rocks glass with ice.
Garnish: peach salt half-rim (p 507) and peach wedge

Picante
Chris Ojeda, Soho House, West Hollywood
2 oz (60 ml) reposado tequila
1 oz (30 ml) lime juice
¾ oz (22 ml) agave syrup (p 494)
10 coriander (cilantro) leaves, stems attached
1 small slice birdseye chilli
Serve in a frozen double rocks glass with ice.
Garnish: birdseye chilli slice

Port of Spain
Dominic Alling, Beretta, San Francisco, 2013
1½ oz (45 ml) mezcal
¾ oz (22 ml) lime juice
¾ oz (22 ml) orgeat
½ oz (15 ml) Angostura Bitters
Garnish: lime wedge

Quinceañera
Karin Stanley, Dutch Kills, NYC
1 oz (30 ml) blanco tequila
1 oz (30 ml) Amontillado Sherry
½ oz (15 ml) lime juice
½ oz (15 ml) simple syrup
2 drops Bittermens Xocolatl Mole Bitters
Garnish: orange half-wheel

Red Grasshopper
Michael Madrusan, The Everleigh, Melbourne, 2011
(Tequila Honeysuckle with smoked paprika)
2 oz (60 ml) blanco tequila
1 oz (30 ml) lime juice
¾ oz (22 ml) honey syrup (p 496)
Garnish: dusting of smoked paprika

Robert Rodriguez
Lorenzo Antinori, Bar Leone, Hong Kong, 2023
1½ oz (45 ml) reposado tequila
½ oz (15 ml) Cynar
¾ oz (22 ml) pineapple juice
¾ oz (22 ml) lime juice
⅜ oz (11ml) simple syrup
1 teaspoon (5 ml) Ancho Reyes Verde
1 drop sesame oil
Serve in a frozen double rocks glass with ice.
Garnish: pineapple wedge

Rosalita
Dylan O'Brien, Prizefighter, Emeryville, 2015
2 oz (60 ml) reposado tequila
½ oz (15 ml) Amaro Montenegro
¾ oz (22 ml) lime juice
¾ oz (22 ml) agave syrup (p 494)
Serve in a frozen double rocks glass with ice.
Garnish: salt rim

Sandia Watermelon Cocktail
David Valdez, Simbal, Los Angeles
1 oz (30 ml) blanco tequila
1 oz (30 ml) Aperol
1 oz (30 ml) watermelon juice
½ oz (15 ml) lime juice
½ oz (15 ml) ginger syrup (p 496)
2 drops saline solution (p 493)
1 dash Scrappy's Bitters Fire Tincture
Serve in a frozen double rocks glass with ice.
Garnish: mint leaf

Satin Sheet
2 oz (60 ml) blanco tequila
¾ oz (22 ml) lime juice
½ oz (15 ml) falernum
¼ oz (7 ml) simple syrup
Garnish: lime wedge

Add all ingredients to a shaker, then shake with ice and strain into a frozen coupe.

Short Rib
Phil Ward, Death & Co, NYC, 2008
2 oz (60 ml) blanco tequila
¾ oz (22 ml) lime juice
¾ oz (22 ml) grenadine (p 496)
4 dashes hot sauce

Siesta
Katie Stipe, Flatiron Lounge, NYC, 2006
1½ oz (45 ml) blanco tequila
½ oz (15 ml) Campari
½ oz (15 ml) pink grapefruit juice
½ oz (15 ml) lime juice
½ oz (15 ml) simple syrup
2 dashes Angostura Bitters

Silver Monk
Phil Ward, Death & Co, NYC, 2007
1½ oz (45 ml) blanco tequila
¾ oz (22 ml) Yellow Chartreuse
¾ oz (22 ml) lime juice
¼ oz (7 ml) simple syrup
2 cucumber wheels
8 mint leaves
Press cucumber with simple syrup, add remaining ingredients and shake with ice, then strain into a frozen coupe.
2 drops saline solution (p 493)

Sonora
Harry Craddock
Ted Saucier's Bottoms Up, *Ted Saucier, 1951*
2 oz (60 ml) blanco tequila
1 oz (30 ml) pineapple juice
½ oz (15 ml) grenadine (p 496)
¼ oz (7 ml) lime juice
Garnish: lime wedge

Spicy Flamingo
Dan Greenbaum, Diamond Reef, NYC, 2017
2 oz (60 ml) blanco tequila
1 oz (30 ml) watermelon juice
¾ oz (22 ml) lime juice
½ oz (15 ml) agave syrup (p 494)
Serve in a frozen double rocks glass with ice.
Garnish: pinch of chilli salt

Spicy Pineapple Situation
Felix Woods, Black Pearl, Melbourne, 2022
1 oz (30 ml) blanco tequila
½ oz (15 ml) mezcal
¾ oz (22 ml) pineapple juice
½ oz (15 ml) lime juice
½ oz (15 ml) simple syrup
½ teaspoon (1 g) finely chopped fresh habanero chilli
Serve in a frozen double rocks glass with ice.
Garnish: makrut lime leaf and a pinch of salt flakes

Squash
Sebastian Tollius, Eleven Madison Park, NYC, 2023
1 oz (30 ml) squash (pumpkin)-infused reposado tequila (p 504)
½ oz (15 ml) coconut fat-washed Calvados (preferably Manoir de Grandouet Calvados Pays d'Auge Fine; p 502)
½ oz (15 ml) St Germain Elderflower Liqueur
½ oz (15 ml) lime juice
½ oz (15 ml) spiced squash (pumpkin) syrup (p 501)
1 teaspoon (5 ml) Ancho Reyes Verde
1 teaspoon (5 ml) yuzu juice
Serve in a frozen double rocks glass with an ice block.
Garnish: 4 pickled squash ribbons, layered atop the ice block

Switchblade
Riley Perrin, Attaboy, Nashville, 2018
2 oz (60 ml) blanco tequila
½ oz (15 ml) white crème de cacao
¾ oz (22 ml) lime juice
¼ oz (7 ml) simple syrup
Garnish: dusting of cayenne pepper

Teal
Harrison Kenney, Cantina OK!, Sydney, 2021
1⅓ oz (40 ml) blanco tequila
⅓ oz (10 ml) Fino Sherry
⅔ oz (20 ml) lime juice
⅔ oz (20 ml) celery juice
½ oz (15 ml) kiwi purée
½ oz (15 ml) simple syrup
Garnish: 3 drops of vanilla olive oil (p 507)

Tequila
(Tequila Shake with pomegranate)
Café Royal Cocktail Book, *W.J. Tarling, 1937*
2 oz (60 ml) blanco tequila
¾ oz (22 ml) lime juice
¾ oz (22 ml) grenadine (p 496)
Garnish: lime wedge

Tequila Cocktail
(Tequila Shake with Angostura Bitters)
Bar La Florida Cocktails, *1935*
2 oz (60 ml) blanco tequila
1 oz (30 ml) lime juice
¾ oz (22 ml) simple syrup
2 dashes Angostura Bitters
Garnish: lime wedge

Tequila Matador
Trader Vic's Bartender's Guide, *Trader Vic, 1972*
2 oz (60 ml) blanco tequila
1 oz (30 ml) pineapple juice
¼ oz (7 ml) lime juice
½ oz (15 ml) simple syrup
Garnish: pineapple wedge

Tijuana Lady
Michael Madrusan, Little Branch, NYC, 2008
1½ oz (45 ml) blanco tequila
1 oz (30 ml) Licor 43
¾ oz (22 ml) lime juice
2 dashes Angostura Bitters
Garnish: lime wedge

Tommy's Margarita
Julio Bermejo, Tommy's Mexican Restaurant, San Francisco, circa 1987
2 oz (60 ml) blanco tequila
1 oz (30 ml) lime juice
½ oz (15 ml) agave syrup (p 494)
Serve in a frozen double rocks glass with ice.
Garnish: salt half-rim (optional) and lime wedge

Add all ingredients to a shaker, then shake with ice and strain into a frozen coupe.

Toreador
Café Royal Cocktail Book, *W.J. Tarling, 1937*
1½ oz (45 ml) blanco tequila
½ oz (15 ml) apricot brandy
¾ oz (22 ml) lime juice
1 teaspoon (5 ml) simple syrup
Garnish: lime wedge

212
Willy Shine, NYC, 2008
2 oz (60 ml) reposado tequila
1 oz (30 ml) Aperol
2 oz (60 ml) pink grapefruit juice
¼ oz (7 ml) lime juice
Serve in a frozen double rocks glass with ice.
Garnish: lime wedge

Viva Villa
(Tequila Shake with salt)
Famous New Orleans Drinks and How to Mix 'Em, *Stanley Clisby Arthur, 1937*
2 oz (60 ml) blanco tequila
1 oz (30 ml) lime juice
¾ oz (22 ml) simple syrup
Garnish: lime wedge and pinch of salt

BRANDY

Bonnie Prince Charlie Cocktail
(aka **Comet**)
The How and When, *Hyman Gale and Gerald F. Marco, 1937*
1½ oz (45 ml) Cognac
¾ oz (22 ml) Drambuie
¾ oz (22 ml) lime juice
Garnish: lime wedge

Chirulín
Tatiana Flores Escalante, Lima
2 oz (60 ml) pisco (preferably acholado)
1½ oz (45 ml) pink grapefruit juice
½ oz (15 ml) cinnamon syrup (p 495)
¼ oz (7 ml) lime juice
Serve in a frozen double rocks glass with ice.
Ganrish: grapefruit half-wheel and cinnamon quill

Doctor Prickly
Vincenzo Errico, L'Artefatto, Forio d'Ischia, 2023
2 oz (60 ml) pisco
⅜ oz (11 ml) maraschino liqueur
1 oz (30 ml) lime juice
⅜ oz (11 ml) simple syrup
2 chunks prickly pear
Muddle prickly pear with simple syrup, add remaining ingredients, then shake with ice and strain into a frozen coupe.

Grand Stand
1700 Cocktails for the Man Behind the Bar, *R. de Fleury, 1934*
1 oz (30 ml) Cognac
1 oz (30 ml) gin
⅜ oz (11 ml) maraschino liqueur
¾ oz (22 ml) lime juice
⅜ oz (11 ml) simple syrup
Garnish: cherry

Jack Rose
Jack's Manual, *J.A. Grohusko, 1908*
2 oz (60 ml) bonded apple brandy
½ oz (15 ml) orange juice
½ oz (15 ml) raspberry syrup (p 500)
⅜ oz (11 ml) lemon juice
⅜ oz (11 ml) lime juice

Jack Rose Cocktail
Drinks, *Jacques Straub, 1914*
2 oz (60 ml) bonded apple brandy
¾ oz (22 ml) lime juice
¾ oz (22 ml) grenadine (p 496)
Garnish: lime wedge
▼ Swap bonded apple brandy for Cognac to make the **Jack Rose No. 3** from *1700 Cocktails for the Man Behind the Bar*, R. de Fleury, 1934.

Mystic Marvel
1700 Cocktails for the Man Behind the Bar, *R. de Fleury, 1934*
¾ oz (22 ml) Cognac
¾ oz (22 ml) Calvados
¾ oz (22 ml) Drambuie
¾ oz (22 ml) lime juice
Garnish: orange twist

Ned King's Gem
Ned King, Easthampton
1 oz (30 ml) Cognac
1 oz (30 ml) Jamaican dark rum
¾ oz (22 ml) lime juice
½ oz (15 ml) pineapple syrup (p 499)
1 dash Angostura Bitters
Garnish: freshly grated cinnamon

Occidental
Occidental Hotel, Washington DC
Ted Saucier's Bottoms Up, *Ted Saucier, 1951*
2 oz (60 ml) Cognac
¾ oz (22 ml) lime juice
¾ oz (22 ml) grenadine (p 496)
6–8 mint leaves

Pan American Clipper
(Jack Rose Cocktail with absinthe)
The Gentleman's Companion, *Charles H. Baker Jr., 1939*
2 oz (60 ml) bonded apple brandy
¾ oz (22 ml) lime juice
¾ oz (22 ml) grenadine (p 496)
2 dashes absinthe
Garnish: lime wedge

Pisco! Pisco!
Bianca Wendt, Bar Que Sera, Sawtell
1½ oz (45 ml) pisco
⅓ oz (10 ml) Suze
¾ oz (22 ml) lime juice
½ oz (15 ml) simple syrup
2 cucumber wheels
Press cucumber with simple syrup, add remaining ingredients and shake with ice, then strain into a frozen coupe.
Garnish: cucumber wheel

Sky Pilot
Jones' Complete Barguide, *Stan Jones, 1977*
¾ oz (22 ml) bonded apple brandy
¾ oz (22 ml) Jamaican dark rum
¾ oz (22 ml) lime juice
¾ oz (22 ml) grenadine (p 496)
Garnish: lime wedge

Add all ingredients to a shaker, then shake with ice and strain into a frozen coupe.

Taj Mahal

¾ oz (22 ml) bonded apple brandy
¾ oz (22 ml) gin
½ oz (15 ml) apricot brandy
¾ oz (22 ml) lime juice
1 teaspoon (5 ml) simple syrup
Garnish: lime wedge

Temple of the Moon

Christy Pope, Midnight Rambler, Dallas, 2015
2 oz (60 ml) jasmine-infused pisco (p 503)
1 oz (30 ml) Crazy Water No. 4 (or strong, full-bodied mineral water)
¾ oz (22 ml) lime juice
¾ oz (22 ml) pineapple syrup (p 499)
2 drops saline solution (p 493)
Garnish: freshly grated nutmeg
Named after the Incan ceremonial temple near Machu Picchu, which comprises six levels, echoed by the number of ingredients.

The Grandpa

(Honeysuckle with bonded apple brandy)
The Saloon in the Home or A Garland of Rumblossoms, *Ridgley Hunt and George S. Chappell, 1930*
2 oz (60 ml) bonded apple brandy
1 oz (30 ml) lime juice
¾ oz (22 ml) honey syrup (p 496)
Garnish: lime wedge

The Yokohama Romance Cocktail

(Cognac Gimlet with cherry)
The Gentleman's Companion, *Charles H. Baker Jr., 1939*
2 oz (60 ml) Cognac
1 oz (30 ml) lime juice
¾ oz (22 ml) simple syrup
2 cherries
Press cherries with simple syrup, add remaining ingredients and shake with ice, then strain into a frozen coupe.
Garnish: cherry

Yellow Jacket

Greg Keesee, Attaboy, Nashville, 2021
¾ oz (22 ml) bonded apple brandy
¾ oz (22 ml) Amaro Nardini
¾ oz (22 ml) lime juice
¾ oz (22 ml) ginger syrup (p 496)
Garnish: candied ginger

AMERICAN WHISKEY

Bone

David Wondrich, 2003
2 oz (60 ml) rye whiskey
½ oz (15 ml) lime juice
½ oz (15 ml) Demerara syrup (p 495)
2 dashes hot sauce (preferably Cholula Original Hot Sauce)
Garnish: lemon twist (discard)

Commodore

(Bourbon Shake with orange bitters)
Phil Gross, Cincinnatti
Hoffman House Bartender's Guide, *Charles S. Mahoney, 1905*
2 oz (60 ml) bourbon
1 oz (30 ml) lime juice
¾ oz (22 ml) simple syrup
2 dashes orange bitters
Garnish: lime wedge

Expat

(Bourbon Shake with mint and Angostura Bitters)
Lauren Schell and Vito Dieterle, Little Branch, NYC, 2010
2 oz (60 ml) bourbon
1 oz (30 ml) lime juice
¾ oz (22 ml) simple syrup
3 dashes Angostura Bitters
6–8 mint leaves
Garnish: mint leaf

Gypsy Gentleman

Eric Johnson, Noble Experiment, San Diego, 2012
2 oz (60 ml) bourbon
¾ oz (22 ml) lime juice
¾ oz (22 ml) grenadine (p 496)
1 teaspoon (5 ml) Fernet-Branca, to rinse
Coat the inside of a frozen coupe with Fernet-Branca. Add remaining ingredients to a shaker, then shake with ice and strain into the coupe.

Jackknife

Jon Nutter, Attaboy, NYC, 2021
1½ oz (45 ml) bourbon
½ oz (15 ml) Amaro Averna
¾ oz (22 ml) watermelon juice
¾ oz (22 ml) lime juice
½ oz (15 ml) simple syrup
"I love Jon's Jackknife: great for folks looking for something like a Paper Plane." – Sam Ross

Junior

Esquire, *1937*
1½ oz (60 ml) rye whiskey
¾ oz (22 ml) Bénédictine
¾ oz (22 ml) lime juice
2 dashes Angostura Bitters
Garnish: lime wedge

Lion's Tail

Café Royal Cocktail Book, *W.J. Tarling, 1937*
2 oz (60 ml) bourbon
1 oz (30 ml) lime juice
¾ oz (22 ml) simple syrup
2 dashes Dale DeGroff's Pimento Aromatic Bitters
2 dashes Angostura Bitters
Garnish: lime wedge
In 1937's *Café Royal Cocktail Book* but was later popularised in Ted Haigh's *Vintage Spirits and Forgotten Cocktails, 2009.*

Mad Hatter

Ted Saucier's Bottoms Up, *Ted Saucier, 1951*
2 oz (60 ml) rye whiskey
¾ oz (22 ml) simple syrup
⅜ oz (11 ml) lemon juice
⅜ oz (11 ml) lime juice
2 dashes absinthe

Add all ingredients to a shaker, then shake with ice and strain into a frozen coupe.

New Yorker

(aka **New York Cocktail** in *The Official Mixer's Manual*, Patrick Gavin Duffy, 1934)
The Fine Art of Mixing Drinks, *David A. Embury, 1948*
2 oz (60 ml) rye whiskey
¾ oz (22 ml) lime juice
¾ oz (22 ml) grenadine (p 496)
Garnish: lime wedge

Quick Draw

David Molyneux, The Everleigh, Melbourne, 2015
1 oz (30 ml) rye whiskey
½ oz (15 ml) Fernet-Branca
1 oz (30 ml) pink grapefruit juice
½ oz (15 ml) lime juice
½ oz (15 ml) simple syrup

Southern Baptist

I'm Just Here for the Drinks, *Sother Teague, 2018*
2 oz (60 ml) rye whiskey
¾ oz (22 ml) lime juice
¾ oz (22 ml) ginger syrup (p 496)
Garnish: candied ginger

SCOTCH

Admiral

(Commodore with Scotch)
Felix Woods, The Everleigh, Melbourne, 2014
2 oz (60 ml) Scotch
1 oz (30 ml) lime juice
¾ oz (22 ml) simple syrup
2 dashes orange bitters
2 dashes absinthe
Garnish: lime wedge

Crown Sour

Callum Rixson
1½ oz (45 ml) Scotch
1 oz (30 ml) pineapple juice
½ oz (15 ml) lime juice
¼ oz (7 ml) falernum
¼ oz (7 ml) simple syrup
2 drops Bittermens Hellfire Habanero Shrub
Garnish: lime wedge

Rubicon

Tom Lasher-Walker, Fresh Kills, NYC, 2017
1½ oz (45 ml) Scotch
1 oz (30 ml) ruby Port
½ oz (15 ml) lime juice
½ oz (15 ml) simple syrup
2 dashes Angostura Bitters

Smoke & Mirrors

Alex Day, Death & Co, NYC, 2010
1 oz (30 ml) Scotch
½ oz (15 ml) Islay Scotch
1 oz (30 ml) lime juice
¾ oz (22 ml) simple syrup
2 dashes absinthe
6–8 mint leaves
Serve in a frozen double rocks glass with ice.

Smokescreen

(Smoke & Mirrors with Green Chartreuse)
Alex Day, Death & Co, NYC, 2010
1½ oz (45 ml) Islay Scotch
¼ oz (7 ml) Green Chartreuse
1 oz (30 ml) lime juice
¾ oz (22 ml) simple syrup
6–8 mint leaves
Serve in a frozen double rocks glass with ice.

The Prospector

(Honeysuckle with Scotch)
Lewis Cooke, Black Pearl, Melbourne 2018
2 oz (60 ml) Scotch
¾ oz (22 ml) lime juice
¾ oz (22 ml) honey syrup (p 496)
Garnish: lime wedge

WORLD WHISK(E)Y

Wild Eyed Rose

(Irish Whiskey Shake with pomegranate on the rocks)
Recipes for Mixed Drinks, *Hugo R. Ensslin, 1917*
2 oz (60 ml) Irish whiskey
¾ oz (22 ml) lime juice
¾ oz (22 ml) grenadine (p 496)
Serve in a frozen double rocks glass with ice.
Garnish: lime wedge
▼ Originally a Rickey.

FORTIFIED & LIQUEUR

Alpine Start

Michael McCollum, Attaboy, Nashville, 2022
1½ oz (45 ml) Amaro Braulio
½ oz (15 ml) génépy
1 oz (30 ml) lime juice
½ oz (15 ml) simple syrup
6–8 mint leaves
3 dashes Angostura Bitters
Serve in a frozen double rocks glass with ice.
Garnish: mint sprig

Drink of Laughter & Forgetting

Michael Yusko
Cure: New Orleans Drinks and How to Mix 'Em, *Neal Bodenheimer and Emily Timberlake, 2022*
1½ oz (45 ml) Cynar
½ oz (15 ml) Green Chartreuse
¾ oz (22 ml) lime juice
½ oz (15 ml) Demerara syrup (p 495)
3 dashes Angostura Bitters

Add all ingredients to a shaker, then shake with ice and strain into a frozen coupe.

DAIQUIRI

Hemingway Daiquiri p 228

Daiquiri

A short, sharp Cuban cocktail shaken with rum, fresh lime and sugar, served in a frozen coupe.

rum + lime + sugar

Add all ingredients to a shaker, then shake with ice and strain into a frozen coupe.

Even though the people of the Caribbean had been combining rum with lime and sugar for centuries prior, the earliest printed recipe for the modern Daiquiri is found in *Straub's Manual of Mixed Drinks* by Jacques Straub in 1913, where it goes by the name of the Daiguiri (p 230). This most quintessential of Cuban cocktails is thought to have taken shape nearly two decades earlier, however, in 1898, thanks to American mining engineer Jennings Stockton Cox Jr., who ran the Spanish-American Iron Company near Daiquiri, a small harbour village on Cuba's east coast.

Fresh out of gin while entertaining some fellow Americans, Cox Jr. poured a local rum from Santiago, Bacardí Carta Blanca, into a jug with ice and used some fresh limes from his garden and a little sugar to disguise it. The drink, which he called a Rum Sour, was such a hit that he introduced it to the bars of Santiago, where it was reworked and renamed by various bartenders. Before long, the drink made its way to Havana, and it became the Daiquiri we know and love today.

Much like the Manhattan (p 334) and Martini (p 304) before it, the Daiquiri has truly stood the test of time, with many milestone moments in its history. The invention of the electric blender ushered in a new era for the drink in 1922, spawning countless frozen, or frappé, variations around the world. In the 1930s, Ernest Hemingway customised his own rum-heavy and sugar-free variant, the Papa Doble (p 232). It was also the drink former US President John F. Kennedy famously called for before dinner.

In essence, a Daiquiri is a basic Sour (p 152) with rum at its core. Rum has so many different profiles, not just light or aged, and we specify various rums for different drinks throughout the chapter for this very reason. As simple as the original three-ingredient cocktail may be, it is a true test of a bartender's mettle and there's a real sense of mastery that comes with achieving a perfect balance of flavour. For best results, we encourage the use of freshly squeezed lime juice (no exceptions!) and a damn hard shake for that trademark zestful finish.

Hotel Nacional Special

Wil P. Taylor
The Gentleman's Companion, *Charles H. Baker Jr., 1939*
1¾ oz (52 ml) light rum
½ oz (15 ml) apricot brandy
1 oz (30 ml) pineapple juice
¼ oz (7 ml) lime juice
¼ oz (7 ml) Demerara syrup (p 495)

Add all ingredients to a shaker then shake with ice and strain into a frozen coupe.
Garnish: pineapple wedge

The Hotel Nacional Special – referred to by author Charles H. Baker Jr. as 'one of the three finest Bacardí drinks known to science' – is a tropical Daiquiri variation named after Havana's historic Hotel Nacional de Cuba. Now a national monument and UNESCO site, the hotel was established late in 1930 and sadly destroyed only three years later in the Battle of the Hotel Nacional de Cuba. When it finally reopened in 1939, it quickly hit its stride as a top pick for sun-seeking tourists, celebrities and politicians from across the globe. The hotel also played host to major mafia bosses for the Havana Conference in 1946, a meeting that was famously re-created in Francis Ford Coppola's landmark sequel, *The Godfather Part II*.

In all likelihood, the hotel's namesake drink derived from the National Cocktail, a similar concoction from the 1934 pamphlet *Bar La Florida Cocktails*. Crucially, this earlier rendition did not include lime juice, a defining feature of the recipe in *The Gentleman's Companion*, which Baker Jr. credits to cruise-line publicist Wil P. Taylor. Simply put, it is a drink with abundant personality, which dances between sweet and sour effortlessly on the palate. Interestingly, Baker recommends using 'Gold Label Bacardí' (Bacardí Carta Oro), commenting that lighter rum styles are too delicate to stand up against the richness of apricot and pineapple. We suggest you experiment with both light and dark styles, or even a split of the two if you have them on hand.

If you're looking for even more out-of-office energy, try the Cobra's Fang (p 447) or Champagne Colada (p 447) in the Tropical collection (p 442).

Hemingway Daiquiri

(aka **Daiquiri Num. 3 {Maidique Style}** in *Bar La Florida Cocktails*, 1934)
Constantino Ribalaigua Vert, El Floridita, Havana, 1930s
1¾ oz (52 ml) light rum
¼ oz (7 ml) maraschino liqueur
1 oz (30 ml) pink grapefruit juice
½ oz (15 ml) lime juice
¼ oz (7 ml) simple syrup

Add all ingredients to a shaker then shake with ice and strain into a frozen coupe.
Garnish: cherry

Originally blended and served as a frappé, the Daiquiri Num. 3 – now more commonly known as the Hemingway Daiquiri – is a citrusy, bittersweet classic combining light rum, maraschino liqueur, fresh grapefruit juice and lime. Created by Constantino Ribalaigua Vert at Havana's historic fish restaurant and cocktail bar El Floridita in the early 1930s, this Daiquiri variation was said to be a favourite of one of the venue's most recognisable regulars, American novelist Ernest Hemingway.

First established in 1817, El Floridita was originally called La Piña de Plata (The Silver Pineapple). Constantino, or "Constante" as he was more commonly known, emigrated from Catalunya to Cuba as a teenager and began working at the bar in 1914. After four years behind the stick, Constante successfully purchased the business in 1918 and went on to build the venue's reputation as 'la cuna del Daiquiri' (the birthplace of the Daiquiri), schooling a legion of highly skilled cantineros (bartenders) in the process. Constante is also credited as an unofficial ambassador of the electric blender, popularising the frozen Daiquiri in the 1930s.

While Hemingway supposedly enjoyed Constante's original creation, he is said to have requested a stronger version with double the rum and without sugar because he had hemochromatosis, a rare genetic condition that can lead to diabetes. Hemingway was affectionately known as "Papa" at El Floridita, and so, with twice the rum and little more than a squeeze of fresh lime, the Papa Doble (p 232) was born. The Hemingway Daiquiri we know today was further adapted by head bartender Antonio Meilan a few years later, who balanced the dry and rum-heavy version with grapefruit juice and a splash of maraschino liqueur.

The Daiquiri Num. 3 is one of a handful of Daiquiri variations recorded by Constante in a small booklet of the bar's recipes, titled *Bar La Florida Cocktails*, first published in 1934. For similar short, sharp and citrusy cocktails in the drier style, try the Jasmine (p 192), which combines gin, Campari, triple sec and lemon juice, or the Dovetail (p 217) by The Everleigh alumnus Andy Chu.

Hotel Nacional Special

Daiquiri

LIGHT RUM & CANE SPIRIT

Alabaster
Jake Powell, Death & Co, Denver, 2022
¾ oz (22 ml) light rum
¾ oz (22 ml) aloe vera liqueur
¾ oz (22 ml) lime juice
¾ oz (22 ml) falernum
Garnish: lime wedge

Beachcomber
The Official Mixer's Manual, *Patrick Gavin Duffy, 1956*
2 oz (60 ml) light rum
⅜ oz (11 ml) maraschino liqueur
⅜ oz (11 ml) triple sec
¾ oz (22 ml) lime juice
1 teaspoon (5 ml) simple syrup
Garnish: cherry

Boukman Daiquiri
Alex Day, Death & Co, NYC, 2008
1½ oz (45 ml) light rum (preferably Flor de Caña Extra Seco Blanco)
½ oz (15 ml) Cognac
¾ oz (22 ml) lime juice
¾ oz (22 ml) cinnamon syrup (p 495)

Casa Blanca
Jones' Complete Barguide, *Stan Jones, 1977*
2 oz (60 ml) light rum
⅜ oz (11 ml) maraschino liqueur
⅜ oz (11 ml) orange curaçao (p 498)
¾ oz (22 ml) lime juice
2 dashes Angostura Bitters
Garnish: cherry

Casa Blanca No. 2
(Daiquiri No. 5 with Angostura Bitters)
Michael Madrusan, Little Branch, NYC, 2008
1½ oz (45 ml) light rum
¾ oz (22 ml) lime juice
⅜ oz (11 ml) maraschino liqueur
⅜ oz (11 ml) grenadine
2 dashes Angostura Bitters
Garnish: cherry

Cuban Peach
The Fine Art of Mixing Drinks, *David A. Embury, 1948*
2 oz (60 ml) light rum
½ oz (15 ml) Giffard Crème de Pêche de Vigne
¾ oz (22 ml) lime juice
1 teaspoon (5 ml) simple syrup
Garnish: lime wedge
▼ Swap peach liqueur for apricot brandy to make a **Cuban Apricot**.

Daiquiri Cocktail
(aka **Daiguiri**)
Straub's Manual of Mixed Drinks, *Jacques Straub, 1913*
2 oz (60 ml) light rum
1 oz (30 ml) lime juice
¾ oz (22 ml) simple syrup
Garnish: lime wedge
▼ Originally called for inverse proportions, of ⅔ lime juice to ⅓ light rum.

Daiquiri De Luxe
The Fine Art of Mixing Drinks, *David A. Embury, 1948*
2 oz (60 ml) light rum
¾ oz (22 ml) lime juice
½ oz (15 ml) orgeat
▼ "No decoration should be used with the Daiquiri because it is a cloudy cocktail."

Daiquiri No. 5 (Pink)
Bar La Florida Cocktails, *1939*
2 oz (60 ml) light rum
⅜ oz (11 ml) maraschino liqueur
¾ oz (22 ml) lime juice
⅜ oz (11 ml) grenadine (p 496)
Garnish: lime wedge

Daiquiri Num. 2
Bar La Florida Cocktails, *1934*
2 oz (60 ml) light rum
¾ oz (22 ml) orange curaçao (p 498)
1 oz (30 ml) orange juice
¼ oz (7 ml) lime juice
Garnish: lime wedge

Daiquiri Num. 4 (Florida Style)
(aka **El Floridita Daiquiri**)
Bar La Florida Cocktails, *1934*
2 oz (60 ml) light rum
⅜ oz (11 ml) maraschino liqueur
¾ oz (22 ml) lime juice
⅜ oz (11 ml) simple syrup
Garnish: cherry

Defend Arrack
Maksym Pazuniak, Cure, New Orleans
1½ oz (45 ml) Batavia-Arrack van Oosten
½ oz (15 ml) apricot brandy
¾ oz (22 ml) lime juice
1 teaspoon (5 ml) simple syrup
½ teaspoon (2.5 ml) pimento (allspice) dram
Garnish: orange twist (discard)

Del Monte Cocktail
(aka **Santiago Cocktail** in *Sloppy Joe's Cocktails Manual*, 1932, and *The Savoy Cocktail Book*, Harry Craddock, 1930, or Pomegranate Daiquiri)
Trader Vic's Bartender's Guide, *Trader Vic, 1947*
2 oz (60 ml) light rum
¾ oz (22 ml) lime juice
¾ oz (22 ml) grenadine (p 496)
Garnish: lime wedge

Doris Diesel
Evan Stroeve, The Waratah, Sydney, 2024
1½ oz (45 ml) light rum
¾ oz (22 ml) pineapple juice
½ oz (15 ml) lime juice
⅓ oz (10 ml) yuzu syrup (p 502)

Dry Daiquiri
Kevin Armstrong, Match Bar, London, 2005
1½ oz (45 ml) light rum
½ oz (15 ml) Campari
¾ oz (22 ml) lime juice
½ oz (15 ml) simple syrup
1 teaspoon (5 ml) passionfruit syrup (p 499)
Garnish: orange twist (preferably flamed)

Add all ingredients to a shaker, then shake with ice and strain into a frozen coupe.

Dry Pornstar Daiquiri
Julian de Féral, Kindred, London, 2022
1½ oz (45 ml) light rum
½ oz (15 ml) Bonanto
1 oz (30 ml) lime juice
¼ oz (7 ml) passionfruit syrup (p 499)
¼ oz (7 ml) vanilla syrup (p 502)

French Daiquiri
(Daiquiri with crème de cassis and mint)
The Stork Club Bar Book, *Lucius Beebe, 1946*
2 oz (60 ml) light rum
½ oz (15 ml) crème de cassis
¾ oz (22 ml) lime juice
1 teaspoon (5 ml) simple syrup
6–8 mint leaves
Garnish: mint leaf

Havana Beach
Bar La Florida Cocktails, *1934*
2 oz (60 ml) light rum
1 oz (30 ml) pineapple juice
½ oz (15 ml) simple syrup
¼ oz (7 ml) lime juice
Garnish: lime wedge

Honeysuckle
(Bee's Knees with light rum and lime)
The Fine Art of Mixing Drinks, *David A. Embury, 1948*
2 oz (60 ml) light rum
1 oz (30 ml) lime juice (originally lemon juice)
¾ oz (22 ml) honey syrup (p 496)
Garnish: lime wedge
▼ Likely an improvement on the **Southern Honeysuckle**, a recipe that calls for equal parts of all three ingredients in *Here's How Again!*, Judge Jr., 1929.

I'm No Angel
(Cuban Apricot with Angostura Bitters)
Jayne's Bartender's Guide, *1934*
2 oz (60 ml) light rum
½ oz (15 ml) apricot brandy
¾ oz (22 ml) lime juice
1 teaspoon (5 ml) simple syrup
2 dashes Angostura Bitters
Garnish: lime wedge

Jockey Club Cocktail
Miramar Hotel, La Guaira
The South American Gentleman's Companion, *Charles H. Baker Jr., 1951*
1 oz (30 ml) Diamond Reserve 151 Aged Rum
½ oz (15 ml) Green Chartreuse
1 oz (30 ml) lime juice
¾ oz (22 ml) simple syrup
2 dashes Angostura Bitters
Garnish: orange twist (discard)

Larchmont
(Daiquiri with orange curaçao)
The Fine Art of Mixing Drinks, *David A. Embury, 1948*
2 oz (60 ml) light rum
¾ oz (22 ml) orange curaçao (p 498)
¾ oz (22 ml) lime juice
Garnish: lime wedge

Latina Daisy
The Connaught Bar, *Agostino Perrone, Giorgio Bargiani & Maura Milia, 2024*
1½ oz (45 ml) light rum
½ oz (15 ml) white crème de cacao
⅓ oz (10 ml) Galliano L'Autentico
¾ oz (22 ml) lime juice
1 teaspoon white (granulated) sugar
1 teaspoon fennel seeds
Muddle fennel seeds in a shaker, then add sugar and lime juice and stir to combine. Add remaining ingredients, shake with ice, and fine strain into a frozen coupe.
Garnish: cocoa powder rim

Maison Charles
(Daiquiri with mint)
The Fine Art of Mixing Drinks, *David A. Embury, 1948*
2 oz (60 ml) light rum
1 oz (30 ml) lime juice
¾ oz (22 ml) simple syrup
6–8 mint leaves
Garnish: mint leaf

Miami
The Fine Art of Mixing Drinks, *David A. Embury, 1948*
2 oz (60 ml) light rum
¾ oz (22 ml) lime juice
¾ oz (22 ml) simple syrup
1 teaspoon (5 ml) white crème de menthe
Garnish: mint leaf

Mexicane Banana Daiquiri
Chad Solomon, Midnight Rambler, Dallas, 2019
¾ oz (22 ml) Paranubes Blanco
¾ oz (22 ml) Uruapan Charanda Blanco
½ oz (15 ml) blanc vermouth
⅜ oz (11 ml) Giffard Banane du Brésil et des Caraïbes
¾ oz (22 ml) lime juice
⅜ oz (11 ml) simple syrup
2 drops saline solution (p 493)

Motomami
Alicia Perry and Anthony Schmidt, Quixote, San Diego, 2025
1 oz (30 ml) pineapple-infused mezcal (p 504)
½ oz (15 ml) San Bartolo Mezcal
½ oz (15 ml) Cañada Rum
½ oz (15 ml) iichiko shochu
¾ oz (22 ml) lime juice
½ oz (15 ml) butter gardenia (p 506)
¼ oz (7 ml) rich Demerara syrup (p 500)
Garnish: lime wedge

Nacional
The Fine Art of Mixing Drinks, *David A. Embury, 1948*
2 oz (60 ml) light rum
½ oz (15 ml) apricot brandy
¾ oz (22 ml) lime juice
1 teaspoon (5 ml) simple syrup
Garnish: lime wedge

Add all ingredients to a shaker, then shake with ice and strain into a frozen coupe.

Nacional (Louis P. De Gouy Recipe)

(Hotel Nacional Special without apricot brandy)
The Cocktail Hour, *Louis P. De Gouy, 1951*
2 oz (60 ml) light rum
1 oz (30 ml) pineapple juice
½ oz (15 ml) Demerara syrup (p 495)
¼ oz (7 ml) lime juice
Garnish: lime or pineapple wedge

New Moon

Michael Madrusan, Milk & Honey, NYC, 2008
2 oz (60 ml) light rum
¾ oz (22 ml) lime juice
½ oz (15 ml) simple syrup
1 teaspoon (5 ml) crème de violette
2 dashes orange bitters
Garnish: lime wedge

Nuclear Daiquiri

Gregor de Gruyther, LAB Bar, London, 2005
1 oz (30 ml) Wray & Nephew White Overproof Rum
¾ oz (22 ml) Green Chartreuse
1 oz (30 ml) lime juice
¼ oz (7 ml) falernum
Garnish: lime wedge

Pandan-quiri

Nico de Soto, Mace, NYC, 2012
2 oz (60 ml) light rum (preferably Planteray 3 Stars)
¾ oz (22 ml) lime juice
¾ oz (22 ml) pandan syrup (p 499)

Papa Doble

El Floridita, Havana
3 oz (90 ml) light rum
½ oz (15 ml) maraschino liqueur
1½ oz (45 ml) pink grapefruit juice
¾ oz (22 ml) lime juice
½ oz (15 ml) simple syrup
Blend all ingredients and pour into a frozen Spritz glass.
Garnish: cherry

Periodista

El Arte del Cantinero, *Hilario Alonso Sanchez, 1948*
2 oz (60 ml) light rum
⅜ oz (11 ml) orange curaçao (p 498)
⅜ oz (11 ml) apricot brandy
¾ oz (22 ml) lime juice
Garnish: lime twist (discard) and cherry
▾ Swapping light rum for aged dark rum also works a treat.

Pineapple Daiquiri

Nico de Soto, Mace, NYC, 2019
1 oz (30 ml) pineapple rum
½ oz (15 ml) light rhum agricole (preferably Père Labat 40)
½ oz (15 ml) light rum
¾ oz (22 ml) pineapple juice
½ oz (15 ml) lime juice
¼ oz (7 ml) cane syrup (p 494)
Garnish: pineapple wedge

Princess Cup

2 oz (60 ml) light rum
¾ oz (22 ml) lime juice
¾ oz (22 ml) simple syrup
2 cucumber wheels
1 strawberry, halved
Muddle strawberry and cucumber with lime juice and simple syrup, add rum, then shake with ice and strain into a frozen double rocks glass with ice.
Garnish: cucumber wheel and strawberry half

Royal Bermuda Yacht Club Cocktail

Crosby Gaige's Cocktail Guide and Ladies' Companion, *Crosby Gaige, 1941*
2 oz (60 ml) light rum
⅜ oz (11 ml) triple sec
¾ oz (22 ml) lime juice
⅜ oz (11 ml) falernum
Garnish: lime wedge

Ruby Cane

Erik Lorincz, Kwãnt Mayfair, London, 2023
1½ oz (45 ml) light rum (preferably Bacardí Carta Blanca)
½ oz (15 ml) ruby Port
⅔ oz (20 ml) lime juice
½ oz (15 ml) simple syrup
⅓ oz (10 ml) lapsang souchong vinegar (p 497)
3 dashes Peychaud's Aromatic Cocktail Bitters

Scorpion Kick

Dan Greenbaum, Diamond Reef, NYC, 2017
2 oz (60 ml) light rum
½ oz (15 ml) white crème de cacao
1 oz (30 ml) lime juice
¼ oz (7 ml) cane syrup (p 494)
6–8 mint leaves
Garnish: mint leaf

Snaquiri

Karin Stanley, Dutch Kills, NYC, 2010
¾ oz (22 ml) light rum
½ oz (15 ml) lime juice
⅜ oz (11 ml) simple syrup
Serve in a frozen mini coupe.

The Monarch

Jenna Hemsworth, Sydney, 2018
1½ oz (45 ml) light rum (preferably Bacardí Carta Blanca)
⅓ oz (10 ml) Bénédictine
1 oz (30 ml) mandarin juice
¾ oz (22 ml) lime juice
8 basil leaves
1 mandarin skin
Press mandarin, add remaining ingredients and shake with ice, then strain into a frozen coupe.
Garnish: basil leaf
▾ This cocktail needs to be fine strained.

Add all ingredients to a shaker, then shake with ice and strain into a frozen coupe.

The Nevada Cocktail
The Savoy Cocktail Book,
Harry Craddock, 1930
1¾ oz (52 ml) light rum
1 oz (30 ml) pink grapefruit juice
½ oz (15 ml) lime juice
½ oz (15 ml) simple syrup
2 dashes Angostura Bitters
Garnish: lime wedge

The Sun Also Rises
(Hemingway Daiquiri with absinthe)
Jim Meehan, Portland
1½ oz (45 ml) light rum
⅜ oz (11 ml) maraschino liqueur
1 oz (30 ml) pink grapefruit juice
½ oz (15 ml) lime juice
⅜ oz (11 ml) simple syrup
4 dashes absinthe
Garnish: lime wedge

Tiger Special
Princeton Club of New York, NYC
Ted Saucier's Bottoms Up,
Ted Saucier, 1951
2 oz (60 ml) light rum
½ oz (15 ml) triple sec
¾ oz (22 ml) lime juice
1 teaspoon (5 ml) simple syrup
Garnish: lime wedge

From *Harry Johnson's Bartenders' Manual* (1900):

May your heart be light, your glass be full, and your hangover be brief!

Voyager
Robert Hess, DrinkBoy, 2006
1¾ oz (52 ml) light rum
½ oz (15 ml) Bénédictine
¾ oz (22 ml) lime juice
½ oz (15 ml) falernum
2 dashes Angostura Bitters
Serve in a frozen double rocks glass with ice.
Garnish: lime wedge

Weekend at the Waldorf
Ted Saucier's Bottoms Up,
Ted Saucier, 1951
2 oz (60 ml) light rum
½ oz (15 ml) triple sec
¾ oz (22 ml) lime juice
1 teaspoon (5 ml) simple syrup
1 strawberry, halved
Muddle strawberry with simple syrup, add remaining ingredients, then shake with ice and strain into a frozen coupe.
Garnish: strawberry half

DARK RUM & CANE SPIRIT

Another Time
Riley Perrin, Attaboy, Nashville, 2018
2 oz (60 ml) Goslings Black Seal Rum
1 oz (30 ml) pineapple juice
½ oz (15 ml) Coco López
¼ oz (7 ml) lime juice
Garnish: lime twist (discard)

Beehive
Brandon Bramhall, Attaboy, NYC, 2015
1½ oz (45 ml) Jamaican dark rum
½ oz (15 ml) Fernet-Branca
¾ oz (22 ml) lime juice
¾ oz (22 ml) honey syrup (p 496)
Garnish: lime wedge

Brugal Cocktail
(Aged Dark Rum Daiquiri with mint)
Trader Vic's Bartender's Guide,
Trader Vic, 1947
2 oz (60 ml) aged dark rum
(preferably Brugal 1888)
1 oz (30 ml) lime juice
¾ oz (22 ml) simple syrup
6–8 mint leaves
Garnish: mint leaf

Cantineros Cóctel
Nathan Beasley, Black Pearl, Melbourne, 2014
1½ oz (45 ml) aged dark rum
½ oz (15 ml) orange curaçao (p 498)
½ oz (15 ml) falernum
½ oz (15 ml) lime juice
1 teaspoon (5 ml) ginger syrup (p 496)
2 dashes Angostura Bitters
Garnish: long lime twist

Captain's Blood
(Jamaican Dark Rum Daiquiri with Angostura Bitters)
The Fine Art of Mixing Drinks,
David A. Embury, 1948
2 oz (60 ml) Jamaican dark rum
¾ oz (22 ml) lime juice
¾ oz (22 ml) simple syrup
3 dashes Angostura Bitters
Garnish: lime wedge

Centre of the Galaxy
Smuggler's Cove: Exotic Cocktails, Rum and the Cult of Tiki, *Martin and Rebecca Cate, 2016*
2 oz (60 ml) aged dark rum
¾ oz (22 ml) lime juice
½ oz (15 ml) honey syrup (p 496)
¼ oz (7 ml) Demerara syrup (p 495)
2 raspberries
Muddle raspberries and honey syrup in a shaker. Add remaining ingredients and shake with ice, then strain into a frozen coupe.
Garnish: raspberry and freshly grated cinnamon

Charley Royal's Reserve Cocktail
Crosby Gaige's Cocktail Guide and Ladies' Companion,
Crosby Gaige, 1941
1 oz (30 ml) Jamaican dark rum
1 oz (30 ml) aged dark rum
⅜ oz (11 ml) maraschino liqueur
¾ oz (22 ml) lime juice
⅜ oz (11 ml) falernum
Garnish: lime wedge

Add all ingredients to a shaker, then shake with ice and strain into a frozen coupe.

Cloak & Dagger
Ted Saucier's Bottoms Up, *Ted Saucier, 1951*
1 oz (30 ml) Goslings Black Seal Rum
1 oz (30 ml) aged dark rum
1 oz (30 ml) lime juice
¾ oz (22 ml) simple syrup
Garnish: lime wedge

Daiquilroy
Michael McIlroy, Attaboy, NYC, 2015
2 oz (60 ml) aged dark rum
1 oz (30 ml) pineapple juice
½ oz (15 ml) lime juice
½ oz (15 ml) simple syrup
Garnish: lime wedge

Detroit Daisy
(Aged Dark Rum Daiquiri with pomegranate and mint)
The Stork Club Bar Book, *Lucius Beebe, 1946*
2 oz (60 ml) aged dark rum
¾ oz (22 ml) lime juice
¾ oz (22 ml) grenadine (p 496)
6–8 mint leaves
Garnish: lime wedge

El Draque
Sir Francis Drake, 1500s
Smuggler's Cove: Exotic Cocktails, Rum and the Cult of Tiki, *Martin and Rebecca Cate, 2016*
2 oz (60 ml) aged cachaça (preferably pot still)
¾ oz (22 ml) lime juice
¾ oz (22 ml) Demerara syrup (p 495)
6–8 mint leaves
Garnish: mint leaf
▼ Thought by some to be the world's very first cocktail, devised by none other than English explorer Sir Francis Drake, who concocted the drink with a crude spirit called aguardiente to treat illness on ships.

El InterAmericano Cocktail
(Hemingway Daiquiri with Jamaican dark rum and mint)
The South American Gentleman's Companion, *Charles H. Baker Jr., 1951*
1¾ oz (52 ml) Jamaican dark rum
¼ oz (7 ml) maraschino liqueur
1 oz (30 ml) pink grapefruit juice
½ oz (15 ml) lime juice
¼ oz (7 ml) simple syrup
6–8 mint leaves
Garnish: cherry

Flamingo
The Flamingo Hotel, Las Vegas
Ted Saucier's Bottoms Up, *Ted Saucier, 1951*
2 oz (60 ml) aged dark rum
1 oz (30 ml) pineapple juice
½ oz (15 ml) grenadine (p 496)
¼ oz (7 ml) lime juice
Garnish: lime wedge

Flock of Seagulls
Greg Keesee, Attaboy, Nashville, 2021
1½ oz (45 ml) aged dark rum
½ oz (15 ml) Select Aperitivo
¾ oz (22 ml) pineapple juice
½ oz (15 ml) lime juice
½ oz (15 ml) Coco López
Serve in a frozen double rocks glass with ice.
Garnish: orange half-wheel

Heart Throb
Scott Teague, 2014
Death & Co Welcome Home, *Alex Day, Nick Fauchald and David Kaplan, 2021*
2 oz (60 ml) aged dark rum
½ oz (15 ml) Giffard Crème de Pamplemousse Rose
¾ oz (22 ml) lime juice
¼ oz (7 ml) cinnamon syrup (p 495)
Garnish: lime twist (discard)

Honey Bee
(aka **Jamaica Honey Bee** in *Trader Vic's Bartender's Guide*, Trader Vic, 1947 or Honeysuckle with Jamaican dark rum)
The Fine Art of Mixing Drinks, *David A. Embury, 1948*
2 oz (60 ml) Jamaican dark rum
1 oz (30 ml) lime juice (originally lemon)
¾ oz (22 ml) honey syrup (p 496)
Garnish: lime wedge
▼ Add 2 dashes of Angostura Bitters to make the **Brooklynite** from *The Stork Club Bar Book*, Lucius Beebe, 1946.

Honey Pot
Michael Madrusan, The Everleigh, Melbourne, 2011
1 oz (30 ml) Jamaican dark rum
1 oz (30 ml) aged dark rum
1 oz (30 ml) lime juice
¾ oz (22 ml) honey syrup (p 496)
Garnish: lime wedge

Hoptoad
Old Waldorf Bar Days, *Albert Stevens Crockett, 1931*
1¾ oz (52 ml) Jamaican dark rum
½ oz (15 ml) apricot brandy
¾ oz (22 ml) lime juice
1 teaspoon (5 ml) simple syrup
Garnish: lime wedge

Jack & Bone
Oska Whitehart, The Everleigh, Melbourne, 2016
1½ oz (45 ml) Jamaican dark rum
½ oz (15 ml) Cynar
¾ oz (22 ml) lime juice
½ oz (15 ml) orgeat
Garnish: lime wedge

Add all ingredients to a shaker, then shake with ice and strain into a frozen coupe.

Knickerbocker
The Bar-Tenders‘ Guide, Jerry Thomas, *1862*
2 oz (60 ml) aged dark rum
⅜ oz (11 ml) orange curaçao (p 498)
¾ oz (22 ml) lime juice
⅜ oz (11 ml) raspberry syrup (p 500)
Garnish: raspberry

▼ Serve in a double rocks glass with ice to make the **White Lion** from the *New and Improved Bartender's Manual*, Harry Johnson, 1882.

Millionaire Cocktail
Recipes for Mixed Drinks, *Hugo R. Ensslin, 1916*
1½ oz (45 ml) Jamaican dark rum
½ oz (15 ml) apricot brandy
½ oz (15 ml) sloe gin
¾ oz (22 ml) lime juice
1 teaspoon (5 ml) grenadine (p 496)
Garnish: lime wedge

Vazquez Daiquiri
Bartender's Sixth Sense, *Jose Maria Vazquez, 1940s*
2 oz (60 ml) aged dark rum
½ oz (15 ml) white crème de cacao
¾ oz (22 ml) lime juice
¼ oz (7 ml) Demerara syrup (p 495)
Garnish: lime wedge

Navy Grog
(See p 450)

Ned King's Gem
Ned King, Gigantic, Easthampton
1 oz (30 ml) Jamaican dark rum
1 oz (30 ml) Cognac
¾ oz (22 ml) lime juice
½ oz (15 ml) pineapple syrup (p 499)
1 dash Angostura Bitters
Garnish: freshly grated cinnamon

No Show Me State
Kathryn "Pepper" Stashek, Attaboy, NYC
2 oz (60 ml) Jamaican dark rum
1 oz (30 ml) Red Gala apple juice
½ oz (15 ml) lime juice
½ oz (15 ml) honey syrup (p 496)
2 dashes Angostura Bitters
Garnish: apple fan

Quarter-Deck Cocktail
"Harry" of Ciro's ABC of Mixing Cocktails, *Harry MacElhone, 1923*
2 oz (60 ml) Jamaican dark rum
½ oz (15 ml) Pedro Ximénez
¾ oz (22 ml) lime juice
1 teaspoon (5 ml) simple syrup
Garnish: orange twist (discard)

Rum Club Daiquiri
Kevin Ludwig, Rum Club, Portland
2 oz (60 ml) aged dark rum
¼ oz (7 ml) maraschino liqueur
¾ oz (22 ml) lime juice
½ oz (15 ml) Demerara syrup (p 495)
3 dashes absinthe
2 dashes Angostura Bitters
Garnish: lime wedge

Spanish Daiquiri
Tom Richter, The Beagle, NYC, 2011
1½ oz (45 ml) aged dark rum
1 oz (30 ml) Pedro Ximénez
¾ oz (22 ml) lime juice
Garnish: lime wedge

Spiced Pineapple Daiquiri
Naren Young, Sweet Liberty, Miami, 2024
½ oz (15 ml) aged dark rum (preferably Angostura 1919)
½ oz (15 ml) spiced rum
½ oz (15 ml) pineapple rum (preferably Planteray Stiggins' Fancy Pineapple Rum)
½ oz (15 ml) Giffard Caribbean Pineapple
½ oz (15 ml) pineapple juice
½ oz (15 ml) lime juice
¼ oz (7 ml) spiced pineapple syrup (p 501)
1 teaspoon (5 ml) pineapple vinegar
3 drops saline solution (p 493)
Garnish: pineapple half-ring

Tahitian Honey Bee
(Honeysuckle with Puerto Rican dark rum)
Trader Vic's Bartender's Guide, *Trader Vic, 1947*
2 oz (60 ml) Puerto Rican dark rum
1 oz (30 ml) lime juice
¾ oz (22 ml) honey syrup (p 496)
Garnish: lime wedge

The Chunky Dunk
Hilary Hestead and Lamar Kumangi, False Idol, San Diego, 2023
¾ oz (22 ml) overproof Jamaican dark rum
¾ oz (22 ml) Giffard Banane du Brésil et des Caraïbes
¾ oz (22 ml) Amontillado Sherry
¾ oz (22 ml) lime juice
¾ oz (22 ml) condensed syrup (p 495)
Garnish: freshly grated cinnamon

Vailee Hi
George St. John, Half Step, Austin, 2016
1 oz (30 ml) aged dark rhum agricole
½ oz (15 ml) pot still Jamaican dark rum (preferably Smith & Cross Traditional Jamaica Rum)
½ oz (15 ml) Rhum Clément Mahina Coco
¾ oz (22 ml) pineapple juice
¾ oz (22 ml) lime juice
½ oz (15 ml) Demerara syrup (p 495)
Garnish: freshly grated cinnamon

From *The Old Waldorf-Astoria Bar Book* (1935):

An optimist sees the glass as half full, a pessimist sees it as half empty, and a bartender sees someone who needs a refill.

Add all ingredients to a shaker, then shake with ice and strain into a frozen coupe.

BATIDA

Caipirinha p 242

Batida

A rustic 'shake-and-dump' cocktail with muddled citrus and cracked ice. Creamy variations with coconut or condensed/evaporated milk are often blended and served on crushed ice.

spirit + lime chunks + sugar

↓

Muddle fruit and sugar in a shaker, then add remaining ingredients and cracked ice. Shake briefly and empty into a frozen double rocks glass.

Described as 'the most Brazilian of all cocktails' by Brazilian bartender João Zarattini in his 1944 book, *Coquetel em Suas Diversas Fórmulas* (*Cocktail in Its Many Forms*), the Batida represents a class of rustic, refreshing cocktails comprising spirit (traditionally cachaça), sugar and fresh citrus chunks, shaken and served on cracked ice. While it's assumed that cachaça, citrus fruits and sugar were being consumed together in Brazil for some time prior, it was in the first half of the 20th century that the Batida Paulista – roughly translating to 'São Paulo Shake' – firmly established its place in the cocktail kingdom. By the 1950s, the drink had evolved even further thanks to a growing demand for iced cocktails and the widespread influence of increasingly sophisticated American mixology. Now commonly known as the Caipirinha (p 242), this rather unassuming cocktail began crossing continents with travelling journalists and enthusiasts. It wasn't until the 1980s that the drink really made a name for itself in Europe, where the original cachaça recipe and popular variations dominated cocktail lists for a decade or more. Intriguingly, this cohort never saw quite the same success in the United States.

Caipirinha translates loosely to 'little hillbilly', a term to describe someone from the rural hinterlands, and the eponymous cocktail is considered the archetype of all Batidas – batida being Portuguese for 'shake' or 'crash'. Bartenders have referred to Batidas as 'country-style' cocktails or 'peasant drinks' due to the industrious method of muddling then lightly shaking citrus chunks with spirits and sweeteners, and dumping them directly into the glass rather than straining. The result is a textured cocktail with a singular depth of flavour, far from refined but brimming with personality.

→

The Caipirinha introduced the world to cachaça, also known as 'pinga', a sugarcane-based spirit made in Brazil. It's the base of most Brazilian cocktails, as it's had such a high production volume in the country since the 16th century. Historically likened to New World rum, cachaça has a reputation as an accessible and affordable spirit, usually distilled at lower strength, with more impurities and therefore a more aromatic or funky character. That distinct flavour, combined with ripe, zesty citrus, is exactly what makes the Caipirinha so remarkable. Over the past 50 years, variations with light rum (the Caipirissima, p 242) and vodka (the Caipiroska, p 242) have become icons in their own right, while fruity riffs with berries, mango or guava have also proven to be hits.

In contemporary culture, Batida seems to be the most appropriate term to categorise shaken and blended cocktails of this kind, featuring cachaça or an alternative spirit, sugar and chunks of citrus and/or other fruits. The category also encompasses milkshake-like variations featuring coconut or condensed/evaporated milk. These drinks have a more unpretentious, no-frills feel to them than most, and while the Brazilian originals tend to be fruit-forward, sweet or creamy, modern variations are often clean, crisp or even savoury.

ESSENTIAL VARIATION

Gordon's Cup

Sasha Petraske, East Side Company Bar, NYC, 2005
2 oz (60 ml) gin
¾ oz (22 ml) simple syrup
6 lime chunks
3 cucumber wheels

Add lime, cucumber and simple syrup to a shaker and press. Add remaining ingredients with cracked ice and shake 4–5 times, then empty into a frozen double rocks glass.
Garnish: 3 cucumber wheels and pinches of salt and pepper

Sasha Petraske was a New York City native and a true visionary credited with spearheading the classic cocktail renaissance at his first bar, the now-closed Milk & Honey, which opened on December 31st, 1999. Petraske was many things to many people, but above all he was a man of integrity. He believed we all could and should be better people – better to each other and the very best at our trade.

Because of its purist, methodical approach to every detail of the drink and its delivery, Milk & Honey remains a leading authority in modern bartending culture, pioneering the use of large block ice for shaking, measured pouring, a strict adherence to fresh ingredients and a renewed focus on simple, timeless cocktails. Petraske's 'neo-speakeasy' was well regarded all over the world and sparked a plethora of bar openings in its likeness, including The Everleigh, where he was Michael's mentor and partner until his untimely death at age 42, in August 2015. The Everleigh was proud to carry the bloodline of Milk & Honey and honour Petraske's most treasured beliefs and ideals. As the man always said, 'There are only two crimes: stealing and not trying.'

Created by Petraske in the early 2000s, the Gordon's Cup is a clean, refreshing and slightly savoury cocktail inspired by Batidas like Brazil's Caipirinha (p 242). Cucumber makes for a cool, slightly sweet and herbaceous addition, its crispness juxtaposed with the hearty texture of muddled lime and rounded out by the subtle spice of salt and pepper as a garnish. For more savoury citrus cocktails, explore Gordon's Cup riffs by Milk & Honey alumni, such as the Gordon's Breakfast (p 243), which features Cholula Original Hot Sauce and Worcestershire sauce, or the El Guapo (p 242), a tequila variation with Cholula – both by Sam Ross – or the Square Meal (p 243), a bourbon-based riff with chipotle by Michael.

Batida

Batida
Tiki Drinks: Tropical Cocktails for the Modern Bar, *Nicole Weston and Robert Sharp, 2015*
2 oz (60 ml) cachaça
1 oz (30 ml) coconut cream
1 oz (30 ml) condensed milk
¼ oz (7 ml) lime juice
Shake briefly with ice and strain into a Spritz glass with crushed ice.
Garnish: edible orchid

Batida de Carnaval
Difford's Guide
2 oz (60 ml) cachaça
1½ oz (45 ml) mango purée
1 oz (30 ml) orange juice
1 oz (30 ml) condensed milk
¼ oz (7 ml) lime juice
Shake briefly with ice and strain into a Spritz glass with crushed ice.
Garnish: dehydrated mango slice

Batida de Coco
Igor Renovato
2 oz (60 ml) cachaça
1½ oz (45 ml) cloudy apple juice
1 oz (30 ml) coconut cream
1 oz (30 ml) condensed milk
¼ oz (7 ml) lime juice
Shake briefly with ice and strain into a Spritz glass with crushed ice.
Garnish: apple fan

Batida de Morango
Difford's Guide
2 oz (60 ml) cachaça
¾ oz (22 ml) simple syrup
½ oz (15 ml) condensed milk
¼ oz (7 ml) lime juice
3 strawberries, halved
Muddle strawberries with simple syrup and lime juice, add remaining ingredients, then shake and strain into a frozen double rocks glass with crushed ice.
Garnish: strawberry half

Brazilian Mojito
2 oz (60 ml) cachaça
¾ oz (22 ml) simple syrup
5–6 lime chunks
1 white sugar cube
8–10 mint leaves
Garnish: mint bouquet

Caipirinha
2 oz (60 ml) cachaça
¾ oz (22 ml) simple syrup
5–6 lime chunks
1 white sugar cube

Caipirissima
(Caipirinha with light rum)
2 oz (60 ml) light rum
¾ oz (22 ml) simple syrup
5–6 lime chunks
1 white sugar cube

Caipiroska
(Caipirinha with vodka)
2 oz (60 ml) vodka
¾ oz (22 ml) simple syrup
6 lime chunks
1 white sugar cube

Caipiruva
Dale DeGroff
2 oz (60 ml) cachaça
4 lime chunks
4 green grapes
½ oz (15 ml) Demerara syrup (p 495)

Chilean Mojito
Sam Ross, Milk & Honey, NYC, 2008
2 oz (60 ml) pisco
¾ oz (22 ml) simple syrup
5–6 lime chunks
1 raw sugar cube 8–10 mint leaves
Garnish: mint bouquet

Criolla
Hillary Hestead and Lamar Kumangi, False Idol, San Diego, 2023
1 oz (30 ml) light rum
½ oz (15 ml) overproof rhum agricole (preferably Paranubes)
¾ oz (22 ml) simple syrup
5–6 lime chunks
1 raw sugar cube
8–10 coriander (cilantro) leaves

Early Supper
Tom Lasher-Walker, Fresh Kills, NYC, 2016
1½ oz (45 ml) Scotch
½ oz (15 ml) Islay Scotch
¾ oz (22 ml) honey syrup (p 496)
5–6 lime chunks
4 dashes Cholula Original Hot Sauce
2 dashes Worcestershire sauce
3 cucumber wheels
3 cocktail onions (p 506)
Press cucumber and cocktail onions with honey syrup, add remaining ingredients and cracked ice. Shake briefly, then empty into a frozen double rocks glass with ice.
Garnish: 3 cucumber wheels and pinches of salt and cracked pepper

El Guapo
(Gordon's Cup with tequila and Cholula)
Sam Ross, Little Branch, NYC, 2008
2 oz (60 ml) blanco tequila
¾ oz (22 ml) simple syrup
6 lime chunks
3 cucumber wheels
5 dashes Cholula Original Hot Sauce
Muddle lime and cucumber with simple syrup in a shaker. Add remaining ingredients and cracked ice. Shake briefly, then empty into a frozen double rocks glass with ice.
Garnish: 3 cucumber wheels and pinches of salt and cracked pepper

El Niño
Sam Ross, Milk & Honey, NYC, 2016
2 oz (60 ml) blanco tequila
¾ oz (22 ml) simple syrup
5–6 lime chunks
1 strawberry, halved
1 dash rosewater
Muddle lime and strawberry with simple syrup, add remaining ingredients and cracked ice. Shake briefly, then empty into a frozen double rocks glass with ice.

Muddle fruit and sugar in a shaker, then add remaining ingredients and cracked ice. Shake briefly and empty into a frozen double rocks glass.

Gordon's Breakfast
(Gordon's Cup with Cholula and Worcestershire)
Sam Ross, Little Branch, NYC, 2008
2 oz (60 ml) gin
¾ oz (22 ml) simple syrup
5–6 lime chunks
3 cucumber wheels
5 dashes Cholula Original Hot Sauce
2 dashes Worcestershire sauce
Garnish: 3 cucumber wheels and dashes of salt and cracked pepper

Lemon Batida Cocktail
India Stevens, Cinder House, St. Louis
2 oz (60 ml) cachaça
¾ oz (22 ml) falernum
¾ oz (22 ml) lime juice
½ oz (15 ml) coconut milk
½ oz (15 ml) simple syrup
Shake briefly with ice and strain into a Spritz glass with crushed ice.
Garnish: freshly grated nutmeg and toasted coconut flakes

Mojo Criollo
Libro de Cocktail, *Juan A. Lasa, 1929*
2 oz (60 ml) light rum
¾ oz (22 ml) simple syrup
3 dashes Angostura Bitters
1 dash soda, to top
1 raw sugar cube
5–6 lime chunks
8–10 mint leaves
Garnish: mint bouquet

Mojito Criollo No. 3
Bar La Florida Cocktails, 1934
2 oz (60 ml) Cognac
¾ oz (22 ml) simple syrup
1 dash soda, to top
1 raw sugar cube
5–6 lime chunks
8–10 mint leaves
Garnish: mint bouquet

Mojo de Ginebra
Libro de Cocktail, *Juan A. Lasa, 1929*
2 oz (60 ml) gin
¾ oz (22 ml) simple syrup
1 dash soda, to top
1 raw sugar cube
5–6 lime chunks
8–10 mint leaves
Garnish: mint bouquet
▼ Originally Old Tom gin.

Mojo de Ron
Libro de Cocktail, *Juan A. Lasa, 1929*
2 oz (60 ml) light rum
¾ oz (22 ml) simple syrup
5–6 lime chunks
1 dash soda
1 raw sugar cube
8–10 mint leaves
Garnish: mint bouquet
▼ Add 3 dashes of Angostura Bitters to make the **Mojo Criollo**.

Passionfruit Batida
2 oz (60 ml) cachaça
¾ oz (22 ml) passionfruit syrup (p 499)
½ oz (15 ml) coconut cream
5–6 lime chunks
Shake briefly with ice and strain into a frozen Spritz glass with crushed ice.
Garnish: thinly sliced passionfruit skin

Square Meal
(Gordon's Cup with bourbon and chipotle)
Michael Madrusan, The Everleigh, Melbourne, 2016
2 oz (60 ml) bourbon
¾ oz (22 ml) simple syrup
5–6 lime chunks
3 cucumber wheels
3 dashes Cholula Chipotle Hot Sauce
Garnish: 3 cucumber wheels and pinches of salt and cracked pepper

Tequila Cup
2 oz (60 ml) blanco tequila
¾ oz (22 ml) simple syrup
5–6 lime chunks
3 cucumber wheels
Garnish: 3 cucumber wheels and pinches of salt and cracked pepper

From *Harry Johnson's Bartenders' Manual* (1900):

Here's to those who love us well, and those who don't can go to—hell!

Watermelon Batida
Jorge Balbontin, Barcelona, 2015
2 oz (60 ml) cachaça
2 oz (60 ml) evaporated milk
2 oz (60 ml) coconut water
¾ oz (22 ml) agave syrup (p 494)
3–4 1 in (2.5 cm) watermelon chunks
Press watermelon with agave syrup, add remaining ingredients, then shake and strain into a frozen Spritz glass with crushed ice.
Garnish: watermelon wedge

Muddle fruit and sugar in a shaker, then add remaining ingredients and cracked ice. Shake briefly and empty into a frozen double rocks glass.

FIX & SWIZZLE

Up All Night Swizzle p 261 (left), Frantic Atlantic p 255 (right)

Fix & Swizzle

Thirst-quenching citrus cocktails served on crushed ice and distinguished by technique, often invigorated with pressed or muddled fruit and/or fresh mint.

spirit + citrus + sugar
and/or liqueur/s or syrup/s

FIX

Build all ingredients in a shaker, then pour into a frozen double rocks glass with crushed ice. Shimmy and top with more crushed ice.

SWIZZLE

Build all ingredients in a shaker, then pour into a frozen Collins glass with crushed ice. Swizzle and top with more crushed ice.

A Fix, in short, is a Non-Traditional Sour (p 155) (spirit, lemon and sugar, shaken and served up) served on crushed ice, often with an ornate fruit garnish. The category arose in the mid-19th century, when its first iteration, the Gin Fix, appeared in print in 1841. By the late 1880s, bartenders had taken to sweetening Fixes with liqueurs and syrups, much like Sours (p 152) were sweetened to become Daisies (p 184); in the case of the Fix, however, this shift marked the start of the style's downfall.

By the turn of the 20th century, Fixes were found in cocktail books rather than bars, and few bartenders today can be expected to know the drink by name. This is not to say that spirit-driven drinks served on crushed ice have had their day, however. World-famous modern classics like the Bramble (p 248) by Dick Bradsell – a Fix in the traditional sense – still make a strong case for the category's ongoing relevance.

In the Caribbean, a similar albeit lesser-known cocktail dubbed the Swizzle originated around the same time as the Fix. Traditionally a combination of rum or gin, sugar or falernum, bitters and often lime, the Swizzle is defined by the distinctive technique employed to briskly mix, chill, dilute and aerate the ingredients in the glass using an eponymous tool: the swizzle stick. The most famous drinks in this family, such as the Queen's Park Swizzle (p 250), hail from Trinidad and 'because of their origin, call for rum' according to the king of tiki, Trader Vic. Yet, Vic also noted that 'nearly all punches can be swizzled', which speaks to the diversity of the Swizzles that follow.

As big believers in the power of fresh produce, we've rejigged some of the older recipes that call for syrups and fruit liqueurs to feature real fruit instead. We've also developed our own method for crafting these drinks, the

→

Madrusan method, which differs somewhat from the industry standard. Our technique begins by building the wet ingredients in one tin, then adds a splash of that mixture to another tin with the fresh produce to be muddled together. The muddled mixture is then poured into the glass, prior to adding the crushed ice. Finally, the remaining wet ingredients are poured through the centre of the crushed ice, creating a vibrant and glamorous gradient effect that turns heads every time.

ESSENTIAL VARIATIONS

Bramble

Dick Bradsell, Fred's Club, London, 1980s
2 oz (60 ml) gin
¾ oz (22 ml) lemon juice
¾ oz (22 ml) simple syrup
3 blackberries

Swirl the liquids together in a shaker, then muddle blackberries with a splash of the swirled liquids in a separate shaker. Pour the muddled mixture into a frozen double rocks glass, add crushed ice, then pour in the remaining liquids, shimmy and top with more crushed ice.
Garnish: blackberry

The Bramble is a modern classic created in the mid-1980s by the late Dick Bradsell, the renowned English bartender responsible for the Espresso Martini (p 464) among other benchmarks. Bradsell was the bar manager at Fred's Club in London's Soho, a debaucherous member's club owned by Fred Taylor and frequented by pop stars and supermodels. Setting out to invent a truly British cocktail, he thought back to his upbringing on the Isle of Wight, where he played among the thorny brambles and feasted on their seasonal delights. In the end, Bradsell was the first to acknowledge that both the crème de mûre and likely Spanish-grown lemons he selected as supporting players weren't native to England. Even so, his cocktail succeeded in capturing the understated elegance of English summer: a simple gin-based Sour with blackberry, lengthened by a heap of crushed ice.

Our preferred Bramble recipe utilises fresh, ripe blackberries, which are succulent, sweet and tangy when in season, and bring a gratifyingly earthy richness to the drink. Those with a fondness for that flavour should try the Blackout (p 214), a similar Gimlet variation in Lucius Beebe's *The Stork Club Bar Book* from 1946. And while Bradsell was staunchly against swapping the gin for other spirits (especially vodka), we wholeheartedly recommend the Rumble (p 254), a rum-based riff by our dear friend Michael McIlroy.

Queen's Park Swizzle

Queen's Park Hotel, Trinidad, circa 1895
Trader Vic's Book of Food and Drink, *Trader Vic, 1946*
2 oz (60 ml) light rum (preferably Demerara rum)
1 oz (30 ml) lime juice
¾ oz (22 ml) simple syrup
8–10 mint leaves
1 white sugar cube
3 dashes Angostura Bitters, to float
3 dashes Peychaud's Aromatic Cocktail Bitters, to float

Press mint with lime juice and sugar in a shaker, then add rum and simple syrup and swirl to combine. Pour into a frozen Collins glass, add crushed ice, then float bitters, swizzle and top with more crushed ice.
Garnish: mint bouquet
● For optimal presentation, try to make sure the mint remains gathered at the bottom of the glass, and use a bar spoon to push down rogue leaves.

The recipe for the Queen's Park Swizzle was first published in *Trader Vic's Book of Food and Drink* in 1946. Named after the Queen's Park Hotel in Port of Spain, Trinidad, which opened in 1895, the cocktail is best thought of as a drier, more complex Mojito with Demerara rum and Angostura Bitters, swizzled in true Trinidadian fashion. In his tropical tome, Trader Vic endorsed the drink with vigour, describing it as 'the most delightful form of anaesthesia given out' in its day, and the drink has stood tall as a staple of tiki culture ever since. Curiously, despite bearing the Queen's Park name, it is believed that the Green Swizzle (p 259) – an intriguing marriage of rum or gin, falernum and wormwood bitters – was actually the hotel's more famous cocktail.

For more righteous rum cocktails on the dry to bitter side, try the El InterAmericano Cocktail (p 234), a Jamaican dark rum twist on the Hemingway Daiquiri (p 228) in Charles H. Baker Jr's *The South American Gentleman's Companion* from 1951, or Trader Vic's Dr. Funk (p 87), a Rickey-style mixture of aged dark rum, lime, grenadine, absinthe and soda from 1946.

Fix

Build all ingredients in a shaker, then pour into a frozen double rocks glass with crushed ice. Shimmy and top with more crushed ice.

GIN

Bin-'n'-Gitters
J.K.L. Ponsonby-Foulcques
The South American Gentleman's Companion, *Charles H. Baker Jr., 1951*
1¾ oz (52 ml) gin
¾ oz (22 ml) lime juice
½ oz (15 ml) simple syrup
4 dashes Angostura Bitters, to float
Build all ingredients in a shaker, then pour into a frozen double rocks glass with crushed ice. Float bitters, shimmy and top with more crushed ice.
Garnish: mint sprig and lime wedge

Cosmic Dancer
Tony Roehr, Raised by Wolves, San Diego, 2021
1 oz (30 ml) gin
1 oz (30 ml) Cappelletti Pasubio Vino Amaro
¾ oz (22 ml) lemon juice
¾ oz (22 ml) simple syrup
3 raspberries
Swirl the liquids together in a shaker, then muddle raspberries with a splash of the swirled liquids in a separate shaker. Pour the muddled mixture into a frozen double rocks glass, add crushed ice, then pour in the remaining liquids, shimmy and top with more crushed ice.
Garnish: raspberry

Hocus Pocus
(Chelsea Sidecar with crushed ice)
Jones' Complete Barguide, *Stan Jones, 1977*
1½ oz (45 ml) gin
½ oz (15 ml) triple sec
¾ oz (22 ml) lemon juice
1 teaspoon (5 ml) simple syrup
Garnish: lemon wedge and cherry

Honeysuckle Julep
Damon Boelte, Grand Army, NYC
2 oz (60 ml) Old Tom gin
¼ oz (7 ml) Yellow Chartreuse
½ oz (15 ml) honey syrup
2 slices white peach
Swirl the liquids together in a shaker, then muddle peaches with a splash of the swirled liquids in a separate shaker. Pour the muddled mixture into a frozen double rocks glass, add crushed ice, then pour in the remaining liquids, shimmy and top with more crushed ice.
Garnish: lemon half-wheel and fragrant flower

Jitterbug
David Molyneux, The Everleigh, Melbourne, 2018
¾ oz (22 ml) gin
¾ oz (22 ml) St Germain Elderflower Liqueur
¾ oz (22 ml) Aperol
¾ oz (22 ml) lime juice
Garnish: mint bouquet

From *Here's How!* (1927):

Here's to the nights we'll never remember, with the friends we'll never forget!

Lemon Popsicle
Naren Young, Sweet Liberty, Miami, 2024
1½ oz (45 ml) gin (preferably Bombay Sapphire Premier Cru Murcian Lemon Gin)
½ oz (15 ml) limoncello
½ oz (15 ml) Nardini Acqua di Cedro
½ oz (15 ml) Sanpellegrino Limonata
½ oz (15 ml) lemon juice
¼ oz (7 ml) simple syrup
1 teaspoon (6 g) lemon curd
2 dashes lemon bitters
Add Limonata to a frozen double rocks glass with crushed ice. Dry shake remaining ingredients, pour into the frozen double rocks glass, then shimmy and top with more crushed ice.
Garnish: freshly grated lemon zest

Ramble
Phil Ward, Death & Co, NYC, 2008
1¾ oz (50 ml) gin
¾ oz (22 ml) lemon juice
¾ oz (22 ml) simple syrup
4 raspberries
Swirl the liquids together in a shaker, then muddle raspberries with a splash of the swirled liquids in a separate shaker. Pour the muddled mixture into a frozen double rocks glass, add crushed ice, then pour in the remaining liquids, shimmy and top with more crushed ice.
Garnish: raspberry

The Chaperone
Andrew Cordero, Seneca, San Diego, 2022
1 oz (30 ml) gin
1 oz (30 ml) Amaro Montenegro
¾ oz (22 ml) lime juice
½ oz (15 ml) honey syrup (p 496)
4 cucumber wheels
Muddle cucumber with honey syrup, add remaining ingredients, then toss and pour into a frozen double rocks glass with crushed ice. Shimmy and top with more crushed ice.
Garnish: celery stalk

Build all ingredients in a shaker, then pour into a frozen double rocks glass with crushed ice. Shimmy and top with more crushed ice.

RUM & CANE SPIRIT

Barracuda
Felix Woods, The Everleigh, Melbourne, 2018
¾ oz (22 ml) light rum
¾ oz (22 ml) Manzanilla Sherry
¾ oz (22 ml) lime juice
¾ oz (22 ml) simple syrup
2 dashes orange bitters
Garnish: lime wedge

Blitzer
Greg Keesee, Attaboy, Nashville, 2021
2 oz (60 ml) light rum
¾ oz (22 ml) lime juice
¾ oz (22 ml) Coco López
6–8 mint leaves
¼ oz (7 ml) overproof Jamaican dark rum, to float
Press mint, lime juice and Coco López in a shaker, then add light rum and swirl to combine. Toss and strain into a frozen Collins glass with crushed ice, then float Jamaican dark rum, shimmy and top with more crushed ice.
Garnish: mint bouquet

Deep Purple Punch
Trader Vic's Bartender's Guide, *Trader Vic, 1947*
1½ oz (45 ml) light rum
¾ oz (22 ml) lime juice
¾ oz (22 ml) passionfruit syrup (p 499)
5 red grapes
Swirl the liquids together in a shaker, then muddle grapes with a splash of the swirled liquids in a separate shaker. Pour the mixture into a frozen double rocks glass, add crushed ice, then pour in the remaining liquids, shimmy and top with more crushed ice.
Garnish: red grape

Golden Glove
(Jamaican Rum Sidecar with crushed ice)
Bar La Florida Cocktails, *1934*
1½ oz (45 ml) Jamaican dark rum
½ oz (15 ml) triple sec
¾ oz (22 ml) lemon juice
1 teaspoon (5 ml) simple syrup
Garnish: lemon wedge and cherry

Havana Fix
(Light Rum Fix with pineapple and Green Chartreuse)
Eric Alperin, The Varnish, Los Angeles
1¼ oz (37 ml) light rum
¾ oz (22 ml) simple syrup
¾ oz (22 ml) pineapple juice
¼ oz (7 ml) lemon juice
¼ oz (7 ml) Green Chartreuse, to float
Build all ingredients in a shaker, then pour into a frozen double rocks glass with crushed ice. Shimmy, top with more crushed ice, then float Green Chartreuse.
Garnish: mint sprig

Mojito
Sloppy Joe's Cocktails Manual, *1932*
2 oz (60 ml) light rum
1 oz (30 ml) lime juice
¾ oz (22 ml) simple syrup
1 raw sugar cube
8–10 mint leaves
Press mint with lime juice and sugar in a shaker, then add rum and swirl to combine. Pour into a frozen double rocks glass with crushed ice, then shimmy and top with more crushed ice.
Garnish: mint bouquet
● First published in Spanish as <u>Mojo Criollo</u> in *Libro de Cocktail*, Juan A. Lasa, 1929.

Motor City Mojito
Greg Keesee, Attaboy, Nashville, 2021
1 oz (30 ml) aged dark rum
1 oz (30 ml) Laird's Straight Applejack 86
¾ oz (22 ml) lime juice
½ oz (15 ml) cane syrup (p 494)
½ oz (15 ml) falernum
1 raw sugar cube
8–10 mint leaves
Press mint with lime juice and sugar in a shaker, then add rum and swirl to combine. Pour into a frozen double rocks glass with crushed ice, then shimmy and top with more crushed ice.
Garnish: mint bouquet

Night Flight Cocktail
Trader Vic's Bartender's Guide, *Trader Vic, 1947*
1¾ oz (50 ml) Jamaican dark rum
1 oz (30 ml) lime juice
½ oz (15 ml) maple syrup
Garnish: mint bouquet

Rich Man's Mojito
(Mojito with blended aged rums)
Toby Maloney, Milk & Honey, NYC, 2004
1 oz (30 ml) Goslings Black Seal Rum
1 oz (30 ml) aged dark rum
1 oz (30 ml) lime juice
¾ oz (22 ml) simple syrup
1 raw sugar cube
8–10 mint leaves
Press mint with lime juice and sugar in a shaker, then add rum and swirl to combine. Pour into a frozen double rocks glass with crushed ice, then shimmy and top with more crushed ice.
Garnish: mint bouquet

Build all ingredients in a shaker, then pour into a frozen double rocks glass with crushed ice. Shimmy and top with more crushed ice.

Rumble

Michael McIlroy, Milk & Honey, NYC, 2006

2 oz (60 ml) light rum
¾ oz (22 ml) lemon juice
¾ oz (22 ml) simple syrup
3 blackberries

Swirl the liquids together in a shaker, then muddle blackberries with a splash of the swirled liquids in a separate shaker. Pour the muddled mixture into a frozen double rocks glass, add crushed ice, then pour in the remaining liquids, shimmy and top with more crushed ice.

Garnish: blackberry

Santa Cruz Fix

The Bar-Tender's Guide, *Jerry Thomas, 1862*

2 oz (60 ml) Cruzan Aged Dark Rum
¾ oz (22 ml) lemon juice
¾ oz (22 ml) simple syrup
Garnish: lemon half-wheel and 3–4 assorted seasonal berries

Santa Cruz Fix (1887 Recipe)

(Santa Cruz Fix with orange curaçao)
The Bar-Tender's Guide, *Jerry Thomas, 1887*

2 oz (60 ml) Cruzan Aged Dark Rum
¾ oz (22 ml) orange curaçao (p 498)
¾ oz (22 ml) lemon juice
Garnish: orange half-wheel, pineapple wedge and cherry

St. Croix Fix

(Santa Cruz Fix with pineapple syrup)
New and Improved Bartender's Manual, *Harry Johnson, 1882*

2 oz (60 ml) Cruzan Aged Dark Rum
¾ oz (22 ml) lemon juice
¾ oz (22 ml) pineapple syrup (p 499)
Garnish: 2 pineapple fronds and cherry

Surfer Rosa

Adele Stratton, Noble Experiment, San Diego, 2016

1½ oz (45 ml) Jamaican dark rum
½ oz (15 ml) Suze
1 oz (30 ml) pineapple juice
¼ oz (7 ml) lime juice
½ oz (15 ml) orgeat
Garnish: 2 pineapple fronds and cherry

Yacht Club Punch

Jones' Complete Barguide, *Stan Jones, 1977*

2 oz (60 ml) light rum
¾ oz (22 ml) lime juice
¾ oz (22 ml) grenadine (p 496)
2 dashes absinthe
Garnish: mint bouquet

AGAVE

Armillita Chico

The Gentleman's Companion, *Charles H. Baker Jr., 1939*

2 oz (60 ml) blanco tequila
¾ oz (22 ml) lime juice
¾ oz (22 ml) grenadine (p 496)
1 drop orange blossom water
Garnish: lime wedge and cherry

▼ "Armillita is the idol of Mexico, their foremost, most finished, most graceful, most dramatic bullfighter."

Catamaran

Brandon Bramhall, Last Saint, Charleston, 2023

1½ oz (45 ml) blanco tequila
½ oz (15 ml) Amaro Meletti
¾ oz (22 ml) lime juice
¾ oz (22 ml) passionfruit syrup (p 499)
1 teaspoon (5 ml) cane syrup (p 494)
8–10 mint leaves

Press mint with cane syrup in a shaker, add remaining ingredients, then toss and pour into a frozen double rocks glass with crushed ice. Shimmy and top with more crushed ice.

Garnish: mint bouquet

Cocodrilo

Anthony Jayasekera, Bar Tobalá, Melbourne, 2023

1 oz (30 ml) mezcal
½ oz (15 ml) pear liqueur
1 oz (30 ml) pineapple juice
½ oz (15 ml) lime juice
½ oz (15 ml) orgeat
Garnish: orange wedge and cherry

London Scramble

Dre Masso and Henry Besant, 2007

1½ oz (45 ml) blanco tequila
⅜ oz (11 ml) lemon juice
⅜ oz (11 ml) lime juice
½ oz (15 ml) agave syrup (p 494)
3 blackberries

Swirl the liquids together in a shaker, then muddle blackberries with a splash of the swirled liquids in a separate shaker. Pour the muddled mixture into a frozen double rocks glass, add crushed ice, then pour in the remaining liquids, shimmy and top with more crushed ice.

Garnish: lemon wedge and blackberry

Loner's Club

Alicia Perry, The Gutter, San Diego, 2023

1½ oz (45 ml) mezcal
½ oz (15 ml) Cocchi Americano
1 oz (30 ml) lime juice
¾ oz (22 ml) simple syrup
6–8 mint leaves
2 cucumber wheels

Press cucumber and mint in a shaker. Add remaining ingredients, then toss and pour into a frozen double rocks glass with crushed ice. Shimmy and top with more crushed ice.

Garnish: mint sprig and cucumber fan

Build all ingredients in a shaker, then pour into a frozen double rocks glass with crushed ice. Shimmy and top with more crushed ice.

Perfect Timing
Andrew Cordero, Seneca, San Diego, 2022
1½ oz (45 ml) blanco tequila
½ oz (15 ml) Cynar
¾ oz (22 ml) lemon juice
¾ oz (22 ml) passionfruit syrup (p 499)
2 orange half-wheels
Muddle orange and passionfruit syrup in a shaker. Add remaining ingredients, then toss and pour into a frozen double rocks glass with crushed ice. Shimmy and top with more crushed ice.
Garnish: orange wedge

Pilot Light
Michael McCollum, Attaboy, Nashville, 2021
2 oz (60 ml) blanco tequila
¾ oz (22 ml) lime juice
¾ oz (22 ml) Coco López
2 dashes Scrappy's Bitters Fire Tincture
2 drops saline solution (p 493)
2 cucumber wheels
Press cucumber with coconut syrup, add remaining ingredients, then toss and pour into a frozen double rocks glass with crushed ice. Shimmy and top with more crushed ice.
Garnish: cucumber fan and dusting of cayenne pepper

Tia Mia
Ivy Mix, Leyenda, NYC
1 oz (30 ml) espadín mezcal (preferably Del Maguey Vida)
1 oz (30 ml) Jamaican dark rum (preferably Appleton Estate Reserve)
½ oz (15 ml) Pierre Ferrand Dry Curaçao
¾ oz (22 ml) lime juice
½ oz (15 ml) orgeat
Garnish: mint sprig, lime wedge and edible orchid

Two Step
Kathryn "Pepper" Stashek, Attaboy, NYC, 2017
¾ oz (22 ml) blanco tequila
¾ oz (22 ml) Cocchi Americano
¾ oz (22 ml) lemon juice
¾ oz (22 ml) simple syrup
3 strawberry halves
Swirl the liquids together in a shaker, then muddle strawberries with a splash of the swirled liquids in a separate shaker. Pour the muddled mixture into a frozen double rocks glass, add crushed ice, then pour in the remaining liquids, shimmy and top with more crushed ice.
Garnish: half a strawberry

Vernita Green
Alicia Perry and Anthony Schmidt, Quixote, San Diego, 2024
1½ oz (45 ml) reposado tequila
½ oz (15 ml) raicilla
1½ oz (45 ml) verdita (p 507)
1 oz (30 ml) mango syrup (p 498)
¾ oz (22 ml) lime juice
Add all ingredients to a shaker and pebble whip, then pour into a frozen Spritz glass with crushed ice, shimmy, then top with more crushed ice.
Garnish: pineapple wedge dipped in Tajín Clásico, mint bouquet and marigold

BRANDY

Autumn in Jersey
Anthony Schmidt, Noble Experiment, San Diego, 2011
2 oz (60 ml) bonded apple brandy
¾ oz (22 ml) lemon juice
½ oz (15 ml) orgeat
2 dashes orange bitters
Garnish: apple fan and freshly grated cinnamon

Brandy Fix
New and Improved Bartender's Manual, *Harry Johnson, 1882*
1½ oz (45 ml) Cognac
¼ oz (7 ml) Green Chartreuse
¾ oz (22 ml) lemon juice
¾ oz (22 ml) pineapple syrup (p 499)
Garnish: 3–4 assorted seasonal berries

Frantic Atlantic
(aka **Quick Fix**)
Michael Madrusan, Little Branch, NYC, 2007
1 oz (30 ml) pisco (preferably Acholado)
1 oz (30 ml) St Germain Elderflower Liqueur
1 oz (30 ml) pink grapefruit juice
½ oz (15 ml) lime juice
Garnish: mint sprig and cherry

Mendez Vigo-Special
(Aviation No. 2 with Cognac on crushed ice)
Bar La Florida Cocktails, 1935
1½ oz (45 ml) Cognac
⅜ oz (11 ml) maraschino liqueur
¾ oz (22 ml) lemon juice
⅜ oz (11 ml) simple syrup
Garnish: cherry

Patio Vibes
Half Step, Austin, 2016
1 oz (30 ml) pisco
¾ oz (22 ml) Galliano L'Autentico
1 oz (30 ml) pink grapefruit juice
½ oz (15 ml) lemon juice
½ oz (15 ml) simple syrup
Garnish: grapefruit wedge

Pisco-Apricot Tropicáls
Lima Country Club, Lima
The South American Gentleman's Companion, *Charles H. Baker Jr., 1951*
1½ oz (45 ml) pisco
½ oz (15 ml) apricot brandy
¾ oz (22 ml) lime juice
1 teaspoon (5 ml) simple syrup
2 dashes Angostura Bitters
Garnish: mint sprig and cherry

Build all ingredients in a shaker, then pour into a frozen double rocks glass with crushed ice. Shimmy and top with more crushed ice.

Pompeii
Oska Whitehart, The Everleigh, Melbourne, 2017
1½ oz (45 ml) Cognac
¾ oz (22 ml) lemon juice
¾ oz (22 ml) simple syrup
2 dashes absinthe
3 strawberry halves
Swirl the liquids together in a shaker, then muddle strawberry with a splash of the swirled liquids in a separate shaker. Pour the mixture into a frozen double rocks glass, add crushed ice, then pour in the remaining liquids, shimmy and top with more crushed ice.
Garnish: mint sprig and strawberry half

St. Stephen's Sour
Jeffrey Morgenthaler, Clyde Common, Portland, 2014
1 oz (30 ml) Cognac
1 oz (30 ml) aged dark rum
¾ oz (22 ml) lemon juice
½ oz (15 ml) orgeat
Garnish: lemon twist

Vanilla Punch
The Bar-Tender's Guide, *Jerry Thomas, 1862*
1½ oz (45 ml) Cognac
¾ oz (22 ml) Giffard Vanille de Madagascar
½ oz (15 ml) lemon juice
Garnish: orange wedge and cherry

AMERICAN WHISKEY

Breakfast Manhattan
Andy Chu, The Everleigh, Melbourne, 2017
1 oz (30 ml) bourbon
¾ oz (22 ml) sweet vermouth
¾ oz (22 ml) lemon juice
½ oz (15 ml) simple syrup
Garnish: orange wedge and cherry

Fedora
New and Improved Illustrated Bartender's Manual, *Harry Johnson, 1888*
½ oz (15 ml) bourbon
½ oz (15 ml) Cognac
½ oz (15 ml) Jamaican dark rum
¾ oz (22 ml) orange curaçao (p 498)
¾ oz (22 ml) lemon juice
Garnish: mint sprig, raspberry and blackberry

Midnight Stinger
Sam Ross, Attaboy, NYC, 2008
1 oz (30 ml) bourbon
1 oz (30 ml) Fernet-Branca
¾ oz (22 ml) lemon juice
¾ oz (22 ml) simple syrup
Garnish: mint bouquet

Mississippi Jones
Alicia Perry and Anthony Schmidt, The Gutter, San Diego, 2023
1½ oz (45 ml) rye whiskey
½ oz (15 ml) Scotch
¼ oz (7 ml) apricot brandy
¼ oz (7 ml) Giffard Crème de Pêche de Vigne
¾ oz (22 ml) lemon juice
½ oz (15 ml) orgeat
Garnish: mint sprig and grapefruit twist

Mixed Berry Fix
Michael Madrusan, The Everleigh, 2023
¾ oz (22 ml) bourbon
¾ oz (22 ml) Cognac
¾ oz (22 ml) lemon juice
¾ oz (22 ml) simple syrup
2 blackberries
2 raspberries
8–10 mint leaves
Swirl the liquids together in a shaker, then muddle mint and berries with a splash of the swirled liquids in a separate shaker. Pour the muddled mixture into a frozen double rocks glass, add crushed ice, then pour in the remaining liquids, shimmy and top with more crushed ice.
Garnish: blackberry and raspberry
● Based on Dre Masso's Mixed Berry Julep, 2009.

The Separatist
Daniel Zacharczuk, The Varnish, Los Angeles, 2024
1 oz (30 ml) bourbon
1 oz (30 ml) Amaro CioCiaro
¾ oz (22 ml) lemon juice
¾ oz (22 ml) simple syrup
1 orange half-wheel
Press orange with simple syrup, add remaining ingredients, then toss and pour into a frozen double rocks glass with crushed ice. Shimmy and top with more crushed ice.
Garnish: orange half-wheel and cherry

SCOTCH

Irresponsible Husband
Brian Lee, Noble Experiment, San Diego, 2013
1½ oz (45 ml) Scotch
⅜ oz (11 ml) apricot brandy
¾ oz (22 ml) lemon juice
⅜ oz (11 ml) orgeat
Garnish: freshly grated nutmeg

The Dissident
Daniel Zacharczuk, The Varnish, Los Angeles, 2024
1 oz (30 ml) Scotch
1 oz (30 ml) Amaro CioCiaro
¾ oz (22 ml) lemon juice
¾ oz (22 ml) simple syrup
1 orange half-wheel
Press orange with simple syrup, add remaining ingredients, then toss and pour into a frozen double rocks glass with crushed ice. Shimmy and top with more crushed ice.
Garnish: orange wedge

Build all ingredients in a shaker, then pour into a frozen double rocks glass with crushed ice. Shimmy and top with more crushed ice.

Whisky Snapper
(Scotch Fix with raspberry and honey)
Bariana, *Louis Fouquet, 1896*
1¾ oz (52 ml) Scotch
¾ oz (22 ml) lemon juice
½ oz (15 ml) simple syrup
3 raspberries
¼ oz (7 ml) honey syrup (p 496), to float
Swirl the liquids together in a shaker, then muddle raspberries with a splash of the swirled liquids in a separate shaker. Pour the muddled mixture into a frozen double rocks glass, add crushed ice, then pour in the remaining liquids. Shimmy, top with more crushed ice and float honey syrup.
Garnish: raspberry

FORTIFIED & LIQUEUR

Cádiz Bramble
Ryan Gannon
Cure: New Orleans Drinks and How to Mix 'Em, *Neal Bodenheimer and Emily Timberlake, 2022*
1½ oz (45 ml) Fino Sherry
¾ oz (22 ml) lemon juice
¾ oz (22 ml) simple syrup
¼ oz (7 ml) crème de cassis, to float
Build all ingredients in a shaker, then pour into a frozen double rocks glass with crushed ice. Shimmy, top with more crushed ice, then float crème de cassis.
Garnish: lemon wedge

From *Harry Johnson's Bartenders' Manual* (1900):

Never trust a bartender who refuses to taste his own drinks.

Midnight Bramble
Leo Robitschek, The NoMad Bar, NYC
1 oz (30 ml) Fino Sherry
¾ oz (22 ml) Bonal Gentiane-Quina
¾ oz (22 ml) lemon juice
¾ oz (22 ml) simple syrup
3 blackberries
Swirl the liquids together in a shaker, then muddle blackberries with a splash of the swirled liquids in a separate shaker. Pour the muddled mixture into a frozen double rocks glass, add crushed ice, then pour in the remaining liquids, shimmy and top with more crushed ice.
Garnish: blackberry

OTHER

Berry Dangerous Fix
Jane Danger, The NoMad Bar, NYC
1½ oz (45 ml) aquavit
¼ oz (7 ml) Campari
¾ oz (22 ml) lemon juice
¾ oz (22 ml) cane syrup (p 494)
3 drops orange blossom water
3 strawberry halves
Swirl the liquids together in a shaker, then muddle strawberries with a splash of the swirled liquid in a separate shaker. Pour the mixture into a frozen double rocks glass, add crushed ice, then pour in the remaining liquid, shimmy and top with more crushed ice.
Garnish: strawberry half

Sway Reduction
Ewan Bennie, Part Time Lover, San Diego, 2022
1 oz (30 ml) shochu
1 oz (30 ml) St Germain Elderflower Liqueur
1 oz (30 ml) pink grapefruit juice
½ oz (15 ml) lime juice
Garnish: grapefruit twist, mint sprig and spritz of orange blossom water

Swizzle

Build all ingredients in a shaker, then pour into a frozen Collins glass with crushed ice. Swizzle and top with more crushed ice.

VODKA

Hazards of Love
Mike Perez, Death & Co, Los Angeles, 2023
1 oz (30 ml) vodka
¾ oz (22 ml) mezcal
¼ oz (7 ml) pear brandy
¾ oz (22 ml) lime juice
¾ oz (22 ml) grenadine (p 496)
2 dashes absinthe
2 drops Addition Jalapeño Cocktail Spice
2 cucumber wheels
Press cucumber, add remaining ingredients, then toss and pour into a frozen Collins glass with crushed ice. Swizzle and top with more crushed ice.
Garnish: cucumber fan

GIN

Chill in the Air
Kathryn "Pepper" Stashek, Attaboy, NYC
1½ oz (45 ml) gin
1 oz (30 ml) Red Gala apple juice
½ oz (15 ml) lime juice
½ oz (15 ml) orgeat
½ oz (15 ml) Madeira, to float
Build all ingredients in a shaker, then pour into a frozen Collins glass with crushed ice. Float Madeira, then swizzle and top with more crushed ice.
Garnish: mint bouquet and freshly grated nutmeg

Build all ingredients in a shaker, then pour into a frozen Collins glass with crushed ice. Swizzle and top with more crushed ice.

Death in the Gulf Stream

Ernest Hemingway
The Gentleman's Companion, *Charles H. Baker Jr., 1939*
2 oz (60 ml) genever
1 oz (30 ml) lime juice
½ oz (15 ml) simple syrup
5 dashes Angostura Bitters, to float
Build all ingredients in a shaker, then pour into a frozen Collins glass with crushed ice. Float bitters, then swizzle and top with more crushed ice.

Garden Park Swizzle

Jon Armstrong, Death & Co, Los Angeles, 2014
1½ oz (45 ml) gin
½ oz (15 ml) Suze
¾ oz (22 ml) lemon juice
¾ oz (22 ml) ginger syrup (p 496)
¼ oz (7 ml) falernum
3 dashes Angostura Bitters, to float
3 dashes Peychaud's Aromatic Cocktail Bitters, to float
Build all ingredients in a shaker, then pour into a frozen Collins glass with crushed ice. Float bitters, then swizzle and top with more crushed ice.
Garnish: mint bouquet

Green Thumb

Oska Whitehart, The Everleigh, Melbourne, 2017
1½ oz (45 ml) gin
½ oz (15 ml) Liquore Strega
¾ oz (22 ml) lime juice
½ oz (15 ml) simple syrup
2 dashes peach bitters
Garnish: mint sprig and lime wedge

Hyde Park Swizzle

(Queen's Park Swizzle with gin)
Phil Ward, Death & Co, NYC, 2008
2 oz (60 ml) gin
1 oz (30 ml) lime juice
¾ oz (22 ml) simple syrup
8–10 mint leaves
1 white sugar cube
3 dashes Angostura Bitters, to float
3 dashes Peychaud's Aromatic Cocktail Bitters, to float
Press mint with lime juice and sugar in a shaker, then add gin and simple syrup and swirl to combine. Pour into a frozen Collins glass, add crushed ice, then float bitters, swizzle and top with more crushed ice.
Garnish: mint bouquet

Lovers Rock

Brandon Bramhall and Michael McIlroy, Attaboy, Nashville, 2018
1 oz (30 ml) navy strength gin
1 oz (30 ml) Fino Sherry
1 oz (30 ml) pineapple juice
½ oz (15 ml) lime juice
½ oz (15 ml) simple syrup
4 dashes Angostura Bitters, to float
Build all ingredients in a shaker, then pour into a frozen Collins glass with crushed ice. Float bitters, then swizzle and top with more crushed ice.
Garnish: 2 pineapple fronds and a cherry

Red Swizzle

(aka **Bennett Swizzle**)
Jones' Complete Barguide, *Stan Jones, 1977*
2 oz (60 ml) gin
1 oz (30 ml) lime juice
¾ oz (22 ml) simple syrup
4 dashes Angostura Bitters
Build all ingredients in a shaker, then pour into a frozen Collins glass with crushed ice. Float bitters, then swizzle and top with more crushed ice.
Garnish: mint bouquet

Sleeping Lotus

Sierra Kirk, Portland
2 oz (60 ml) gin
¾ oz (22 ml) lemon juice
¾ oz (22 ml) orgeat
2 dashes orange bitters
Garnish: mint sprig and edible orchid

Something More Comfortable

Zachary Gelnaw-Rubin, Lion Lion, NYC, 2018
1½ oz (45 ml) gin
¼ oz (7 ml) crème de cassis
¼ oz (7 ml) pimento (allspice) dram
¾ oz (22 ml) lemon juice
½ oz (15 ml) simple syrup
Garnish: cherry and freshly grated nutmeg

Stone's Throw Swizzle

Felix Woods, Black Pearl, Melbourne, 2022
¾ oz (22 ml) gin
¾ oz (22 ml) genever
½ oz (15 ml) apricot brandy
¾ oz (22 ml) lime juice
1 teaspoon (5 ml) simple syrup
5 dashes Angostura Bitters, to float
Build all ingredients in a shaker, then pour into a frozen Collins glass with crushed ice. Float bitters, then swizzle and top with more crushed ice.
Garnish: lime wedge

Trinidaddy

Malcom Peters
Approved Cocktails, *United Kingdom Bartenders' Guild, 1937*
2 oz (60 ml) gin
1 oz (30 ml) pink grapefruit juice
¾ oz (22 ml) honey syrup (p 496)
½ oz (15 ml) lemon juice
Garnish: 3 assorted seasonal berries

Build all ingredients in a shaker, then pour into a frozen Collins glass with crushed ice. Swizzle and top with more crushed ice.

RUM & CANE SPIRIT

Bajan Swizzle
Joseph Schwartz, Little Branch, NYC
1½ oz (45 ml) Doorly's XO Fine Old Barbados Rum
1 oz (30 ml) kola tonic
½ oz (15 ml) lime juice
¼ oz (7 ml) falernum
Garnish: mint bouquet

Barbados Swizzle
2 oz (60 ml) aged dark rum
1 oz (30 ml) lime juice
¾ oz (22 ml) simple syrup
Garnish: mint bouquet

Blanc de Funk
Felix Woods, Black Pearl, Melbourne, 2020
½ oz (15 ml) rhum agricole
1 oz (30 ml) simple syrup
½ oz (15 ml) lime juice
2 dashes absinthe
6–8 mint leaves
1½ oz (45 ml) Champagne, to top
Press mint with absinthe and simple syrup, add remaining ingredients, then toss and pour into a chilled Collins glass with crushed ice. Top with Champagne, then swizzle and top with more crushed ice.
Garnish: mint bouquet

Freight Train Swizzle
Sam Ross, Attaboy, NYC, 2017
1½ oz (45 ml) aged dark rum
¾ oz (22 ml) Green Chartreuse
¾ oz (22 ml) lime juice
¾ oz (22 ml) falernum
3 dashes Angostura Bitters, to float
Build all ingredients in a shaker, then pour into a frozen Collins glass with crushed ice. Float bitters, then swizzle and top with more crushed ice.
Garnish: mint sprig and freshly grated nutmeg

Fu Manchu
The Fine Art of Mixing Drinks, *David A. Embury, 1948*
2 oz (60 ml) Jamaican dark rum
1 oz (30 ml) lime juice
½ oz (15 ml) simple syrup
1 teaspoon (5 ml) white crème de menthe
2 dashes orange bitters
Garnish: mint bouquet

Green Swizzle
Barbados, 1890s
1½ oz (45 ml) overproof aged Barbados dark rum
¾ oz (22 ml) lime juice
¾ oz (22 ml) falernum
1 teaspoon (5 ml) wormwood bitters
3 dashes Angostura Bitters, to float
Build all ingredients in a shaker, then pour into a frozen Collins glass with crushed ice. Float Angostura Bitters, then swizzle and top with more crushed ice.
Garnish: mint bouquet
Made famous in *The Rummy Affair of Old Biffy*, P.G. Wodehouse, 1924.

Hot in the Shade
Dan Greenbaum, Diamond Reef, NYC, 2017
1½ oz (45 ml) aged dark rum
1 oz (30 ml) pineapple juice
½ oz (15 ml) lime juice
½ oz (15 ml) orgeat
½ oz (15 ml) Madeira, to float
Build all ingredients in a shaker, then pour into a frozen Collins glass with crushed ice. Float Madeira, then swizzle and top with more crushed ice.
Garnish: mint bouquet and freshly grated nutmeg

Independence Swizzle
(aka **Tahitian Honey Bee Swizzle**)
Jones' Complete Barguide, *Stan Jones, 1977*
2 oz (60 ml) aged dark rum
1 oz (30 ml) lime juice
¾ oz (22 ml) honey syrup (p 496)
Garnish: mint bouquet

Iz Bananaz
Rob Krueger, Extra Fancy, NYC, 2014
1¼ oz (37 ml) cachaça
¾ oz (22 ml) Amaro Montenegro
¾ oz (22 ml) Giffard Banane du Brésil et des Caraïbes
¾ oz (22 ml) lemon juice
3 dashes Angostura Bitters, to float
Build all ingredients in a shaker, then pour into a frozen Collins glass with crushed ice. Float bitters, then swizzle and top with more crushed ice.
Garnish: long orange twist

Ola Swizzle
Antonello Arzedi, Sydney, 2024
1¼ oz (37 ml) cachaça
¼ oz (7 ml) amaretto
¼ oz (7 ml) Brookie's Mac. (or Giffard Noix de Macadamia)
1¼ oz (37 ml) rockmelon (cantaloupe) juice
¾ oz (22 ml) lime juice
¼ oz (7 ml) orgeat
Garnish: rockmelon (cantaloupe) wedge and tarragon sprig

Philadelphia Boating Punch
The Modern Bartenders' Guide, *O.H. Byron, 1884*
1¼ oz (37 ml) Goslings Gold Seal Rum
¾ oz (22 ml) Cognac
¾ oz (22 ml) lemon juice
¾ oz (22 ml) simple syrup
Garnish: orange wedge and 3 assorted seasonal berries
Use a 50/50 blend of lemon and lime juice instead to make **The Old Delaware Fishing Punch**, *New and Improved Illustrated Bartender's Manual*, Harry Johnson, 1888.

Rum Swizzle
Georgetown Club, Georgetown, 1870s
2 oz (60 ml) aged dark rum
½ oz (15 ml) simple syrup
⅜ oz (11 ml) lemon juice
⅜ oz (11 ml) lime juice
¼ oz (7 ml) falernum
2 dashes Angostura Bitters
Garnish: mint bouquet

Build all ingredients in a shaker, then pour into a frozen Collins glass with crushed ice. Swizzle and top with more crushed ice.

Samson Swizzle

Sam Miller, Zombie Village, San Francisco

1 oz (30 ml) Jamaican gold rum
1 oz (30 ml) Barbados light rum
¾ oz (22 ml) lime juice
⅓ oz (10 ml) passionfruit syrup (p 499)
⅓ oz (10 ml) cinnamon syrup (p 495)
8–10 mint leaves
3 dashes Angostura Bitters, to float

Press mint with lime and syrups in a shaker, then add rums and swirl to combine. Pour into a frozen Collins glass, add crushed ice, then float bitters, swizzle and top with more crushed ice.

Garnish: mint bouquet

Schnorkel Cocktail

Trader Vic's Bartender's Guide, *Trader Vic, 1947*

2 oz (60 ml) aged dark rum
1 oz (30 ml) lime juice
¾ oz (22 ml) simple syrup
3 dashes absinthe

Garnish: mint bouquet

Soho Swizzle

1 oz (30 ml) aged dark rum
½ oz (15 ml) Goslings Black Seal Rum
½ oz (15 ml) lime juice
½ oz (15 ml) simple syrup
¼ oz (7 ml) falernum
2 dashes Angostura Bitters, to float

Build all ingredients in a shaker, then pour into a frozen Collins glass with crushed ice. Float bitters, then swizzle and top with more crushed ice.

Garnish: mint bouquet

Surf School Swizzle

John Fry, Rumba, Seattle

1 oz (30 ml) Barbados gold rum
½ oz (15 ml) Giffard Banane du Brésil et des Caraïbes
¾ oz (22 ml) lemon juice
½ oz (15 ml) Angostura Bitters
½ oz (15 ml) orgeat

Garnish: mint bouquet

White Witch

Trader Vic's Bartender's Guide, Revised, *Trader Vic, 1972*

1½ oz (45 ml) Jamaican light rum
½ oz (15 ml) triple sec
½ oz (15 ml) white crème de cacao
¾ oz (22 ml) lime juice
1 teaspoon (5 ml) Demerara syrup (p 495)

Garnish: mint bouquet and dusting of icing (confectioners') sugar

AGAVE

Alameda Swizzle

(Queen's Park Swizzle with tequila)
Zara Madrusan, Bar Margaux, Melbourne, 2020

2 oz (60 ml) blanco tequila
1 oz (30 ml) lime juice
¾ oz (22 ml) simple syrup
8–10 mint leaves
1 white sugar cube
3 dashes Angostura Bitters, to float
3 dashes Peychaud's Aromatic Cocktail Bitters, to float

Press mint with lime and sugar in a shaker, then add tequila and simple syrup and swirl to combine. Pour into a frozen Collins glass, add crushed ice, then float bitters, swizzle and top with more crushed ice.

Garnish: mint bouquet

Beach Cruiser

Erick Castro, Polite Provisions, San Diego

1 oz (30 ml) blanco tequila
1 oz (30 ml) mezcal
¾ oz (22 ml) lime juice
¾ oz (22 ml) grenadine (p 496)
2 dashes orange bitters
2 dashes absinthe

Garnish: orange half-wheel and cherry

Death in the Valley

Michael Madrusan, Heartbreaker, Melbourne, 2024

1 oz (30 ml) blanco tequila
½ oz (15 ml) mezcal
½ oz (15 ml) Ancho Reyes Original
1 oz (30 ml) lime juice
½ oz (15 ml) agave syrup (p 494)
2 drops saline solution (p 493)
5 dashes Angostura Bitters, to float

Build all ingredients in a shaker, then pour into a frozen Collins glass with crushed ice. Float bitters, then swizzle and top with more crushed ice.

Garnish: dusting of smoked paprika

Jalisco Swizzle

Phil Ward, Death & Co, NYC, 2008

1½ oz (45 ml) blanco tequila
½ oz (15 ml) mezcal
¾ oz (22 ml) lime juice
½ oz (15 ml) cane syrup (p 494)

Garnish: lime wedge

La Bandera Swizzle

Daniel Zacharczuk, The Varnish, Los Angeles, 2024

2 oz (60 ml) mezcal
¾ oz (22 ml) Campari
¾ oz (22 ml) lime juice
½ oz (15 ml) simple syrup

Garnish: lime wedge, orange wedge and light dusting of icing (confectioners') sugar

Build all ingredients in a shaker, then pour into a frozen Collins glass with crushed ice. Swizzle and top with more crushed ice.

'Spicy with Tequila'
Bobby Heugel, Houston
2 oz (60 ml) blanco tequila
½ oz (15 ml) Green Chartreuse
1 oz (30 ml) lime juice
½ oz (15 ml) agave syrup (p 494)
10–12 mint leaves
2 dashes Scrappy's Bitters Fire Tincture
Press mint with lime juice and agave syrup in a shaker, then add remaining ingredients and swirl to combine. Pour into a frozen Collins glass, add crushed ice, then swizzle and top with more crushed ice.
Garnish: mint sprig and dusting of Tajín Clásico

Up All Night Swizzle
Michael Madrusan, The Everleigh, Melbourne, 2024
1½ oz (45 ml) jalapeño-infused blanco tequila (p 503)
½ oz (15 ml) mezcal
1½ oz (45 ml) pineapple juice
½ oz (15 ml) lime juice
½ oz (15 ml) passionfruit syrup (p 499)
2 drops saline solution (p 493)
Garnish: 2 pineapple fronds and a cherry

From *The Ideal Bartender* (Tom Bullock, 1917):

May your joys be as deep as the ocean, your troubles as light as its foam.

BRANDY

Asbury Park Swizzle
Chad Solomon and Christy Pope, 2015
2 oz (60 ml) Laird's Jersey Lightning Apple Brandy
¼ oz (7 ml) apple liqueur (preferably Berentzen)
¾ oz (22 ml) lemon juice
¾ oz (22 ml) honey syrup (p 496)
2 drops saline solution (p 493)
8–10 mint leaves
2 dashes Angostura Bitters, to float
2 dashes Peychaud's Aromatic Cocktail Bitters, to float
2 dashes Dale DeGroff's Pimento Aromatic Bitters, to float
Press mint with lemon juice and sugar in a shaker, then add remaining ingredients and swirl to combine. Pour into a frozen Collins glass, add crushed ice, then float bitters, swizzle and top with more crushed ice.
Garnish: mint bouquet

Brandy Marguerite
Jayne's Bartender's Guide, *1934*
1½ oz (45 ml) Cognac
¾ oz (22 ml) Yellow Chartreuse
¾ oz (22 ml) lemon juice
Garnish: mint bouquet

AMERICAN WHISKEY

Chrissy Pud
Toby Callaghan, The Waratah, Sydney, 2024
1 oz (30 ml) rye whiskey
⅓ oz (10 ml) Tempus Fugit Crème de Cacao
⅓ oz (10 ml) coffee-infused Pedro Ximénez (p 503)
¾ oz (22 ml) lemon juice
½ oz (15 ml) raspberry syrup (p 500)
Garnish: raspberry

Fishtail Punch
Felix Woods, Black Pearl, Melbourne, 2022
1½ oz (45 ml) bourbon
½ oz (15 ml) Fino Sherry
½ oz (15 ml) simple syrup
½ oz (15 ml) pineapple juice
¼ oz (7 ml) lemon juice
5 dashes Angostura Bitters, to float
Build all ingredients in a shaker, then pour into a frozen Collins glass with crushed ice. Float bitters, then swizzle and top with more crushed ice.
Garnish: 2 pineapple fronds

Florida Punch
The Fine Art of Mixing Drinks, *David A. Embury, 1948*
1½ oz (45 ml) bourbon
1 oz (30 ml) pineapple juice
¾ oz (22 ml) simple syrup
½ oz (15 ml) lemon juice
Garnish: mint bouquet

Mississippi Punch
The Fine Art of Mixing Drinks, *David A. Embury, 1948*
1½ oz (45 ml) bourbon
¾ oz (22 ml) Cognac
¾ oz (22 ml) lemon juice
¾ oz (22 ml) simple syrup
½ oz (15 ml) pot still Jamaican dark rum, to float
Build all ingredients in a shaker, then pour into a frozen Collins glass with crushed ice. Swizzle, then top with more crushed ice and float rum.
Garnish: mint bouquet

The Democrat
Jon Santer, Bourbon & Branch, San Francisco, 2007
2 oz (60 ml) bourbon
½ oz (15 ml) Giffard Crème de Pêche de Vigne
¾ oz (22 ml) lemon juice
½ oz (15 ml) honey syrup (p 496)
Garnish: mint sprig and lemon wedge

Build all ingredients in a shaker, then pour into a frozen Collins glass with crushed ice. Swizzle and top with more crushed ice.

FORTIFIED & LIQUEUR

Congress Park Swizzle
Keely Sutherland, Death & Co, Denver, 2019
1 oz (30 ml) blanc vermouth
½ oz (15 ml) Jamaican dark rum (preferably Appleton Estate Signature Blend)
½ oz (15 ml) Giffard Mangue
¾ oz (22 ml) lime juice
½ oz (15 ml) pineapple syrup (p 499)
8–10 mint leaves
5 dashes Peychaud's Aromatic Cocktail Bitters, to float
Press mint with lime juice and pineapple syrup in a shaker, then add remaining ingredients and swirl to combine. Pour into a frozen Collins glass with crushed ice, float bitters, then swizzle and top with more crushed ice.
Garnish: mint bouquet

Frozen Italian Mojito
Session Cocktails, *Drew Lazor, 2018*
2½ oz (75 ml) Cocchi Americano
1 oz (30 ml) lime juice
½ oz (15 ml) simple syrup
8–10 mint leaves
Press mint with lime juice and simple syrup in a shaker, then add Cocchi Americano and swirl to combine. Pour into a frozen double rocks glass with crushed ice, then shimmy and top with more crushed ice.
Garnish: mint bouquet

Mississippi Punch (Jerry Thomas Recipe)
The Bar-Tender's Guide, *Jerry Thomas, 1862*
1 oz (30 ml) Cognac
½ oz (15 ml) aged dark rum
½ oz (15 ml) bourbon
¾ oz (22 ml) lemon juice
¾ oz (22 ml) simple syrup
Pebble whip and pour into a frozen double rocks glass with crushed ice, then shimmy and top with more crushed ice.
Garnish: orange half-wheel, blackberry and raspberry

Surfside Swizzle
Sam Ross, Ad Lib, Miami, 2019
1 oz (30 ml) Manzanilla Sherry
¾ oz (22 ml) St Germain Elderflower Liqueur
1½ oz (45 ml) Granny Smith apple juice
¼ oz (7 ml) lemon juice
2 oz (60 ml) Champagne, to top
Pebble whip, then pour into a chilled Collins glass with crushed ice and top with Champagne. Swizzle gently and top with more crushed ice.
Garnish: apple fan

From *Crosby Gaige's Cocktail Guide and Ladies' Companion* (1941):

The secret to a great cocktail? Pour it with confidence, drink it with pleasure, and never ask what's in it.

Build all ingredients in a shaker, then pour into a frozen Collins glass with crushed ice. Swizzle and top with more crushed ice.

COBBLER

Sherry Cobbler p 268

Cobbler

A citrus cocktail on crushed ice, often low in alcohol, with a lavish garnish and straw.

wine/fortified wine and/or spirit
+ sugar and/or liqueur
+ citrus

Muddle citrus and sugar in a shaker, then add remaining ingredients. Toss and strain into a frozen Spritz glass, then top with crushed ice. Shimmy, then top with more crushed ice.

Likely taking its name from the 'cobbles' or pebbles of ice upon which it's built, the Cobbler is a 19th-century American cocktail that was designed to be light, brisk and simple. The Cobbler rose to prominence in the 1830s, featuring predominantly wine or fortified wine, sugar and citrus peel or slices, shaken with ice and dressed elaborately with seasonal fruits. It is significant to note that these drinks feature little to no citrus juice, relying on the peels and/or slices of fruit to liven the recipe instead. What's more, the Cobbler is also credited with prompting the advent of iced cocktails around the world and was among the first drinks to call for a straw. Although its precise origins are unclear, it is possible that native New Yorker Martha King Niblo was responsible for its creation, or at the very least for its rise to fame. Together with her husband, William, Niblo ran an outdoor pleasure garden and performance space, and legend has it that her Cobblers were the most sought after in New York City.

The most famous recipe of the bunch is arguably the Sherry Cobbler (p 268), which first appeared in a diary entry by Katherine Jane Ellice, who documented her experiences travelling the United States during the summer of 1838. The drink went on to inspire a number of popular variations throughout the 1840s, earning a reputation as a cooling American cocktail across the globe. While stronger, spirit-driven riffs such as the Brandy Cobbler became commonplace in Europe, and the Whisky Cobbler (p 272) took hold in the United States, many contend that the Cobbler was intended to be easy-drinking and lower in alcohol above all. Low-ABV or spirited, the Cobbler was a perennially popular pick in warm weather, at least until the late 19th century when it was largely replaced by other iced styles such as the Rickey (p 78) and the Collins (p 62).

Contemporary Cobbler variations are few and far between due to the category's waning popularity, but we consider this family of drinks highly relevant to today's discerning drinker and strongly believe it shouldn't be overlooked.

Sherry Cobbler (Jerry Thomas Recipe)

The Bar-Tender's Guide, *Jerry Thomas, 1862*
3 oz (90 ml) Amontillado Sherry
½ oz (15 ml) simple syrup
2 orange wedges
1 lemon wedge

Muddle citrus with simple syrup in a shaker, add sherry then toss and strain into a frozen Spritz glass and top with crushed ice.
Garnish: mint bouquet and 3–4 mixed berries

An American icon in its prime, the Sherry Cobbler would have once been considered one of the most influential American-style cocktails. This crisp, refreshing drink made waves around the world in the 1840s, distinct in its employment of the modern-day straw. After close to half a decade of success, the Sherry Cobbler was described by influential American bartender and author Harry Johnson, in 1888, as 'without a doubt the most popular beverage in the country, with ladies as well as with gentlemen.' By the turn of the century, however, the drink had been superseded by its contemporaries to the extent that modern American bartenders were rarely familiar with the original recipe.

It is a surprise that the Sherry Cobbler has not been revived in the recent classic cocktail renaissance given its low-alcohol composition and the rising demand for low-alcohol cocktails and non-alcoholic drinks more broadly. While Sherries and other fortified wines were undoubtedly less profitable to the Prohibition-era bootlegger – and less exciting to the thirsty post-Prohibition reveller – they do play a prominent role in modern cocktail culture. In this recipe, Amontillado Sherry offers a full-bodied base with nutty, herbal notes, whereas lighter, drier styles such as Manzanilla and Fino add a touch of salinity to a drink's overall balance. Sherry Cobbler fans should also explore the stunningly simple Spanish sherry lemonade, the Rebujito (p 77), or the Sherry Colada (p 458), for a more tropical treat.

Cobbler

Averna Cobbler
Stacey Swenson, Dante, NYC
1½ oz (45 ml) Amaro Averna
½ oz (15 ml) sweet vermouth
½ oz (15 ml) lemon juice
1 teaspoon (6 g) orange marmalade
Toss and strain into a frozen footed Delmonico glass with crushed ice, shimmy, then top with more crushed ice.
Garnish: mint bouquet, blackberries and pinch of cracked pepper

Champagne Cobbler
The Bar-Tender's Guide, *Jerry Thomas, 1862*
3 oz (90 ml) Champagne
½ oz (15 ml) simple syrup
1 lemon wheel
1 orange half-wheel
Muddle citrus with simple syrup then add Champagne and stir gently. Strain into a frozen Spritz glass with crushed ice, shimmy, then top with more crushed ice.
Garnish: mint bouquet and 3–4 mixed berries

Champagne Cobbler
Dale DeGroff, Blackbird, NYC, 1999
4 oz (120 ml) Champagne
⅜ oz (11 ml) maraschino liqueur
⅜ oz (11 ml) simple syrup
1 lemon wheel
1 orange half-wheel
1 chunk pineapple
Muddle fruit with maraschino liqueur, add Champagne and ice, then stir and strain into a chilled flute, shimmy, then top with more crushed ice.

Chelsea Cobbler
1½ oz (45 ml) Fino Sherry
¾ oz (22 ml) orange curaçao (p 498)
½ oz (15 ml) pineapple juice
½ oz (15 ml) lemon juice
Toss and strain into a frozen Spritz glass with crushed ice, shimmy, then top with more crushed ice.
Garnish: 2 pineapple fronds

Coastal Groove
Dan Greenbaum, Diamond Reef, NYC
3 oz (90 ml) dry rosé
¾ oz (22 ml) falernum
1 blood orange half-wheel
1 navel orange half-wheel
1 lime wheel
Garnish: mint bouquet and 3–4 mixed berries

Coffee Cobbler
The Fine Art of Mixing Drinks, *David A. Embury, 1948*
1½ oz (45 ml) Cognac
1 oz (30 ml) tawny Port
1 teaspoon (5 ml) simple syrup
Toss and strain into a frozen footed Delmonico glass with crushed ice, shimmy, then top with more crushed ice.
Garnish: lemon twist

Colonial Cooler
The Gentleman's Companion, *Charles H. Baker Jr., 1939*
1½ oz (45 ml) gin
1½ oz (45 ml) sweet vermouth
¼ oz (7 ml) Picon Amer
2 dashes Angostura Bitters
Toss and strain into a frozen Spritz glass with crushed ice, shimmy, then top with more crushed ice.
Garnish: mint sprig

Dunmore Cobbler
Ryan Fitzgerald and Todd Smith, ABV, San Francisco
2 oz (60 ml) Amontillado Sherry
½ oz (15 ml) Scotch
¾ oz (22 ml) lemon juice
½ oz (15 ml) pineapple syrup (p 499)
1 dash Angostura Bitters
Toss and strain into a frozen Spritz glass with crushed ice, shimmy, then top with more crushed ice.
Garnish: pineapple wedge and 3 dashes of Angostura Bitters

English Cobbler
1½ oz (45 ml) Jamaican dark rum
¾ oz (22 ml) black tea (brewed and cooled)
½ oz (15 ml) lemon juice
½ oz (15 ml) simple syrup
Toss and strain into a frozen Spritz glass with crushed ice, shimmy, then top with more crushed ice.
Garnish: mint bouquet

Gran Cobbler
Jacques Bezuidenhout, Forgery, San Francisco
3 oz (90 ml) sweet vermouth
½ oz (15 ml) lime juice
¼ oz (7 ml) absinthe
6 raspberries
Garnish: lime wheel and raspberries

Half Court Cobbler
Dan Greenbaum, Diamond Reef, NYC
2½ oz (75 ml) Amontillado Sherry
½ oz (15 ml) Cynar
½ oz (15 ml) honey syrup (p 496)
1 lemon wedge
1 orange half-wheel
Garnish: orange half-wheel and lemon wedge

Jane Stanley
Leo Robitschek, The NoMad Bar, NYC
1½ oz (45 ml) Amontillado Sherry
1 oz (30 ml) Amaro CioCiaro
¾ oz (22 ml) lemon juice
½ oz (15 ml) cane syrup (p 494)
1 orange half-wheel
Garnish: orange half-wheel

Muddle citrus and sugar in a shaker, then add remaining ingredients. Toss and strain into a frozen Spritz glass, then top with crushed ice. Shimmy, then top with more crushed ice.

Juicebox Cobbler
Dan Greenbaum, Diamond Reef, NYC
3 oz (90 ml) Carpano Antica Formula
½ oz (15 ml) passionfruit syrup (p 499)
1 orange half-wheel
1 lemon wedge
1 pineapple chunk
Garnish: mint bouquet and 3–4 mixed berries

Keep Your Dream a Burnin'
Kirk Estopinal, Cure, New Orleans
2½ oz (75 ml) Manzanilla Sherry
½ oz (15 ml) overproof pot still Jamaican dark rum
½ oz (15 ml) orgeat
2 dashes Angostura Bitters
2 lemon peels
Muddle peels, add remaining ingredients, then toss and strain into a frozen Spritz glass with crushed ice.
Garnish: lemon wheel and cinnamon stick

Ma Cherie
Leo Robitscheck, The NoMad Bar, NYC
2½ oz (75 ml) Fino Sherry
¼ oz (7 ml) Green Chartreuse
½ oz (15 ml) lime juice
½ oz (15 ml) pineapple syrup (p 499)
¼ oz (7 ml) falernum
10 drops saline solution (p 493)
1 cucumber wheel
Press cucumber, add remaining ingredients, then toss and strain into a frozen Collins glass with crushed ice. Shimmy, then top with more crushed ice.
Garnish: cucumber ribbon around the inside of the glass

Netherlands Cobbler
Inspired by American and Other Drinks, *Charlie Paul, 1884*
Michael Madrusan, 2025
1½ oz (45 ml) genever
¾ oz (22 ml) Giffard Vanille de Madagascar
¾ oz (22 ml) lemon juice
½ oz(15 ml) tawny Port, to float
Toss and strain into a frozen Spritz glass with crushed ice, shimmy, then top with more crushed ice. Float Port.
Garnish: 3–4 mixed berries

Orgeat Punch
The Bar-Tender's Guide, *Jerry Thomas, 1862*
1½ oz (45 ml) Cognac
¾ oz (22 ml) lemon juice
¾ oz (22 ml) orgeat
½ oz (15 ml) tawny Port, to float
Toss and strain into a frozen Spritz glass with crushed ice, shimmy, then top with more crushed ice. Float Port.
Garnish: 3–4 mixed berries

Port Cobbler
2 oz (60 ml) ruby Port
½ oz (15 ml) orange curaçao (p 498)
1 lemon wedge
1 lime wedge
1 orange wedge
1 strawberry, halved
Garnish: strawberry half, blackberry and mint sprig

Sherry Cobbler (Dan Greenbaum Recipe)
Dan Greenbaum, Diamond Reef, NYC
3 oz (90 ml) Amontillado Sherry
½ oz (15 ml) simple syrup
4 raspberries
1 lemon wedge
Garnish: mint bouquet and 3–4 mixed berries

Sherry Cobbler (Difford's Recipe)
Difford's Guide
2 oz (60 ml) Oloroso Sherry
½ oz (15 ml) Pedro Ximénez
¼ oz (7 ml) pineapple juice
¼ oz (7 ml) orange juice
1 teaspoon (5 ml) maraschino liqueur
1 teaspoon (5 ml) simple syrup
Toss and strain into a frozen Spritz glass with crushed ice, shimmy, then top with more crushed ice.
Garnish: mint bouquet, 3–4 mixed berries and pineapple wedge

Sherry Cobbler (Harrison Ginsberg Recipe)
Harrison Ginsberg
1 oz (30 ml) Manzanilla Sherry
½ oz (15 ml) Oloroso Sherry
½ oz (15 ml) Pedro Ximénez
½ oz (15 ml) lemon juice
½ oz (15 ml) simple syrup
4 raspberries
Garnish: mint bouquet, 3–4 mixed berries and a dusting of icing (confectioners') sugar

Sherry Cobbler (Jim Meehan Recipe)
Jim Meehan
1¾ oz (52 ml) Cream Sherry
1 oz (30 ml) Manzanilla Sherry
¼ oz (7 ml) East India Sherry
Garnish: orange half-wheel and 3–4 mixed berries

Sherry Cobbler (Sweet Liberty Recipe)
John Lermayer, Sweet Liberty,Miami
2½ oz (75 ml) Fino Sherry
½ oz (15 ml) St Germain Elderflower Liqueur
1 oz (30 ml) pink grapefruit juice
½ oz (15 ml) pineapple juice
½ oz (15 ml) honey syrup (p 496)
Toss and strain into a frozen Spritz glass with crushed ice, shimmy, then top with more crushed ice.
Garnish: mint bouquet and 3 raspberries

Muddle citrus and sugar in a shaker, then add remaining ingredients. Toss and strain into a frozen Spritz glass, then top with crushed ice. Shimmy, then top with more crushed ice.

Shoemaker
Felix Woods, The Everleigh, Melbourne, 2018
2 oz (60 ml) Fino Sherry
¾ oz (22 ml) honey syrup (p 496)
½ oz (15 ml) lime juice
2 dashes orange bitters
Toss and strain into a frozen double rocks glass with crushed ice, shimmy, then top with more crushed ice.
Garnish: orange half-wheel and mint sprig

Taxi Cocktail
Straub's Manual of Mixed Drinks, *Jacques Straub, 1913*
1½ oz (45 ml) gin
1½ oz (45 ml) dry vermouth
½ oz (15 ml) lime cordial (p 497)
3 dashes absinthe
Toss and strain into a frozen Spritz glass with crushed ice, shimmy, then top with more crushed ice.
Garnish: 3–4 mixed berries

The Mexican Gentleman
Sean Kenyon, Williams & Graham, Denver
1 oz (30 ml) Manzanilla Sherry
1 oz (30 ml) reposado tequila
½ oz (15 ml) mezcal
½ oz (15 ml) Pedro Ximénez
2 blackberries
2 raspberries
1 strawberry, halved
1 orange wheel
Garnish: mint bouquet, blackberry, raspberry and strawberry half

Traction
Devon Tarby, Death & Co, Los Angeles, 2014
1½ oz (45 ml) Amontillado Sherry
½ oz (15 ml) aged dark rum (preferably Santa Teresa 1796 Solera Rum)
¾ oz (22 ml) orange curaçao (p 498)
2 lemon wedges
1 strawberry, halved
Garnish: lemon wedge, strawberry half and mint sprig

Treasury Cocktail
Straub's Manual of Mixed Drinks, *Jacques Straub, 1913*
1½ oz (45 ml) gin
1½ oz (45 ml) sweet vermouth
2 orange half-wheels
Toss and strain into a frozen Spritz glass with crushed ice, shimmy, then top with more crushed ice.
Garnish: orange half-wheel and cherry

Tuxedo Cobbler
Chantal Tseng, Washington D.C.
2 oz (60 ml) Manzanilla Sherry
½ oz (15 ml) gin
¼ oz (7 ml) maraschino liqueur
¼ oz (7 ml) simple syrup
5 dashes absinthe
2 dashes orange bitters
3 lemon half-wheels
1 orange half-wheel
Garnish: lemon half-wheel and cherry

Vanilla Cobbler
The Fine Art of Mixing Drinks, *David A. Embury, 1948*
1½ oz (45 ml) Cognac
1 oz (30 ml) Giffard Vanille de Madagascar
½ oz (15 ml) house cream (p 506)
Toss and strain into a frozen Spritz glass with crushed ice, shimmy, then top with more crushed ice.
Garnish: freshly grated nutmeg

Vitamin C Cobbler
Colin Bugbee, Cure, New Orleans, 2021
1½ oz (45 ml) Manzanilla Sherry
¼ oz (7 ml) bonded apple brandy
¾ oz (22 ml) orange juice
½ oz (15 ml) orgeat
1 teaspoon (5 ml) lemon juice
2 dashes orange bitters
Toss and strain into a frozen Spritz glass with crushed ice, shimmy, then top with more crushed ice.
Garnish: mint bouquet

Whisky Cobbler
The Fine Art of Mixing Drinks, *David A. Embury, 1948*
1½ oz (45 ml) Scotch
¼ oz (7 ml) Pierre Ferrand Dry Curaçao
¼ oz (7 ml) Giffard Crème de Pêche de Vigne
¼ oz (7 ml) lemon juice
¼ oz (7 ml) pineapple syrup (p 499)
Toss and strain into a frozen Spritz glass with crushed ice, shimmy, then top with more crushed ice.
Garnish: mint bouquet and 3–4 mixed berries

From *Café Royal Cocktail Book* (1937):

May your drinks be stiff, your spirits be high, and your hangovers be merciful.

Muddle citrus and sugar in a shaker, then add remaining ingredients. Toss and strain into a frozen Spritz glass, then top with crushed ice. Shimmy, then top with more crushed ice.

JULEP, SMASH & STINGER

Ztinger p 287 (left),Whiskey Julep p 285 (middle), Stinger p287 (right)

Julep, Smash & Stinger

Spirit-driven cocktails enlivened by the freshness and fragrance of mint.

JULEP
spirit + sugar + mint

Press mint with sugar and/or syrup and/or liqueur in a frozen Julep cup, then add remaining ingredients. Fill the cup with crushed ice, then swizzle and top with more crushed ice.

SMASH
spirit + sugar + fresh mint + muddled fruit*

Muddle mint (plus other fruits in modern variations) with sugar and/or syrup in a shaker. Add spirit, then shake with ice and strain into a frozen double rocks glass with cracked ice.

*Contemporary Smashes include muddled citrus and other fruits.

STINGER
spirit + crème de menthe**

Build all ingredients in a frozen double rocks glass, then fill the glass with crushed ice.

**Contemporary variations often incorporate other minty digestifs.

When it comes to essential ingredients and execution, the Julep, Smash and Stinger have a lot in common.

Regarded as one of the oldest American mixed drinks, the spirited Julep is commonly recognised as a Southern cocktail, stemming back to Virginia in the 1700s. Traditionally, the drink is made by pressing mint into the base of a tumbler with sugar before adding the spirit. The name 'Julep', however, is derived from a Persian word for 'rosewater'; prior to the American additions of liquor and fresh mint, the drink had a long history as a medicinal mixture of water and infused syrup. In the early 1800s, when ice became more readily available in American bars, the iced Julep emerged – a combination of water, sugar, mint and rum – and began evolving into the drink we know today.

In the 1862 edition of *The Bar-Tender's Guide*, Jerry Thomas includes six Julep recipes: two interpretations of

→

the Mint Julep (p 285), followed by variations with brandy, gin, whiskey and pineapple. Thomas credits British naval officer and novelist Frederick Marryat for the 'real Mint Julep' recipe, as Marryat described it in his second series of *A Diary in America* (1840), and Marryat is deemed responsible for introducing the all-American cocktail to England, where it became 'quite a favourite'.

By 1939, whiskey had become the base spirit of choice for the Julep, and that year the bourbon-led Mint Julep was named the official cocktail of the Kentucky Derby, one of the world's most prestigious horseraces. The drink was presented in polished silver cups with a tapered base and beaded rim, popular gifts and collector's items for wealthy enthusiasts, which have since become integral to the Julep's identity. The Derby now serves approximately 120,000 Mint Juleps each year, and the drink continues to be an emblem of Southern hospitality.

The Smash is another all-American cocktail, thought to have originated in the South in the 1840s. In *The Bar-Tender's Guide* from 1862, Jerry Thomas described the drink as 'simply a julep on a small plan'. Unlike the Julep, where ingredients are pressed and layered, the Smash (also known as a Smasher or Smash-Up) generally calls for the components to be muddled all together then stirred or shaken, giving it a heartier texture. The name alone indicates that the drink was perceived as a somewhat less elegant cocktail, designed to be enjoyed with vigour.

The Stinger – a cool combination of Cognac and crème de menthe, classically shaken and served up, but often served on crushed or cracked ice – has been associated with after-dinner drinking in elite circles since the 1890s, and became known as a cocktail during the Prohibition, having been preceded by The Judge (p 287). Versions of the cocktail went under many names until the 1910s when Stinger stuck, thought to reference a boxing term for a sharp jab to the head. The cocktail remained popular until the 1980s, spawning a number of variations that called for alternative spirits to VSOP Cognac as it became increasingly expensive and consequently inaccessible. Even though most classic Stingers are shaken and served up, Milk & Honey alumni have always maintained that the cocktail should be served over crushed ice – not only to accentuate the menthol flavour, but also to ensure that the drink remains ice cold until the last sip.

While different, the Julep, Smash and Stinger all traditionally avoid citrus, making the spirit and mint the stars of the show. Thus, we've united these three styles on behalf of those searching for herbacous bracers that are brisk and spirituous in equal measure.

ESSENTIAL VARIATIONS

Continental Julep

(Cognac Julep with muddled strawberry and Jamaican dark rum)
Jayne's Bartender's Guide, *1934*
2 oz (60 ml) Cognac
½ oz (15 ml) simple syrup
1 strawberry, halved
6–8 mint leaves
½ oz (15 ml) Jamaican dark rum, to float

Muddle strawberry and mint with simple syrup in a frozen Julep cup, then add Cognac. Fill the cup with crushed ice, swizzle, then top with more crushed ice and float rum.
Garnish: mint bouquet

The Continental Julep from *Jayne's Bartender's Guide* is a bold and vibrant cocktail reminiscent of a summertime picnic Punch, with the spice of Cognac and sweetness of strawberry enlivened by fresh mint and a potent punch of rich, spicy Jamaican dark rum. Contrary to popular belief, early renditions of the Julep rarely featured whiskey. Instead, the innovative cocktail more often comprised brandy, gin or wine combined with fresh seasonal fruits, as well as a rum float and abundant garnishes.

Published by Dr. D. Jayne and Son, *Jayne's Bartender's Guide* was one of many cocktail books released in a bid to revive cocktail culture shortly after the repeal of Prohibition. Far from a bartender – or qualified doctor according to records of the time – Dr. D. Jayne was a patent medicine manufacturer based in Philadelphia. The 'Jayne's' brand used this book and other marketing tools such as an annual almanac to advertise a variety of beauty products, pills and tonics to the American market. Ads for these appear between recipes for cocktails and mixed drinks that had become popular prior to Prohibition, along with long-lost formulas for multiple bitters and cordials.

Jayne's introduction explains: 'Of the making of drinks there is no end. Even to classify all known mixed drinks into headings would be a formidable task. However, since the blending of liquors, wines and other delectable beverages into satisfying drinks has been more or less a secret art for the past decade or more, our happy escape from the restrictions of the Eighteenth Amendment (may it rest in peace!) calls for some sudden expert knowledge of these mixtures.'

Cognac dilutes elegantly, making it a great fit in cocktails with crushed ice, such as the Mojito Criollo No. 3 (p 243). If it's the Jamaican dark rum that floats your boat, steer towards the English Cobbler (p 270), which combines the spirit with citrus and black tea.

Whiskey Smash

Dale DeGroff, Bar Americain, NYC, 2005
2 oz (60 ml) bourbon
¾ oz (22 ml) simple syrup
4 lemon wedges
6–8 mint leaves

Muddle all ingredients in a shaker, then shake with ice and strain into a frozen double rocks glass with cracked ice.
Garnish: mint bouquet

The Brandy Smash was America's go-to cocktail in the 1850s, though once the style, method and formula became established, variations with other spirits and ingredients began to appear. Along with the Julep and Cobbler, the Smash marked a new era of iced cocktails, a revolutionary development in American drinking. These drinks all called for elaborate garnishes such as slices of orange and lemon, berries and mint sprigs, ensuring that they were, as Jerry Thomas put it, 'acceptable to the eye, as well as the palate'. Despite its prevalence, however, the Smash's heyday turned out to be short-lived, and it lost traction by the turn of the 20th century.

Roughly 100 years later, the Smash was given a new lease on life in 2005 when American bartender, author and expert Dale DeGroff, nicknamed "King Cocktail", created his version of the Whiskey Smash for the opening menu of Bobby Flay's Bar Americain in New York City. DeGroff, 'a little bored of Mint Juleps', decided to muddle some lemon with the mint and, lo and behold, the modern Smash was born. In contrast to the crushed ice or pebbles in Juleps and Cobblers, contemporary Smashes feature muddled slices of fruit or juice alongside the fresh mint, shaken and strained over cracked ice.

Whiskey, citrus and fresh mint make a glorious combination, especially in the Whiskey Freezer (p 82) from Crosby Gaige circa 1944, or contemporary Whiskey Buck variation, Poppa's Pride (p 105), a huge hit by Jay Zimmerman at the now-closed Ba'sik in Brooklyn. DeGroff's summer variation, the Whiskey Peach Smash (p 286) adds half a peach to the equation and proves other fruits can get in on the fun, too.

Devil's Cocktail

(Stinger with cayenne pepper)
Cocktails: How to Mix Them, *Robert Vermeire, 1922*
2 oz (60 ml) Cognac
¾ oz (22 ml) white crème de menthe

Build all ingredients in a frozen double rocks glass, then fill the glass with crushed ice.
Garnish: mint bouquet and light dusting of cayenne pepper

First published by Belgian bartender Robert Vermeire in 1922's *Cocktails: How to Mix Them*, the Devil's Cocktail is a stunningly simple variation on the classic Stinger, accented with a light dusting of cayenne pepper for a savoury, spicy finish. Among the most commercially successful cocktail books of its era, Vermeire's text captured the culture of European drinking in the early 20th century and added a vast number of new European cocktails to the repertoire of bartenders around the world.

This cocktail persevered into the late 1930s, appearing once again in *The How and When* by Hyman Gale and Gerald F. Marco in 1937. Marco was the co-owner of Marco Liquors, a retail outlet with multiple stores across downtown Chicago. *The How and When* is a beautiful hardbound book that was 'intended as an authoritative reference guide', containing 1000 cocktail recipes, as well as information on the origins of myriad wines and spirits, plus a collection of dishes to pair with alcoholic beverages. Careful attention was paid to the book's details and design, and it is thought that versions of the cover were even customised for the purchaser.

If you're curious about cocktails cleverly invigorated with cayenne pepper, a spice that adds a little heat and brightens other flavours such as fresh citrus, try Michael's Non-Traditional Sour variation, the Chelsea Smile (p 170), or Dan Greenbaum's Tequila Gimlet variation, the Mexican Razor Blade (p 218) – both derived from the Holland Razor Blade (p 171), published by Charles H. Baker Jr. in 1939.

Julep

Press mint with sugar and/or syrup and/or liqueur in a frozen Julep cup, then add remaining ingredients. Fill the cup with crushed ice, then swizzle and top with more crushed ice.

Aperitivo Julep

Alex Day, Death & Co, NYC, 2009

2 oz (60 ml) dry vermouth
¾ oz (22 ml) Amaro CioCiaro
1 teaspoon (5 ml) Giffard Crème de Pêche de Vigne
6–8 mint leaves
Garnish: mint bouquet

Brandy Julep

The Bar-Tender's Guide, *Jerry Thomas, 1862*

2½ oz (75 ml) Cognac
¼ oz (7 ml) simple syrup
1 white sugar cube
6–8 mint leaves
Garnish: mint bouquet

Brandy Mist

American Club, Buenos Aires
The South American Gentleman's Companion, *Charles H. Baker Jr., 1951*

2 oz (60 ml) Cognac
½ oz (15 ml) Giffard Crème de Pêche de Vigne
2 dashes Angostura Bitters
6–8 mint leaves
Garnish: mint bouquet

Breakfast Julep

Michael Madrusan, The Everleigh, Melbourne, 2016

2 oz (60 ml) bourbon
¾ oz (22 ml) orange marmalade syrup (p 499)
6–8 mint leaves
Stir marmalade syrup with bourbon to mix. Add mint, press gently, then fill the cup with crushed ice, swizzle and top with more crushed ice.
Garnish: mint bouquet

Champagne Julep

New and Improved Bartender's Manual, *Harry Johnson, 1882*

¼ oz (7 ml) simple syrup
1 white sugar cube
6–8 mint leaves
3 oz (90 ml) Champagne, to top
Press mint with sugar in a Julep cup, then top with Champagne. Fill the cup with crushed ice, swizzle and top with more crushed ice.
Garnish: mint bouquet and strawberry

Champagne Julep (Punch Recipe)

Punch

½ oz (15 ml) Cognac
¼ oz (7 ml) simple syrup
2 dashes Angostura Bitters
1 white sugar cube
6–8 mint leaves
3 oz (90 ml) Champagne, to top
Press mint with sugar, simple syrup and bitters in a Julep cup. Add Cognac and mix. Top with Champagne and fill the cup with crushed ice. Swizzle, then top with more crushed ice.
Garnish: mint bouquet

Cider Julep

Chris Bostick, Half Step, Austin, 2014

2 oz (60 ml) dry apple cider
½ oz (15 ml) Calvados
¼ oz (7 ml) soda
1 teaspoon (5 ml) simple syrup
2 dashes Angostura Bitters
1 white sugar cube
6–8 mint leaves
Garnish: mint bouquet dusted with icing (confectioners') sugar

Cleopatra's Julep

Michael Madrusan, The Everleigh, Melbourne, 2019

1½ oz (45 ml) Cocchi Americano
1½ oz (45 ml) Brachetto d'Acqui
1 strawberry, halved
6–8 mint leaves
Muddle strawberry and mint with Cocchi Americano in a frozen Julep cup, then add Brachetto d'Acqui. Fill the cup with crushed ice, then swizzle briefly and top with more crushed ice.
Garnish: mint bouquet dusted with icing (confectioners') sugar

Colonial Julep

Rosina Cocktail Lounge, Las Vegas, 2017

1½ oz (45 ml) pineapple rum
1 oz (30 ml) rye whiskey
¼ oz (7 ml) cane syrup (p 494)
1 dash absinthe
6–8 mint leaves
Garnish: mint bouquet

Cynar Julep

Session Cocktails, *Drew Lazor, 2018*

1½ oz (45 ml) Cynar
1 oz (30 ml) pink grapefruit juice
½ oz (15 ml) lemon juice
½ oz (15 ml) simple syrup
1½ oz (45 ml) soda
6–8 mint leaves
Garnish: mint bouquet and dusting of ras el hanout

Don't Mind if I Do Julep

Sam Ross, Milk & Honey, NYC, 2009

1½ oz (45 ml) bonded apple brandy
1 oz (30 ml) bourbon
¼ oz (7 ml) cane syrup (p 494)
6–8 mint leaves
¼ oz (7 ml) Jamaican dark rum, to float
Press mint with cane syrup in a frozen Julep cup, then add brandy and bourbon. Fill the cup with crushed ice, swizzle, then top with more crushed ice and float rum.
Garnish: mint bouquet

Press mint with sugar and/or syrup and/or liqueur in a frozen Julep cup, then add remaining ingredients. Fill the cup with crushed ice, then swizzle and top with more crushed ice.

Georgia Mint Julep
Famous New Orleans Drinks and How to Mix 'Em, *Stanley Clisby Arthur, 1937*
2 oz (60 ml) Cognac
½ oz (15 ml) Giffard Crème de Pêche de Vigne
1 teaspoon (5 ml) simple syrup
6–8 mint leaves
1 white sugar cube

High Plains Julep
Travis Hernandez, Half Step, Austin, 2017
1 oz (30 ml) rye whiskey
½ oz (15 ml) Amaro Braulio
½ oz (15 ml) amaretto
6–8 mint leaves
Garnish: mint bouquet dusted with icing (confectioners') sugar

Last One Standing
Natasha David, Nitecap, NYC, 2014
1 oz (30 ml) Cognac
¾ oz (22 ml) Amaro CioCiaro
½ oz (15 ml) Jamaican gold rum
1 teaspoon (5 ml) Giffard Crème de Pêche de Vigne
6–8 mint leaves
Garnish: peach slice and mint bouquet dusted with icing (confectioners') sugar

Major Bailey
(aka **Gin Julep**)
Irvin S. Cobb's Own Recipe Book, *Irvin S. Cobb, 1936*
2½ oz (75 ml) gin
¼ oz (7 ml) simple syrup
1 white sugar cube
6–8 mint leaves
Garnish: mint bouquet

Maple Julep
2½ oz (75 ml) rye whiskey
¼ oz (7 ml) maple syrup
1 white sugar cube
6–8 mint leaves
Garnish: mint bouquet

Ment-Julep (Mexican Style)
Bar La Florida Cocktails, *1935*
2 oz (60 ml) Cognac
½ oz (15 ml) tawny Port
1 teaspoon (5 ml) maraschino liqueur
2 dashes Angostura Bitters
1 white sugar cube
6–8 mint leaves
Garnish: cherry, mint bouquet and lemon twist

Mint Julep
(aka **Southern Mint Julep** in *Burke's Complete Cocktail & Drinking Recipes*, Harman Burney Burke, 1934 or Cognac Julep with Jamaican rum)
The Bar-Tender's Guide, *Jerry Thomas, 1862*
2½ oz (75 ml) Cognac
¼ oz (7 ml) simple syrup
1 white sugar cube
6–8 mint leaves
½ oz (15 ml) Jamaican dark rum, to float
Press mint with sugar and simple syrup in a frozen Julep cup, then add Cognac. Fill the cup with crushed ice, swizzle, then top with more crushed ice and float rum.
Garnish: 3 seasonal berries and mint bouquet dusted with icing (confectioners') sugar

Mint Julep (Charlie Paul Recipe)
Recipes of American and Other Iced Drinks, *Charlie Paul, 1902*
1 oz (30 ml) Cognac
½ oz (15 ml) Yellow Chartreuse
½ oz (15 ml) aged dark rum
6–8 mint leaves
¼ oz (7 ml) tawny Port, to float
Press mint with Yellow Chartreuse in a frozen Julep cup, then add remaining ingredients. Fill the cup with crushed ice, swizzle, then top with more crushed ice and float Port.
Garnish: 3 seasonal berries and mint bouquet dusted with icing (confectioners') sugar
▼ "This is a drink fit for a king." The more common julep with whiskey is called a **Whiskey Julep** (opposite).

Prescription Julep
Harper's New Monthly Magazine, *1857*
1½ oz (45 ml) Cognac
½ oz (15 ml) rye whiskey
¼ oz (7 ml) simple syrup
1 white sugar cube
6–8 mint leaves
Garnish: mint bouquet

Smoked Julep
Phil Ward, Death & Co, NYC, 2008
1 oz (30 ml) Islay Scotch
1 oz (30 ml) bonded apple brandy
¼ oz (7 ml) maple syrup
6–8 mint leaves
Garnish: mint bouquet

St. Regis Mint Julep
J. Swago
Famous New Orleans Drinks and How to Mix 'Em, *Stanley Clisby Arthur, 1937*
1¼ oz (37 ml) aged dark rum
1¼ oz (37 ml) rye whiskey
¼ oz (7 ml) grenadine (p 496)
6–8 mint leaves
Garnish: mint bouquet

The Real Georgia Mint Julep
The Bar-Tender's Guide, *Jerry Thomas, 1887*
2 oz (60 ml) Cognac
½ oz (15 ml) Giffard Crème de Pêche de Vigne
1 teaspoon (5 ml) simple syrup
1 white sugar cube
6–8 mint leaves
Garnish: mint bouquet

Whiskey Julep
The Bar-Tender's Guide, *Jerry Thomas, 1862*
2½ oz (75 ml) bourbon
¼ oz (7 ml) simple syrup
1 white sugar cube
6–8 mint leaves
Garnish: mint bouquet
▼ Swap bourbon for rye whiskey to make the **Yankee Julep**.

Press mint with sugar and/or syrup and/or liqueur in a frozen Julep cup, then add remaining ingredients. Fill the cup with crushed ice, then swizzle and top with more crushed ice.

Smash

Muddle mint and syrup (plus other fruits in modern variations) in a shaker. Add spirit, then shake with ice and strain into a frozen double rocks glass with cracked ice.

Harvest Smash
Chip Tyndale, Dutch Kills, NYC
2 oz (60 ml) bonded apple brandy
½ oz (15 ml) Demerara syrup (p 495)
3 lemon wedges
3–5 blueberries
8–10 mint leaves
Garnish: mint sprig and blueberry

Mulberry Smash
Good Things to Drink with Mr. Lyan & Friends, *Ryan Chetiyawardana, 2015*
2 oz (60 ml) gin
¾ oz (22 ml) lemon juice
2 teaspoons (12 g) mulberry jam
8–10 mint leaves
Add gin and mulberry jam to a shaker and stir to combine. Add remaining ingredients, muddle, then shake with ice and strain into a frozen double rocks glass with cracked ice.
Garnish: mint bouquet

Perfidia
Lauren Schell, The Everleigh, Melbourne, 2011
2 oz (60 ml) aged dark rum
½ oz (15 ml) simple syrup
3 dashes Angostura Bitters
3 lemon wedges
2 orange wedges
6–8 mint leaves
Garnish: mint bouquet
▾ Swap aged dark rum for spiced rum to make the **Perfidia #2** by Lauren Schell, The Everleigh, Melbourne, 2011.

Strawberry Watermelon Smash
2 oz (60 ml) gin
¾ oz (22 ml) simple syrup
1 strawberry, halved
2 watermelon chunks
4 lemon wedges
6–8 mint leaves
Garnish: mint sprig and watermelon wedge

Tequila Smash
2 oz (60 ml) blanco tequila
½ oz (15 ml) agave syrup (p 494)
4 lemon wedges
6–8 mint leaves
Garnish: mint bouquet

Whiskey Peach Smash
Dale DeGroff, Bar Americain, NYC, 2005
2 oz (60 ml) bourbon
¾ oz (22 ml) simple syrup
3 lemon wedges
½ peach, quartered
6–8 mint leaves
Garnish: mint sprig and peach slice

Wry Grin
Sam Ross, Milk & Honey, NYC, 2010
1½ oz (45 ml) rye whiskey
½ oz (15 ml) Fernet-Branca
¾ oz (22 ml) simple syrup
4 lemon wedges
6–8 mint leaves
Garnish: mint bouquet

Stinger

Build all ingredients in a frozen double rocks glass, then fill the glass with crushed ice.

Apotheke
"Harry" of Ciro's ABC of Mixing Cocktails, *Harry MacElhone, 1986*
1 oz (30 ml) Fernet-Branca
1 oz (30 ml) white crème de menthe
1 oz (30 ml) sweet vermouth
Garnish: mint bouquet

Apotheke Cocktail (Original)
Der Perfekte Mixer, *Martin Heile, 1950*
1½ oz (45 ml) sweet vermouth
¾ oz (22 ml) Cognac
¾ oz (22 ml) white crème de menthe
4 dashes Angostura Bitters

Après Souper
The Flowing Bowl: What and When to Drink, *William Schmidt, 1891*
2 oz (60 ml) Cognac
¾ oz (22 ml) white crème de menthe
¼ oz (7 ml) maraschino liqueur
Garnish: mint bouquet

Brant Cocktail
(Stinger served up with Angostura Bitters and a lemon twist)
Jack's Manual, *J.A. Grohusko, 1916*
2 oz (60 ml) Cognac
¾ oz (22 ml) white crème de menthe
2 dashes Angostura Bitters
Stir with ice and strain into a frozen coupe.
Garnish: lemon twist

Dry Stinger
The Fine Art of Mixing Drinks, *David A. Embury, 1948*
1½ oz (45 ml) Cognac
¾ oz (22 ml) white crème de menthe
¾ oz (22 ml) lime juice
Garnish: mint bouquet

Muddle mint (plus other fruits in modern variations) with sugar and/or syrup in a shaker. Add spirit, then shake with ice and strain into a frozen double rocks glass with cracked ice.

Gin Stinger
Cesar Romero
The South American Gentleman's Companion, *Charles H. Baker Jr., 1951*
1½ oz (45 ml) gin
½ oz (15 ml) Cognac
¾ oz (22 ml) white crème de menthe
¼ oz (7 ml) grenadine (p 496), to float
Build all ingredients in a frozen double rocks glass, then fill the glass with crushed ice and float grenadine.
Garnish: mint bouquet

Good Night & Good Luck
Chad Solomon, Midnight Rambler, Dallas, 2014
¾ oz (22 ml) Cognac
¾ oz (22 ml) Branca Menta
¾ oz (22 ml) rye whiskey
2 drops saline solution (p 493)
Garnish: mint bouquet
▼ Named after American broadcaster Edward R. Murrow's signature sign-off phrase.

Half Past Midnight
Sam Ross, Attaboy, NYC, 2015
2 oz (60 ml) Cognac
½ oz (15 ml) Fernet-Branca
½ oz (15 ml) white crème de menthe
Garnish: mint bouquet

Midnight Stinger
Sam Ross, Attaboy, NYC, 2008
1 oz (30 ml) bourbon
1 oz (30 ml) Fernet-Branca
¾ oz (22 ml) lemon juice
¾ oz (22 ml) simple syrup
Garnish: mint bouquet

Morning After Cocktail
J.P. Mitchell
Barflies and Cocktails, *Harry MacElhone, 1927*
1½ oz (45 ml) Fernet-Branca
1 oz (30 ml) white crème de menthe
½ oz (15 ml) crème de cassis
Garnish: mint bouquet
▼ "Guaranteed to bring the bloom back to your nose."

Port Stinger
2½ oz (75 ml) tawny Port
½ oz (15 ml) white crème de menthe
Garnish: mint bouquet

Stinger
Straub's Manual of Mixed Drinks, *Jacques Straub, 1913*
2 oz (60 ml) Cognac
¾ oz (22 ml) white crème de menthe
1 lemon twist
Shake with ice and strain into a frozen coupe glass.
Garnish: lemon twist

Stinger Cocktail
(aka **Stinger Royal** in *The How and When*, Hyman Gale and Gerald F. Marco, 1938)
Cocktails: How to Mix Them, *Robert Vermeire, 1922*
2 oz (60 ml) Cognac
¾ oz (22 ml) white crème de menthe
3 dashes absinthe
Garnish: mint bouquet

Stinger (Double Deuce Lounge Recipe)
Double Deuce Lounge, Sydney
2 oz (60 ml) Cognac
⅓ oz (10 ml) white crème de menthe
1 teaspoon (5 ml) Fernet-Branca
1 teaspoon (5 ml) Branca Menta
3 dashes absinthe
Stir with ice and strain into a frozen coupe.
Garnish: mint leaf and two drops of peppermint and avocado oil

The Judge
The Flowing Bowl, *William Schmidt, 1891*
2 oz (60 ml) Cognac
¾ oz (22 ml) white crème de menthe
Stir ingredients and pour into a frozen coupe.
Garnish: mint bouquet
▼ The original Stinger.

White Spider
(aka **Vodka Stinger**)
Jones' Complete Bartending Guide, *Stan Jones, 1977*
2 oz (60 ml) vodka
¾ oz (22 ml) white crème de menthe
Garnish: mint bouquet

From *Here's How!* (1927):

May all your troubles last as long as your resolutions!

White Way Cocktail
(aka **Gin Stinger**)
Classic Cocktails: A Modern Shake, *Mark Kingwell, 2007*
2 oz (60 ml) gin
¾ oz (22 ml) white crème de menthe
Garnish: mint bouquet

Ztinger
(aka **Mezcal Stinger**)
Robert Simonson, NYC, 2020
2½ oz (75 ml) mezcal
¾ oz (22 ml) white crème de menthe
Garnish: mint bouquet

Build all ingredients in a frozen double rocks glass, then fill the glass with crushed ice.

NEGRONI

Negroni p 292

Negroni

A bittersweet aperitivo cocktail classically comprising gin, sweet vermouth and Italian bitters, built and served on the rocks.

gin + sweet vermouth + Campari

↓

Build all ingredients in an Old Fashioned glass, then add ice.

Undeniably Italy's most celebrated contribution to the cocktail canon, the Negroni is a harmonious mix of gin, sweet vermouth and Italian bitters served on ice, and in its country of origin, often finished with a splash of soda. This stunningly foolproof cocktail first made a stir at Caffè Casoni in Florence around 1919 when Italian aristocrat Count Camillo Negroni asked bartender Fosco Scarselli to liven up his Americano, and he responded by swapping out the soda for gin. Whether Camillo Negroni was in fact a Count is questionable, but we do know that he was a flamboyant character, said to have ventured to the United States and spent time as a cowboy in the Wild West, as a gambler in New York City, and, quite unpredictably, as a fencing instructor.

Around the same time in Paris, the French were enjoying a fashionable cocktail that they dubbed the Camparinete (p 299), a blend of gin, sweet vermouth and Italian bitters predominantly served up sans soda. This drink also made the rounds in New York City during the 1920s and 1930s. Interestingly, it wasn't until the end of World War II that the Negroni truly took its place as the confident, cosmopolitan Italian aperitivo we recognise today.

Its enchanting colour and effortless bittersweet balance appealed to the discerning drinker, and it developed an identity as the cocktail for connoisseurs around the world. If interest in the drink did waver at any point during the latter half of the 20th century, the classic cocktail renaissance of the early 2000s reinstated the Negroni as the epitome of fine drinking culture – the drink you drink if you know about drinks, if you will.

→

Our preferred Negroni uses a lighter, fruitier style vermouth from Torino with a moscato base. Whereas most Negroni recipes are equal parts gin, vermouth and Campari, we increase the amount of vermouth to allow its delicate profile to stand up against the others. It is worth noting that the Campari of today is a wildly different product to the one Scarselli mixed with in 1919.

As products and palates evolve, we advocate interrogating classic recipes and continuously considering whether they need recalibration to cater to contemporary ingredients and modern tastes. It is truly remarkable how, with revision and subtle revitalisation of recipes, the appetite for simple, classic drinks like the Negroni, born over one hundred years ago, continues to soar, and this in turn inspires a growing number of exciting variations.

Negroni (House Recipe)

1 oz (30 ml) sweet vermouth
¾ oz (22 ml) gin
¾ oz (22 ml) Campari

Build all ingredients in an Old Fashioned glass, then add ice.
Garnish: orange twist
● Originally credited to Fosco Scarselli of Caffé Casoni, Florence, 1919.

ESSENTIAL VARIATIONS

White Negroni

Wayne Collins, 2001
1 oz (30 ml) gin
¾ oz (22 ml) Cocchi Americano
¾ oz (22 ml) Suze

Build all ingredients in an Old Fashioned glass, then add ice.
Garnish: grapefruit twist

Born out of necessity by a pair of British hospitality heavyweights in 2001, the White Negroni is a modern classic celebrated by the bar community worldwide. This Negroni *a la française* came to fruition when Nick Blacknell (then managing director of Plymouth Gin) and bartender Wayne Collins worked up a competitive thirst on a trip to Bordeaux. Collins suggested they make Negronis, but with French ingredients in the spirit of their trip. From a sea of obscure local products, the pair picked out a bottle of Suze – a refreshingly bitter and bright yellow gentian liqueur – and another of Lillet Blanc, a light and citrusy fortified wine. Blacknell supplied the gin and Collins finished the drink with a pink grapefruit twist.

Although Blacknell and Collins had high hopes of splashing their creation around the United Kingdom, the White Negroni took some time to catch on. It wasn't until 2012, when industry advocates pushed for Pernod Ricard to export Suze to the United States, that the drink really found its feet. With the Negroni at the height of its popularity, variations were in high demand in New York City bars, and supporters such as Jim Meehan of PDT and Audrey Saunders of Pegu Club delivered the White Negroni with pride.

Our preferred recipe features Cocchi Americano instead of Lillet Blanc, the former delightfully crisp and citrusy with a delicate floral aroma and subtle bitterness to finish. After other memorable classics with a dash of French flair? Try the Daisy variation the Champs-Élysées (p 178), or the Saint-Germain-des-Prés (p 162), a twist on a Traditional Sour.

Cynarita

Michael Madrusan, The Everleigh, Melbourne, 2011
1½ oz (45 ml) blanco tequila
½ oz (15 ml) Cynar
½ oz (15 ml) Campari

Build all ingredients in an Old Fashioned glass, then add ice.
Garnish: lemon twist

The Cynarita is a bold tequila-based Negroni variation that uses Cynar instead of sweet vermouth, which I came up with in 2011. Having recently returned to Australia from New York City to open The Everleigh that same year, I was behind the bar most nights, taking spare moments to nip out back and do the ordering and invoicing. I remember my brother-in-law, Greg, coming by one slow Monday night. I was there picking mint; he sat down in front of me and asked for something boozy with tequila. He liked Negronis, and I was drinking a lot of Cynar at the time. Greg's face entertains me at the best of times, but I think I laughed out loud at his expression when he took that first sip.

The Everleigh team's appreciation for tequila was a big part of the bar's reputation after it arrived on Fitzroy's Gertrude Street, with talented alumni crafting a number of excellent original cocktails using the spicier spirit over the years. The Cynarita is a pre-dinner drink that's full of life, an adventurous next step for the Negroni lover. The tequila's earthiness combined with the bittersweetness of Campari and savouriness of the artichoke-based Cynar results in a robust cocktail geared for savvy drinkers.

Cynar has been embraced by the bartending community in several recent additions to the cocktail world. Some favourites include the Bensonhurst from Chad Solomon (p 346) and the Little Italy (p 344) from Audrey Saunders – both variations on the Manhattan – as well as the Chin Up (p 315), a Martini riff by Sam Ross. Fans of the Cynarita should also explore other Old Fashioned variants with tequila, such as The Coffee House (Heartbreaker Recipe; p 380), with coffee liqueur and orange bitters.

Boulevardier Cocktail

Barflies and Cocktails, *Harry MacElhone, 1927*
1½ oz (45 ml) bourbon
¾ oz (22 ml) sweet vermouth
¾ oz (22 ml) Campari

Add all ingredients to a mixing glass, then stir with ice and strain into a frozen coupe.
Garnish: orange twist
● This drink is traditionally built and served on ice.

The Boulevardier Cocktail first popped up in Harry MacElhone's *Barflies and Cocktails* in 1927. MacElhone was a Scottish bartender, born in 1890 in Dundee. He began his career in Paris before heading to the United States, with stints behind the stick in Connecticut and New York City prior to World War I, when he served in the air force. After the war, MacElhone returned to the United Kingdom and achieved renown as the head bartender at London's Ciro's, a successful nightclub in Leicester Square with locations across Europe and in Los Angeles. This is where he published his first book, *"Harry" of Ciro's ABC of Mixing Cocktails* in 1923, which spawned a whopping twelve revised editions in the three decades that followed. In 1923, MacElhone purchased the New York Bar in Paris and stuck his name on it.

MacElhone is credited with many immortal cocktails, including the Monkey Gland (p 172), as well as two influential cocktail books, but it was his knack for building Harry's New York Bar into a brand that is perhaps most significant. MacElhone was a true pioneer in the bar industry, using merchandise and media relationships to market his establishment and develop an internationally acclaimed phenomenon – not just *an* American bar in Paris, but *the* American bar in Paris. Following his death in 1958, MacElhone's son, grandson and great-grandson have all carried on his legacy and, remarkably, the bar is still operating over one hundred years since it first opened.

Curiously, the Boulevardier was listed not within the recipe pages of *Barflies and Cocktails*, but instead in a short chapter entitled 'Cocktails Round Town' by Arthur Moss. A columnist of the *New York Herald*, Moss attributes the drink to barfly Erskinne Gwynne, one of a group of so-called 'Men-About-Town' who not only 'clamor for every possible liquid combination; they even invent their own'.

While the original recipe calls for equal parts bourbon, Italian vermouth and Campari, we prefer to emphasise the bourbon and make the drink in the style of a Manhattan (p 334), stirred and served up. This adaptation allows the dark spirit's complexity to shine, contoured by the supporting players, and culminates in a whiskey-driven, Negroni-esque cocktail.

Today's drinker is no stranger to Campari thanks to the worldwide success of the Negroni and the Americano (p 112), but modern riffs on the Boulevardier continue to appear, proving it is an equally popular choice. For a drier twist on this classic using rye whiskey, try another of MacElhone and Moss's benchmarks, the My Old Pal (p 298). Or, give another close and slightly more contemporary relative a go: the Left Hand (p 302) by Sam Ross, spiced with mole bitters.

Negroni

FORTIFIED & LIQUEUR

Charente White Negroni
Simon Difford and Matthias Lataille, 2014
1 oz (30 ml) Suze
1 oz (30 ml) Lillet Blanc
½ oz (15 ml) gin
½ oz (15 ml) Cognac
Garnish: grapefruit twist

Chinotto Negroni
Darren Leaney, Caretaker's Cottage, Melbourne, 2024
1 oz (30 ml) Amaro Amarót
¾ oz (22 ml) gin (preferably Tanqueray London Dry Gin)
¾ oz (22 ml) Punt e Mes
½ oz (15 ml) Campari
Garnish: orange twist (discard) and orange half-wheel

Coffee Negroni
1 oz (30 ml) sweet vermouth
¾ oz (22 ml) gin
¾ oz (22 ml) Campari
½ oz (15 ml) coffee liqueur
Garnish: orange twist

Cold Brew Negroni (Edd Siu Recipe)
Edd Siu, Vespr Coffee Bar, Orlando
1 oz (30 ml) Campari
1 oz (20 ml) sweet vermouth
1½ oz (45 ml) cold brew concentrate
Garnish: orange twist
● Alternate option in gin (p 299).

Ghosts of My Life
Turk Dietrich, Cure, New Orleans
1½ oz (45 ml) Zucca Rabarbaro
1 oz (30 ml) overproof gin
½ oz (15 ml) Campari
3 dashes orange bitters
Garnish: lemon twist

Gloria
Cocktails de Paris, *Georges Gabriel Thenon, 1929*
1 oz (30 ml) gin
1 oz (30 ml) dry vermouth
½ oz (15 ml) Campari
½ oz (15 ml) triple sec
Garnish: lemon twist

House Negroni (Torrisi Recipe)
Nathan McCarley-O'Neill, Torrisi, NYC, 2024
1½ oz (45 ml) Campari
1 oz (30 ml) gin (preferably The Boatyard Distillery Boatyard Double Gin)
1 oz (30 ml) Carpano Antica Formula
¼ oz (7 ml) Punt e Mes
Garnish: orange twist (discard) and orange half-wheel

Intruder
ms. franky marshall, Le Boudoir, NYC, 2015
1 oz (30 ml) reposado tequila
1 oz (30 ml) Byrrh Grand Quinquina
¾ oz (22 ml) Tempus Fugit Gran Classico Bitter
Garnish: grapefruit twist

Marianito
Originated in Bilbao, Spain
2½ oz (75 ml) sweet vermouth (preferably Lustau Vermut Rojo)
½ oz (15 ml) gin
½ oz (15 ml) Campari
2 dashes Angostura Bitters
Garnish: orange twist and green olive

My Old Pal
(Negroni with rye whiskey)
"Sparrow" Robertson
Barflies and Cocktails, *Harry MacElhone, 1927*
1 oz (30 ml) sweet vermouth
¾ oz (22 ml) rye whiskey
¾ oz (22 ml) Campari
Garnish: orange twist

Negroni Sbagliato
Mirko Stocchetto, Bar Basso, 1972
1 oz (30 ml) sweet vermouth
1 oz (30 ml) Campari
2 oz (60 ml) Prosecco, to top
Build in a chilled double rocks glass with ice, then top with Prosecco.
Garnish: orange half-wheel

Negroni Svegliato
Cicala, Philadelphia
1 oz (30 ml) gin
1 oz (30 ml) Campari
1 oz (30 ml) coffee-brewed sweet vermouth (p 503)
Garnish: orange twist

Polka Dot Negroni
Toby Maloney, The Violet Hour, Chicago
1½ oz (45 ml) Salers Gentiane
1 oz (30 ml) gin
1 oz (30 ml) bianco vermouth
3 dashes grapefruit bitters
Stir with ice and strain into a frozen coupe.
Garnish: lemon twist and cherry

Quill Cocktail
(aka **Ritz Negroni** or Negroni with absinthe)
Frank C. Payne, Harry's New York Bar, Paris
1 oz (30 ml) sweet vermouth
¾ oz (22 ml) gin
¾ oz (22 ml) Campari
2 dashes absinthe
Garnish: orange twist
● An Everleigh favourite.

Sharon
Session Cocktails, *Drew Lazor, 2018*
1½ oz (45 ml) Manzanilla Sherry
1 oz (30 ml) sweet vermouth
¾ oz (22 ml) Campari
Stir with ice and strain into a frozen coupe.
Garnish: orange twist

White Negroni Sbagliato
(See p 419)

Build all ingredients in an Old Fashioned glass, then add ice.

VODKA

Valentino
The Joy of Mixology, *Gary Regan, 2003*
2 oz (60 ml) vodka
½ oz (15 ml) sweet vermouth
½ oz (15 ml) Campari
Stir with ice and strain into a frozen coupe.
Garnish: orange twist

GIN

Alpine Negroni
Jack Schramm, NYC
¾ oz (22 ml) gin
¾ oz (22 ml) sweet vermouth
¾ oz (22 ml) Campari
¾ oz (22 ml) Amaro Braulio
¼ oz (7 ml) Champagne acid (p 505)
Garnish: lemon twist

Belfast Bastard
Jack McGarry, The Dead Rabbit, NYC
The Negroni: Drinking to La Dolce Vita, with Recipes & Lore, *Gary Regan, 2015*
2 oz (60 ml) gin
½ oz (15 ml) dry vermouth
½ oz (15 ml) Campari
½ oz (15 ml) Giffard Crème de Pamplemousse Rose
2 dashes orange bitters
Stir with ice and strain into a frozen coupe.
Garnish: grapefruit twist

Bench Warmer
Sean O'Connor-Combee, J & Tony's Discount Cured Meats and Negroni Warehouse, San Diego, 2022
1 oz (30 ml) gin
1 oz (30 ml) bianco vermouth
½ oz (15 ml) Luxardo Bitter Bianco
½ oz (15 ml) Fino Sherry
1 dash absinthe
Garnish: lemon twist (discard) and mint sprig

Bergamot Negroni
Naren Young, Dante, NYC, 2019
1 oz (30 ml) gin
¾ oz (22 ml) Campari
¾ oz (22 ml) dry vermouth
¼ oz (7 ml) Italicus Rosolio di Bergamotto
Garnish: orange half-wheel

Berlioni
Gonçalo de Sousa Monteiro, 2004
1¾ oz (52 ml) gin
¾ oz (22 ml) dry vermouth
½ oz (15 ml) Cynar
Stir with ice and strain into a frozen coupe.
Garnish: orange twist
● An Everleigh fav'.

Camparinete
"Albert", Chatham
Cocktails de Paris, *Georges Gabriel Thenon, 1929*
2 oz (60 ml) gin
½ oz (15 ml) Campari
½ oz (15 ml) sweet vermouth
Stir with ice and strain into a frozen coupe.
Garnish: orange twist

Cardinal
Jones' Complete Barguide, *Stan Jones, 1977*
1½ oz (45 ml) gin
¾ oz (22 ml) dry vermouth
¾ oz (22 ml) Campari
Stir with ice and strain into a frozen coupe.
Garnish: lemon twist
● A great dry Negroni variation.

Cardinale (Original Recipe)
Cocktails Portfolio, *Amedeo Gandiglio, 1947*
1 oz (30 ml) gin
1 oz (30 ml) dry vermouth
1 oz (30 ml) Campari
Stir with ice and strain into a frozen coupe.
Garnish: lemon twist

Cardinale (Excelsior Hotel Recipe)
Giovanni Raimondo, Excelsior Hotel, Rome, 1950
2 oz (60 ml) gin
1 oz (30 ml) riesling
½ oz (15 ml) Campari
Garnish: clove-studded orange twist

Cavalier
Sam Ross, Attaboy, NYC, 2017
1 oz (30 ml) gin
1 oz (30 ml) dry vermouth
1 oz (30 ml) Amaro Montenegro
Garnish: lemon twist

Coffee Negroni!
Lorenzo Antinori, Bar Leone, Hong Kong
¾ oz (22 ml) coffee-washed gin (p 503)
¾ oz (22 ml) sweet vermouth (preferably Mancino Vermouth di Torino Rosso Amaranto)
¾ oz (22 ml) Campari
1 teaspoon (5 ml) mezcal
Garnish: grapefruit twist

Cold Brew Negroni
Kristine Bocchino, Lunetta, Santa Monica
1 oz (30 ml) gin
¾ oz (22 ml) sweet vermouth
¾ oz (22 ml) Cappelletti Vino Aperitivo Americano Rosso
½ oz (15 ml) Mr Black Cold Brew Coffee Liqueur
Garnish: orange twist
● Swap Mr Black for Cold Brew Coffee to get Simon Difford's **Version 2021**.

Cynartown
Phil Ward, Death & Co, NYC, 2008
1¾ oz (52 ml) gin
¾ oz (22 ml) sweet vermouth
½ oz (15 ml) Cynar
Stir with ice and strain into a frozen coupe.
Garnish: cherry

Build all ingredients in an Old Fashioned glass, then add ice.

Dear Jane
Zachary Gelnaw-Rubin, Attaboy, NYC, 2015
1 oz (30 ml) gin
1 oz (30 ml) Campari
¾ oz (22 ml) sweet vermouth
¼ oz (7 ml) St Germain Elderflower Liqueur
Garnish: orange twist

Dirty Negroni
Travis Tober, Nickel City, Austin, 2017
1 oz (30 ml) olive oil-infused gin (p 504)
1 oz (30 ml) sweet vermouth
1 oz (30 ml) Campari
3 dashes The Bitter Truth Olive Bitters
3 drops saline solution (p 493)
Garnish: olive

Dr Pepper Negroni
Travis Tober, Nickel City, Austin, 2017
1 oz (30 ml) almond-infused gin (p 502)
1 oz (30 ml) Select Aperitivo
1 oz (30 ml) Amaro Montenegro
¼ oz (7 ml) Dr Pepper syrup (p 495)
Garnish: cherry

Gaz Regan's Negroni
Gary "Gaz" Regan, NYC
1 oz (30 ml) gin (preferably Tanqueray London Dry Gin)
1 oz (30 ml) sweet vermouth (preferably Dolin Rouge)
1 oz (30 ml) Jägermeister
Garnish: orange twist

John Perona
John Perona
Ted Saucier's Bottoms Up, *Ted Saucier, 1951*
1½ oz (45 ml) gin
1¼ oz (37 ml) sweet vermouth
1 teaspoon (5 ml) Campari
Stir with ice and strain into a frozen coupe.
Garnish: lemon twist
Great variation for those wanting something a little less bitter.

Kula Negroni
Julie Reiner, Clover Club, NYC, 2017
1 oz (30 ml) gin (preferably Tanqueray London Dry Gin)
1 oz (30 ml) bianco vermouth
1 oz (30 ml) strawberry-infused Campari (p 504)
Garnish: half a strawberry

Leg Before Wicket
Café Royal Cocktail Guide, *W.J. Tarling, 1937*
1½ oz (45 ml) gin
¾ oz (22 ml) sweet vermouth
½ oz (15 ml) Campari
½ oz (15 ml) lime cordial (p 497)
Stir with ice and strain into a frozen coupe.
Garnish: lime twist

Liberty Negroni
Michael Bascetta and Nick Tesar, Bar Liberty, Melbourne
1 oz (30 ml) gin (preferably Reed & Co. Distillery Remedy Australian Dry Gin)
1 oz (30 ml) sweet vermouth (preferably Maidenii Classic Vermouth)
¾ oz (22 ml) Campari
1 teaspoon (5 ml) Picon Amer
Garnish: orange twist

Lucien-Gaudin
"Charlie", Cheval Pie
Cocktails de Paris, *Georges Gabriel Thenon, 1929*
1½ oz (45 ml) gin
½ oz (15 ml) dry vermouth
½ oz (15 ml) Campari
½ oz (15 ml) triple sec
Stir with ice and strain into a frozen coupe.
Garnish: lemon twist

Negroni Frappé
Naren Young, Dante, NYC
¾ oz (22 ml) gin
¾ oz (22 ml) Meletti 1870 Bitter Aperitivo
¾ oz (22 ml) sweet vermouth
¾ oz (22 ml) orange juice
3 dashes orange bitters
Whip and pour into a frozen double rocks glass with crushed ice.
Garnish: freshly grated orange zest

Negroni Tredici
Toby Maloney, 2009
1½ oz (45 ml) gin
1 oz (30 ml) sweet vermouth
¼ oz (7 ml) Campari
¼ oz (7 ml) Cynar
2 dashes orange bitters
Stir with ice and strain into a frozen coupe.
Garnish: lemon twist

Nico
Matty Eggleston, Nico Osteria, Chicago
1¼ oz (37 ml) gin
1¼ oz (37 ml) Cocchi Americano
½ oz (15 ml) Amaro Braulio
¾ oz (22 ml) sparkling mineral water
Stir with ice and strain into a frozen coupe.
Garnish: lemon peel

Old Flame
(aka **Fancy Nancy**)
Dale DeGroff, NYC, 2001
1 oz (30 ml) gin
½ oz (15 ml) triple sec
½ oz (15 ml) sweet vermouth
½ oz (15 ml) Campari
1 oz (30 ml) orange juice
1 teaspoon (5 ml) lemon juice
Shake with ice and strain into a frozen coupe.
Garnish: flamed orange twist
Winner of the 'Fancy Cocktail' category at the 2001 Martini & Rossi Grand Prix.

Build all ingredients in an Old Fashioned glass, then add ice.

Palm Sunday
Brandon Bramhall, Attaboy, Nashville, 2017
1½ oz (45 ml) gin
½ oz (15 ml) dry vermouth
½ oz (15 ml) Suze
½ oz (15 ml) Aperol
Garnish: grapefruit twist

Tailspin
Old Mr. Boston Deluxe Official Bartender's Guide, *Leo Cotton, 1936*
1 oz (30 ml) gin
1 oz (30 ml) sweet vermouth
1 oz (30 ml) Green Chartreuse
1 teaspoon (5 ml) Campari
Stir with ice and strain into a frozen coupe.
Garnish: lemon twist

The Contessa
John Gertsen, Drink, Boston
1 oz (30 ml) gin
1 oz (30 ml) dry vermouth
1 oz (30 ml) Aperol
Garnish: lemon twist

Tony's Negroni
Anthony Schmidt, J & Tony's Discount Cured Meats and Negroni Warehouse, San Diego, 2020
1 oz (30 ml) gin
1 oz (30 ml) Carpano Antica Formula
1 oz (30 ml) Campari
¼ oz (7 ml) lemon juice
Stir briefly with ice and strain into an Old Fashioned glass with ice.
Garnish: lemon twist (discard) and orange half-wheel

Tunnel
"Bob", Harry's New York Bar
Cocktails de Paris, *Georges Gabriel Thenon, 1929*
1½ oz (45 ml) gin
½ oz (15 ml) dry vermouth
½ oz (15 ml) Campari
½ oz (15 ml) Punt e Mes
Garnish: lemon twist

Unusual Negroni
Charlotte Voisey, 2011
1 oz (30 ml) gin
1 oz (30 ml) Lillet Blanc
1 oz (30 ml) Campari
Garnish: orange twist

Winterized Negroni
Brian Evans, Sunday Hospitality, NYC
1 oz (30 ml) gin
¾ oz (22 ml) sweet vermouth
¾ oz (22 ml) Campari
½ teaspoon (2.5 ml) Islay Scotch
Stir with ice and strain into a frozen coupe.

Yuzu Negroni (Bar Leone Recipe)
Lorenzo Antinori, Bar Leone, Hong Kong
¾ oz (22 ml) gin
¾ oz (22 ml) Suze
½ oz (15 ml) Cocchi Americano
¼ oz (7 ml) yuzushu
Garnish: lemon twist

Yuzu Negroni (Sager + Wilde Recipe)
Marcis Dzelzainis, Sager + Wilde, London
¾ oz (22 ml) gin
¾ oz (22 ml) yuzushu
¾ oz (22 ml) Campari
½ oz (15 ml) Punt e Mes
Garnish: lemon twist

RUM & CANE SPIRIT

East India Negroni
Jim Meehan, PDT, NYC, 2010
2 oz (60 ml) light rum (preferably Banks 5 Island Rum)
¾ oz (22 ml) Lustau East India Solera Sherry
¾ oz (22 ml) Campari
Garnish: orange twist

Kingston Negroni
Joaquín Simó, Death & Co, NYC, 2009
1 oz (30 ml) overproof Jamaican dark rum
1 oz (30 ml) sweet vermouth
1 oz (30 ml) Campari
Garnish: orange twist
● A fantastic rum Negroni.

Right Hand
(Boulevardier with aged dark rum and mole bitters)
Michael McIlroy, Milk & Honey, NYC, 2008
1½ oz (45 ml) aged dark rum
¾ oz (22 ml) sweet vermouth
¾ oz (22 ml) Campari
2 drops Bittermens Xocolatl Mole Bitters
Stir with ice and strain into a frozen coupe.
Garnish: orange twist

Shadow Boxer
Spirits of Latin America, *Ivy Mix, 2020*
1½ oz (45 ml) cachaça
¾ oz (22 ml) dry vermouth
¾ oz (22 ml) Campari
¼ oz (7 ml) apricot eau de vie
¼ oz (7 ml) Giffard Crème de Pamplemousse Rose
Garnish: orange twist

The Black Stallion Sets Sail
John Parra and Kyle Hankin, Fox Liquor Bar, Raleigh
1 oz (30 ml) Cruzan Black Strap Rum
1 oz (30 ml) sweet vermouth
½ oz (15 ml) Campari
½ oz (15 ml) Fernet-Branca
3 drops saline solution (p 493)
Garnish: orange twist

Toffee Negroni
Lynnette Marrero, 2016
1 oz (30 ml) aged dark rum
1 oz (30 ml) Aperol
1 oz (30 ml) Amontillado Sherry
Garnish: grapefruit twist

Tropicale
Lorenzo Antinori, Bar Leone, Hong Kong, 2023
¾ oz (22 ml) Jamaican dark rum
¾ oz (22 ml) Campari
½ oz (15 ml) sweet vermouth
⅜ oz (11 ml) Oloroso Sherry
1 teaspoon (5 ml) Giffard Banane du Brésil et des Caraïbes
Garnish: orange wedge

Build all ingredients in an Old Fashioned glass, then add ice.

Walrus
Simon Aukett, Keefer Bar, Vancouver
1 oz (30 ml) Goslings Black Seal Rum
1 oz (30 ml) dry vermouth
1 oz (30 ml) Campari
Garnish: lemon twist

AGAVE

Charming Man
Joaquín Simó, Pouring Ribbons, NYC, 2017
1 oz (30 ml) mezcal
1 oz (30 ml) Lustau East India Solera Sherry
1 oz (30 ml) Cappelletti Amaro Sfumato Rabarbaro
2 drops Bittermens Xocolatl Mole Bitters
Garnish: orange twist

Luca Brazi
Lorenzo Antinori, Bar Leone, Hong Kong, 2023
1 oz (30 ml) reposado tequila (preferably Tequila Ocho Reposado)
¾ oz (22 ml) Punt e Mes
½ oz (15 ml) Campari
⅓ oz (10 ml) Cynar
5 drops Bittermens Xocolatl Mole Bitters
Garnish: grapefruit twist

Pandan Negroni
Liana Oster, NoMad London, London, 2021
1 oz (30 ml) pandan-infused reposado tequila (p 504)
¾ oz (22 ml) sweet vermouth
¾ oz (22 ml) Campari
½ oz (15 ml) unfiltered coconut water
1 teaspoon (5 ml) cold-brew coffee

Rainy Day Fund
Courtney McKamey, Weather Up, NYC
1½ oz (45 ml) mezcal
¾ oz (22 ml) dry vermouth
¾ oz (22 ml) Italicus Rosolio di Bergamotto
2 dashes orange bitters
Garnish: orange twist

Rosita
Old Mr. Boston Deluxe Official Bartender's Guide, *Leo Cotton, 1974*
1½ oz (45 ml) blanco tequila
½ oz (15 ml) sweet vermouth
½ oz (15 ml) dry vermouth
½ oz (15 ml) Campari
1 dash Angostura Bitters
Stir with ice and strain into a frozen coupe.
Garnish: lemon twist
● Originally served on the rocks.

Scorched Earth No. 2
Nicholas Hearin, Restaurant Eugene, Atlanta, 2006
1 oz (30 ml) mezcal
1 oz (30 ml) Cynar
1 oz (30 ml) Campari
2 dashes orange bitters
Garnish: orange twist

Thou Shall Not be Named
Alicia Perry, San Diego
1½ oz (45 ml) reposado tequila
½ oz (15 ml) sweet vermouth
½ oz (15 ml) mezcal
½ oz (15 ml) Cappelletti Amaro Sfumato Rabarbaro
Garnish: lemon twist

Tia Juano
(Tequila Old Pal with an orange twist)
Café Royal Cocktail Book, *W.J. Tarling, 1937*
1½ oz (45 ml) blanco tequila
¾ oz (22 ml) dry vermouth
¾ oz (22 ml) Campari
Stir with ice and strain into a frozen coupe.
Garnish: orange twist

AMERICAN WHISKEY

All In
(Old Pal with white crème de cacao)
Natasha David, Nitecap, NYC
1½ oz (45 ml) rye whiskey
¾ oz (22 ml) dry vermouth
¾ oz (22 ml) Campari
¼ oz (7 ml) white crème de cacao
Stir with ice and strain into a frozen coupe.
Garnish: lemon twist (discard)

Banana Boulevardier
Terry Williams, Anvil, Houston, 2016
1 oz (30 ml) bourbon
1 oz (30 ml) sweet vermouth
½ oz (15 ml) Campari
¼ oz (7 ml) Giffard Banane du Brésil et des Caraïbes
Garnish: orange twist

Boulevardier
Attributed to Erskine Gwynne, an American expat who frequented Harry's New York Bar and edited a monthly magazine called The Boulevardier
Barflies and Cocktails, *Harry MacElhone, 1927*
1½ oz (45 ml) bourbon
¾ oz (22 ml) sweet vermouth
¾ oz (22 ml) Campari
Stir with ice and strain into a frozen coupe.
Garnish: cherry
● Traditionally served on the rocks.

Left Hand
(Boulevardier with mole bitters)
Sam Ross, Milk & Honey, NYC, 2006
1½ oz (45 ml) bourbon
¾ oz (22 ml) sweet vermouth
¾ oz (22 ml) Campari
2 drops Bittermens Xocolatl Mole Bitters
Stir with ice and strain into a frozen coupe.
Garnish: cherry

Build all ingredients in an Old Fashioned glass, then add ice.

Old Gal
Phil Ward, The Long Island Bar, NYC
1 oz (30 ml) rye whiskey
1 oz (30 ml) bianco vermouth
1 oz (30 ml) Campari
Garnish: orange twist

"Old Pal" Cocktail
"Sparrow" Robertson
Harry's ABC of Mixing Cocktails,
Harry MacElhone, 1923
1½ oz (45 ml) rye whiskey
¾ oz (22 ml) dry vermouth
¾ oz (22 ml) Campari
Garnish: lemon twist

Pincushion
Hunter Orahood, Attaboy, NYC, 2018
1½ oz (45 ml) rye whiskey
¾ oz (22 ml) sweet vermouth
¾ oz (22 ml) Campari
1 dash absinthe
Garnish: orange twist

Spin-Off
1¾ oz (52 ml) rye whiskey
½ oz (15 ml) sweet vermouth
½ oz (15 ml) Green Chartreuse
¼ oz (7 ml) Campari
Stir with ice and strain into a frozen coupe.
Garnish: lemon twist

Top Rope
Sean O'Connor-Combee, J & Tony's Discount Cured Meats and Negroni Warehouse, San Diego, 2022
1 oz (30 ml) bourbon
1 oz (30 ml) Campari
¾ oz (22 ml) Fino Sherry
¼ oz (7 ml) Pedro Ximénez
1 dash black walnut bitters
Garnish: orange twist

SCOTCH

Sin Cyn
Paul Dellevigne, Red Owl Tavern, Philadelphia
1 oz (30 ml) single malt Scotch
1 oz (30 ml) Cynar
1 oz (30 ml) sweet vermouth
Garnish: orange twist

WORLD WHISK(E)Y

Cancomp
(Old Pal with Canadian whisky)
Jones' Complete Barguide,
Stan Jones, 1977
1½ oz (45 ml) Canadian whisky
¾ oz (22 ml) dry vermouth
¾ oz (22 ml) Campari
Stir with ice and strain into a frozen coupe.
Garnish: lemon twist

BRANDY

La Mela Rossa
Hisanori Miyazaki, Bar TRIAD, Tokyo, 2023
1 oz (30 ml) Calvados
¾ oz (22 ml) sweet vermouth
½ oz (15 ml) Campari
1 teaspoon (5 ml) amaretto
2 dashes Angostura Bitters
Garnish: lemon twist

Leeward Negroni
Kevin Diedrich, Pacific Cocktail Haven, San Francisco
1 oz (30 ml) Campari
½ oz (15 ml) navy strength gin
¾ oz (22 ml) pandan syrup (p 499)
3 drops Bittermens Elemakule Tiki Bitters, to coat
Swirl 3 drops of Bittermens Elemakule Tiki Bitters around the inside of a frozen coupe, then stir remaining ingredients with ice and strain into the coupe.
Garnish: pandan leaf

Scorched Earth
Nicholas Hearin, Restaurant Eugene, Atlanta, 2006
2 oz (60 ml) Cognac
½ oz (15 ml) sweet vermouth
½ oz (15 ml) Cynar
Stir with ice and strain into a frozen coupe.
Garnish: lemon twist

The Enzo
Oliver Churcher, Double Deuce Lounge, Sydney, 2021
1 oz (30 ml) Cognac
1 oz (30 ml) sweet vermouth
1 oz (30 ml) Campari
1 dash absinthe
Garnish: orange twist

From *The Complete Buffet Guide or How to Mix All Kinds of Drinks* (1903):

Happy are we met, happy have we been, happy may we part, and happy meet again.

Build all ingredients in an Old Fashioned glass, then add ice.

MARTINI

Hoffman House Cocktail p 318

Martini

An elegant, spirit-forward cocktail generally combining gin or vodka with vermouth/fortified wine and bitters, stirred and served up.

spirit + vermouth + bitters

Add all ingredients to a mixing glass, then stir with ice and strain into a frozen coupe.

American journalist and scholar H.L. Mencken memorably described the Martini as 'the only American invention as perfect as the sonnet'. Indeed, the cocktail's iconic status and association with purity and perfection has continued to resonate throughout history, thanks largely to its unfailingly simple formula and elegant appearance. Famously featured in literature and film, the drink has become synonymous with sophistication and quiet luxury, its bold, spirituous character juxtaposed by a silken texture and diamond-like look that lures both discerning and image-conscious drinkers alike. It is a bona fide icon, a pillar of the canon that has inspired countless interpretations and resulted in a broad category of outstanding drinks in varying styles.

A commonly held belief is that the Martini derived from the Martinez Cocktail (p 308), an early variation on the Manhattan (p 334) that first appeared in the 1860s. Although the Martinez Cocktail is now commonly distinguished by its celebration of sweet (Italian) vermouth, initial iterations used sweet and dry (French) vermouths interchangeably. Whether the Martinez, Martini or Martine – as it was also known – was invented at San Francisco's Occidental Hotel (a short trip from the gold-rush town of Martinez), Julio's Bar on Ferry Street in Martinez itself (and paid for with a gold nugget) or, as some argue, at New York City's Knickerbocker Hotel (and perhaps stirred up by bartender Martini di Arma di Taggia) remains debatable. What we do know is that the Martini, as it eventually came to be known, saw a sharp rise in popularity and stole the cocktail crown from the

→

Manhattan in the 1890s, and it is still garnished with it to this day.

The cocktail's life in print began in 1884 in O.H. Byron's *The Modern Bartenders' Guide*. The author's name is thought to be a pseudonym, and we know little of their history, though we can deduce from the publisher that they lived in New York City. Byron lists the Martinez Cocktail as the 'same as Manhattan, only you substitute gin for whisky'. Notably his versions of both cocktails included curaçao and Angostura Bitters. At the time, both sweet (Italian) and dry (French) vermouths were being employed to soften gin and whiskey in New York City's executive clubs and hotel bars, and as the preference for drier drinks developed by the turn of the century, the Dry Martini came into the world.

The sheer variety and degree of creativity at work in the Martini world is something to behold, but at its core, this is a drink centred on a very simple question: 'How do you take yours?' It's a question that invites a rare degree of personalisation, running from choice of spirit(s) and vermouth(s) to ratios, flavour profiles and garnishes, all of which bless the Martini with a unique ability to expand its audience and evolve as a category long into the future. As for our preference? The Hoffman House Cocktail (p 318), a wet style with a 2:1 ratio of gin to dry vermouth and the addition of orange bitters, finished with a lemon twist.

ESSENTIAL VARIATIONS

Martinez Cocktail

The Bar-Tender's Guide, *Jerry Thomas, 1887*
1½ oz (45 ml) gin
1¼ oz (37 ml) sweet vermouth
¼ oz (7 ml) maraschino liqueur
2 dashes orange bitters

Add all ingredients to a mixing glass then stir with ice and strain into a frozen coupe.
Garnish: orange twist

Though *The Modern Bartenders' Guide* by O.H. Byron marked the Martinez Cocktail's first print appearance in 1884, the recipe most closely aligned with the cocktail we make today comes from the 1887 edition of *The Bar-Tender's Guide* by Jerry Thomas. Jeremiah P. Thomas was born in Sackets Harbor, New York, in 1830. Thomas began bartending in New Haven, Connecticut, when he was 16, before becoming a sailor until the age of 19, when he stopped in San Francisco to mine for gold. There, he tended bar and ran a minstrel show before heading back to New York City with $16,000 in his pocket, to run a bar under Barnum's American Museum.

Over the years, Thomas – often referred to as "The Professor" – became something of a celebrity behind the stick across the United States. His knack for elaborate showmanship and ostentatious sense of style gave rise to theatrical cocktails such as the Blue Blazer (p 406) and laid the foundations for flair bartending. In 1858, he took on the role of head bartender at New York City's Metropolitan Hotel and the following year jetted off to Europe, with a custom-made set of silver bar utensils in tow, thought to be worth $4000.

Thomas found himself back in California in 1862 and started running the bar at San Francisco's famous Occidental Hotel, established the year prior, where he earned $100 a week – more than the Vice President at the time. It was here that he put the finishing touches on *How to Mix Drinks* – also known as *The Bon-Vivant's Companion* and *The Bar-Tender's Guide* – credited as the first ever printed compilation of cocktail recipes. This text, and the numerous editions that followed, cemented Thomas as one of the most influential figures in the history of cocktail bartending.

Though Martini variations featuring sweet (Italian) vermouth are not the dominant style nowadays, the Martinez and its offspring remain worthy recommendations. Standouts include the Manhattan-adjacent Death & Taxes (p 350), which features both gin and Scotch, as well as the Hanky Panky Cocktail (p 325), a Fernet-Branca fan favourite. Variations that utilise both sweet and dry vermouth, such as the Rolls Royce (p 326), are also worthwhile detours.

Tuxedo

(aka **Tussetto Cocktail** in *Straub's Manual of Mixed Drinks*, Jacques Straub, 1913)
Old Waldorf Bar Days, *Albert Stevens Crockett, 1931*
2 oz (60 ml) gin
1 oz (30 ml) Fino Sherry
2 dashes orange bitters

Add all ingredients to a mixing glass, then stir with ice and strain into a frozen coupe.
Garnish: lemon twist

In his book *Old Waldorf Bar Days*, journalist Albert Stevens Crockett captures the spirit and recipes of the bar inside New York City's Waldorf-Astoria hotel in the 1890s, ahead of its 1929 closure and subsequent demolition to make room for the Empire State Building. The Waldorf-Astoria housed one of the United States' most internationally regarded bars, which had significant influence even after it shuttered and moved to 301 Park Avenue. The bar was known for the high quality of its classic drinks, simple in form and strong in spirit, mixed by a cohort of charming Irish-American bartenders.

One of the go-to cocktails at the 'Old Waldorf Bar' was the Tuxedo, a wet Martini variation spiked with Sherry. Over time, the Tuxedo has been listed under many names and spellings, originally appearing as the Tussetto Cocktail in *Straub's Manual of Mixed Drinks* by Jacques Straub, published in 1913. The drink is thought to have taken its name from Tuxedo Park, a gated community near Jersey City for affluent New Yorkers founded in the 1880s, which also incidentally lent its name to the formal dinner jacket.

Quite a few cocktails mixing Sherry and gin surfaced during the twilight years of the 19th century, then reappeared in various forms over the next few decades. Request a drink featuring the two today, and it's likely your bartender will offer plenty of suggestions. Our go-to is the Sidecar variation known as the Sherry Lady (p 204).

Of course, no discussion of the Tuxedo is complete without mentioning an earlier recipe from *The New and Improved Illustrated Bartenders' Manual* by Harry Johnson in 1900. Johnson's Tuxedo Cocktail (p 322) is a vastly different proposition than its Sherry-scented cousin, comprising equal parts Old Tom gin and dry vermouth, with splashes of maraschino liqueur, absinthe and orange bitters. Three decades later, we find the same recipe listed as Tuxedo Cocktail (No. 2) (p 322) in *The Savoy Cocktail Book* by Harry Craddock, utilising gin instead of Old Tom. In our humble opinion, Craddock's recipe is one of the finest Martini variations out there when the specs are adjusted to highlight the gin; maraschino liqueur lends cherry sweetness to the dryness of the spirit and vermouth, while the combo of absinthe and orange bitters makes for a fragrant, spicy finish.

Richmond No. 1

The Savoy Cocktail Book, *Harry Craddock, 1930*
2 oz (60 ml) gin
1 oz (30 ml) Cocchi Americano

Add all ingredients to a mixing glass, then stir with ice and strain into a frozen coupe.
Garnish: lemon twist

Stunningly simple Martini variation, The Richmond, first appeared in Harry Craddock's, *The Savoy Cocktail Book*, published in 1930. Craddock called for Plymouth Gin and Kina Lillet to be shaken and strained into a cocktail glass before squeezing a lemon peel on top. The result is a dry-style Martini, meaning it is gin-dominant, balanced with Kina Lillet, a popular quinine-based aromatised wine of the time.

The birthplace of this cocktail, The American Bar at The Savoy Hotel, where British bartender, Harry Craddock (aka the dean of cocktail shakers) held court for almost twenty years, is undoubtedly one of the most monumental bars in classic cocktail history. Having honed his skills at some of the most reputable establishments in America prior to Prohibition, including New York City's Hoffman House Hotel and Knickerbocker Hotel, Craddock established The American Bar as the London home of American mixology. In his remarkable collection, *The Savoy Cocktail Book*, Craddock documents classic pre-Prohibition drinks that might otherwise have been lost, alongside new and influential European cocktails of the era. This book remains one of the most impressive and important drinks books of the 20th century.

This drink appears again with the same specification in R. de Fleury's *1700 Cocktails for the Man Behind the Bar*, a comprehensive British cocktail guide published in 1934. This time, the drink is listed as the Richmond No. 1, with a Richmond No. 2 sitting alongside it – a contrasting wet-style Martini (French vermouth-dominant) featuring a dash of curaçao. In his preface, de Fleury declared his manual to be the largest collection of recipes ever included in one book – an achievement he would top a few years later when he released a second edition with a further 100 cocktails added.

Since Kina Lillet was discontinued in 1986, our recipe defers to a close relative, Cocchi Americano: a fortified and aromatised Italian white wine from Piedmont, known for its high levels of cinchona, the bitter bark used to make quinine. Cocchi Americano adds a golden hue to the drink, together with subtle spice and notes of honey, zesty citrus and bitter gentian.

Fans of Cocchi Americano and the reformulated Lillet Blanc will likely be familiar with the Vesper (p 322) made famous by Ian Fleming in the first James Bond novel, *Casino Royale*, along with the legendary bracer, the Corpse Reviver No. 2 (p 203), which is another of Craddock's creations. Other favourites in varying styles that benefit from Cocchi Americano's singular character include the White Negroni (p 292) and Cleopatra's Julep (p 284).

Martini

CORE STYLES:

Dirty Gin Martini
2 oz (60 ml) gin
½ oz (15 ml) dry vermouth
½ oz (15 ml) olive brine
Garnish: Cerignola olive

Dry Gin Martini
2 oz (60 ml) gin
½ oz (15 ml) dry vermouth
Garnish: lemon twist or Cerignola olive

Dusty Gin Martini
2 oz (60 ml) gin
¾ oz (22 ml) dry vermouth
¼ oz (7 ml) olive brine
Garnish: Cerignola olive

Extra Dry Gin Martini
2½ oz (75 ml) gin
1 teaspoon (5 ml) dry vermouth
Garnish: orange twist

Filthy Gin Martini
2 oz (60 ml) gin
¼ oz (7 ml) dry vermouth
¾ oz (22 ml) olive brine
Garnish: Cerignola olive

Freezer Gin Martini
Serves 6
10 oz (300 ml) Tanqueray No. 10 gin
4 oz (120 ml) Tanqueray London Dry gin
3½ oz (100 ml) dry vermouth
5 oz (150 ml) filtered water
6 dashes orange bitters
6 drops saline solution (p 493)
Add ingredients to a clean 24 oz (700 ml) bottle and store in freezer overnight. To serve, pour 3½ oz (110 ml) into a frozen coupe.
Garnish: lemon twist or Cerignola olive

Gibson
(2:1 Gin Martini with a cocktail onion)
Bohemian Club, San Francisco, 1890s
2 oz (60 ml) gin
1 oz (30 ml) dry vermouth
Garnish: cocktail onion
▼ While the first printed recipe for the drink appeared in 1908's *The World's Drinks and How to Mix Them* by Wm. T. Boothby, it made no mention of the onion, which only emerged in recipes after Prohibition.

Perfect Martini
(aka **Perfect Gin Martini** and **Martini (Medium) Cocktail** in *The Savoy Cocktail Book*, Harry Craddock, 1930)
2 oz (60 ml) gin
½ oz (15 ml) dry vermouth
½ oz (15 ml) sweet vermouth
Garnish: lemon twist

Smoky Gin Martini
2 oz (60 ml) gin
¾ oz (22 ml) dry vermouth
¼ oz (7 ml) Islay Scotch
Garnish: lemon twist

Sweet Gin Martini
2 oz (60 ml) gin
1 oz (30 ml) sweet vermouth
Garnish: cherry

Wet Gin Martini
2 oz (60 ml) gin
1 oz (30 ml) dry vermouth
2 dashes orange bitters
Garnish: lemon twist or Cerignola olive

GIN (DRY)

Alberto
A. J. Smith
Café Royal Cocktail Guide, *W.J. Tarling, 1937*
1 oz (30 ml) gin
¾ oz (22 ml) Cocchi Americano
¾ oz (22 ml) Manzanilla Sherry
1 teaspoon (5 ml) triple sec
Garnish: orange twist

Allies Cocktail
(2:1 Gin Martini with Kummel)
Recipes for Mixed Drinks, *Hugo R. Ensslin, 1917*
2 oz (60 ml) gin
1 oz (30 ml) dry vermouth
1 teaspoon (5 ml) kümmel
Garnish: lemon twist

Anchorage
Sam Ross, Attaboy, NYC, 2017
2 oz (60 ml) gin
½ oz (15 ml) Fino Sherry
½ oz (15 ml) Yellow Chartreuse
2 dashes orange bitters
Garnish: lemon twist

Anderson
(2:1 Plymouth Gin Martini with an orange twist)
1700 Cocktails for the Man Behind the Bar, *R. de Fleury, 1934*
2 oz (60 ml) Plymouth Gin
1 oz (30 ml) dry vermouth
2 dashes orange bitters
Garnish: orange twist

Arsenic & Old Lace
(aka **Atty Cocktail** in *The Savoy Cocktail Book*, Harry Craddock, 1930)
Cocktail Guide and Ladies' Companion, *Crosby Gaige, 1941*
2 oz (60 ml) gin
¾ oz (22 ml) dry vermouth
¼ oz (7 ml) crème de violette
2 dashes absinthe
Garnish: lemon twist
▼ A descendant of the **Attention Cocktail** in *Recipes for Mixed Drinks*, Hugo R. Ensslin, 1917, originally comprising equal parts of all four ingredients.

Astoria Bianco
Jim Meehan, Gramercy Tavern, NYC, 2005
2 oz (60 ml) gin
¾ oz (22 ml) Martini Bianco
2 dashes orange bitters
Garnish: orange twist

Add all ingredients to a mixing glass, then stir with ice and strain into a frozen coupe.

Astoria Cocktail
(aka **2:1 Old Tom Martini**)
Straub's Manual of Mixed Drinks, *Jacques Straub, 1913*
2 oz (60 ml) Old Tom gin
1 oz (30 ml) dry vermouth
2 dashes orange bitters
Garnish: orange twist

Atlas Martini
Jason Williams, Atlas, Singapore, 2017
2 oz (60 ml) gin
¾ oz (22 ml) blanc vermouth
2 dashes orange bitters
5 dashes Champagne vinegar
Garnish: lemon twist

Atta Boy Cocktail
The Savoy Cocktail Book, *Harry Craddock, 1930*
2 oz (60 ml) gin
¾ oz (22 ml) dry vermouth
¼ oz (7 ml) grenadine (p 496)
Garnish: lemon twist

Ballantine's Cocktail
Trader Vic's Bartender's Guide, *Victor Bergeron, 1947*
2 oz (60 ml) Plymouth Gin
¾ oz (22 ml) dry vermouth
2 dashes absinthe
2 dashes orange bitters
Garnish: lemon twist

Baron
Jones' Complete Barguide, *Stan Jones, 1977*
2 oz (60 ml) gin
½ oz (15 ml) dry vermouth
¼ oz (7 ml) sweet vermouth
¼ oz (7 ml) Pierre Ferrand Dry Curaçao
Garnish: lemon twist

Blonde on Blonde
Jane June, Raines Law Room, NYC, 2019
1½ oz (45 ml) gin (preferably New York Distilling Company Dorothy Parker American Gin)
½ oz (15 ml) blanc vermouth
½ oz (15 ml) Fino Sherry
½ oz (15 ml) St Germain Elderflower Liqueur
1 grapefruit twist, in mixing glass
Garnish: grapefruit twist

Bonnie Prince
Jones' Complete Barguide, *Stan Jones, 1977*
2¼ oz (67 ml) gin
½ oz (15 ml) Cocchi Americano
¼ oz (7 ml) Drambuie
Garnish: lemon twist

Boomerang
(Perfect Gin Martini with maraschino liqueur and bitters)
The Fine Art of Mixing Drinks, *David A. Embury, 1948*
2 oz (60 ml) gin
½ oz (15 ml) dry vermouth
½ oz (15 ml) sweet vermouth
1 teaspoon (5 ml) maraschino liqueur
2 dashes orange bitters
2 dashes Angostura Bitters
Garnish: lemon twist

Bradford à la Martini
The New and Improved Illustrated Bartenders' Manual, *Harry Johnson, 1900*
2½ oz (75 ml) gin
½ oz (15 ml) dry vermouth
2 dashes orange bitters
1 lemon twist
Shake with ice and strain into a frozen coupe.
Garnish: Cerignola olive

Caprice
(Dry Gin Martini with Bénédictine)
The How and When, *Hyman Gale and Gerald F. Marco, 1937*
2 oz (60 ml) gin
½ oz (15 ml) dry vermouth
½ oz (15 ml) Bénédictine
2 dashes orange bitters
Garnish: lemon twist
▼ Poet's Dream variation.

Charlie O.
(Dry Gin Martini with triple sec and orange curaçao)
Jones' Complete Barguide, *Stan Jones, 1977*
2 oz (60 ml) gin
½ oz (15 ml) dry vermouth
¼ oz (7 ml) triple sec
¼ oz (7 ml) Pierre Ferrand Dry Curaçao
Garnish: lemon twist

Chelsea Special
(Dry Gin Martini with orange curaçao)
1700 Cocktails for the Man Behind the Bar, *R. de Fleury, 1934*
2 oz (60 ml) gin
½ oz (15 ml) dry vermouth
½ oz (15 ml) Pierre Ferrand Dry Curaçao
2 dashes Angostura Bitters
Garnish: lemon twist

Chin Up
(Dry Gin Martini with Cynar and cucumber)
Sam Ross, Milk & Honey, NYC, 2005
2 oz (60 ml) gin
½ oz (15 ml) dry vermouth
½ oz (15 ml) Cynar
1 cucumber wheel
Press cucumber in mixing glass, add remaining ingredients and stir with ice, then strain into a frozen coupe.
Garnish: lemon twist

Add all ingredients to a mixing glass, then stir with ice and strain into a frozen coupe.

Comet
Dorothy Perosino
Approved Cocktails, *United Kingdom Bartenders' Guild, 1937*
2 oz (60 ml) gin
¾ oz (22 ml) Cocchi Americano
1 teaspoon (5 ml) maraschino liqueur
2 dashes orange bitters
Garnish: lemon twist

Cooperstown
(Perfect Gin Martini with mint)
The Fine Art of Mixing Drinks, *David A. Embury, 1948*
2 oz (60 ml) gin
½ oz (15 ml) dry vermouth
½ oz (15 ml) sweet vermouth
3–4 mint leaves
Garnish: lemon twist

Deep Blue Sea
Michael Madrusan, Little Branch, NYC, 2007
2 oz (60 ml) gin
¾ oz (22 ml) Cocchi Americano
¼ oz (7 ml) crème de violette
2 dashes orange bitters
Garnish: lemon twist

Deep Sea Cocktail
Cocktails: How to Mix Them, *Robert Vermeire, 1922*
2¼ oz (67 ml) gin
¾ oz (22 ml) dry vermouth
2 dashes absinthe
2 dashes orange bitters
Garnish: lemon twist

Delmonico
Old Waldorf Bay Days, *Albert Stevens Crockett, 1931*
1½ oz (45 ml) Plymouth Gin
1½ oz (45 ml) dry vermouth
1 orange twist
Shake with ice and strain into a frozen coupe.
▾ "Adopted from the bar of Delmonico's, a long-famous New York restaurant."
Garnish: orange twist

Depth Charge Cocktail
(Richmond No. 1 with absinthe)
The Savoy Cocktail Book, *Harry Craddock, 1930*
2 oz (60 ml) gin
1 oz (30 ml) Cocchi Americano
2 dashes absinthe
Garnish: lemon twist

Derby Cocktail
The Savoy Cocktail Book, *Harry Craddock, 1930*
2½ oz (75 ml) gin
2 dashes peach bitters
3–4 mint leaves, in mixing glass
Garnish: lemon twist

Dope AF Lychee Martini
Naren Young, Sweet Liberty, Miami, 2024
¾ oz (22 ml) gin (preferably Fords Gin)
¾ oz (22 ml) vodka (preferably Grey Goose vodka)
¾ oz (22 ml) sauvignon blanc (preferably from Marlborough or Sancerre)
½ oz (15 ml) St Germain Elderflower Liqueur
½ oz (15 ml) Giffard Lichi-Li
¼ oz (7 ml) Martini Fiero
2 drops saline solution (p 493)
3 dashes Peychaud's Aromatic Cocktail Bitters
Garnish: frozen lychee and spritz of rosewater

Dot
Approved Cocktails, *United Kingdom Bartenders' Guild, 1937*
1½ oz (45 ml) gin
½ oz (15 ml) Manzanilla Sherry
½ oz (15 ml) Pierre Ferrand Dry Curaçao
½ oz (15 ml) apricot brandy
Garnish: lemon twist

Douglas Cocktail
(2:1 Gin Martini with an orange and lemon twist)
The Savoy Cocktail Book, *Harry Craddock, 1930*
2 oz (60 ml) gin
1 oz (30 ml) dry vermouth
Garnish: orange twist and lemon twist

Du Barry Cocktail
(2:1 Gin Martini with absinthe and Angostura Bitters)
Harry's ABC of Mixing Drinks, *Harry MacElhone, 1923*
2 oz (60 ml) gin
1 oz (30 ml) dry vermouth
2 dashes absinthe
2 dashes Angostura Bitters
Garnish: orange twist

Dukes Martini
(aka **Direct Martini**)
Salvatore Calabrese, Dukes Bar, London, 1985
2½ oz (75 ml) gin, frozen
½ teaspoon (2.5 ml) dry vermouth
1 teaspoon (5 ml) chilled filtered water, to coat
Pour water into a frozen coupe, then swirl gently to coat the glass and return it to the freezer for at least two hours. To serve, pour dry vermouth into the coupe, swirl gently to coat the glass, then add the gin.
Garnish: lemon twist or Cerignola olive

Dundee
(2:1 Gin Martini with marmalade syrup)
Cocktails by "Jimmy" Late of Ciro's London, *1930*
2 oz (60 ml) gin
1 oz (30 ml) dry vermouth
1 teaspoon (5 ml) orange marmalade syrup (p 499)
Garnish: lemon twist

Fascinator Cocktail
The Savoy Cocktail Book, *Harry Craddock, 1930*
1¾ oz (52 ml) gin
¾ oz (22 ml) dry vermouth
2 dashes absinthe
1 mint sprig, in mixing glass
Garnish: lemon twist

Add all ingredients to a mixing glass, then stir with ice and strain into a frozen coupe.

Fifty-Fifty Cocktail
Recipes for Mixed Drinks, *Hugo R. Ensslin, 1917*
1½ oz (45 ml) gin
1½ oz (45 ml) dry vermouth
Garnish: lemon twist or Cerignola olive

Fire Lily
Eric Alperin, The Varnish, Los Angeles
1½ oz (45 ml) gin (preferably Fords Gin)
½ oz (15 ml) mezcal
½ oz (15 ml) dry vermouth
¼ oz (7 ml) triple sec
¼ oz (7 ml) crème de violette
1 dash Thai chilli firewater tincture (p 505)
Garnish: orange twist

Fitzroy Martini
Felix Woods and Oisín Conneely, Black Pearl, Melbourne, 2021
1½ oz (45 ml) Australian gin
1 oz (30 ml) dry riesling
½ oz (15 ml) St Germain Elderflower Liqueur
1 dash orange bitters
Garnish: lemon twist (discard) and Cerignola olive

Floral Martini
Serves 6
Darren Leaney, Caretaker's Cottage, Melbourne, 2024
9½ oz (290 ml) gin (preferably Tanqueray No. 10)
4 oz (120 ml) dry vermouth (preferably Noilly Prat Original Dry)
2¾ oz (85 ml) umeshu
1⅓ oz (40 ml) RinQuinQuin à la Pêche
2 oz (60 ml) filtered water
0.05 oz (1.5 g) salt
Add all ingredients to a jug and stir to dissolve salt, then decant into an insulated flask and store overnight in the freezer. To serve, pour 3½ oz (100 ml) into a frozen Martini glass.
Garnish: grapefruit twist (discard) and baby's breath flower

Ford Cocktail
Modern American Drinks, *George J. Kappeler, 1895*
1½ oz (45 ml) Old Tom gin
1½ oz (45 ml) dry vermouth
1 teaspoon (5 ml) Bénédictine
2 dashes orange bitters
Garnish: orange twist

Fourth Degree Cocktail
(aka **Tammany Cocktail** in *What Shall We Drink?*, Magnus Bredenbek, 1934)
Harry's ABC of Mixing Drinks, *Harry MacElhone, 1923*
1 oz (30 ml) gin
1 oz (30 ml) dry vermouth
1 oz (30 ml) sweet vermouth
3 dashes absinthe
Garnish: lemon twist

Frank's Special
The Artistry of Mixing Drinks, *Frank Meier, 1936*
2 oz (60 ml) gin
¾ oz (22 ml) dry vermouth
¼ oz (7 ml) Giffard Crème de Pêche de Vigne
Garnish: lemon twist

Fresh Cut
Summer Goff, Death & Co, Denver, 2021
1½ oz (45 ml) gin
¾ oz (22 ml) blanc vermouth
½ oz (15 ml) aquavit
¼ oz (7 ml) mango eau de vie (preferably Rhine Hall Mango Eau de Vie)
2 dashes orange bitters
1 drop saline solution (p 493)
Garnish: lemon twist

Gibson (Matt Young Recipe)
Matt Young, Ante, Sydney, 2022
2 oz (60 ml) Japanese gin
⅔ oz (20 ml) usunigori (lightly cloudy) sake
⅓ oz (10 ml) dry vermouth
Garnish: rakkyozuke (pickled onion)

Gin & Sin
(Dry Gin Martini with apricot brandy and absinthe)
Sam Ross, Attaboy, NYC, 2017
2 oz (60 ml) gin
½ oz (15 ml) dry vermouth
½ oz (15 ml) apricot brandy
1 dash absinthe
Garnish: lemon twist

Gin Blossom
Julie Reiner, Flatiron Lounge, NYC, 2008
1¼ oz (37 ml) Plymouth Gin
1¼ oz (37 ml) blanc vermouth
½ oz (15 ml) apricot eau de vie
2 dashes orange bitters
Garnish: orange twist

Golf Cocktail
(2:1 Gin Martini with Angostura Bitters)
Straub's Manual of Mixed Drinks, *Jacques Straub, 1913*
2 oz (60 ml) gin
1 oz (30 ml) dry vermouth
2 dashes Angostura Bitters
Garnish: lemon twist

Great Secret Cocktail
(Richmond with Angostura Bitters and an orange twist)
The Savoy Cocktail Book, *Harry Craddock, 1930*
2 oz (60 ml) gin
1 oz (30 ml) Cocchi Americano
2 dashes Angostura Bitters
Garnish: orange twist

Headlong Hall
Crosby Gaige's Cocktail Guide and Ladies' Companion, *Crosby Gaige, 1941*
1¼ oz (37 ml) gin
1¼ oz (37 ml) dry vermouth
½ oz (15 ml) Bénédictine
2 dashes absinthe
Garnish: lemon twist

Add all ingredients to a mixing glass, then stir with ice and strain into a frozen coupe.

Hoffman House Cocktail

(aka **Amsterdam** in *Old Waldorf Bar Days*, Albert Stevens Crockett, 1931 or 2:1 Gin Martini with orange bitters)
Harry's ABC of Mixing Drinks, *Harry MacElhone, 1923*
2 oz (60 ml) gin
1 oz (30 ml) dry vermouth
2 dashes orange bitters
Garnish: lemon twist
▼ Supposedly the house cocktail at NYC's Hoffman House in the 1880s, originally garnished with an orange twist.

Hong Kong

(Dry Gin Martini with Angostura Bitters, sugar and lime cordial)
The Fine Art of Mixing Drinks, *David A. Embury, 1948*
2 oz (60 ml) gin
½ oz (15 ml) dry vermouth
1 teaspoon (5 ml) simple syrup
1 teaspoon (5 ml) lime cordial (p 497)
2 dashes Angostura Bitters
Garnish: lime twist

Imperial Cocktail

Daly's Bartenders' Encyclopedia, *Tim Daly, 1903*
2 oz (60 ml) Plymouth Gin
¾ oz (22 ml) dry vermouth
¼ oz (7 ml) maraschino liqueur
2 dashes Angostura Bitters
Garnish: lemon twist and Cerignola olive
▼ "Very popular with Europeans of the better class, particularly the French..."

Jabberwock

1700 Cocktails for the Man Behind the Bar, *R. de Fleury, 1934*
1 oz (30 ml) Plymouth Gin
1 oz (30 ml) Manzanilla Sherry
1 oz (30 ml) Cocchi Americano
2 dashes orange bitters
Garnish: lemon twist

Jenks Cocktail

Drinks, *Jacques Straub, 1914*
1½ oz (45 ml) gin
1½ oz (45 ml) dry vermouth
¼ oz (7 ml) Bénédictine
Garnish: lemon twist

Jimmie Lee

Old Waldorf Bar Days, *Albert Stevens Crockett, 1931*
1 oz (30 ml) gin
1 oz (30 ml) dry vermouth
1 oz (30 ml) sweet vermouth
2 dashes Peychaud's Aromatic Cocktail Bitters
Garnish: orange twist

Joy Division

Phil Ward, Death & Co, NYC, 2008
2 oz (60 ml) gin
¾ oz (22 ml) dry vermouth
¼ oz (7 ml) triple sec
3 dashes absinthe
Garnish: lemon twist

Kemble House Cocktail

(Dry Gin Martini with Fernet-Branca)
The Cocktail Book: A Sideboard Manual for Gentlemen, *1926*
2 oz (60 ml) gin
½ oz (15 ml) dry vermouth
½ oz (15 ml) Fernet-Branca
2 dashes orange bitters
Garnish: orange twist

Lafayette Martini

(aka **Lobby Martini** or Dry Gin Martini with Fino Sherry and Green Chartreuse)
Alicia Perry, The Lafayette Hotel and Club, San Diego, 2023
2 oz (60 ml) gin
½ oz (15 ml) blanc vermouth
¼ oz (7 ml) Fino Sherry
¼ oz (7 ml) Green Chartreuse
1 dash orange bitters
Garnish: lemon twist

Last Round

The Artistry of Mixing Drinks, *Frank Meier, 1936*
1¼ oz (37 ml) gin
1¼ oz (37 ml) dry vermouth
½ oz (15 ml) Cognac
2 dashes absinthe
Garnish: lemon twist

Le Diamant

Jake Powell, Death & Co, Denver, 2022
1½ oz (45 ml) gin (preferably Tanqueray No. 10)
½ oz (15 ml) apple eau de vie
½ oz (15 ml) blanc vermouth
½ oz (15 ml) Dolin Génépi des Alpes
2 dashes orange bitters
Garnish: lemon twist

Leek

Sebastian Tollius, Eleven Madison Park, NYC, 2021
1 oz (30 ml) Roku Gin
½ oz (15 ml) The Boatyard Distillery Boatyard Double Gin
½ oz (15 ml) caramelised leek-infused dry vermouth (p 502)
¼ oz (7 ml) Salers Gentiane
¼ oz (7 ml) Comoz Blanc Vermouth de Chambéry
¼ oz (7 ml) Château de Laubade Blanche Armagnac
¼ oz (7 ml) Pale Cream Sherry
5 drops cocktail onion brine
Garnish: cocktail onion (p 506)

Lifetime Ban

Dan Greenbaum, Attaboy, NYC, 2016
1 oz (30 ml) navy strength gin
1 oz (30 ml) Cocchi Americano
1 oz (30 ml) Fino Sherry
2–3 mint leaves, in mixing glass
Garnish: lemon twist

Add all ingredients to a mixing glass, then stir with ice and strain into a frozen coupe.

Lone Tree Cocktail
(Perfect Gin Martini with orange bitters)
Recipes for Mixed Drinks, *Hugo R. Ensslin, 1917*
2 oz (60 ml) gin
½ oz (15 ml) dry vermouth
½ oz (15 ml) sweet vermouth
2 dashes orange bitters
Garnish: lemon twist
▼ Use Plymouth Gin to make the **Sunshine Cocktail** from *The World's Drinks and How to Mix Them*, Wm. T. Boothby, 1908.

McHenry Cocktail
Straub's Manual of Mixed Drinks, *Jacques Straub, 1913*
2 oz (60 ml) gin
¾ oz (22 ml) dry vermouth
¼ oz (7 ml) apricot brandy
2 dashes orange bitters
Garnish: lemon twist

Mahoney Cocktail
(Fifty-Fifty Cocktail with orange bitters and an orange twist)
Hoffman House Bartender's Guide, *Charles S. Mahoney, 1905*
1½ oz (45 ml) gin
1½ oz (45 ml) dry vermouth
2 dashes orange bitters
Garnish: orange twist

March Hare
Nat Yao, Bar Margaux, Melbourne, 2022
¾ oz (22 ml) gin
¾ oz (22 ml) bianco vermouth
¾ oz (22 ml) Manzanilla Sherry
¼ oz (7 ml) Calvados
1 teaspoon (5 ml) maraschino liqueur
2 dashes orange bitters
Garnish: orange twist

Marguerite Cocktail
The New and Improved Illustrated Bartenders' Manual, *Harry Johnson, 1900*
1½ oz (45 ml) Plymouth Gin
1½ oz (45 ml) dry vermouth
2 dashes absinthe
2 dashes orange bitters
Garnish: lemon twist and cherry

Marguerite Cocktail (Thomas Stuart Recipe)
(2:1 Plymouth Gin Martini with orange bitters and a lemon twist)
Stuart's Fancy Drinks and How to Mix Them, *Thomas Stuart, 1904*
2 oz (60 ml) Plymouth Gin
1 oz (30 ml) dry vermouth
2 dashes orange bitters
Garnish: lemon twist

Martinelle
ms. franky marshall, Le Boudoir, NYC, 2017
1 oz (30 ml) gin
1 oz (30 ml) Vieux Pineau des Charentes Blanc
½ oz (15 ml) Dolin Génépi des Alpes
1 dash absinthe
1 dash orange bitters
Garnish: lemon twist (discard)

Maxim
(Dry Gin Martini with crème de cacao)
Esquire Drink Book, *1956*
2 oz (60 ml) gin
½ oz (15 ml) dry vermouth
½ oz (15 ml) white crème de cacao
Garnish: lemon twist

Merry Widow Cocktail
Recipes for Mixed Drinks, *Hugo R. Ensslin, 1917*
2 oz (60 ml) gin
¾ oz (22 ml) dry vermouth
¼ oz (7 ml) Bénédictine
2 dashes absinthe
2 dashes Peychaud's Aromatic Cocktail Bitters
Garnish: lemon twist

Millionaire's Martini
1½ oz (45 ml) gin
1½ oz (45 ml) dry vermouth
1 oz (30 ml) Champagne, to top
Stir with ice and strain into a frozen coupe, then top with Champagne.
Garnish: lemon twist

Molly Picon
Cocktail Guide and Ladies' Companion, *Crosby Gaige, 1941*
1½ oz (45 ml) gin
¾ oz (22 ml) sweet vermouth
½ oz (15 ml) Picon Amer
1 teaspoon (5 ml) Pierre Ferrand Dry Curaçao
Garnish: lemon twist

Montauk
Old Waldorf Bar Days, *Albert Stevens Crockett, 1931*
1 oz (30 ml) gin
¾ oz (22 ml) dry vermouth
¾ oz (22 ml) sweet vermouth
2 dashes Peychaud's Aromatic Cocktail Bitters
Serve in a double rocks glass with ice.
Garnish: lemon twist

Monte Leon
Dana Skinner, Dutch Kills, NYC, 2018
1½ oz (45 ml) gin
½ oz (15 ml) blanc vermouth
½ oz (15 ml) Tempus Fugit Gran Classico Bitter
½ oz (15 ml) Fino Sherry
2 dashes orange bitters
Garnish: lemon twist

Montgomery Martini (15:1 Ratio)
(aka **Extra Dry Gin Martini**, shaken)
Harry's Bar, Venice
2½ oz (75 ml) gin
1 teaspoon (5 ml) dry vermouth
Shake with ice and strain into a frozen coupe.
Garnish: orange twist
▼ Supposedly Ernest Hemingway's preferred ratio and named after British Field Marshal Bernard Montgomery, who aimed to outnumber his enemies in World War II battles by 15 soldiers to one.

Add all ingredients to a mixing glass, then stir with ice and strain into a frozen coupe.

Moser Martini
Robert Simonson, 2024
2 oz (60 ml) Reisetbauer Blue Gin
½ oz (15 ml) dry vermouth
½ oz (15 ml) blanc vermouth
½ teaspoon (2.5 ml) aquavit, to coat
Pour aquavit into a frozen coupe and swirl gently to coat, then stir remaining ingredients with ice and strain into the coupe.

Needles & Pins
David Molyneux, The Everleigh, Melbourne, 2015
2 oz (60 ml) gin
½ oz (15 ml) Manzanilla Sherry
½ oz (15 ml) Cocchi Americano
1 teaspoon (5 ml) Bénédictine
Garnish: lemon twist

Newman Cocktail
Straub's Manual of Mixed Drinks, *Jacques Straub, 1913*
1½ oz (45 ml) gin
1½ oz (45 ml) dry vermouth
1 teaspoon (5 ml) Picon Amer
Garnish: lemon twist

Obituary
Lafitte's Blacksmith Shop, New Orleans, 1940s
2½ oz (75 ml) gin
½ oz (15 ml) dry vermouth
6 dashes absinthe
Garnish: lemon twist
▼ Also good on the rocks.

Olivette Cocktail
The New and Improved Illustrated Bartenders' Manual, *Harry Johnson, 1900*
2½ oz (75 ml) Plymouth Gin
1 teaspoon (5 ml) simple syrup
2 dashes absinthe
2 dashes orange bitters
Garnish: lemon twist and Cerignola olive

Olivette Cocktail (John Applegreen Recipe)
(2:1 Gin Martini with Peychaud's and orange bitters)
Applegreen's Barkeeper's Guide, *John Applegreen, 1904*
2 oz (60 ml) gin
1 oz (30 ml) dry vermouth
2 dashes Peychaud's Aromatic Cocktail Bitters
2 dashes orange bitters
Garnish: lemon twist

Onion Cocktail
The University Club, Portland
Beverages de Luxe, *George R. Washburne, 1914*
1¾ oz (52 ml) gin
¾ oz (22 ml) dry vermouth
½ teaspoon (2.5 ml) cocktail onion brine
2 dashes orange bitters
Garnish: cocktail onion

Ott's Special
(Dry Gin Martini with Liquore Strega)
Jack Powell
Café Royal Cocktail Guide, *W.J. Tarling, 1937*
2 oz (60 ml) gin
½ oz (15 ml) dry vermouth
½ oz (15 ml) Liquore Strega
Garnish: lemon twist

Oxford Comma
Jeremy Oertel, Dram, NYC
2 oz (60 ml) gin
¾ oz (22 ml) dry vermouth
¼ oz (7 ml) Green Chartreuse
1 teaspoon (5 ml) maraschino liqueur
1 dash Bittermens Orchard Street Celery Shrub
Garnish: lemon twist

Pastiche Martini
Jason Williams, 2019
2 oz (60 ml) gin
⅓ oz (10 ml) dry vermouth
⅓ oz (10 ml) Green Chartreuse
⅓ oz (10 ml) Pierre Ferrand Dry Curaçao
Garnish: orange twist

Paulista Cocktail
Automóvel Clube, São Paulo
The South American Gentleman's Companion, *Charles H. Baker Jr., 1951*
2 oz (60 ml) gin
¾ oz (22 ml) Fernet-Branca
1 teaspoon (5 ml) simple syrup
2 dashes orange bitters
Garnish: orange twist

Paul's Own
Café Royal Cocktail Guide, *W.J. Tarling, 1937*
1 oz (30 ml) gin
1 oz (30 ml) dry vermouth
½ oz (15 ml) triple sec
½ oz (15 ml) Pierre Ferrand Dry Curaçao
1 teaspoon (5 ml) Fernet-Branca
Garnish: orange twist

Perfect Martini (Nathan McCarley-O'Neill Recipe)
Nathan McCarley-O'Neill, Torrisi, NYC, 2024
1½ oz (45 ml) Plymouth Gin
1 oz (30 ml) Contratto Vermouth Bianco
1 oz (30 ml) Cocchi Storico Vermouth di Torino
Serve in a frozen double rocks glass with ice.
Garnish: grapefruit twist, orange twist and Castelvetrano olive

Philadelphia Special
Straub's Manual of Mixed Drinks, *Jacques Straub, 1913*
2 oz (60 ml) gin
¾ oz (22 ml) dry vermouth
¼ oz (7 ml) orange curaçao (p 498)
Garnish: lemon twist

Pickle Martini
Kyle Jamieson, Nauticus, Edinburgh
1½ oz (45 ml) gin (preferably Hendrick's Gin)
¾ oz (22 ml) dry vermouth
½ oz (15 ml) Nautilus pickle brine (p 498)
Garnish: cornichon

Add all ingredients to a mixing glass, then stir with ice and strain into a frozen coupe.

Pickle Martini (Antonello Arzedi Recipe)
Antonello Arzedi, Sydney, 2024
2 oz (60 ml) Tanqueray London Dry Gin
½ oz (15 ml) filtered water
1 teaspoon (5 ml) dry vermouth
1 teaspoon (5 ml) Manzanilla Sherry
1 teaspoon (5 ml) pickle water (p 499)
Garnish: cocktail onion, cornichon, pickled carrot coin and green olive on a skewer

Pink Gibson
Hawksmoor, London
1¾ oz (52 ml) gin
½ oz (15 ml) vodka
⅓ oz (10 ml) dry vermouth
¾ oz (22 ml) filtered water
¼ oz (7 ml) pink cocktail onion brine (p 500)
Add all ingredients to an insulated flask and store overnight in the freezer. To serve, pour into a frozen coupe.
Garnish: pink cocktail onion

Pink Gin
1700 Cocktails for the Man Behind the Bar, *R. de Fleury, 1934*
2½ oz (75 ml) gin
5 dashes Angostura Bitters
Garnish: lemon twist

Plymouth Gin Cocktail
Modern American Drinks, *George J. Kappeler, 1895*
2¾ oz (82 ml) Plymouth Gin
1 teaspoon (5 ml) simple syrup
2 dashes orange bitters
Garnish: lemon twist

Poet's Dream
Café Royal Cocktail Book, *W.J. Tarling, 1937*
The How and When, *Hyman Gale and Gerald Marco, 1937*
2 oz (60 ml) gin
¾ oz (22 ml) dry vermouth
¼ oz (7 ml) Bénédictine
2 dashes orange bitters
Garnish: lemon twist

Polaris
Brandon Bramhall, Attaboy, Nashville, 2018
1½ oz (45 ml) gin
1 oz (30 ml) Manzanilla Sherry
½ oz (15 ml) Aperol
2 cucumber wheels
Press cucumber, add remaining ingredients and stir with ice, then strain into a frozen coupe.
Garnish: lemon twist

Prince Henry
(2:1 Gin Martini with white crème de menthe)
Old Waldorf Bar Days, *Albert Stevens Crockett, 1931*
2 oz (60 ml) gin
1 oz (30 ml) dry vermouth
½ teaspoon (2.5 ml) white crème de menthe
Garnish: lemon twist

Puritan Cocktail
The Cocktail Book: A Sideboard Manual for Gentlemen, *1926*
2 oz (60 ml) gin
¾ oz (22 ml) dry vermouth
¼ oz (7 ml) Yellow Chartreuse
2 dashes orange bitters
Garnish: lemon twist

Racquet Club Cocktail
Modern American Drinks, *George J. Kappeler, 1895*
1½ oz (45 ml) Old Tom gin
1½ oz (45 ml) dry vermouth
2 dashes orange bitters
Garnish: lemon twist

Salt & Pepper Martini
Michael McIlroy, Temple Bar, NYC, 2023
1¾ oz (52 ml) gin
½ oz (15 ml) blanc vermouth
½ oz (15 ml) Manzanilla Sherry
¼ oz (7 ml) Giffard Piment d'Espelette
8 dashes celery bitters
3 drops saline solution (p 493)
Garnish: pickled biquinho pepper

Savoy Hotel Special Cocktail (No. 1)
The Savoy Cocktail Book, *Harry Craddock, 1930*
2 oz (60 ml) gin
¾ oz (22 ml) dry vermouth
¼ oz (7 ml) grenadine (p 496)
2 dashes absinthe
Garnish: lemon twist

Sculpture Garden
Jack Stevenson, Death & Co, Los Angeles, 2024
2 oz (60 ml) gin (preferably Roku Gin)
½ oz (15 ml) Cocchi Americano
½ oz (15 ml) umeshu
3 dashes peach bitters
Garnish: orange twist
▼ Originally with peach blossom white tea instead of peach bitters.

Self-Starter Cocktail
The Savoy Cocktail Book, *Harry Craddock, 1930*
2 oz (60 ml) gin
¾ oz (22 ml) Cocchi Americano
¼ oz (7 ml) apricot brandy
2 dashes absinthe
Garnish: lemon twist

Silver Cocktail
The New and Improved Illustrated Bartenders' Manual, *Harry Johnson, 1900*
2 oz (60 ml) gin
¾ oz (22 ml) dry vermouth
¼ oz (7 ml) maraschino liqueur
2 dashes orange bitters
Garnish: lemon twist

Some Moth Cocktail
(Gibson with absinthe)
The Savoy Cocktail Book, *Harry Craddock, 1930*
2 oz (60 ml) gin
1 oz (30 ml) dry vermouth
2 dashes absinthe
Garnish: cocktail onion

Add all ingredients to a mixing glass, then stir with ice and strain into a frozen coupe.

Stirred 29

Michael Madrusan, The Everleigh, 2017
2 oz (60 ml) gin
¾ oz (22 ml) Cocchi Americano
1 teaspoon (5 ml) maraschino liqueur
1 teaspoon (5 ml) crème de violette
Garnish: edible purple flower
▼ Created for Le Labo, Melbourne.

The Bartender

Approved Cocktails, *United Kingdom Bartenders' Guild, 1937*
1½ oz (45 ml) gin
½ oz (15 ml) dry vermouth
½ oz (15 ml) sweet vermouth
½ oz (15 ml) Manzanilla Sherry
1 teaspoon (5 ml) Pierre Ferrand Dry Curaçao
Garnish: lemon twist

The Cappa

ms. franky marshall, The Tippler, NYC, 2012
1½ oz (45 ml) gin
1½ oz (45 ml) Vieux Pineau des Charentes Blanc
½ oz (15 ml) maraschino liqueur
Garnish: lemon twist (discard)

Third Degree Cocktail

"Harry" of Ciro's ABC of Mixing Cocktails, *Harry MacElhone, 1923*
1½ oz (45 ml) gin
¾ oz (22 ml) dry vermouth
2 dashes absinthe
Serve in an Old Fashioned glass with ice.
Garnish: lemon twist

Trinity Cocktail

The Savoy Cocktail Book, *Harry Craddock, 1930*
1 oz (30 ml) gin
1 oz (30 ml) dry vermouth
1 oz (30 ml) sweet vermouth
Garnish: lemon twist

Turf Cocktail

The New and Improved Illustrated Bartenders' Manual, *Harry Johnson, 1900*
1½ oz (45 ml) Plymouth Gin
1½ oz (45 ml) dry vermouth
1 teaspoon (5 ml) maraschino liqueur
2 dashes absinthe
2 dashes orange bitters
Garnish: Cerignola olive

Turncoat

Brandon Bramhall, Attaboy, NYC, 2015
1½ oz (45 ml) gin
½ oz (15 ml) dry vermouth
½ oz (15 ml) sweet vermouth
½ oz (15 ml) Fino Sherry
Garnish: lemon twist

Tuxedo Cocktail (Harry Johnson Recipe)

The New and Improved Illustrated Bartenders' Manual, *Harry Johnson, 1900*
1½ oz (45 ml) Old Tom gin
1½ oz (45 ml) dry vermouth
1 teaspoon (5 ml) maraschino liqueur
2 dashes absinthe
2 dashes orange bitters
Garnish: lemon twist and cherry

Tuxedo Cocktail (No. 1)

The Savoy Cocktail Book, *Harry Craddock, 1930*
1½ oz (45 ml) gin
1½ oz (45 ml) dry vermouth
3 dashes absinthe
Garnish: lemon twist

Tuxedo Cocktail (No. 2)

The Savoy Cocktail Book, *Harry Craddock, 1930*
2 oz (60 ml) gin
¾ oz (22 ml) dry vermouth
¼ oz (7 ml) maraschino liqueur
2 dashes absinthe
2 dashes orange bitters
Garnish: lemon twist and cherry

Undertaker's Cocktail

(aka **Russian Cocktail**)
Trader Vic's Bartender's Guide, *Trader Vic, 1947*
1¼ oz (37 ml) gin
1 oz (30 ml) vodka
¾ oz (22 ml) white crème de cacao

From *The Savoy Cocktail Book* (1930):

A dry martini is like a good speech: short enough to be interesting, but strong enough to leave an impact.

Van Zandt Cocktail

Straub's Manual of Mixed Drinks, *Jacques Straub, 1913*
2 oz (60 ml) gin
¾ oz (22 ml) dry vermouth
¼ oz (7 ml) apricot brandy
Garnish: lemon twist

Vesper

Casino Royale, *Ian Fleming, 1953*
2 oz (60 ml) gin
½ oz (15 ml) vodka
½ oz (15 ml) Cocchi Americano
Garnish: lemon twist

Wallick

(2:1 Gin Martini with orange blossom water)
Recipes for Mixed Drinks, *Hugo R. Ensslin, 1917*
2 oz (60 ml) gin
1 oz (30 ml) dry vermouth
2 dashes orange bitters
Garnish: lemon twist and a spritz of orange blossom water

Zephyr

Benjamin Schwartz, Little Branch, NYC, 2010
2 oz (60 ml) gin
½ oz (15 ml) Cocchi Americano
½ oz (15 ml) Green Chartreuse
Garnish: lemon twist

Add all ingredients to a mixing glass, then stir with ice and strain into a frozen coupe.

GIN (SWEET)

Air Service
What'll You Have?, *Julien J. Proskauer, 1933*
2 oz (60 ml) gin
¾ oz (22 ml) sweet vermouth
¼ oz (7 ml) triple sec
Garnish: orange twist

Alaska Cocktail
Straub's Manual of Mixed Drinks, *Jacques Straub, 1913*
2¼ oz (67 ml) gin
¾ oz (22 ml) Yellow Chartreuse
2 dashes orange bitters
Garnish: lemon twist

Amsterdam Sunshine
(Sweet Gin Martini with a lemon twist)
2 oz (60 ml) gin
1 oz (30 ml) sweet vermouth
Garnish: lemon twist

Angel Face Cocktail
The Savoy Cocktail Book, *Harry Craddock, 1930*
1½ oz (45 ml) gin
1 oz (30 ml) Calvados
½ oz (15 ml) apricot brandy
Garnish: lemon twist

Anniversary
The Fine Art of Mixing Drinks, *David A. Embury, 1948*
1 oz (30 ml) gin
1 oz (30 ml) Cognac
1 oz (30 ml) sweet vermouth
2 dashes orange bitters
Garnish: lemon twist

Archangel
Richard Boccato and Michael McIlroy, Milk & Honey, NYC, 2006
2¼ oz (67 ml) gin
¾ oz (22 ml) Aperol
1 cucumber wheel
Press cucumber, add remaining ingredients, then shake with ice and strain into a frozen coupe.
Garnish: lemon twist

Argentina Cocktail
Jones' Complete Barguide, *Stan Jones, 1977*
2 oz (60 ml) gin
½ oz (15 ml) dry vermouth
¼ oz (7 ml) Bénédictine
¼ oz (7 ml) triple sec
2 dashes orange bitters
2 dashes Angostura Bitters
Garnish: lemon twist

Artillery Cocktail
(Sweet Gin Martini with Angostura Bitters)
The Savoy Cocktail Book, *Harry Craddock, 1930*
2 oz (60 ml) gin
1 oz (30 ml) sweet vermouth
2 dashes Angostura Bitters
Garnish: lemon twist

Aunt Eleanor
Zachary Pease, My Friend Duke, NYC, 2018
2 oz (60 ml) gin
½ oz (15 ml) sweet vermouth
½ oz (15 ml) Cocchi Americano
1 teaspoon (5 ml) Yellow Chartreuse
Garnish: lemon twist

Automobile Cocktail
Hoffman House Bartender's Guide, *Charles S. Mahoney, 1905*
1 oz (30 ml) gin
1 oz (30 ml) sweet vermouth
1 oz (30 ml) Scotch
2 dashes orange bitters
Garnish: lemon twist

Barry Cocktail
Jack's Manual, *J.A. Grohusko, 1933*
1½ oz (45 ml) gin
1½ oz (45 ml) sweet vermouth
1 teaspoon (5 ml) white crème de menthe
2 dashes Angostura Bitters
Garnish: lemon twist

Berry Wall Cocktail
The Savoy Cocktail Book, *Harry Craddock, 1930*
1½ oz (45 ml) gin
1¼ oz (37 ml) sweet vermouth
¼ oz (7 ml) Pierre Ferrand Dry Curaçao
Garnish: lemon twist

Bijou Cocktail
(aka **Jewel** from Just Cocktails, *W.C. Whitfield, 1939*)
The New and Improved Illustrated Bartenders' Manual, *Harry Johnson, 1900*
1½ oz (45 ml) gin
¾ oz (22 ml) sweet vermouth
¾ oz (22 ml) Green Chartreuse
2 dashes orange bitters
Garnish: lemon twist and cherry

Bloodhound Cocktail
"Harry" of Ciro's ABC of Mixing Cocktails, *Harry MacElhone, 1923*
1 oz (30 ml) gin
1 oz (30 ml) sweet vermouth
1 oz (30 ml) dry vermouth
2 strawberries, halved
Muddle strawberries, add remaining ingredients, then shake with ice and strain into a frozen coupe.
Garnish: strawberry half

Bloodhound Cocktail
(Harry Craddock Recipe)
(Perfect Gin Martini with muddled strawberry)
The Savoy Cocktail Book, *Harry Craddock, 1930*
2 oz (60 ml) gin
½ oz (15 ml) sweet vermouth
½ oz (15 ml) dry vermouth
2 strawberries, halved
Muddle strawberries, add remaining ingredients, then shake with ice and strain into a frozen coupe.
Garnish: strawberry

Add all ingredients to a mixing glass, then stir with ice and strain into a frozen coupe.

Bloomsbury
Robert Hess, DrinkBoy, *2003*
2 oz (60 ml) gin
½ oz (15 ml) Cocchi Americano
½ oz (15 ml) Licor 43
2 dashes Peychaud's Aromatic Cocktail Bitters
Garnish: lemon twist

Bridal
The Old Waldorf-Astoria Bar Book, *Albert Stevens Crockett, 1935*
2 oz (60 ml) gin
¾ oz (22 ml) sweet vermouth
¼ oz (7 ml) maraschino liqueur
2 dashes orange bitters
Garnish: orange twist

Campden Cocktail
The Savoy Cocktail Book, *Harry Craddock, 1930*
2 oz (60 ml) gin
½ oz (15 ml) Cocchi Americano
½ oz (15 ml) triple sec
Garnish: cherry

Charlie Lindberg (Stan Jones Recipe)
Jones' Complete Barguide, *Stan Jones, 1977*
2 oz (60 ml) gin
½ oz (15 ml) Cocchi Americano
½ oz (15 ml) apricot brandy
2 dashes orange bitters
Garnish: lemon twist

Chinatown Cocktail
Trader Vic's Bartender's Guide, *Trader Vic, 1947*
1½ oz (45 ml) gin
½ oz (15 ml) dry vermouth
½ oz (15 ml) sweet vermouth
½ oz (15 ml) Cognac
Garnish: lemon twist
▼ Swap the lemon twist for an orange twist to make the **Machu Picchu Special** from *The South American Gentleman's Companion*, Charles H. Baker Jr., 1951.

Claridge Cocktail
(aka **The Frankenjack Cocktail** in *The Savoy Cocktail Book*, Harry Craddock, 1930)
Leon, Bartender, Claridge's Hotel, Paris
Barflies and Cocktails, *Harry MacElhone, 1927*
1½ oz (45 ml) gin
½ oz (15 ml) dry vermouth
½ oz (15 ml) apricot brandy
½ oz (15 ml) triple sec
Garnish: orange twist

Club Cocktail
The Flowing Bowl, *William Schmidt, 1891*
2 oz (60 ml) gin
¾ oz (22 ml) sweet vermouth
¼ oz (7 ml) Green Chartreuse
2 dashes orange bitters
Garnish: cherry

Constantine
Pioneers of Mixing at Elite Bars: 1903–1933, *Charles Christopher Mueller, 1936*
2 oz (60 ml) gin
¾ oz (22 ml) sweet vermouth
¼ oz (7 ml) maraschino liqueur
2 dashes absinthe
2 dashes orange bitters
Garnish: cherry

Death & Taxes
(See p 350)

Defender
Old Waldorf Bar Days, *Albert Stevens Crockett, 1931*
2 oz (60 ml) gin
¾ oz (22 ml) sweet vermouth
1 teaspoon (5 ml) Crème Yvette
2 dashes orange bitters
Garnish: lemon twist

DeGroff Martini
The Book of Cocktail Ratios, *Michael Ruhlman, 2023*
1½ oz (45 ml) Old Tom gin
1 oz (30 ml) blanc vermouth
½ oz (15 ml) sweet vermouth
2 dashes Dale DeGroff's Pimento Aromatic Bitters

Delmonico Special
The Fine Art of Mixing Drinks, *David A. Embury, 1948*
1¾ oz (52 ml) gin
½ oz (15 ml) dry vermouth
½ oz (15 ml) sweet vermouth
¼ oz (7 ml) Cognac
2 dashes Angostura Bitters
Garnish: orange twist

Demeanour
Jones' Complete Barguide, *Stan Jones, 1977*
2 oz (60 ml) gin
¾ oz (22 ml) sweet vermouth
¼ oz (7 ml) crème de violette
2 dashes orange bitters
Garnish: lemon twist

Don't Give Up the Ship
Trader Vic's Bartender's Guide, *Trader Vic, 1947*
1½ oz (45 ml) gin
½ oz (15 ml) sweet vermouth
½ oz (15 ml) Fernet-Branca
½ oz (15 ml) Pierre Ferrand Dry Curaçao
Garnish: orange twist
▼ Substitute gin for rye whiskey for a great variation.

Dorchester Cocktail
Ernest of The Dorchester
An Anthology of Cocktails, *1930s*
2 oz (60 ml) gin
½ oz (15 ml) Cocchi Americano
¼ oz (7 ml) sweet vermouth
¼ oz (7 ml) Pierre Ferrand Dry Curaçao
Garnish: orange twist

Ethiopia
The Fine Art of Mixing Drinks, *David A. Embury, 1948*
2 oz (60 ml) gin
¾ oz (22 ml) sweet vermouth
¼ oz (7 ml) Fernet-Branca
Garnish: lemon twist

Add all ingredients to a mixing glass, then stir with ice and strain into a frozen coupe.

European Union
Alex Day, Death & Co, NYC, 2009
1½ oz (45 ml) Old Tom gin
¾ oz (22 ml) sweet vermouth
½ oz (15 ml) Calvados (preferably VSOP)
1 teaspoon (5 ml) Liquore Strega
1 dash The Bitter Truth Old Time Aromatic Bitters
Garnish: cherry

Fin de Siècle
The Old Waldorf-Astoria Bar Book, *Albert Stevens Crockett, 1935*
2 oz (60 ml) gin
½ oz (15 ml) sweet vermouth
½ oz (15 ml) Picon Amer
2 dashes orange bitters
Garnish: lemon twist

Fox Shot Cocktail
Straub's Manual of Mixed Drinks, *Jacques Straub, 1913*
1½ oz (45 ml) gin
¾ oz (22 ml) sweet vermouth
¾ oz (22 ml) Cognac
3 dashes Angostura Bitters
Garnish: lemon twist

Gin & It
The Artistry of Mixing Drinks, *Frank Meier, 1936*
1½ oz (45 ml) gin
1½ oz (45 ml) sweet vermouth
Garnish: lemon twist

Good Times Cocktail
(Sweet Old Tom Gin Martini with a lemon twist)
A Life-Time Collection of 688 Recipes for Drinks, *1934*
2 oz (60 ml) Old Tom gin
1 oz (30 ml) sweet vermouth
Garnish: lemon twist

Grand Street
Alex Day, Death & Co, NYC, 2009
2 oz (60 ml) gin
¾ oz (22 ml) Punt e Mes
¼ oz (7 ml) Cynar
1 teaspoon (5 ml) maraschino liqueur
1 grapefruit twist

Greenwich
The Fine Art of Mixing Drinks, *David A. Embury, 1948*
1¼ oz (37 ml) gin
1¼ oz (37 ml) bonded apple brandy
½ oz (15 ml) white crème de cacao

Hanky Panky Cocktail
Ada Coleman, American Bar, The Savoy, London, circa 1921
The Savoy Cocktail Book, *Harry Craddock, 1930*
1½ oz (45 ml) gin
1½ oz (45 ml) sweet vermouth
¼ oz (7 ml) Fernet-Branca
Garnish: orange twist

Hearst Cocktail
Straub's Manual of Mixed Drinks, *Jacques Straub, 1913*
1½ oz (45 ml) gin
1½ oz (45 ml) sweet vermouth
2 dashes Angostura Bitters
2 dashes orange bitters
Garnish: lemon twist

Hell Diver
How to Properly Mix Drinks, *1930s*
2 oz (60 ml) gin
¾ oz (22 ml) sweet vermouth
¼ oz (7 ml) white crème de cacao
2 dashes absinthe
Garnish: orange twist

Hillside Cocktail
Chris Bostick, The Varnish, Los Angeles
1½ oz (45 ml) gin
¾ oz (22 ml) dry vermouth
¾ oz (22 ml) Amaro Nonino
1 teaspoon (5 ml) Élixir Végétal de la Grande-Chartreuse
Garnish: lemon twist

Honolulu Cocktail
Recipes for Mixed Drinks, *Hugo R. Ensslin, 1917*
2¼ oz (75 ml) gin
⅜ oz (11 ml) Bénédictine
⅜ oz (11 ml) maraschino liqueur
Garnish: lemon twist
▼ The Honolulu Cocktail appears in both the 1908 edition of *Jack's Manual* by J.A. Grohusko and 1914's *Drinks* by Jacques Straub as a Bourbon Highball.

Lamb's Club Cocktail
(Perfect Gin Martini with Bénédictine)
Trader Vic's Bartender's Guide, *Trader Vic, 1947*
2 oz (60 ml) gin
½ oz (15 ml) sweet vermouth
½ oz (15 ml) dry vermouth
¼ oz (7 ml) Bénédictine
Garnish: lemon twist

L'Aurore
The Flowing Bowl, *William Schmidt, 1891*
1½ oz (45 ml) gin
1¼ oz (37 ml) sweet vermouth
¼ oz (7 ml) maraschino liqueur
2 dashes orange bitters
2 dashes absinthe
Garnish: orange twist and lemon twist

Le Bateleur
Alex Day, Death & Co, NYC, 2008
1¾ oz (52 ml) gin
¾ oz (22 ml) Punt e Mes
⅓ oz (10 ml) Liquore Strega
¼ oz (7 ml) Cynar

Lord Helpus Cocktail
Crosby Gaige's Cocktail Guide and Ladies' Companion, *Crosby Gaige, 1941*
2 oz (60 ml) gin
½ oz (15 ml) sweet vermouth
¼ oz (7 ml) maraschino liqueur
¼ oz (7 ml) triple sec
Garnish: lemon twist

Maiden's Wish
The Fine Art of Mixing Drinks, *David A. Embury, 1948*
1 oz (30 ml) gin
1 oz (30 ml) Cocchi Americano
½ oz (15 ml) bonded apple brandy
½ oz (15 ml) apricot brandy
Garnish: lemon twist

Add all ingredients to a mixing glass, then stir with ice and strain into a frozen coupe.

Martinez (Buck and Breck Recipe)
Buck and Breck, Berlin
1½ oz (45 ml) gin
¾ oz (22 ml) sweet vermouth
½ oz (15 ml) genever
1 teaspoon (5 ml) maraschino liqueur
2 dashes Peychaud's Aromatic Cocktail Bitters
Garnish: orange twist

Mercy Mercy
Joseph Schwartz, Little Branch, NYC, 2008
2 oz (60 ml) gin
½ oz (15 ml) Cocchi Americano
½ oz (15 ml) Aperol
2 dashes Angostura Bitters
Garnish: orange twist

Milady's Martini
Julie Reiner, Milady's, NYC, 2022
1½ oz (45 ml) gin
¾ oz (22 ml) Fino Sherry
¾ oz (22 ml) Cocchi Rosa
½ teaspoon (2.5 ml) Amaro Ramazzotti
Garnish: black olive

Opera Cocktail
Drinks, *Jacques Straub, 1914*
2 oz (60 ml) gin
¾ oz (22 ml) sweet vermouth
¼ oz (7 ml) mandarin liqueur
Garnish: orange twist

Opera Cocktail (Harry Craddock Recipe)
The Savoy Cocktail Book, *Harry Craddock, 1930*
2 oz (60 ml) gin
½ oz (15 ml) Dubonnet
½ oz (15 ml) maraschino liqueur
Garnish: orange twist

Ox Blood
R. Emmerich
Café Royal Cocktail Book, *W.J. Tarling, 1937*
1½ oz (45 ml) gin
½ oz (15 ml) sweet vermouth
½ oz (15 ml) Pierre Ferrand Dry Curaçao
½ oz (15 ml) Heering Cherry Liqueur
2 dashes orange bitters
Garnish: cherry

Ozone
1700 Cocktails for the Man Behind the Bar, *R. de Fleury, 1934*
2 oz (60 ml) gin
½ oz (15 ml) Cocchi Americano
½ oz (15 ml) Licor 43
Garnish: lemon twist

Passion
Ted Saucier's Bottoms Up, *Ted Saucier, 1951*
1 oz (30 ml) gin
1 oz (30 ml) Cognac
1 oz (30 ml) Green Chartreuse
1 teaspoon (5 ml) Picon Amer
2 dashes absinthe
Garnish: cherry

Pippin No. 2
Jason E. Clapham, St. Edward's MCR, Oxford
1½ oz (45 ml) gin
1 oz (30 ml) Dubonnet
¼ oz (7 ml) maraschino liqueur
¼ oz (7 ml) Campari
Shake with ice and strain into a frozen coupe.
Garnish: orange twist
▼ Swap gin for Cognac to make the **Pippin No. 1**.

Princeton Cocktail
Modern American Drinks, *George J. Kappeler, 1895*
2½ oz (75 ml) Old Tom gin
2 dashes orange bitters
½ oz (15 ml) tawny Port, to finish
Shake the gin and bitters with ice and strain into a frozen coupe, then float Port and allow it to settle on the bottom of the glass before serving.
Garnish: cherry

Psychopathia Sexualis
Cocktail Guide and Ladies' Companion, *Crosby Gaige, 1941*
¾ oz (22 ml) gin
¾ oz (22 ml) Palo Cortado Sherry
¾ oz (22 ml) sweet vermouth
¾ oz (22 ml) dry vermouth
1 dash orange bitters
Garnish: orange twist

Rolls Royce
(aka **Football Hero** from "What'll You Have? A Not Too Dry Text Book About Cocktails", *Julien J. Proskauer, 1933*, or Perfect Plymouth Gin Martini with Bénédictine)
1700 Cocktails for the Man Behind the Bar, *R. de Fleury, 1934*
2 oz (60 ml) Plymouth Gin
½ oz (15 ml) sweet vermouth
½ oz (15 ml) dry vermouth
1 teaspoon (5 ml) Bénédictine
Garnish: lemon twist

Royal Cocktail
The Art of Mixing, *James A. Wiley and Helene M. Griffith, 1932*
2 oz (60 ml) gin
½ oz (15 ml) dry vermouth
¼ oz (7 ml) maraschino liqueur
¼ oz (7 ml) Heering Cherry Liqueur
Garnish: cherry

San Martin Cocktail
Cocktails: How to Mix Them, *Robert Vermeire, 1922*
2 oz (60 ml) gin
½ oz (15 ml) sweet vermouth
½ oz (15 ml) Yellow Chartreuse
Garnish: lemon twist

Six Cylinder
Raymond Latour
½ oz (15 ml) gin
½ oz (15 ml) sweet vermouth
½ oz (15 ml) dry vermouth
½ oz (15 ml) Dubonnet
½ oz (15 ml) Campari
½ oz (15 ml) Heering Cherry Liqueur
Garnish: lemon twist
▼ Winning cocktail at the Paris Cocktail Championship in 1928.

Add all ingredients to a mixing glass, then stir with ice and strain into a frozen coupe.

Tailspin
Old Mr. Boston De Luxe Official Bartender's Guide, *Leo Cotton, 1935*
1 oz (30 ml) gin
1 oz (30 ml) sweet vermouth
1 oz (30 ml) Green Chartreuse
1 teaspoon (5 ml) Campari
Garnish: lemon twist
▼ See **Spin-Off** (p 303) for rye variation.

Tango Cocktail
(Sweet Gin Martini with apricot brandy)
A Life-Time Collection of 688 Recipes for Drinks, *1934*
2 oz (60 ml) gin
1 oz (30 ml) sweet vermouth
1 teaspoon (5 ml) apricot brandy
Garnish: lemon twist

The Queen Mother Cocktail
Jake Burger, Portobello Star, London, 2014
1 oz (30 ml) gin
1 oz (30 ml) Dubonnet
¾ oz (22 ml) Aperol
1 teaspoon (5 ml) Jamaican dark rum
Garnish: orange twist and lemon twist

Tulane Cocktail
Drinks, *Jacques Straub, 1914*
1½ oz (45 ml) Plymouth Gin
1½ oz (45 ml) sweet vermouth
1 teaspoon (5 ml) Dolin Chambéryzette
Garnish: strawberry half

Turf Club Cocktail
How to Mix Drinks, *George Winter, 1884*
1½ oz (45 ml) Old Tom gin
1½ oz (45 ml) sweet vermouth
3 dashes Angostura Bitters
Garnish: cherry

Vancouver
About Town Cocktail Book, *1925*
2 oz (60 ml) gin
¾ oz (22 ml) sweet vermouth
¼ oz (7 ml) Bénédictine
2 dashes orange bitters
Garnish: cherry

Van Wyck Cocktail
A Life-Time Collection of 688 Recipes for Drinks, *1934*
2 oz (60 ml) gin
1 oz (30 ml) sloe gin
2 dashes orange bitters
Garnish: lemon twist

Warday's Cocktail
(aka **Waxen** from A Life-Time Collection of 688 Recipes for Drinks, *Herbert Jenkins Ltd, 1934*)
Harry's ABC of Mixing Cocktails, *Harry MacElhone, 1923*
1 oz (30 ml) gin
1 oz (30 ml) bonded apple brandy
¾ oz (22 ml) sweet vermouth
¼ oz (7 ml) Yellow Chartreuse
Garnish: lemon twist

Warday's No. 2
Sam Ross, Milk & Honey, NYC, 2008
1 oz (30 ml) gin
1 oz (30 ml) bonded apple brandy
¾ oz (22 ml) sweet vermouth
¼ oz (7 ml) Green Chartreuse
Garnish: lemon twist

White Bear Cocktail
Burke's Complete Cocktail & Drinking Recipes, *Harman Burney Burke, 1934*
1½ oz (45 ml) gin
½ oz (15 ml) sweet vermouth
½ oz (15 ml) dry vermouth
½ oz (15 ml) Pierre Ferrand Dry Curaçao
2 dashes Angostura Bitters
Garnish: lemon twist

Wiffin
David Wondrich
1½ oz (45 ml) gin
¾ oz (22 ml) sweet vermouth
¾ oz (22 ml) Cognac
1 dash absinthe
Garnish: lemon twist
▼ Wondrich's interpretation of a cocktail from a P.G. Wodehouse short story, named after its protagonist.

Yale Fence
The Fine Art of Mixing Drinks, *David A. Embury, 1948*
1 oz (30 ml) gin
1 oz (30 ml) sweet vermouth
1 oz (30 ml) bonded apple brandy
Garnish: lemon twist

Zimmy
1700 Cocktails for the Man Behind the Bar, *R. de. Fleury, 1934*
2 oz (60 ml) gin
½ oz (15 ml) sweet vermouth
½ oz (15 ml) dry vermouth
1 teaspoon (5 ml) Bénédictine
2 dashes orange bitters
Garnish: lemon twist

VODKA

CORE STYLES:

Dirty Vodka Martini
2 oz (60 ml) vodka
½ oz (15 ml) dry vermouth
½ oz (15 ml) olive brine
Garnish: olive

Dry Vodka Martini
2½ oz (75 ml) vodka
½ oz (15 ml) dry vermouth
Garnish: lemon twist or olive

Wet Vodka Martini
1¾ oz (52 ml) vodka
¾ oz (22 ml) dry vermouth
Garnish: lemon twist or olive

Briny Bay
Michael Bascetta, Bar Liberty, Melbourne, 2021
2 oz (60 ml) vodka
⅓ oz (10 ml) dry vermouth
1 teaspoon (5 ml) olive brine
Garnish: bay leaf

Add all ingredients to a mixing glass, then stir with ice and strain into a frozen coupe.

Dreamy Dorini Smoking Martini
Audrey Saunders, Beacon, NYC, 2003
2 oz (60 ml) vodka
¼ oz (7 ml) Islay Scotch
½ teaspoon (2.5 ml) pastis
Garnish: lemon twist

Flame of Love
Pepe Ruiz, Chasen's, Los Angeles, 1970
2½ oz (75 ml) vodka
2 orange twists
1 teaspoon (5 ml) Fino Sherry, to coat
Pour Sherry into a frozen coupe and swirl to coat, then flame both orange twists to express oils into the glass. Shake the vodka with ice and strain into the glass.
Garnish: orange twist
▾ Created for Dean Martin.

Flatiron Martini
Julie Reiner, Flatiron Lounge, NYC
1¼ oz (37 ml) vodka
1¼ oz (37 ml) Lillet Blanc
1 teaspoon (5 ml) triple sec
Garnish: orange twist

Gilda Martini
Dave Spanton, Vermuteria, Sydney, 2023
1¼ oz (37 ml) vodka
1¼ oz (37 ml) dry vermouth
2 dashes Angostura Bitters
Garnish: Gilda (white anchovy, Gordal olive and guindilla on a skewer)

Houndstooth
Serves 6
Darren Leaney, Caretaker's Cottage, Melbourne, 2024
12 oz (350 ml) Hartshorn Sheep Whey Vodka
2¼ oz (70 ml) Cocchi Americano
2¼ oz (70 ml) Fino Sherry
2¼ oz (70 ml) junmai sake
1⅔ oz (50 ml) filtered water
Add all ingredients to an insulated flask and store overnight in the freezer. To serve, pour 3½ oz (100 ml) into a frozen coupe.
Garnish: orange twist and Sicilian olive

Jackalope
Michael Madrusan, Jackalope Hotel, Mornington Peninsula, 2018
2 oz (60 ml) vodka
1 oz (30 ml) dry vermouth
2 drops pink peppercorn bitters
1 drop fennel bitters
Garnish: cucumber wheel

Kangaroo Kicker
(aka **Kangaroo** in *The Standard Cocktail Guide*, Crosby Gaige, 1944)
Cocktail and Wine Digest, *Oscar Haimo, 1943*
2 oz (60 ml) vodka
¾ oz (22 ml) dry vermouth
1 dash orange bitters
Garnish: lemon twist

Royal Toast
W.E. Edwards
Approved Cocktails, *United Kingdom Bartenders' Guild, 1937*
2 oz (60 ml) vodka
½ oz (15 ml) dry vermouth
½ oz (15 ml) Heering Cherry Liqueur
Garnish: lemon twist

Salty Martini
Salvatore Calabrese, Fifty, London, 2009
2 oz (60 ml) vodka
¼ oz (7 ml) dry vermouth
¼ oz (7 ml) Fino Sherry
1 teaspoon (5 ml) caper brine
Garnish: caperberry

Sfusato Martini
Alessandro Palazzi, Dukes Bar, London, 2023
2¾ oz (82 ml) lemon verbena-infused vodka (p 503), frozen
⅜ oz (11 ml) limoncello (preferably Pallini Limoncello), frozen
3 drops pineapple bitters
Add the bitters to a frozen coupe, followed by the vodka and the limoncello.
Garnish: lemon twist (preferably an Amalfi lemon)

Soviet Salute
The How and When, *Hyman Gale and Gerald F. Marco, 1937*
1½ oz (45 ml) vodka
¾ oz (22 ml) dry vermouth
¾ oz (22 ml) Oloroso Sherry
Garnish: lemon twist

Straitjacket
(aka **Vodka Tussetto**)
David Molyneux, The Everleigh, Melbourne, 2017
2 oz (60 ml) vodka
1 oz (30 ml) Fino Sherry
2 dashes orange bitters
Garnish: lemon twist

The Cut
Felix Woods, The Everleigh, Melbourne, 2018
2¼ oz (67 ml) rye vodka
½ oz (15 ml) Fino Sherry
¼ oz (7 ml) Cocchi Americano
2 dashes absinthe
1 lemon twist

The Noble Experiment Dirty Program
Adele Stratton and Ryan Kuntz, Noble Experiment, San Diego, 2016
2 oz (60 ml) vodka
¼ oz (7 ml) Fino Sherry
½ oz (15 ml) olive brine
¾ teaspoon (3.75 ml) cornichon brine
¾ teaspoon (3.75 ml) cocktail onion brine
Garnish: lemon twist (discard), olive, cocktail onion and dill sprig

Vodkatini
(aka **Vodka Gibson**)
Jerome Zerbe
Ted Saucier's Bottoms Up, *Ted Saucier, 1951*
2 oz (60 ml) vodka
½ oz (15 ml) dry vermouth
Garnish: cocktail onion

Add all ingredients to a mixing glass, then stir with ice and strain into a frozen coupe.

GENEVER

Improved Holland Gin Cocktail

The Bar-Tender's Guide, *Jerry Thomas, 1876*

2 oz (60 ml) genever
¾ oz (22 ml) Pierre Ferrand Dry Curaçao or maraschino liqueur
2 dashes absinthe
2 dashes Angostura Bitters
Garnish: lemon twist

Le Subtil

Toby Cecchini, 2009

2 oz (60 ml) genever
½ oz (15 ml) Carpano Antica Formula
½ oz (15 ml) Cardamaro
2 drops Bittermens Hopped Grapefruit Bitters
Garnish: grapefruit twist

Martinez Cocktail (O.H. Byron Recipe)

The Modern Bartenders' Guide, *O.H. Byron, 1884*

1½ oz (45 ml) genever
1¼ oz (37 ml) sweet vermouth
¼ oz (7 ml) Pierre Ferrand Dry Curaçao
2 dashes Angostura Bitters
Garnish: orange twist

▾ Widely considered the original Martinez, modelled after Byron's Manhattan Cocktail, No. 2, "only you substitute gin for whisky".

Smith Cocktail

Modern American Drinks, *George J. Kappeler, 1895*

1½ oz (45 ml) genever
1½ oz (45 ml) dry vermouth
2 dashes Angostura Bitters
Garnish: lemon twist

Smugglers' Eye-Opener Cocktail

Señor Bode, Cafe Plaza, Maracaibo
The South American Gentleman's Companion, *Charles H. Baker Jr., 1951*

2 oz (60 ml) genever
1 oz (30 ml) gin
1 teaspoon (5 ml) simple syrup
2 dashes Angostura Bitters
Garnish: lemon twist

AGAVE

Bad Date

Alastair Walker, Caretaker, Auckland, 2021

1½ oz (45 ml) blanco tequila
½ oz (15 ml) dry vermouth
½ oz (15 ml) Suze
½ oz (15 ml) Yellow Chartreuse
2 dashes absinthe
Garnish: lime twist

Camisado

Brandon Bramhall, Attaboy, Nashville, 2021

1½ oz (45 ml) mezcal
½ oz (15 ml) blanc vermouth
½ oz (15 ml) Suze
½ oz (15 ml) Yellow Chartreuse
2 dashes absinthe
Garnish: grapefruit twist

Desert Bloom

Jake Powell, Death & Co, Denver, 2021

¾ oz (22 ml) mezcal (preferably espadín)
¾ oz (22 ml) blanc vermouth
¾ oz (22 ml) pear eau de vie
½ oz (15 ml) raicilla
¼ oz (7 ml) white Port
1 dash orange bitters
Garnish: grapefruit twist

Don Silvio

Cameron Parish, The Everleigh, Melbourne, 2018

1 oz (30 ml) blanco tequila
1 oz (30 ml) Cocchi Rosa
½ oz (15 ml) mezcal
½ oz (15 ml) Amaro Meletti
3 dashes Angostura Bitters
Garnish: lemon twist

El Chapo

Lynnette Marrero and Jessica Gonzalez, 2015

¾ oz (22 ml) reposado tequila
¾ oz (22 ml) pisco acholado
¾ oz (22 ml) dry vermouth
¾ oz (22 ml) Cocchi Americano
Garnish: lemon twist

Firmin's Folly

Dylan O'Brien, Prizefighter, Emeryville, 2019

1½ oz (45 ml) mezcal
¾ oz (22 ml) dry vermouth
¼ oz (7 ml) Tempus Fugit Crème de Banane
2 drops Bittermens Xocolatl Mole Bitters

Hocus Pocus (Christy Pope and Chad Solomon Recipe)

Christy Pope and Chad Solomon, Midnight Rambler, Dallas, 2014

1½ oz (45 ml) blanco tequila
1¼ oz (37 ml) ancho-chilli-infused Lustau East India Solera Sherry (p 502)
¾ teaspoon (3.7 ml) Tempus Fugit Crème de Cacao
½ teaspoon (2.5 ml) Bigallet China-China
½ teaspoon (2.5 ml) Ancho Reyes Original
¼ teaspoon (1.25 ml) kümmel
2 drops saline solution (p 493)
Garnish: whole star anise

▾ A nod to Ada Coleman's Hanky Panky Cocktail.

La Bandera

Eric Alperin, The Varnish, Los Angeles

2 oz (60 ml) mezcal
¼ oz (7 ml) Campari
¾ oz (22 ml) lime cordial (p 497)
Garnish: lime twist

La Chinesca

Paul Hammond and Priscilla Leong

1¼ oz (37 ml) blanco tequila
¾ oz (22 ml) Cynar
½ oz (15 ml) sweet vermouth
⅜ oz (11 ml) mezcal
Garnish: orange twist

La Perla

Jacques Bezuidenhout, Tres Agaves, San Francisco, 2005

1¼ oz (37 ml) reposado tequila
1¼ oz (37 ml) Manzanilla Sherry
½ oz (15 ml) Poire Williams
Garnish: lemon twist

Add all ingredients to a mixing glass, then stir with ice and strain into a frozen coupe.

La Rosita
Mr. Boston DeLuxe Official Bartender's Guide, *Leo Cotton, 1974*
1½ oz (45 ml) blanco tequila
½ oz (15 ml) dry vermouth
½ oz (15 ml) sweet vermouth
½ oz (15 ml) Campari
1 dash Angostura Bitters
Garnish: lemon twist
▾ Originally on the rocks.

Maiden Voyage
Brandon Bramhall, Last Saint, Charleston, 2024
1½ oz (45 ml) mezcal
½ oz (15 ml) Fino Sherry
½ oz (15 ml) Yellow Chartreuse
½ oz (15 ml) Amaro Montenegro
Garnish: lemon twist

Matador
Café Royal Cocktail Book, *W.J. Tarling, 1937*
2 oz (60 ml) blanco tequila
½ oz (15 ml) dry vermouth
½ oz (15 ml) Pierre Ferrand Dry Curaçao
Garnish: lemon twist

Mexican Monk
Eric Alperin, The Varnish, Los Angeles
2 oz (60 ml) reposado tequila
½ oz (15 ml) Amontillado Sherry
¼ oz (7 ml) Bénédictine
¼ oz (7 ml) coffee liqueur

Mezcaletti Gimlet
Daniel Zacharczuk, The Varnish, Los Angeles, 2024
1 oz (30 ml) mezcal
1 oz (30 ml) Amaro Meletti
1 oz (30 ml) lime cordial (p 497)
Garnish: lime twist

Midnight Marauder
Joaquín Simó, Pouring Ribbons, NYC, 2018
1 oz (30 ml) mezcal
1 oz (30 ml) Bonal Gentiane-Quina
1 oz (30 ml) Cynar
1 dash Bittermens Xocolatl Mole Bitters

Quick Step
Natasha David, Nitecap, NYC, 2015
1½ oz (45 ml) mezcal
1 oz (30 ml) blanc vermouth
½ oz (15 ml) jalapeño-infused blanco tequila (p 503)
1 teaspoon (5 ml) Giffard Crème de Pêche de Vigne

Reposado Martinez
Steven Robbins, Half Step, Austin
2 oz (60 ml) reposado tequila
1 oz (30 ml) Punt e Mes
1 teaspoon (5 ml) maraschino liqueur
2 drops Bittermens Xocolatl Mole Bitters
Garnish: grapefruit twist

Sombrero
(aka **Perfect Tequila Martini**)
Café Royal Cocktail Book, *W.J. Tarling, 1937*
2 oz (60 ml) blanco tequila
½ oz (15 ml) dry vermouth
½ oz (15 ml) sweet vermouth
Garnish: lemon twist

Spicy Martini
Nathan McCarley-O'Neill, Torrisi, NYC, 2024
2 oz (60 ml) jalapeño-infused blanco tequila (p 503)
½ oz (15 ml) blanc vermouth
¼ oz (7 ml) Grappa Nonino Lo Chardonnay Bianco
½ oz (15 ml) Castelvetrano olive brine
Garnish: Castelvetrano olive

The Last Mechanical Art
Maks Pazuniak, Cure, New Orleans, 2011
¾ oz (22 ml) mezcal
¾ oz (22 ml) Punt e Mes
¾ oz (22 ml) Cynar
¾ oz (22 ml) Campari
Garnish: orange twist

Tia Juano
Café Royal Cocktail Book, *W.J. Tarling, 1937*
1½ oz (45 ml) blanco tequila
¾ oz (22 ml) dry vermouth
¾ oz (22 ml) Campari
Garnish: orange twist

White Walker
Sky Huo, Earl's Juke Joint, Sydney
1½ oz (45 ml) blanco tequila
¾ oz (22 ml) blanc vermouth
⅓ oz (10 ml) maraschino liqueur
1 dash Fee Brothers Lemon Bitters
Garnish: lemon twist

BRANDY

Fair Harvard
(aka **2:1 Pisco Martini**)
Robert Simonson, 2016
2 oz (60 ml) pisco
1 oz (30 ml) blanc vermouth
3 dashes orange bitters
Garnish: lemon twist

FORTIFIED & LIQUEUR

Abbot Kinney
Devon Tarby, 2015
1½ oz (45 ml) blanc vermouth
¾ oz (22 ml) gin
¼ oz (7 ml) Suze
¼ oz (7 ml) St Germain Elderflower Liqueur
¼ oz (7 ml) verjus
2 dashes celery bitters
Garnish: celery ribbon

Adonis **(Difford's Recipe)**
Difford's Guide
1 oz (30 ml) Palo Cortado Sherry
1 oz (30 ml) Amontillado Sherry
1 oz (30 ml) sweet vermouth
½ teaspoon (2.5 ml) Campari
2 dashes orange bitters
Garnish: orange twist

Add all ingredients to a mixing glass, then stir with ice and strain into a frozen coupe.

Adonis Cocktail

Straub's Manual of Mixed Drinks, *Jacques Straub, 1913*
2 oz (60 ml) Amontillado Sherry
1 oz (30 ml) sweet vermouth
2 dashes orange bitters
Garnish: orange twist

Created in NYC by Joseph F. McKone at NYC's Hoffman House in 1884 or 1885 to honour a popular Broadway show of the same name and originally made with a 2:1 ratio of sweet vermouth to Sherry.

Andalusia

Invented by Aurélie Panhelleux, co-founder of the Parisian bar CopperBay
2 oz (60 ml) Amontillado Sherry
½ oz (15 ml) Cognac
½ oz (15 ml) light rum
2 dashes Angostura Bitters
Garnish: lemon twist

Armour Cocktail

Modern American Drinks, *George J. Kappeler, 1895*
1½ oz (45 ml) Oloroso Sherry
1½ oz (45 ml) sweet vermouth
2 dashes orange bitters
Garnish: orange twist

Astoria

(aka **Reverse Gin Martini**)
Old Waldorf Bar Days, *Albert Stevens Crockett, 1931*
2 oz (60 ml) dry vermouth
1 oz (30 ml) gin
2 dashes orange bitters
Garnish: lemon twist

Bamboo Cocktail (Harry Craddock Recipe)

The Savoy Cocktail Book, *Harry Craddock, 1930*
1½ oz (45 ml) Fino Sherry
¾ oz (22 ml) dry vermouth
¾ oz (22 ml) sweet vermouth

Bamboo Cocktail (Thomas Stuart Recipe)

Stuart's Fancy Drinks and How to Mix Them, *Thomas Stuart, 1904*
2 oz (60 ml) Fino Sherry
1 oz (30 ml) sweet vermouth
2 dashes orange bitters
Garnish: lemon twist

The drink's first written mention appeared in the *Western Kansas World* newspaper in 1886.

Bamboo Cocktail (Wm. T. Boothby Recipe)

Louis Eppinger, Yokohama
The World's Drinks and How to Mix Them, *Wm. T. Boothby, 1908*
1½ oz (45 ml) Fino Sherry
1½ oz (45 ml) dry vermouth
2 dashes orange bitters
2 dashes Angostura Bitters
Garnish: lemon twist

Add 2 dashes of absinthe to make the **Brazil Cocktail** from *Cocktails: How to Mix Them*, Robert Vermeire, 1922.

Blackthorn Cocktail

Wm. Smith, Esq., Royal Hawaiian Hotel, Honolulu
The World's Drinks and How to Mix Them, *Wm. T. Boothby, 1908*
1 oz (30 ml) sweet vermouth
1 oz (30 ml) dry vermouth
1 oz (30 ml) sloe gin
2 dashes Angostura Bitters
2 dashes orange bitters
Garnish: lemon twist (discard)

Catavino

Brandon Bramhall, Attaboy, Nashville, 2017
1¼ oz (37 ml) Amontillado Sherry
1¼ oz (37 ml) Cocchi Americano
2 dashes Angostura Bitters
2 dashes orange bitters
Garnish: grapefruit twist

Chrysanthemum Cocktail

Recipes for Mixed Drinks, *Hugo R. Ensslin, 1917*
2 oz (60 ml) dry vermouth
¾ oz (22 ml) Bénédictine
3 dashes absinthe
1 dash orange bitters
Garnish: orange twist

Coronation Cocktail

Joseph Rose, Murray Bros.' Café, Newark
Hoffman House Bartender's Guide, *Charles S. Mahoney, 1905*
2 oz (60 ml) Manzanilla Sherry
1 oz (30 ml) dry vermouth
1 teaspoon (5 ml) maraschino liqueur
2 dashes orange bitters
Garnish: lemon twist (discard) and olive

Won second prize at the Police Gazette Bartenders' Contest in 1903.

Diplomate Cocktail

Cocktails: How to Mix Them, *Robert Vermeire, 1922*
2 oz (60 ml) dry vermouth
1 oz (30 ml) sweet vermouth
1 teaspoon (5 ml) maraschino liqueur
2 dashes orange bitters
2 dashes Angostura Bitters
Garnish: lemon twist and cherry

Greenbriar Cocktail

Harry's ABC of Mixing Cocktails, *Harry MacElhone, 1923*
2 oz (60 ml) Oloroso Sherry
1 oz (30 ml) dry vermouth
2 dashes peach bitters
3–4 mint leaves, in mixing glass
Garnish: lemon twist

Haberdasher

Josh Harris and Scott Baird, Trick Dog, San Francisco, 2011
1 oz (30 ml) Amontillado Sherry
1 oz (30 ml) sweet vermouth
1 oz (30 ml) Tempus Fugit Gran Classico Bitter
2 dashes orange bitters
Garnish: lemon twist

Add all ingredients to a mixing glass, then stir with ice and strain into a frozen coupe.

Improved Sherry Cocktail
Midnight Rambler, Dallas, 2014
2½ oz (75 ml) Fino Sherry
½ oz (15 ml) Amontillado Sherry
¼ oz (7 ml) mineral syrup (p 498)
¾ teaspoon maraschino liqueur
¼ teaspoon absinthe
1 dash orange bitters
2 drops Angostura Bitters
2 drops mineral saline solution
Garnish: lemon twist

Little Egypt
The New and Improved Illustrated Bartenders' Manual, *Harry Johnson, 1900*
2½ oz (75 ml) Oloroso Sherry
½ oz (15 ml) sweet vermouth
2 dashes absinthe
2 dashes Angostura Bitters
Garnish: cherry

Minneapolis
(Perfect Sloe Gin Martini with orange bitters and a lemon twist)
The How and When, *Hyman Gale and Gerald F. Marco, 1938*
2 oz (60 ml) sloe gin
½ oz (15 ml) sweet vermouth
½ oz (15 ml) dry vermouth
2 dashes orange bitters
Garnish: lemon twist

Model Citizen
Tony Roehr and Anthony Schmidt, Raised by Wolves, San Diego, 2021
1½ oz (45 ml) Cocchi Americano
¾ oz (22 ml) Fino Sherry
¾ oz (22 ml) Italicus Rosolio di Bergamotto
Garnish: grapefruit twist (discard) and lemon twist

Orchid Thief
Chip Tyndale, Dutch Kills, NYC
1½ oz (45 ml) Fino Sherry
1 oz (30 ml) dry vermouth
½ oz (15 ml) Bénédictine
Garnish: lemon twist

Oxygénée Cocktail
Cocktails de Paris, *Georges Gabriel Thenon, 1929*
2 oz (60 ml) dry vermouth
½ oz (15 ml) absinthe
½ oz (15 ml) mandarin liqueur
Garnish: lemon twist

Prima Donna
Tess Anne Sawyer, Mother's Ruin, NYC, 2015
¾ oz (22 ml) Amontillado Sherry
¾ oz (22 ml) Lustau East India Solera Sherry
¾ oz (22 ml) dry vermouth
¾ oz (22 ml) sweet vermouth
2 dashes Angostura Bitters
2 dashes orange bitters
Garnish: lemon twist

Reform Cocktail
The New and Improved Illustrated Bartenders' Manual, *Harry Johnson, 1900*
1½ oz (45 ml) Fino Sherry
1½ oz (45 ml) dry vermouth
2 dashes Angostura Bitters
2 dashes orange bitters
Garnish: lemon twist and cherry

Seventh Heaven
Bar La Florida Cocktails, *1934*
1½ oz (45 ml) sloe gin
1 oz (30 ml) sweet vermouth
½ oz (15 ml) Fernet-Branca
Garnish: lemon twist and several walnuts or almonds on the side

Sherry Cocktail
Harry's ABC of Mixing Cocktails, *Harry MacElhone, 1923*
2½ oz (75 ml) Fino Sherry
½ oz (15 ml) dry vermouth
2 dashes orange bitters
2 dashes peach bitters
Garnish: lemon twist

Sweet Mezcal Martini
Robert Simonson, NYC, 2020
2 oz (60 ml) blanc vermouth
1 oz (30 ml) mezcal
2 dashes orange bitters
Garnish: cherry

Tiptop Cocktail
Jack's Manual, *J.A. Grohusko, 1933*
2½ oz (75 ml) dry vermouth
¼ oz (7 ml) Bénédictine
2 dashes orange bitters
2 dashes Angostura Bitters
Garnish: lemon twist

Vermouth Panaché
To Have and Have Another, *Philip Greene, 2012*
2 oz (60 ml) dry vermouth
1 oz (30 ml) sweet vermouth
3 dashes Angostura Bitters
Build in a frozen double rocks glass with ice.
Garnish: lemon twist

Xeres Cocktail
Harry's ABC of Mixing Cocktails, *Harry MacElhone, 1923*
3 oz (90 ml) Fino Sherry
1 teaspoon (5 ml) simple syrup
2 dashes orange bitters
2 dashes peach bitters
Garnish: lemon twist

Zaza Cocktail
The World's Drinks and How to Mix Them, *Wm. T. Boothby, 1908*
1¾ oz (52 ml) Dubonnet
1½ oz (45 ml) gin
Shake then strain into a frozen coupe.
Garnish: orange twist
▼ If stirred, this drink becomes a **Dubonnet Cocktail No. 1**.

From *The Savoy Cocktail Book* (1930):

One martini is all right. Two are too many, and three are not enough.
– James Thurber

Add all ingredients to a mixing glass, then stir with ice and strain into a frozen coupe.

OTHER

Falling Leaves

Audrey Saunders, Bemelmans Bar, NYC, 2004

1½ oz (45 ml) dry riesling
¾ oz (22 ml) Poire Williams
½ oz (15 ml) Pierre Ferrand Dry Curaçao
1 teaspoon (5 ml) honey syrup (p 496)
2 dashes Peychaud's Aromatic Cocktail Bitters
Garnish: whole star anise

▼ Swap Poire Williams for Pommeau de Normandie to make the **Falling Leaves No. 2** by Michael Madrusan, The Everleigh, Melbourne, 2013.

Holy Fuji

Michael Madrusan, The Everleigh, 2021

1¾ oz (52 ml) sake
¾ oz (22 ml) gin
½ oz (15 ml) Manzanilla Sherry
Garnish: lemon twist

Rosalind Russell

(aka Sweet Aquavit Martini)
The Stork Club Bar Book, *Lucius Beebe, 1946*

2 oz (60 ml) aquavit
1 oz (30 ml) sweet vermouth
3 dashes Angostura Bitters
Garnish: cherry

Sakura Martini

Kenta Goto, Bar Goto, NYC, 2015

1¾ oz (52 ml) sake
¾ oz (22 ml) gin
½ teaspoon (2.5 ml) maraschino liqueur
Garnish: salted cherry blossom

Trident

Robert Hess, DrinkBoy, circa 2000

1 oz (30 ml) aquavit
1 oz (30 ml) Manzanilla Sherry
1 oz (30 ml) Cynar
2 dashes peach bitters
Garnish: lemon twist

Add all ingredients to a mixing glass, then stir with ice and strain into a frozen coupe.

MANHATTAN

Sweet Manhattan p 342

Manhattan

A rich, smooth and spirituous cocktail that traditionally combines American whiskey, vermouth and bitters, stirred and served up.

spirit + vermouth + bitters

Add all ingredients to a mixing glass, then stir with ice and strain into a frozen coupe.

This virile sipper is believed to be the first 'modern' cocktail, if you will. The act of mixing aromatised and fortified wine with American whiskey and bitters likely began in New York City, sometime during the late 1870s. While both the Manhattan Club (originally on 5th Avenue, then Madison Square) and the lesser-known Manhattan Inn on Broadway claimed to be the drink's birthplace, what we know for sure is that by the early 1880s the Manhattan was considered the cocktail to beat. Soon thereafter, the drink began appearing in various publications and cocktail books, with its first written mention as the 'Manhattan Cocktail, No. 1' in *The Modern Bartenders' Guide* by O.H. Byron in 1884. Before long, the cocktail was being served in bars around the world.

Although today's preferred ratio is 2:1 rye whiskey to Italian (sweet) vermouth, early renditions were often heavier on the vermouth and used rye whiskey and bourbon interchangeably, as well as a lemon twist garnish. However, both Jerry Thomas and Harry Johnson published Manhattan recipes with rye whiskey, which proved highly influential, and by the end of the 19th century it is thought that New Yorkers had developed a proclivity for the spicier spirit. Much like the Martini (p 304) that followed, a bartender of the time might've asked if you preferred your Manhattan 'sweet' (using Italian, or sweet, vermouth) 'dry' (using dry vermouth), or 'perfect' (using an equal split of the two). The cherry first came into play in 1891 and is typically the garnish of choice for sweet Manhattans, while the lemon twist is reserved for dry and perfect versions.

For us, the Manhattan is one of the all-time greats and wildly underrated in modern drinking culture, likely due to its ill treatment in the latter half of the 20th century. We must salute those who led the classic cocktail renaissance of the early 2000s for revisiting and repairing this glorious cocktail, inspiring a new wave of expertly balanced and creative variations.

Cocktail à La Louisiane

(aka **De La Louisiane** or **La Louisiane**)
Famous New Orleans Drinks and How to Mix 'Em,
Stanley Clisby Arthur, 1937
2 oz (60 ml) rye whiskey
½ oz (15 ml) sweet vermouth
½ oz (15 ml) Bénédictine
2 dashes absinthe
2 dashes Peychaud's Aromatic Cocktail Bitters

Add all ingredients to a mixing glass, then stir with ice and strain into a frozen coupe.
Garnish: lemon twist

Recorded by journalist and historian Stanley Clisby Arthur in his 1937 book, *Famous New Orleans Drinks and How to Mix 'Em*, this rich Manhattan variation was the house cocktail at Restaurant de la Louisiane in New Orleans. Arthur, a native of California, arrived in Louisiana in 1915 and dedicated much of his life to documenting his new home, compiling books on various aspects of the region's culture and history. Arthur captured pre-Prohibition drinking culture in New Orleans with passion and flair, often describing how older drinks hailing from cities like New York have been evolved or improved by New Orleans' best bartenders.

Arthur was one of the first authors to show such a specific interest in the origin stories and backgrounds of individual drinks. Quite unlike the no-nonsense, trade-orientated and pocket-sized books by the era's influential American bartenders, Arthur's volume offers half a page to each cocktail, publishing the recipe along with a short paragraph detailing his understanding and opinion of the drink's ancestry and influence. According to Arthur, the Restaurant de la Louisiane was 'long the rendezvous of those who appreciate the best in Creole cuisine' and the eponymous cocktail was 'as out-of-the-ordinary as the many distinctive dishes that grace its menu'.

The De La Louisiane – as it is more commonly known today – appeals to fans of both the Manhattan and the Sazerac (p 366). Peychaud's Aromatic Cocktail Bitters and absinthe enhance the sting of the rye, while Bénédictine offers an earthy roundness. Try Jerry Thomas's Improved Whiskey Cocktail (p 366) from the 1876 edition of *The Bar-Tender's Guide* for something similarly spicy with a little more punch.

Brooklyn Cocktail

Jack's Manual, *J.A. Grohusko, 1908*
2 oz (60 ml) rye whiskey
½ oz (15 ml) dry vermouth
¼ oz (7 ml) maraschino liqueur
¼ oz (7 ml) Picon Amer

Add all ingredients to a mixing glass, then stir with ice and strain into a frozen coupe.
Garnish: cherry

The Brooklyn Cocktail is thought to be an original from Jacob A. Grohusko, first published in *Jack's Manual* in 1908. *Jack's Manual* was a substantial contribution to the annals of the cocktail world, with more than 1000 recipes including percentages for glass, bowl or barrel scaling.

Born in 1876 to a Russian-Jewish family in England, Grohusko moved to the United States with his parents at an early age and is known to have worked at a handful of New York City venues prior to settling at Baracca's, an Italian restaurant on Stone Street, where he forged his reputation as a skilled bartender and finalised the first edition of the book. The man loved liquor in all forms, and his book is something of a drink encyclopaedia compared to the usual bartender's guide.

Likely inspired in part by the well-established Manhattan and Bronx cocktails, the Brooklyn is a dry Manhattan variation featuring maraschino and Picon Amer, a bittersweet French apéritif flavoured with orange zest, gentian and quinine. The product's name is a portmanteau of the French word for 'bitter' and the surname of its inventor, scholar-cum-infantry-horseman-and-distiller Gaétan Picon, who devised the original formula in Algeria in 1837 to ward off malaria.

While we can't necessarily attest to its disease-busting benefits, we can confirm that Picon Amer is an absolute asset to cocktails. Fans of the orange-scented apéritif should try the New Deal (p 344), a rye Manhattan with Picon Amer instead of vermouth. If it's dry rye Manhattans you're interested in, seek out some lesser-known recipes, such as the Manhattan No. 6 Extra Dry (p 346) featuring Cocchi Americano, and the Vail Cocktail (p 347) with Bénédictine.

Manhattan

CORE STYLES:

Dry Manhattan
2 oz (60 ml) rye whiskey
1 oz (30 ml) dry vermouth
3 dashes Angostura Bitters
Garnish: lemon twist

Perfect Manhattan
2 oz (60 ml) rye whiskey
½ oz (15 ml) sweet vermouth
½ oz (15 ml) dry vermouth
3 dashes Angostura Bitters
Garnish: lemon twist

Sweet Manhattan
2 oz (60 ml) rye whiskey
1 oz (30 ml) sweet vermouth
3 dashes Angostura Bitters
Garnish: cherry

RYE WHISKEY (SWEET)

Black Mamba
Giuseppe Gonzalez, Clover Club, NYC
2 oz (60 ml) rye whiskey
½ oz (15 ml) Green Chartreuse
½ oz (15 ml) Pommeau de Normandie
Garnish: cherry

Black Manhattan
Todd Smith, Bourbon & Branch, San Francisco, 2015
2 oz (60 ml) rye whiskey
1 oz (30 ml) Amaro Averna
1 dash Angostura Bitters
1 dash orange bitters
Garnish: cherry

Blue Collar Cocktail
Michael Madrusan, Milk & Honey, NYC, 2008
2 oz (60 ml) rye whiskey
½ oz (15 ml) sweet vermouth
¼ oz (7 ml) Amaro CioCiaro
¼ oz (7 ml) maraschino liqueur
2 dashes orange bitters
2 dashes Angostura Bitters
Garnish: lemon twist

Boothby
(See p 346)

Bushwick
Phil Ward, Death & Co, NYC, 2009
2 oz (60 ml) rye whiskey
½ oz (15 ml) sweet vermouth
¼ oz (7 ml) Picon Amer
¼ oz (7 ml) maraschino liqueur
Garnish: cherry

Capitol
(Sweet Manhattan with triple sec)
The Fine Art of Mixing Drinks, *David A. Embury, 1948*
2 oz (60 ml) rye whiskey
¾ oz (22 ml) sweet vermouth
1 teaspoon (5 ml) triple sec
Garnish: cherry

Caravan
David Molyneux, The Everleigh, Melbourne, 2018
1½ oz (45 ml) rye whiskey
¾ oz (22 ml) Manzanilla Sherry
⅜ oz (11 ml) sweet vermouth
⅜ oz (11 ml) Cynar
Garnish: lemon twist

Caravan #2
Felix Woods, The Everleigh, Melbourne, 2018
1½ oz (45 ml) rye whiskey
¾ oz (22 ml) Cynar
¾ oz (22 ml) Amontillado Sherry
Garnish: cherry

Carroll Gardens
Joaquín Simó, Death & Co, NYC, 2008
2 oz (60 ml) rye whiskey
½ oz (15 ml) sweet vermouth
½ oz (15 ml) Amaro Nardini
1 teaspoon (5 ml) maraschino liqueur
Garnish: lemon twist (discard)

Columbia Heights
Rob Libecans, Caretaker's Cottage, Melbourne, 2022
1¼ oz (37 ml) rye whiskey
1¼ oz (37 ml) sweet vermouth
¼ oz (7 ml) maraschino liqueur
1 dash absinthe
Garnish: lemon twist

Creole Cocktail
Recipes for Mixed Drinks, *Hugo R. Ensslin, 1917*
2 oz (60 ml) rye whiskey
½ oz (15 ml) sweet vermouth
¼ oz (7 ml) Picon Amer
¼ oz (7 ml) Bénédictine
Garnish: lemon twist
● Swap sweet vermouth for Campari to make the **Prizefighter** by Jakob Etzold, The Everleigh, Melbourne, 2015.

Creole Cocktail (Chad Solomon and Christy Pope Recipe)
Chad Solomon and Christy Pope
2 oz (60 ml) rye whiskey
½ oz (15 ml) sweet vermouth
¼ oz (7 ml) Bénédictine
½ teaspoon (2.5 ml) Bigallet China-China
½ teaspoon (2.5 ml) Luxardo Amaro Abano
2 drops saline solution (p 493)
Garnish: lemon twist

Deshler Cocktail
Recipes for Mixed Drinks, *Hugo R. Ensslin, 1917*
2 oz (60 ml) rye whiskey
¾ oz (22 ml) sweet vermouth
¼ oz (7 ml) triple sec
2 dashes Peychaud's Aromatic Cocktail Bitters
1 lemon twist
1 orange twist
Garnish: orange twist

Diamondback Cocktail
Murray Stenson, Zig Zag Cafe, Seattle
1½ oz (45 ml) rye whiskey
¾ oz (22 ml) bonded apple brandy
¾ oz (22 ml) Green Chartreuse
Garnish: cherry
● Riff on Diamondback Lounge from Bottoms Up, Ted Sauciers, 1951

Add all ingredients to a mixing glass, then stir with ice and strain into a frozen coupe.

Dirk Diggler
Lorenzo Antinori, Bar Leone, Hong Kong, 2023
1½ oz (45 ml) rye whiskey
1½ oz (45 ml) Punt e Mes
1 teaspoon (5 ml) Fernet-Branca
2 dashes peach bitters
1 dash Angostura Bitters
Garnish: orange twist

DuBoudreau Cocktail
Jim Meehan, PDT, NYC, 2009
2 oz (60 ml) bonded rye whiskey
¾ oz (22 ml) Dubonnet
¼ oz (7 ml) Fernet-Branca
¼ oz (7 ml) St Germain Elderflower Liqueur
Garnish: lemon twist
Named after famed Seattle bartender Jamie Boudreau.

Evans
The Artistry of Mixing Drinks, *Frank Meier, 1936*
2 oz (60 ml) rye whiskey
½ oz (15 ml) Pierre Ferrand Dry Curaçao
½ oz (15 ml) apricot brandy
Garnish: lemon twist

Fall Back
Sasha Petraske, The John Dory, NYC, 2012
1 oz (30 ml) rye whiskey
1 oz (30 ml) bonded apple brandy
½ oz (15 ml) sweet vermouth
½ oz (15 ml) Amaro Nonino
2 dashes Peychaud's Aromatic Cocktail Bitters
Garnish: lemon twist

Fancy Manhattan Cocktail
American and Other Iced Drinks, *Charlie Paul, 1902*
2 oz (60 ml) rye whiskey
½ oz (15 ml) sweet vermouth
½ oz (15 ml) Pierre Ferrand Dry Curaçao or maraschino liqueur
3 dashes Angostura Bitters
Garnish: lemon twist

Floridita Special
Bar La Florida Cocktails, *1935*
2 oz (60 ml) rye whiskey
½ oz (15 ml) sweet vermouth
¼ oz (7 ml) Picon Amer
¼ oz (7 ml) Pierre Ferrand Dry Curaçao
2 dashes Angostura Bitters
Garnish: lemon twist

Fogerty
Ryan Fitzgerald, ABV, San Francisco
2 oz (60 ml) rye whiskey
½ oz (15 ml) Campari
¼ oz (7 ml) Tempus Fugit Crème de Cacao
2 dashes orange bitters
Garnish: orange twist

Foreign Ministry
Brandon Bramhall, Attaboy, Nashville, 2021
1½ oz (45 ml) rye whiskey
1 oz (30 ml) Select Aperitivo
½ oz (15 ml) Green Chartreuse
Garnish: orange twist

Fourth Regiment Cocktail
Straub's Manual of Mixed Drinks, *Jacques Straub, 1913*
1½ oz (45 ml) rye whiskey
1½ oz (45 ml) sweet vermouth
2 dashes Angostura Bitters
2 dashes orange bitters
2 dashes celery bitters
Garnish: lemon twist

Greenpoint
Michael McIlroy, Milk & Honey, NYC, 2005
2 oz (60 ml) rye whiskey
½ oz (15 ml) sweet vermouth
½ oz (15 ml) Yellow Chartreuse
2 dashes Angostura Bitters
2 dashes orange bitters
Garnish: lemon twist

Habitant (Michael Madrusan Recipe)
Michael Madrusan, Milk & Honey, NYC, 2008
2 oz (60 ml) rye whiskey
¾ oz (22 ml) sweet vermouth
1 teaspoon (5 ml) maple syrup
3 dashes Angostura Bitters
Garnish: cherry
Originally a "Sweet Martini with the addition of as much maple syrup as Italian vermouth" in *The Fine Art of Mixing Drinks*, David A. Embury, 1948.

Harvest Moon
Daniel Eun, PDT, NYC, 2007
1¼ oz (37 ml) rye whiskey
1 oz (30 ml) Cocchi Americano
½ oz (15 ml) bonded apple brandy
¼ oz (7 ml) Green Chartreuse
2 drops Bob's Bitters Abbotts Bitters
Garnish: orange twist

Hawthorne
The Fine Art of Mixing Drinks, *David A. Embury, 1948*
2 oz (60 ml) rye whiskey
½ oz (15 ml) sweet vermouth
½ oz (15 ml) Dubonnet
1 teaspoon (5 ml) Pierre Ferrand Dry Curaçao
3 dashes Angostura Bitters
Garnish: cherry

Hoffman House No. 2
1700 Cocktails for the Man Behind the Bar, *R. de Fleury, 1934*
2¼ oz (67 ml) rye whiskey
¾ oz (22 ml) Pierre Ferrand Dry Curaçao
2 dashes absinthe
2 dashes Angostura Bitters
2 dashes Peychaud's Aromatic Cocktail Bitters
Garnish: lemon twist and cherry

La Viña
Alex Day, Death & Co, NYC, 2009
1 oz (30 ml) rye whiskey
1 oz (30 ml) Amaro Nonino
1 oz (30 ml) Lustau East India Solera Sherry
1 dash orange bitters

Add all ingredients to a mixing glass, then stir with ice and strain into a frozen coupe.

Lazy Riff
Elijah Harriss, The Everleigh, Melbourne, 2024
1 oz (30 ml) rye whiskey
1 oz (30 ml) Cognac
1 oz (30 ml) Amaro Averna
3 dashes Angostura Bitters
4 dashes absinthe
Garnish: lemon twist

Liberal Cocktail
Modern American Drinks, *George J. Kappeler, 1895*
2¼ oz (67 ml) rye whiskey
½ oz (15 ml) sweet vermouth
¼ oz (7 ml) Picon Amer
2 dashes orange bitters
Garnish: lemon twist

Little Italy
Audrey Saunders, Pegu Club, NYC, 2006
2 oz (60 ml) rye whiskey
½ oz (15 ml) sweet vermouth
½ oz (15 ml) Cynar
Garnish: cherry

Made Man
Ali Reynolds, Hawksmoor, London
2 oz (60 ml) rye whiskey
½ oz (15 ml) Yellow Chartreuse
½ oz (15 ml) Heering Cherry Liqueur
1 teaspoon (5 ml) Fernet-Branca
Garnish: cherry

Manhattan Cocktail (Jerry Thomas Recipe)
The Bar-Tender's Guide, *Jerry Thomas, 1862*
2 oz (60 ml) rye whiskey
¾ oz (22 ml) sweet vermouth
¼ oz (7 ml) maraschino liqueur or Pierre Ferrand Dry Curaçao
3 dashes Angostura Bitters
Garnish: lemon twist

Manhattan Jr. Cocktail
(Sweet Manhattan with an orange twist)
A Life-Time Collection of 688 Recipes for Drinks, *1934*
2 oz (60 ml) rye whiskey
1 oz (30 ml) sweet vermouth
3 dashes Angostura Bitters
Garnish: orange twist

Man Maker
Hayden S. Lambert, Above Board, Melbourne
¾ oz (22 ml) rye whiskey
¾ oz (22 ml) Cognac
¾ oz (22 ml) Amaro Averna
¾ oz (22 ml) Bénédictine
1 dash Angostura Bitters
1 dash orange bitters
Garnish: lemon twist

Mergers & Acquisitions
Shrimp Toast, Craft & Commerce, San Diego, 2019
1½ oz (45 ml) rye whiskey
¾ oz (22 ml) sweet vermouth
½ oz (15 ml) aquavit
¼ oz (7 ml) Bénédictine
1 dash Angostura Bitters
1 dash Peychaud's Aromatic Cocktail Bitters
Garnish: orange twist

Meteor
(aka **Sherman Cocktail** in *Straub's Manual of Mixed* Drinks, Jacques Straub, 1913 or Sweet Manhattan with absinthe)
Harry Craddock
Ted Saucier's Bottoms Up, *Ted Saucier, 1951*
2 oz (60 ml) rye whiskey
1 oz (30 ml) sweet vermouth
2 dashes absinthe
2 dashes Angostura Bitters
Garnish: cherry

Milwaukee Cocktail
The How and When, *Hyman Gale and Gerald F. Marco, 1937*
2¼ oz (67 ml) rye whiskey
¾ oz (22 ml) apricot brandy
Garnish: lemon twist

Momosé Manhattan
The Way of the Cocktail, *Julia Momosé, 2021*
1½ oz (45 ml) rye whiskey
½ oz (15 ml) sweet vermouth
½ oz (15 ml) Amaro Braulio
½ oz (15 ml) Pineau des Charentes
Garnish: lemon twist

Morning Glory Cocktail
The Bar-Tender's Guide, *Jerry Thomas, 1887*
1 oz (30 ml) rye whiskey
1 oz (30 ml) Cognac
¾ oz (22 ml) Pierre Ferrand Dry Curaçao
2 dashes absinthe
2 dashes Angostura Bitters
Garnish: lemon twist

Mountain
(See p 167)

New Deal
The Fine Art of Mixing Drinks, *David A. Embury, 1948*
2 oz (60 ml) rye whiskey
¾ oz (22 ml) Picon Amer
1 teaspoon (5 ml) simple syrup
Garnish: orange twist

Nirvana Cocktail
The Canon Cocktail Book, *Jamie Boudreau and James O. Fraioli, 2016*
2 oz (60 ml) rye whiskey
¾ oz (22 ml) Picon Amer
1 teaspoon (5 ml) maraschino liqueur
1 teaspoon (5 ml) Bénédictine
2 dashes Angostura Bitters
Garnish: orange twist

Police Gazette Cocktail
Hoffman House Bartender's Guide, *Charles S. Mahoney, 1905*
2 oz (60 ml) rye whiskey
½ oz (15 ml) sweet vermouth
¼ oz (7 ml) Pierre Ferrand Dry Curaçao
¼ oz (7 ml) maraschino liqueur
3 dashes Angostura Bitters
Garnish: cherry

Add all ingredients to a mixing glass, then stir with ice and strain into a frozen coupe.

Preakness
Just Cocktails, *W.C. Whitfield, 1939*
2 oz (60 ml) rye whiskey
¾ oz (22 ml) sweet vermouth
¼ oz (7 ml) Bénédictine
3 dashes Angostura Bitters
Garnish: lemon twist

Prospect Park
Tom Schlesinger-Guidelli, Eastern Standard, Boston
1½ oz (45 ml) rye whiskey
1 oz (30 ml) Aperol
¼ oz (7 ml) sweet vermouth
¼ oz (7 ml) maraschino liqueur
Garnish: cherry

Red Hook
Vincenzo Errico, Milk & Honey, NYC, 2003
2 oz (60 ml) rye whiskey
½ oz (15 ml) Punt e Mes
½ oz (15 ml) maraschino liqueur
Garnish: cherry
● The beginning of the modern neighbourhood variations.

Remember the Maine
(aka **McKinley's Delight**)
The Gentleman's Companion, *Charles H. Baker Jr., 1939*
2 oz (60 ml) rye whiskey
¾ oz (22 ml) sweet vermouth
¼ oz (7 ml) Heering Cherry Liqueur
2 dashes absinthe
2 dashes Angostura Bitters
Garnish: lemon twist (discard) and cherry
● "Treat this one with the respect it deserves, gentlemen."

Saratoga Cocktail
The Bar-Tender's Guide, *Jerry Thomas, 1887*
1 oz (30 ml) rye whiskey
1 oz (30 ml) Cognac
1 oz (30 ml) sweet vermouth
3 dashes Angostura Bitters
Garnish: lemon twist

Sheepshead Bay
The Fine Art of Mixing Drinks, *David A. Embury, 1948*
1¾ oz (52 ml) rye whiskey
¾ oz (22 ml) sweet vermouth
1 teaspoon (5 ml) Bénédictine
3 dashes Angostura Bitters
Garnish: cherry

Sir Francis Drake
Hotel Sir Francis Drake, San Francisco
Ted Saucier's Bottoms Up, *Ted Saucier, 1951*
1 oz (30 ml) rye whiskey
1 oz (30 ml) gin
½ oz (15 ml) Green Chartreuse
½ oz (15 ml) triple sec
Garnish: lemon twist

Southern Club Manhattan Cocktail
Hoffman House Bartender's Guide, *Charles S. Mahoney, 1905*
2 oz (60 ml) rye whiskey
½ oz (15 ml) sweet vermouth
¼ oz (7 ml) Pierre Ferrand Dry Curaçao
1 teaspoon (5 ml) maraschino liqueur
2 dashes Peychaud's Aromatic Cocktail Bitters
Garnish: orange twist (discard)

Spider
Louis' Mixed Drinks, *Louis Muckensturm, 1906*
2 oz (60 ml) rye whiskey
¾ oz (22 ml) sweet vermouth
¼ oz (7 ml) Pierre Ferrand Dry Curaçao
2 dashes Angostura Bitters
2 dashes orange bitters
Garnish: cherry

Stingray
Felix Woods, The Everleigh, Melbourne, 2018
2 oz (60 ml) rye whiskey
¾ oz (22 ml) sweet vermouth
¼ oz (7 ml) Fernet-Branca
2 drops Bittermens Xocolatl Mole Bitters
Garnish: orange twist

Stood Up
Michael McIlroy, Milk & Honey, NYC, 2010
1½ oz (45 ml) rye whiskey
1½ oz (45 ml) sweet vermouth
1 teaspoon (5 ml) Luxardo Bitter Rosso
Garnish: grapefruit twist

Sunset Park
Michael Madrusan, Milk & Honey, NYC, 2009
2 oz (60 ml) rye whiskey
½ oz (15 ml) sweet vermouth
½ oz (15 ml) dry vermouth
2 dashes Angostura Bitters
1 teaspoon (5 ml) Giffard Crème de Pêche de Vigne
Garnish: lemon twist

The Slope
Julie Reiner, Clover Club, NYC
2 oz (60 ml) rye whiskey
¾ oz (22 ml) sweet vermouth
¼ oz (7 ml) apricot brandy
2 dashes Angostura Bitters
Garnish: cherry

Uptown Manhattan
(Sweet Manhattan with a dash of lemon)
The Fine Art of Mixing Drinks, *David A. Embury, 1948*
2 oz (60 ml) rye whiskey
¾ oz (22 ml) sweet vermouth
½ teaspoon (2.5 ml) lemon juice
2 dashes Angostura Bitters
Garnish: lemon twist
● Add 2 dashes of kümmel to make the **Piccadilly**, also from *The Fine Art of Mixing Drinks*, David A. Embury, 1948.

Wicked Kiss
Phil Ward, Death & Co, NYC, 2007
1⅓ oz (40 ml) rye whiskey
1⅓ oz (40 ml) bonded apple brandy
¼ oz (7 ml) Yellow Chartreuse
¼ oz (7 ml) Bénédictine
1 dash Angostura Bitters

Add all ingredients to a mixing glass, then stir with ice and strain into a frozen coupe.

RYE WHISKEY (DRY)

Bensonhurst
Chad Solomon, Pegu Club and Milk & Honey, NYC, 2006
2 oz (60 ml) rye whiskey
¾ oz (22 ml) dry vermouth
¼ oz (7 ml) maraschino liqueur
¼ oz (7 ml) Cynar
2 drops saline solution (p 493)

Boothby
(Sweet Manhattan topped with Champagne)
The World's Drinks and How to Mix Them, Wm. T. Boothby, 1908
1½ oz (45 ml) rye whiskey
¾ oz (22 ml) sweet vermouth
2 dashes Angostura Bitters
2 dashes orange bitters
Champagne, to top
Toss and strain into a chilled flute, then top with Champagne.
Garnish: cherry

Boulevard
The Fine Art of Mixing Drinks, *David A. Embury, 1948*
2 oz (60 ml) rye whiskey
¾ oz (22 ml) dry vermouth
¼ oz (7 ml) Pierre Ferrand Dry Curaçao
2 dashes orange bitters
Garnish: lemon twist

Brooklyn Heights
Maxwell Britten, NYC, 2011
1½ oz (45 ml) rye whiskey
½ oz (15 ml) dry vermouth
½ oz (15 ml) maraschino liqueur
¼ oz (7 ml) Luxardo Amaro Abano
1 teaspoon (5 ml) Campari
2 dashes orange bitters

Clifton Cocktail
Straub's Manual of Mixed Drinks, *Jacques Straub, 1913*
1½ oz (45 ml) rye whiskey
1½ oz (45 ml) dry vermouth
¼ oz (7 ml) Pierre Ferrand Dry Curaçao
2 dashes Angostura Bitters
Garnish: lemon twist

Cobble Hill
Sam Ross, Milk & Honey, NYC, 2005
2 oz (60 ml) rye whiskey
½ oz (15 ml) dry vermouth
½ oz (15 ml) Amaro Montenegro
1 cucumber wheel
Press cucumber, add remaining ingredients and stir with ice, then strain into a frozen coupe.
Garnish: lemon twist

Cockpit
Ferdy Tuohy
Barflies and Cocktails, *Harry MacElhone, 1927*
1 oz (30 ml) rye whiskey
1 oz (30 ml) Irish whiskey
½ oz (15 ml) dry vermouth
½ oz (15 ml) sweet vermouth
Garnish: cherry

Country Cocktail
Modern American Drinks, *George J. Kappeler, 1895*
2½ oz (75 ml) rye whiskey
2 dashes orange bitters
2 dashes Angostura Bitters
1 lemon twist
Garnish: lemon twist

Double-Barrel Cocktail
Modern American Drinks, *George J. Kappeler, 1895*
1 oz (30 ml) rye whiskey
1 oz (30 ml) dry vermouth
1 oz (30 ml) sweet vermouth
2 dashes Angostura Bitters
2 dashes orange bitters
Garnish: lemon twist

Filthy Rich
Zachary Gelnaw-Rubin, Dutch Kills, NYC, 2012
1 oz (30 ml) rye whiskey
1 oz (30 ml) dry vermouth
½ oz (15 ml) Bénédictine
½ oz (15 ml) Cynar
Garnish: lemon twist

Ipanema Majestic
Rogerio Igarashi, Bar Trench, Tokyo, 2023
1½ oz (45 ml) Nikka Miyagikyo Single Malt Whisky
1 oz (30 ml) coconut water
1 teaspoon (5 ml) maraschino liqueur
1 teaspoon (5 ml) Koko Kanu
3 drops Bob's Bitters Abbotts Bitters
Garnish: lemon twist

Last Man Standing
Benjamin Hash, Horse Inn of Lancaster, Pennsylvania
¾ oz (22 ml) rye whiskey
¾ oz (22 ml) gin
¾ oz (22 ml) Fernet-Branca
¾ oz (22 ml) Campari
2 orange twists
Add all ingredients to a mixing glass with ice, express orange twists and discard one, then stir and strain into a frozen coupe.
Garnish: orange twist

Locksmith
Ingrid Archer and David Molyneux, The Everleigh, Melbourne, 2018
1½ oz (45 ml) rye whiskey
1 oz (30 ml) Cocchi Americano
½ oz (15 ml) Islay Scotch
Garnish: lemon twist

Manhattan No. 6 Extra Dry
1700 Cocktails for the Man Behind the Bar, *R. de Fleury, 1934*
2 oz (60 ml) rye whiskey
½ oz (15 ml) dry vermouth
½ oz (15 ml) Cocchi Americano
Garnish: lemon twist

Manhattan Transfer
Phil Ward, Mayahuel, NYC, 2013
1½ oz (45 ml) rye whiskey
1 oz (30 ml) dry vermouth
1 oz (30 ml) Amaro Ramazzotti
1 dash orange bitters
1 orange twist
Garnish: cherry

Add all ingredients to a mixing glass, then stir with ice and strain into a frozen coupe.

New 1920 Cocktail
(Perfect Manhattan with orange bitters)
The Savoy Cocktail Book, *Harry Craddock, 1930*
2 oz (60 ml) rye whiskey
½ oz (15 ml) dry vermouth
½ oz (15 ml) sweet vermouth
2 dashes Angostura Bitters
2 dashes orange bitters
Garnish: lemon twist
Add 2 dashes of absinthe to make the **Cotton Cocktail** from *Jack's Manual*, J.A. Grohusko, 1933.

Packard Twins
"The Hotel Barclay"
Angostura Recipes, *Charles Scotto, 1934*
2 oz (60 ml) rye whiskey
¾ oz (22 ml) Manzanilla Sherry
¼ oz (7 ml) maraschino liqueur
2 dashes Angostura Bitters
2 dashes orange bitters
Garnish: orange twist

Perfect BQE
Ivy Mix, Leyenda, NYC
2 oz (60 ml) rye whiskey
½ oz (15 ml) dry vermouth
½ oz (15 ml) sweet vermouth
¼ oz (7 ml) Green Chartreuse
½ teaspoon (2.5 ml) maraschino liqueur
Garnish: cherry

Sidney
Cocktails by "Jimmy" Late of Ciro's London, *1930*
2 oz (60 ml) rye whiskey
½ oz (15 ml) dry vermouth
½ oz (15 ml) Yellow Chartreuse
Garnish: cherry

Simpson's Cocktail
Louis' Mixed Drinks, *Louis Muckensturm, 1906*
1½ oz (45 ml) rye whiskey
¾ oz (22 ml) Manzanilla Sherry
½ oz (15 ml) Pierre Ferrand Dry Curaçao
2 dashes orange bitters
2 dashes Angostura Bitters
Garnish: lemon twist

Swiss Family
(Dry Manhattan with absinthe)
Irvin S. Cobb's Own Recipe Book, *Irvin S. Cobb, 1936*
2 oz (60 ml) rye whiskey
1 oz (30 ml) dry vermouth
2 dashes absinthe
2 dashes Angostura Bitters
Garnish: lemon twist

The Intrepid
Eryn Reece, Sons & Daughters, NYC, 2016
1½ oz (45 ml) rye whiskey
¾ oz (22 ml) blanc vermouth
¾ oz (22 ml) Cynar
½ oz (15 ml) mezcal
1 dash celery bitters

Toronto
The Fine Art of Mixing Drinks, *David A. Embury, 1948*
2 oz (60 ml) rye whiskey
¾ oz (22 ml) Fernet-Branca
¼ oz (7 ml) simple syrup
2 dashes Angostura Bitters
Garnish: orange twist

Vail Cocktail
Trader Vic's Bartender's Guide, *Trader Vic, 1947*
2 oz (60 ml) rye whiskey
¾ oz (22 ml) dry vermouth
¼ oz (7 ml) Bénédictine
Garnish: lemon twist

Van Brunt
1¾ oz (52 ml) rye whiskey
¾ oz (22 ml) dry vermouth
¼ oz (7 ml) maraschino liqueur
¼ oz (7 ml) Barolo Chinato
Garnish: cherry

White Collar
Zachary Gelnaw-Rubin, Dutch Kills, NYC, 2014
2 oz (60 ml) rye whiskey
½ oz (15 ml) blanc vermouth
½ oz (15 ml) Amaro CioCiaro
1 teaspoon (5 ml) maraschino liqueur
2 dashes orange bitters
Garnish: lemon twist

BOURBON

Bourbonella
W. Whitfield
Approved Cocktails, *United Kingdom Bartenders' Guild, 1937*
2 oz (60 ml) bourbon
½ oz (15 ml) dry vermouth
½ oz (15 ml) Pierre Ferrand Dry Curaçao
1 teaspoon (5 ml) grenadine (p 496)
Garnish: orange twist and cherry

Brown Bomber
Jim Meehan, PDT, NYC, 2008
1¾ oz (52 ml) bourbon
¾ oz (22 ml) Lillet Blanc
½ oz (15 ml) Suze
Garnish: lemon twist
Named after American boxer Joe Louis, aka the "Brown Bomber".

Brown Cocktail
(Dry Manhattan with bourbon and orange bitters)
Jack's Manual, *J.A. Grohusko, 1933*
1¾ oz (52 ml) bourbon
1¼ oz (37 ml) dry vermouth
2 dashes orange bitters
2 dashes Angostura Bitters
Garnish: orange twist

Country Life
Crosby Gaige's Cocktail Guide and Ladies' Companion, *Crosby Gaige, 1941*
1½ oz (45 ml) bourbon
¾ oz (22 ml) Jamaican dark rum
¾ oz (22 ml) tawny Port
2 dashes orange bitters
2 dashes Angostura Bitters
Garnish: cherry

Country Life #2
Sam Ross, Milk & Honey, NYC, 2009
1¼ oz (37 ml) bourbon
1 oz (30 ml) sweet vermouth
¾ oz (22 ml) Jamaican dark rum
3 dashes Angostura Bitters
Garnish: orange twist

Add all ingredients to a mixing glass, then stir with ice and strain into a frozen coupe.

Crescent Cocktail
Drinks, *Jacques Straub, 1914*
1 oz (30 ml) bourbon
1 oz (30 ml) Picon Amer
¾ oz (22 ml) sweet vermouth
1 teaspoon (5 ml) raspberry syrup (p 500)
Garnish: lemon twist

Dobbs
(Sweet Manhattan with bourbon and Fernet-Branca)
Matt Dawson, Brooklyn Social, NYC
2 oz (60 ml) bourbon
1 oz (30 ml) sweet vermouth
1 teaspoon (5 ml) Fernet-Branca
Garnish: cherry
Originally called a 'Fedora', but Sam Ross changed the name as it was already taken (2005).

Doberman
David Molyneux, The Everleigh, Melbourne, 2018
1½ oz (45 ml) bourbon
½ oz (15 ml) sweet vermouth
½ oz (15 ml) Bénédictine
½ oz (15 ml) Fernet-Branca
Garnish: lemon twist

Endeavour
P.F. Chinsall
Approved Cocktails, *United Kingdom Bartenders' Guild, 1937*
2 oz (60 ml) bourbon
½ oz (15 ml) Green Chartreuse
½ oz (15 ml) Cocchi Americano
3 dashes Angostura Bitters
Garnish: orange twist

Fanciulli
Old Waldorf Bar Days, *Albert Stevens Crockett, 1931*
1½ oz (45 ml) bourbon
¾ oz (22 ml) sweet vermouth
¼ oz (7 ml) Fernet-Branca
Serve in a frozen double rocks glass with crushed ice.
Garnish: mint bouquet

Grandfather
Sam Ross, Milk & Honey, NYC, 2006
1 oz (30 ml) bourbon
1 oz (30 ml) bonded apple brandy
1 oz (30 ml) sweet vermouth
2 dashes Peychaud's Aromatic Cocktail Bitters
2 dashes Angostura Bitters
Garnish: cherry

Hague
The How and When, *Hyman Gale and Gerald F. Marco, 1937*
2 oz (60 ml) bourbon
½ oz (15 ml) Green Chartreuse
½ oz (15 ml) dry vermouth
Garnish: cherry

H.G. Wells Cocktail
(Dry Manhattan with bourbon and absinthe)
Trader Vic's Bartender's Guide, *Trader Vic, 1947*
2 oz (60 ml) bourbon
1 oz (30 ml) dry vermouth
2 dashes absinthe
3 dashes Angostura Bitters
Garnish: lemon twist

Hollow Point
Michael Madrusan, The Everleigh, Melbourne, 2013
1¾ oz (52 ml) bourbon
½ oz (15 ml) sweet vermouth
⅜ oz (11 ml) Campari
⅜ oz (11 ml) apricot brandy
Garnish: lemon twist

Left Hand
(See p 302)

Loose Cannon
Brandon Bramhall, Last Saint, Charleston
1½ oz (45 ml) bourbon
½ oz (15 ml) Punt e Mes
½ oz (15 ml) Fernet-Vallet
½ oz (15 ml) Pierre Ferrand Dry Curaçao
Garnish: orange twist

Mirage
Joyce Chang, Bar Margaux, Melbourne, 2024
1 oz (30 ml) bourbon
1 oz (30 ml) Oloroso Sherry
½ oz (15 ml) aged dark rum
½ oz (15 ml) maple syrup
2 dashes orange bitters
Garnish: lemon twist

Present Company
David Yee, Watershed Kitchen + Bar, Columbus
2 oz (60 ml) bourbon
½ oz (15 ml) Cynar
¼ oz (7 ml) Manzanilla Sherry
¼ oz (7 ml) honey syrup (p 496)
1 dash Angostura Bitters
Garnish: lemon twist

Ristretto Manhattan
(See p 467)

Robinson Cocktail
Modern American Drinks, *George J. Kappeler, 1895*
2½ oz (75 ml) bourbon
2 dashes Peychaud's Aromatic Cocktail Bitters
2 dashes Angostura Bitters
1 lemon twist
Garnish: lemon twist

Shrapnel
Jones' Complete Barguide, *Stan Jones, 1977*
1¾ oz (52 ml) bourbon
½ oz (15 ml) sweet vermouth
½ oz (15 ml) dry vermouth
¼ oz (7 ml) apricot brandy
Garnish: orange twist

The Caretaker
Lisa Kempen, Caretaker, Auckland, 2021
2 oz (60 ml) bourbon
½ oz (15 ml) dry vermouth
¼ oz (7 ml) Amaro Ramazzotti
½ oz (7 ml) maraschino liqueur
1 mint leaf
Garnish: mint leaf

Boulevardier
(See p 302)

Add all ingredients to a mixing glass, then stir with ice and strain into a frozen coupe.

The Master
Michael Madrusan, The Everleigh, Melbourne, 2019
2 oz (60 ml) bourbon
½ oz (15 ml) sweet vermouth
½ oz (15 ml) tawny Port
2 dashes Angostura Bitters
Garnish: cherry

The Mother-in-Law Cocktail
Vintage Spirits and Forgotten Cocktails, *Ted Haigh, 2004*
2¼ oz (67 ml) bourbon
¼ oz (7 ml) maraschino liqueur
¼ oz (7 ml) Pierre Ferrand Dry Curaçao
¼ oz (7 ml) Picon Amer
2 dashes Angostura Bitters
2 dashes Peychaud's Aromatic Cocktail Bitters
Garnish: orange twist
● Swap Picon Amer for Amaro CioCiaro to make the **Son-in-Law** by Michael Madrusan, Little Branch, NYC, 2007.

Three Graces
John La Gatta
Ted Saucier's Bottoms Up, *Ted Saucier, 1951*
2½ oz (75 ml) bourbon
½ oz (15 ml) simple syrup
6–8 mint leaves
Garnish: mint leaf

Time & Place
Summer Goff, Death & Co, Denver, 2021
1¼ oz (37 ml) overproof bourbon
1 oz (30 ml) tawny Port
¾ oz (22 ml) Cocchi Rosa
1 teaspoon (5 ml) Reisetbauer Karotte
2 dashes The Bitter Truth Old Time Aromatic Bitters
Garnish: lemon twist

Up to Date Cocktail
Recipes for Mixed Drinks, *Hugo R. Ensslin, 1917*
2 oz (60 ml) bourbon
½ oz (15 ml) Oloroso Sherry
½ oz (15 ml) Pierre Ferrand Dry Curaçao
2 dashes Angostura Bitters
Garnish: orange twist

Verrazano
Leo Robitscheck, Eleven Madison Park, NYC
1½ oz (45 ml) bourbon
¾ oz (22 ml) Punt e Mes
¾ oz (22 ml) Cynar
1 teaspoon (5 ml) mezcal
Garnish: lemon twist

Waldorf Cocktail
(Sweet Manhattan with bourbon and absinthe)
Straub's Manual of Mixed Drinks, *Jacques Straub, 1913*
2 oz (60 ml) bourbon
1 oz (30 ml) sweet vermouth
3 dashes Angostura Bitters
2 dashes orange bitters
2 dashes absinthe
Garnish: cherry
● Add 3 dashes Peychaud's Aromatic Cocktail Bitters to make the **Satan Cocktail** from *Trader Vic's Bartender's Guide*, Trader Vic, 1947.

Woolworth Manhattan
Toby Maloney, 2008
2 oz (60 ml) bourbon
¾ oz (22 ml) sweet vermouth (preferably Carpano Antica Formula)
¼ oz (7 ml) Cynar
1 dash Angostura Bitters
Garnish: cherry and 2 drops of Bittercube Root Beer Bitters

York Cocktail
Modern American Drinks, *George J. Kappeler, 1895*
1½ oz (45 ml) bourbon
1½ oz (45 ml) sweet vermouth
2 dashes orange bitters
Garnish: cherry

SCOTCH

.38 Special
Michael Madrusan, Little Branch, NYC, 2007
2¼ oz (67 ml) Scotch
⅜ oz (11 ml) Picon Amer
⅜ oz (11 ml) Yellow Chartreuse
3 dashes Angostura Bitters
Garnish: lemon twist
● Michael's first fight with Sasha Petraske was over the name of this drink.

Affinity Cocktail
(Perfect Manhattan with Scotch)
Recipes for Mixed Drinks, *Hugo R. Ensslin, 1917*
2 oz (60 ml) Scotch
½ oz (15 ml) sweet vermouth
½ oz (15 ml) dry vermouth
3 dashes Angostura Bitters
Garnish: lemon twist
● Serve in a frozen double rocks glass with ice to make the **Beals Cocktail** from *Straub's Manual of Mixed Drinks*, Jacques Straub, 1913.

Automobile Cocktail
Hoffman House Bartender's Guide, *Charles S. Mahoney, 1905*
1 oz (30 ml) Scotch
1 oz (30 ml) sweet vermouth
1 oz (30 ml) gin
2 dashes orange bitters
Garnish: lemon twist

Beadleston
(Rob Roy Cocktail with dry vermouth)
The Fine Art of Mixing Drinks, *David A. Embury, 1948*
2 oz (60 ml) Scotch
1 oz (30 ml) dry vermouth
3 dashes Angostura Bitters
Garnish: lemon twist

Add all ingredients to a mixing glass, then stir with ice and strain into a frozen coupe.

Benton Cocktail
(aka **Express** in *The Old Waldorf-Astoria Bar Book*, Albert Stevens Crockett, 1935, or **Ohio** in *Approved Cocktails*, United Kingdom Bartenders' Guild, 1937)
Louis' Mixed Drinks, *Louis Muckensturm, 1906*
1½ oz (45 ml) Scotch
1½ oz (45 ml) sweet vermouth
2 dashes Angostura Bitters
2 dashes orange bitters
Garnish: lemon twist

Bobbie Burns
The Fine Art of Mixing Drinks, *David A. Embury, 1948*
1¾ oz (52 ml) Scotch
¾ oz (22 ml) sweet vermouth
¼ oz (7 ml) Drambuie
3 dashes Angostura Bitters
Serve in an Old Fashioned glass with ice.
Garnish: lemon twist

Bobby Burns Cocktail
Recipes for Mixed Drinks, *Hugo R. Ensslin, 1916*
1¾ oz (52 ml) Scotch
¾ oz (22 ml) sweet vermouth
¼ oz (7 ml) Bénédictine
3 dashes Angostura Bitters
Garnish: lemon twist
Serve in an Old Fashioned glass with ice.
● Popular variation on the Baby Burns from *Fancy Drinks: How They Are Mixed*, 1902.

Bobby Burns No. 2
1700 Cocktails for the Man Behind the Bar, *R. de Fleury, 1934*
1¾ oz (52 ml) Scotch
¾ oz (22 ml) sweet vermouth
¼ oz (7 ml) maraschino liqueur
3 dashes Angostura Bitters
Serve in an Old Fashioned glass with ice.
Garnish: orange twist

Both Ways
Tom Lasher-Walker, Fresh Kills, NYC, 2016
1½ oz (45 ml) Scotch
¾ oz (22 ml) sweet vermouth
½ oz (15 ml) Islay Scotch
¼ oz (7 ml) white crème de menthe
2 dashes orange bitters
Garnish: lemon twist

Bow Bells
C. Frey
Approved Cocktails, *United Kingdom Bartenders' Guild, 1937*
2 oz (60 ml) Scotch
¾ oz (22 ml) dry vermouth
¼ oz (7 ml) Yellow Chartreuse
2 dashes Angostura Bitters
Garnish: lemon twist

Broadmoor
Andreas Noren, The Player, London, 2001
2 oz (60 ml) Scotch
¾ oz (22 ml) Green Chartreuse
1 teaspoon (5 ml) simple syrup
2 dashes orange bitters
Garnish: whole star anise

Chancellor
Esquire Drink Book, *1956*
1½ oz (45 ml) Scotch
1 oz (30 ml) tawny Port
½ oz (15 ml) dry vermouth
3 dashes Angostura Bitters
Garnish: cherry
● Swap dry vermouth for sweet vermouth to make the **Chancellor No. 2** by Joseph Schwartz, Little Branch, NYC.

City to City
(See p 467)

Coffee and Cigarettes
(See p 467)

Crimson Glory
Michael Madrusan, The Everleigh, Melbourne, 2020
2 oz (60 ml) Scotch
½ oz (15 ml) Lillet Rouge
½ oz (15 ml) Amaro Montenegro
Garnish: cherry

Crux of the Matter
Michael Bascetta, Capitano, Melbourne
1 oz (30 ml) Scotch
½ oz (15 ml) sweet vermouth
½ oz (15 ml) fortified muscat
3 dashes Australian Bitters Company Aromatic Bitters or Angostura Bitters

Death & Taxes
Michael Madrusan, Milk & Honey, NYC, 2009
1 oz (30 ml) Scotch
1 oz (30 ml) gin
¾ oz (22 ml) sweet vermouth
¼ oz (7 ml) Bénédictine
2 dashes Angostura Bitters
2 dashes orange bitters
Garnish: lemon twist

Fitzroy
(Rob Roy Cocktail with Islay Scotch)
Sam Ross, Milk & Honey, NYC, 2005
1½ oz (45 ml) Scotch
1 oz (30 ml) sweet vermouth
½ oz (15 ml) Islay Scotch
3 dashes Angostura Bitters
Garnish: lemon twist

Gentle John
Jones' Complete Barguide, *Stan Jones, 1977*
2 oz (60 ml) Scotch
¾ oz (22 ml) dry vermouth
¼ oz (7 ml) triple sec
3 dashes Angostura Bitters
Garnish: orange twist

Glasgow
Esquire Drink Book, *1956*
2 oz (60 ml) Scotch
1 oz (30 ml) dry vermouth
2 dashes absinthe
2 dashes Angostura Bitters
Garnish: lemon twist

"Hoots Mon" Cocktail
The Savoy Cocktail Book, *Harry Craddock, 1930*
2 oz (60 ml) Scotch
½ oz (15 ml) sweet vermouth
½ oz (15 ml) Cocchi Americano
Garnish: lemon twist

Add all ingredients to a mixing glass, then stir with ice and strain into a frozen coupe.

Monte Burns
Tim Philips-Johansson, Milk & Honey, London
2 oz (60 ml) Scotch
¾ oz (22 ml) sweet vermouth
1 teaspoon (5 ml) Amaro Montenegro
Garnish: orange twist

Mr Burns
Richard Elgar
1½ oz (45 ml) single malt Scotch
¾ oz (22 ml) sweet vermouth
½ oz (15 ml) Bénédictine
2 dashes Peychaud's Aromatic Cocktail Bitters
1 dash absinthe
Garnish: lemon twist

Northern Lights
Sam Ross, Attaboy, NYC, 2017
1½ oz (45 ml) Islay Scotch
¾ oz (22 ml) Fino Sherry
¾ oz (22 ml) Aperol
Garnish: lemon twist

Ohio (Michael Madrusan Recipe)
Michael Madrusan, The Everleigh, 2012
¾ oz (22 ml) Scotch
¾ oz (22 ml) Irish whiskey
1 oz (30 ml) sweet vermouth
2 dashes Angostura Bitters
2 dashes peach bitters
Garnish: cherry

Old Alhambra
Leo Robitschek, The NoMad Bar, NYC
1½ oz (45 ml) Islay Scotch
¾ oz (22 ml) blanc vermouth
½ oz (15 ml) Lustau East India Solera Sherry
¼ oz (7 ml) Tempus Fugit Crème de Cacao
Garnish: grapefruit twist

Rapscallion
Adeline Shepard and Craig Harper, Ruby, Copenhagen, 2007
1¾ oz (52 ml) single malt Scotch (preferably Talisker 10yr Single Malt Scotch Whisky)
¾ oz (22 ml) Pedro Ximénez
3 dashes absinthe
Garnish: lemon twist

Robert Burns
The Old Waldorf-Astoria Bar Book, *Albert Stevens Crockett, 1935*
2 oz (60 ml) Scotch
1 oz (30 ml) sweet vermouth
2 dashes absinthe
2 dashes orange bitters
Garnish: cherry

Rob Roy Cocktail
(aka **Sweet Scotch Manhattan**)
Stuart's Fancy Drinks and How to Mix Them, *Thomas Stuart, 1904*
2 oz (60 ml) Scotch
1 oz (30 ml) sweet vermouth
3 dashes Angostura Bitters
2 dashes orange bitters
Garnish: cherry
Swap the cherry for a Cerignola olive to make **The Highland Fling** from *What'll You Have?*, Julien J. Proskauer, 1933.

Rob Roy No. 2
1700 Cocktails for the Man Behind the Bar, *R. de Fleury, 1934*
2 oz (60 ml) Scotch
½ oz (15 ml) dry vermouth
½ oz (15 ml) Pierre Ferrand Dry Curaçao
3 dashes Angostura Bitters
Garnish: lemon twist

Rob Roy No. 3
1700 Cocktails for the Man Behind the Bar, *R. de Fleury, 1934*
1½ oz (45 ml) Scotch
½ oz (15 ml) sweet vermouth
½ oz (15 ml) dry vermouth
½ oz (15 ml) Pierre Ferrand Dry Curaçao
2 dashes Angostura Bitters
2 dashes Peychaud's Aromatic Cocktail Bitters
Garnish: cherry

Rob Roy Holiday Style
(Perfect Rob Roy Cocktail with Drambuie)
Jones' Complete Barguide, *Stan Jones, 1977*
2 oz (60 ml) Scotch
½ oz (15 ml) sweet vermouth
½ oz (15 ml) dry vermouth
1 teaspoon (5 ml) Drambuie
3 dashes Angostura Bitters
Garnish: lemon twist

Scoundrel
Yao Wong, The Elysian, Melbourne, 2021
1½ oz (45 ml) Scotch
½ oz (15 ml) Islay Scotch
¾ oz (22 ml) Pedro Ximénez
¼ oz (7 ml) Green Chartreuse
1 dash orange bitters
Garnish: lemon twist

Straight Up
Oska Whitehart, The Everleigh, Melbourne, 2016
2 oz (60 ml) Scotch
½ oz (15 ml) Cocchi Americano
¼ oz (7 ml) Amaro Meletti
1 dash Peychaud's Aromatic Cocktail Bitters
Garnish: cherry

The Hundred Pipers
Michael Madrusan, The Everleigh, Melbourne, 2012
2 oz (60 ml) Scotch
½ oz (15 ml) Cocchi Americano
½ oz (15 ml) Drambuie
2 dashes absinthe
Garnish: cherry

Training Day
Daniel Eun, The Varnish, Los Angeles, 2010
2 oz (60 ml) Scotch
1 oz (30 ml) Amaro Nonino
3 dashes Angostura Bitters
Garnish: lemon twist

Add all ingredients to a mixing glass, then stir with ice and strain into a frozen coupe.

Trilby Cocktail

The New and Improved Illustrated Bartenders' Manual, *Harry Johnson, 1900*

2 oz (60 ml) Scotch
¾ oz (22 ml) sweet vermouth
1 teaspoon (5 ml) parfait amour
2 dashes absinthe
2 dashes orange bitters
Garnish: cherry

Whiz-Bang

Cocktails: How to Mix Them, *Robert Vermeire, 1922*

2 oz (60 ml) Scotch
¾ oz (22 ml) dry vermouth
1 teaspoon (5 ml) grenadine (p 496)
2 dashes absinthe
2 dashes orange bitters
Garnish: lemon twist

William Wallace

Joe Schofield, Schofield's Bar, Manchester, 2018

1¾ oz (52 ml) Scotch
½ oz (15 ml) Pedro Ximénez
⅓ oz (10 ml) sweet vermouth
3 dashes orange bitters
Garnish: orange twist

Woolworth

John Deragon, PDT, NYC, 2007

2 oz (60 ml) Scotch
¾ oz (22 ml) Manzanilla Sherry
¼ oz (7 ml) Bénédictine
2 dashes orange bitters
Garnish: lemon twist

From old British drinking traditions:

May you be in heaven half an hour before the devil knows you're dead!

IRISH WHISKEY

Blackthorn Cocktail

The Savoy Cocktail Book, *Harry Craddock, 1930*

2¼ oz (67 ml) Irish whiskey
¾ oz (22 ml) dry vermouth
2 dashes absinthe
2 dashes Angostura Bitters
Garnish: cherry

Brain Storm Cocktail

Recipes for Mixed Drinks, *Hugo R. Ensslin, 1917*

2 oz (60 ml) Irish whiskey
½ oz (15 ml) dry vermouth
½ oz (15 ml) Bénédictine
Garnish: orange twist

Emerald Cocktail

Straub's Manual of Mixed Drinks, *Jacques Straub, 1913*

1½ oz (45 ml) Irish whiskey
1½ oz (45 ml) sweet vermouth
2 dashes orange bitters
Garnish: cherry

Psycho Killer

Jillian Vose, The Dead Rabbit, NYC, 2014

2 oz (60 ml) Irish whiskey
½ oz (15 ml) Campari
¼ oz (7 ml) Giffard Banane du Brésil et des Caraïbes
¼ oz (7 ml) Tempus Fugit Crème de Cacao
1 dash absinthe

Rory O'More

(Sweet Manhattan with Irish whiskey)
The Old Waldorf-Astoria Bar Book, *Albert Stevens Crockett, 1935*

2 oz (60 ml) Irish whiskey
1 oz (30 ml) sweet vermouth
3 dashes Angostura Bitters
Garnish: cherry

Shamrock Cocktail

Recipes for Mixed Drinks, *Hugo R. Ensslin, 1917*

2 oz (60 ml) Irish whiskey
½ oz (15 ml) dry vermouth
½ oz (15 ml) Green Chartreuse
1 teaspoon (5 ml) white crème de menthe
Garnish: cherry

Tipperary Cocktail

Recipes for Mixed Drinks, *Hugo R. Ensslin, 1917*

2 oz (60 ml) Irish whiskey
½ oz (15 ml) sweet vermouth
½ oz (15 ml) Green Chartreuse
Garnish: cherry

Weeski

David Wondrich, NYC, 2004

2 oz (60 ml) Irish whiskey
1 oz (30 ml) Cocchi Americano
1 teaspoon (5 ml) triple sec
2 dashes orange bitters
Garnish: lemon twist

WORLD WHISK(E)Y

Rose Manhattan

The Way of the Cocktail, *Julia Momosé, 2021*

1½ oz (45 ml) Japanese whisky
¾ oz (22 ml) Oloroso Sherry
½ oz (15 ml) Cocchi Rosa
1 teaspoon (5 ml) cane syrup (p 494)
½ teaspoon (2.5 ml) rose liqueur
Garnish: lime twist

BRANDY

Anniversary

The Fine Art of Mixing Drinks, *David A. Embury, 1948*

1 oz (30 ml) Cognac
1 oz (30 ml) gin
1 oz (30 ml) sweet vermouth
2 dashes orange bitters
Garnish: lemon twist

● Swap sweet vermouth for dry vermouth to make the **Bermuda**, also from *The Fine Art of Mixing Drinks*, David A. Embury, 1948.

Add all ingredients to a mixing glass, then stir with ice and strain into a frozen coupe.

Ante
1700 Cocktails for the Man Behind the Bar, *R. de Fleury, 1934*
2 oz (60 ml) Calvados
¾ oz (22 ml) triple sec
2 dashes absinthe
2 dashes orange bitters
2 dashes Angostura Bitters
Garnish: cherry

Antilles Cocktail
Jack's Manual, *J.A. Grohusko, 1908*
2 oz (60 ml) Cognac
½ oz (15 ml) sweet vermouth
½ oz (15 ml) dry vermouth
1 dash orange blossom water
Garnish: cherry

Association
G.R. Woollard
Approved Cocktails, *United Kingdom Bartenders' Guild, 1937*
1½ oz (45 ml) bonded apple brandy
¾ oz (22 ml) dry vermouth
¾ oz (22 ml) Pierre Ferrand Dry Curaçao
1 teaspoon (5 ml) Fernet-Branca
Garnish: cherry

Athos
(Sweet Manhattan with Armagnac)
Harry's American Bar, Paris, 1920s
2 oz (60 ml) Armagnac
1 oz (30 ml) sweet vermouth
Garnish: cherry

Bentley
1700 Cocktails for the Man Behind the Bar, *R. de Fleury, 1934*
1½ oz (45 ml) bonded apple brandy
1½ oz (45 ml) sweet vermouth
3 dashes Angostura Bitters
Garnish: cherry

Betsy Ross
The Fine Art of Mixing Drinks, *David A. Embury, 1948*
2 oz (60 ml) Cognac
½ oz (15 ml) tawny Port
¼ oz (7 ml) Pierre Ferrand Dry Curaçao
3 dashes Angostura Bitters
Garnish: lemon twist

Black Feather
Robert Hess, DrinkBoy, *2000*
2 oz (60 ml) Cognac
¾ oz (22 ml) dry vermouth
¼ oz (7 ml) triple sec
3 dashes Angostura Bitters
Garnish: lemon twist

Block & Tackle
The How and When, *Hyman Gale and Gerald F. Marco, 1937*
2 oz (60 ml) Cognac
½ oz (15 ml) bonded apple brandy
½ oz (15 ml) triple sec
2 dashes absinthe
Garnish: cherry

Blue Paradise
Bar La Florida Cocktails, *1935*
2 oz (60 ml) Cognac
¾ oz (22 ml) Dubonnet
¼ oz (7 ml) crème de violette
Garnish: lemon twist

Bombay Cocktail (No. 2)
The Savoy Cocktail Book, *Harry Craddock, 1930*
1½ oz (45 ml) Cognac
½ oz (15 ml) sweet vermouth
½ oz (15 ml) dry vermouth
¼ oz (7 ml) Pierre Ferrand Dry Curaçao
2 dashes absinthe
Garnish: lemon twist

Brant
Old Waldorf Bar Days, *Albert Stevens Crockett, 1931*
2¼ oz (67 ml) Cognac
¾ oz (22 ml) white crème de menthe
3 dashes Angostura Bitters
Garnish: lemon twist

Bughouse
(Harvard Cocktail with absinthe)
The Fine Art of Mixing Drinks, *David A. Embury, 1948*
2 oz (60 ml) Cognac
1 oz (30 ml) sweet vermouth
2 dashes absinthe
2 dashes Angostura Bitters
Garnish: cherry

Button Hook Cocktail
Recipes for Mixed Drinks, *Hugo R. Ensslin, 1916*
2 oz (60 ml) Cognac
½ oz (15 ml) white crème de menthe
½ oz (15 ml) apricot brandy
2 dashes absinthe
Garnish: lemon twist

Carrol Cocktail
"Harry" of Ciro's ABC of Mixing Cocktails, *Harry MacElhone, 1923*
2 oz (60 ml) Cognac
¾ oz (22 ml) sweet vermouth
Garnish: pickled walnut

Carrol Cocktail (Stan Jones Recipe)
Jones' Complete Barguide, *Stan Jones, 1977*
2 oz (60 ml) Cognac
¾ oz (22 ml) sweet vermouth
¼ oz (7 ml) maraschino liqueur
Garnish: cherry

Catastrophe
Just Cocktails, *W.C. Whitfield, 1939*
2 oz (60 ml) Cognac
½ oz (15 ml) bonded apple brandy
½ oz (15 ml) Bénédictine
2 dashes absinthe
Garnish: lemon twist

Ce Soir
Nicole Lebedevitch, The Hawthorne, Boston, 2011
2 oz (60 ml) Cognac
¾ oz (22 ml) Cynar
½ oz (15 ml) Yellow Chartreuse
1 dash Angostura Bitters
1 dash orange bitters
Garnish: lemon twist (discard)

Cho-Cho
Drinks – Long & Short, *Nina Toye and A. H. Adair, 1925*
2 oz (60 ml) Cognac
½ oz (15 ml) dry vermouth
½ oz (15 ml) Pierre Ferand Dry Curaçao
2 dashes absinthe
Garnish: lemon twist

Add all ingredients to a mixing glass, then stir with ice and strain into a frozen coupe.

Chocolate Soldier Cocktail
The South American Gentleman's Companion, *Charles H. Baker Jr., 1951*
1 oz (30 ml) Cognac
1 oz (30 ml) dry vermouth
1 oz (30 ml) Tempus Fugit Crème de Cacao
2 dashes orange bitters
Garnish: lemon twist

Clove Cocktail
(aka **Clare** from the same book)
A Life-Time Collection of 688 Recipes for Drinks, *1934*
1 oz (30 ml) Cognac
1 oz (30 ml) sweet vermouth
1 oz (30 ml) sloe gin
Garnish: lemon twist

Copperhead
Pegu Club, NYC
2 oz (60 ml) bonded apple brandy
½ oz (15 ml) rye whiskey
½ oz (15 ml) Yellow Chartreuse
Garnish: cherry

Coronation
Old Waldorf Bar Days, *Albert Stevens Crockett, 1931*
1¾ oz (52 ml) bonded apple brandy
½ oz (15 ml) sweet vermouth
½ oz (15 ml) dry vermouth
¼ oz (7 ml) apricot brandy
Garnish: lemon twist

Coronation Cocktail – No. 1
The How and When, *Hyman Gale and Gerald F. Marco, 1937*
1¾ oz (52 ml) bonded apple brandy
½ oz (15 ml) sweet vermouth
½ oz (15 ml) dry vermouth
2 dashes peach bitters
Garnish: lemon twist

Corpse Reviver (No. 1)
The Savoy Cocktail Book, *Harry Craddock, 1930*
1½ oz (45 ml) Cognac
¾ oz (22 ml) Calvados
¾ oz (22 ml) sweet vermouth
Garnish: lemon twist
"To be taken before 11 a.m., or whenever steam and energy are needed."

Dragon's Breath
1700 Cocktails for the Man Behind the Bar, *R. de Fleury, 1934*
1½ oz (45 ml) Calvados
1 oz (30 ml) dry vermouth
½ oz (15 ml) apricot brandy
3 dashes hot sauce
Garnish: pickled walnut

El Capitán
Peru, 1920s
2 oz (60 ml) pisco
1 oz (30 ml) sweet vermouth
2 dashes Angostura Bitters
Garnish: cherry

Expatriate
2 oz (60 ml) Cognac
½ oz (15 ml) dry vermouth
¼ oz (7 ml) St Germain Elderflower Liqueur
2 dashes Angostura Bitters
2 dashes absinthe
Garnish: lemon twist

Fair Weather Cocktail
Trader Vic's Bartender's Guide, *Trader Vic, 1947*
1½ oz (45 ml) bonded apple brandy
¾ oz (22 ml) sweet vermouth
2 dashes orange bitters
2 dashes Angostura Bitters
Garnish: lemon twist
Originally served on the rocks.

Fallen Leaves
American Bar, *Charles Schumann, 1991*
1¼ oz (37 ml) bonded apple brandy
¾ oz (22 ml) sweet vermouth
½ oz (15 ml) dry vermouth
½ oz (15 ml) Cognac
Garnish: cherry

Fernet Cocktail
Cocktails: How to Mix Them, *Robert Vermeire, 1922*
2 oz (60 ml) Cognac
¾ oz (22 ml) Fernet-Branca
¼ oz (7 ml) simple syrup
2 dashes Angostura Bitters
Garnish: lemon twist

Flushing Cocktail
(Harvard Cocktail on the rocks)
Jack's Manual, *J.A. Grohusko, 1933*
2 oz (60 ml) Cognac
1 oz (30 ml) sweet vermouth
3 dashes Angostura Bitters
Serve in a double rocks glass with ice.
Garnish: cherry

Full House
Old Waldorf Bar Days, *Albert Stevens Crockett, 1931*
2 oz (60 ml) bonded apple brandy
½ oz (15 ml) Yellow Chartreuse
½ oz (15 ml) Bénédictine
3 dashes Angostura Bitters
Garnish: lemon twist

Greenwich
The Fine Art of Mixing Drinks, *David A. Embury, 1948*
1 oz (30 ml) bonded apple brandy
1 oz (30 ml) gin
1 oz (30 ml) Tempus Fugit Crème de Cacao
Garnish: lemon twist

Hand in Glove
Tom Lasher-Walker, Fresh Kills, NYC, 2018
2 oz (60 ml) Cognac
½ oz (15 ml) Cocchi Americano
½ oz (15 ml) white crème de cacao
A boozier version of the Velvet Glove (p 361) from the *Café Royal Cocktail Book*, W.J. Tarling, 1937.

Add all ingredients to a mixing glass, then stir with ice and strain into a frozen coupe.

Harvard Cocktail

(aka **Royal Fox Cocktail** in *Hoffman House Bartender's Guide*, Charles S. Mahoney, 1905, or Sweet Manhattan with Cognac)
Straub's Manual of Mixed Drinks, *Jacques Straub, 1913*
2 oz (60 ml) Cognac
1 oz (30 ml) sweet vermouth
3 dashes Angostura Bitters
Garnish: cherry
● This works equally well by swapping Cognac for Oloroso Sherry and adding two drops of orange bitters.

Harvard Law

(Boothby with Cognac)
David Molyneux, The Everleigh, Melbourne, 2016
1½ oz (45 ml) Cognac
¾ oz (22 ml) sweet vermouth
2 dashes Angostura Bitters
Champagne, to top
Toss and strain into a chilled coupe, then top with Champagne.
Garnish: cherry

Hot-Kiss

Bar La Florida Cocktails, *1935*
2 oz (60 ml) Cognac
½ oz (15 ml) sweet vermouth
½ oz (15 ml) Pierre Ferand Dry Curaçao
Garnish: cherry

Hunky Dory

(Somewhere between a Stinger and a Hanky Panky Cocktail)
Tom Lasher-Walker, American Bar at The Savoy, London, 2013
1½ oz (45 ml) Cognac
1½ oz (45 ml) sweet vermouth
¼ oz (7 ml) Branca Menta
Garnish: lemon twist

Kiss from Heaven

The How and When, *Hyman Gale and Gerald F. Marco, 1937*
2 oz (60 ml) Cognac
½ oz (15 ml) dry vermouth
½ oz (15 ml) Drambuie
Garnish: lemon twist

Los Saicos

Chad Solomon, Midnight Rambler, Dallas, 2015
1¾ oz (52 ml) pisco
1¼ oz (37 ml) Punt e Mes
¾ teaspoon (3.75 ml) maraschino liqueur
½ teaspoon (2.5 ml) Giffard Crème de Pamplemousse
¼ teaspoon (1.25 ml) absinthe
2 drops saline solution (p 493)
Garnish: grapefruit twist
● Named after the 1960s Peruvian garage rock/proto-punk band.

Marconi Wireless

(Sweet Manhattan with bonded apple brandy)
Old Waldorf Bar Days, *Albert Stevens Crockett, 1931*
2 oz (60 ml) bonded apple brandy
1 oz (30 ml) sweet vermouth
2 dashes Angostura Bitters
2 dashes orange bitters
Garnish: cherry

Metropole (Southern Style)

1700 Cocktails for the Man Behind the Bar, *R. de Fleury, 1934*
2 oz (60 ml) Cognac
1 oz (30 ml) dry vermouth
2 dashes orange bitters
Garnish: cherry
● Add 2 dashes of absinthe to make the Lusitania Cocktail from *Drinks*, Jacques Straub, 1914.

Metropolitan Cocktail

Modern American Drinks, *George J. Kappeler, 1895*
1½ oz (45 ml) Cognac
1½ oz (45 ml) dry vermouth
3 dashes Angostura Bitters
Garnish: lemon twist

Montgomery Smith

Nate Dumas, PDT, NYC, 2007
2 oz (60 ml) Cognac
½ oz (15 ml) Bénédictine
¼ oz (7 ml) Fernet-Branca
Garnish: lemon twist

Moonraker Cocktail

The Savoy Cocktail Book, *Harry Craddock, 1930*
2 oz (60 ml) Cognac
½ oz (15 ml) Byrrh Grand Quinquina or Bonal Gentiane-Quina
¼ oz (7 ml) peach brandy
2 dashes absinthe
Garnish: lemon twist

Morning Cocktail

The New and Improved Illustrated Bartenders' Manual, *Harry Johnson, 1900*
2 oz (60 ml) Cognac
½ oz (15 ml) sweet vermouth
¼ oz (7 ml) maraschino liqueur
¼ oz (7 ml) Pierre Ferrand Dry Curaçao
2 dashes absinthe
2 dashes Angostura Bitters
Garnish: lemon twist and cherry

Morning Cocktail (Jacques Straub Recipe)

Straub's Manual of Mixed Drinks, *Jacques Straub, 1913*
1½ oz (45 ml) Cognac
1½ oz (45 ml) sweet vermouth
2 dashes absinthe
2 dashes Angostura Bitters
Build in a frozen double rocks glass with crushed ice, then shimmy and top with more crushed ice.
Garnish: cherry

Morning Cocktail (Harman Burney Burke Recipe)

Burke's Complete Cocktail & Drinking Recipes, *Harman Burney Burke, 1934*
2 oz (60 ml) Cognac
½ oz (15 ml) dry vermouth
¼ oz (7 ml) maraschino liqueur
¼ oz (7 ml) Tempus Fugit Crème de Cacao
2 dashes absinthe
2 dashes Angostura Bitters
Garnish: lemon twist and cherry

Add all ingredients to a mixing glass, then stir with ice and strain into a frozen coupe.

Naramata
The Canon Cocktail Book, *Jamie Boudreau and James O. Fraioli, 2016*
1½ oz (45 ml) Cognac
¾ oz (22 ml) sweet vermouth
¾ oz (22 ml) Pommeau de Normandie
2 dashes peach bitters
2 dashes Angostura Bitters
Garnish: flamed orange twist

Netherland
Old Waldorf Bar Days, *Albert Stevens Crockett, 1931*
2 oz (60 ml) Cognac
¾ oz (22 ml) Pierre Ferrand Dry Curaçao
2 dashes orange bitters
Garnish: lemon twist

Newark
Jim Meehan and John Deragon, PDT, NYC, 2007
1¾ oz (52 ml) bonded apple brandy
¾ oz (22 ml) sweet vermouth
¼ oz (7 ml) Fernet-Branca
¼ oz (7 ml) maraschino liqueur

Night Owl
Alex Day, Death & Co, NYC, 2009
2 oz (60 ml) Cognac
½ oz (15 ml) sweet vermouth
½ oz (15 ml) Lustau East India Solera Sherry
¼ oz (7 ml) Batavia-Arrack van Oosten

North Atlantic
Dan Greenbaum, The Beagle, NYC
1¾ oz (52 ml) Calvados
¾ oz (22 ml) Madeira
½ oz (15 ml) Bénédictine
5 dashes Angostura Bitters
Garnish: freshly grated nutmeg

Passion
Ted Saucier's Bottoms Up, *Ted Saucier, 1951*
1 oz (30 ml) Cognac
1 oz (30 ml) gin
1 oz (30 ml) Green Chartreuse
1 teaspoon (5 ml) Picon Amer
2 dashes absinthe
Garnish: orange twist

Pick Me Up
(Dry Cognac Manhattan with absinthe)
2 oz (60 ml) Cognac
1 oz (30 ml) dry vermouth
2 dashes absinthe
2 dashes Angostura Bitters
Garnish: lemon twist

Pippin No. 1
Jason E. Clapham, St. Edward's MCR, Oxford
1½ oz (45 ml) Cognac
1 oz (30 ml) Dubonnet
¼ oz (7 ml) maraschino liqueur
¼ oz (7 ml) Campari
Garnish: orange twist
Swap Cognac for gin to make a **Pippin No. 2** (p 326).

Réveillon
Chuck Taggart and Wesley Moore, 2005
2 oz (60 ml) bonded apple brandy
½ oz (15 ml) sweet vermouth
½ oz (15 ml) pear brandy
¼ oz (7 ml) pimento (allspice) dram
2 dashes Angostura Bitters
Garnish: cinnamon quill

Scobeyville
Chad Solomon, Midnight Rambler, Dallas
2 oz (60 ml) bonded apple brandy
¾ oz (22 ml) blanc vermouth
¼ oz (7 ml) Campari
¼ oz (7 ml) maraschino liqueur
2 drops saline solution (p 493)
Garnish: orange twist

Seesaw
The Fine Art of Mixing Drinks, *David A. Embury, 1948*
2 oz (60 ml) Cognac
½ oz (15 ml) dry vermouth
½ oz (15 ml) Bénédictine
3 dashes Angostura Bitters
Garnish: lemon twist

Serpent's Kiss
Michael Madrusan, The Everleigh, Melbourne, 2018
1½ oz (45 ml) Pommeau de Normandie
½ oz (15 ml) Cognac
½ oz (15 ml) Islay Scotch
¼ oz (7 ml) Bénédictine
Garnish: cherry

Sidecar Special
Burke's Complete Cocktail & Drinking Recipes, *Harman Burney Burke, 1934*
1½ oz (45 ml) Cognac
½ oz (15 ml) Pierre Ferrand Dry Curaçao
¼ oz (7 ml) maraschino liqueur
¼ oz (7 ml) triple sec
Garnish: lemon twist

Sidewinder
Phil Ward, Death & Co, NYC, 2008
2 oz (60 ml) Cognac
½ oz (15 ml) bonded apple brandy
¼ oz (7 ml) Bénédictine
¼ oz (7 ml) Yellow Chartreuse
1 dash absinthe
1 dash Peychaud's Aromatic Cocktail Bitters

Sir Knight
The How and When, *Hyman Gale and Gerald F. Marco, 1937*
2 oz (60 ml) Cognac
½ oz (15 ml) Green Chartreuse
½ oz (15 ml) triple sec
3 dashes Angostura Bitters
Garnish: orange twist

Star
(aka **Klondike** or **Farmer's Wife**)
The Fine Art of Mixing Drinks, *David A. Embury, 1948*
2 oz (60 ml) bonded apple brandy
1 oz (30 ml) dry vermouth
3 dashes Angostura Bitters
Garnish: lemon twist

Add all ingredients to a mixing glass, then stir with ice and strain into a frozen coupe.

Starboy
Zachary Gelnaw-Rubin, Lion Lion, NYC, 2018
1 oz (30 ml) bonded apple brandy
1 oz (30 ml) rye whiskey
1 oz (30 ml) Cocchi Americano
2 dashes Angostura Bitters
Garnish: lemon twist

Star Cocktail
Hoffman House Bartender's Guide, *Charles S. Mahoney, 1905*
2 oz (60 ml) bonded apple brandy
¾ oz (22 ml) dry vermouth
¼ oz (7 ml) Pierre Ferrand Dry Curaçao
2 dashes Angostura Bitters
Garnish: lemon twist

Vanderbilt Cocktail
Cocktails: How to Mix Them, *Robert Vermeire, 1922*
2¼ oz (67 ml) Cognac
¾ oz (22 ml) Heering Cherry Liqueur
3 dashes Angostura Bitters
Garnish: lemon twist

Wells Cocktail
Louis' Mixed Drinks, *Louis Muckensturm, 1906*
1½ oz (45 ml) Cognac
½ oz (15 ml) white crème de menthe
½ oz (15 ml) Fernet-Branca
½ oz (15 ml) crème de cassis
Garnish: lemon twist

Widow's Kiss
Modern American Drinks, *George J. Kappeler, 1895*
2 oz (60 ml) bonded apple brandy
½ oz (15 ml) Yellow Chartreuse
½ oz (15 ml) Bénédictine
3 dashes Angostura Bitters
Garnish: cherry
▼ Swap Yellow Chartreuse for Green Chartreuse to make the **Widow's Kiss No. 2**.

Yale Fence
The Fine Art of Mixing Drinks, *David A. Embury, 1948*
1 oz (30 ml) bonded apple brandy
1 oz (30 ml) sweet vermouth
1 oz (30 ml) gin
Garnish: lemon twist

Young Man's Cocktail
The How and When, *Hyman Gale and Gerald F. Marco, 1937*
2 oz (60 ml) Cognac
¾ oz (22 ml) dry vermouth
¼ oz (7 ml) Pierre Ferrand Dry Curaçao
2 dashes Angostura Bitters
Garnish: cherry

RUM & CANE SPIRIT

Arawak
Bartender's Guide, *Trader Vic, 1947*
2 oz (60 ml) Jamaican dark rum
1 oz (30 ml) Cream Sherry
2 dashes Angostura Bitters
Garnish: cherry

Beachcomber's Gold
(Perfect Manhattan with dark rum)
Jones' Complete Barguide, *Stan Jones, 1977*
2 oz (60 ml) aged dark rum
½ oz (15 ml) sweet vermouth
½ oz (15 ml) dry vermouth
3 dashes Angostura Bitters
Garnish: lemon twist

Betsy Flanagan
(Sweet Manhattan with Jamaican dark rum)
The Fine Art of Mixing Drinks, *David A. Embury, 1948*
2 oz (60 ml) Jamaican dark rum
1 oz (30 ml) sweet vermouth
3 dashes Angostura Bitters
Garnish: cherry

Bywater
Chris Hannah, Arnaud's, New Orleans, 2007
1¾ oz (52 ml) aged dark rum
¾ oz (22 ml) Amaro Averna
½ oz (15 ml) Green Chartreuse
¼ oz (7 ml) falernum
1 orange twist, in mixing glass
2 dashes Peychaud's Aromatic Cocktail Bitters
2 dashes orange bitters
Garnish: cherry

Chairman's Refresher
Jim Meehan, PDT, NYC, 2010
1½ oz (45 ml) light rum
½ oz (15 ml) Frangelico
2 oz (60 ml) coconut water
3 cucumber wheels
Press cucumber with Frangelico in a mixing glass, add remaining ingredients, then stir with ice and fine strain into a frozen coupe.
Garnish: cucumber wheel

Chinese Cocktail
Frank P. Newman
"Harry" of Ciro's ABC of Mixing Cocktails, *Harry MacElhone, 1923*
1½ oz (45 ml) Jamaican dark rum
¼ oz (7 ml) Pierre Ferrand Dry Curaçao
¼ oz (7 ml) maraschino liqueur
½ oz (15 ml) grenadine (p 496)
3 dashes Angostura Bitters
Garnish: cherry

Cigalon
Jones' Complete Barguide, *Stan Jones, 1977*
2 oz (60 ml) aged dark rum
¾ oz (22 ml) sweet vermouth
¼ oz (7 ml) maraschino liqueur
2 dashes orange bitters
Garnish: cherry

Club Cocktail
1¾ oz (52 ml) aged dark rum
½ oz (15 ml) sweet vermouth
½ oz (15 ml) dry vermouth
¼ oz (7 ml) maraschino liqueur
3 dashes Angostura Bitters
Garnish: cherry

Add all ingredients to a mixing glass, then stir with ice and strain into a frozen coupe.

Dark Hand
Yao Wong, The Elysian, Melbourne, 2020
2 oz (60 ml) aged dark rum
¾ oz (22 ml) sweet vermouth
⅜ oz (11 ml) Amaro Lucano
1 dash orange bitters
Garnish: orange twist

Dunlop Cocktail
"Harry" of Ciro's ABC of Mixing Cocktails, *Harry MacElhone, 1923*
1 oz (30 ml) aged dark rum
1 oz (30 ml) Manzanilla Sherry
¾ oz (22 ml) Jamaican dark rum
¼ oz (7 ml) simple syrup
3 dashes Angostura Bitters
Garnish: lemon twist

Dust Jacket
David Molyneux, The Everleigh, Melbourne, 2017
1¾ oz (52 ml) aged dark rum
¾ oz (22 ml) Manzanilla Sherry
½ oz (15 ml) Amaro Ramazzotti
1 teaspoon (5 ml) maraschino liqueur

East India Trading Co.
Brian Miller, Death & Co, NYC, 2009
1¾ oz (52 ml) Jamaican dark rum
¾ oz (22 ml) Lustau East India Solera Sherry
½ oz (15 ml) Amaro Ramazzotti
2 drops Bittermens Xocolatl Mole Bitters

Fair and Warmer Cocktail
Recipes for Mixed Drinks, *Hugo R. Ensslin, 1916*
2 oz (60 ml) light rum
½ oz (15 ml) sweet vermouth
½ oz (15 ml) Pierre Ferrand Dry Curaçao
Garnish: lemon twist

Flapper
(Dry Manhattan with Jamaican dark rum)
The Old Waldorf-Astoria Bar Book, *Albert Stevens Crockett, 1935*
2 oz (60 ml) Jamaican dark rum
1 oz (30 ml) dry vermouth
3 dashes Angostura Bitters
Garnish: orange twist and cherry

Fluffy Ruffles
(Sweet Manhattan with aged dark rum and a lime twist)
Recipes for Mixed Drinks, *Hugo R. Ensslin, 1916*
2 oz (60 ml) aged dark rum
1 oz (30 ml) sweet vermouth
3 dashes Angostura Bitters
Garnish: lime twist
● Add 2 dashes of orange bitters to make the **Palmer Cocktail** from *A Life-Time Collection of 688 Recipes for Drinks*, 1934.

Foreign Legion
Brandon Bramhall, Attaboy, Nashville, 2021
1½ oz (45 ml) Jamaican dark rum
1 oz (30 ml) Select Aperitivo
½ oz (15 ml) Green Chartreuse
Garnish: orange twist

Georgetown Club Cocktail
The South American Gentleman's Companion, *Charles H. Baker Jr., 1951*
2 oz (60 ml) aged dark rum
¾ oz (22 ml) dry vermouth
1 teaspoon (5 ml) falernum
Garnish: orange twist

Guatemalan Square
I'm Just Here for the Drinks, *Sother Teague, 2018*
1 oz (30 ml) aged dark rum (preferably Ron Zacapa No. 23)
½ oz (15 ml) rye whiskey
½ oz (15 ml) Carpano Antica Formula
¼ oz (7 ml) Pierre Ferrand Dry Curaçao
2 dashes Angostura Bitters
2 dashes Peychaud's Aromatic Cocktail Bitters
Garnish: orange twist

Handyman
Alastair Walker and Heather Garland, Caretaker, Auckland, 2020
1½ oz (45 ml) aged dark rum
¾ oz (22 ml) sweet vermouth
⅜ oz (11 ml) Campari
⅜ oz (11 ml) Tempus Fugit Crème de Cacao
Garnish: orange twist

Kingston
Felix Woods, The Everleigh, Melbourne, 2016
2 oz (60 ml) Jamaican dark rum
½ oz (15 ml) dry vermouth
¼ oz (7 ml) Amaro Montenegro
1 teaspoon (5 ml) Pierre Ferrand Dry Curaçao
Garnish: orange twist

Linchpin
David Molyneux, The Everleigh, Melbourne, 2017
1 oz (30 ml) Jamaican dark rum
1 oz (30 ml) aged dark rum
½ oz (15 ml) Pedro Ximénez
2 dashes orange bitters
Garnish: grapefruit twist

Palmetto Cocktail
The Savoy Cocktail Book, *Harry Craddock, 1930*
1½ oz (45 ml) aged dark rum
1½ oz (45 ml) sweet vermouth
2 dashes orange bitters

Presidente Cocktail
Manual del Cantinero, *John B. Escalante, 1915*
2 oz (60 ml) light rum
½ oz (15 ml) dry vermouth
½ oz (15 ml) Pierre Ferrand Dry Curaçao
1 teaspoon (5 ml) grenadine (p 496)
Garnish: orange twist and cherry

Prince
Cocktails by "Jimmy" Late of Ciro's London, *1930*
1¾ oz (52 ml) aged dark rum
¾ oz (22 ml) sweet vermouth
1 teaspoon (5 ml) white crème de menthe

Professor
Michael Madrusan, PDT, NYC, 2007
2 oz (60 ml) aged dark rum
¾ oz (22 ml) tawny Port
¼ oz (7 ml) sweet vermouth
1 dash Angostura Bitters
1 dash orange bitters
Garnish: orange twist
● Inspired by the Chancellor (p 350).

Add all ingredients to a mixing glass, then stir with ice and strain into a frozen coupe.

Right Hand
(See p 301)

Right-Hand Man
Alastair Walker, Caretaker, Auckland, 2020
2 oz (60 ml) aged dark um
½ oz (15 ml) dry vermouth
½ oz (15 ml) Cynar
Garnish: orange twist

Ron-Cacao Cocktail
Trader Vic's Bartender's Guide, *Trader Vic, 1947*
2 oz (60 ml) Jamaican dark rum
½ oz (15 ml) dry vermouth
½ oz (15 ml) Tempus Fugit Crème de Cacao

Sevilla Cocktail – 1
(Sweet Manhattan with light rum and an orange twist)
Trader Vic's Bartender's Guide, *Trader Vic, 1947*
2 oz (60 ml) light rum
1 oz (30 ml) sweet vermouth
3 dashes Angostura Bitters
Garnish: orange twist
● Swap the orange twist for a lime twist to make the **Chaparra** from *Bar La Florida Cocktails*, 1935.

Soundsystem
Chad Solomon, Midnight Rambler, Dallas, 2014
1½ oz (45 ml) Jamaican dark rum (preferably Hamilton Jamaican Pot Still Black Rum)
1¼ oz (37 ml) blanc vermouth
1 teaspoon (5 ml) Pierre Ferrand Dry Curaçao
¾ teaspoon (3.75 ml) kümmel
¼ teaspoon (1.25 ml) pimento (allspice) dram
2 drops saline solution (p 493)

The Chadburn
Martin Cate
Smuggler's Cove: Exotic Cocktails, Rum and the Cult of Tiki, *Martin and Rebecca Cate, 2016*
2 oz (60 ml) aged dark rum
½ oz (15 ml) tawny Port
½ oz (15 ml) pear liqueur
2 drops Bittermens Xocolatl Mole Bitters

The Mixologist
Elijah Harriss, The Everleigh, Melbourne, 2024
1½ oz (45 ml) aged dark rum
1 oz (30 ml) Amaro Averna
½ oz (15 ml) mezcal
3 dashes Angostura Bitters
Garnish: orange twist

Transmigration
Tom Lasher-Walker, Fresh Kills, NYC, 2017
¾ oz (22 ml) Goslings Black Seal Rum
¾ oz (22 ml) Cruzan Black Strap Rum
½ oz (15 ml) sweet vermouth
½ oz (15 ml) Cynar
½ oz (15 ml) coffee liqueur
Garnish: orange twist

Whist Cocktail
The Stork Club Bar Book, *Lucius Beebe, 1946*
1½ oz (45 ml) light rum
¾ oz (22 ml) sweet vermouth
¾ oz (22 ml) bonded apple brandy
Garnish: cherry

Yacht Club
The Fine Art of Mixing Drinks, *David A. Embury, 1948*
2 oz (60 ml) light rum
½ oz (15 ml) sweet vermouth
½ oz (15 ml) apricot brandy
Garnish: lemon twist

AGAVE

All Hands on Deck
Andrew Rice, Attaboy, NYC, 2015
1½ oz (45 ml) mezcal
½ oz (15 ml) sweet vermouth
½ oz (15 ml) Pierre Ferrand Dry Curaçao
½ oz (15 ml) Fernet-Branca
Garnish: orange twist

Añejo Manhattan
Ryan Magarian, Suite 410, Seattle, 2006
2 oz (60 ml) añejo tequila
½ oz (15 ml) sweet vermouth
¼ oz (7 ml) Licor 43
2 dashes orange bitters
2 dashes Angostura Bitters
Garnish: cherry

Another Sunken Boat
Phil Ward, The Long Island Bar, NYC, 2022
1½ oz (45 ml) mezcal
¾ oz (22 ml) Punt e Mes
½ oz (15 ml) Heering Cherry Liqueur
2 dashes absinthe
Garnish: cherry

Augie March
Phil Ward, Death & Co, NYC, 2008
2 oz (60 ml) reposado tequila
¾ oz (22 ml) sweet vermouth (preferably Carpano Antica Formula)
½ oz (15 ml) Cynar
Garnish: cherry

Black Dahlia
Liana Oster, NoMad London, London, 2021
1 oz (30 ml) mezcal
¾ oz (22 ml) Lustau Moscatel Emilín Sherry
½ oz (15 ml) overproof rye whiskey (preferably Rittenhouse Straight Rye Whisky)
½ oz (15 ml) Amaro Nardini
½ oz (15 ml) Grand Marnier
1 dash grapefruit bitters
Garnish: grapefruit twist

Add all ingredients to a mixing glass, then stir with ice and strain into a frozen coupe.

Blood of My Enemies (Alastair Walker Recipe)
Alastair Walker, Caretaker, Auckland, 2020
2 oz (60 ml) mezcal
½ oz (15 ml) Punt e Mes
½ oz (15 ml) Cappelletti Aperitivo
Garnish: cherry

Broken Oath
Eryn Reece, Death & Co, NYC, 2013
1½ oz (45 ml) mezcal
¾ oz (22 ml) sweet vermouth
¾ oz (22 ml) Amontillado Sherry
½ oz (15 ml) coffee liqueur
2 drops Bittermens Xocolatl Mole Bitters

Darkness Calls
Trevor Shores, Death & Co, Denver, 2023
1¼ oz (37 ml) reposado tequila
¾ oz (22 ml) Punt e Mes
½ oz (15 ml) Demerara rum
½ oz (15 ml) Campari
¼ oz (7 ml) Tempus Fugit Crème de Cacao
Garnish: orange twist

Elefante
Leo Robitschek, The NoMad Bar, NYC
1½ oz (45 ml) blanco tequila
½ oz (15 ml) blanc vermouth
½ oz (15 ml) triple sec
½ oz (15 ml) Punt e Mes
¼ oz (7 ml) Luxardo Amaro Abano

Nighthawks
Eryn Reece, Banzarbar, NYC, 2018
1½ oz (45 ml) mezcal
¾ oz (22 ml) Amontillado Sherry
½ oz (15 ml) sweet vermouth
¼ oz (7 ml) coffee liqueur
1 teaspoon (5 ml) Ancho Reyes Original
1 dash Bittermens Xocolatl Mole Bitters
● Riff on her own 'Broken Oath' cocktail.

No. 8
Daniel Eun, PDT, NYC, 2008
1¾ oz (52 ml) reposado tequila
¾ oz (22 ml) Palo Cortado Sherry
½ oz (15 ml) Bärenjäger Honey Liqueur
2 dashes orange bitters
Garnish: lemon twist

Palo Negro
Spirits of Latin America, *Ivy Mix, 2020*
2 oz (60 ml) reposado tequila
1 oz (30 ml) Palo Cortado Sherry
½ oz (15 ml) Cruzan Black Strap Rum
1 teaspoon (5 ml) Grand Marnier
1 teaspoon (5 ml) Demerara syrup (p 495)
Garnish: orange twist

Remember the Alamo
The Canon Cocktail Book, *Jamie Boudreau and James O. Fraioli, 2016*
1¾ oz (52 ml) reposado tequila
1 oz (30 ml) sweet vermouth
¼ oz (7 ml) Heering Cherry Liqueur
2 dashes absinthe
2 dashes Angostura Bitters
Garnish: cherry

Teatro
I'm Just Here for the Drinks, *Sother Teague, 2018*
1½ oz (45 ml) blanco tequila
¾ oz (45 ml) Green Chartreuse
¾ oz (22 ml) sweet vermouth
2 dashes orange bitters
Garnish: cherry

The Real Deal
Eryn Reece, Mayahuel, NYC, 2005
1½ oz (45 ml) mezcal
¾ oz (22 ml) Punt e Mes
¾ oz (22 ml) sweet vermouth
1 teaspoon (5 ml) Fernet-Branca

FORTIFIED & LIQUEUR

Among Dreams
Turk Dietrich, Cure, New Orleans
2 oz (60 ml) Carpano Antica Formula
½ oz (15 ml) rye whiskey
½ oz (15 ml) Green Chartreuse
9 drops Bittermens Elemakule Tiki Bitters
3 dashes Fee Brothers Old Fashion Aromatic Bitters

Cease and Desist
Maksym Pazuniak, Cure, New Orleans, 2009
2 oz (60 ml) Punt e Mes
1 oz (30 ml) rye whiskey
1 teaspoon (5 ml) Fernet-Branca
Garnish: orange twist

Guggenheimer Cocktail
Jack's Manual, *J.A. Grohusko, 1908*
2¾ oz (82 ml) sweet vermouth
¼ oz (7 ml) Fernet-Branca
Garnish: lemon twist

Long-Range Cocktail
Modern American Drinks, *George J. Kappeler, 1895*
2 oz (60 ml) sweet vermouth
1 oz (30 ml) Cognac
3 dashes absinthe
3 dashes Peychaud's Aromatic Cocktail Bitters
Garnish: lemon twist

Manhattan Reverse
Michael Madrusan, The Everleigh, Melbourne, 2021
1½ oz (45 ml) sweet vermouth
1 oz (30 ml) Scotch
½ oz (15 ml) full-bodied dry red wine (preferably durif or shiraz)
Garnish: cherry

1910
Ezra Star, Drink, Boston, 2010
1 oz (30 ml) sweet vermouth
¾ oz (22 ml) mezcal
¾ oz (22 ml) Cognac
½ oz (15 ml) maraschino liqueur
2 dashes Peychaud's Aromatic Cocktail Bitters
Garnish: orange twist

Add all ingredients to a mixing glass, then stir with ice and strain into a frozen coupe.

Power Move
ms. franky marshall, NYC, 2024
1½ oz (45 ml) Pineau des Charentes Rouge
1¼ oz (37 ml) rye whiskey
¼ teaspoon (1.25 ml) Cappelletti Amaro Sfumato Rabarbaro
Garnish: candied grapefruit (optional)

Royalist
Café Royal Cocktail Book, *W.J. Tarling, 1937*
1 oz (45 ml) dry vermouth
¾ oz (22 ml) bourbon
¾ oz (22 ml) Bénédictine
2 dashes peach bitters
Garnish: lemon twist

Session Manhattan
Session Cocktails, *Drew Lazor, 2018*
1 oz (30 ml) sweet vermouth
¾ oz (22 ml) rye whiskey
¾ oz (22 ml) Amontillado Sherry
½ oz (15 ml) dry vermouth
3 dashes Angostura Bitters
Garnish: lemon twist

Stifferino
W.C. Weaver
Barflies and Cocktails, *Harry MacElhone, 1927*
¾ oz (22 ml) Fernet-Branca
¾ oz (22 ml) dry vermouth
¾ oz (22 ml) sweet vermouth
¼ oz (7 ml) Cognac
Garnish: orange twist

The Dunaway
Misty Kalkofen, Boston, 2010
2¼ oz (67 ml) Fino Sherry
½ oz (15 ml) Cynar
¼ oz (7 ml) maraschino liqueur
2 dashes Angostura Bitters
Garnish: lemon twist (discard)

Vanishing Point
Alicia Perry and Anthony Schmidt, The Gutter, San Diego, 2023
1½ oz (45 ml) Amontillado Sherry
1 oz (30 ml) sweet vermouth
½ oz (15 ml) Fino Sherry
1 teaspoon (5 ml) Islay Scotch
Garnish: grapefruit twist

Velvet Glove
L.V. Battersby
Café Royal Cocktail Book, *W.J. Tarling, 1937*
1½ oz (45 ml) Cocchi Americano
1 oz (30 ml) Cognac
½ oz (15 ml) Tempus Fugit Crème de Cacao
Garnish: lemon twist

Washington Cocktail
Hoffman House Bartender's Guide, *Charles S. Mahoney, 1905*
2 oz (60 ml) dry vermouth
1 oz (30 ml) Cognac
3 dashes Angostura Bitters
Garnish: lemon twist

From *The Old Waldorf-Astoria Bar Book* (1935):

Drink today, and drown all sorrow.
You shall perhaps not do it tomorrow.
Best while you have it, use your breath—
there is no drinking after death!

Add all ingredients to a mixing glass, then stir with ice and strain into a frozen coupe.

OLD FASHIONED & SAZERAC

Old Fashioned p 366 (left), Sazerac p 366 (right)

Old Fashioned & Sazerac

Robust, traditionally whisk(e)y-led cocktails balanced with sugar and bitters.

OLD FASHIONED

spirit + sugar + bitters

Build all ingredients in an Old Fashioned glass, then add ice.

SAZERAC

rye whiskey/Cognac + sugar + bitters + absinthe

Fill a small Old Fashioned glass with crushed ice, add four dashes of absinthe and set aside to chill. Add the sugar cube, bitters and soda to a frozen mixing glass and crush the sugar. Add spirit and ice, then stir until ice cold, ensuring that sugar granules are well mixed but take care not to over-dilute. Strain the absinthe into a chilled shot glass, discard the ice and strain the cocktail into the small Old Fashioned glass. Express a lemon twist over the cocktail, then lay the peel across the rim and serve the cocktail along with the absinthe shot as a sidecar.

The Old Fashioned is the original cocktail in its simplest form: a combination of spirit, sugar, water and bitters, first defined as such in 1806. Back then, what we now recognise as an Old Fashioned was known simply as a Whiskey Cocktail, which featured American whiskey, although gin and brandy variants were popular alternatives. By 1850, bartenders were experimenting with the format, giving rise to 'Fancy Cocktails', enhanced by the inclusion of liqueurs like curaçao and maraschino, or even Chartreuse and absinthe, many of which were served up with a citrus twist. This marked the start of the Whiskey Cocktail's evolution.

By the 1870s, American mixology was in full force, and the Old Fashioned was commonplace, made with a split base of spirit and vermouth – a formula that sparked two era-defining classics, the Manhattan (p 334) and the Martini (p 304). Those who preferred their cocktail with the traditional proportions would ask for an 'Old Fashioned Cocktail', a name that became synonymous with the spirituous drink served over ice in a weighted tumbler, which soon became known as an Old Fashioned glass.

Not even 100 years on, by the second half of the 1900s, the Old Fashioned had taken the form of a drink built on cheap whiskey and low-quality ice, with muddled citrus and maraschino cherries. What was once a cornerstone of cocktail culture had been severely diluted, but this dip in popularity didn't last long. By the start of the 21st century, old had become new again, and leading bartenders became invested in revisiting the early recipes and restoring the drink to its former glory. Today, the Old Fashioned is a cocktail that channels the ageless spirit of the 1806 original, one that sits proudly on bar menus worldwide and holds court among the most celebrated drinks in modern drinking culture.

→

The Sazerac might be considered a cousin of the Old Fashioned, a 'Fancy' deviation of the Whiskey Cocktail with an aromatic mix of rye whiskey and/or Cognac, plus sugar and bitters, served in an absinthe-rinsed glass. First stirred up in New Orleans sometime in the mid-1800s, it has become a totem of The Big Easy and a firm favourite among the cocktail cognoscenti. While the Sazerac and its variations are prepared and served somewhat differently to those in the Old Fashioned family, the similarities between the two in style, formula and origin are impossible to ignore.

This collection also includes a vast assortment of other cocktails that don't necessarily stick to the traditional Old Fashioned script, but will no doubt appeal to those who like their drinks direct, bold and precise, served on the rocks with little fanfare.

Old Fashioned

Early 1800s
2 oz (60 ml) spirit
1 white sugar cube
3 dashes Angostura Bitters
1 teaspoon (5 ml) soda

Press sugar cube with soda in an Old Fashioned glass, then build all ingredients and add ice.
Garnish: orange twist and lemon twist

Sazerac

Merchants Exchange Coffee House, New Orleans, mid-1800s
2 oz (60 ml) rye whiskey or Cognac
1 white sugar cube
3 dashes Peychaud's Aromatic Cocktail Bitters
1 teaspooon (5 ml) soda
4 dashes absinthe, to rinse

Fill a small Old Fashioned glass with crushed ice, add four dashes of absinthe and set aside to chill. Add the sugar cube, bitters and soda to a frozen mixing glass and crush the sugar. Add spirit and ice, then stir until ice cold, ensuring that sugar granules are well mixed but take care not to over-dilute. Strain the absinthe into a chilled shot glass, discard the ice and strain the cocktail into the small Old Fashioned glass. Express a lemon twist over the cocktail, then lay the peel across the rim and serve the cocktail along with the absinthe shot as a sidecar.
Garnish: lemon twist (expressed and rested on the glass)

ESSENTIAL VARIATIONS

Improved Whiskey Cocktail

The Bar-Tender's Guide, *Jerry Thomas, 1876*
2 oz (60 ml) rye whiskey
¼ oz (7 ml) maraschino liqueur
2 dashes absinthe
2 dashes Peychaud's Aromatic Cocktail Bitters

Build all ingredients in an Old Fashioned glass, then add ice.
Garnish: lemon twist

The Improved Whiskey Cocktail is included in an appendix to the 1876 edition of *The Bar-Tender's Guide* by Jerry Thomas. He applied a novel way of categorising well-known drinks to this edition, incorporating adaptations of classics he described as 'Improved' or 'Fancy'. As there were far fewer cocktails in circulation during these early days of American mixology, this new classification was significant; essentially, Thomas was formalising a process many bartenders were likely already experimenting with by the late 1800s, subtly altering original drinks to cater to different palates or requests. Given the modest repertoire at the time, the drinks didn't necessarily demand original names, and any of them could be 'Improved' or made 'Fancy' by subtle additions like small measures of liqueur and/or bitters. By the end of the century, as the canon grew, these terms faded as each cocktail variation received its own unique name for clarity.

The evolution of the cocktail, of course, has largely depended on simple but substantial riffs to straightforward, well-balanced formulas. When a drink only requires two or three core ingredients, adding even a dash or two of bitters, liqueur or absinthe can make a tremendous difference to flavour and overall balance. The Improved Whiskey Cocktail advances the traditional Old Fashioned with a bit of maraschino liqueur, and a few drops of absinthe bring it closer to the New Orleans specialty, the Sazerac. It's a drink that's tailor-made for those who appreciate dry and spicy whiskey cocktails, with a preference for them over ice. Topflight variations include Dan Greenbaum's Improved New York Cocktail (p 377) from 2016 – which splits the base between rye whiskey and Cognac – as well as the Mardi Gras (p 378) from Irvin S. Cobb's 1936 recipe book, a Sazerac sibling featuring the addition of Angostura Bitters, served on the rocks.

Vieux Carré Cocktail

Walter Bergeron, Hotel Monteleone, New Orleans, 1930s
Famous New Orleans Drinks and How to Mix 'Em, *Stanley Clisby Arthur, 1937*

1 oz (30 ml) rye whiskey
1 oz (30 ml) Cognac
1 oz (30 ml) sweet vermouth
1 teaspoon (5 ml) Bénédictine
2 dashes Angostura Bitters
2 dashes Peychaud's Aromatic Cocktail Bitters

Build all ingredients in an Old Fashioned glass, then add ice.
Garnish: lemon twist and cherry
▼ Switch out the Cognac for Jamaican Pot Still rum to get **Près du Quai**.

This is the cocktail that Walter Bergeron, Head Bartender of the Hotel Monteleone Cocktail Lounge, takes special pride in mixing. He originated it, he says, to do honour to the famed Vieux Carré, that part of New Orleans where the antique shops and the iron lace balconies give sightseers a glimpse into the romance of another day.

With an assertive base comprising rye whiskey, Cognac and sweet vermouth, the Vieux Carré Cocktail is an indulgent sipper that argues you can in fact have it all. The drink is an obvious descendant of the Manhattan and the 'Improved' or 'Fancy' Whiskey Cocktail, created in the 1930s by Walter Bergeron, the legendary head bartender at the Hotel Monteleone in New Orleans. What sets it apart is a splash of Bénédictine, which brings herbal complexity to the core trio of ingredients, and the use of both Angostura and Peychaud's Aromatic Cocktail Bitters for even more depth.

Although the bracer is classified by the International Bartenders Association as an 'unforgettable' classic, it remains one of the lesser-known heroes in New Orleans' rich cocktail history. 'Vieux Carré' is French for 'old square' and is a reference to the Crescent City's famed French Quarter, alleged to be Bergeron's source of inspiration. In 1937's *Famous New Orleans Drinks and How to Mix 'Em* – where the recipe was first published – columnist and historian Stanley Clisby Arthur notes that Bergeron took 'special pride in mixing' the drink and originated it 'to do honor to ... that part of New Orleans where the antique shops and the iron lace balconies give sightseers a glimpse into the romance of another day'.

For another equally classy and characterful New Orleans cocktail, try the impeccable Manhattan variation, Cocktail à La Louisiane (p 338), which also features Bénédictine and Peychaud's Aromatic Cocktail Bitters and appears in Arthur's 1937 volume. For a simpler drink with a little spice, look to Crosby Gaige's The Battle of New Orleans (p 379), an Old Fashioned with bourbon, absinthe and both Peychaud's and orange bitters from 1941.

Old Fashioned

Build all ingredients in an Old Fashioned glass, then add ice.

GIN

Alberto
A.J. Smith
Café Royal Cocktail Book, *W.J. Tarling, 1937*
1 oz (30 ml) gin
¾ oz (22 ml) Manzanilla Sherry
¾ oz (22 ml) Cocchi Americano
1 teaspoon (5 ml) triple sec
Garnish: orange twist

Angler's Cocktail
Bariana, *Louis Fouquet, 1896*
2 oz (60 ml) gin (or genever)
½ oz (15 ml) raspberry syrup (p 500)
2 dashes orange bitters
2 dashes Angostura Bitters
Garnish: lemon twist

Arrow Through Me
Andrew Cordero, Seneca, San Diego, 2022
1 oz (30 ml) gin
1 oz (30 ml) Cappelletti Pasubio Vino Amaro
1 oz (30 ml) Cocchi Americano
Garnish: lemon twist

Berkeley Hotel Cocktail
"Dick" of the Berkeley
An Anthology of Cocktails, *1930s*
¾ oz (22 ml) gin
¾ oz (22 ml) dry vermouth
¾ oz (22 ml) Liquore Strega
Garnish: lemon twist

Coaster
(Pink Gin on the rocks)
"Harry" of Ciro's ABC of Mixing Cocktails, *Harry MacElhone, 2006*
2 oz (60 ml) gin
5 dashes Angostura Bitters
Garnish: lemon twist
● Michael's drink of 2013.

Derby No. 2
2 oz (60 ml) gin
2 dashes Peychaud's Aromatic Cocktail Bitters
Garnish: lemon twist and mint sprig

Elder Fashion
Phil Ward, Death & Co, NYC, 2007
2 oz (60 ml) gin
½ oz (15 ml) St Germain Elderflower Liqueur
2 dashes orange bitters
Garnish: grapefruit twist

Gin Bride-on-the-Rocks
The South American Gentleman's Companion, *Charles H. Baker Jr., 1951*
2 oz (60 ml) gin
2 dashes orange bitters
1 dash orange blossom water
Garnish: orange twist

"K.T."
Approved Cocktails, *United Kingdom Bartenders' Guild, 1937*
2 oz (60 ml) gin
¾ oz (22 ml) kola tonic
3 dashes Angostura Bitters
Garnish: lemon twist

Navy Strength Old Fashioned
Dan Smith, Queen Mary Tavern, Chicago
1 oz (30 ml) navy strength gin (preferably Hayman's Royal Dock Gin)
1 oz (30 ml) Jamaican dark rum (preferably Smith & Cross Traditional Jamaica Rum)
¾ teaspoon (3.75 ml) Demerara syrup (p 495)
2 dashes Angostura Bitters
1 drop saline solution (p 493)
Garnish: orange twist

Nice Legs
Chris Bostick, Half Step, Austin, 2011
1½ oz (45 ml) gin
¾ oz (22 ml) Barolo Chinato
½ oz (15 ml) Suze
Garnish: orange twist

Promises Promises
Nick Jarrett, Cure, New Orleans, 2015
1½ oz (45 ml) gin
¾ oz (22 ml) Cocchi Americano
¼ oz (7 ml) Giffard Crème de Pamplemousse Rose
1 dash Bittermens Grapefruit Bitters
Garnish: orange twist

Secret Service
I'm Just Here for the Drinks, *Sother Teague, 2018*
1½ oz (45 ml) Plymouth Gin
¾ oz (22 ml) Maurin Quina
¾ oz (22 ml) Ancho Reyes Original
2 drops Bittermens Xocolatl Mole Bitters
Garnish: orange twist

Spanish Steps
David Molyneux, The Everleigh, Melbourne, 2016
¾ oz (22 ml) gin
¾ oz (22 ml) Campari
½ oz (15 ml) coffee liqueur
½ oz (15 ml) tawny Port
Garnish: orange twist

Yellow Submarine
The Connaught Bar, *Agostino Perrone, Giorgio Bargiani & Maura Milia, 2024*
1¾ oz (52 ml) gin
¾ oz (22 ml) Fino Sherry
½ oz (15 ml) Galliano L'Autentico
2 dashes celery bitters
Garnish: lemon twist and cucumber ribbon

RUM & CANE SPIRIT

Archbishop
Brandon Bramhall, Attaboy, Nashville, 2017
1½ oz (45 ml) pot still Jamaican dark rum (preferably Smith & Cross Traditional Jamaica Rum)
1 oz (30 ml) Campari
½ oz (15 ml) Green Chartreuse
Garnish: orange twist

Build all ingredients in an Old Fashioned glass, then add ice.

Away Colours
Zachary Gelnaw-Rubin, Lion Lion, NYC, 2016
1½ oz (45 ml) aged dark rum
⅜ oz (11 ml) Fernet-Branca
⅜ oz (11 ml) Tempus Fugit Crème de Banane
Garnish: orange twist

Batiste
Jones' Complete Barguide, *Stan Jones, 1977*
¾ oz (22 ml) Jamaican dark rum
¾ oz (22 ml) aged dark rum
½ oz (15 ml) Pierre Ferrand Dry Curaçao
3 dashes Angostura Bitters
Garnish: orange twist

BBC
Marian Beke, Artesian, London, 2009
2 oz (60 ml) aged dark rum
½ oz (15 ml) Becherovka Original
1 dash wormwood bitters
Garnish: apple fan

Blood of My Enemies
Erick Castro, Boilermaker, NYC, 2014
1 oz (30 ml) aged dark rum
1 oz (30 ml) Amaro Montenegro
1 oz (30 ml) Punt e Mes
Garnish: lemon twist

Caribbean Cricket
Matt Clark, Dutch Kills, NYC, 2019
1 oz (30 ml) Cruzan Black Strap Rum
1 oz (30 ml) sweet vermouth
½ oz (15 ml) aged dark rum
½ oz (15 ml) Fernet-Branca
¼ oz (7 ml) Tempus Fugit Crème de Cacao
Garnish: mint sprig and orange twist

Chet Baker
Sam Ross, Milk & Honey, NYC, 2005
1½ oz (45 ml) aged dark rum
⅓ oz (10 ml) sweet vermouth
1 teaspoon (5 ml) honey syrup (p 496)
3 dashes Angostura Bitters
Garnish: orange twist

Chet Faker
Tom Lasher-Walker, Fresh Kills, NYC, 2016
2 oz (60 ml) aged dark rum
⅓ oz (10 ml) Tempus Fugit Crème de Banane
1 teaspoon (5 ml) honey syrup (p 496)
3 drops Bittermens Xocolatl Mole Bitters
2 drops saline solution (p 493)
Garnish: orange twist

Corn 'n' Oil
Barbados, 1700s
2 oz (60 ml) Aged Barbados dark rum
½ oz (15 ml) falernum
3 dashes Angostura Bitters
2 lime wedges
Squeeze a lime wedge and drop it into an Old Fashioned glass. Add the remaining ingredients, except the second lime wedge, and stir to combine. Add cracked ice and stir. Squeeze the second lime wedge and drop it into the drink.
Garnish: lime wedge

Cuevas
Dane Barca
Smuggler's Cove: Exotic Cocktails, Rum and the Cult of Tiki, *Martin and Rebecca Cate, 2016*
2 oz (60 ml) aged dark rum
½ oz (15 ml) sweet vermouth
¼ oz (7 ml) tawny Port
¼ oz (7 ml) cinnamon syrup (p 495)
Garnish: cherry

Double Agent
(aka **New Caledonia**)
Michael Madrusan, The Everleigh, Melbourne, 2013
1 oz (30 ml) aged dark rum
1 oz (30 ml) Cognac
1 brown sugar cube
2 dashes orange bitters
2 dashes Angostura Bitters
1 teaspooon (5 ml) soda
Garnish: orange twist

Encino Man
Brandon Bramhall, Attaboy, Nashville, 2021
¾ oz (22 ml) pot still Jamaican dark rum (preferably Smith & Cross Traditional Jamaica Rum)
¾ oz (22 ml) Cocchi Americano
¾ oz (22 ml) dry vermouth
¾ oz (22 ml) Amaro dell'Etna
Garnish: lemon twist

Expense Account
Peter Hill, Albert Street Cocktail Company, Winnipeg, 2015
½ oz (15 ml) aged dark rum
½ oz (15 ml) Cruzan Black Strap Rum
½ oz (15 ml) bonded apple brandy
¼ oz (7 ml) Bénédictine
¼ oz (7 ml) maple syrup
3 dashes absinthe
3 dashes orange bitters
Garnish: orange twist

Haitian Divorce
Tom Richter, The Beagle, NYC, 2011
1½ oz (45 ml) aged dark rum
¾ oz (22 ml) mezcal
½ oz (15 ml) Pedro Ximénez
3 dashes Angostura Bitters
Garnish: orange twist and lime twist

Hat in Hand
Alicia Lombardo and Meaghan Dorman, Raines Law Room at The William, NYC, 2015
1½ oz (45 ml) aged dark rum (preferably Ron Zacapa No. 23)
¾ oz (22 ml) Giffard Banane du Brésil et des Caraïbes
½ oz (15 ml) Cognac
2 dash Angostura Bitters
1 drop saline solution (p 493)
Garnish: orange twist

Island Old Fashioned
Michael Madrusan and Joseph Schwartz, Little Branch, NYC, 2009
2 oz (60 ml) aged dark rum
¼ oz (7 ml) falernum
2 dashes Angostura Bitters
2 dashes Dale DeGroff's Pimento Aromatic Bitters
Garnish: orange twist

Build all ingredients in an Old Fashioned glass, then add ice.

Linchpin

David Molyneux, The Everleigh, Melbourne, 2017

1 oz (30 ml) Jamaican dark rum
1 oz (30 ml) aged dark rum
½ oz (15 ml) Pedro Ximénez
2 dashes orange bitters
Garnish: grapefruit twist

Lion Tamer

Paul Hammond and Priscilla Leong

1¼ oz (37 ml) Goslings Black Seal Rum
⅓ oz (10 ml) pear eau de vie
½ oz (15 ml) pimento (allspice) dram
⅓ oz (10 ml) maple syrup
Garnish: gingersnap

Migration

Milk & Honey, NYC

¾ oz (22 ml) Goslings Black Seal Rum
¾ oz (22 ml) Cruzan Black Strap Rum
¾ oz (22 ml) Cynar
¾ oz (22 ml) sweet vermouth
Garnish: orange twist

Old Spice

Michael Madrusan, The Everleigh, Melbourne, 2020

2 oz (60 ml) spiced rum
¼ oz (7 ml) falernum (preferably Snug Harbor Company Old World Falernum)
¼ oz (7 ml) Demerara syrup (p 495)
2 dashes Angostura Bitters
2 drops Bittermens Elemakule Tiki Bitters
Garnish: orange twist and lime twist

Plátanos en Mole Old Fashioned

Jim Meehan, PDT, NYC, 2010

2 oz (60 ml) aged dark rum (preferably Ron Zacapa No. 23)
¼ oz (7 ml) Giffard Banane du Brésil et des Caraïbes
12 drops Bittermens Xocolatl Mole Bitters
Garnish: pinch of chilli powder

Près du Quai

(See p 368)

Rabo de Galo

São Paulo, 1950s

1¾ oz (52 ml) aged cachaça
¾ oz (22 ml) sweet vermouth
⅓ oz (10 ml) Cynar
Garnish: lime twist

Rum River Mystic

Paul McGee, Lost Lake, Chicago

1 oz (30 ml) aged dark rum
1 oz (30 ml) rye whiskey
¾ oz (22 ml) Byrrh Grand Quinquina
¼ oz (7 ml) Bénédictine
2 dashes Angostura Bitters
Garnish: orange twist (discard) and 2 dashes Bittermens Elemakule Tiki Bitters

Shadow Boxer

Ivy Mix, Leyenda, NYC, 2016

1½ oz (45 ml) cachaça (preferably Novo Fogo Silver Cachaça)
¾ oz (22 ml) dry vermouth
¾ oz (22 ml) Campari
¼ oz (7 ml) apricot eau de vie (preferably Blume Marillen)
¼ oz (7 ml) Giffard Crème de Pamplemousse Rose
Garnish: orange twist

Smuggler's Notch

Eric Alperin, The Varnish, Los Angeles

2 oz (60 ml) aged dark rum
1 brown sugar cube
2 dashes orange bitters
2 dashes absinthe
Garnish: orange twist

Spanish Town

Approved Cocktails, *United Kingdom Bartenders' Guild, 1937*

1½ oz (45 ml) aged dark rum
½ oz (15 ml) Pierre Ferrand Dry Curaçao
Garnish: freshly grated nutmeg

Tango Nuevo

The One-Bottle Cocktail, *Maggie Hoffman, 2018*

1½ oz (45 ml) aged dark rum
½ oz (15 ml) coffee liqueur
½ oz (15 ml) honey syrup (p 496)
Garnish: lemon twist and a pinch of smoked salt

Testadura

Richard Boccato, Dutch Kills, NYC, 2017

1½ oz (45 ml) aged dark rum
½ oz (15 ml) Cynar
¼ oz (7 ml) cinnamon syrup (p 495)
2 drops Bittermens Xocolatl Bitters
Garnish: orange twist

The Affiliate

Charles Joly, The Aviary, Chicago, 2013

1½ oz (45 ml) aged Cuban dark rum
¾ oz (22 ml) Fino Sherry
¾ oz (22 ml) Heering Cherry Liqueur
2 dashes Angostura Bitters
2 dashes orange bitters
Garnish: orange twist

Treacle

Dick Bradsell, London, 1990s

2 oz (60 ml) pot still Jamaican dark rum
¼ oz (7 ml) simple syrup
3 dashes Angostura Bitters
½ oz (15 ml) Royal Gala apple juice, to float

Build rum, simple syrup and bitters in a frozen double rocks glass, then add a large block of ice and float apple juice.

Garnish: orange twist

Worried About the Weather

Trevor Shores, Death & Co, Denver 2022

1½ oz (45 ml) light rum
¾ oz (22 ml) blanc vermouth
½ oz (15 ml) Blanche Armagnac
1 teaspoon (5 ml) génépy
1 teaspoon (5 ml) St. George Spiced Pear Liqueur
1 dash orange bitters
Garnish: grapefruit twist

Build all ingredients in an Old Fashioned glass, then add ice.

AGAVE

Aces and Eights
Jarred Weigand, Death & Co, NYC, 2016
2 oz (60 ml) reposado tequila
½ oz (15 ml) Amaro Meletti
1 teaspoon (5 ml) coffee liqueur (preferably Galliano Espresso)
1 teaspoon (5 ml) vanilla syrup (p 502)
1 dash Bittermens Xocolatl Mole Bitters
Garnish: orange twist

Agave Bravo
Chad Solomon, The Tar Pit, Los Angeles, 2008
1½ oz (45 ml) reposado tequila (preferably El Tesoro Reposado Tequila)
½ oz (15 ml) reposado mezcal (preferably Los Danzantes Reposado)
1 teaspoon (5 ml) Demerara syrup (p 495)
2 dashes Angostura Bitters
2 drops saline solution (p 493)
Garnish: grapefruit twist

Arinato
Spirits of Latin America: A Celebration of Culture & Cocktails, *Ivy Mix, 2020*
1½ oz (45 ml) mezcal (preferably espadín)
¾ oz (22 ml) Lillet Blanc
½ oz (15 ml) dry vermouth
¼ oz (7 ml) Yellow Chartreuse
½ teaspoon (2.5 ml) maraschino liqueur
2 dashes Peychaud's Aromatic Cocktail Bitters
Garnish: grapefruit twist

The Coffee House (Heartbreaker Recipe)
(See p 380)

Cover Cocktail
Zachary Pease, Attaboy, NYC
1½ oz (45 ml) blanco tequila
½ oz (15 ml) sweet vermouth
½ oz (15 ml) Amaro Braulio
½ oz (15 ml) Yellow Chartreuse
Garnish: orange twist
▼ Swap blanco tequila for reposado tequila to make the **Inside Job** by Zachary Pease, Attaboy, NYC.

Daydreamer
Joyce Chang, Bar Margaux, Melbourne, 2024
1½ oz (45 ml) blanco tequila
½ oz (15 ml) Liquore Strega
½ oz (15 ml) Pavan
2 dashes orange bitters
Garnish: grapefruit twist

Del Rio
Sam Ross, Attaboy, NYC, 2017
¾ oz (22 ml) blanco tequila
¾ oz (22 ml) Cocchi Americano
¾ oz (22 ml) St. George Bruto Americano
Garnish: lemon twist

El Barrio
Paul Hammond and Priscilla Leong
1 oz (30 ml) añejo tequila
¾ oz (22 ml) coffee liqueur
⅓ oz (10 ml) mezcal
⅓ oz (10 ml) Campari
⅓ oz (10 ml) Punt e Mes
Garnish: orange twist

Guillotine
ms. franky marshall, Le Boudoir, NYC, 2015
1 oz (30 ml) mezcal
¾ oz (22 ml) Scotch
¼ oz (7 ml) Giffard Banane du Brésil et des Caraïbes
¼ oz (7 ml) honey syrup (p 496)
Garnish: lemon twist (discard)

Mance Rayder
Erick Castro, Polite Provisions, San Diego, 2013
1½ oz (45 ml) reposado tequila
½ oz (15 ml) mezcal
½ oz (15 ml) sweet vermouth
½ oz (15 ml) Pierre Ferrand Dry Curaçao
2 dashes Angostura Bitters
2 dashes orange bitters
Garnish: lemon twist

Maravilla
José Cardenas, Raines Law Room, NYC, 2017
2 oz (60 ml) mezcal
½ oz (15 ml) white crème de cacao
¼ oz (7 ml) Cappelletti Amaro Sfumato Rabarbaro
2 dashes orange bitters
2 drops Bittermens Xocolatl Mole Bitters
Garnish: orange twist

Mezcaletti
Richard Boccato, Dutch Kills, NYC, 2015
1 oz (30 ml) mezcal
1 oz (30 ml) Amaro Meletti
2 dashes orange bitters
Garnish: lemon twist

Montañista
Brandon Bramhall, Attaboy, Nashville, 2017
1½ oz (45 ml) mezcal
¾ oz (22 ml) blanc vermouth
¾ oz (22 ml) Amaro Braulio
Garnish: grapefruit twist

Monte Carlos
Chris Bostick, The Varnish, Los Angeles
1½ oz (45 ml) blanco tequila
½ oz (15 ml) Bénédictine
2 dashes Angostura Bitters
Garnish: lemon twist

Nouveau Carré
Jonny Raglin, Absinthe Brasserie & Bar, San Francisco, 2005
1½ oz (45 ml) blanco tequila
½ oz (15 ml) Cocchi Americano
1 teaspoon (5 ml) Bénédictine
2 dashes Peychaud's Aromatic Cocktail Bitters
Garnish: lemon twist

Build all ingredients in an Old Fashioned glass, then add ice.

Oaxaca Old Fashioned
Phil Ward, Death & Co, NYC, 2008
1½ oz (45 ml) reposado tequila
½ oz (15 ml) mezcal
1 teaspoon (5 ml) agave syrup (p 494)
2 dashes Angostura Bitters
Garnish: orange twist

San Miguel
Jim Meehan, PDT, NYC, 2014
2 oz (60 ml) blanco tequila
1 teaspoon (5 ml) agave syrup (p 494)
2 dashes celery bitters
Garnish: grapefruit twist

Six Figure
Dan Greenbaum, Attaboy, NYC, 2016
1¼ oz (37 ml) mezcal
1¼ oz (37 ml) blanc vermouth
¼ oz (7 ml) Yellow Chartreuse
2 dashes orange bitters
Garnish: grapefruit twist

Spaghetti Western
Jessica Gonzalez, Death & Co, NYC, 2011
1 oz (30 ml) reposado tequila
¾ oz (22 ml) Amaro Nonino
½ oz (15 ml) mezcal
1 dash orange bitters
Garnish: grapefruit twist

Speedy Ximénez
Chris Bostick, Half Step, Austin, 2017
1½ oz (45 ml) blanco tequila
¾ oz (22 ml) Pedro Ximénez
Garnish: lemon twist

Spring Blossom
Gordan Bellaver, The Varnish, Los Angeles, 2018
1½ oz (45 ml) mezcal
¾ oz (22 ml) Suze
¾ oz (22 ml) blanc vermouth
2 dashes Bittermens Xocolatl Mole Bitters
Garnish: grapefruit twist

Tequila Gumption
Phil Ward, Mayahuel, NYC, 2010
1 oz (30 ml) blanco tequila
1 oz (30 ml) mezcal
¼ oz (7 ml) maraschino liqueur
2 dashes orange bitters
2 dashes Angostura Bitters
Garnish: lemon twist

Tequila Old Fashioned
Jake Down, This Must Be the Place, Sydney, 2017
1½ oz (45 ml) añejo tequila
½ oz (15 ml) agave syrup (p 494)
2 drops Bittermens Xocolatl Mole Bitters
½ oz (15 ml) Islay Scotch, to float
Build tequila, bitters and agave syrup in an Old Fashioned glass, then add ice and float Scotch.
Garnish: lemon twist

The Obligatory
Tim Philips-Johansson, Bulletin Place, Sydney
1 oz (30 ml) añejo tequila
¾ oz (22 ml) Punt e Mes
½ oz (15 ml) cold-brew coffee
¼ oz (7 ml) maple syrup
Garnish: orange twist

Villa Nova
Brynn Smith, Bar Next Door, Los Angeles, 2023
1 oz (30 ml) mezcal
1 oz (30 ml) Cocchi Americano
½ oz (15 ml) Amaro Meletti
½ oz (15 ml) Luxardo Bitter Bianco
Garnish: grapefruit twist and 2 smacked basil leaves
▼ Named for the famed restaurant now known as The Rainbow Bar & Grill.

Yerba Agave
Kirk Estopinal
2 oz (60 ml) añejo tequila
⅓ oz (10 ml) white crème de menthe
¼ oz (7 ml) agave syrup (p 494)
1 teaspoon (5 ml) Bénédictine
2 dashes Angostura Bitters
Garnish: mint sprig

Zone Amarillo
Mike Dolfini, Attaboy, Nashville, 2019
1 oz (30 ml) mezcal
1 oz (30 ml) reposado tequila
¾ oz (22 ml) Punt e Mes
¼ oz (7 ml) Yellow Chartreuse
2 dashes Angostura Bitters
2 dashes Peychaud's Aromatic Cocktail Bitters
Garnish: orange twist and cherry

AMERICAN WHISKEY

Act of Pardon
Andrew Cordero, The Reading Club, San Diego, 2022
1½ oz (45 ml) bourbon
½ oz (15 ml) pot still Jamaican dark rum
½ oz (15 ml) Pedro Ximénez
2 dashes orange bitters

African Flower
Becky McFalls-Schwartz, Little Branch, NYC, 2008
1½ oz (45 ml) bourbon
⅜ oz (11 ml) Amaro CioCiaro
⅜ oz (11 ml) Tempus Fugit Crème de Cacao
2 dashes orange bitters
Garnish: orange twist

Alcazar Cocktail
100 Cocktails: How to Mix Them, *"Bernard", 1958*
1½ oz (45 ml) rye whiskey
½ oz (15 ml) Bénédictine
2 dashes orange bitters
Garnish: lemon twist

Amber Old Fashioned
Meaghan Dorman, Raines Law Room, NYC, 2013
1 oz (30 ml) bourbon
1 oz (30 ml) aged dark rum
¼ oz (7 ml) simple syrup
2 dashes Angostura Bitters
1 dash peach bitters
Garnish: orange twist

Build all ingredients in an Old Fashioned glass, then add ice.

American Trilogy
Richard Boccato and Michael McIlroy, Milk & Honey, NYC, 2006
1 oz (30 ml) rye whiskey
1 oz (30 ml) bonded apple brandy
1 raw sugar cube
2 dashes orange bitters
1 teaspooon (5 ml) soda
Garnish: orange twist

Amor Amore
Wolf Alexander, The Varnish, Los Angeles, 2023
1½ oz (45 ml) rye whiskey
¾ oz (22 ml) Campari
¾ oz (22 ml) Amaro Ramazzotti
Garnish: orange twist

Approve
Approved Cocktails, *United Kingdom Bartenders' Guild, 1937*
1½ oz (45 ml) rye whiskey
¼ oz (7 ml) Pierre Ferrand Dry Curaçao
3 dashes Angostura Bitters
Garnish: lemon twist
● Swap rye whiskey for bourbon to make the **Talent Scout** from *Ted Saucier's Bottoms Up*, Ted Saucier, 1951.

Autumn Leaves
Jeffrey Morgenthaler, Clyde Common, Portland, 2007
¾ oz (22 ml) rye whiskey
¾ oz (22 ml) bonded apple brandy
¾ oz (22 ml) sweet vermouth
¼ oz (7 ml) Liquore Strega
1 dash Angostura Bitters
Garnish: orange twist

Back Stop
Dan Greenbaum, Diamond Reef, NYC, 2017
1½ oz (45 ml) bourbon
⅜ oz (11 ml) Amargo-Vallet
⅜ oz (11 ml) coffee liqueur
Garnish: orange twist

Base Camp
Matty Clark, Attaboy, NYC, 2017
1½ oz (45 ml) bourbon
⅜ oz (11 ml) Islay Scotch
¼ oz (7 ml) Tempus Fugit Crème de Cacao
¼ oz (7 ml) pimento (allspice) dram
2 dashes orange bitters
Garnish: lemon twist

Beekeeper
Giuseppe Gonzalez
2 oz (60 ml) bourbon
1 teaspoon (5 ml) honey syrup (p 496)
3 dashes Angostura Bitters
2 dashes absinthe
Garnish: lemon twist

Bellshire Old Fashioned
Mitchell Taylor, Attaboy, Nashville, 2018
1 oz (30 ml) rye whiskey
1 oz (30 ml) Cognac
1 teaspoon (5 ml) Bénédictine
1 teaspoon (5 ml) honey syrup (p 496)
2 dashes absinthe
Garnish: lemon twist

Black Barrel
Mitchell Taylor, Attaboy, Nashville, 2018
1½ oz (45 ml) rye whiskey
⅜ oz (11 ml) Amontillado Sherry
⅜ oz (11 ml) Amaro Averna
3 dashes Angostura Bitters
Garnish: lemon twist

Black Hawk
1700 Cocktails for the Man Behind the Bar, *R. de Fleury, 1934*
1½ oz (45 ml) rye whiskey
¾ oz (22 ml) sloe gin
Garnish: cherry

Blood, Sweat & Tears
Yao Wong, The Elysian, Melbourne, 2021
2 oz (60 ml) rye whiskey
⅜ oz (11 ml) Fernet-Branca
⅜ oz (11 ml) simple syrup
1 dash chocolate bitters
1 dash absinthe
Garnish: lemon twist

Campfire Old Fashioned
I'm Just Here for the Drinks, *Sother Teague, 2018*
¾ oz (22 ml) rye whiskey
¾ oz (22 ml) bourbon
¼ oz (7 ml) Islay Scotch
¼ oz (7 ml) cane syrup (p 494)
1 dash Angostura Bitters
1 dash Bittermens Hellfire Habanero Shrub
Garnish: orange twist

Carajillo Old Fashioned
Sean O'Connor-Combee, J & Tony's Discount Cured Meats and Negroni Warehouse, San Diego, 2022
1 oz (30 ml) rye whiskey
1 oz (30 ml) Cognac
¼ oz (7 ml) coffee liqueur
¼ oz (7 ml) Licor 43
Garnish: 3 coffee beans

Chamberlain
American Bar, *Frank P. Newman, 1900*
2 oz (60 ml) bourbon
¼ oz (7 ml) grenadine (p 496)
2 dashes absinthe
Garnish: orange twist

Coast Guard
Evan Hosaka, Electra Cocktail Club, Las Vegas, 2018
1½ oz (45 ml) rye whiskey
½ oz (15 ml) pear brandy
¼ oz (7 ml) Licor 43
1 teaspoon (5 ml) cane syrup (p 494)
2 dashes Angostura Bitters
Garnish: lemon twist and freshly grated cinnamon

Cock 'n Bull Special
The Cock 'n Bull, Los Angeles
Ted Saucier's Bottoms Up, *Ted Saucier, 1951*
1 oz (30 ml) bourbon
½ oz (15 ml) Cognac
½ oz (15 ml) Bénédictine
¼ oz (7 ml) triple sec
Garnish: orange twist
● Home of the Moscow Mule.

Build all ingredients in an Old Fashioned glass, then add ice.

Country Livin'
Evan Stroeve, The Waratah, Sydney, 2024
1½ oz (45 ml) bourbon
¾ oz (22 ml) Jamaican dark rum
¾ oz (22 ml) mandarin skin Port (p 504)
¼ oz (7 ml) honey syrup (p 496)
3 dashes orange bitters
Garnish: mandarin twist (discard)

Cut & Polish
(Rye Old Fashioned with Campari and absinthe)
David Molyneux and Cameron Parish, The Everleigh, Melbourne, 2019
1½ oz (45 ml) rye whiskey
¼ oz (7 ml) Campari
1 white sugar cube
3 dashes Angostura Bitters
2 dashes absinthe
1 teaspooon (5 ml) soda
Press sugar cube with soda in an Old Fashioned glass, then build all ingredients and add ice.
Garnish: orange twist

Dead Man's Hand
Greg Keesee, Attaboy, Nashville, 2022
1½ oz (45 ml) bourbon
½ oz (15 ml) sweet vermouth
½ oz (15 ml) Campari
½ oz (15 ml) Yellow Chartreuse
2 drops Bittermens Xocolatl Mole Bitters
Garnish: orange twist

Dealing Despair
Trevor Shores, Death & Co, Denver, 2023
1 oz (30 ml) bourbon
1 oz (30 ml) Armagnac
¾ oz (22 ml) sweet vermouth
1 teaspoon (5 ml) Giffard Crème de Pêche de Vigne
1 teaspoon (5 ml) Amaro Averna
2 dashes Angostura Bitters
Garnish: orange twist

Diamondback Lounge
Lord Baltimore Hotel, Baltimore
Ted Saucier's Bottoms Up, *Ted Saucier, 1951*
1½ oz (45 ml) rye whiskey
⅜ oz (11 ml) bonded apple brandy
⅜ oz (11 ml) Yellow Chartreuse
Garnish: cherry

Donkey Kong
Holly Graham, Tokyo Confidential, Tokyo, 2023
1½ oz (45 ml) bourbon (preferably Woodford Reserve Kentucky Straight Bourbon Whiskey)
¾ oz (22 ml) Tempus Fugit Crème de Banane
⅓ oz (10 ml) Marsala
2 drops The Japanese Bitters Umami Bitters
Garnish: dried banana chip

Double Header
Dan Greenbaum, Diamond Reef, NYC, 2017
1½ oz (45 ml) bourbon
½ oz (15 ml) Amontillado Sherry
½ oz (15 ml) apricot brandy
2 dashes Angostura Bitters
Garnish: lemon twist

Ed Dexter
Irvin S. Cobb's Own Recipe Book, *Irvin S. Cobb, 1936*
1½ oz (45 ml) bourbon
½ oz (15 ml) Pierre Ferrand Dry Curaçao
Garnish: orange twist and lemon twist
▼ "Named for a sincere drinker, and recommended only for such."

Fairbanks Cocktail
Jack's Manual, *J.A. Grohusko, 1908*
1½ oz (45 ml) rye whiskey
½ oz (15 ml) apricot brandy
3 dashes Angostura Bitters
1 teaspoon (5 ml) simple syrup
Garnish: lemon twist

Fancy Free
Crosby Gaige's Cocktail Guide and Ladies' Companion, *Crosby Gaige, 1941*
1½ oz (45 ml) bourbon
¼ oz (7 ml) maraschino liqueur
1 teaspoon (5 ml) simple syrup
2 dashes Angostura Bitters
2 dashes orange bitters
Garnish: orange twist

Fashionably Late
Brian Lee, Noble Experiment, San Diego, 2014
2 oz (60 ml) bourbon
½ oz (15 ml) Licor 43
2 dashes Angostura Bitters
Garnish: orange twist

Fedora
New and Improved Illustrated Bartender's Manual, *Harry Johnson, 1888*
¾ oz (22 ml) bourbon
¾ oz (22 ml) Jamaican dark rum
¾ oz (22 ml) Cognac
½ oz (15 ml) Pierre Ferrand Dry Curaçao
Garnish: lemon twist, orange twist and cherry

Five Year Plan
Summer Goff, Death & Co, Denver, 2023
1¼ oz (37 ml) bourbon
½ oz (15 ml) Armagnac (preferably Delord Armagnac VSOP)
¼ oz (7 ml) nocino
1 teaspoon (5 ml) cinnamon syrup (p 495)
1 dash The Bitter Truth Old Time Aromatic Bitters
Garnish: orange twist and lemon twist

Build all ingredients in an Old Fashioned glass, then add ice.

Fox River Cocktail

The Official Mixer's Manual, *Patrick Gavin Duffy, 1934*
1½ oz (45 ml) rye whiskey
½ oz (15 ml) Tempus Fugit Crème de Cacao
2 dashes peach bitters
Garnish: lemon twist
Swap rye whiskey for bourbon to make the **Kentucky River** in *Just Cocktails*, W. C. Whitfield, 1939.

Fredo Corleone

Lorenzo Antinori, Bar Leone, Hong Kong, 2023
1 oz (30 ml) rye whiskey
1 oz (30 ml) Jamaican dark rum
⅜ oz (11 ml) Amaro Nonino
1 teaspoon (5 ml) Pedro Ximénez
2 drops Bittermens Xocolatl Mole Bitters
Garnish: orange twist

Gentleman's Exchange

Leo Robitschek, The NoMad Bar, NYC, 2016
1½ oz (45 ml) rye whiskey
¾ oz (22 ml) sweet vermouth
½ oz (15 ml) Suze
½ oz (15 ml) Amaro Averna
1 teaspoon (5 ml) coffee liqueur
3 dashes absinthe
2 dashes Angostura Bitters
Garnish: grapefruit twist

Ghostwriter

Leigh Lacap, Ironside Fish & Oyster, San Diego, 2016
2 oz (60 ml) bourbon
½ oz (15 ml) Amaro Meletti
2 dashes walnut bitters
Garnish: orange twist

Governor's Club

Greg Keesee, Attaboy, Nashville
2 oz (60 ml) bourbon
½ oz (15 ml) Stambecco Maraschino Cherry Amaro
1 teaspoon (5 ml) cane syrup (p 494)
Garnish: orange twist and cherry

Grimes & Petty

Martin McConnell and Liam Murphy, Frog's Hollow Saloon, Brisbane, 2022
1¼ oz (37 ml) bourbon
1 oz (30 ml) Amaro Montenegro
½ oz (15 ml) coffee liqueur
⅓ oz (10 ml) sweet vermouth
2 dashes orange bitters
Garnish: orange half-wheel

Harry Dean Stanton

Steven Robbins and Ben Sprouse, Half Step, Austin
2 oz (60 ml) rye whiskey
¼ oz (7 ml) pimento (allspice) dram
¼ oz (7 ml) falernum
2 dashes orange bitters
Garnish: orange twist

Hendrick Cocktail

(aka **Zazarack**, Jack's Manual, *J.A. Grohusko, 1910*, Old Fashioned with absinthe)
The Mixicologist, *C.F. Lawlor, 1895*
2 oz (60 ml) bourbon
1 white sugar cube
3 dashes Angostura Bitters
3 dashes absinthe
1 teaspooon (5 ml) soda
Press sugar cube, build all ingredients in an Old Fashioned glass, then add ice.
Garnish: orange twist and lemon twist

Home on the Range

Crosby Gaige's Cocktail Guide and Ladies' Companion, *Crosby Gaige, 1941*
1½ oz (45 ml) rye whiskey
½ oz (15 ml) sweet vermouth
¼ oz (7 ml) triple sec
3 dashes Angostura Bitters
Garnish: orange twist and lemon twist

Hunter Cocktail

A Life-Time Collection of 688 Recipes for Drinks, *1934*
1½ oz (45 ml) rye whiskey
½ oz (15 ml) Heering Cherry Liqueur
Garnish: lemon twist

Improved New York Cocktail

(Improved Whiskey Cocktail with rye whiskey and Cognac)
Dan Greenbaum, Attaboy, NYC, 2016
1 oz (30 ml) rye whiskey
1 oz (30 ml) Cognac
½ oz (15 ml) maraschino liqueur
3 dashes Peychaud's Aromatic Cocktail Bitters
1 dashes absinthe
Garnish: lemon twist

Kentucky Colonel

(aka **Kentucky Cole**)
Straub's Manual of Mixed Drinks, *Jacques Straub, 1913*
1½ oz (45 ml) bourbon
½ oz (15 ml) Bénédictine
3 dashes Angostura Bitters (optional)
Garnish: lemon twist

King Cole Cocktail

Recipes for Mixed Drinks, *Hugo R. Ensslin, 1917*
1½ oz (45 ml) bourbon
½ oz (15 ml) Fernet-Branca
¼ oz (7 ml) simple syrup
Garnish: orange twist

King Kong

Sam Ross, Attaboy, NYC, 2015
1½ oz (45 ml) bourbon
½ oz (15 ml) pot still Jamaican dark rum (preferably Smith & Cross Traditional Jamaica Rum)
½ oz (15 ml) Tempus Fugit Crème de Banane
3 dashes Angostura Bitters
Garnish: lemon twist

Made to Measure

Felix Woods, The Everleigh, Melbourne, 2017
1 oz (30 ml) rye whiskey
1 oz (30 ml) Cognac
1 teaspoon (5 ml) maple syrup
2 dashes Angostura Bitters
2 dashes Peychaud's Aromatic Cocktail Bitters
Garnish: orange twist and lemon twist

Build all ingredients in an Old Fashioned glass, then add ice.

Mardi Gras
Irvin S. Cobb's Own Recipe Book, *Irvin S. Cobb, 1936*
2 oz (60 ml) rye whiskey
1 white sugar cube
2 dashes Peychaud's Aromatic Cocktail Bitters
2 dashes Angostura Bitters
2 dashes absinthe
1 teaspoon (5 ml) soda
Press sugar cube with soda in an Old Fashioned glass, then build all ingredients and add ice.
Garnish: lemon twist

Midnight Rambler
Chad Solomon and Christy Pope, Midnight Rambler, Dallas, 2019
2 oz (60 ml) bourbon (preferably Balcones Texas Pot Still Bourbon)
2½ teaspoons (12.5 ml) Ancho Reyes Original
½ teaspoon (2.5 ml) Demerara syrup (p 495)
1 dash Bittermens Xocolatl Mole Bitters
1 dash Angostura Bitters
2 drops saline solution (p 493)
Garnish: grapefruit twist

Mid-Term
Daniel Zacharczuk, Kitchen, Los Angeles, 2011
2 oz (60 ml) Tennessee whiskey
½ oz (15 ml) Cynar
1 teaspoon (5 ml) simple syrup
Garnish: orange twist

Monte Carlo
The How and When, *Hyman Gale and Gerald F. Marco, 1937*
1½ oz (45 ml) rye whiskey
½ oz (15 ml) Bénédictine
3 dashes Angostura Bitters
Garnish: lemon twist

Mr. Brown
ms. franky marshall, Clover Club, NYC, 2011
2 oz (60 ml) bourbon
¾ oz (22 ml) coffee liqueur
1 teaspoon (5 ml) vanilla syrup (p 502)
1 dash Angostura Bitters
1 dash orange bitters
Garnish: orange twist

New York Old Fashioned
(Old Fashioned with equal parts rye whiskey and Cognac)
1 oz (30 ml) rye whiskey
1 oz (30 ml) Cognac
1 white sugar cube
3 dashes Angostura Bitters
1 teaspoon (5 ml) soda
Press sugar cube with soda in an Old Fashioned glass, then build all ingredients and add ice.
Garnish: orange twist and lemon twist

Nova Scotia
Paul Hammond and Priscilla Leong
1½ oz (45 ml) bourbon
⅓ oz (10 ml) Islay Scotch
¼ oz (7 ml) Fernet-Branca
¼ oz (7 ml) honey syrup (p 496)
Garnish: lemon twist

Old Barrel
Benjamin Schwartz, Little Branch, NYC, 2014
1½ oz (45 ml) rye whiskey
⅜ oz (11 ml) Amontillado Sherry
⅜ oz (11 ml) Bénédictine
3 dashes Angostura Bitters
Garnish: lemon twist

Old Bay Ridge
David Wondrich, 5 Ninth, NYC, 2005
1 oz (30 ml) rye whiskey
1 oz (30 ml) aquavit
1 white sugar cube
3 dashes Angostura Bitters
1 teaspoon (5 ml) soda
Garnish: lemon twist

Old Fashioned (Nathan McCarley-O'Neill Recipe)
Nathan McCarley-O'Neill, Torrisi, NYC, 2024
2¼ oz (67 ml) bourbon (preferably Michter's Kentucky Straight Rye Whiskey)
½ oz (15 ml) Nardini Mandorla
¼ oz (7 ml) cane syrup (p 494)
2 dashes Angostura Bitters
Garnish: orange twist

Old Hat
Benjamin Schwartz, Little Branch, NYC, 2010
2 oz (60 ml) rye whiskey
¼ oz (7 ml) sweet vermouth
1 white sugar cube
5 dashes Angostura Bitters
1 teaspoon (5 ml) soda
Press sugar cube with soda in an Old Fashioned glass, then build all ingredients and add ice.
Garnish: orange twist and lemon twist

Old Timber
Ryan Kuntz, Noble Experiment, San Diego, 2016
2 oz (60 ml) bourbon
¼ oz (7 ml) Amaro Averna
¼ oz (7 ml) falernum
1 teaspoon (5 ml) orgeat
2 dashes orange bitters
8–10 mint leaves
½ oz (15 ml) pot still Jamaican dark rum, to float
Add liquids to a mixing glass and stir with ice. Place the mint in an Old Fashioned glass, add ice, then strain the mixed liquids on top and float rum.
Garnish: mint sprig

Paige Ellis
(Nice Legs with bourbon)
Chris Bostick, Half Step, Austin, 2014
1½ oz (45 ml) bourbon
¾ oz (22 ml) Barolo Chinato
¾ oz (22 ml) Suze
Garnish: lemon twist

Build all ingredients in an Old Fashioned glass, then add ice.

Pay Cut
Dan Greenbaum, Attaboy, NYC, 2015
2 oz (60 ml) bourbon
¾ oz (22 ml) Amargo-Vallet
¼ oz (7 ml) honey syrup (p 496)
Garnish: orange twist

Pick-Up Cocktail
Bartender's Guide, *Trader Vic, 1947*
2 oz (60 ml) rye whiskey
½ oz (15 ml) Fernet-Branca
1 teaspoon (5 ml) simple syrup
2 dashes absinthe
Garnish: lemon twist

Pop Quiz
Devon Tarby, Death & Co, NYC, 2010
1½ oz (45 ml) bourbon
½ oz (15 ml) Amaro Ramazzotti
1 teaspoon (5 ml) simple syrup
2 drops Bittermens Xocolatl Mole Bitters
Garnish: orange twist

Professional
Benjamin Schwartz, Little Branch, NYC, 2010
1½ oz (45 ml) bourbon
1 oz (30 ml) Campari
½ oz (15 ml) overproof Jamaican dark rum
Garnish: orange twist

Revolver
Jon Santer, Bruno's, San Francisco, 2004
2¼ oz (67 ml) bourbon
½ oz (15 ml) coffee liqueur
2 dashes orange bitters
Garnish: orange twist

Sherpa
Matt Clark, Dutch Kills, NYC, 2010
2 oz (60 ml) bourbon
¼ oz (7 ml) Pierre Ferrand Dry Curaçao
¼ oz (7 ml) pimento (allspice) dram
2 drops Bittermens Xocolatl Mole Bitters
Garnish: orange twist

Smoke and a Pancake
Jason Crawley, Sydney, 2015
2 oz (60 ml) Jack Daniel's Gentleman Jack
⅓ oz (10 ml) Tempus Fugit Crème de Banane
1 teaspoon (5 ml) maple syrup
3 dashes Angostura Bitters
3 dashes chocolate bitters
Garnish: orange twist, lemon twist and 2 spritzes of Islay Scotch

Social Animal
Tony Roehr, Raised By Wolves, San Diego
2 oz (60 ml) bourbon
½ oz (15 ml) Tempus Fugit Crème de Banane
1 teaspoon (5 ml) nocino
2 dashes Angostura Bitters
Garnish: lemon twist

Red Ant
Thomas Waugh, The Alembic, San Francisco, 2011
1½ oz (45 ml) rye whiskey
½ oz (15 ml) mezcal
½ oz (15 ml) Heering Cherry Liqueur
2 drops Bittermens Xocolatl Mole Bitters
Garnish: cherry and freshly grated cinnamon

Rhymes with Orange
Toby Maloney, Violet Hour, Chicago, 2011
2 oz (60 ml) rye whiskey
1 oz (30 ml) sweet vermouth
½ oz (15 ml) Amaro Ramazzotti
1 teaspoon (5 ml) Islay Scotch
3 dashes orange bitters
Garnish: flamed orange twist

Rich Pickings
Jason Williams, Apollonia, Sydney, 2021
1½ oz (45 ml) rye whiskey
⅓ oz (10 ml) sweet vermouth
⅓ oz (10 ml Pedro Ximénez
⅓ oz (10 ml) Amaro Averna
1 teaspoon (5 ml) fig balsamic vinegar
1 dash Angostura Bitters
Garnish: orange twist

Shinola
Greg Keesee, Attaboy, Nashville, 2021
2 oz (60 ml) rye whiskey
¼ oz (7 ml) Amaro Nardini
¼ oz (7 ml) Green Chartreuse
1 teaspoon (5 ml) cane syrup (p 494)
2 dashes orange bitters
Garnish: lemon twist

Shirley Jane
The Fine Art of Mixing Drinks, *David A. Embury, 1948*
2 oz (60 ml) rye whiskey
½ oz (15 ml) grenadine (p 496)
Garnish: lemon twist

Stingrye
Tom Lasher-Walker, Bramble, Edinburgh, 2012
2 oz (60 ml) rye whiskey
1 oz (30 ml) Branca Menta
Garnish: lemon twist

Stone Fence
The Bar-Tender's Guide, *Jerry Thomas, 1862*
2 oz (60 ml) bourbon
1½ oz (45 ml) non-alcoholic still apple cider (or cloudy apple juice)
Garnish: apple fan

The Battle of New Orleans
Crosby Gaige's Cocktail Guide and Ladies' Companion, *Crosby Gaige, 1941*
2 oz (60 ml) bourbon
1 teaspoon (5 ml) simple syrup
2 dashes orange bitters
2 dashes Peychaud's Aromatic Cocktail Bitters
2 dashes absinthe
Garnish: lemon twist

The Bee Bee
Jones' Complete Barguide, *Stan Jones, 1977*
2 oz (60 ml) bourbon
½ oz (15 ml) honey syrup (p 496)
3 lemon twists
3 orange twists
Press the citrus twists with honey syrup in a Old Fashioned glass, then add bourbon and ice.

Build all ingredients in an Old Fashioned glass, then add ice.

The Bell Keeper
Sky Huo, Happiness Forgets, London
1½ oz (45 ml) Michter's Original Sour Mash Whiskey
1 oz (30 ml) apple liqueur (preferably The Somerset Cider Brandy Company Kingston Black Apple Aperitif (Available in the UK)
1 teaspoon (5 ml) Pierre Ferrand Dry Curaçao
½ teaspoon (2.5 ml) simple syrup
2 dashes Fee Brothers Rhubarb Bitters

The Boss
(Godfather with bourbon)
Jones' Complete Barguide, *Stan Jones, 1977*
1½ oz (45 ml) bourbon
½ oz (15 ml) amaretto
Garnish: lemon twist

The Coffee House
The Saloon in the Home or A Garland of Rumblossoms, *Ridgley Hunt and George S. Chappell, 1930*
1½ oz (45 ml) rye whiskey
1 oz (30 ml) coffee liqueur
2 dashes orange bitters
Garnish: orange twist
● Swap rye whiskey for blanco tequila to make **The Coffee House (Heartbreaker Recipe)**, Heartbreaker, Melbourne, 2015.

The Erin
Toby Cecchini, The Long Island Bar, NYC, 2015
2 oz (60 ml) rye whiskey
½ oz (15 ml) sweet vermouth
½ oz (15 ml) Suze
½ oz (15 ml) Bigallet China-China
3 dashes pimento (allspice) dram
Garnish: orange twist and lemon twist
● "Invented for Greg Pasquarelli."

Tombstone
Imbibe!, *David Wondrich, 2007*
2 oz (60 ml) bourbon
1 teaspoon (5 ml) Demerara syrup (p 495)
3 dashes Angostura Bitters
Garnish: lemon twist

Truth Teller
Andrew Cordero, Seneca, 2022
2 oz (60 ml) bourbon
¼ oz (7 ml) coffee liqueur
¼ oz (7 ml) white sambuca
1 dash Peychaud's Aromatic Cocktail Bitters
1 dash orange bitters
Garnish: lemon twist

Vieux Pompier
Rhachel Shaw
A Quick Drink: The Speed Rack Guide to Winning Cocktails For Any Mood, *Lynnette Marrero and Ivy Mix, 2024*
¾ oz (22 ml) rye whiskey
¾ oz (22 ml) bonded apple brandy
½ oz (15 ml) Palo Cortado Sherry
½ oz (15 ml) Tempus Fugit Crème de Banane
2 dashes Peychaud's Aromatic Cocktail Bitters
Garnish: lemon twist

Wagon Train
Matt Clark, Dutch Kills, NYC
1½ oz (45 ml) rye whiskey
½ oz (15 ml) Amontillado Sherry
⅜ oz (11 ml) Amaro Braulio
1 teaspoon (5 ml) maple syrup
Garnish: orange twist

We Will, We Will Roku
Jim Meehan, Takibi, Portland, 2021
1 oz (30 ml) rye whiskey
1 oz (30 ml) sweet vermouth
½ oz (15 ml) Japanese gin (preferably Roku Gin)
½ oz (15 ml) Campari
½ oz (15 ml) Aperol
¼ oz (7 ml) apricot eau de vie
2 dashes Angostura Bitters
Garnish: orange twist

SCOTCH

Always Betz on Black
Leo Robitschek, The NoMad Bar, NYC
1 oz (30 ml) single malt Scotch (preferably The Macallan Double Cask 12yr Highland Single Malt Scotch Whisky)
1 oz (30 ml) Jameson Irish Whiskey
¾ oz (22 ml) Pedro Ximénez
½ oz (15 ml) aged dark rum (preferably Mount Gay XO Triple Cask Blend)
2 dashes coffee liqueur
3 dashes absinthe
Garnish: pinch of salt flakes

Backwards Point
Andrew Rice, Attaboy, NYC, 2017
2 oz (60 ml) Scotch
¾ oz (22 ml) Cynar
½ oz (15 ml) sweet vermouth
Garnish: orange twist

Beals Cocktail
(Affinity Cocktail on the rocks)
Drinks, *Jacques Straub, 1914*
2 oz (60 ml) Scotch
½ oz (15 ml) sweet vermouth
½ oz (15 ml) dry vermouth
3 dashes Angostura Bitters
Garnish: lemon twist

Benedict Arnold
Jones' Complete Barguide, *Stan Jones, 1977*
1½ oz (45 ml) Scotch
½ oz (15 ml) Bénédictine
3 dashes Angostura Bitters
Garnish: lemon twist

Beth's Going to Town
Daniel Zacharczuk, 2015
1 oz (30 ml) single malt Scotch
1 oz (30 ml) gin
½ oz (15 ml) sweet vermouth
¼ oz (7 ml) Amaro Ramazzotti
¼ oz (7 ml) apricot brandy
Garnish: mint leaf

Build all ingredients in an Old Fashioned glass, then add ice.

Black Watch
Jones' Complete Barguide,
Stan Jones, 1977
1½ oz (45 ml) Scotch
¾ oz (22 ml) coffee liqueur
Garnish: lemon twist

Bobbie Burns
The Fine Art of Mixing Drinks,
David A. Embury, 1948
1½ oz (45 ml) Scotch
½ oz (15 ml) sweet vermouth
¼ oz (7 ml) Drambuie
3 dashes Angostura Bitters
Garnish: lemon twist

Bobby Burns Cocktail
Recipes for Mixed Drinks,
Hugo R. Ensslin, 1917
1½ oz (45 ml) Scotch
½ oz (15 ml) sweet vermouth
¼ oz (7 ml) Bénédictine
3 dashes Angostura Bitters
Garnish: lemon twist

Bobby Burns No. 2
1700 Cocktails for the Man Behind the Bar, *R. de Fleury, 1934*
1½ oz (45 ml) Scotch
½ oz (15 ml) sweet vermouth
¼ oz (7 ml) maraschino liqueur
3 dashes Angostura Bitters
Garnish: orange twist

Bonnie Prince Charlie No. 2
Brandon Bramhall, Attaboy, NYC, 2018
1½ oz (45 ml) Scotch
⅜ oz (11 ml) Drambuie
⅜ oz (11 ml) Amontillado Sherry
2 dashes Angostura Bitters
Garnish: lemon twist

Bonny Scot
1700 Cocktails for the Man Behind the Bar, *R. de Fleury, 1934*
1½ oz (45 ml) Scotch
¾ oz (22 ml) Drambuie
½ oz (15 ml) Calvados
¼ oz (7 ml) Giffard Crème de Fruit de la Passion
Garnish: lemon twist and cherry

Buena Vista
Paul Hammond and Priscilla Leong
1¼ oz (37 ml) Scotch
¾ oz (22 ml) coffee liqueur
½ oz (15 ml) Islay Scotch
⅓ oz (10 ml) Punt e Mes
3 drops Bittermens Xocolatl Mole Bitters
Garnish: lemon twist

Built 33
Michael Madrusan, Melbourne, 2017
1½ oz (45 ml) Highland Scotch
1 teaspoon (5 ml) sapin liqueur
1 teaspoon (5 ml) honey syrup (p 496)
Garnish: spritz of Scotch rosewater (1:1 Islay Scotch and rosewater)
● Created for LeLabo, Melbourne.

Cherry Whisky
(John McClain with grenadine)
100 Cocktails: How to Mix Them,
"Bernard", 1958
2 oz (60 ml) Scotch
1 white sugar cube
3 dashes Angostura Bitters
1 teaspoon (5 ml) grenadine (p 496)
1 teaspooon (5 ml) soda
Press sugar cube with soda in an Old Fashioned glass, then build all ingredients and add ice.
Garnish: lemon twist

Chief Executive
Brandon Bramhall, Attaboy, Nashville, 2017
1½ oz (45 ml) Islay Scotch
1 oz (30 ml) Tempus Fugit Gran Classico Bitter
½ oz (15 ml) pot still Jamaican dark rum (preferably Smith & Cross Traditional Jamaica Rum)
Garnish: orange twist

Choker Old Fashioned
(John McClain with absinthe)
Trader Vic's Bartender's Guide,
Trader Vic, 1947
2 oz (60 ml) Scotch
1 white sugar cube
3 dashes Angostura Bitters
3 dashes absinthe
1 teaspooon (5 ml) soda
Press sugar cube with soda in an Old Fashioned glass, then build all ingredients and add ice.
Garnish: orange twist and lemon twist

Clandestine
Simon Difford, Cabinet Room, London, 2017
1½ oz (45 ml) Scotch
½ oz (15 ml) Suze
⅓ oz (10 ml) Italicus Rosolio di Bergamotto
1 teaspoon (5 ml) honey syrup (p 496)
Garnish: orange twist

Coastal Brew
Kyle Jamieson, Nauticus, Edinburgh
1⅓ oz (40 ml) single malt Scotch (preferably Talisker 10yr Single Malt Scotch Whisky)
½ oz (15 ml) coffee liqueur (preferably Mr Black Cold Brew Coffee Liqueur)
½ oz (15 ml) Tempus Fugit Crème de Cacao
3 dashes Angostura Bitters
Garnish: orange twist

Crimson Chin
Aidan Tibbins, The Waratah, Sydney, 2024
1½ oz (45 ml) Scotch
⅔ oz (20 ml) apple cordial (p 494)
⅓ oz (10 ml) grenadine (p 496)
1 teaspoon (5 ml) raspberry eau de vie
Garnish: lemon twist

Build all ingredients in an Old Fashioned glass, then add ice.

Deadbolt

Michael McCollum, Attaboy, Nashville, 2021

1 oz (30 ml) Islay Scotch
1 oz (30 ml) Tempus Fugit Gran Classico Bitters
1 oz (30 ml) Bonal Gentiane-Quina
2 drops Bittermens Xocolatl Mole Bitters
Garnish: orange twist

Don Lockwood

Abraham Hawkins, Dutch Kills, NYC, 2012

1 oz (30 ml) Islay Scotch
1 oz (30 ml) bourbon
¼ oz (7 ml) maple syrup
2 drops Bittermens Xocolatl Mole Bitters
Garnish: orange twist

Edinburgh

Mike Dolfini, Attaboy, Nashville, 2019

1½ oz (45 ml) Scotch
½ oz (15 ml) Islay Scotch
½ oz (15 ml) Amaro Braulio
1 teaspoon (5 ml) honey syrup (p 496)
2 drops saline solution (p 493)
Garnish: lemon twist

Full Windsor

Erick Castro, Rickhouse, San Francisco, 2009

1 oz (30 ml) Scotch
1 oz (30 ml) bonded apple brandy
¾ oz (22 ml) sweet vermouth
¼ oz (7 ml) Bénédictine
2 dashes Angostura Bitters
2 dashes Peychaud's Aromatic Cocktail Bitters
Garnish: orange twist

Godfather

Brian's Booze Guide, *Brian F. Rea, 1976*

1½ oz (45 ml) Scotch
½ oz (15 ml) amaretto
Garnish: lemon twist

Highlander

Eric Alperin, The Varnish, Los Angeles

2 oz (60 ml) Scotch
½ oz (15 ml) Heering Cherry Liqueur
Garnish: lemon twist

Huntsman

Zachary Pease, Attaboy, NYC, 2018

¾ oz (22 ml) Islay Scotch
¾ oz (22 ml) Scotch
¾ oz (22 ml) Amargo-Vallet
¾ oz (22 ml) Pedro Ximénez
Garnish: orange twist

John McClain

(aka **Scotch Old Fashioned**)
Jones' Complete Barguide, *Stan Jones, 1977*

2 oz (60 ml) Scotch
1 white sugar cube
3 dashes Angostura Bitters
1 teaspooon (5 ml) soda
Press sugar cube with soda in an Old Fashioned glass, then build all ingredients and add ice.
Garnish: orange twist and lemon twist

From The Savoy Cocktail Book (1930):

A bartender is just a pharmacist with a limited inventory.

Kinkade

Tom Lasher-Walker, Fresh Kills, NYC, 2016

1½ oz (45 ml) Scotch
½ oz (15 ml) Islay Scotch
½ oz (15 ml) Tempus Fugit Crème de Banane
Garnish: orange twist

Nova Scotia

Tom Lasher-Walker, Fresh Kills, NYC, 2016

2¼ oz (67 ml) single malt Scotch
½ oz (15 ml) Yellow Chartreuse
2 dashes orange bitters
Garnish: lemon twist

Raspberry

Sebastian Tollius, Eleven Madison Park, NYC, 2022

1½ oz (45 ml) pandan-infused The Macallan 12yr Sherry Oak Cask Highland Single Malt Scotch Whisky (p 504)
½ oz (15 ml) white chocolate fat-washed aged cachaça (p 505)
½ oz (15 ml) raspberry-infused Campari (p 504)
½ oz (15 ml) blanc vermouth
1 teaspoon (5 ml) coffee liqueur (preferably Mr Black Cold Brew Coffee Liqueur)
1 teaspoon (5 ml) Demerara syrup (p 495)
4 dashes Peychaud's Aromatic Cocktail Bitters
Stir with ice and strain into an Old Fashioned glass with ice.
Garnish: raspberry pâte de fruit

Rolex

(John McClain with Galliano L'Autentico)
Michael Madrusan, The Everleigh, Melbourne, 2011

2 oz (60 ml) Scotch
1 white sugar cube
3 dashes Angostura Bitters
1 teaspoon (5 ml) Galliano L'Autentico
1 teaspoon (5 ml) soda
Press sugar cube with soda in an Old Fashioned glass, then build all ingredients and add ice.
Garnish: orange twist
Named after a famous scene from the 1988 film *Die Hard*.

Rustiest Nail

Sam Ross, Attaboy, NYC, 2015

1¼ oz (37 ml) Highland Scotch
1 oz (30 ml) Islay Scotch
½ oz (15 ml) Drambuie
3 dashes Angostura Bitters
Garnish: orange twist

Rusty Nail

1½ oz (45 ml) Scotch
¾ oz (22 ml) Drambuie
Garnish: lemon twist
Created in 1937, but popularised at NYC's 21 Club in the 1950s.

Build all ingredients in an Old Fashioned glass, then add ice.

Rusty Nail (Leo Robitschek Recipe)
Leo Robitschek, The NoMad Bar, NYC
1 oz (30 ml) single malt Scotch (preferably Aberfeldy 12yr Highland Single Malt Scotch Whisky)
½ oz (15 ml) Japanese whisky (preferably Suntory Toki)
¼ oz (7 ml) Drambuie
⅔ oz (20 ml) lacto-fermented mango honey (p 497)
Garnish: lemon twist (discard)

Stingray
Tom Lasher-Walker, Bramble, Edinburgh, 2012
2 oz (60 ml) Islay Scotch
1 oz (30 ml) Branca Menta
Garnish: lemon twist

Strongman
Martin Lange, Cobbler, Brisbane, 2016
1⅓ oz (40 ml) Islay Scotch (preferably Lagavulin 16yr Single Malt Scotch Whisky)
½ oz (15 ml) Fino Sherry
¼ oz (7 ml) Tempus Fugit Crème de Cacao
2 dashes Angostura Orange Bitters
2 drops Bittermens Xocolatl Mole Bitters
Garnish: orange twist (discard)

Swanson
Nathan Beasley, Black Pearl, Melbourne, 2015
1 oz (30 ml) Islay Scotch (preferably Lagavulin 16yr Single Malt Scotch Whisky)
¾ oz (22 ml) Becherovka Original
¾ oz (22 ml) Pedro Ximénez
3 dashes orange bitters
Garnish: freshly grated coffee bean

Tattletale
Sam Ross, Milk & Honey, NYC, 2010
1½ oz (45 ml) Scotch
½ oz (15 ml) Islay Scotch
1 teaspoon (5 ml) honey syrup (p 496)
3 dashes Angostura Bitters
Garnish: lemon twist

The Bairn
Jones' Complete Barguide, *Stan Jones, 1977*
1½ oz (45 ml) Scotch
¼ oz (7 ml) triple sec
2 dashes orange bitters
Garnish: lemon twist

Trejo
Charlie Ainsbury, 2009
1⅓ oz (40 ml) Scotch
⅓ oz (10 ml) agave syrup (p 494)
3 drops Bittermens Xocolatl Mole Bitters
⅓ oz (10 ml) Del Maguey Santa Caterina Minas Minero Mezcal, to float
Build Scotch, agave syrup and bitters in an Old Fashioned glass, then add ice and float mezcal.

WORLD WHISK(E)Y

Isle Old Fashioned
Conor Johns, Red Hook Tavern, NYC, 2021
1½ oz (45 ml) Japanese whisky
½ oz (15 ml) Giffard Caribbean Pineapple
¼ oz (7 ml) Cocchi Americano
¼ oz (7 ml) pimento (allspice) dram
2 drops Bitter End Jamaican Jerk Bitters
Garnish: pineapple wedge and freshly ground pimento (allspice)

Kombu Old Fashioned
Matt Young, Ante, Sydney, 2023
2 oz (60 ml) kombu-infused Japanese whisky (p 503)
⅔ oz (20 ml) umeshu
⅓ oz (10 ml) simple syrup
3 dashes Peychaud's Aromatic Cocktail Bitters
1 dash orange bitters
1 orange twist
Press orange twist with simple syrup in an Old Fashioned glass, then build all ingredients and add ice. Stir briefly to combine.

Loop of Love
Sky Huo
1 oz (30 ml) Japanese whisky (preferably Nikka Miyagikyo Single Malt)
¾ oz (22 ml) umeshu
¾ oz (22 ml) Amontillado Sherry
2 dashes orange bitters
2 dashes chocolate bitters

Safety Word
Chris Bostick, The Varnish, Los Angeles, 2009
1½ oz (45 ml) Irish whiskey
½ oz (15 ml) Yellow Chartreuse
3 dashes Angostura Bitters
Garnish: lemon twist

Toki Bout It
Jim Meehan, Takibi, Portland, 2022
¾ oz (22 ml) Japanese whisky (preferably Suntory Toki)
¾ oz (22 ml) yuzushu
2 oz (60 ml) buckwheat tea, chilled
⅜ oz (11 ml) maple syrup
Stir with ice and strain into a double rocks glass with ice.
Garnish: freshly grated nutmeg

Tokyo Conference
Haley Traub, Attaboy, NYC
1 oz (30 ml) Japanese whisky
1 oz (30 ml) mezcal
¼ oz (7 ml) Tempus Fugit Crème de Banane
¼ oz (7 ml) Amaro Nardini
Garnish: orange twist

Build all ingredients in an Old Fashioned glass, then add ice.

BRANDY

Banana Bliss (Caitlin Laman Recipe)
E. Angerosa
Café Royal Cocktail Book, *W.J. Tarling, 1937*
1 oz (30 ml) Cognac
¾ oz (22 ml) Oloroso Sherry
½ oz (7 ml) Tempus Fugit Crème de Banane
Garnish: orange twist

Bayonet
Jake Powell, Death & Co, Denver, 2021
¾ oz (22 ml) Cognac
¾ oz (22 ml) sweet vermouth
½ oz (15 ml) Calvados
½ oz (15 ml) apricot eau de vie
½ oz (15 ml) Cynar
Garnish: orange twist

Belafonte
Steven Robbins, Half Step, Austin, 2018
1¼ oz (37 ml) Calvados
1 oz (30 ml) aquavit
¾ oz (22 ml) Cocchi Rosa
2 dashes Angostura Bitters
Garnish: lemon twist

Beverly Hills Cocktail
(aka **Calvados Old Fashioned**)
100 Cocktails: How to Mix Them, *"Bernard", 1958*
2 oz (60 ml) Calvados
1 white sugar cube
3 dashes Angostura Bitters
1 teaspooon (5 ml) soda
Press sugar cube with soda in an Old Fashioned glass, then build all ingredients and add ice.
Garnish: orange twist and lemon twist

B.V.D. Cocktail
The Stork Club Bar Book, *Lucius Beebe, 1946*
1½ oz (45 ml) bonded apple brandy
¾ oz (22 ml) sweet vermouth
3 dashes Angostura Bitters
Garnish: lemon twist

Eau Claire Old Fashioned
Robert Simonson, NYC, 2014
2 oz (60 ml) Cognac (preferably Pierre Ferrand 1840 Original Formula)
1 teaspoon (5 ml) simple syrup
3 dashes Bittercube Cherry Bark Vanilla Bitters
Garnish: orange twist

Fair Weather Cocktail
Trader Vic's Bartender's Guide, *Trader Vic, 1947*
1½ oz (45 ml) bonded apple brandy
¾ oz (22 ml) sweet vermouth
2 dashes Angostura Bitters
2 dashes orange bitters
Garnish: lemon twist

Flushing Cocktail
(Harvard Cocktail on the rocks with a lemon twist)
Jack's Manual, *J.A. Grohusko, 1908*
1½ oz (45 ml) Cognac
¾ oz (22 ml) sweet vermouth
3 dashes Angostura Bitters
Garnish: lemon twist

Folk Hero
Jake Powell, Death & Co, Denver, 2024
¾ oz (22 ml) bonded apple brandy
¾ oz (22 ml) rye whiskey
1 teaspoon (5 ml) aquavit
1 teaspoon (5 ml) Amaro Nonino
1 teaspoon (5 ml) Bénédictine
1 teaspoon (5 ml) honey syrup (p 496)
1 dash Angostura Bitters
Garnish: lemon twist

Frank Hill Cocktail
A Life-Time Collection of 688 Recipes for Drinks, *1934*
1½ oz (45 ml) Cognac
½ oz (15 ml) Heering Cherry Liqueur
Garnish: lemon twist

French Canadian
Alastair Walker, Caretaker, Auckland, 2021
1½ oz (45 ml) Cognac
½ oz (15 ml) coffee liqueur
¼ oz (7 ml) maple syrup
Garnish: orange twist

Good Fellow Cocktail
Bartender's Guide, *Trader Vic, 1947*
1½ oz (45 ml) Cognac
½ oz (15 ml) Bénédictine
3 dashes Angostura Bitters
Garnish: lemon twist

Japanese Cocktail
The Bar-Tender's Guide, *Jerry Thomas, 1862*
2 oz (60 ml) Cognac
½ oz (15 ml) orgeat
3 dashes Angostura Bitters
Garnish: lemon twist
Be sure to try the **La Japonaise**, a fantastic variation by Toby Cecchini on p 181.

Jersey Lightning
Trader Vic's Bartender's Guide, *Trader Vic, 1947*
2 oz (60 ml) bonded apple brandy
¼ oz (7 ml) simple syrup
3 dashes Angostura Bitters
Garnish: orange twist

Mikado Cocktail
Cocktails: How to Mix Them, *Robert Vermeire, 1922*
2 oz (60 ml) Cognac
1 teaspoon (5 ml) Pierre Ferrand Dry Curaçao
1 teaspoon (5 ml) Tempus Fugit Crème de Noyaux
1 teaspoon (5 ml) orgeat
3 dashes Angostura Bitters
Garnish: lemon twist and cherry

Milk & Money
The South American Gentleman's Companion, *Charles H. Baker Jr., 1951*
1½ oz (45 ml) Cognac
½ oz (15 ml) white crème de cacao
1 teaspoon (5 ml) orgeat
Garnish: orange twist

My Hope
The Flowing Bowl, *William Schmidt, 1891*
2 oz (60 ml) Cognac
½ oz (15 ml) tawny Port
3 dashes Angostura Bitters
Garnish: pinch of cayenne pepper

Build all ingredients in an Old Fashioned glass, then add ice.

New Caledonia
(aka **Double Agent**)
Michael Madrusan, Little Branch, NYC, 2009
1 oz (30 ml) Cognac
1 oz (30 ml) aged dark rum
1 raw sugar cube
2 dashes Angostura Bitters
Press sugar cube with soda in an Old Fashioned glass, then build all ingredients and add ice.
Garnish: orange twist

Newton's Special
Approved Cocktails, *United Kingdom Bartenders' Guild, 1937*
1½ oz (45 ml) Cognac
½ oz (15 ml) triple sec
3 dashes Angostura Bitters
Garnish: orange twist

Old Timer
Lorenzo Antinori, Bar Leone, Hong Kong, 2023
¾ oz (22 ml) Calvados
¾ oz (22 ml) bourbon
⅜ oz (11 ml) mezcal
⅜ oz (11 ml) Oloroso Sherry
¼ oz (7 ml) maple syrup
2 dashes Angostura Bitters
Garnish: lemon twist

Ontario
Sam Ross, Attaboy, NYC, 2018
1 oz (30 ml) bonded apple brandy
1 oz (30 ml) rye whiskey
¾ oz (22 ml) Fernet-Branca
¼ oz (7 ml) simple syrup
Garnish: orange twist

Panamericano
Leo Robitschek, The NoMad Bar, NYC
1 oz (30 ml) pisco (preferably quebranta)
1 oz (30 ml) Cocchi Americano
1 oz (30 ml) blanc vermouth
Garnish: orange twist

Pay Day
Brandon Bramhall, Attaboy, Nashville, 2017
2 oz (60 ml) bonded apple brandy
¾ oz (22 ml) Amaro Nardini
¼ oz (7 ml) honey syrup (p 496)
Garnish: orange twist

Peach and Honey
New and Improved Bartender's Manual, *Harry Johnson, 1882*
1½ oz (45 ml) Cognac
½ oz (15 ml) Giffard Crème de Pêche de Vigne
1 teaspoon (5 ml) honey syrup (p 496)
Garnish: lemon twist

Peacock Cocktail
The How and When, *Hyman Gale and Gerald F. Marco, 1937*
1½ oz (45 ml) Cognac
½ oz (15 ml) Picon Amer
2 dashes absinthe
Garnish: lemon twist

Place de la Concorde
Brittini Rae Peterson, 2015
1¾ oz (52 ml) Cognac
¾ oz (22 ml) sweet vermouth
½ oz (15 ml) maple syrup
2 dashes peach bitters
2 dashes Peychaud's Aromatic Cocktail Bitters
Garnish: orange twist and lemon twist

Pork Pie Hat
Wolf Alexander, The Varnish, Los Angeles, 2024
2 oz (60 ml) bonded apple brandy
½ oz (15 ml) Amaro CioCiaro
½ teaspoon (2.5 ml) maple syrup
Garnish: orange twist and freshly grated cinnamon

Primos
"Antoine", Primo's
Cocktails de Paris, *Georges Gabriel Thenon, 1929*
¾ oz (22 ml) Cognac
¾ oz (22 ml) Scotch
¾ oz (22 ml) orange curaçao
Garnish: lemon twist
● Swap Scotch for bourbon to make the **Primos Cocktail** from *Trader Vic's Bartender's Guide*, Trader Vic, 1947.

Rusty Ringo
Kenta Goto, Bar Goto, NYC
1¾ oz (52 ml) Calvados
½ oz (15 ml) Drambuie
¼ oz (7 ml) single malt Scotch (preferably Talisker 10yr Single Malt Scotch Whisky)
Garnish: gold leaf

Second Marriage
Dan Greenbaum, Attaboy, NYC, 2015
1 oz (30 ml) Calvados
1 oz (30 ml) bourbon
½ oz (15 ml) Pedro Ximénez
2 dashes Angostura Bitters
Garnish: orange twist

The French Connection
(Godfather with Cognac)
Jones' Complete Barguide, *Stan Jones, 1977*
1½ oz (45 ml) Cognac
½ oz (15 ml) amaretto
Garnish: lemon twist

Valedictorian
Parker Marvin, Attaboy, NYC, 2017
2¼ oz (67 ml) bonded apple brandy
½ oz (15 ml) Cynar
1 teaspoon (5 ml) cane syrup (p 494)
Garnish: lemon twist

Vizier's Tale
John Sinclair, Death & Co, Washington D.C., 2024
1½ oz (45 ml) pisco
¾ oz (22 ml) Salers Gentiane
½ oz (15 ml) Bonal Gentiane-Quina
½ oz (15 ml) Sauternes
½ oz (7 ml) Campari
Garnish: fresh bay leaf

Build all ingredients in an Old Fashioned glass, then add ice.

Ward's Cocktail
Trader Vic's Bartender's Guide, *Trader Vic, 1947*
1½ oz (45 ml) Cognac
½ oz (15 ml) Green Chartreuse
Garnish: orange twist

FORTIFIED & LIQUEUR

Backwoods
Andy Chu, The Everleigh, Melbourne, 2017
1 oz (30 ml) Barolo Chinato
¾ oz (22 ml) mezcal
¾ oz (22 ml) Cynar
2 dashes Angostura Bitters
2 dashes orange bitters
Garnish: orange twist

Bitter Giuseppe
Stephen Cole, Violet Hour, Chicago, 2007
2 oz (60 ml) Cynar
¾ oz (22 ml) sweet vermouth (preferably Carpano Antica Formula)
1 teaspoon (5 ml) lemon juice
Garnish: lemon twist (discard) and lemon wheel

Brut Cocktail
Jack's Manual, *J.A. Grohusko, 1908*
1½ oz (45 ml) dry vermouth
¾ oz (22 ml) Picon Amer
2 dashes Angostura Bitters
2 dashes orange bitters
Garnish: lemon twist

Cab Calloway
Tiffanie Barriere, Atlanta
1½ oz (45 ml) Oloroso Sherry
½ oz (15 ml) rye whiskey
¼ oz (7 ml) dry vermouth
¼ oz (7 ml) apricot brandy
2 dashes Angostura BItters
2 dashes orange bitters
Garnish: lemon twist

Catavino
Brandon Bramhall, Attaboy, Nashville, 2017
1¼ oz (37 ml) Amontillado Sherry
1¼ oz (37 ml) Cocchi Americano
2 dashes Angostura Bitters
2 dashes orange bitters
Garnish: grapefruit twist

Cortland
1 oz (30 ml) bonded apple brandy
1½ oz (45 ml) Cocchi Americano
½ oz (15 ml) dry vermouth
4 dashes Peychaud's Aromatic Cocktail Bitters
Garnish: lemon half-wheel

Fernet Cocktail
Cocktails: How to Mix Them, *Robert Vermeire, 1922*
1 oz (30 ml) Fernet-Branca
1 oz (30 ml) Cognac
1 teaspoon (5 ml) simple syrup
3 dashes Angostura Bitters
Garnish: orange twist

Florentine
Sam Ross, Attaboy, NYC, 2017
1 oz (30 ml) dry vermouth
1 oz (30 ml) Cocchi Americano
1 oz (30 ml) Cynar
Garnish: orange twist

Jump the Gun
Mitchell Taylor, Attaboy, Nashville, 2018
1½ oz (45 ml) Cocchi Americano
¾ oz (22 ml) Jamaican dark rum
2 dashes Angostura Bitters
Garnish: lemon twist

L'Appetit
The Flowing Bowl, *William Schmidt, 1891*
1½ oz (45 ml) sweet vermouth
1 oz (30 ml) Fernet-Branca
Garnish: orange twist

Madame Devalier
Genevieve Mashburn
1½ oz (45 ml) Cocchi Rosa
1 oz (30 ml) Old Tom gin
½ oz (15 ml) Salers Gentiane
7 dashes The Bitter Truth Old Time Aromatic Bitters
Garnish: lemon twist

Natoma St.
Caitlin Laman, Trick Dog, San Francisco
1 oz (30 ml) Amontillado Sherry
1 oz (30 ml) dry vermouth
1 oz (30 ml) Tempus Fugit Gran Classico Bitter
Garnish: lemon twist

Peach Bamboo
All Day Cocktails, *Shaun Byrne and Nick Tesar, 2019*
1½ oz (45 ml) dry vermouth
¾ oz (22 ml) Giffard Crème de Pêche de Vigne
2 dashes orange bitters
Garnish: lemon half-wheel

Remember the Alimony
Dan Greenbaum, Attaboy, NYC, 2016
1¼ oz (37 ml) Fino Sherry
1¼ oz (37 ml) Cynar
¾ oz (22 ml) gin
Garnish: orange twist

Vecchietto
Paul Hammond and Priscilla Leong
¾ oz (22 ml) dry vermouth
¾ oz (22 ml) Cynar
¾ oz (22 ml) Amaro Ramazzotti
½ oz (15 ml) Amontillado Sherry
3 dashes cardamom bitters
Garnish: lemon twist

Zeus
Jones' Complete Barguide, *Stan Jones, 1977*
1½ oz (45 ml) Campari
1 oz (30 ml) vodka
Garnish: lemon twist

Build all ingredients in an Old Fashioned glass, then add ice.

OTHER

North Sea Oil
Leo Robitschek, The NoMad Bar, NYC
1½ oz (45 ml) aquavit
¾ oz (22 ml) Cocchi Americano
½ oz (15 ml) Islay Scotch (preferably Laphroaig 10yr Single Malt Scotch Whisky)
¼ oz (7 ml) triple sec (preferably L'Original Combier)
Garnish: grapefruit twist

Sazerac

Fill a small Old Fashioned glass with crushed ice, add four dashes of absinthe and chill. Add sugar, bitters and soda to a frozen mixing glass and crush the sugar. Add spirit and ice, then stir until ice cold, ensuring sugar is well mixed, but take care not to over-dilute. Strain the absinthe into a chilled shot glass, discard the ice and strain into the Old Fashioned glass. Express a lemon twist over the top, lay it across the rim and serve with the absinthe shot as a sidecar.

Bailiff
Alastair Walker, Caretaker, Auckland, 2021
1 oz (30 ml) Scotch
½ oz (15 ml) Islay Scotch
½ oz (15 ml) Aperol
3 dashes Angostura Bitters
4 dashes absinthe, to rinse
Garnish: lemon twist

Colonial Ties
Eric Alperin, The Varnish, Los Angeles, 2010
1 oz (30 ml) rye whiskey
1 oz (30 ml) Jamaican dark rum
1 raw sugar cube
2 dashes orange bitters
2 dashes Angostura Bitters
1 teaspoon (5 ml) soda
4 dashes absinthe, to rinse
Garnish: lemon twist

Lotus Club Special
(aka **Weylin** or Sazerac with Angostura Bitters)
The Fine Art of Mixing Drinks, *David A. Embury, 1948*
2 oz (60 ml) rye whiskey
1 white sugar cube
2 dashes Peychaud's Aromatic Cocktail Bitters
2 dashes Angostura Bitters
1 teaspooon (5 ml) soda
4 dashes absinthe, to rinse
Garnish: lemon twist

New York Sazerac
(aka **50/50 Sazerac** or Sazerac with equal parts Cognac and rye whiskey)
1 oz (30 ml) rye whiskey
1 oz (30 ml) Cognac
1 white sugar cube
3 dash Peychaud's Aromatic Cocktail Bitters
1 teaspoon (5 ml) soda
4 dashes absinthe, to rinse
Garnish: lemon twist

Rye Witch
Jim Meehan, PDT, NYC, 2007
2 oz (60 ml) rye whiskey
¼ oz (7 ml) Liquore Strega
¼ oz (7 ml) Amontillado Sherry
1 white sugar cube
2 dashes orange bitters
Garnish: orange twist

Tide-Breaker (Sazerac Style)
Eric Alperin, The Varnish, Los Angeles
1 oz (30 ml) aged dark rum
½ oz (15 ml) Rittenhouse Straight Rye Whisky
½ oz (15 ml) Old Overholt Straight Rye Whiskey
1 raw sugar cube
2 dashes orange bitters
4 dashes absinthe, to rinse
Garnish: lemon twist

Whiskey Cocktail
The Bar-Tender's Guide, *Jerry Thomas, 1862*
2 oz (60 ml) rye whiskey
1 white sugar cube
3 dashes Angostura Bitters
1 teaspoon (5 ml) soda
Garnish: lemon twist

From *The Cocktail Hour* (1938):

Men are like fish: neither would get into trouble if they kept their mouths shut.

Fill a small Old Fashioned glass with crushed ice, add four dashes of absinthe and chill. Add sugar, bitters and soda to a frozen mixing glass and crush the sugar. Add spirit and ice, then stir until ice cold, ensuring sugar is well mixed, but take care not to over-dilute. Strain the absinthe into a chilled shot glass, discard the ice and strain into the Old Fashioned glass. Express a lemon twist over the top, lay it across the rim and serve with the absinthe shot as a sidecar.

FLIP

Café con Leche p 394

Flip

A creamy, full-bodied cocktail shaken with a whole egg or egg yolk, often including cream, and served in a frozen footed cocktail glass.

spirit + whole egg or egg yolk + sugar

Add all ingredients to a shaker and dry shake vigorously to emulsify. Add ice, then shake again and strain into a frozen footed cocktail glass.

Dating all the way back to the 1600s, the Flip was originally a warm cocktail combining beer and spirit with sweeteners and often spices, served in a large-format pitcher. The drink was said to be heated with a red-hot iron rod known as a loggerhead, pulled straight from the fire, and served to English sailors – a technique that became popular both in England and North America as colonists travelled across the Atlantic. This unique method made for a foamy cocktail characterised by caramelised sugars and bitter burnt hops.

The Flip was redefined at the end of the 18th century, when various recipes appeared with a whole egg in the mix. By this stage, the loggerhead method had been retired and the drink was being made 'by repeated pouring back and forth between two vessels', according to trailblazing bartender and author Jerry Thomas in 1862. By the late 1800s, ale disappeared from the formula and the simple combination of spirit, sugar and egg, shaken with ice, remained.

Given the modern preference for lighter, brighter cocktails, contemporary Flip variations are few and far between. Some excellent iterations have cropped up in recent years, however, often calling for dark spirits, fortified wines, liqueurs, cream and/or coffee. These are great drinks to keep up your sleeve for after dinner, perfect to replace – or even accompany – dessert.

East New York Flip

(New York Flip with honey syrup)
Jose Gil, Milk & Honey, NYC, 2006
1 oz (30 ml) bourbon
¾ oz (22 ml) tawny Port
½ oz (15 ml) honey syrup (p 496)
½ oz (15 ml) house cream (p 506)
1 egg yolk

Add all ingredients to a shaker and dry shake to emulsify. Add ice, then shake again and strain into a frozen footed cocktail glass.
Garnish: freshly grated nutmeg

The East New York Flip is a clever riff on the well-known New York Flip (p 397), a drink that combines bourbon with tawny Port, sugar, cream and an egg yolk. This 2006 variation by Jose Gil of New York City's Milk & Honey switches simple syrup for honey syrup, a warm and welcome ingredient in the hearty dessert-style cocktail. Gil was a barback at Milk & Honey at the time and requested his New York Flip with honey as a preference. The bartenders saluted the results and the rest, as they say, is history.

In this cocktail, the cream and egg yolk come together to create a smooth, custard-like texture, while tawny Port adds syrupy richness and flavours of dried fruits and herbs. The honey syrup, meanwhile, highlights the bourbon's caramel and vanilla characters, and the garnish of freshly grated nutmeg puts you right by a roaring fire on a winter's night. If you're searching for other dessert-style cocktails enriched with Port, we suggest both the Porto Flip (p 399) and the curiously named Coffee Cocktail (p 395), which is actually coffee-free.

Flip

GIN

Negroni Flip
Difford's Guide
1 oz (30 ml) gin
1 oz (30 ml) Campari
1 oz (30 ml) sweet vermouth
1 teaspoon (5 ml) simple syrup
2 drops saline solution (p 493)
1 whole egg
Garnish: orange twist

RUM & CANE SPIRIT

Brennan's Bracer
Brandon Bramhall, Attaboy, Nashville, 2017
1 oz (30 ml) Cruzan Black Strap Rum
¾ oz (22 ml) Tempus Fugit Crème de Banane
¾ oz (22 ml) orgeat
¾ oz (22 ml) house cream (p 506)
1 egg yolk
Garnish: freshly grated nutmeg

Café con Leche
Sam Ross, Milk & Honey, NYC, 2009
1 oz (30 ml) Goslings Black Seal Rum
¾ oz (22 ml) coffee liqueur
½ oz (15 ml) simple syrup
½ oz (15 ml) house cream (p 506)
1 egg yolk
Garnish: freshly grated nutmeg

East Melbourne Flip
Michael Madrusan, The Everleigh, Melbourne, 2011
1 oz (30 ml) aged dark rum
¾ oz (22 ml) Pedro Ximénez
½ oz (15 ml) honey syrup (p 496)
½ oz (15 ml) house cream (p 506)
1 egg yolk
Garnish: freshly grated nutmeg

Georgetown Demerara Rum Flip
The South American Gentleman's Companion, *Charles H. Baker Jr., 1951*
1 oz (30 ml) Goslings 151 Proof Black Seal Rum
½ oz (15 ml) Pedro Ximénez
½ oz (15 ml) simple syrup
½ oz (15 ml) house cream (p 506)
Garnish: freshly grated nutmeg

Jean Laffite Cocktail
Famous New Orleans Drinks and How to Mix 'Em, *Stanley Clisby Arthur, 1937*
2 oz (60 ml) aged dark rum
¾ oz (22 ml) orange curaçao (p 498)
1 teaspoon (5 ml) simple syrup
2 dashes absinthe
1 egg yolk

Reincarnation Flip
(aka **Resurrection Flip**)
Tim Philips-Johansson
2 oz (60 ml) aged dark rum (preferably Ron Zacapa No. 23)
1 teaspoon (5 ml) Islay Scotch
1 teaspoon (5 ml) lemon juice
1 teaspoon (6 g) fig jam
1 whole egg
Shake the jam and lemon juice, add remaining ingredients and dry shake. Add ice, then shake again and strain into a frozen footed cocktail glass.
Garnish: freshly grated nutmeg

Stout & Sons #2
(See p 440)

Three Storms Flip
Ryan Chetiyawardana, Dandelyan, London, 2015
1¾ oz (52 ml) gold rum
¼ oz (7 ml) Islay Scotch
¾ oz (22 ml) falernum
2 dashes orange bitters
2 drops saline solution (p 493)
Pinch of black pepper
1 whole egg
Garnish: freshly grated nutmeg

AGAVE

Confortador Flip
1½ oz (45 ml) blanco tequila
¾ oz (22 ml) tawny Port
½ oz (15 ml) simple syrup
½ oz (15 ml) house cream (p 506)
1 egg yolk
Garnish: freshly grated nutmeg

Death Flip
Chris Hysted-Adams, Black Pearl, Melbourne, 2010
1 oz (30 ml) blanco tequila
½ oz (15 ml) Jägermeister
½ oz (15 ml) Yellow Chartreuse
¼ oz (7ml) cane syrup (p 494)
1 whole egg
Garnish: freshly grated nutmeg

Dulce de Leche
Jim Meehan, PDT, NYC, 2008
1½ oz (45 ml) añejo tequila
¾ oz (22 ml) Pedro Ximénez
½ oz (15 ml) house cream (p 506)
1 whole egg
Garnish: freshly grated cinnamon

BRANDY

Ale Flip
(See p 439)

Apricot Flip
John Deragon, PDT, NYC, 2007
2 oz (60 ml) Cognac
¾ oz (22 ml) apricot brandy (preferably Rothman & Winter Orchard Apricot Fruit Liqueur)
½ oz (15 ml) simple syrup
1 whole egg
Garnish: freshly grated nutmeg

B.A.C Flip
Michael Madrusan, Little Branch, NYC, 2008
1 oz (30 ml) bonded apple brandy
¾ oz (22 ml) bourbon
½ oz (15 ml) honey syrup (p 496)
½ oz (15 ml) house cream (p 506)
1 whole egg
Garnish: freshly grated cinnamon

Add all ingredients to a shaker and dry shake to emulsify. Add ice, then shake again and strain into a frozen footed cocktail glass.

Bosom Caresser
American & Other Drinks, *Leo Engel, 1878*
2 oz (60 ml) Cognac
¾ oz (22 ml) simple syrup
1 strawberry, halved
1 whole egg
Muddle strawberry with simple syrup, then add remaining ingredients. Dry shake, then add ice, shake again and strain into a frozen footed cocktail glass.
Garnish: strawberry half

Bosom Caresser (George J. Kappeler Recipe)
Modern American Drinks, *George J. Kappeler, 1895*
2 oz (60 ml) Cognac
¾ oz (22 ml) simple syrup
½ oz (15 ml) house cream (p 506)
3 raspberries
1 whole egg
Muddle raspberry with simple syrup, then add remaining ingredients. Dry shake, then add ice, shake again and strain into a frozen footed cocktail glass.
Garnish: raspberry

Bosom Caresser Cocktail (aka "Bobby Jones" Cocktail or "Francis Ouimet" Cocktail)
The Savoy Cocktail Book, *Harry Craddock, 1930*
1½ oz (45 ml) Cognac
¾ oz (22 ml) orange curaçao (p 498)
½ oz (15 ml) grenadine (p 496)
1 egg yolk

Bossom [*sic*] Caresser
"Harry" of Ciro's ABC of Mixing Cocktails, *Harry MacElhone, 1923*
1½ oz (45 ml) Cognac
½ oz (15 ml) Madeira
½ oz (15 ml) orange curaçao (p 498)
½ oz (15 ml) grenadine (p 496)
1 egg yolk

Butterfly Flip
Jas. H. O'Brien, 1891
The World's Drinks and How to Mix Them, *Wm. T. Boothby, 1908*
1½ oz (45 ml) Cognac
¾ oz (22 ml) white crème de cacao
¾ oz (22 ml) house cream (p 506)
1 egg yolk
Garnish: freshly grated nutmeg
▼ Originally without egg yolk.

Caledonia
Bar La Florida Cocktails, *1935*
1½ oz (45 ml) Cognac
¾ oz (22 ml) white crème de cacao
¾ oz (22 ml) house cream (p 506)
2 dashes Angostura Bitters
1 egg yolk
Serve in a frozen double rocks glass with crushed ice.
Garnish: freshly grated cinnamon and finely grated lemon zest

Champagne Flip
Daly's Bartender Encyclopedia, *Tim Daly, 1903*
¾ oz (22 ml) Cognac
¼ oz (7 ml) triple sec
¼ oz (7 ml) simple syrup
¼ oz (7 ml) house cream (p 506)
2 oz (60 ml) Champagne, to top
1 egg yolk
Dry shake all ingredients, except Champagne, add ice, then shake again. Strain into a frozen footed cocktail glass and top with Champagne.

Charleston Bracer
(New York Flip with Cognac)
"Cheerio!", *Charles formerly of Delmonico's, 1928*
1 oz (30 ml) Cognac
¾ oz (22 ml) tawny Port
½ oz (15 ml) simple syrup
½ oz (15 ml) house cream (p 506)
1 egg yolk
Garnish: freshly grated nutmeg

Chocolate Flip
Jack's Manual, *J.A. Grohusko, 1916*
1½ oz (45 ml) Cognac
1½ oz (45 ml) sloe gin
1 egg yolk
Garnish: freshly grated nutmeg

Coffee Cocktail
The Bar-Tender's Guide, *Jerry Thomas, 1887*
1½ oz (45 ml) Cognac
1½ oz (45 ml) tawny Port
¼ oz (7 ml) muscovado syrup (p 498)
1 whole egg
Garnish: freshly grated nutmeg
▼ "...coffee and bitters are not to be found among its ingredients, but it looks like coffee when it has been properly concocted..."

Eye Opener
American and Other Iced Drinks, *Charlie Paul, 1902*
1 oz (30 ml) Cognac
1 oz (30 ml) aged dark rum
½ oz (15 ml) simple syrup
1 whole egg

French Kiss
Parker Marvin, Attaboy, NYC, 2017
1½ oz (45 ml) Cognac
¾ oz (22 ml) pimento (allspice) dram
¾ oz (22 ml) simple syrup
½ oz (15 ml) house cream (p 506)
1 egg yolk
Garnish: freshly grated nutmeg

Golden Slipper
Hotel Last Frontier, Las Vegas
Ted Saucier's Bottoms Up, *Ted Saucier, 1951*
1 oz (30 ml) Cognac
¾ oz (22 ml) Heering Cherry Liqueur
½ oz (15 ml) simple syrup
½ oz (15 ml) house cream (p 506)
1 egg yolk
Garnish: freshly grated nutmeg

Itchiban
Trader Vic's Bartender's Guide, *Trader Vic, 1947*
1½ oz (45 ml) Cognac
½ oz (15 ml) Bénédictine
½ oz (15 ml) white crème de cacao
1 whole egg
Garnish: freshly grated nutmeg

Add all ingredients to a shaker and dry shake to emulsify. Add ice, then shake again and strain into a frozen footed cocktail glass.

Josephine Baker
El Floridita, Havana, 1930s
Bar La Florida Cocktails, *1935*
1½ oz (45 ml) Cognac
¾ oz (22 ml) tawny Port
½ oz (15 ml) apricot brandy
½ oz (15 ml) house cream (p 506)
1 egg yolk
Garnish: freshly grated cinnamon
▼ Originally without cream.

Kinsley's Invigorator
Applegreen's Barkeeper's Guide, *John Applegreen, 1899*
1 oz (30 ml) Cognac
¾ oz (22 ml) tawny Port
1 oz (30 ml) cold-brew coffee
½ oz (15 ml) simple syrup
½ oz (15 ml) house cream (p 506)
1 egg yolk

Lazy Man Flip
(New York Flip with applejack)
Chris Jepson, Milk & Honey, London, 2007
1 oz (30 ml) bonded apple brandy
¾ oz (22 ml) tawny Port
½ oz (15 ml) simple syrup
½ oz (15 ml) house cream (p 506)
1 egg yolk
Garnish: freshly grated nutmeg

Magnolia
Bariana, *Louis Fouquet, 1896*
1½ oz (45 ml) Cognac
½ oz (15 ml) maraschino liqueur
1 egg yolk
Champagne, to top
Dry shake all ingredients, except Champagne, add ice, then shake again. Strain into a frozen footed cocktail glass and top with Champagne.

Magnolia (à la Simmons)
American & Other Drinks, *Leo Engel, 1875*
2 oz (60 ml) Cognac
½ oz (15 ml) orange curaçao (p 498)
¼ oz (7 ml) simple syrup
1 whole egg
Champagne, to top
Dry shake all ingredients, except Champagne, add ice, then shake again. Strain into a frozen footed cocktail glass and top with Champagne.
Garnish: orange half-wheel

Pan-American Flip
American Embassy, Quito
The South American Gentleman's Companion, *Charles H. Baker Jr., 1951*
2 oz (60 ml) Cognac
½ oz (15 ml) white crème de menthe
½ oz (15 ml) house cream (p 506)
1 teaspoon (5 ml) orgeat
1 egg yolk

Pit Stop Flip
Alex Day, Death & Co, NYC, 2008
1½ oz (45 ml) bonded apple brandy
½ oz (15 ml) Madeira
½ oz (15 ml) maple syrup
½ oz (15 ml) house cream (p 506)
1 egg yolk
Garnish: apple fan and freshly grated nutmeg

Promenade
What'll You Have?, *Julien J. Proskauer, 1933*
1 oz (30 ml) Cognac
¾ oz (22 ml) white crème de cacao
½ oz (15 ml) tawny Port
¾ oz (22 ml) house cream (p 506)
1 whole egg

Revolutionary Flip
Markus Olsen, Ziloufs, London, 2015
1½ oz (45 ml) Cognac
1 oz (30 ml) English bitter ale, stirred and flattened
½ oz (15 ml) tawny Port
½ oz (15 ml) Demerara syrup (p 495)
1 whole egg
Add ale to a shaker and stir to decarbonate, then add the remaining ingredients. Dry shake, then add ice, shake again and strain into a frozen footed Delmonico glass.
Garnish: freshly grated nutmeg

Sunday Morning Cocktail No. II
The Gentleman's Companion, *Charles H. Baker Jr., 1939*
1½ oz (45 ml) Cognac
½ oz (15 ml) tawny port
½ oz (15 ml) coffee liqueur
1 whole egg
Garnish: freshly grated cinnamon

Sunday Vespers
The Gentleman's Companion, *Charles H. Baker Jr., 1939*
1½ oz (45 ml) Cognac
¾ oz (22 ml) tawny Port
1 oz (30 ml) espresso
½ oz (15 ml) simple syrup
½ oz (15 ml) house cream (p 506)
1 egg yolk
Garnish: whole clove and freshly grated nutmeg

The Bridge Bracer
The Flowing Bowl, *William Schmidt, 1891*
2 oz (60 ml) Cognac
½ oz (15 ml) ginger syrup (p 496)
½ oz (15 ml) simple syrup
1 whole egg
Garnish: Angostura Bitters stripe

Add all ingredients to a shaker and dry shake to emulsify. Add ice, then shake again and strain into a frozen footed cocktail glass.

Thunder and Lightning Cocktail
The Savoy Cocktail Book, *Harry Craddock, 1930*
2 oz (60 ml) Cognac
¾ oz (22 ml) simple syrup
1 whole egg
Garnish: pinch of cayenne pepper

Tiger's Milk
Difford's Guide
1½ oz (45 ml) Cognac
½ oz (15 ml) Licor 43
½ oz (15 ml) simple syrup
½ oz (15 ml) house cream (p 506)
1 whole egg
Garnish: freshly grated cinnamon
▼ Based on the Tiger's Milk No. 1 in *The Gentleman's Companion*, Charles H. Baker Jr., 1939.

Tropical Thunder Cocktail
Don Eduardo Lopéz
The South American Gentleman's Companion, *Charles H. Baker Jr., 1951*
1½ oz (45 ml) Cognac
½ oz (15 ml) pastis
½ oz (15 ml) simple syrup
½ oz (15 ml) house cream (p 506)
1 egg yolk
Garnish: whole clove and a pinch of ground ginger

White Tiger's Milk
The Bar-Tender's Guide, *Jerry Thomas, 1862*
1½ oz (45 ml) bonded apple brandy
1 oz (30 ml) Giffard Crème de Pêche de Vigne
¾ oz (22 ml) house cream (p 506)
2 dashes Angostura Bitters
1 whole egg
Garnish: freshly grated nutmeg

AMERICAN WHISKEY

Boston Flip
The How and When, *Hyman Gale and Gerald F. Marco, 1937*
1½ oz (45 ml) rye whiskey
1½ oz (45 ml) Madeira
¼ oz (7 ml) simple syrup
1 egg yolk
Garnish: freshly grated nutmeg

Bourbon Banana Flip
Sam Ross, Attaboy, NYC, 2016
1½ oz (45 ml) bourbon
¾ oz (22 ml) Tempus Fugit Crème de Banane
¾ oz (22 ml) simple syrup
½ oz (15 ml) house cream (p 506)
1 egg yolk
Garnish: freshly grated nutmeg

Chicago Flip
Toby Maloney, Violet Hour, Chicago, 2007
2 oz (60 ml) bourbon
¾ oz (22 ml) 20yr tawny Port
¾ oz (22 ml) Licor 43
¼ oz (7 ml) simple syrup
1 whole egg
Garnish: 3 drops pimento (allspice) dram and freshly grated nutmeg

Flip Williams
Julian de Féral, Milk & Honey, London, 2007
1½ oz (45 ml) bourbon
¾ oz (22 ml) Poire Williams
½ oz (15 ml) simple syrup
½ oz (15 ml) house cream (p 506)
2 dashes Angostura Bitters
1 egg yolk

Lafayette Flip
The Flowing Bowl, *William Schmidt, 1891*
1½ oz (45 ml) rye whiskey
½ oz (15 ml) Green Chartreuse
½ oz (15 ml) orange curaçao (p 498)
½ oz (15 ml) house cream (p 506)
1 egg yolk

London Cocktail
Trader Vic's Bartender's Guide, *Trader Vic, 1947*
2 oz (60 ml) rye whiskey
¾ oz (22 ml) orgeat
2 dashes orange blossom water
1 whole egg
Garnish: freshly grated nutmeg

New York Flip
1 oz (30 ml) bourbon
¾ oz (22 ml) tawny Port
½ oz (15 ml) simple syrup
½ oz (15 ml) house cream (p 506)
1 egg yolk
Garnish: freshly grated nutmeg

Rebel Flip
Sam Ross, Milk & Honey, NYC, 2008
1½ oz (45 ml) bourbon
1 oz (30 ml) Licor 43
½ oz (15 ml) honey
½ oz (15 ml) house cream (p 506)
1 oz (30 ml) Champagne, to top
Garnish: freshly grated nutmeg

SCOTCH

Bridal Cocktail
Oska Whitehart, The Everleigh, Melbourne
1 oz (30 ml) Scotch
½ oz (15 ml) Tempus Fugit Crème de Banane
½ oz (15 ml) tawny Port
½ oz (15 ml) honey syrup (p 496)
½ oz (15 ml) house cream (p 506)
1 egg yolk
Garnish: freshly grated cinnamon

Add all ingredients to a shaker and dry shake to emulsify. Add ice, then shake again and strain into a frozen footed cocktail glass.

Fireside Flip
Good Things to Drink with Mr. Lyan & Friends, *Ryan Chetiyawardana, 2015*
1 oz (30 ml) single malt Scotch
1 oz (30 ml) sloe gin
½ oz (15 ml) honey syrup (p 496)
1 slice fresh ginger
1 dash Angostura Bitters
1 whole egg
Muddle ginger and honey syrup, add remaining ingredients, dry shake, add ice, shake again and strain into a frozen footed cocktail glass.
Garnish: freshly grated nutmeg

Fumigator Flip
Julian de Féral, Bureau, London, 2008
1½ oz (45 ml) Scotch
½ oz (15 ml) Islay Scotch
¾ oz (22 ml) Heering Cherry Liqueur
¼ oz (7 ml) simple syrup
1 egg yolk
Garnish: cherry and freshly grated nutmeg

Morning Star
(New York Flip with Scotch)
Straub's Manual of Mixed Drinks, *Jacques Straub, 1913*
1 oz (30 ml) Scotch
¾ oz (22 ml) tawny Port
½ oz (15 ml) simple syrup
½ oz (15 ml) house cream (p 506)
1 egg yolk
Garnish: freshly grated nutmeg
● Originally made with a whole egg and topped with soda.

Peanut Malt Flip
Angus Winchester, M Bar, Mandarin Oriental, Hong Kong, 2004
1¾ oz (52 ml) single malt Scotch
¾ oz (22 ml) house cream (p 506)
½ oz (15 ml) simple syrup
1 teaspoon (6 g) smooth peanut butter
1 egg yolk
Stir peanut butter and Scotch, then add remaining ingredients. Dry shake, then add ice, shake again and strain into a frozen footed cocktail glass.
Garnish: freshly grated nutmeg

Singer's Flip
Aneka Saxon, Violet Hour, Chicago, 2018
2 oz (60 ml) Scotch
½ oz (15 ml) orgeat
¼ oz (7 ml) cinnamon syrup (p 495)
1 whole egg
Garnish: pinch of salt flakes

Smoke Show
Lynnette Marrero, NYC
1 oz (30 ml) Islay Scotch
1 oz (30 ml) Oloroso Sherry
¾ oz (22 ml) Coco López
½ oz (15 ml) Demerara syrup (p 495)
1 whole egg
Garnish: freshly grated nutmeg

FORTIFIED & LIQUEUR

Amaretto Apricot Flip
All Day Cocktails, *Shaun Byrne and Nick Tesar, 2019*
¾ oz (22 ml) amaretto
½ oz (15 ml) Sauternes
½ oz (15 ml) house cream (p 506)
1 tablespoon (6 g) apricot jam
2 dashes Angostura Bitters
1 egg yolk
Stir jam and amaretto, add remaining ingredients and dry shake. Add ice, shake again, and strain into a frozen footed cocktail glass.

Banana Cream Flip
Anthony Schmidt, Raised by Wolves, San Diego, 2021
2 oz (60 ml) Giffard Banane du Brésil
1 oz (30 ml) house cream (p 506)
1 dash absinthe
1 egg yolk
Garnish: freshly grated nutmeg

Chocolate Cocktail
Modern American Drinks, *George J. Kappeler, 1895*
2 oz (60 ml) tawny Port
½ oz (15 ml) simple syrup
2 dashes Angostura Bitters
1 whole egg

Chocolate Cocktail (Harry MacElhone Recipe)
"Harry" of Ciro's ABC of Mixing Cocktails, *Harry MacElhone, 1923*
1½ oz (45 ml) tawny Port
½ oz (15 ml) Yellow Chartreuse
½ oz (15 ml) simple syrup
1 teaspoon (2.5 g) cocoa powder
1 egg yolk

Chocolate Punch
Jack's Manual, *J.A. Grohusko, 1908*
1½ oz (45 ml) tawny Port
½ oz (15 ml) orange curaçao (p 498)
½ oz (15 ml) simple syrup
½ oz (15 ml) house cream (p 506)
1 whole egg
Garnish: freshly grated nutmeg

Clyde Common Eggnog
Jeffrey Morgenthaler, Clyde Common, Portland, 2009
1¼ oz (37 ml) Amontillado Sherry
1 oz (30 ml) añejo tequila
½ oz (15 ml) simple syrup
½ oz (15 ml) house cream (p 506)
1 whole egg
Garnish: freshly grated nutmeg

Count of Monte Cristo
The South American Gentleman's Companion, *Charles H. Baker Jr., 1951*
2 oz (60 ml) Amontillado Sherry
1 oz (30 ml) Cognac
½ oz (15 ml) simple syrup
1 whole egg
Garnish: spritz of rosewater

Cynar Flip
Ben Sandrof, Boston, 2008
2½ oz (75 ml) Cynar
½ oz (15 ml) simple syrup
1 whole egg
5 drops Fee Brothers Whiskey Barrel-Aged Bitters, swirled

Dewey Flip
American Bar, *Frank P. Newman, 1900*
1½ oz (45 ml) white Port
½ oz (15 ml) maraschino liqueur
½ oz (15 ml) simple syrup
1 egg yolk
Garnish: freshly grated nutmeg

Add all ingredients to a shaker and dry shake to emulsify. Add ice, then shake again and strain into a frozen footed cocktail glass.

Duke No. 1
1700 Cocktails for the Man Behind the Bar, *R. de Fleury, 1934*
1 oz (30 ml) Drambuie
½ oz (15 ml) lemon juice
½ oz (15 ml) orange juice
1 whole egg
Champagne, to top
Dry shake all ingredients, except Champagne, add ice, then shake again. Strain into a frozen Sour glass while pouring Champagne simultaneously.
Garnish: lemon twist (discard)

Elephant Flip
(See p 437)

French Toast Flip
Erick Castro, Polite Provisions, San Diego
1 oz (30 ml) Oloroso Sherry
¾ oz (22 ml) Scotch
¾ oz (22 ml) bonded apple brandy
½ oz (15 ml) maple syrup
¼ oz (7 ml) pimento (allspice) dram
2 dashes Fee Brothers Whiskey Barrel-Aged Bitters
1 whole egg
Garnish: freshly grated cinnamon

Miss Mazie
Daly's Bartenders' Encyclopaedia, *Tim Daly, 1903*
2 oz (60 ml) tawny Port
½ oz (15 ml) grenadine (p 496)
½ oz (15 ml) house cream (p 506)
1 whole egg
Garnish: freshly grated cinnamon

Grenoble Flip
Milk & Honey, London
1 oz (30 ml) Green Chartreuse
½ oz (15 ml) maraschino liqueur
½ oz (15 ml) simple syrup
1 whole egg
Garnish: freshly grated nutmeg

Port Wine Flip
The Bar-Tender's Guide, *Jerry Thomas, 1887*
2 oz (60 ml) tawny Port
½ oz (15 ml) simple syrup
1 whole egg
Garnish: freshly grated nutmeg

Porto Flip
Army & Navy Club, Manila, 1931
The Gentleman's Companion, *Charles H. Baker Jr., 1939*
1½ oz (45 ml) tawny Port
½ oz (15 ml) Cognac
½ oz (7 ml) house cream (p 506)
¼ oz (7 ml) simple syrup
1 teaspoon (5 ml) Yellow Chartreuse
1 whole egg
Garnish: freshly grated nutmeg

Sherry Flip
The Flowing Bowl, *William Schmidt, 1891*
2 oz (60 ml) Oloroso Sherry
1 oz (30 ml) house cream (p 506)
½ oz (15 ml) simple syrup
1 whole egg
Garnish: freshly grated nutmeg

Sherry Wine Flip
The Bar-Tender's Guide, *Jerry Thomas, 1887*
2 oz (60 ml) Oloroso Sherry
½ oz (15 ml) simple syrup
1 whole egg
Garnish: freshly grated nutmeg
▼ Add 1 oz (30 ml) house cream (p 506) to make the **Sherry Flip** (above) from *The Flowing Bowl*, William Schmidt, 1891.

OTHER

L'Alligator C'est Vert
Nico de Soto, Mace, NYC, 2015
1 oz (30 ml) absinthe
1 oz (30 ml) pandan syrup (p 499)
1 oz (30 ml) coconut milk
1 whole egg
Garnish: freshly grated nutmeg

From *The Bon Vivant's Companion* (Jerry Thomas, 1862, still referenced in 1900s books):

Drink moderately, for drunkenness neither keeps a secret, nor observes a promise.

Add all ingredients to a shaker and dry shake to emulsify. Add ice, then shake again and strain into a frozen footed cocktail glass.

TODDY

Gin Cling p 406

Toddy

A soothing, warmly spiced cocktail, typically made with bolder spirits and often served hot.

spirit + sugar (predominantly honey) + boiling water

↓

Warm a Toddy glass by filling with boiling water. Empty water, then build ingredients in the glass and top with fresh boiling water. Alternatively, add room-temperature filtered water and use a milk frother or steamer to steam all ingredients until hot. Stir to combine.

The Toddy first appeared in print in England in 1741 and is best understood as a streamlined Punch (a category of spirit-driven drinks with multiple ingredients and spices, see p 122), served hot in winter and cold in summer. Unlike Punches, however, Toddies don't rely on citrus, although many variations employ lemon or lime and ginger. Due to their high water content, Toddies have traditionally featured bold, flavoursome spirits, such as Scotch, brandy or Jamaican dark rum, all of which can withstand the dilution.

Toddies are most often associated with cold winter nights and tickly sore throats, so it's somewhat unsurprising that the Whisky Toddy – also known as the Hot Whisky, Hot Scotch or Whiskey Skin in Ireland, where a lemon peel is added – had become the most popular variation by the 1870s. These soothing drinks typically featured a spoonful of sugar, plus a clove or a sprinkle of nutmeg, and were thought to have medicinal benefits. The classic Hot Toddy (p 407) preparation involved mixing spirit and sugar, dissolving the sugar with hot water, and then stirring to create a long, comforting drink. Contemporary methods, however, often combine the ingredients in the glass before steaming them all together, allowing for better control of the serving temperature.

While traditional European glöggs and mulled wines don't sit cleanly in this category because they are predominantly wine based, we've included spirit-driven riffs on the style, such as the modern Cognac-spiked English Bishop (p 406), which evolved from the 18th-century English Port-based Punch, and the Bishop (p 406), a 20th-century American Toddy that calls for Jamaican dark rum and red wine.

Indoor heating in today's cocktail bars has reduced the demand for hot drinks, meaning Toddies are appreciated less out of necessity and more as expertly balanced cocktails in their own right – equally as impressive as their ice-cold counterparts. When served in appropriate glassware with a handle or stem, at a perfect temperature that doesn't scald the ingredients or drinker's lips, the Toddy is an undeniably enjoyable choice in any season.

ESSENTIAL VARIATION

Hot Buttered Rum

2 oz (60 ml) aged dark rum
1 oz (30 ml) honey syrup (p 496)
1½ teaspoons (7 g) unsalted butter
2 oz (60 ml) boiling water

Warm a toddy glass with boiling water. Empty the glass then build all ingredients and top with fresh boiling water. Alternatively, add the water and steam all the ingredients together. Stir.
Garnish: freshly grated nutmeg

Dating back to the 1700s, the Hot Buttered Rum is a simple Toddy that has stood the test of time: a harmonious combination of aged dark rum, honey and hot water made silky smooth by a pat of butter, finished with freshly grated nutmeg. The butter melts into the drink, creating a luxuriously creamy texture and is enhanced by the rum's full body and the honey's fragrance. Traditionally enjoyed throughout the frosty festive season in the northern hemisphere, it's a hearty and indulgent treat akin to crumbly Scottish shortbread.

Many contemporary bars have revived the Hot Buttered Rum, or HBR as it's now known, utilising modern techniques such as fat-washing spirits to combine the butter and spices ahead of time. In these recipes, the flavour and texture of the butter is infused into the rum and excess fats are excluded, appealing to the 21st century, health-conscious drinker. Creative twists include aromatic spiced butters using allspice, cinnamon and even cayenne pepper, while coconut oil proves a worthy replacement in vegan variations.

If warm and buttery is what you're looking for, don't look past the bourbon-and-Port-based Toddy, Southern Hospitality (p 407), from The Everleigh alumnus Felix Woods. For occasions that call for something cooler, try a Non-Traditional Sour called the Beehive Sour (p 180), featuring rum, lemon and honey.

Toddy

Apple & Ginger Toddy
Felix Woods, The Everleigh, Melbourne, 2018
2 oz (60 ml) Pommeau de Normandie
1 oz (30 ml) lemon juice
½ oz (15 ml) ginger syrup (p 496)
½ oz (15 ml) honey syrup (p 496)
2 oz (60 ml) boiling water
Garnish: dried apple slice, candied ginger and freshly grated cinnamon
▼ Switch out Pommeau for Calvados for an **Apple & Ginger Toddy No. 2**.

A Sure Relief
What'll You Have?, *Julien J. Proskauer, 1933*
2 oz (60 ml) Cognac
½ oz (15 ml) ginger syrup (p 496)
½ oz (15 ml) grenadine (p 496)
2 drops peppermint bitters
2 oz (60 ml) boiling water
Garnish: candied ginger

Bishop
Daly's Bartenders' Encyclopedia, *Tim Daly, 1903*
2 oz (60 ml) Jamaican dark rum
½ oz (15 ml) red wine
¾ oz (22 ml) lime juice
¾ oz (22 ml) simple syrup
2 dashes orange bitters
2 oz (60 ml) boiling water
Garnish: lime wedge
▼ Originally served cold but has found a lot of success as a Toddy.

Blue Blazer
The Bar-Tender's Guide, *Jerry Thomas, 1862*
2 oz (60 ml) cask-strength Scotch
1 teaspoon (6 g) white (granulated) sugar
2 oz (60 ml) boiling water
Warm a snifter with boiling water and set aside. Using two silver-plated mugs or tankards, add Scotch and boiling water to one and ignite the liquid with fire. While blazing, transfer the mixture from one mug to the other four to five times. Empty the water from the snifter, pour the mixture in, add sugar and swirl to combine.
Garnish: lemon twist

Dirty Banana (Hot)
(See p 465)

English Bishop
Serves 6
Ezra Star, Drink, Boston
6 oz (180 ml) Cognac
34 oz (1 litre) ruby Port
1 cup (250 g) white (granulated) sugar
2 sour oranges
30 whole cloves
2 oz (60 ml) boiling water
Stud oranges with cloves and place in a 200°C (400° F) oven until browned (around 30 minutes). Quarter oranges and place in a saucepan with Port to simmer for 30 minutes. Remove and discard orange quarters and strain liquid. Add Cognac and sugar, stirring to dissolve. Serve warm in mugs.
Garnish: grated nutmeg

Fireside Toddy
Jayne's Bartender's Guide, *1934*
1 oz (30 ml) aged dark rum
1 oz (30 ml) Cognac
1 oz (30 ml) honey syrup (p 496)
¾ oz (22 ml) lemon juice
2 dashes Dale DeGroff's Pimento Aromatic Bitters
2 oz (60 ml) boiling water
Garnish: freshly grated cinnamon and freshly grated nutmeg

Gin Cling
Bariana, *Louis Fouquet, 1896*
2 oz (60 ml) gin
¾ oz (22 ml) lemon juice
¾ oz (22 ml) honey syrup (p 496)
1 dash eucalyptus bitters
2 oz (60 ml) boiling water
Garnish: lemon half-wheel

Ginger Toddy
2 oz (60 ml) bourbon
¾ oz (22 ml) lemon juice
½ oz (15 ml) honey syrup (p 496)
½ oz (15 ml) ginger syrup (p 496)
2 oz (60 ml) boiling water
Garnish: freshly grated cinnamon

Glühwein
1½ oz (45 ml) red wine
½ oz (15 ml) Armagnac
½ oz (15 ml) tawny Port
½ oz (15 ml) honey syrup (p 496)
3 dashes Dale DeGroff's Pimento Aromatic Bitters
2 oz (60 ml) boiling water
Garnish: cinnamon quill, star anise and freshly grated nutmeg

Gorilla Sweat
(Hot Buttered Tequila with agave)
Jones' Complete Barguide, *Stan Jones, 1977*
2 oz (60 ml) blanco tequila
¾ oz (22 ml) agave syrup (p 494)
1½ teaspoons (7 g) unsalted butter
2 oz (60 ml) boiling water
Garnish: freshly grated nutmeg

Gun Club Toddy
Alex Day, Death & Co, NYC, 2012
1½ oz (45 ml) chamomile-infused Calvados (p 502)
1 oz (30 ml) Pineau des Charentes
½ oz (15 ml) honey syrup (p 496)
¼ oz (7 ml) lemon juice
2 oz (60 ml) boiling water
Garnish: apple fan

Hot 'n' Stormy
2 oz (60 ml) Gosling's Black Seal Rum
½ oz (15 ml) lime juice
¾ oz (22 ml) ginger syrup (p 496)
2 oz (60 ml) boiling water
Garnish: candied ginger

Warm a Toddy glass by filling with boiling water. Empty water, then build ingredients in the glass and top with fresh boiling water. Alternatively, add room-temperature filtered water and use a milk frother or steamer to steam all ingredients until hot. Stir to combine.

Hot Fruit Cup
2 oz (60 ml) fruit cup (p 126)
½ oz (15 ml) lemon juice
½ oz (15 ml) simple syrup
2 oz (60 ml) boiling water
Garnish: freshly grated cinnamon

Hot Penicillin
1½ oz (45 ml) Scotch
¾ oz (22 ml) lemon juice
½ oz (15 ml) honey syrup (p 496)
½ oz (15 ml) ginger syrup (p 496)
2 oz (60 ml) boiling water
¼ oz (7 ml) Islay Scotch, to float
Add ingredients to a Toddy glass, top with boiling water or add water and steam until hot, then float Islay Scotch.
Garnish: candied ginger

Hot Rum Punch
1 oz (30 ml) aged dark rum
1 oz (30 ml) Cognac
½ oz (15 ml) Fino Sherry
¾ oz (22 ml) lime juice
¾ oz (22 ml) simple syrup
2 oz (60 ml) boiling water
Garnish: freshly grated nutmeg

Hot Toddy
2 oz (60 ml) spirit (rum, whiskey, gin, brandy, etc.)
¾ oz (22 ml) lemon juice
¾ oz (22 ml) honey syrup (p 496)
1 whole clove
2 oz (60 ml) boiling water
Garnish: lemon half-wheel and cinnamon stick

Hot Zombie (Ronrico Rum Co., 1941)
Beachbum Berry's Sippin' Safari, *Jeff Berry, 2007*
2 oz (60 ml) gold rum
1 oz (30 ml) pineapple juice
½ oz (15 ml) lime juice
½ oz (15 ml) passionfruit syrup (p 499)
1 raw sugar cube
1½ teaspoons (7 g) unsalted butter
2 oz (60 ml) boiling water
Garnish: freshly grated nutmeg

In Hot Water
Brittany Fells, 2014
2 oz (60 ml) Cognac
½ oz (15 ml) coffee liqueur
½ oz (15 ml) maple syrup
1 dash Fee Brothers Cardamom Bitters
2 oz (60 ml) boiling water
Garnish: cinnamon quill

Irish Coffee
(See p 467)

Keoke Coffee
(See p 466)

Match Coffee
Michael Butt, 2003
(See p 464)

Southern Hospitality
Felix Woods, The Everleigh, Melbourne
1 oz (30 ml) bourbon
¾ oz (22 ml) tawny Port
¾ oz (22 ml) honey syrup (p 496)
1½ teaspoons (7 g) unsalted butter
2 oz (60 ml) boiling water
Garnish: freshly grated nutmeg

Three 'Hot' Dots and a Dash
1 oz (30 ml) aged dark rum
½ oz (15 ml) Goslings Black Seal Rum
¾ oz (22 ml) lime juice
½ oz (15 ml) orange juice
½ oz (15 ml) honey syrup (p 496)
¼ oz (7 ml) falernum
3 dashes Angostura Bitters
2 dashes Dale DeGroff's Pimento Aromatic Bitters
2 oz (60 ml) boiling water
Garnish: cherry and 2 pineapple fronds

Whiskey Hot Toddy
Graham Heubach, Sportsman's Club, Chicago
1 oz (30 ml) bourbon
1 oz (30 ml) tawny Port
½ oz (15 ml) orange curaçao (p 498)
½ oz (15 ml) lemon juice
½ oz (15 ml) cinnamon syrup (p 495)
2 oz (60 ml) boiling water
Garnish: orange peel

From *The Old Waldorf-Astoria Bar Book* (1935):

Drink to the past with a toast to the future—because the present is already slipping away!

Warm a Toddy glass by filling with boiling water. Empty water, then build ingredients in the glass and top with fresh boiling water. Alternatively, add room-temperature filtered water and use a milk frother or steamer to steam all ingredients until hot. Stir to combine.

BY POPULAR REQUEST

APERITIVO & SPRITZ

Spritz Veneziano p 419 (left), White Negroni Sbagliato p 419 (right)

Aperitivo & Spritz

The Italian tradition of aperitivo – the pre-dinner ritual designed to awaken the appetite – originated in the late 18th century and has evolved into one of Italy's most enduring and exported cultural customs.

The concept is rooted in the belief that bitter, herbal drinks can stimulate digestion, a notion that gained popularity in cities like Turin, where in 1786, distiller Antonio Benedetto Carpano created the first vermouth. By infusing fortified wine with a proprietary blend of botanicals, Carpano launched a beverage category that would become central to aperitivo culture. His innovation quickly caught on, and throughout the 19th century other regions in Italy began producing their own distinct liqueurs – Martini in Pessione, Campari in Milan, Aperol in Padua. The herbaceous, often bitter spirits were typically served with a splash of soda or Prosecco, over ice, and garnished with citrus, forming the basis for what we now recognise as the Spritz. Its modern renaissance was sparked by a 2017 Aperol campaign that branded it as the 'ultimate summer drink', leading to a broader revival of aperitivo hour as a stylish alternative to the more boisterous 'happy hour'. Today, the Spritz is not just a drink but a symbol of balance: bitter and bright, refreshing and complex, casual yet steeped in tradition.

Typically lower in alcohol, ingredients like Aperol, Campari and vermouth create well rounded, layered drinks that are both refreshing and sophisticated. Their bitterness helps balance sweeter elements, while their herbal and citrus notes add aroma and interest.

Aperitivo & Spritz

À Trois
ms. franky marshall, Le Boudoir, NYC, 2016
1½ oz (45 ml) Barolo Chinato
¾ oz (22 ml) Calvados
2 dashes orange bitters
1 oz (30 ml) tonic water, to top
Build in a frozen double rocks glass with ice.
Garnish: bay leaf

Adonis Spritz
Bethany Heinze, Vern's, Charleston
1½ oz (45 ml) Cappelletti Vino Aperitivo Americano Rosso
1½ oz (45 ml) Amontillado Sherry
5 dashes orange bitters
3 oz (90 ml) sparkling wine, to top
Build in a Spritz glass with ice.
Garnish: orange half-wheel

Alpino Spritz
Lachlan Bentley, The Everleigh, Melbourne, 2019
1 oz (30 ml) sweet vermouth
¾ oz (22 ml) dry vermouth
¾ oz (22 ml) Amaro Braulio
2 oz (60 ml) tonic water, to top
Build in a Spritz glass with ice.
Garnish: lemon half-wheel and mint bouquet

Americano (Gaspare Campari Recipe)
(See p 112)

Americano (House Recipe)
(See p 112)

Americano Chinato
Michael Madrusan, The Everleigh, Melbourne, 2020
1¼ oz (37 ml) Barolo Chinato
1 oz (30 ml) Campari
1 oz (30 ml) soda, to top
Build in a frozen double rocks glass with ice.
Garnish: lemon wedge

Americano Perfecto
(See p 436)

Americano Pesca
Felix Woods, Black Pearl, Melbourne, 2021
1¼ oz (37 ml) RinQuinQuin à la Pêche
¾ oz (22 ml) sweet vermouth
¾ oz (22 ml) Campari
Soda, to top
Build in a frozen Collins glass with ice.
Garnish: Cerignola olive

Americano Vergano
Batched & Bottled, *Max and Noel Venning, 2018*
1½ oz (45 ml) dry white wine
½ oz (15 ml) Campari
1½ oz (45 ml) pink grapefruit juice
½ oz (15 ml) lemon juice
½ oz (15 ml) simple syrup
Soda, to top
Shake with ice, then strain into a frozen Spritz glass with ice and top with soda.
Garnish: grapefruit half-wheel

Aperol Spritz
Padua, Veneto, 1950s
2 oz (60 ml) Aperol
3 oz (90 ml) Prosecco, to top
1 oz (30 ml) soda, to top
Build in a Spritz glass with ice.
Garnish: orange half-wheel

Apollo Spritz
Sam Ross, Good Guy's, NYC, 2024
¾ oz (22 ml) Amaro Braulio
1 oz (30 ml) Royal Gala apple juice
¼ oz (7 ml) ginger syrup (p 496)
1 teaspoon (5 ml) lemon juice
3 oz (90 ml) Champagne, to top
Toss and strain into a double rocks glass with ice, then top with Champagne.
Garnish: mint sprig

Belafonte (Charlie Ainsbury Recipe)
Charlie Ainsbury, This Must Be the Place, Sydney, 2015
⅔ oz (20 ml) Fino Sherry
½ oz (15 ml) gin (at least 45% ABV)
⅔ oz (20 ml) lemon juice
⅔ oz (20 ml) simple syrup
2⅓ oz (70 ml) Prosecco, to top
Toss and strain into a Spritz glass with ice, then top with Prosecco.
Garnish: basil sprig

Bellini
Giuseppe Cipriani, Harry's Bar, Venice, 1948
2 oz (60 ml) white peach purée
¼ oz (7 ml) lemon juice
2 oz (60 ml) Prosecco, to top
Toss and strain into a chilled flute, then top with Prosecco very slowly.
▼ Named after 15th century Venetian painter Giovanni Bellini.

Bellini (Vincenzo Errico Recipe)
Vincenzo Errico, L'Artefatto, Forio d'Ischia, 2021
1 scoop peach sorbet
2 oz (60 ml) Prosecco, to top
Add peach sorbet to a chilled coupe, then top with Prosecco and stir gently to combine.
Garnish: a short straw

Betty is Back
The Connaught Bar, *Agostino Perrone, Giorgio Bargiani & Maura Milia, 2024*
½ oz (15 ml) Aperol
1 teaspoon (5 ml) St Germain Elderflower Liqueur
1 teaspoon (5 ml) lemon juice
3⅓ oz (100 ml) Champagne, to top
Stir and strain into a chilled flute, then top with Champagne.
Garnish: cherry

Bicicletta Spritz
Difford's Guide
1½ oz (45 ml) Campari
1½ oz (45 ml) dry Italian white wine
1½ oz (45 ml) soda, to top
Build in a Spritz glass with ice.
Garnish: orange half-wheel

Bitter Intentions

Bobby Heugel, Anvil, Houston

2 oz (60 ml) Campari
¾ oz (22 ml) lemon juice
½ oz (15 ml) simple syrup
1½ oz (45 ml) soda, to top
1 oz (30 ml) Carpano Antica Formula, to float

Toss and strain into a frozen Collins glass with ice, then top with soda and float Carpano Antica Formula.

Garnish: orange half-wheel

Caffè Trentino

Felix Woods, The Everleigh, Melbourne, 2018

1½ oz (45 ml) Cappelletti Vino Aperitivo Americano Rosso
½ oz (15 ml) sweet vermouth
½ oz (15 ml) coffee liqueur
1 oz (30 ml) soda, to top

Build in a frozen double rocks glass with ice.

Garnish: orange half-wheel

Cameron Park Spritz

Christopher Galicia, Las Ramblas at Market Square, Brownsville

1 oz (30 ml) Aperol
¾ oz (22 ml) St Germain Elderflower Liqueur
½ oz (15 ml) mezcal
2 oz (60 ml) sparkling wine, to top
1 oz (30 ml) soda, to top

Build in a Spritz glass with ice.

Garnish: orange half-wheel

Champagne Cup

Cocktails: How to Mix Them, *Robert Vermeire, 1922*

1 oz (30 ml) Cognac
¾ oz (22 ml) orange curaçao
¾ oz (22 ml) apricot brandy
1 oz (30 ml) Champagne, to top
½ oz (15 ml) soda, to top

Build in a double rocks glass with ice.

Garnish: 3–4 seasonal berries

Champino

Audrey Saunders, Beacon, NYC, 2000

1 oz (30 ml) Campari
1 oz (30 ml) sweet vermouth
Champagne, to top

Toss and strain into a chilled flute with ice, then top with Champagne.

Garnish: orange twist

Como Spritz

Sam Ross, Attaboy, NYC, 2018

1 oz (30 ml) Cynar
¾ oz (22 ml) passionfruit syrup (p 499)
¼ oz (7 ml) lemon juice
3 oz (90 ml) Prosecco, to top

Toss in a double rocks glass with ice.

Garnish: orange half-wheel

Cynar Spritz

2 oz (60 ml) Cynar
3 oz (90 ml) Prosecco, to top
1 oz (30 ml) soda, to top

Build in a Spritz glass with ice.

Garnish: lemon wedge (squeezed and dropped into the drink)

Duchesse

ms. franky marshall, Le Boudoir, NYC, 2015

1 oz (30 ml) dry vermouth
¾ oz (22 ml) blanc vermouth
¾ oz (22 ml) génépy
1 oz (30 ml) tonic water, to top

Build in a frozen double rocks glass with ice.

Garnish: lemon twist and rosemary sprig

86 Spritz

Sam Ross, Electra Cocktail Club, Las Vegas, 2018

1 oz (30 ml) Amaro Montenegro
1 oz (30 ml) bianco vermouth
¾ oz (22 m) soda, to top
2 oz (60 ml) Champagne, to top

Build in a double rocks glass with ice.

Garnish: grapefruit twist

Enzo

Greg Keesee, Attaboy, Nashville, 2021

1½ oz (45 ml) sweet vermouth
1 oz (30 ml) Campari
½ oz (15 ml) Fernet-Branca
Soda, to top

Build in a frozen double rocks glass with ice.

Garnish: orange half-wheel

Excelsior Special

Excelsior Bar, Rome

Ted Saucier's Bottoms Up, *Ted Saucier, 1951*

1½ oz (45 ml) sweet vermouth
¾ oz (22 ml) dry vermouth
¾ oz (22 ml) Campari
Soda, to top

Build in a frozen Spritz glass with cracked ice.

Garnish: orange twist

Famiglia Reale

(Negroni topped with Champagne)

Sam Ross, Milk & Honey, NYC, 2010

1 oz (30 ml) sweet vermouth
¾ oz (22 ml) gin
¾ oz (22 ml) Campari
1 oz (30 ml) Champagne, to top.

Build in a double rocks glass with ice.

Garnish: grapefruit twist

Frozen Sgroppino

Joe Campanale, Alta Linea, NYC

1 oz (30 ml) vodka
1 oz (30 ml) limoncello
1 oz (30 ml) Prosecco
1 scoop lemon sorbet

Gently whisk all ingredients in a bowl until smooth and pour into a frozen coupe.

Garnish: lemon wheel

Garibaldi
1½ oz (45 ml) Campari
4 oz (120 ml) fresh orange juice, to top
Cube whip the orange juice until fluffy, then add remaining ingredients to a frozen Highball glass with ice and top with orange juice.
Garnish: orange wedge
▼ Named after Giuseppe Garibaldi, the Italian revolutionary and military hero who led the movement to unification.

Garibaldi Royale
Nathan McCarley-O'Neill, Torrisi, NYC, 2024
1½ oz (45 ml) Campari
½ oz (15 ml) Aperol
3 oz (90 ml) orange juice
1 oz (30 ml) Prosecco, to top
Cube whip Campari, Aperol and orange juice until fluffy, then pour into a Collins glass with ice, top with Prosecco and stir briefly to combine.
Garnish: orange half-wheel

Have it All Spritz
Michael Madrusan, The Everleigh, Melbourne, 2018
¾ oz (22 ml) Cocchi Americano
¾ oz (22 ml) Aperol
½ oz (15 ml) Cocchi Rosa
1 oz (30 ml) Prosecco, to top
1 oz (30 ml) soda, to top
Build in a Spritz glass with ice.
Garnish: orange half-wheel and lemon half-wheel

Heavy Handed
Sam Ross, Good Guy's, NYC, 2024
1 oz (30 ml) sweet vermouth (preferably Carpano Antica Formula)
1 oz (30 ml) Campari
3 dashes absinthe
3 drops Bittermens Xocolatl Mole Bitters
3 oz (90 ml) Lambrusco, to top
Build in a Spritz glass with ice.
Garnish: orange half-wheel

Hightower Spritz
David Molyneux, The Everleigh, Melbourne, 2018
1½ oz (45 ml) Barolo Chinato
1 oz (30 ml) Suze
2 oz (60 ml) Champagne, to top
Build in a Spritz glass with ice.
Garnish: lemon horse's neck

Hugo Spritz
"Roland 'Ak' Gruber", San Zeno Wine and Cocktail Bar, Tyrol, Italy, 2005
¾ oz (22 ml) St Germain Elderflower Liqueur
4 oz (120 ml) Prosecco, to top
1 oz (30 ml) soda, to top
Build in a Spritz glass with ice.
Garnish: lemon half-wheel and mint sprig

Il Carretto No. 1
Paul Hammond, Connie's Italian Diner, Melbourne, 2022
1 oz (30 ml) Aperol
½ oz (15 ml) Cynar
¼ oz (7 ml) Galliano Vanilla
¼ oz (7 ml) lemon juice
2 oz (60 ml) Prosecco, to top
1 oz (30 ml) soda, to top
Toss and strain into a Spritz glass with ice, then top with Prosecco and soda.
Garnish: orange half-wheel and Sicilian olive

Il Carretto No. 2
Paul Hammond, Connie's Italian Diner, Melbourne, 2022
¾ oz (22 ml) Campari
⅜ oz (11 ml) coffee liqueur
½ teaspoon (2.5 ml) Fernet-Branca
2 oz (60 ml) Lambrusco, to top
1 oz (30 ml) soda, to top
Toss and strain into a Spritz glass with ice, then top with Lambrusco and soda.
Garnish: mint bouquet

Il Carretto No. 3
Paul Hammond, Connie's Italian Diner, Melbourne, 2022
¾ oz (22 ml) Manzanilla Sherry
½ oz (15 ml) apricot brandy
¼ oz (7 ml) Suze
¼ oz (7 ml) lemon juice
2½ oz (75 ml) moscato, to top
1 oz (30 ml) soda, to top
Toss and strain into a Spritz glass with ice, then top with moscato and soda.
Garnish: cucumber fan

Kingston Americano
Tyson Buhler, Death & Co, 2019
1 oz (30 ml) Jamaican dark rum (preferably Wray & Nephew)
1 oz (30 ml) Campari
4 oz (120 ml) pink grapefruit soda, to top
Build in a Spritz glass with ice.
Garnish: grapefruit half-wheel and pinch of salt

Lac Leman
Alastair Walker, Caretaker, Auckland, 2021
1½ oz (45 ml) Cocchi Americano
1 oz (30 ml) Suze
3 dashes absinthe
Soda, to top
Build in a frozen footed Delmonico glass with ice and stir briefly to combine.
Garnish: lemon twist

Ladybird
Oska Whitehart, The Everleigh, Melbourne, 2017
1½ oz (45 ml) Cappelletti Vino Aperitivo Americano Rosso
½ oz (15 ml) coffee liqueur
¼ oz (7 ml) Heering Cherry Liqueur
Soda, to top
Dry shake, then pour into a frozen footed Delmonico glass with ice and top with soda.
Garnish: orange half-wheel and cherry

Layover in Paris

Alicia Perry, Polite Provisions, San Diego, 2017

¾ oz (22 ml) Giffard Crème de Pamplemousse Rose
¾ oz (22 ml) pink grapefruit juice
2 dashes absinthe
3 oz (90 ml) sparkling rosé, to top

Toss all ingredients, then strain into a Spritz glass with ice.

Garnish: grapefruit twist and 3 seasonal berries

Limoncello Spritz

1½ oz (45 ml) limoncello
1 oz (30 ml) Prosecco, to top
¾ oz (22 ml) soda, to top

Build in a Spritz glass with ice.

Garnish: orange half-wheel

Long Legs

Sam Ross, Good Guy's, NYC, 2024

¾ oz (22 ml) Luxardo Bitter
¼ oz (7 ml) Tempus Fugit Crème de Cacao
¼ oz (7 ml) raspberry liqueur (preferably Giffard Crème de Framboise)
1 oz (30 ml) pineapple juice
¼ oz (7 ml) lemon juice
3 oz (90 ml) Lambrusco, to top

Toss all ingredients then strain into a Spritz glass with ice.

Garnish: pineapple frond and cocktail umbrella

Mauresque

1830s

1 oz (30 ml) pastis
¾ oz (22 ml) orgeat
4 oz (120 ml) cold filtered water, served on the side

Add pastis and orgeat to a frozen footed Delmonico glass with ice and top with water to taste.

▼ Allegedly invented by French soldiers serving in the Batallions of Light Infantry of Africa.

Mid-Morning Americano

Felix Woods, Black Pearl, Melbourne, 2020

1½ oz (45 ml) sweet vermouth
¾ oz (22 ml) Campari
¾ oz (22 ml) coffee liqueur
Soda, to top

Dry shake, then pour into a frozen footed Delmonico glass with ice and top with soda.

Garnish: orange half-wheel

Milano-Torino

(aka **Mi-To**)

Gaspare Campari, Milan, 1860s

1½ oz (45 ml) Campari
1½ oz (45 ml) sweet vermouth

Build in a frozen footed Delmonico glass with ice.

Garnish: orange half-wheel

▼ Considered the precursor to the Americano.

Negroni Frappé

(See p 300)

Negroni Sbagliato

Mirko Stocchetto, Bar Basso, 1972

1 oz (30 ml) Campari
1 oz (30 ml) sweet vermouth
2 oz (60 ml) Prosecco, to top

Build in a Spritz glass with ice.

Garnish: orange half-wheel

No Hands

Brandon Bramhall, Attaboy, Nashville, 2017

1¼ oz (37 ml) Campari
1¼ oz (37 ml) sweet vermouth
2 drops Bittermens Xocolatl Mole Bitters
1 oz (30 ml) soda, to top

Build in a frozen footed Delmonico glass with ice and stir briefly to combine.

Garnish: orange twist

Old Hickory Cocktail

Famous New Orleans Drinks and How to Mix 'Em, *Stanley Clisby Arthur, 1937*

1½ oz (45 ml) sweet vermouth
1 oz (30 ml) dry vermouth
4 dashes Peychaud's Aromatic Cocktail Bitters
4 dashes orange bitters

Build in a frozen Old Fashioned glass with ice.

Garnish: orange twist

Pacific Coast Highway

Parker Marvin, Attaboy, NYC, 2017

1 oz (30 ml) Bruto Americano
1 oz (30 ml) blanc vermouth
1 oz (30 ml) lime juice
¾ oz (22 ml) simple syrup
Soda, to top

Cube whip and pour into a frozen Highball glass with ice, then top with soda and stir briefly to combine.

Garnish: orange half-wheel

Palazzo Spritz

Ingrid Archer and David Molyneux, The Everleigh, Melbourne, 2018

1 oz (30 ml) Cocchi Rosa
¾ oz (22 ml) Cap Corse Mattei Blanc
¾ oz (22 ml) Campari
2 dashes peach bitters
Soda, to top

Cube whip and pour into a frozen footed Delmonico glass with ice, then top with soda and stir briefly to combine.

Garnish: grapefruit twist

Palomar Americano

(See p 468)

Passionfruit Sgroppino

Stacey Swenson, Dante, NYC

1½ oz (45 ml) Prosecco
1 oz (30 ml) Contratto Aperitif
1 scoop passionfruit sorbet

Gently whisk all ingredients in a bowl until smooth and pour into a frozen coupe.

Pear & Pastis

Batched & Bottled, *Max and Noel Venning, 2018*

1½ oz (45 ml) vodka
½ oz (15 ml) pear liqueur
1 oz (30 ml) lemon juice
½ oz (15 ml) simple syrup
½ teaspoon (2.5 ml) pastis
1 oz (30 ml) soda, to top

Cube whip and pour into a frozen footed Delmonico glass with ice, then top with soda and stir briefly to combine.

Garnish: lemon half-wheel

Pomponella

Matthew Thorp, Bar Louise, NYC

1½ oz (45 ml) Amaro Nonino
4 dashes orange bitters
3 oz (90 ml) Lambrusco, to top
1 oz (30 ml) soda, to top

Build in a Spritz glass with ice.

Garnish: orange half-wheel and Cerignola olive

Rome with a View

(See p 84)

Sakuranbō Americano

The Way of the Cocktail, *Julia Momosé, 2021*

1½ oz (45 ml) Campari
¾ oz (22 ml) Barolo Chinato
½ oz (15 ml) Heering Cherry Liqueur

Build in a frozen footed Delmonico glass with crushed ice and stir briefly to combine.

Garnish: cherry

Sbagliato (Nathan McCarley-O'Neill Recipe)

Nathan McCarley-O'Neill, Torrisi, NYC, 2024

1½ oz (45 ml) Punt e Mes
1½ oz (45 ml) Aperol
1½ oz (45 ml) Lambrusco, to top

Build in a double rocks glass with ice and stir briefly to combine.

Garnish: orange twist (discard) and orange half-wheel

Sbagliato Rosa

Tom Macy, Clover Club, NYC

1 oz (30 ml) Cappelletti Vino Aperitivo Americano Rosso
1 oz (30 ml) Cocchi Rosa
1 oz (30 ml) Rosé Champagne, to top

Build in a frozen footed Delmonico glass with ice.

Garnish: orange and grapefruit twist

Seven Hills

Chip Tyndale, Dutch Kills, NYC

1 oz (30 ml) Cocchi Americano
1 oz (30 ml) Amaro CioCiaro
½ oz (15 ml) apricot brandy
¾ oz (22 ml) lemon juice
¼ oz (7 ml) simple syrup
Soda, to top

Cube whip and pour into a frozen Highball glass with ice, then top with soda and stir briefly to combine.

Garnish: orange half-wheel and freshly grated cinnamon

Sgroppino

Venice, Italy

2 oz (60 ml) Prosecco
1 oz (30 ml) vodka
1 scoop lemon sorbet

Gently whisk all ingredients in a bowl until smooth and pour into a frozen coupe.

Garnish: mint sprig

Sinking Spritz

Hawksmoor, London

1½ oz (45 ml) sauvignon blanc
1½ oz (45 ml) Aperol
¼ oz (7 ml) Lillet Rouge
¼ oz (7 ml) Picon Amer
¼ oz (7 ml) St Germain Elderflower Liqueur

Build in a frozen Spritz glass with ice and stir briefly to combine.

Garnish: orange twist

▼ Based on 'A Sinking Cocktail' by Rich Hunt, Quo Vadis, London, 2009.

South Pacific Spritz

Ella Diaz, Ironside Fish & Oyster, San Diego, 2019

1½ oz (45 ml) blanco tequila
½ oz (15 ml) Cocchi Americano
¾ oz (22 ml) lemon juice
¾ oz (22 ml) passionfruit syrup (p 499)
1½ oz (45 ml) Champagne, to top
1 oz (30 ml) soda, to top

Toss and strain into a Spritz glass with ice, then top with Champagne and soda and stir briefly to combine.

Garnish: orange half-wheel and edible orchid

Spritz Cup

Chris Bostick, Half Step, Austin, 2015

1 oz (30 ml) Aperol
1 oz (30 ml) sweet vermouth
1 oz (30 ml) fruit cup (p 126)
1 oz (30 ml) Prosecco, to top

Build in a Spritz glass with ice.

Garnish: cucumber fan

Spritz Fagio

Mitshel Ibrahim, Ombra, London

1 oz (30 ml) Cynar
1 oz (30 ml) Campari
2 oz (60 ml) Prosecco, to top
1 oz (30 ml) soda, to top

Build in a Spritz glass with ice.

Garnish: orange half-wheel and Cerignola olive

Spritz Torrisi

Nathan McCarley-O'Neill, Torrisi, NYC, 2024

1½ oz (45 ml) Aperol
½ oz (15 ml) Giffard Rhubarb Liqueur
¼ oz (7 ml) Giffard Crème de Pêche de Vigne
¼ oz (7 ml) lemon juice
Prosecco, to top

Toss and strain into a frozen footed Delmonico glass with ice, then top with Prosecco and stir briefly to combine.

Garnish: 3 thin orange slices wrapped around the inside of the glass

Spritz Veneziano
(aka **Venetian Spritz**)
2 oz (60 ml) Select Aperitivo
3 oz (90 ml) Prosecco, to top
1 oz (30 ml) soda, to top
Build in a Spritz glass with ice and stir briefly to combine.
Garnish: Cerignola olive

Sunday Spritz
Felix Woods, The Everleigh, Melbourne, 2018
2 oz (60 ml) Cocchi Americano
2 dashes absinthe
2 dashes orange bitters
3 oz (90 ml) soda, to top
Build in a frozen double rocks glass with ice.
Garnish: mint sprig and grapefruit twist

Sussudio
Sam Ross, Temple Bar, NYC, 2023
¾ oz (22 ml) Cappelletti Amaro Pasubio
1 oz (30 ml) watermelon juice
¼ oz (7 ml) lime juice
¼ oz (7 ml) agave syrup (p 494)
3 oz (90 ml) Prosecco, to top
Toss and strain into a Spritz glass with ice, then top with Prosecco and stir briefly to combine.
Garnish: lime wheel and freshly cracked black pepper

Tan Line Spritz
Stacey Swenson, Dante, NYC
1 oz (30 ml) dry vermouth
1 oz (30 ml) Cappelletti Vino Aperitivo Americano Rosso
1 oz (30 ml) watermelon juice
3 drops saline solution (p 493)
3 oz (90 ml) Prosecco, to top
Toss and strain into a Spritz glass with ice, then top with Prosecco and stir briefly to combine.
Garnish: lemon wheel

Trap Queen
Erick Castro, Raised By Wolves, San Diego
1½ oz (45 ml) Cappelletti Vino Aperitivo Americano Rosso
½ oz (15 ml) Giffard Lichi-Li
3 oz (90 ml) Prosecco, to top
1 oz (30 ml) soda, to top
Build in a Spritz glass with ice.
Garnish: grapefruit twist (discard) and grapefruit half-wheel

Watermelon Sgroppino
Michael Madrusan, The Everleigh, Melbourne, 2025
1½ oz (45 ml) blanco tequila
1 scoop watermelon sorbet
½ oz (15 ml) lime juice
1½ oz (45 ml) sparkling wine
Stir gently in a shaker tin and pour into a frozen Sour glass.
Garnish: light dusting of cayenne pepper

West End
Cameron Parish, The Everleigh, Melbourne, 2017
1 oz (30 ml) Cocchi Americano
¾ oz (22 ml) Cynar
2 dashes peach bitters
3 oz (90 ml) Champagne, to top
Build in a Spritz glass with ice.
Garnish: orange twist

White Negroni Sbagliato
Toby Cecchini, The Long Island Bar, NYC, 2018
1 oz (30 ml) Carpano Bianco
1 oz (30 ml) Avèze (or Suze)
4 oz (120 ml) Prosecco, to top
Build in a double rocks glass with ice.
Garnish: long cucumber ribbon
▼ Made for Michael Manfredi and Claire Weiss.

White Peach Sgroppino
Toby Cecchini, Long Island Bar, NYC
4 oz (120 ml) Prosecco
1 oz (30 ml) vodka
½ oz (15 ml) Giffard Crème de Pêche de Vigne
2 scoops white peach sorbet
Gently whisk vodka, Giffard Crème de Pêche de Vigne and 1 oz (30 ml) Prosecco in a bowl until smooth, then pour into a Sour glass and top with remaining Prosecco.

From *Irish and English bar toasts of the early 1900s*:

To the wise, the wild, and the ones who make life worthwhile!

Young American
Michael Madrusan, Milk & Honey, NYC, 2009
1½ oz (45 ml) sweet vermouth
½ oz (15 ml) Campari
½ oz (15 ml) Aperol
3 dashes absinthe
1 oz (30 ml) soda, to top
Build in a frozen footed Delmonico glass with ice.
Garnish: lemon twist (discard) and lemon half-wheel

Yuzu Shakerato
Lorenzo Antinori, Bar Leone, Hong Kong, 2023
1½ oz (45 ml) Campari
¾ oz (22 ml) yuzushu (preferably Heiwa Shuzo Tsuru-ume Yuzushu)
½ oz (15 ml) Amaro Santoni
⅔ oz (20 ml) pink grapefruit juice
1 teaspoon (5 ml) lime juice
Shake with ice and strain into a frozen coupe.

SPARKLING

Millionaire's Martini p 319 (left), The French "75" p 425 (right)

Sparkling

Cocktails with sparkling wine are delightful and are often chosen to mark moments of celebration.

Lively and decadent, sparkling wines and Champagnes add a bright effervescence and sophistication to a multitude of different cocktail styles, with recipes spanning categories such as Sours (p 152), Collins (p 62) and Fizzes (p 134), amongst others.

Bubbles – usually Champagne or sparkling wine – are often used to counter herbal or bittersweet ingredients from the aperitivo family, resulting in bright and balanced drinks with broad appeal.

This ingredient also plays well with tart and bitter citrus by lifting and softening flavours such as orange, grapefruit, pineapple and peach. When employed as a base, Sparkling cocktails also appeal to the health-conscious, low-alcohol drinker, offering elegant and attractive alternatives to the spiritous sipper.

Sparkling

CHAMPAGNE

Buck's Fizz
Pat McGarry, Buck's Club, London, 1921
3½ oz (105 ml) Champagne, to top
2 oz (60 ml) fresh orange juice
Cube whip the orange juice until fluffy, then pour into a chilled flute and top with Champagne.

Barbotage of Champagne
The Artistry of Mixing Drinks, *Frank Meier, 1936*
4 oz (120 ml) Champagne, to top
½ oz (15 ml) lemon juice
½ oz (15 ml) simple syrup
1 dash Angostura Bitters
Pebble whip, then pour into a frozen footed Delmonico glass with ice.
Garnish: orange twist

Champagne Cobbler
(See p 270)

Champagne Cobbler (Dale DeGroff's Recipe)
(See p 270)

Champagne Cocktail
The Bar-Tender's Guide, *Jerry Thomas, 1862*
4 oz (120 ml) Champagne
1 white sugar cube
5 dashes Angostura Bitters
Soften sugar cube with bitters in a small dish, then gently drop the cube into a chilled flute of Champagne.
Garnish: lemon twist

Champagne Julep
(See p 284)

Champagne Punch
(See p 131)

Honey Rider
Alicia Perry, Starlite, San Diego, 2024
½ oz (15 ml) Cocchi Americano
1 oz (30 ml) chenin blanc cordial (p 494)
¾ oz (22 ml) lemon juice
½ oz (15 ml) grapefruit piña syrup (p 496)
2 oz (60 ml) sparkling wine, to top
Shake with ice and strain into a small wine glass with ice.
Garnish: 2–3 edible flowers

Mimosa
Frank Meier, Ritz Paris, Paris, 1925
2 oz (60 ml) Champagne, to top
2 oz (60 ml) fresh orange juice
Cube whip the orange juice until fluffy, then pour into a chilled flute and top with Champagne.

VODKA

Only Fans
Leo Robitschek, The NoMad Bar, NYC
1 oz (30 ml) vodka
1 oz (30 ml) Fino Sherry
¾ oz (22 ml) lime juice
½ oz (15 ml) falernum
½ oz (15 ml) passionfruit syrup (p 499)
½ oz (15 ml) vanilla syrup (p 502)
1 egg white
¾ oz (22 ml) Champagne, to top
Dry shake, add ice and shake again, then strain into a chilled Sour glass and top with Champagne.

Russian Spring Punch
Dick Bradsell, London, 1980s
1½ oz (45 ml) vodka
½ oz (15 ml) crème de cassis
¾ oz (22 ml) lemon juice
½ oz (15 ml) simple syrup
2 oz (60 ml) Champagne, to top
Toss and strain into a chilled Collins glass with ice, then top with Champagne.
Garnish: lemon wedge and raspberry

Silver Angel
1 oz (30 ml) vodka
¼ oz (7 ml) Giffard Crème de Pêche de Vigne
¾ oz (22 ml) cloudy apple juice
¼ oz (7 ml) passionfruit syrup (p 499)
2 oz (60 ml) Champagne, to top
Toss and strain into a chilled flute, then top with Champagne.

GIN

Baker's Dozen
Sam Ross, Attaboy, NYC, 2012
1 oz (30 ml) gin
½ oz (15 ml) apricot brandy
½ oz (15 ml) lemon juice
¼ oz (7 ml) orgeat
2 oz (60 ml) Champagne, to top
Toss and strain into a chilled flute, then top with Champagne.
Garnish: lemon twist

Beverley Hills Iced Tea
¾ oz (22 ml) gin
¾ oz (22 ml) vodka
½ oz (15 ml) triple sec
½ oz (15 ml) lime juice
½ oz (15 ml) simple syrup
2 oz (60 ml) Champagne, to top
Toss and strain into a chilled flute with ice, then top with Champagne.
Garnish: lime twist

Bitter French
Phil Ward, Death & Co, NYC, 2008
1 oz (30 ml) gin
¼ oz (7 ml) Campari
½ oz (15 ml) lemon juice
½ oz (15 ml) simple syrup
2 oz (60 ml) Champagne, to top
Toss and strain into a chilled flute, then top with Champagne.
Garnish: grapefruit twist

Champagne-Ginebra
The South American Gentleman's Companion, *Charles H. Baker Jr., 1951*
1 oz (30 ml) gin
½ oz (15 ml) triple sec
½ oz (15 ml) lemon juice
2 dashes Angostura Bitters
2 oz (60 ml) Champagne, to top
Toss and strain into a chilled Spritz glass with ice, then top with Champagne.
Garnish: lemon twist

Diamond Cocktail
1 oz (30 ml) gin
½ oz (15 ml) lemon juice
½ oz (15 ml) grenadine (p 496)
2 oz (60 ml) Champagne, to top
Toss and strain into a chilled flute with ice, then top with Champagne.

Diamond Fizz
(See p 138)

Diamond Hitch
(Pink Gin with ice and Champagne)
Bar La Florida Cocktails, *1935*
1½ oz (45 ml) gin
5 dashes Angostura Bitters
2 oz (60 ml) Champagne, to top
Build in an Old Fashioned glass with cracked ice.
Garnish: lemon twist

Dinosaur
Louis Wilson, Dingo Bar
Barflies and Cocktails, *Harry MacElhone, 1927*
1 oz (30 ml) gin
½ oz (15 ml) Cognac
½ oz (15 ml) Heering Cherry Liqueur
2 dashes absinthe
2 oz (60 ml) Champagne, to top
Toss and strain into a chilled flute, then top with Champagne.

Elder Fashion Royale
Phil Ward, Death & Co, NYC, 2008
1½ oz (45 ml) gin
½ oz (15 ml) St Germain Elderflower Liqueur
1 dash orange bitters
2 oz (60 ml) Champagne, to top
Toss and strain into a chilled flute with ice, then top with Champagne.
Garnish: grapefruit twist

Falconet
Oscar Shaw, The Everleigh, Melbourne, 2021
1 oz (30 ml) gin
¾ oz (22 ml) lime juice
½ oz (15 ml) simple syrup
2 dashes absinthe
1 cucumber wheel
2 oz (60 ml) Champagne, to top
Press cucumber with simple syrup, add remaining ingredients and toss. Strain into a chilled flute with ice, then top with Champagne.
Garnish: cucumber wheel

Foreplay in the Foyer
Adele Stratton, Noble Experiment, San Diego, 2016
¾ oz (22 ml) gin
¼ oz (7 ml) raspberry eau de vie
½ oz (15 ml) lemon juice
½ oz (15 ml) simple syrup
1 dash pastis
2 oz (60 ml) Champagne, to top
Toss and strain into a chilled flute with ice, then top with Champagne.
Garnish: raspberry

Last Laugh
(Last Word with Champagne)
Abigail Gullo, Compère Lapin, New Orleans
½ oz (15 ml) gin
½ oz (15 ml) Green Chartreuse
½ oz (15 ml) maraschino liqueur
½ oz (15 ml) lime juice
1 oz (30 ml) Champagne, to top
Shake with ice and strain into a chilled coupe, then top with Champagne.
Garnish: cherry

Millionaire's Martini
(See p 319)

Passionfruit "75"
1 oz (30 ml) gin
¾ oz (22 ml) passionfruit syrup (p 499)
½ oz (15 ml) lemon juice
2 oz (60 ml) Champagne, to top
Toss and strain into a chilled flute, then top with Champagne.

Radio Days
Alex Day, Death & Co, NYC, 2013
1 oz (30 ml) gin
¾ oz (22 ml) Salers Gentiane
¾ oz (22 ml) lemon juice
½ oz (15 ml) honey syrup (p 496)
2 oz (60 ml) Champagne, to top
Shake with ice and strain into a chilled coupe, then top with Champagne.
Garnish: orange twist (discard)

The French "75"
(aka **French 75**)
Here's How!, *Judge Jr., 1927*
1 oz (30 ml) gin
½ oz (15 ml) lemon juice
½ oz (15 ml) simple syrup
2 oz (60 ml) Champagne, to top
Toss and strain into a chilled flute with ice, then top with Champagne,
Garnish: lemon twist
▼ *"This drink is really what won the War for the Allies."*

The Seaplane
(French 75 with absinthe and orange bitters)
Joseph Schwartz, Little Branch, NYC
1 oz (30 ml) gin
½ oz (15 ml) lemon juice
½ oz (15 ml) simple syrup
2 dashes absinthe
2 dashes orange bitters
2 oz (60 ml) Champagne, to top
Toss and strain into a chilled flute, then top with Champagne.
Garnish: lemon twist

Trench 75
Rogerio Igarashi, Bar Trench, Tokyo, 2017
1 oz (30 ml) gin (preferably Nikka Coffey Gin)
½ oz (15 ml) lemon juice
⅓ oz (10 ml) honey syrup (p 496)
1 oz (30 ml) sparkling sake, to top
Shake with ice and strain into a chilled coupe, then top with sparkling sake.
Garnish: lime wheel

RUM & CANE SPIRIT

Air Mail
Bacardí y sus Muchos Usos, *1930*
1 oz (30 ml) light rum
½ oz (15 ml) lime juice
½ oz (15 ml) honey syrup (p 496)
2 oz (60 ml) Champagne, to top
Toss and strain into a chilled flute, then top with Champagne.

Blanc de Funk
(See p 259)

Champagne Colada
(See p 447)

Crimean Cup, à la Marmora
The Bar-Tender's Guide, *Jerry Thomas, 1862*
1 oz (30 ml) Jamaican dark rum
1 oz (30 ml) Cognac
¼ oz (7 ml) maraschino liqueur
¾ oz (22 ml) lemon juice
¾ oz (22 ml) orgeat
2 oz (60 ml) Champagne, to top
Toss and strain into a chilled wine glass with ice, then top with Champagne.
Garnish: lemon twist (discard) and cherry
▼ "The celebrated Soyer". Named after Italian general and statesman Alfonso Ferrero La Marmora, a hero of the Crimean War.

In Sheep's Clothing
Tony Roehr and Anthony Schmidt, Raised by Wolves, San Diego, 2021
½ oz (15 ml) aged rhum agricole
½ oz (15 ml) bonded apple brandy
½ oz (15 ml) lime juice
½ oz (15 ml) honey syrup (p 496)
2 oz (60 ml) Champagne, to top
Toss and strain into a chilled double rocks glass with ice, then top with Champagne.
Garnish: mint sprig

Mai Tai Spritz
(See p 449)

Old Cuban
Audrey Saunders, Bemelmans Bar, NYC, 2001
1 oz (30 ml) aged dark rum
½ oz (15 ml) lime juice
½ oz (15 ml) simple syrup
4–6 mint leaves
2 dashes Angostura Bitters
2 oz (60 ml) Champagne, to top
Shake briefly and strain into a chilled flute, then top with Champagne.

Rocky Mountain Punch
The Bar-Tender's Guide, Jerry Thomas, 1862
1 oz (30 ml) Jamaican dark rum
¼ oz (7 ml) maraschino liqueur
¾ oz (22 ml) lemon juice
¼ oz (7 ml) simple syrup
2 oz (60 ml) Champagne, to top
Toss and strain into a chilled wine glass with ice, then top with Champagne.
Garnish: mint sprig, orange half-wheel and lemon half-wheel

Rum & Roses
Davide Segat, NoMad London, London
1½ oz (45 ml) light rum
¾ oz (22 ml) St Germain Elderflower Liqueur
½ oz (15 ml) simple syrup
¼ oz (7 ml) lemon juice
2 dashes absinthe
1 oz (30 ml) sparkling rosé, to top
Toss and strain into a chilled wine glass with ice, then top with sparkling rosé.

Sparkling Mai Tai
(See p 451)

AGAVE

Beautiful Stranger
Erick Castro, 2007
1 oz (30 ml) blanco tequila
½ oz (15 ml) lemon juice
½ oz (15 ml) grenadine (p 496)
2 oz (60 ml) Champagne, to top
Toss and strain into a chilled flute, then top with Champagne.

Hail Mary
Spirits of Latin America, *Ivy Mix, 2020*
1 oz (30 ml) blanco tequila
¾ oz (22 ml) Salers Gentiane
¼ oz (7 ml) Giffard Crème de Pêche de Vigne
½ oz (15 ml) lemon juice
½ oz (15 ml) raspberry syrup (p 500)
1 dash orange bitters
2 oz (60 ml) cava, to top
Toss and strain into a chilled flute, then top with cava.
Garnish: grapefruit twist

Lone Ranger
Jeffrey Morgenthaler, Portland, 2012
1½ oz (45 ml) blanco tequila
¾ oz (22 ml) lemon juice
¾ oz (22 ml) simple syrup
Brut rosé Champagne, to top
Toss and strain into a chilled Collins glass with ice, then top with Brut rosé Champagne.
Garnish: long lemon twist

Margarita Royale
Dré Masso, Green & Red Mexican Cantina, London, 2005
1 oz (30 ml) blanco tequila
½ oz (15 ml) lime juice
¼ oz (7 ml) agave syrup (p 494)
2 oz (60 ml) Champagne, to top
Toss and strain into a chilled flute, then top with Champagne.

Palomita
(Paloma with Champagne)
Michael and Zara Madrusan, The Everleigh Bottling Co., 2020
¾ oz (22 ml) blanco tequila
1½ oz (45 ml) pink grapefruit juice
¼ oz (7 ml) lime juice
¼ oz (7 ml) agave syrup (p 494)
2 drops saline solution (p 493)
1½ oz (45 ml) soda, to top
1 oz (30 ml) Champagne, to top
Toss and strain into a chilled Collins glass with ice, then top with soda and Champagne.
Garnish: grapefruit half-wheel and pinch of salt

Pinche Cocktail
Michael Madrusan, Milk & Honey, NYC, 2008
1½ oz (45 ml) blanco tequila
¾ oz (22 ml) Aperol
¾ oz (22 ml) lime juice
¾ oz (22 ml) pink grapefruit juice
½ oz (15 ml) simple syrup
2 oz (60 ml) Champagne, to top
1 oz (30 ml) soda, to top
Toss and strain into a chilled Collins glass with ice, then top with soda and Champagne.
Garnish: lime wedge

AMERICAN WHISKEY

Boothby
(See p 346)

French 95
(French 75 with bourbon)
Jones' Complete Barguide, *Stan Jones, 1977*
1 oz (30 ml) bourbon
½ oz (15 ml) lemon juice
½ oz (15 ml) simple syrup
2 oz (60 ml) Champagne, to top
Toss and strain into a chilled flute with ice, then top with Champagne.
Garnish: lemon twist

Rebel Flip
(See p 398)

WORLD WHISK(E)Y

Rosy Cheeks
Jim Meehan, PDT, NYC, 2012
¾ oz (22 ml) Irish whiskey (preferably Redbreast 12yr Single Pot Still Irish Whiskey)
½ oz (15 ml) sloe gin
½ oz (15 ml) Tempus Fugit Crème de Cacao
½ oz (15 ml) lemon juice
2 oz (60 ml) Champagne, to top (preferably Blanc de Blancs)
Stir with ice and strain into a chilled wine glass with ice, then top with Champagne.
Garnish: lemon wheel

BRANDY

A Pink Agenda
A Quick Drink, *Lynnette Marrero and Ivy Mix with Megan Krigbaum, 2024*
1 oz (30 ml) pisco
½ oz (15 ml) pink grapefruit juice
½ oz (15 ml) raspberry syrup (p 500)
1 teaspoon (5 ml) lemon juice
1 drop saline solution (p 493)
2 oz (60 ml) Sparkling rosé, to top
Toss and strain into a chilled flute, then top with sparkling rosé.
Garnish: raspberry

Ambrosia
Famous New Orleans Drinks and How to Mix 'Em, *Stanley Clisby Arthur, 1937*
¾ oz (22 ml) Cognac
¾ oz (22 ml) bonded apple brandy
½ oz (15 ml) triple sec
½ oz (15 ml) lemon juice
2 oz (60 ml) Champagne, to top
Toss and strain into a chilled flute, then top with Champagne.
Garnish: lemon twist

Ambrosia (Xavier Herit Recipe)
Xavier Herit, Wallflower, NYC
1 oz (30 ml) Spanish brandy (preferably Cardenal Mendoza Solera Gran Reserva Brandy de Jerez)
½ oz (15 ml) Pedro Ximénez
½ oz (15 ml) Oloroso Sherry
¼ oz (7 ml) maraschino liqueur
½ oz (15 ml) verjus
2 dashes orange bitters
1½ oz (45 ml) Champagne, to top
Toss and strain into a chilled flute, then top with Champagne.
Garnish: cherry

American 25
Robert Simonson, 2014
1 oz (30 ml) bonded apple brandy
¼ oz (7 ml) Islay Scotch (preferably Laphroaig 10yr)
½ oz (15 ml) lemon juice
½ oz (15 ml) simple syrup
2 oz (60 ml) Champagne, to top
Toss and strain into a chilled flute, then top with Champagne.
Garnish: lemon twist

Boomin' Granny
Jillian Vose, Death & Co, NYC, 2012
1½ oz (45 ml) Cognac
1 oz (30 ml) Granny Smith apple juice
½ oz (15 ml) lime juice
½ oz (15 ml) honey syrup (p 496)
1 oz (30 ml) Champagne, to top
Toss and strain into a chilled flute, then top with Champagne
Garnish: apple fan

Champagne Cocktail No. II
(aka **Jimmie Roosevelt**)
The Gentleman's Companion, *Charles H. Baker Jr., 1939*
1 oz (30 ml) Cognac
¼ oz (7 ml) cane syrup (p 494)
3 dashes Angostura Bitters
1 white sugar cube
2 oz (60 ml) Champagne, to top
¼ oz (7 ml) Green Chartreuse, to float
Add the sugar cube and bitters to a shaker, then crush the sugar. Add remaining ingredients, stir to combine, then pour into a chilled small wine glass with ice, top with Champagne and float Green Chartreuse.
Garnish: lemon twist

Champagne Flip
(See p 395)

Champagne Socialist
Felix Woods, Black Pearl, Melbourne, 2021
1 oz (30 ml) Cognac
⅜ oz (11 ml) Yellow Chartreuse
3 dashes Angostura Bitters
½ white sugar cube
1½ oz (45 ml) Champagne, to top
Add the sugar cube and bitters to a chilled Old Fashioned glass, then crush the sugar. Add remaining ingredients, stir to combine, then add ice and top with Champagne.
Garnish: lemon twist (discard)

Chicago Cocktail
The Savoy Cocktail Book, *Harry Craddock, 1930*
1 oz (30 ml) Cognac
½ oz (15 ml) orange curaçao (p 498)
2 dashes Angostura Bitters
2½ oz (80 ml) Champagne, to top
Toss and strain into a chilled flute with ice, then top with Champagne.
Garnish: sugar rim and lemon twist

Corpse Reviver (W.J. Tarling Recipe)
Café Royal Cocktail Book, *W.J. Tarling, 1937*
1½ oz (45 ml) Cognac
1 oz (30 ml) orange juice
¾ oz (22 ml) grenadine (p 496)
½ oz (15 ml) lemon juice
2 oz (60 ml) Champagne, to top
Toss and strain into a chilled wine glass with ice, then top with Champagne.
Garnish: lemon twist (discard)

Daydream Cocktail
(Classic Cocktail topped with Champagne)
100 Cocktails: How to Mix Them, *"Bernard", 1970*
1½ oz (45 ml) Cognac
½ oz (15 ml) orange curaçao (p 498)
½ oz (15 ml) maraschino liqueur
½ oz (15 ml) lemon juice
1 oz (30 ml) Champagne, to top
Shake with ice, then strain into a chilled coupe and top with Champagne.
Garnish: lemon twist (discard)

False Alarm
Spirits of Latin America, *Ivy Mix, 2020*
1 oz (30 ml) pisco
¼ oz (7 ml) Campari
½ oz (15 ml) lemon juice
½ oz (15 ml) raspberry syrup (p 500)
2 oz (60 ml) Champagne, to top
Toss and strain into a small chilled wine glass with ice, then top with Champagne.
Garnish: 3 raspberries on a cocktail skewer

Fancy Brandy Cocktail
New and Improved Bartender's Manual, *Harry Johnson, 1882*
1½ oz (45 ml) Cognac
½ oz (15 ml) orange curaçao (p 498)
2 dashes Angostura Bitters
2½ oz (80 ml) Champagne, to top
Toss and strain into a small chilled wine glass with ice, then top with Champagne.
Garnish: lemon twist

Fantino
(French 125 with Italicus)
Felix Woods, The Everleigh, Melbourne, 2018
1 oz (30 ml) Cognac
½ oz (15 ml) lemon juice
½ oz (15 ml) simple syrup
1 teaspoon (5 ml) Italicus Rosolio di Bergamotto
2 oz (60 ml) Champagne, to top
Toss and strain into a chilled wine glass with ice, then top with Champagne.
Garnish: lemon twist

Fleurissimo
The Connaught Bar, *Agostino Perrone, Giorgio Bargiani & Maura Milia, 2024*
½ oz (15 ml) Cognac
1 teaspoon (5 ml) crème de violette
2 dashes Peychaud's Aromatic Cocktail Bitters
1 white sugar cube
3½ oz (105 ml) Champagne, to top
Soften sugar cube with bitters in a small dish, then build remaining ingredients in a chilled coupe. Gently drop the cube into the coupe and top with Champagne.
Garnish: rose petal
▾ Created in honour of Princess Grace of Monaco, a former guest.

Fortune Cocktail
Michael Madrusan, Milk & Honey, NYC, 2007
1 oz (30 ml) bonded apple brandy
½ oz (15 ml) lemon juice
½ oz (15 ml) simple syrup
6–8 mint leaves
2 oz (60 ml) Champagne, to top
Toss and strain into a chilled flute, then top with Champagne.
Garnish: mint leaf

French 125
(French 75 with Cognac)
Jones' Complete Barguide, *Stan Jones, 1977*
1 oz (30 ml) Cognac
½ oz (15 ml) lemon juice
½ oz (15 ml) simple syrup
2 oz (60 ml) Champagne, to top
Toss and strain into a chilled flute with ice, then top with Champagne.
Garnish: lemon twist

Harry's Pick-Me-Up
Approved Cocktails, *United Kingdom Bartenders' Guild, 1937*
1 oz (30 ml) Cognac
½ oz (15 ml) lemon juice
½ oz (15 ml) grenadine (p 496)
2 oz (60 ml) Champagne, to top
Toss and strain into a chilled flute, then top with Champagne
Garnish: lemon twist

Harvard Law
(See p 355)

I.B.F. Pick-Me-Up Cocktail
The Official Mixer's Manual, *Patrick Gavin Duffy, 1934*
1 oz (30 ml) Cognac
½ oz (15 ml) Fernet-Branca
½ oz (15 ml) orange curaçao (p 498)
2½ oz (80 ml) Champagne, to top
Toss and strain into a chilled flute, then top with Champagne.
Garnish: lemon twist

Inca Sol
1½ oz (45 ml) pisco
½ oz (15 ml) pear liqueur
½ oz (15 ml) lemon juice
¼ oz (7 ml) simple syrup
8–10 mint leaves
2 dashes Angostura Bitters
2 oz (60 ml) Champagne, to top
Shake with ice and strain into a chilled coupe, then top with Champagne.

Livener
(French 125 with raspberry and Angostura Bitters)
Recipes of American and Other Iced Drinks, *Charlie Paul, 1902*
1 oz (30 ml) Cognac
½ oz (15 ml) lemon juice
½ oz (15 ml) simple syrup
2 raspberries
2 dashes Angostura Bitters
2 oz (60 ml) Champagne, to top
Press raspberries with simple syrup, add remaining ingredients and toss. Strain into a chilled flute, then top with Champagne.
Garnish: raspberry

Magnolia
(See p 396)

Magnolia (à la Simmons)
(See p 396)

Magnolia Highball
(See p 147)

Monte Carlo Casino Special
Monte Carlo Casino, Monte Carlo
Ted Saucier's Bottoms Up, *Ted Saucier, 1951*
1½ oz (45 ml) Cognac
¼ oz (7 ml) Demerara syrup (p 495)
3 dashes absinthe
2½ oz (80 ml) Champagne, to top
Toss and strain into a chilled flute, then top with Champagne.
Garnish: orange twist

Napoleon's Cocktail
American Bar, *Frank P. Newman, 1900*
1½ oz (45 ml) Cognac
½ oz (15 ml) Giffard Crème de Pêche de Vigne
2 dashes peach bitters
2½ oz (80 ml) Champagne, to top
Toss and strain into a chilled flute, then top with Champagne.
Garnish: lemon twist

Pacific Union Club Punch
The World's Drinks and How to Mix Them, *Wm. T. Boothby, 1908*
1 oz (30 ml) Cognac
½ oz (15 ml) orange curaçao (p 498)
½ oz (15 ml) lemon juice
2 oz (60 ml) Champagne, to top
Toss and strain into a chilled flute, then top with Champagne.
Garnish: lemon twist

Pisco Punch No. 2
1½ oz (45 ml) pisco
1 oz (30 ml) pineapple juice
½ oz (15 ml) lemon juice
½ oz (15 ml) simple syrup
¼ oz (7 ml) falernum
2 oz (60 ml) Champagne, to top
Toss and strain into a frozen double rocks glass with ice, then top with Champagne.
Garnish: pineapple wedge

Pistolet
Andy Chu, The Everleigh, Melbourne, 2017
1 oz (30 ml) Cognac
½ oz (15 ml) lemon juice
½ oz (15 ml) simple syrup
1 teaspoon (5 ml) Suze
2 oz (60 ml) Champagne, to top
Toss and strain into a chilled flute, then top with Champagne.
Garnish: lemon twist

Prince of Wales
Bariana, *Louis Fouquet, 1896*
1 oz (30 ml) Cognac
½ oz (15 ml) orange curaçao (p 498)
½ oz (15 ml) lemon juice
3 dashes Angostura Bitters
2 oz (60 ml) Champagne, to top
Toss and strain into a chilled flute, then top with Champagne.
Garnish: lemon twist

Ritz Cocktail
Dale DeGroff, Aurora, NYC, 1985
¾ oz (22 ml) Cognac
½ oz (15 ml) triple sec
⅓ oz (10 ml) maraschino liqueur
⅓ oz (10 ml) lemon juice
2 oz (60 ml) Champagne, to top
Toss and strain into a chilled flute, then top with Champagne.
Garnish: orange twist

Seven Year Itch
Eryn Reece, Death & Co, NYC, 2014
1½ oz (45 ml) Calvados
½ oz (15 ml) Yellow Chartreuse
¾ oz (22 ml) lemon juice
½ oz (15 ml) cane syrup (p 494)
1½ oz (45 ml) Champagne, to top
Shake with ice and strain into a chilled coupe, then top with Champagne.

Shaken 22
Michael Madrusan, The Everleigh, Melbourne, 2017
½ oz (15 ml) Cognac
½ oz (15 ml) gin
½ oz (15 ml) apricot brandy
½ oz (15 ml) lemon juice
2 oz (60 ml) Champagne, to top
Toss and strain into a chilled flute, then top with Champagne.
Garnish: lemon twist

"The Evening Sun"
(See p 166)

Trouble No More
Alicia Perry and Anthony Schmidt, The Gutter, San Diego, 2023
½ oz (15 ml) Cognac
½ oz (15 ml) gin
¼ oz (7 ml) Pierre Ferrand Dry Curaçao
½ oz (15 ml) lemon juice
½ oz (15 ml) simple syrup
1 strawberry, halved
2 oz (60 ml) Champagne, to top
Muddle strawberry with lemon juice and simple syrup, add remaining ingredients, then shake with ice, strain into a chilled flute and top with Champagne.
Garnish: half a strawberry

Valencia Cocktail (No. 2)
The Savoy Cocktail Book, Harry Craddock, *1930*
1 oz (30 ml) apricot brandy
1½ oz (45 ml) orange juice
¼ oz (7 ml) lemon juice
2 oz (60 ml) Champagne, to top
Toss and strain into a chilled flute, then top with Champagne.
Garnish: orange twist (discard)

FORTIFIED & LIQUEUR

Amara
Alicia Perry, The Lafayette Hotel and Club, San Diego, 2023
½ oz (15 ml) Angeleno Amaro (or Aperol)
½ oz (15 ml) Giffard Lichi-Li
¾ oz (22 ml) lemon juice
¾ oz (22 ml) passionfruit syrup (p 499)
1½ oz (45 ml) Prosecco, to top
1 oz (30 ml) soda, to top
Toss and strain into a small chilled wine glass with ice, then top with Prosecco and soda.
Garnish: edible orchid

Boston Club Punch
Davide Segat, NoMad London, London
1/3 oz (10 ml) Cognac
1/3 oz (10 ml) light rum
1/3 oz (10 ml) Pierre Ferrand Dry Curaçao
1/3 oz (10 ml) maraschino liqueur (preferably Havana Club 3yr)
1/2 oz (15 ml) strawberry syrup (p 501)
1/3 oz (10 ml) pineapple syrup (p 499)
1 teaspoon (5 ml) lemon juice
3 oz (90 ml) Champagne, to top
Toss and strain into a chilled Spritz glass with ice, then top with Champagne.
Garnish: redcurrant

Champ de Mars
Michael Madrusan, The Everleigh, Melbourne, 2017
1½ oz (45 ml) Cocchi Americano
1 oz (30 ml) St Germain Elderflower Liqueur
2 dashes absinthe
1 dash orange bitters
3 oz (90 ml) Champagne, to top
Build in a chilled Spritz glass with ice then top with Champagne.
Garnish: mint bouquet and lemon half-wheel

Champagne Daisy
Paul Hammond, Seamstress, Melbourne, 2008
3/4 oz (22 ml) orange curaçao (p 498)
1/2 oz (15 ml) Cognac
1/2 oz (15 ml) lemon juice
3 raspberries
1 egg white
2 oz (60 ml) Champagne, to top
Muddle raspberries with lemon juice then add all ingredients, except Champagne, and dry shake. Add ice and shake again, then strain into a frozen Sour glass and top with Champagne.
Garnish: lemon twist (discard) and raspberry

Chatham Cocktail
Devon Tarby, Death & Co, NYC, 2015
3/4 oz (22 ml) Fino Sherry
3/4 oz (22 ml) Cocchi Americano
1/4 oz (7 ml) Grand Marnier
1/2 oz (15 ml) lemon juice
1/4 oz (7 ml) simple syrup
2 drops saline solution (p 493)
1½ oz (45 ml) Champagne, to top
Toss and strain into a chilled Spritz glass with ice, then top with Champagne.
Garnish: grapefruit twist

Corpse Reviver No. 3 (Patrick Gavin Duffy Recipe)
The Official Mixer's Manual, *Patrick Gavin Duffy, 1956*
1½ oz (45 ml) pastis
3/4 oz (22 ml) lemon juice
1/2 oz (15 ml) simple syrup
3 oz (90 ml) Champagne, to top
Toss and strain into a chilled Spritz glass with ice, then top with Champagne.
Garnish: lemon half-wheel

Duke No. 1
(See p 399)

Kir Pêche
(Kir Royale with peach liqueur)
1/2 oz (15 ml) Giffard Crème de Pêche
4 oz (120 ml) Champagne, to top
Build in a chilled flute, then top with Champagne.
Garnish: lemon twist
▼ Swap peach liqueur for raspberry liqueur to make a **Kir Impérial**.

Kir Royale
1/2 oz (15 ml) crème de cassis
4 oz (120 ml) Champagne, to top
Build in a chilled flute, then top with Champagne.
Garnish: lemon twist
▼ A twist on the original Kir cocktail, created in Dijon in 1904 and originally made with white Burgundy instead of Champagne. Named after Félix Kir, a Catholic priest, politician and World War II resistance hero.

Kohinoor
(See p 149)

"Orange Wine"
Punch
1 oz (30 ml) Contratto Bianco vermouth
1/2 oz (15 ml) strega
1/4 oz (7 ml) Carpano Antica Formula
3/4 oz (22 ml) tangerine juice
3 oz (90 ml) Prosecco, to top
Build in a chilled Spritz glass with ice then top with Prosecco.
Garnish: white grapes

Puccini
1/2 oz (15 ml) Giffard Mandarin Liqueur
2 oz (60 ml) mandarin juice
3 oz (90 ml) Prosecco, to top
Shake short and strain into a chilled flute then top with Prosecco.

Surfside Swizzle
(See p 262)

The Tramp
The Canon Cocktail Book, *Jamie Boudreau and James O. Fraioli, 2016*
1 oz (30 ml) sloe gin
1/2 oz (15 ml) apricot brandy
1/2 oz (15 ml) lime juice
2 oz (60 ml) Champagne, to top
Toss and strain into chilled flute, then top with Champagne

From *The Savoy Cocktail Book* (1930):

To my friends: If we ever go to jail together, let's remember who has the best lawyer.

OTHER

Death in the Afternoon

Ernest Hemingway, 1935

½ oz (15 ml) absinthe
1 teaspoon (5 ml) simple syrup
4 oz (120 ml) Champagne, to top
Build in a chilled flute, then top with Champagne.
Garnish: lemon twist

Full Monte

Audrey Saunders, Pegu Club, NYC

½ oz (15 ml) light rum
½ oz (15 ml) gin
½ oz (15 ml) vodka
½ oz (15 ml) blanco tequila
½ oz (15 ml) maraschino liqueur
1 oz (30 ml) lemon juice
¼ oz (7 ml) simple syrup
2 dashes Angostura Bitters
2 oz (60 ml) Champagne, to top
Toss and strain into a chilled Spritz glass with ice, then top with Champagne.
Garnish: lemon half-wheel

Imperial Plaza Cocktail

Chad Solomon, The Plaza, NYC, 2008

1 oz (30 ml) apricot eau de vie
½ oz (15 ml) lemon juice
½ oz (15 ml) honey syrup (p 496)
2 drops saline solution (p 493)
2 oz (60 ml) Champagne, to top
Toss and strain into a chilled flute, then top with Champagne.
Garnish: lemon twist (discard)

BEER

Chelada p 437 (left), Americano Perfecto p 436 (middle), Black Velvet p 440 (right)

Beer

Beer is an intriguing ingredient in cocktails, able to add weight, complexity and fizz to many different drink styles.

It can act as both a textural, refreshing base and a stand-in for soda or sparkling wine, to top. As a lengthener, beer has a way of lifting the other alcoholic ingredients and citrus characters while also introducing its own flavours – hoppy, malty, fruity, bitter, sweet, sour – according to the specific brewing style. The frothiness factor adds its own liveliness and even a slight creaminess to the mouthfeel in some cases, too.

Generally, lighter spirits pair well with crisp pilsners and pale ales, whereas heftier IPAs and stouts are better off enriching rum- and whisk(e)y-based recipes. Due to the proliferation of craft brewing over the last several decades, today's bartenders have a vast array of flavour profiles with which to experiment, providing them with opportunities aplenty for innovating modern cocktails. More often than not, beer cocktails have a playfulness that resonates with drinkers seeking more unconventional options, but they also hold substantial appeal for those looking for lower-alcohol alternatives.

Beer

LIGHTER

Accidental Guru
Natasha David, Nitecap, NYC, 2014
1 oz (30 ml) Irish whiskey
½ oz (15 ml) Giffard Crème de Pêche de Vigne
½ oz (15 ml) lime juice
½ oz (15 ml) ginger syrup (p 496)
Wheat beer, to top
Pebble whip and pour into a frozen pilsner glass with ice, then top with wheat beer.
Garnish: lime wheel

Americano Perfecto
Damon Boelte, Prime Meats, NYC
1½ oz (45 ml) sweet vermouth
1½ oz (45 ml) Campari
Pilsner, to top
Build in a frozen pilsner glass with ice, then top with pilsner.
Garnish: orange half-wheel

Andy Shandy
Alastair Walker, The Everleigh, Melbourne, 2013
1 oz (30 ml) gin
½ oz (15 ml) lemon juice
½ oz (15 ml) simple syrup
1 egg white
Amber ale, to top
Dry shake, then add ice and shake again. Strain into a frozen footed Delmonico glass, then top with amber ale.

Aperitivo Buck
Michael Madrusan, The Everleigh, Melbourne, 2018
1½ oz (45 ml) Cynar
¾ oz (22 ml) ginger syrup
½ oz (15 ml) lime juice
Pilsner, to top
Cube whip and pour into a frozen pilsner glass with ice, then top with pilsner.
Garnish: candied ginger

Arrowhead Limited
Damon Boelte, Grand Army, NYC
1 oz (30 ml) sweet vermouth
½ oz (15 ml) mezcal
½ oz (15 ml) Campari
IPA, to top
Build in a frozen pilsner glass with ice, then top with IPA.
Garnish: grapefruit half-wheel

Aura Frame
Lacy Hawkins
A Quick Drink, *Lynnette Marrero and Ivy Mix with Megan Krigbaum, 2024*
1¼ oz (37 ml) Scotch
1 oz (30 ml) passionfruit liqueur
½ oz (15 ml) lime juice
½ oz (15 ml) ginger syrup
Light lager, to top
Pebble whip and pour into a frozen pilsner glass with ice, then top with light lager
Garnish: Tajín Clásico rim and lime wheel

Beerhive
Alastair Walker, The Everleigh, Melbourne, 2013
1 oz (30 ml) bourbon
¾ oz (22 ml) lemon juice
¾ oz (22 ml) honey syrup (p 496)
Pale ale, to top
Pebble whip and pour into a frozen pilsner glass with ice, then top with pale ale.

Beertini
Punch
12 oz (350 ml) lager
Serve in a frozen beer mug, adding olives and brine to taste.
Garnish: 4–5 green olives and ½ oz (15 ml) olive brine, served on the side
● The Midwestern bar room staple.

Beggars Banquet
Aisha Sharpe, NYC, 2010
2 oz (60 ml) bourbon
1 oz (30 ml) lemon juice
¾ oz (22 ml) maple syrup
2 dashes Angostura Bitters
Lager, to top
Pebble whip and pour into a frozen pilsner glass with ice, then top with lager.
Garnish: orange half-wheel

From *The Old Waldorf-Astoria Bar Book* (1935):

A good cocktail should be cold as the Arctic, dry as the Sahara, and smooth as a diplomat.

Bubble Fiction
Lynnette Marrero, Llama San, NYC
½ oz (15 ml) yuzu liqueur
½ oz (15 ml) ginger syrup (p 496)
½ oz (15 ml) lemon juice
¼ oz (7 ml) yuzu juice
Wheat beer, to top
Pebble whip and pour into a frozen pilsner glass with ice, then top with wheat beer.

Chaperone
Michael Madrusan, The Everleigh, Melbourne, 2020
1½ oz (45 ml) gin
½ oz (15 ml) Campari
1 oz (30 ml) pink grapefruit juice
½ oz (15 ml) lemon juice
½ oz (15 ml) simple syrup
2 oz (60 ml) pilsner, to top
Pebble whip and pour into a frozen pilsner glass with ice, then top with pilsner.
Garnish: grapefruit half-wheel

Chelada

Mexico

12 oz (350 ml) can of Mexican beer (preferably lager or pilsner)
2 lime wedges
Pinch of salt flakes

Pour out a splash of beer from the can then squeeze lime wedges into the can and sprinkle with salt flakes. Alternatively, squeeze lime wedges into a salt-rimmed frozen pilsner glass and fill with beer.

● The first drink after a shift (or during pack down) at Milk & Honey. Add a few dashes of hot sauce, and this is often referred to as a **Dressed** or **Dressed-Up Beer**.

Coo-Ee

Martin McConnell, Frog's Hollow Saloon, Brisbane, 2022

1½ oz (45 ml) gin
½ oz (15 ml) Giffard Crème de Pêche de Vigne
½ oz (15 ml) Campari
¾ oz (22 ml) passionfruit purée
½ oz (15 ml) lemon juice
¼ oz (7 ml) simple syrup
Lager (preferably XXXX Gold), to top

Shake with ice and strain into a frozen pilsner glass with ice, then top with lager.

Dark 'n' Hoppy No. 1

Zara Madrusan, The Everleigh, Melbourne, 2014

1½ oz (45 ml) Goslings Black Seal Rum
½ oz (15 ml) lime juice
½ oz (15 ml) ginger syrup
IPA, to top

Pebble whip and pour into a frozen pilsner glass with ice and top with IPA.

Garnish: candied ginger

Dark 'n' Hoppy No. 2

Zara Madrusan, The Everleigh, Melbourne, 2014

1½ oz (45 ml) rye
½ oz (15 ml) lime juice
½ oz (15 ml) ginger syrup
3 oz (90 ml) pale ale, to top

Pebble whip and pour into a frozen pilsner glass with ice, then top with pale ale.

Garnish: candied ginger

Elephant Flip

Christina Rando, The Franklin Mortgage & Investment Co., Philadelphia

1 oz (30 ml) Amaro Ramazzotti
½ oz (15 ml) overproof Jamaican dark rum
½ oz (15 ml) bourbon
½ oz (15 ml) Demerara syrup (p 495)
1 dash Angostura Bitters
6 drops Bittermens Xocolatl Mole Bitters
2 drop saline solution (p 493)
1 whole egg
IPA, to top

Dry shake, then add ice and shake again. Strain into a frozen footed Delmonico glass and top with IPA.

Garnish: 5 drops The Bitter Truth Old Time Aromatic Bitters

Every Cloud

Batch & Bottled, *Max and Noel Venning, 2018*

1½ oz (45 ml) blanco tequila
¾ oz (22 ml) lemon juice
¾ oz (22 ml) simple syrup
Saison, to top

Pebble whip and pour into a frozen pilsner glass with ice, then top with saison.

Garnish: lemon half-wheel

Golden Hour

Davide Segat, Side Hustle, London

½ oz (15 ml) yuzushu
¾ oz (22 ml) lemon sherbet (p 497)
½ oz (15 ml) lemon juice
2 drops saline solution (p 493)
Pilsner, to top

Pebble whip and pour into a frozen pilsner glass with ice, then top with pilsner.

Garnish: lemon wheel and lemon leaf

Grail Ale

The Bartender's Pantry, *Jim Meehan and Bart Sasso with Emma Janzen, 2024*

6 oz (180 ml) American pale ale, chilled
5 oz (150 ml) grapefruit soda, chilled

Build in a frozen pilsner glass with ice.

Garnish: grapefruit half-wheel

● Inspired by the great Austrian beer, Stiegl-Radler Naturtrüb Grapefruit.

Haymarket

Leo Robitschek, The NoMad Bar, NYC

1 oz (30 ml) Suze
¾ oz (22 ml) lemon juice
¾ oz (22 ml) simple syrup
1 cucumber wheel
Pale ale, to top

Press cucumber with simple syrup, add remaining ingredients and pebble whip. Pour into a frozen pilsner glass with ice, then top with pale ale.

Garnish: cucumber fan

Here Comes the Sun

Roofers Union, Washington D.C.

1½ oz (45 ml) rye whiskey
½ oz (15 ml) lemon juice
½ oz (15 ml) ginger syrup
Wheat beer, to top

Pebble whip and pour into a frozen pilsner glass with ice, then top with wheat beer.

Garnish: candied ginger

Joy Ride

Liana Oster, Side Hustle, London, 2021

1 oz (30 ml) Aperol
1 oz (30 ml) lemon juice
¾ oz (22 ml) spicy agave syrup (p 501)
1 cucumber wheel
Chilled Mexican sour beer (or citrusy gose), to top

Press cucumber with spicy agave syrup, add remaining ingredients, toss and strain into a frozen pilsner glass with ice, then top with beer.

Garnish: long cucumber ribbon

Lagerita

1½ oz (45 ml) blanco tequila
¾ oz (22 ml) lime juice
½ oz (15 ml) agave syrup (p 494)
Mexican lager, to top

Toss and strain into a frozen pilsner glass with ice, then top with lager.

Garnish: salt rim and lime wedge

La Valentina

Thomas Waugh, Death & Co, NYC, 2009

1½ oz (45 ml) blanco tequila
1 oz (30 ml) pink grapefruit juice
¾ oz (22 ml) lime juice
¾ oz (22 ml) simple syrup
3 raspberries
Pinch of sea salt
Wheat beer, to top

Muddle raspberry with simple syrup, add remaining ingredients, then toss and strain into a frozen pilsner glass with ice and top with wheat beer.

Garnish: 3 raspberries on a cocktail skewer

Michelada

Mexico

1 oz (30 ml) tomato juice or sangrita
½ oz (15 ml) lime juice
5 dashes Cholula Original Hot Sauce
1 × 12 oz (350 ml) can Mexican lager, to top

Build in a frozen pilsner glass with ice, then top with lager.

Garnish: salt rim, lime wedge and pinch of black pepper

Michelada Cubana

½ oz (15 ml) lime juice
½ teaspoon (2.5 ml) Worcestershire sauce
½ teaspoon (2.5 ml) Maggi Original Seasoning
5 dashes Cholula Original Hot Sauce (or Valentina Salsa Picante)
12 oz (350 ml) Mexican lager, to top

Build in a frozen pilsner glass with ice, then top with lager.

Garnish: lime wedge and pinch of black pepper

Picon Bière

1 oz (30 ml) Picon Amer
5 oz (150 ml) pilsner, to top

Build in a frozen pilsner glass with ice, then top with pilsner.

Garnish: orange wedge

Radler

Franz Kugler, 1920s

1 oz (30 ml) lemon juice
¾ oz (22 ml) simple syrup
3 oz (90 ml) lager, to top
1½ oz (45 ml) soda, to top

Toss and strain into a frozen pilsner glass with ice, then top with lager and soda.

● German for 'Cyclist', this drink came about because Franz needed to stretch his beer supply with sparkling lemonade.

Reality Check

Simone Caporale, Artesian, London, 2013

¾ oz (22 ml) vodka
¾ oz (22 ml) Becherovka
⅓ oz (10 ml) simple syrup
¼ oz (7 ml) lime juice
1 dash Angostura Bitters
5 raspberries
Pilsner, to top

Muddle raspberry with simple syrup, add remaining ingredients, then toss and strain into a frozen pilsner glass with ice and top with pilsner.

Garnish: lime twist

Red Beer

4 oz (120 ml) tomato juice
8 oz (240 ml) American lager, to top

Build in a frozen beer mug, then top with lager.

Garnish: 5 green olives, served on the side

Red-Eye

8 oz (240 ml) American lager
4 oz (120 ml) tomato juice
½ oz (15 ml) lemon juice
4 dashes Worcestershire sauce
3 dashes Cholula Original Hot Sauce
1 whole egg

Add liquid ingredients to a frozen beer mug and stir to combine, then crack the egg into the mug and drink immediately.

Garnish: pinch of salt and pepper

● Feel free to experiment with additional ingredients such as Old Bay Seasoning, A.1. Steak Sauce, HP Sauce or fresh horseradish.

Rustic Fruit Cup

Chantal Tseng, Washington D.C.

2 oz (60 ml) fruit cup (p 126)
½ oz (15 ml) ginger syrup
3 cucumber wheels
1 lemon wedge
1 lime wedge
Wheat beer, to top

Press cucumber with ginger syrup, add remaining ingredients then shake with ice and strain into a frozen pilsner glass with ice. Top with wheat beer and stir briefly.

Garnish: cucumber fan and lemon half-wheel

Savage Islands

Tyson Buhler, Death & Co, NYC, 2016

2 oz (60 ml) Madeira
1 oz (30 ml) pineapple juice
½ oz (15 ml) lemon juice
½ oz (15 ml) simple syrup
1 dash Angostura Bitters
2 drops saline solution (p 493)
American IPA, to top

Toss and strain into a frozen pilsner glass, then top with IPA.

Garnish: dehydrated pineapple slice

Shaky Pete's Ginger Brew

Pete Jeary, Hawksmoor, London, 2012

1½ oz (45 ml) gin
¾ oz (22 ml) lemon juice
¾ oz (22 ml) ginger syrup (p 496)
Pale ale, to top

Toss and strain into a frozen pilsner glass with ice, then top with pale ale.

Garnish: candied ginger

Shandygaff

England, 1800s

1 oz (30 ml) lime juice
¾ oz (22 ml) ginger syrup (p 496)
Pale ale, to top

Whip, pour into a frozen pilsner glass, then top with pale ale.

Garnish: candied ginger

● Comes from Cockney slang for a pint of beer: 'shant of gatter'.

Spaghett

Reed Cahill, Wet City Brewery, Baltimore, 2016

12 oz (350 ml) Miller High Life
1 oz (30 ml) Aperol
½ oz (15 ml) lemon juice

Build in a frozen Spritz glass with ice.

Garnish: lemon half-wheel

● Switch out for Budweiser to get the NASCAR Spritz.

Spaghett 75

Adam Phelps, EZ Inn, Chicago, 2024

¾ oz (22 ml) gin
¾ oz (22 ml) Aperol
½ oz (15 ml) lemon juice
Miller High Life, to top

Shake briefly, then strain into a frozen coupe. Top with High Life and serve the remainder on the side.

The Detroiter

Jacob Grier, 320 Main, Seal Beach

1 oz (30 ml) Cynar
¾ oz (22 ml) bonded apple brandy
¾ oz (22 ml) lemon juice
¾ oz (22 ml) honey syrup (p 496)
American IPA, to top

Toss and strain into a frozen pilsner glass with ice, then top with IPA.

Garnish: grapefruit twist (discard)

Winter Fruit Cup

Winter Drinks, *Editors of Punch, 2018*

2 oz (60 ml) fruit cup (p 126)
½ oz (15 ml) ginger syrup
3 cucumber wheels
1 lemon wedge
1 lime wedge
1 orange half-wheel
1 strawberry
6–8 mint leaves
Lager, to top

Press cucumber with ginger syrup, add remaining ingredients to a shaker and shake with ice, then strain into a frozen pilsner glass with ice. Top with lager and stir briefly.

Garnish: cucumber wheel, mint sprig and candied ginger

DARKER

Ale Flip

An Universal Etymological English Dictionary, *Nathan Bailey, 1721*

1½ oz (45 ml) Cognac
1 oz (30 ml) Demerara syrup (p 495)
1 whole egg
8 oz (240 ml) brown ale, to top

Warm a Toddy glass with boiling water. Meanwhile, heat the brown ale in a saucepan, being careful not to boil. Whisk Cognac, egg and Demerara syrup together in a heatproof jug, then slowly add the warm brown ale to the mixture while whisking so as not to cook the egg. Transfer the mixture between the jug and the saucepan 3–4 times until frothy, then pour into the Toddy glass.

Garnish: freshly grated nutmeg

● *"A sort of Sailor's Drink."*

Black and Tan

(aka **"Arf and Arf"** in *The Bar-Tender's Guide*, Jerry Thomas, 1862)

The Modern Bartenders' Guide, *O.H. Byron, 1884*

6 oz (180 ml) ale
6 oz (180 ml) porter, to float

Pour the ale into a chilled beer mug, then slowly float porter by pouring it over the back of a spoon into the mug.

Black Flip

Jim Meehan, PDT, NYC, 2007

2 oz (60 ml) stout (preferably Brooklyn Brewery Black Chocolate Stout)
1½ oz (45 ml) Cruzan Black Strap Rum
½ oz (15 ml) Demerara syrup (p 495)
1 whole egg

Add stout to a shaker and stir vigorously until decarbonated, then add the remaining ingredients. Dry shake, then add ice, shake again and strain into a frozen footed Delmonico glass.

Garnish: freshly grated nutmeg

Black Velvet

Brooks's, London, 1861

2½ oz (75 ml) Champagne
2½ oz (75 ml) Guinness, to float

Pour the Champagne into a flute, then slowly float Guinness by pouring it over the back of a spoon into the flute.

Irish Breakfast Stout

Leandro DiMonriva and Bryan Tetorakis, Cole's French Dip, Los Angeles

1½ oz (45 ml) Irish whiskey
½ oz (15 ml) coffee liqueur
1 oz (30 ml) cold-brew coffee
½ oz (15 ml) cinnamon syrup (p 495)
1½ oz (45 ml) Guinness, to top
Cacao cream, to float (p 506)

Shake with ice and strain into a frozen pilsner glass with ice, then top with Guinness and float cacao cream.

Garnish: freshly grated chocolate dark chocolate

Rattle Skull

1700s

1½ oz (45 ml) aged dark rum
½ oz (15 ml) lime juice
¾ oz (22 ml) Demerara syrup (p 495)
4 dashes Angostura Bitters
Porter, to top

Toss and strain into a frozen pilsner glass with ice, then top with porter.

Garnish: lime wedge and freshly grated nutmeg

"Root Beer Float"

Punch

2 oz (60 ml) stout
1 oz (30 ml) Amaro Ramazzotti
½ oz (15 ml) Branca Menta
1 oz (30 ml) house cream (p 506)
½ oz (15 ml) simple syrup
1 egg white
Soda, to top

Add stout to a shaker and stir vigorously until decarbonated. Add remaining ingredients to a separate shaker, dry shake, then add ice and stout and shake again. Strain into frozen pilsner glass with ice and top with soda.

Garnish: 2 drops Honest John Sarsaparilla Bitters

Stout & Sons #2

Jason Crawley, Sydney, 2018

2 oz (60 ml) stout
1½ oz (45 ml) aged dark rum
½ oz (15 ml) falernum
1 whole egg

Add stout to a shaker and stir vigorously until decarbonated, then add the remaining ingredients. Dry shake, then add ice, shake again and strain into a frozen footed Delmonico glass.

Garnish: freshly grated nutmeg

From *Rollo, Duke of Normandy - or, The Bloody Brother* by John Fletcher (1617), found in *Harry's Bar: 1911-2011* by Harrys New York Bar Paris:

Drink today and drown all sorrow,
You shall perhaps not do it tomorrow.
Best while you have it use your breath,
There is no drinking after death.

Black Velvet

TROPICAL

Saturn p 446 (left), Three Dots and a Dash p 453 (right)

Tropical

Tropical or Tiki cocktails are a vibrant and popular category with widespread appeal.

These drinks are exotic and exciting, evoking escape and adventure – a vacation in a glass. Tropical fruits and flavours are full of texture and personality. Mixing with brightly coloured juices like pineapple and passionfruit creates aesthetically alluring drinks that are generally finished with playful and elaborate garnishes. Fresh juice adds weight and texture to these drinks, and, depending on the season, these ingredients can add a range of sweet, sour, tangy and refreshing profiles. While Tiki drinks celebrate rum predominantly, tropical flavours can be combined with various spirits with ease. These drinks are less simplistic than their classical counterparts, often calling for multiple fruits, syrups, liqueurs and spices to create a layered and complex cocktail that ignites all the senses.

The Tropical genre is an education in itself. These are often large serves built with crushed ice that can cause the drink to dilute quickly. To execute them well, get your ratios exactly right, serve them quickly and bring plenty of theatre with flamboyant glassware and garnishes in abundance.

Tropical

GIN

Saturn
J. "Popo" Galsini, 1967
2 oz (60 ml) gin
¾ oz (22 ml) lemon juice
½ oz (15 ml) passionfruit syrup (p 499)
¼ oz (7 ml) falernum
¼ oz (7 ml) orgeat
Pebble whip and pour into a frozen double rocks glass with crushed ice, then shimmy and top with more crushed ice.
Garnish: lime twist wrapped around a cherry on a cocktail skewer, in the style of Saturn
▼ Originally blended, and the winner of the IBA World Cocktail Championship in 1967.

Singapore Sling
Ngiam Tong Boon, Raffles, Singapore, 1915
1½ oz (45 ml) gin
½ oz (15 ml) Heering Cherry Liqueur
¼ oz (7 ml) Bénédictine
¼ oz (7 ml) triple sec
1½ oz (45 ml) pineapple juice
½ oz (15 ml) lime juice
1 teaspoon (5 ml) grenadine (p 496)
2 dashes Angostura Bitters
Shake with ice and strain into a frozen Spritz glass with ice.
Garnish: pineapple wedge and cherry

Solomon Sling
Chad Solomon, Pegu Club, NYC, 2006
1½ oz (45 ml) gin
½ oz (15 ml) kirsch
¼ oz (7 ml) Heering Cherry Liqueur
¾ oz (22 ml) lemon juice
½ oz (15 ml) simple syrup
2 dashes Angostura Bitters
2 drops saline solution (p 493)
Soda, to top
Shake with ice and strain into a frozen Spritz glass with ice.
Garnish: 2 cherries
▼ To serve this 'Gonzo Style', accompany with a 7 oz Miller High Life and a half-shot (½ oz or 15 ml) of mezcal.

Special Forces
Sam Ross, Attaboy, NYC, 2017
1 oz (30 ml) navy strength gin
1 oz (30 ml) Fino Sherry
¾ oz (22 ml) lemon juice
¾ oz (22 ml) orgeat
1 dash absinthe
Shake with ice and strain into a frozen coupe.
Garnish: lemon twist (discard)

Starlet Sling
The Canon Cocktail Book, *Jamie Boudreau and James O. Fraioli, 2016*
2 oz (60 ml) gin
¼ oz (7 ml) Heering Cherry Liqueur
¾ oz (22 ml) lemon juice
½ oz (15 ml) orgeat
3 dashes orange bitters
Soda, to top
Shake with ice and strain into a frozen Spritz glass with ice, then top with soda.
Garnish: cherry

Third Man Up
Andrew Rice, Attaboy, NYC, 2017
2 oz (60 ml) gin
½ oz (15 ml) apricot brandy
1 oz (30 ml) lime juice
½ oz (15 ml) orgeat
Dry shake, then pour into a frozen double rocks glass with crushed ice, shimmy and top with more crushed ice.
Garnish: lime wedge, mint bouquet and freshly grated nutmeg

RUM & CANE SPIRIT

Air Balloon
ms. franky marshall, Le Boudoir, NYC, 2015
1½ oz (45 ml) rhum agricole
¾ oz (22 ml) Nardini Acqua di Cedro
¼ oz (7 ml) Green Chartreuse
½ oz (15 ml) lime juice
¼ oz (7 ml) simple syrup
Pebble whip and pour into a frozen Spritz glass with crushed ice, then shimmy and top with more crushed ice.
Garnish: sage leaf

Ancient Mariner
Jeff "Beachbum" Berry, Beachbum Berry's Latitude 29, New Orleans
1 oz (30 ml) Demerara rum
1 oz (30 ml) Jamaican dark rum
¾ oz (22 ml) lime juice
½ oz (15 ml) white grapefruit juice
½ oz (15 ml) simple syrup
¼ oz (7 ml) pimento (allspice) dram
Pebble whip and pour into a frozen double rocks glass with crushed ice, then shimmy and top with more crushed ice.
Garnish: mint bouquet

Another Time
(See p 233)

From *The Gentleman's Companion* (1939):

May your drinks be cold, your jokes be bold, and your adventures never get old.

Artichoke Hold

Jeremy Oertel, Donna, NYC

¾ oz (22 ml) Jamaican dark rum
¾ oz (22 ml) Cynar
½ oz (15 ml) St Germain Elderflower Liqueur
¾ oz (22 ml) lime juice
½ oz (15 ml) orgeat

Pebble whip and pour into a frozen double rocks glass with crushed ice, then shimmy and top with more crushed ice.

Garnish: mint bouquet

Banana Daiquiri

Antonello Arzedi, Sydney, 2024

1½ oz (45 ml) Jamaican dark rum
¾ oz (22 ml) Tempus Fugit Crème de Banane
⅓ oz (10 ml) Madeira (preferably Henriques & Henriques Single Harvest Sercial 2001)
⅓ oz (10 ml) lime juice
½ banana
1 scoop of crushed ice

Blend and pour into a frozen Sour glass.

Garnish: pinch of charcoal salt

Banana Hammock

Dan Greenbaum, Attaboy, NYC, 2016

1½ oz (45 ml) light rum
½ oz (15 ml) Tempus Fugit Crème de Banane
1 oz (30 ml) lime juice
½ oz (15 ml) orgeat
¼ oz (7 ml) overproof Jamaican dark rum, to float

Pebble whip, pour into a frozen tiki mug with crushed ice, then swizzle, top with more crushed ice and float rum.

Garnish: mint bouquet and freshly grated nutmeg

Bitter Mai Tai

Jeremy Oertel, Dram, NYC, 2011

¾ oz (22 ml) Jamaican dark rum
¾ oz (22 ml) Campari
½ oz (15 ml) Pierre Ferrand Dry Curaçao
¾ oz (22 ml) lime juice
½ oz (15 ml) orgeat

Pebble whip and pour into a frozen double rocks glass with crushed ice, then shimmy and top with more crushed ice.

Garnish: lime wheel, mint bouquet and freshly grated nutmeg

Breakfast Mai Tai

Fanny Chu, Donna, NYC

¾ oz (22 ml) Jamaican dark rum
¾ oz (22 ml) aged dark rum
½ oz (15 ml) Giffard Banane du Brésil et des Caraïbes
1 oz (30 ml) lime juice
½ oz (15 ml) orgeat
¼ oz (7 ml) cinnamon syrup (p 495)
¼ oz (7 ml) overproof Jamaican dark rum, to float

Pebble whip and pour into a frozen double rocks glass with crushed ice, then swizzle, top with more crushed ice and float rum.

Garnish: mint bouquet and cherry

Café Colada

Brandon Bramhall, Attaboy, Nashville, 2018

1½ oz (45 ml) Jamaican dark rum
½ oz (15 ml) Giffard Banane du Brésil et des Caraïbes
½ oz (15 ml) coffee liqueur
1½ oz (45 ml) pineapple juice
¾ oz (22 ml) Coco López
½ oz (15 ml) orange juice
¼ oz (7 ml) lime juice

Toss and strain into a frozen Spritz glass with crushed ice, then shimmy and top with more crushed ice.

Garnish: freshly grated nutmeg

Carta Switchel

Iain Griffiths, Dandelyan, London, 2016

1 oz (30 ml) light rum
1 oz (30 ml) Bacardí Carta Oro
1 oz (30 ml) pink grapefruit juice
½ oz (15 ml) simple syrup
1 teaspoon (5 ml) Fernet-Branca
½ teaspoon (2.5 ml) apple-cider vinegar

Pebble whip and pour into a frozen pilsner glass with crushed ice, then shimmy and top with more crushed ice.

Garnish: mint bouquet and grapefruit twist

▼ Winner of the Bacardí Legacy Cocktail Competition, 2016.

Champagne Colada

Chris Moore, Coupette, London, 2017

¾ oz (22 ml) light rum
½ oz (15 ml) pineapple rum
¼ oz (7 ml) light rhum agricole
1½ oz (45 ml) pineapple juice
2 scoops coconut sorbet
1 scoop (4 oz) crushed ice
1½ oz (45 ml) sparkling wine, to top

Blend all but the sparkling wine, pour into a frozen Spritz glass and top with sparkling wine.

Garnish: toasted coconut flakes

Cobra's Fang

Donn Beach, 1937

¾ oz (22 ml) Goslings Black Seal Rum
¾ oz (22 ml) Jamaican dark rum
½ oz (15 ml) Goslings 151 Proof Black Seal Rum
½ oz (15 ml) orange juice
½ oz (15 ml) lime juice
½ oz (15 ml) passionfruit syrup (p 499)
¼ oz (7 ml) falernum
2 dashes absinthe
2 dashes Angostura Bitters

Pebble whip and pour into a frozen pilsner glass with crushed ice, then shimmy and top with more crushed ice.

Garnish: freshly grated cinnamon, mint bouquet and an orange twist with poked 'eyes' (meant to resemble a snake)

Dance of Dragons

Toby Maloney, 2018

1 oz (30 ml) overproof Jamaican dark rum
1 oz (30 ml) Amaro di Angostura
¾ oz (22 ml) lime juice
½ oz (15 ml) honey syrup (p 496)
¼ oz (7 ml) falernum
5–6 mint leaves

Press the mint with honey syrup, lime juice and falernum, then add rum and amaro and stir to combine. Pour into a frozen Collins glass and top with crushed ice, then shimmy and top with more crushed ice.

Garnish: mint bouquet and orange half-wheel

Disgruntled Mai Tai

Sam Ross, Electra Cocktail Club, Las Vegas, 2018

1 oz (30 ml) pot still Jamaican dark rum (preferably Smith & Cross Traditional Jamaica Rum)
1 oz (30 ml) Aperol
½ oz (15 ml) Pierre Ferrand Dry Curaçao
1 oz (30 ml) lime juice
½ oz (15 ml) orgeat

Pebble whip and pour into a frozen double rocks glass with crushed ice, then shimmy and top with more crushed ice.

Garnish: 0.67 oz (20 ml) Underberg bottle (opened and upended into the drink), cocktail umbrella, mint bouquet and freshly grated nutmeg

From *Crosby Gaige's Cocktail Guide and Ladies' Companion* (1941):

To staying single, drinking double, and seeing triple!

Elusive Dreams

Demi Natoli, The Patterson House, Nashville

1 oz (30 ml) pineapple rum
1 oz (30 ml) light rum
½ oz (15 ml) coffee liqueur
¼ oz (7 ml) Giffard Banane du Brésil et des Caraïbes
1 oz (30 ml) pineapple juice
½ oz (15 ml) lime juice
½ oz (15 ml) cinnamon syrup (p 495)

Pebble whip and pour into a frozen double rocks glass with crushed ice, then shimmy and top with more crushed ice.

Garnish: pineapple half-wheel and edible orchid

Fog Cutter

Trader Vic's Book of Food and Drink, *Trader Vic, 1946*

1 oz (30 ml) aged dark rum
¾ oz (22 ml) Cognac
½ oz (15 ml) gin
½ oz (15 ml) orange juice
½ oz (15 ml) lemon juice
½ oz (15 ml) orgeat
¼ oz (7 ml) Cream Sherry, to float

Toss then strain into a frozen tiki mug with ice and float Sherry.

Garnish: mint bouquet

▼ *"This is delicious but a triple threat. You can get pretty stinking on these, no fooling."*

Gold Cup

The Hukilau, Long Beach, circa 1962

1½ oz (45 ml) Jamaican dark rum
⅜ oz (11 ml) maraschino liqueur
¾ oz (22 ml) lime juice
⅜ oz (11 ml) orgeat
3 dashes absinthe

Pebble whip and pour into a frozen double rocks glass with crushed ice, then shimmy and top with more crushed ice.

Garnish: mint bouquet

Hurricane (Pat O'Brien's Recipe)

Pat O'Brien's, New Orleans, 1940s

2 oz (60 ml) Jamaican dark rum
¾ oz (22 ml) lemon juice
¾ oz (22 ml) passionfruit syrup (p 499)

Pebble whip and pour into a frozen Hurricane glass with crushed ice, then swizzle briefly and top with more crushed ice.

Garnish: lemon half-wheel and a cherry

Hurricane

¾ oz (22 ml) aged dark rum
¾ oz (22 ml) light rum
½ oz (15 ml) Goslings Black Seal Rum
¼ oz (7 ml) Giffard Vanille de Madagascar
¾ oz (22 ml) pineapple juice
¾ oz (22 ml) orange juice
½ oz (15 ml) lime juice
½ oz (15 ml) simple syrup
¼ oz (7 ml) passionfruit syrup (p 499)
2 dashes Angostura Bitters

Pebble whip and pour into a frozen Hurricane glass with crushed ice, then swizzle briefly and top with more crushed ice.

Garnish: pineapple wedge and cherry

Hurricane Punch

The How and When, *Hyman Gale and Gerald F. Marco, 1940*

1 oz (30 ml) Jamaican dark rum
1 oz (30 ml) light rum
¾ oz (22 ml) lime juice
¾ oz (22 ml) passionfruit syrup (p 499)

Pebble whip and pour into a frozen Spritz glass with crushed ice, then swizzle and top with more crushed ice.

Garnish: orange half-wheel and cherry

Jungle Bird

Jeffrey Ong, Hilton Kuala Lumpur, Kuala Lumpur, 1973

The New American Bartender's Guide, *John J. Poister, 1989*

1½ oz (45 ml) Jamaican dark rum
¾ oz (22 ml) Campari
1½ oz (45 ml) pineapple juice
½ oz (15 ml) lime juice
½ oz (15 ml) simple syrup

Shake with ice and strain into a frozen double rocks glass with ice.

Garnish: pineapple wedge, 2 pineapple fronds and a cherry

Jungle Slow Cruise

Spirits of Latin America, *Ivy Mix, 2020*

1 oz (30 ml) Jamaican dark rum (preferably Appleton Estate Reserve)
¾ oz (22 ml) Cognac
½ oz (15 ml) Campari
¼ oz (7 ml) Wray & Nephew White Overproof Rum
¼ oz (7 ml) Cruzan Black Strap Rum
¾ oz (22 ml) pineapple juice
½ oz (15 ml) lime juice
½ oz (15 ml) cane syrup (p 494)
¼ oz (7 ml) passionfruit syrup (p 499)

Pebble whip and pour into a frozen Collins glass with crushed ice, then shimmy and top with more crushed ice.

Garnish: pineapple wedge and 2 pineapple fronds

Karaoke Honeymoon

Zachary Gelnaw-Rubin, Attaboy, NYC

¾ oz (22 ml) spiced rum
¾ oz (22 ml) amaretto
½ oz (15 ml) overproof Jamaican dark rum
½ oz (15 ml) ginger syrup (p 496)
½ oz (15 ml) orange juice
½ oz (15 ml) lemon juice

Pebble whip and pour into a frozen tiki mug with crushed ice, then swizzle and top with more crushed ice.

Garnish: orange half-wheel and freshly grated nutmeg

La Maison Piña

Michael Madrusan, Bar Margaux, Melbourne, 2019

1 oz (30 ml) aged dark rum
1 oz (30 ml) Cognac
1½ oz (45 ml) pineapple juice
¾ oz (22 ml) Coco López
¼ oz (7 ml) lime juice
3 dashes absinthe

Toss and strain into a frozen Spritz glass with crushed ice, then swizzle and top with more crushed ice.

Garnish: 2 pineapple fronds and cherry

Last Rites

Mariano Licudine, Mai-Kai, Fort Lauderdale, 1950s

2 oz (60 ml) dark rhum agricole
¾ oz (22 ml) lime juice
¾ oz (22 ml) passionfruit syrup (p 499)
½ oz (15 ml) falernum

Pebble whip and pour into a frozen double rocks glass with crushed ice, then swizzle and top with more crushed ice.

Garnish: mint bouquet and freshly grated cinnamon

Lost Lake

Paul McGee, Lost Lake, Chicago

1½ oz (45 ml) Jamaican dark rum
¼ oz (7 ml) maraschino liqueur
¼ oz (7 ml) Campari
½ oz (15 ml) pineapple juice
½ oz (15 ml) lime juice
½ oz (15 ml) passionfruit syrup (p 499)

Pebble whip and pour into a frozen Hurricane glass or tiki mug with crushed ice, then swizzle and top with more crushed ice.

Garnish: 2 pineapple fronds, edible orchid and cocktail umbrella

Mai Tai

Trader Vic's, 1944

1½ oz (45 ml) Jamaican dark rum
½ oz (15 ml) orange curaçao (p 498)
¾ oz (22 ml) lime juice
½ oz (15 ml) orgeat
¼ oz (7 ml) 151 overproof rum, to float

Pebble whip and pour into a frozen double rocks glass with crushed ice, then swizzle, top with more crushed ice and float rum.

Garnish: mint bouquet and cherry

Mai Tai Spritz

Martin Cate, Smuggler's Cove

1 oz (30 ml) Jamaican dark rum
½ oz (15 ml) Pierre Ferrand Dry Curaçao
½ oz (15 ml) lime juice
½ oz (15 ml) orgeat
2 oz (60 ml) Champagne, to top

Pebble whip and pour into a frozen Spritz glass with crushed ice, then top with Champagne, swizzle and top with more crushed ice.

Garnish: mint bouquet, lime wheel and cherry

Miami Vice
(Piña Colada and Strawberry Daiquiri in one)
Part 1: Piña Colada
½ oz (15 ml) aged dark rum
½ oz (15 ml) Jamaican dark rum
¾ oz (22 ml) Coco López
¾ oz (22 ml) pineapple juice
¼ oz (7 ml) lime juice
1 scoop (4 oz) crushed ice
Part 2: Strawberry Daiquiri
1 oz (30 ml) light rum
½ oz (22 ml) lime juice
¼ oz (7 ml) simple syrup
2 strawberries
1 scoop (4 oz) crushed ice
Blend the Piña Colada with 1½ cups of crushed ice and pour into a frozen Hurricane glass.
Using the same blender jug, blend the Strawberry Daiquiri with another 1½ cups (350 g) of crushed ice and pour it down the side of the Hurricane glass to try to push the Piña Colada up. Ideally, the result will look like two frozen drinks side by side in the same glass.
Garnish: mint bouquet and strawberry

Missionary's Downfall
Donn Beach, "Don the Beachcomber", 1930s
1½ oz (45 ml) light rum
½ oz (15 ml) Giffard Crème de Pêche de Vigne
½ oz (15 ml) pineapple juice
½ oz (15 ml) lime juice
½ oz (15 ml) honey syrup (p 496)
6–8 mint leaves
Press the mint with honey syrup and lime juice, then add the remaining ingredients and stir to combine. Pour into a frozen Spritz glass then add crushed ice, swizzle and top with more crushed ice.
Garnish: mint bouquet

Montego Bay
Donn Beach, Hotel Sahara, Las Vegas, 1940s
2 oz (60 ml) Jamaican dark rum
¾ oz (22 ml) white grapefruit juice
½ oz (15 ml) lime juice
½ oz (15 ml) honey syrup (p 496)
¼ oz (7 ml) pimento (allspice) dram
2 dashes absinthe
2 dashes Angostura Bitters
Pebble whip and pour into a frozen Spritz glass with crushed ice, then shimmy and top with more crushed ice.
Garnish: mint bouquet and freshly grated nutmeg

Navy Grog
Donn Beach, 1941
¾ oz (22 ml) light rum
¾ oz (22 ml) Demerara dark rum
¾ oz (22 ml) Jamaican dark rum
½ oz (15 ml) white grapefruit juice
½ oz (15 ml) lime juice
½ oz (15 ml) honey syrup (p 496)
Pebble whip and pour into a frozen double rocks glass with crushed ice, then shimmy and top with more crushed ice.
Garnish: mint bouquet and lime wedge

Night Flight Cocktail
Trader Vic's Bartender's Guide, *Trader Vic, 1947*
1½ oz (45 ml) Jamaican dark rum
1 oz (30 ml) lime juice
½ oz (15 ml) maple syrup
Pebble whip and pour into a frozen double rocks glass with crushed ice, then shimmy and top with more crushed ice.
Garnish: mint bouquet

Pago Pago
Beachbum Berry Remixed, *Jeff Berry, 2010*
2 oz (60 ml) Jamaican dark rum
¾ oz (22 ml) honey syrup (p 496)
¾ oz (22 ml) orange juice
¾ oz (22 ml) white grapefruit juice
¼ oz (7 ml) lime juice
2 dashes Angostura Bitters
Pebble whip and pour into a frozen Hurricane glass or tiki mug with crushed ice, then swizzle and top with more crushed ice.
Garnish: orange half-wheel and cherry

Pago Pago Cocktail
The How and When, *Hyman Gale and Gerald F. Marco, 1940*
1½ oz (45 ml) light rum
½ oz (15 ml) white crème de cacao
¼ oz (7 ml) Green Chartreuse
½ oz (15 ml) pineapple juice
½ oz (15 ml) lime juice
Shake with ice and strain into a frozen coupe.
Garnish: pineapple wedge

Painkiller
Soggy Dollar, British Virgin Islands, 1970s
1½ oz (45 ml) aged dark rum
½ oz (15 ml) rhum agricole
1 oz (30 ml) pineapple juice
¾ oz (22 ml) orange juice
¾ oz (22 ml) Coco López
¼ oz (7 ml) lime juice
Shake with ice and strain into a frozen double rocks glass with ice.
Garnish: orange half-wheel and freshly grated nutmeg

Piña Colada
Ramón "Monchito" Marrero Pérez, Caribe Hilton, San Juan, 1954
1 oz (30 ml) Jamaican dark rum
1 oz (30 ml) aged dark rum
1½ oz (45 ml) pineapple juice
¾ oz (22 ml) Coco López
¼ oz (7 ml) lime juice
Toss and strain into a frozen Spritz glass with crushed ice.
Garnish: 2 pineapple fronds, pineapple wedge and cherry

Piña Colada (Tyler Kitzman Recipe)
Tyler Kitzman, Sweet Liberty, Miami
½ oz (15 ml) Planteray Stiggins' Fancy Pineapple Rum
½ oz (15 ml) Cruzan Coconut Rum
½ oz (15 ml) Bacardí Añejo Cuatro Rum
3 oz (90 ml) Coco mix (p 495)
1 oz (30 ml) pineapple juice
1 large pineapple chunk
2 coffee beans
1 scoop (4 oz) crushed ice
¼ oz (7 ml) Pedro Ximénez, to float
Blend all ingredients, then pour into a frozen Hurricane glass and float Pedro Ximénez.
Garnish: mint bouquet, cherry and cocktail umbrella

Pinwheel
Brandon Bramhall, Attaboy, Nashville, 2021
1½ oz (45 ml) Jamaican dark rum
¼ oz (7 ml) Amargo-Vallet
1 oz (30 ml) pineapple juice
¾ oz (22 ml) grenadine (p 496)
½ oz (15 ml) lime juice
Pebble whip and pour into a frozen double rocks glass with crushed ice, then shimmy and top with more crushed ice.
Garnish: mint bouquet and cocktail umbrella

Piranha
Michael McCollum, Attaboy, Nashville, 2021
1 oz (30 ml) Fino Sherry
¾ oz (22 ml) light rum
¼ oz (7 ml) Jamaican dark rum
1 oz (30 ml) lime juice
¾ oz (22 ml) honey syrup (p 496)
1 grapefruit wedge
2 dashes orange bitters
Press grapefruit, add remaining ingredients, toss and pour into a frozen double rocks glass with crushed ice, then shimmy and top with more crushed ice.
Garnish: orange half-wheel and cherry

Queen's Road
Don Beach, 1941
1½ oz (45 ml) aged dark rum
½ oz (15 ml) orange juice
½ oz (15 ml) lime juice
½ oz (15 ml) ginger syrup (p 496)
½ oz (15 ml) honey syrup (p 496)
1 dash Angostura Bitters
Toss and strain into a frozen double rocks glass with ice.
Garnish: orange twist and mint bouquet

Red Rum Club
Mike Perez, Death & Co, Los Angeles, 2023
1 oz (30 ml) pot still Jamaican dark rum (preferably Smith & Cross Traditional Jamaica Rum)
1 oz (30 ml) Madeira Sherry
1 oz (30 ml) agua de Jamaica
¾ oz (22 ml) lime juice
½ oz (15 ml) cinnamon syrup (p 495)
6 dashes absinthe
1 dash Angostura Bitters
Pebble whip and pour into a frozen Hurricane glass or tiki mug with crushed ice, then swizzle briefly and top with more crushed ice.
Garnish: mint bouquet

Scorpion
Trader Vic's Book of Food & Drink, *Trader Vic, 1946*
1½ oz (45 ml) aged dark rum
½ oz (15 ml) Cognac
½ oz (15 ml) gin
1 oz (30 ml) orange juice
½ oz (15 ml) lemon juice
½ oz (15 ml) orgeat
½ oz (15 ml) dry white wine, to top
Shake with ice and strain into a frozen double rocks glass with ice, then top with wine.
Garnish: cherry, orange half-wheel and mint bouquet
▼ Originally a large-format punch, and equally great if you swap white wine with Manzanilla Sherry.

Scorpion (The Luau Recipe)
The Luau, Los Angeles, 1958
1 oz (30 ml) aged dark rum
1 oz (30 ml) gin
½ oz (15 ml) Cognac
1 oz (30 ml) orange juice
½ oz (15 ml) lime juice
½ oz (15 ml) orgeat
¼ oz (7 ml) Demerara syrup (p 495)
Pebble whip and pour into a frozen double rocks glass with crushed ice, then shimmy and top with more crushed ice.
Garnish: gardenia
▼ Originally blended.

Sidewinder's Fang
Lanai, San Mateo, California, 1960s
1½ oz (45 ml) Demerara rum
½ oz (15 ml) pot still Jamaican dark rum (preferably Smith & Cross Traditional Jamaica Rum)
1 oz (30 ml) orange juice
¾ oz (22 ml) lime juice
¾ oz (22 ml) passionfruit syrup (p 499)
Shake with ice and strain into a frozen double rocks glass with ice.
Garnish: long orange twist

Sparkling Mai Tai
Martin Cate
Smuggler's Cove: Exotic Cocktails, Rum and the Cult of Tiki, *Martin and Rebecca Cate, 2016*
½ oz (15 ml) aged dark rum
½ oz (15 ml) Pierre Ferrand Dry Curaçao
¼ oz (7 ml) pot still Jamaican dark rum (preferably Smith & Cross Traditional Jamaica Rum)
½ oz (15 ml) lime juice
¼ oz (7 ml) orgeat
Champagne, to top
Shake with ice and strain into a frozen coupe, then top with Champagne.
Garnish: lime twist, balanced on the rim

Sumatra Kula
Donn Beach, 1930s
1½ oz (45 ml) light rum
½ oz (15 ml) rhum agricole
½ oz (15 ml) lime juice
½ oz (15 ml) pink grapefruit juice
½ oz (15 ml) orange juice
½ oz (15 ml) honey syrup (p 496)
Pebble whip and pour into a frozen Hurricane glass or tiki mug with crushed ice, then swizzle and top with more crushed ice.
Garnish: mint bouquet

Sweet Escape
Toby Callaghan, The Waratah, Sydney, 2024
1 oz (30 ml) light rum
½ oz (15 ml) aged dark rum
½ oz (15 ml) pineapple juice
½ oz (15 ml) lime juice
½ oz (15 ml) coconut and pandan syrup (p 495)
Shake with ice and strain into a frozen coupe.

The Capricorn
Erick Castro, Rickhouse, San Francisco, 2009
1½ oz (45 ml) aged dark rum
½ oz (15 ml) Batavia-Arrack van Oosten
¾ oz (22 ml) lime juice
½ oz (15 ml) falernum
½ oz (15 ml) pineapple syrup (p 499)
Shake with ice and strain into a frozen coupe.
Garnish: lime twist (discard)

The Dead Reckoning
Martin Cate
Smuggler's Cove: Exotic Cocktails, Rum and the Cult of Tiki, *Martin and Rebecca Cate, 2016*
1½ oz (45 ml) aged dark rum
¼ oz (15 ml) tawny Port
¼ oz (15 ml) Licor 43
1½ oz (45 ml) pineapple juice
½ oz (15 ml) lemon juice
½ oz (15 ml) maple syrup
2 dashes Angostura Bitters
1 oz (30 ml) soda, to top
Pebble whip and pour into a frozen Hurricane glass or tiki mug with crushed ice, then add soda, swizzle and top with more crushed ice.
Garnish: 2 pineapple fronds, mint bouquet and lemon pigtail

The Expedition
Martin Cate
Smuggler's Cove: Exotic Cocktails, Rum and the Cult of Tiki, *Martin and Rebecca Cate, 2016*
1½ oz (45 ml) aged dark rum
½ oz (15 ml) bourbon
½ oz (15 ml) Licor 43
¼ oz (7 ml) coffee liqueur
1 oz (30 ml) lime juice
½ oz (15 ml) honey syrup (p 496)
½ oz (15 ml) cinnamon syrup (p 495)
1 oz (30 ml) soda, to top
Pebble whip and pour into a frozen Hurricane glass or tiki mug with crushed ice, then add soda, swizzle briefly and top with more crushed ice.
Garnish: pineapple spear and mint bouquet

The Iron Sheik
Brandon Bramhall, Last Saint, Charleston
1½ oz (45 ml) Demerara dark rum (preferably El Dorado 12yr Rum)
½ oz (15 ml) Amaro Braulio
½ oz (15 ml) coffee liqueur
½ oz (15 ml) lime juice
½ oz (15 ml) Coco López
Toss and strain into a frozen Hurricane glass or tiki mug with crushed ice, then swizzle and top with more crushed ice.
Garnish: mint bouquet and freshly grated cinnamon

The Undead Gentleman
Martin Cate, 2011
Smuggler's Cove: Exotic Cocktails, Rum and the Cult of Tiki, *Martin and Rebecca Cate, 2016*
1½ oz (45 ml) aged dark rum
½ oz (15 ml) pot still Jamaican dark rum (preferably Smith & Cross Traditional Jamaica Rum)
1 oz (30 ml) pink grapefruit juice
½ oz (15 ml) lime juice
¼ oz (7 ml) cinnamon syrup (p 495)
¼ oz (7 ml) falernum
1 dash absinthe
1 dash Angostura Bitters
Shake with ice and strain into a frozen coupe.
Garnish: lime wedge and grapefruit pigtail

Three Dots and a Dash
Donn Beach, 1940s
1 oz (30 ml) aged dark rum
½ oz (15 ml) rhum agriole
½ oz (15 ml) Goslings Black Seal Rum
¾ oz (22 ml) lime juice
½ oz (15 ml) orange juice
½ oz (15 ml) honey syrup (p 496)
¼ oz (7 ml) falernum
½ teaspoon (2.5 ml) pimento (allspice) dram
3 dashes Angostura Bitters
Pebble whip and pour into a frozen Hurricane glass or tiki mug with crushed ice, then swizzle and top with more crushed ice.
Garnish: mint bouquet, orange half-wheel and 3 cherries on a cocktail skewer
▼ Three dots and a dash is Morse code for 'victory'.

Thunder in Paradise
Steve Schneider, Employees Only, NYC
1 oz (30 ml) aged Caribbean dark rum
½ oz (15 ml) Oloroso Sherry
½ oz (15 ml) orgeat
¾ oz (22 ml) lime juice
¾ oz (22 ml) Coco López
5 dashes Peychaud's Aromatic Cocktail Bitters, to float
Toss and strain into a frozen Collins glass with crushed ice, then float bitters, shimmy briefly and top with more crushed ice.
Garnish: cherry

Ti' Punch
Two Years in the French West Indies, *Lafcadio Hearn, 1890*
2 oz (60 ml) rhum agricole
½ oz (15 ml) cane syrup (p 494)
½ lime, cut in half
1 brown sugar cube
Press the lime, cane syrup and sugar cube in an Old Fashioned glass, then add rhum agricole, fill with ice and stir 5–6 times.

Tourist Season
Matt Clark, Dutch Kills, NYC
1 oz (30 ml) clairin
1 oz (30 ml) Amaro Montenegro
¾ oz (22 ml) lime juice
¾ oz (22 ml) passionfruit syrup (p 499)
¼ oz (7 ml) honey syrup (p 496)
Pebble whip and pour into a frozen double rocks glass with crushed ice, then shimmy and top with more crushed ice.
Garnish: orange half-wheel and freshly grated cinnamon

Tourist Trap
Erick Castro, 2014
1½ oz (45 ml) light rum
¾ oz (22 ml) Avèze 18°
1½ oz (45 ml) pineapple juice
½ oz (15 ml) lemon juice
½ oz (15 ml) simple syrup
Shake with ice and strain into a frozen double rocks glass with ice.
Garnish: 2 pineapple fronds and lemon wheel

Trader Vic's Grog
(aka **Beach Boy Grog**)
Trader Vic's Bartender's Guide, Revised, *Trader Vic, 1972*
1 oz (30 ml) Jamaican dark rum
1 oz (30 ml) aged dark rum
1 oz (30 ml) pineapple juice
½ oz (15 ml) lemon juice
½ oz (15 ml) passionfruit syrup (p 499)
3 dashes Angostura Bitters
Pebble whip and pour into a frozen double rocks glass with crushed ice, then shimmy and top with more crushed ice.
Garnish: mint bouquet and cherry

Tradewinds
Jamaica, 1970s
¾ oz (22 ml) Jamaican dark rum
¾ oz (22 ml) light rum
¾ oz (22 ml) apricot brandy
1 oz (30 ml) lemon juice
¾ oz (22 ml) Coco López
Toss and strain into a frozen Hurricane glass or tiki mug with crushed ice, then swizzle and top with more crushed ice.
Garnish: cherry and cocktail umbrella

Voodoo Grog
Trader Vic's Bartender's Guide, Revised, *Trader Vic, 1972*
1 oz (30 ml) gold rum
1 oz (30 ml) rhum agricole
¾ oz (22 ml) lime juice
¾ oz (22 ml) white grapefruit juice
½ oz (15 ml) passionfruit syrup (p 499)
¼ oz (7 ml) pimento (allspice) dram
¼ oz (7 ml) honey syrup (p 496)
1 egg white
Dry shake, then add ice, shake again and strain into a frozen double rocks glass with ice.
Garnish: mint bouquet, pineapple wedge and freshly grated nutmeg
▼ Originally blended.

Yacht Rock
Garret Richard, Brooklyn Luau, NYC
¾ oz (22 ml) Cruzan Black Strap Rum
¾ oz (22 ml) Jamaican dark rum
¾ oz (22 ml) Campari
½ oz (15 ml) blanc vermouth
½ oz (15 ml) white crème de cacao
½ oz (15 ml) orange juice
½ oz (15 ml) lime juice
½ oz (15 ml) simple syrup
Pebble whip and pour into a frozen Spritz glass with crushed ice, then shimmy and top with more crushed ice.
Garnish: lime wedge and edible orchid

Yuzu Painkiller

Alex Boon, Pearl Diver, Melbourne

1 oz (30 ml) nutmeg-infused Havana Club Añejo 7 Anos Rum (p 504)
¾ oz (22 ml) yuzushu
⅓ oz (10 ml) rhum agricole
¾ oz (22 ml) Coco López
¾ oz (22 ml) tiki juice (p 507)
¼ oz (7 ml) yuzu juice

Toss and strain into a frozen tiki mug with crushed ice, then shimmy and top with more crushed ice.

Garnish: orange wedge, mint bouquet and freshly grated nutmeg

Zombie

Donn Beach, Los Angeles, 1934

Beachbum Berry Remixed, *Jeff Berry, 2010*

¾ oz (22 ml) gold rum
¾ oz (22 ml) Jamaican dark rum
½ oz (15 ml) 151 overproof rum (preferably Lemon Hart & Son 151 Rum)
½ oz (15 ml) white grapefruit juice
¾ oz (22 ml) lime juice
¼ oz (7 ml) falernum
1 teaspoon (5 ml) cinnamon syrup (p 495)
1 teaspoon (5 ml) grenadine (p 496)
3 dashes absinthe
3 dashes Angostura Bitters

Dry shake and pour into a frozen Hurricane glass or tiki mug with crushed ice, then swizzle and top with more crushed ice.

Garnish: mint bouquet

Zombie (Barbecue Chef Recipe)

Donn Beach

Barbecue Chef, *Louis A. Spievak, 1950*

¾ oz (22 ml) gold rum
¾ oz (22 ml) light rum
½ oz (15 ml) 151 overproof rum (preferably Lemon Hart & Son 151 Rum)
1 oz (30 ml) pineapple juice
¾ oz (22 ml) passionfruit syrup (p 499)
⅜ oz (11 ml) lemon juice
⅜ oz (11 ml) lime juice
3 dashes Angostura Bitters

Pebble whip and pour into a frozen Hurricane glass or tiki mug with crushed ice, then swizzle briefly and top with more crushed ice.

Garnish: mint bouquet

Zombie (Simplified)

Jeff "Beachbum" Berry, 2007

1 oz (30 ml) Jamaican dark rum
½ oz (15 ml) 151 overproof rum
¾ oz (22 ml) lime juice
1 oz (30 ml) white grapefruit juice
½ oz (15 ml) cinnamon syrup (p 495)

Pebble whip and pour into a frozen Hurricane glass or tiki mug with crushed ice, then swizzle briefly and top with more crushed ice.

Garnish: mint bouquet

AGAVE

Age of Aquarius

Devojka, 2018

1½ oz (45 ml) mezcal
¾ oz (22 ml) lime juice
¾ oz (22 ml) passionfruit syrup (p 499)
¼ oz (7 ml) honey syrup (p 496)
¼ oz (7 ml) Campari, to float

Pebble whip and pour into a frozen double rocks glass with crushed ice, then shimmy, float Campari and top with more crushed ice.

Garnish: mint bouquet

Berlin in the '70s

Billy Dollard, Cure, New Orleans

1 oz (30 ml) mezcal
1 oz (30 ml) blanco tequila
1 oz (30 ml) orange juice
½ oz (15 ml) lemon juice
½ oz (15 ml) cinnamon syrup (p 495)

Pebble whip and pour into a frozen double rocks glass with crushed ice, then shimmy and top with more crushed ice.

Garnish: Fee Brothers Old Fashion Aromatic Bitters crown and orange half-wheel

Bobby Dazzler

Aidan Tibbins, The Waratah, Sydney, 2024

¾ oz (22 ml) light rum
¾ oz (22 ml) blanco tequila
½ oz (15 ml) lime juice
½ oz (15 ml) apple purée (preferably custard apple purée)
2 drops Bittermens Xocolatl Mole Bitters

Toss and strain into a frozen double rocks glass with crushed ice, then shimmy and top with more crushed ice.

Garnish: mint bouquet

Chingona

Kara Greene, Death & Co, Washington D.C., 2024

1½ oz (45 ml) blanco tequila
½ oz (15 ml) raisin eau de vie
¼ oz (7 ml) Cappelletti Amaro Trentino
¾ oz (22 ml) lime juice
½ oz (15 ml) pink grapefruit juice
½ oz (15 ml) honey syrup (p 496)
2 dashes absinthe

Pebble whip and pour into a frozen pilsner glass with crushed ice, then shimmy and top with more crushed ice.

Garnish: mint bouquet

Cyclone Kick
Jeremy Oertel, Death & Co, NYC, 2017
1 oz (30 ml) overproof blanco tequila
1 oz (30 ml) mezcal
¾ oz (22 ml) pineapple juice
¾ oz (22 ml) lime juice
½ oz (15 ml) passionfruit syrup (p 499)
1 teaspoon (5 ml) Giffard Crème de Pêche de Vigne
1 teaspoon (5 ml) ginger syrup (p 496)
Pebble whip and pour into a frozen Spritz glass with crushed ice, then swizzle and top with more crushed ice.
Garnish: 2 pineapple fronds and mint bouquet

Milk Maid
Elizabeth Weiss, Beloved, NYC
2 oz (60 ml) blanco tequila
¾ oz (22 ml) lime juice
¾ oz (22 ml) Coco López
½ oz (15 ml) house cream (p 506)
2 cucumber wheels
2 drops saline solution (p 493)
Press cucumber, add remaining ingredients and shake with ice. Strain into a frozen double rocks glass with ice.
Garnish: cucumber fan

Pineapple Smoke Wreck
Ebby Kurian, Texas
1½ oz (45 ml) mezcal
½ oz (15 ml) overproof Jamaican dark rum
1½ oz (45 ml) pineapple juice
¾ oz (22 ml) ginger syrup (p 496)
½ oz (15 ml) lemon juice
1 dash Angostura Bitters
1 dash Peychaud's Aromatic Cocktail Bitters
Pebble whip and pour into a frozen Hurricane glass or tiki mug with crushed ice, then swizzle and top with more crushed ice.
Garnish: 2 pineapple fronds and cherry

Pinky Gonzalez
Trader Vic, Señor Pico, San Francisco, 1964
2 oz (60 ml) blanco tequila
⅜ oz (11 ml) orange curaçao (p 498)
¾ oz (22 ml) lime juice
⅜ oz (11 ml) orgeat
3 dashes Angostura Bitters
Shake with ice and strain into a frozen double rocks glass with ice.
Garnish: orange half-wheel and mint bouquet

Reef Weasel
Erick Castro, 2016
2 oz (60 ml) mezcal
1½ oz (45 ml) pineapple juice
¾ oz (22 ml) lime juice
¾ oz (22 ml) honey syrup (p 496)
¾ oz (22 ml) house cream (p 506)
Toss and strain into a frozen tiki mug with crushed ice, then shimmy and top with more crushed ice.
Garnish: 2 pineapple fronds and cherry

Sunkissed
Jean Lopez, Weather Up, NYC
1½ oz (45 ml) blanco tequila
¼ oz (7 ml) apricot brandy
1 oz (30 ml) pineapple juice
½ oz (15 ml) lime juice
¼ oz (7 ml) ginger syrup (p 496)
Shake with ice and strain into a frozen double rocks glass with ice.
Garnish: Tajín Clásico half-rim

Top Sider
Sam Ross, Ad Lib, Miami, 2019
1 oz (30 ml) mezcal
1 oz (30 ml) aged rhum agricole
1 oz (30 ml) orange juice
¾ oz (22 ml) Coco López
½ oz (15 ml) lime juice
¼ oz (7 ml) house cream (p 506)
Toss and strain into a frozen Hurricane glass or tiki mug with crushed ice, then swizzle and top with more crushed ice.
Garnish: mint bouquet, freshly grated nutmeg and cocktail umbrella

Vespa
Anthony Schmidt and Alicia Perry, The Lafayette Hotel and Club, San Diego, 2024
1 oz (30 ml) reposado tequila
½ oz (15 ml) overproof Jamaican light rum
¼ oz (7 ml) Amontillado Sherry
¼ oz (7 ml) limoncello
¼ oz (7 ml) Galliano L'Autentico
1 oz (30 ml) coconut Demerara (p 506)
¾ oz (22 ml) lime juice
Toss then pour into a frozen double rocks glass with crushed ice.
Garnish: blue orchid and orange half-wheel

From old British drinking traditions:

Here's to our exes—may they live long so they can see how happy we are without them!

BRANDY

Pisco Punch (John Torrence Recipe)

John Torrence, Bank Exchange, San Francisco, circa 1850s

2 oz (60 ml) pisco
¾ oz (22 ml) lemon juice
¾ oz (22 ml) pineapple syrup (p 499)
¼ oz (7 ml) falernum
2 oz (60 ml) Champagne, to top

Dry shake and pour into a frozen Spritz glass with cracked ice, then top with Champagne.

Garnish: mint bouquet, blackberry, raspberry and strawberry

Stone-Cold Fox

Toby Maloney, 2015

2 oz (60 ml) pisco (preferably acholado)
½ oz (15 ml) Amaro Montenegro
¾ oz (22 ml) orgeat
¾ oz (22 ml) lime juice
½ oz (15 ml) pineapple juice
1 oz (30 ml) soda, to top
½ oz (15 ml) red wine, to float

Pebble whip, pour into a frozen Spritz glass with crushed ice, then add soda, float wine and top with more crushed ice.

Garnish: mint bouquet and orange half-wheel

Tai Du Mai

Erik Hakkinen, Roquette, Seattle

1 oz (30 ml) Cognac
½ oz (15 ml) pot still Jamaican dark rum (preferably Smith & Cross Traditional Jamaica Rum)
¼ oz (7 ml) Pierre Ferrand Dry Curaçao
1 oz (30 ml) lime juice
½ oz (15 ml) pineapple juice
¼ oz (7 ml) orgeat

Pebble whip and pour into a frozen double rocks glass with crushed ice, then shimmy and top with more crushed ice.

Garnish: mint bouquet

The Sexpert

Martin Cate, Smuggler's Cove, San Francisco

1½ oz (45 ml) pisco
½ oz (15 ml) gin
½ oz (15 ml) lemon juice
½ oz (15 ml) passionfruit syrup (p 499)
¼ oz (7 ml) falernum
3 drops Bittermens Burlesque Bitters

Shake with ice and strain into a frozen coupe.

Garnish: edible orchid

Trouble in Paradise

Erick Castro, 2018

2 oz (60 ml) Cognac
1 oz (30 ml) mango juice
¾ oz (22 ml) lime juice
½ oz (15 ml) falernum
½ oz (15 ml) orgeat
4 dashes absinthe
2 dashes Angostura Bitters

Pebble whip and pour into a frozen Hurricane glass or tiki mug with crushed ice, then swizzle and top with more crushed ice.

Garnish: mint bouquet and lime wheel

AMERICAN WHISKEY

Alligator

David Molyneux, Mr. West, Melbourne, 2023

1½ oz (45 ml) rye whiskey
1 oz (30 ml) lime juice
⅜ oz (11 ml) ginger syrup (p 496)
⅜ oz (11 ml) orgeat
1 dash absinthe

Shake with ice and strain into a frozen double rocks glass with ice.

Garnish: mint bouquet

Bird Rights

Sam Ross, Attaboy, NYC, 2019

1½ oz (45 ml) bourbon
½ oz (15 ml) pot still Jamaican dark rum
¾ oz (22 ml) lime juice
¾ oz (22 ml) Coco López
½ oz (15 ml) house cream (p 506)
2 dashes Bittermens Xocolatl Mole Bitters

Toss and strain into a frozen double rocks glass with crushed ice, then shimmy and top with more crushed ice.

Garnish: 2 pineapple fronds, cherry and freshly grated nutmeg

Brokeback Colada

Daniel Waddy, Satan's Whiskers, London

2 oz (60 ml) bourbon
¼ oz (7 ml) Licor 43
1½ oz (45 ml) pineapple juice
¾ oz (22 ml) Coco López
½ oz (15 ml) house cream (p 506)
¼ oz (7 ml) lime juice

Toss and strain into a frozen Spritz glass with crushed ice, then shimmy and top with more crushed ice.

Garnish: 2 pineapple fronds and cherry

Great Bambino
Sam Ross, The Dorsey, Las Vegas, 2018
1½ oz (45 ml) bourbon
½ oz (15 ml) Fernet-Branca
1 oz (30 ml) pear juice
½ oz (15 ml) lemon juice
½ oz (15 ml) orgeat
Pebble whip and pour into a frozen double rocks glass with crushed ice, then shimmy and top with more crushed ice.
Garnish: apple fan and freshly grated cinnamon
▼ Swap pear juice for apple juice to make the Greater Bambino by Sam Ross, The Dorsey, Las Vegas, 2018.

Iron Ranger
Erick Castro, Polite Provisions, San Diego, 2014
2 oz (60 ml) bourbon
1 oz (30 ml) pineapple juice
½ oz (15 ml) falernum
½ oz (15 ml) simple syrup
½ oz (15 ml) lemon juice
2 dashes Angostura Bitters
Pebble whip and pour into a frozen Hurricane glass with crushed ice, then swizzle and top with more crushed ice.
Garnish: mint bouquet and freshly grated cinnamon

Kentucky Sling
Michael Madrusan, The Everleigh, Melbourne, 2024
1½ oz (45 ml) bourbon
½ oz (15 ml) Heering Cherry Liqueur
¼ oz (7 ml) Bénédictine
1½ oz (45 ml) pineapple juice
½ oz (15 ml) lime juice
½ oz (15 ml) ginger syrup (p 496)
¼ oz (7 ml) passionfruit syrup (p 499)
2 dashes Angostura Bitters
Shake with ice and strain into a frozen Spritz glass with ice.
Garnish: pineapple wedge and cherry

Port Light
Beachbum Berry Remixed: A Gallery of Tiki Drinks, *Jeff "Beachbum" Berry, 2010*
2 oz (60 ml) bourbon
¾ oz (22 ml) lemon juice
½ oz (15 ml) passionfruit syrup (p 499)
¼ oz (7 ml) grenadine (p 496)
Pebble whip and pour into a frozen Collins glass with crushed ice. Swizzle briefly, then top with more crushed ice.
Garnish: mint bouquet and cherry

Rye Tai
Toby Maloney, 2013
1½ oz (45 ml) rye whiskey
½ oz (15 ml) pot still Jamaican dark rum (preferably Smith & Cross Traditional Jamaica Rum)
¼ oz (7 ml) Aperol
¾ oz (22 ml) lime juice
½ oz (15 ml) orgeat
¼ oz (7 ml) simple syrup
Pebble whip and pour into a frozen Collins glass with crushed ice, then shimmy and top with more crushed ice.
Garnish: mint bouquet and 3 drops of Angostura Bitters

SCOTCH

Crossfire Cyclone
Angus Payne, Pearl Diver, Melbourne
1 oz (30 ml) Scotch
½ oz (15 ml) Islay Scotch
1 oz (30 ml) lime juice
½ oz (15 ml) passionfruit syrup (p 499)
¼ oz (7 ml) honey syrup (p 496)
Pebble whip and pour into a frozen double rocks glass with crushed ice, then shimmy and top with more crushed ice.
Garnish: Angostura Bitters crown and mint bouquet

Porridge Colada
Kyle Jamieson, Nauticus, Edinburgh
2 oz (60 ml) coconut-washed Scotch (p 505)
1 oz (30 ml) pineapple juice
1 oz (30 ml) oat milk
⅓ oz (10 ml) honey syrup (p 496)
Pebble whip and pour into a frozen Spritz glass with crushed ice, then swizzle and top with more crushed ice.
Garnish: mint bouquet and pinch of oats

WORLD WHISK(E)Y

Birdman
Erick Castro, 2014
2 oz (60 ml) Irish whiskey
¾ oz (22 ml) white grapefruit juice
¾ oz (22 ml) lime juice
½ oz (15 ml) falernum
½ oz (15 ml) honey syrup (p 496)
2 dashes Angostura Bitters
Pebble whip and pour into a frozen tiki mug with crushed ice, then swizzle and top with more crushed ice.
Garnish: mint bouquet and cocktail umbrella

FORTIFIED & LIQUEUR

Brancolada
Jeremy Oertel, NYC
1 oz (30 ml) Branca Menta
1 oz (30 ml) Jamaican dark rum
1½ oz (45 ml) pineapple juice
¼ oz (7 ml) orange juice
1 oz (30 ml) Coco López
1 scoop (4 oz) crushed ice
Blend and pour into a frozen Spritz glass.
Garnish: orange half-wheel and mint bouquet

Howie in the Jungle

Nathan McCarley-O'Neill, The NoMad Bar, NYC

1½ oz (45 ml) Zucca Rabarbaro
¾ oz (22 ml) Aperol
½ oz (15 ml) Heering Cherry Liqueur
¾ oz (22 ml) pineapple juice
¾ oz (22 ml) lime juice
1 teaspoon (5 ml) passionfruit syrup (p 499)
1 oz (30 ml) soda, to top

Shake with ice, then strain into a frozen Collins glass with ice and top with soda.

Garnish: orange half-wheel and mint sprig

Piña Verde

Erick Castro, Polite Provisions, San Diego, 2013

1½ oz (45 ml) Green Chartreuse
1½ oz (45 ml) pineapple juice
¾ oz (22 ml) Coco López
¼ oz (7 ml) lime juice
¼ oz (7 ml) house cream (p 506)

Toss and strain into a frozen Spritz glass with crushed ice, then shimmy and top with more crushed ice.

Garnish: 2 pineapple fronds and freshly grated nutmeg

Poblano Colada

Liam Odien, Playa Provisions, Playa del Rey

1½ oz (45 ml) Ancho Reyes Verde
1½ oz (45 ml) pineapple juice
1 oz (30 ml) Coco López
½ oz (15 ml) lime juice
½ teaspoon (2.5 ml) absinthe

Toss and strain into a frozen Spritz glass with crushed ice, then swizzle and top with more crushed ice.

Garnish: mint bouquet and orange half-wheel

Sherry Colada

Adam Minegar, Raines Law Room, NYC, 2015

2 oz (60 ml) Amontillado Sherry
2 oz (60 ml) pineapple juice
¾ oz (22 ml) Coco López
½ oz (15 ml) house cream (p 506)

Toss and strain into a frozen Spritz glass with crushed ice, then shimmy and top with more crushed ice.

Garnish: 2 pineapple fronds and freshly grated nutmeg

Sherry Painkiller

The Nomad Cocktail Book, *Leo Robitschek, 2019*

2 oz (30 ml) Amontillado Sherry
½ oz (15 ml) aged dark rum (preferably Ron Zacapa 23)
1 oz (30 ml) pineapple juice
½ oz (15 ml) orange juice
¾ oz (22 ml) Coco López
½ oz (15 ml) lime juice

Shake briefly with ice then strain into a frozen Spritz glass. Add crushed ice, shimmy, then top with more crushed ice.

Garnish: orange half-wheel and 3 pineapple fronds

The Turnbuckle

Jen Akin, Seattle, 2018

1 oz (30 ml) Cynar
¾ oz (22 ml) Jamaican dark rum
¾ oz (22 ml) lemon juice
½ oz (15 ml) passionfruit syrup (p 499)
½ oz (7 ml) orgeat

Pebble whip and then pour into a frozen double rocks glass with crushed ice, then shimmy and top with more crushed ice.

Garnish: mint bouquet and edible orchid

Tiki Tak

Andrew Porteus, Montana's Trail House, NYC

1 oz (30 ml) dry vermouth
¼ oz (7 ml) Giffard Banane du Brésil et des Caraïbes
1 oz (30 ml) pineapple juice
½ oz (15 ml) lime juice
¼ oz (7 ml) falernum
2 dashes Peychaud's Aromatic Cocktail Bitters

Pebble whip and pour into a frozen double rocks glass with crushed ice, then shimmy and top with more crushed ice.

Garnish: lime wedge, cherry and cocktail umbrella

Tropical Fluff

Fanny Chu, Donna, NYC

¾ oz (22 ml) Aperol
½ oz (15 ml) Jamaican dark rum
½ oz (15 ml) Giffard Banane du Brésil et des Caraïbes
2 oz (60 ml) pineapple juice
1 oz (30 ml) orange juice
½ oz (15 ml) pink grapefruit juice
¼ oz (7 ml) lime juice

Cube whip and pour into a frozen Highball glass with ice.

Garnish: orange half-wheel

OTHER

Absinthe Colada

Natasha David and Maxwell Britten, Maison Premiere, NYC

1 oz (30 ml) absinthe
½ oz (15 ml) light rhum agricole
1½ oz (45 ml) pineapple juice
1 oz (30 ml) Coco López
¼ oz (7 ml) lime juice
1 teaspoon (5 ml) white crème de menthe

Toss and pour into a frozen Spritz glass with crushed ice, then shimmy and top with more crushed ice.

Garnish: mint bouquet

Beachcomber's Punch
Donn Beach, Los Angeles, 1930s
1½ oz (45 ml) Demerara rum
½ oz (15 ml) apricot brandy
½ oz (15 ml) lime juice
½ oz (15 ml) white grapefruit juice
½ oz (15 ml) simple syrup
2 dashes absinthe
2 dashes Angostura Bitters
Pebble whip and pour into a frozen tiki mug with crushed ice, then swizzle and top with more crushed ice.
Garnish: mint bouquet

Bird of Paradise
(See p 86)

Cooper's Ranch Punch
Trader Vic's Bartender's Guide, *Trader Vic, 1947*
2 oz (60 ml) light rum
¾ oz (22 ml) pineapple juice
¾ oz (22 ml) guava juice
¾ oz (22 ml) grenadine (p 496)
¼ oz (7 ml) lime juice
Pebble whip and pour into a frozen tiki mug with crushed ice, then swizzle and top with more crushed ice.
Garnish: mint bouquet

Dr. Funk
(See p 87)

Freight Train Swizzle
(See p 259)

Ola Swizzle
(See p 259)

Planter's Punch
Fred L. Myers (founder of Myer's Rum), late 1800s; Donn Beach, 1937
2 oz (60 ml) Jamaican dark rum
¾ oz (22 ml) lime juice
½ oz (15 ml) grenadine (p 496)
¼ oz (7 ml) falernum
3 dashes Angostura Bitters
Pebble whip and pour into a frozen double rocks glass with crushed ice, then shimmy and top with more crushed ice.
Garnish: mint bouquet

Planter's Punch (David Embury Recipe)
The Fine Art of Mixing Drinks, *David Embury, 1948*
2 oz (60 ml) Jamaican dark rum
¾ oz (22 ml) lemon juice
¾ oz (22 ml) simple syrup
3 dashes Angostura Bitters
Pebble whip and pour into a frozen double rocks glass with crushed ice, shimmy and top with more crushed ice.
▼ One of sour, two of sweet, three of strong, four of weak.

Planter's Punch (Sloppy Joe's Recipe)
Sloppy Joe's Cocktails Manual, *1932*
2 oz (60 ml) Jamaican dark rum
½ oz (15 ml) orange curaçao (p 498)
¾ oz (22 ml) lemon juice
½ oz (15 ml) grenadine (p 496)
Pebble whip and pour into a frozen double rocks glass with crushed ice, then shimmy and top with more crushed ice.
Garnish: orange half-wheel and cherry

Port Light
(See p 168)

Puka Punch
Tiki-Ti, Los Angeles, 1961
¾ oz (22 ml) light rum
¾ oz (22 ml) aged dark rum
¾ oz (22 ml) Jamaican dark rum
¾ oz (22 ml) lime juice
¾ oz (22 ml) pineapple juice
¾ oz (22 ml) orange juice
½ oz (15 ml) passionfruit syrup (p 499)
½ oz (15 ml) honey syrup (p 496)
¼ oz (7 ml) falernum
1 dash Angostura Bitters
¼ oz (7 ml) overproof dark rum, to float
Toss and strain into a large frozen tiki mug with crushed ice, then swizzle, top with more crushed ice and float rum.
Garnish: mint bouquet

Roman Punch
Trader Vic's Book of Food and Drink, *Trader Vic, 1946*
1 oz (30 ml) Jamaican dark rum
1 oz (30 ml) Cognac
¾ oz (22 ml) lemon juice
½ oz (15 ml) raspberry syrup (p 500)
¼ oz (7 ml) tawny Port, to float
Pebble whip and pour into a frozen double rocks glass with crushed ice, then float Port, shimmy and top with more crushed ice.
Garnish: raspberry, blackberry and strawberry half

From *The Old Waldorf-Astoria Bar Book* (1935):

To those who have seen us at our worst and still claim to be our friends!

Royal Hawaiian
(See p 172)

Soho Swizzle
(See p 260)

Western Sour
(See p 176)

Yacht Club Punch
(See p 254)

COFFEE

Café Frappé p 464 (back), Irish Coffee p 467 (middle), La Dominicana p 465 (front)

Coffee

Whether freshly brewed or in the form of liqueur, coffee plays an invigorating role in modern cocktails, with a power and complexity that stands up to bolder spirits as well as punchy supporting players.

Its natural bitterness often blends well with sweeter ingredients, but its diverse spectrum of characters – chocolatey, earthy, fruity – offers layers of interest to a variety of drink styles.

While it is certainly an unapologetic addition, coffee is surprisingly versatile and aromatic, able to play nice with both light and dark spirits and a wide range of fresh flavours, from pineapple to ginger. The differences in brewing style – be it light-bodied filter brew, syrupy espresso or velvety cold brew – along with serving temperature also allow for plenty of experimentation across several categories, including Spritz (p 410), Old Fashioned (p 362), Toddy (p 400) and Flip (p 388). Factor in the energising effect of caffeine, and it's little wonder these drinks have found such enduring success in bars worldwide.

Coffee

VODKA

Black Magic
Jones' Complete Barguide,
Stan Jones, 1977
1½ oz (45 ml) vodka
¾ oz (22 ml) coffee liqueur
1 teaspoon (5 ml) lemon juice
Build in an Old Fashioned glass with ice.
Garnish: lemon twist

Black Russian
Gustave Tops, Hotel Métropole, Brussels, 1949
1½ oz (45 ml) vodka
1 oz (30 ml) coffee liqueur
Build in an Old Fashioned glass with ice.

Café Frappé
Felix Woods, Black Pearl, Melbourne, 2022
1 oz (30 ml) vodka
¾ oz (22 ml) coffee liqueur
¼ oz (7 ml) Amaro Averna
1 oz (30 ml) espresso
1 teaspoon (5 ml) white crème de menthe
Pebble whip and pour into a frozen double rocks glass with crushed ice, then shimmy and top with more crushed ice.
Garnish: mint sprig

Caffè Espresso
Nathan McCarley-O'Neill, Torrisi, NYC, 2024
1½ oz (45 ml) coffee liqueur (preferably Kahlúa)
1½ oz (45 ml) vodka (preferably Grey Goose vodka)
1½ oz (45 ml) espresso
¼ oz (7 ml) cane syrup (p 494)
Shake with ice and strain into a frozen Sour glass.
Garnish: freshly grated 70% dark chocolate

Charging Station
Sam Ross, Electra Cocktail Club, Las Vegas, 2018
2 oz (60 ml) vodka
¾ oz (22 ml) cold-brew coffee
¾ oz (22 ml) Coco López
½ oz (15 ml) house cream (p 506)
2 dashes habanero bitters
Toss and strain into a frozen Collins glass. Add crushed ice, then shimmy and top with more crushed ice.

Clearwater Espresso
Ali Reynolds, Hawksmoor, London, 2016
1½ oz (45 ml) vodka
½ oz (15 ml) Metté Café Arabica
½ oz (15 ml) Giffard Banane du Brésil et des Caraïbes
½ oz (15 ml) simple syrup
1 dash absinthe
Stir with ice and strain into a frozen coupe.
Garnish: lemon twist (discard)

Espresso Martini
2 oz (45 ml) vodka
½ oz (15 ml) coffee liqueur
1 oz (30 ml) espresso
¼ oz (7 ml) simple syrup
Shake with ice and strain into a frozen coupe.
Garnish: 3 coffee beans

Jerez Espresso Martini
Dave Spanton, Vermuteria, Sydney, 2023
1 oz (30 ml) vodka
1 oz (30 ml) coffee liqueur
1 oz (30 ml) Pedro Ximénez
½ oz (15 ml) Oloroso Sherry
1 teaspoon (5 ml) simple syrup
Shake with ice and strain into a frozen coupe.

Match Coffee
Michael Butt, 2003
1 oz (30 ml) vodka
¾ oz (22 ml) Tempus Fugit Crème de Cacao
3 oz (90 ml) hot filter coffee
½ oz (15 ml) Demerara syrup (p 495)
House cream, to float (p 506)
Build in a Toddy glass, then float cream.
Garnish: dusting of cayenne pepper

Not An Espresso Martini
Frank Audoux, Cravan, Paris, 2024
1½ oz (45 ml) coffee-leaf-infused vodka (p 503)
1½ oz (45 ml) cascara cordial (p 494)
1 drop coffee tincture (p 505)
Shake and strain into a frozen coupe.

Vodka Espresso
Dick Bradsell, London, 1983
1½ oz (45 ml) vodka
¾ oz (22 ml) coffee liqueur
1½ oz (45 ml) espresso
1 teaspoon (5 ml) Demerara syrup (p 495)
Shake with ice and strain into a frozen double rocks glass with ice.
Garnish: 3 coffee beans
▼ Considered the prescursor to the Espresso Martini, and later renamed the Pharmaceutical Stimulant at Pharmacy, Notting Hill, in 1998.

White Russian
1960s
1½ oz (45 ml) vodka
1 oz (30 ml) coffee liqueur
House cream, to float (p 506)
Stir with ice and strain into a frozen coupe, then float cream.
▼ Can be served on the rocks.

GIN

Coffee Negroni!
(See p 298)

Cold Brew Negroni
(See p 299)

Cold Brew Negroni (Edd Siu Recipe)
(See p 298)

New Drop
Leigh Lacap, Polite Provisions, San Diego, 2014
2 oz (60 ml) coffee-washed gin (p 503)
½ oz (15 ml) cacao nib Dolin Blanc (p 506)
¼ oz (7 ml) amaretto
¼ oz (7 ml) white crème de cacao
Stir and strain into a frozen coupe.
Garnish: 3 drops coffee oil

RUM & CANE SPIRIT

Café con Coco
Michael Madrusan, The Everleigh, Melbourne, 2021

1½ oz (45 ml) light rum
¾ oz (22 ml) coffee liqueur
½ oz (15 ml) Coco López
¼ oz (7 ml) house cream (p 506)

Toss and strain into a frozen double rocks glass. Add crushed ice, then shimmy and top with more crushed ice.

Garnish: freshly grated coffee bean

Café Olé
Alastair Walker, Caretaker, Auckland, 2021

1½ oz (45 ml) aged dark rum
¾ oz (22 ml) coffee liqueur
¾ oz (22 ml) house cream (p 506)
½ oz (15 ml) maple syrup

Shake with ice and strain into a frozen coupe.

Calypso Coffee

1½ oz (45 ml) Jamaican dark rum
½ oz (15 ml) coffee liqueur
¾ oz (22 ml) Demerara syrup (p 495)
3 oz (90 ml) hot filter coffee
2 oz (60 ml) house cream, to float (p 506)

Warm a Toddy glass with boiling water. Empty the glass, then build all ingredients and steam together until hot, then float cream.

Coconut Dominicana
Sam Ross, Attaboy, NYC, 2017

1½ oz (45 ml) aged dark rum
1½ oz (45 ml) coffee liqueur
Coconut cream (p 495), to float

Stir with ice and strain into a frozen coupe, then float cream.

Dirty Banana
Jamaica, 1990s

1 oz (30 ml) Jamaican dark rum
½ oz (15 ml) Giffard Banane du Brésil et des Caraïbes
½ oz (15 ml) coffee liqueur
1 oz (30 ml) house cream (p 506)
1 banana, cut into pieces

Muddle banana with rum, add remaining ingredients, then shake with ice and strain into a frozen double rocks glass. Add crushed ice, shimmy and top with more crushed ice.

Dirty Banana (Hot)

1 oz (30 ml) Jamaican dark rum
¾ oz (22 ml) Giffard Banane du Brésil et des Caraïbes
½ oz (15 ml) coffee liqueur
1 oz (30 ml) espresso
House cream, to float (p 506)

Carefully mix all ingredients except cream in a preheated flute, then float cream.

Garnish: freshly grated cinnamon

Espresso Martiki
Martin Hudak, Maybe Sammy, Sydney, 2019

1½ oz (45 ml) pineapple rum
½ oz (15 ml) coffee liqueur
1 oz (30 ml) espresso
1 oz (30 ml) pineapple juice
½ oz (15 ml) orgeat

Shake with ice and strain into a frozen coupe.

Garnish: 3 coffee beans

Habliche
Anthony Jayasekera, Bar Tobalá, Melbourne, 2023

1½ oz (45 ml) aged dark rum
¾ oz (22 ml) Ancho Reyes Original
¾ oz (22 ml) cold-brew coffee
2 dashes Angostura Bitters
2 oz (60 ml) house cream, to float (p 506)

Pebble whip and pour into a frozen double rocks glass with ice, then float cream.

Garnish: freshly grated nutmeg

Jamaican Hop No. 2
Michael Madrusan, Milk & Honey, NYC, 2009

1½ oz (45 ml) Jamaican dark rum
¾ oz (22 ml) coffee liqueur
½ oz (15 ml) Tempus Fugit Crème de Cacao
House cream, to float (p 506)

Stir with ice and strain into a frozen coupe, then float cream.

La Dominicana
Sasha Petraske, Milk & Honey, NYC, 2001

1½ oz (45 ml) aged dark rum
1½ oz (45 ml) coffee liqueur
House cream, to float (p 506)

Stir with ice and strain into a frozen coupe, then float cream.

▼ Swap rum for blanco tequila to make the **La Bestia** by Zara Madrusan, Bar Margaux, Melbourne, 2020.

Tiger Chilled Coffee
(aka **Tigre Chilled Coffee-Grog** in The South American Gentleman's Companion, *Charles H. Baker Jr., 1951) Dutch Kills, NYC*

1 oz (30 ml) aged dark rum
½ oz (15 ml) overproof Jamaican dark rum
2 oz (60 ml) cold-brew coffee
½ oz (15 ml) cinnamon syrup (p 495)
¼ oz (7 ml) pimento (allspice) dram
House cream, to float (p 506)

Pebble whip and pour into a double rocks glass with ice, then float cream.

Garnish: spritz of absinthe

Tiramisù 'Tini
Tony Roehr, Raised by Wolves, San Diego, 2021

1 oz (30 ml) aged dark rum
1 oz (30 ml) coffee liqueur
½ oz (15 ml) aquavit
½ oz (15 ml) cinnamon syrup (p 495)
House cream, to float (p 506)

Stir with ice and strain into a frozen coupe, then float cream.

Garnish: dusting of cocoa powder

Wizard in Black

Jake Powell, Death & Co, Denver, 2022

1½ oz (45 ml) aged dark rum (preferably Ron Zacapa No. 23)
¼ oz (7 ml) Punt e Mes
½ oz (15 ml) cold-brew coffee
1 teaspoon (5 ml) Tempus Fugit Crème de Banane
½ teaspoon (2.5 ml) Demerara syrup (p 495)
1 dash Angostura Bitters
1 drop saline solution (p 493)

Build in an Old Fashioned glass with ice.

Garnish: orange twist

AGAVE

Jalisco Espresso

Henry Besant and Andres Masso, London, 2005

1½ oz (45 ml) blanco tequila
¾ oz (22 ml) coffee liqueur
1 oz (30 ml) espresso
2 drops saline solution (p 493)

Shake with ice and strain into a frozen coupe.

Garnish: 3 coffee beans

The Benevolent

Justin Campbell, Mason, Santa Monica

1½ oz (45 ml) blanco tequila
½ oz (15 ml) Amaro Averna
1 oz (30 ml) cold-brew coffee
½ oz (15 ml) simple syrup
1 dash Bittermens Xocolatl Mole Bitters
1 egg white

Dry shake, then add ice, shake again and strain into a frozen Sour glass.

The Obligatory

(See p 374)

Tiger's Claw

Erick Castro, 2020

2 oz (60 ml) reposado tequila
½ oz (15 ml) coffee liqueur
1 oz (30 ml) pineapple juice
¾ oz (22 ml) lime juice
½ oz (15 ml) cinnamon syrup (p 495)
2 dashes orange bitters
2 drops saline solution (p 493)

Shake, then strain into a frozen Collins glass with ice.

Garnish: mint sprig and orange half-wheel

BRANDY

Affogato Cocktail

Simon Difford, London, 2013

1½ oz (45 ml) grappa di moscato
½ oz (15 ml) coffee liqueur
½ oz (15 ml) Tempus Fugit Crème de Cacao
1 oz (30 ml) espresso
1 scoop vanilla ice cream

Blend with 3 cubes of ice, then pour into a frozen Sour glass.

Garnish: 3 coffee beans

Billy Strut

Luke Whearty, Byrdi, Melbourne, 2022

2 oz (60 ml) apricot brandy
⅓ oz (10 ml) Oloroso Sherry
½ oz (15 ml) chilled filter coffee
House cream, to float (p 506)

Stir with ice and strain into a frozen coupe, then float cream.

Garnish: wattle pollen, grated tonka bean and lemon twist

▼ Fresh take on the classic Irish Coffee named after the 'Billionaire Strut', made famous by UFC fighter Conor McGregor.

Café Royal Frappé

Modern American Drinks, *George J. Kappeler, 1895*

1½ oz (45 ml) Cognac
2 oz (60 ml) espresso
½ oz (15 ml) simple syrup

Toss and strain into a frozen footed Delmonico glass with crushed ice, then shimmy and top with more crushed ice.

Garnish: orange half-wheel and cherry

Carajillo Frappé

¾ oz (22 ml) Cognac
¾ oz (22 ml) aged dark rum
1 oz (30 ml) espresso
¾ oz (22 ml) simple syrup

Pebble whip and pour into a frozen double rocks glass with crushed ice, then shimmy and top with more crushed ice.

Garnish: orange half-wheel and cherry

Coffee Alexander

Jones' Complete Barguide, *Stan Jones, 1977*

1½ oz (45 ml) Cognac
1 oz (30 ml) coffee liqueur
1 oz (30 ml) house cream (p 506)

Shake with ice and strain into a frozen coupe.

Garnish: freshly grated nutmeg

French Canadian

(See p 384)

Keoke Coffee (Jeffrey Morgenthaler Recipe)

George Bullington, Bully's, Del Mar, 1967

Jeffrey Morgenthaler

¾ oz (22 ml) bonded apple brandy
¾ oz (22 ml) Tempus Fugit Crème de Cacao
2 oz (60 ml) hot filter coffee
1 teaspoon (5 ml) Demerara syrup (p 495)
House cream, to float (p 506)

Warm a Toddy glass with boiling water. Empty the glass, then build all ingredients and steam together until hot, then float cream.

Garnish: freshly grated cinnamon

▼ Bullington's original recipe featured coffee liqueur, which Morgenthaler removed in his rework, adding a dash of Demerara syrup in its place.

Kinsley's Invigorator

(See p 396)

Little Death
Felix Woods, Black Pearl, Melbourne, 2021
¾ oz (22 ml) Cognac
½ oz (15 ml) overproof bourbon
⅜ oz (11 ml) Tempus Fugit Crème de Banane
1¼ oz (37 ml) espresso, cooled
½ oz (15 ml) orgeat
Pebble whip and pour into a frozen double rocks glass with ice.
Garnish: freshly grated nutmeg

Stifferino (Louis Muckensturm Recipe)
Louis' Mixed Drinks, *Louis Muckensturm, 1906*
1½ oz (45 ml) Cognac
½ oz (15 ml) Bénédictine
1 oz (30 ml) espresso
¼ oz (7 ml) Demerara syrup (p 495)
Pebble whip and pour into a frozen double rocks glass with crushed ice, then shimmy and top with more crushed ice.
Garnish: freshly grated lemon zest

Sunday Vespers
(See p 396)

Yankee Clipper
(See p 148)

WORLD WHISK(E)Y

City to City
Tom Lasher-Walker, Fresh Kills, NYC, 2017
¾ oz (22 ml) Scotch
¾ oz (22 ml) Islay Scotch
½ oz (15 ml) sweet vermouth
½ oz (15 ml) Cynar
½ oz (15 ml) coffee liqueur
Stir and strain into a frozen coupe.
Garnish: orange twist

Coffee and Cigarettes
Thomas Waugh, Death & Co, NYC, 2011
2 oz (60 ml) Islay Scotch
½ oz (15 ml) coffee liqueur
1 teaspoon (5 ml) Carpano Antica Formula
2 drops Bittermens Xocolatl Mole Bitters
Build in an Old Fashioned glass with ice.

Frozen Irish
Evan Stroeve, The Waratah, Sydney, 2024
1½ oz (45 ml) Australian whisky (preferably Archie Rose Double Malt Whisky)
¾ oz (22 ml) dulce de leche syrup (p 495)
¼ oz (7 ml) simple syrup
1 oz (30 ml) cold-brew coffee
1 scoop crushed ice
Blend with crushed ice, then pour into a frozen Sour glass.
Garnish: freshly grated nutmeg

Irish Breakfast Stout
(See p 440)

Irish Coffee
Joe Sheridan, Foynes Airport, Foynes, 1943
1½ oz (45 ml) Irish whiskey
¾ oz (22 ml) Demerara syrup (p 495)
3 oz (90 ml) hot filter coffee
2 oz (60 ml) house cream, to float (p 506)
Carefully mix all ingredients except the cream in a preheated Toddy glass, then float cream.
Garnish: freshly grated nutmeg (optional)

Irish Coffee (Madrusan Recipe)
Michael Madrusan, Bar Margaux, Melbourne, 2019
1½ oz (45 ml) Irish whiskey
½ oz (15 ml) Guinness
2 oz (60 ml) hot filter coffee
½ oz (15 ml) Demerara syrup (p 495)
2 oz (60 ml) hand-whipped house cream, to float (p 506)
Warm a flute with hot water, then pour out the water, build the cocktail and float cream.

Nickel City Frozen Irish Coffee
Travis Tober, Nickel City, Austin, 2017
2 oz (60 ml) Irish whiskey
2 oz (60 ml) coffee liqueur (preferably Mr Black Cold Brew Coffee Liqueur)
2 scoops vanilla ice cream
Blend with 8 oz (225 g) ice, then pour into a frozen double rocks glass.
Garnish: dusting of finely ground coffee

Revolver
(See p 379)

Ristretto Manhattan
The Connaught Bar, *Agostino Perrone, Giorgio Bargiani & Maura Milia, 2024*
1½ oz (45 ml) bourbon
¾ oz (22 ml) Punt e Mes
⅓ oz (10 ml) coffee liqueur
1 teaspoon (5 ml) crème de mure
2 dashes Angostura Bitters
Stir and strain into a frozen coupe.
Garnish: orange twist (discard) and blackberry

The Coffee House
(See p 380)

FORTIFIED & LIQUEUR

Carajillo (Mexican Recipe)
2 oz (60 ml) Licor 43
1 oz (30 ml) espresso
Toss and strain into an Old Fashioned glass with ice.

Coffee Negroni
(See p 298)

Cup of Joe
Michael Bascetta, Bar Liberty, Melbourne
¾ oz (22 ml) Picon Amer
⅓ oz (10 ml) muscat
¼ oz (7 ml) Tempus Fugit Crème de Cacao
1¾ oz (52 ml) chilled filter coffee
Pebble whip and pour into a frozen double rocks glass with ice.

Espresso + Prosecco
Sam Ross, Good Guy's, NYC, 2024
¾ oz (22 ml) Caffo S. Maria al Monte Elixir di Caffè
¼ oz (7 ml) Amaro Sibilla
1 oz (30 ml) espresso
1 oz (30 ml) orange juice
½ oz (15 ml) vanilla syrup (p 502)
Prosecco, to top
Toss and strain into a frozen footed Delmonico glass with ice, then top with Prosecco.
Garnish: orange half-wheel, mint sprig and 3 coffee beans

Flying Frenchman

Andy Mil, London Cocktail Club, London, 2014

1 oz (30 ml) absinthe
1 oz (30 ml) coffee liqueur
1 oz (30 ml) espresso
Shake with ice and strain into a frozen coupe.
Garnish: whole star anise

Jitterbug (Jamie Boudreau and James O. Fraioli Recipe)

The Canon Cocktail Book, *Jamie Boudreau and James O. Fraioli, 2016*

1 oz (30 ml) Carpano Antica Formula
¼ oz (7 ml) Fernet-Branca
1½ oz (45 ml) cold-brew coffee
½ oz (15 ml) simple syrup
3 dashes orange bitters
Shake with ice and strain into a frozen footed Delmonico glass with cracked ice.
Garnish: freshly grated nutmeg

Palomar Americano

Ricky Gomez, Palomar, Portland

1 oz (30 ml) Campari
1 oz (30 ml) sweet vermouth
1½ oz (45 ml) cold-brew coffee
Dry shake and pour into a frozen Collins glass with crushed ice, then shimmy and top with more crushed ice.
Garnish: orange half-wheel

Pelican

Andrew Rice, Attaboy, NYC, 2015

1 oz (30 ml) coffee liqueur
1 oz (30 ml) Fernet-Branca
1 oz (30 ml) Branca Menta
House cream, to float (p 506)
Stir with ice and strain into a frozen coupe, then float cream.

From *Here's How!* (1927):

Here's to you and here's to me, the best of friends we'll always be. But if we should ever disagree—well, here's to me!

CREAM

Golden Cadillac p 478 (left), Athol Brose No. III p 477 (middle), Alexander Cocktail p 474 (right)

Cream

Often associated with after-dinner and dessert-style drinks, and essential to categories such as Fizz (p 134) and Flip (p 388), cream can be used in a number of ways to transform a cocktail and calibrate its flavour.

When combined with spirits and modifiers, it creates a rich and silky-smooth base that carries substantial weight and feels both luxurious and indulgent. When paired with more potent ingredients, such as whisk(e)y or absinthe, it can have a mellowing effect, taking the edge off otherwise intense cocktails with its subtle lactic sweetness and mouth-coating texture. And when it comes to Fizzes, cream can play an even smaller part, balancing the citrus while adding body and enhancing the drink's aesthetic appeal. Although most cocktails featuring cream are shaken vigorously with ice to integrate the ingredients, floating cream atop a stirred cocktail adds its own magic touch, delivering both an eye-catching layered effect in the glass and a highly sensory drinking experience.

Cream

VODKA

Alexander the Great

The Stork Club Bar Book, *Lucius Beebe, 1946*
1½ oz (45 ml) vodka
½ oz (15 ml) white crème de cacao
½ oz (15 ml) coffee liqueur
1¼ oz (37 ml) house cream (p 506)
Shake with ice and strain into a frozen coupe.
Garnish: freshly grated nutmeg
▾ *"Shake until cold as Siberia."*

Solero

Ross Simon, LAB Bar, London, 2003
1½ oz (45 ml) vodka
½ oz (15 ml) Giffard Vanille de Madagascar
¼ oz (7 ml) passionfruit liqueur
1 oz (30 ml) passionfruit purée
1 oz (30 ml) house cream (p 506)
½ oz (15 ml) passionfruit syrup (p 499)
1 teaspoon (5 ml) passionfruit pulp, to float
Shake with ice and strain into a frozen Spritz glass. Add crushed ice, shimmy, then top with more crushed ice and float passionfruit pulp.
Garnish: mint sprig

White Russian

(See p 464)

GIN

Alexander Cocktail

Recipes for Mixed Drinks, *Hugo R. Ensslin, 1916*
1½ oz (45 ml) gin
1 oz (30 ml) white crème de cacao
1 oz (30 ml) house cream (p 506)
Shake with ice and strain into a frozen coupe.
Garnish: freshly grated nutmeg

Alexander's Sister

Here's How! New and Revised Edition, *Judge Jr., 1928*
1½ oz (45 ml) gin
1 oz (30 ml) white crème de menthe
1¼ oz (37 ml) house cream (p 506)
6–8 mint leaves
Shake with ice and strain into a frozen coupe.
Garnish: mint leaf

Aquamarine Cocktail

Iate Tênis Clube, Belo Horizonte
The South American Gentleman's Companion, *Charles H. Baker Jr., 1951*
1½ oz (45 ml) gin
¾ oz (22 ml) white crème de menthe
¾ oz (22 ml) house cream (p 506)
6–8 mint leaves
1 egg white
Dry shake, then add ice, shake again and strain into a frozen footed Delmonico glass.
Garnish: dusting of icing (confectioners') sugar

Ash Wednesday

Michael McIlroy, Milk & Honey, NYC, 2007
2 oz (60 ml) gin
¾ oz (22 ml) honey syrup (p 496)
¾ oz (22 ml) house cream (p 506)
2 blackberries
Muddle blackberries with honey syrup, add remaining ingredients, shake with ice and strain into a frozen coupe.
Garnish: blackberry

Belmont Cocktail

Recipes for Mixed Drinks, *Hugo R. Ensslin, 1916*
1½ oz (45 ml) gin
¾ oz (22 ml) raspberry syrup (p 500)
¾ oz (22 ml) house cream (p 506)
Shake with ice and strain into a frozen coupe.

Blue Kiss

Michael Madrusan, The Everleigh, Melbourne, 2021
1½ oz (45 ml) gin
¾ oz (22 ml) honey syrup (p 496)
¾ oz (22 ml) house cream (p 506)
3 blueberries
Muddle blueberries with honey syrup, add remaining ingredients, shake with ice and strain into a frozen coupe.
Garnish: blueberry

Café de Paris

Café Royal Cocktail Book, *W.J. Tarling, 1937*
2 oz (60 ml) gin
¼ oz (7 ml) absinthe
½ oz (15 ml) house cream (p 506)
¼ oz (7 ml) simple syrup
1 egg white
Dry shake, then add ice, shake again and strain into a frozen footed Delmonico glass.

Charging Station

(See p 464)

Merengutan

L. Kempen
1 oz (30 ml) gin
½ oz (15 ml) Italicus Rosolio di Bergamotto
¾ oz (22 ml) lemon juice
¾ oz (22 ml) simple syrup
¾ oz (22 ml) house cream (p 506)
1 orange wedge
Press orange with simple syrup, add remaining ingredients, shake with ice, then strain into a frozen coupe.

Mother's Milk Cocktail

The South American Gentleman's Companion, *Charles H. Baker Jr., 1951*
1½ oz (45 ml) gin
¾ oz (22 ml) lemon juice
¾ oz (22 ml) grenadine (p 496)
¾ oz (22 ml) house cream (p 506)
2 dashes orange blossom water
Shake with ice and strain into a frozen coupe.

1915
1½ oz (45 ml) gin
1 oz (30 ml) orange curaçao (p 498)
1 oz (30 ml) house cream (p 506)
Shake with ice and strain into a frozen coupe.

Pepin Rivero
Bar La Florida Cocktails, *1935*
¾ oz (22 ml) gin
¾ oz (22 ml) white crème de cacao
½ oz (15 ml) triple sec
¾ oz (22 ml) house cream (p 506)
Shake with ice and strain into a frozen coupe.

RUM & CANE SPIRIT

Bacardi Zoom
The Artistry of Mixing Drinks, *Frank Meier, 1936*
2 oz (60 ml) Bacardí Carta Blanca
¾ oz (22 ml) honey syrup (p 496)
¾ oz (22 ml) house cream (p 506)
Shake with ice and strain into a frozen coupe.
▾ Zooms can also be made by swapping the light rum for brandy, gin, Scotch or American whiskey.

Bee's Kiss
The Artistry of Mixing Drinks, *Frank Meier, 1936*
1½ oz (45 ml) aged dark rum
¾ oz (22 ml) honey syrup (p 496)
¾ oz (22 ml) house cream (p 506)
Shake with ice and strain into a frozen coupe.

Billy Strut
(See p 466)

Bushwacker
Angie Conigliaro, Ship's Store, St. Thomas, 1975
1 oz (30 ml) aged dark rum
¾ oz (22 ml) coffee liqueur
¾ oz (22 ml) Tempus Fugit Crème de Cacao
¼ oz (7 ml) overproof Jamaican dark rum
¾ oz (22 ml) house cream (p 506)
½ oz (15 ml) Coco López
Shake with ice and strain into a frozen coupe.
▾ This can also be blended as per the original recipe.

Café con Coco
(See p 465)

Café Olé
(See p 465)

Calypso Coffee
(See p 465)

Coconut Dominicana
(See p 465)

Dirty Banana
(See p 465)

Dirty Banana (Hot)
(See p 465)

Habliche
(See p 465)

Jamaican Hop No. 2
(See p 465)

Jamaican Milk Punch
Smuggler's Cove: Exotic Cocktails, Rum and the Cult of Tiki, *Martin and Rebecca Cate, 2016*
1 oz (30 ml) Jamaican dark rum
1½ oz (45 ml) house cream (p 506)
1 oz (30 ml) full cream milk
½ oz (15 ml) Demerara syrup (p 495)
½ oz (15 ml) vanilla syrup (p 502)
1 dash Angostura Bitters
Shake with ice and strain into a frozen double rocks glass with ice.
Garnish: freshly grated nutmeg

La Dominicana
(See p 465)

Lalla Rookh
The How and When, *Hyman Gale and Gerald F. Marco, 1937*
1 oz (30 ml) aged dark rum
1 oz (30 ml) Cognac
¾ oz (22 ml) Giffard Vanille de Madagascar
¾ oz (22 ml) house cream (p 506)
Shake with ice and strain into a frozen coupe.

Montmartre Special
Trader Vic's Bartender's Guide, *Trader Vic, 1947*
1½ oz (45 ml) light rum
¾ oz (22 ml) grenadine (p 496)
¾ oz (22 ml) house cream (p 506)
Shake with ice and strain into a frozen coupe.

Panama Cocktail
Cocktail and Wine Digest, *Oscar Haimo, 1965*
1½ oz (45 ml) aged dark rum
¾ oz (22 ml) white crème de cacao
¾ oz (22 ml) house cream (p 506)
Shake with ice and strain into a frozen coupe.

Parisian Blonde Cocktail
The Savoy Cocktail Book, *Harry Craddock, 1930*
1½ oz (45 ml) Jamaican dark rum
¾ oz (22 ml) Pierre Ferrand Dry Curaçao
¾ oz (22 ml) house cream, to float (p 506)
Stir with ice and strain into a frozen coupe, then float cream.
Garnish: freshly grated cinnamon

Raisin' Cane
Matty Clark, Dutch Kills, NYC, 2019
1½ oz (45 ml) Goslings Black Seal Rum
¾ oz (22 ml) Pedro Ximénez
¾ oz (22 ml) Licor 43
2 drops saline solution (p 493)
2 oz (60 ml) house cream (p 506)
Stir with ice and strain into a frozen coupe.
Garnish: rum-soaked raisin

Tiramisù 'Tini
(See p 465)

AGAVE

Mezcalexander
Robert Simonson, 2020
2 oz (60 ml) mezcal
1 oz (30 ml) Tempus Fugit Crème de Cacao
1 oz (30 ml) house cream (p 506)
Shake with ice and strain into a frozen coupe.
Garnish: freshly grated nutmeg

Silk Stocking
Cocktails for Two, *Helen Spence, 1982*
1½ oz (45 ml) blanco tequila
¾ oz (22 ml) white crème de cacao
¾ oz (22 ml) house cream (p 506)
¼ oz (7 ml) grenadine (p 496)
Shake with ice and strain into a frozen coupe.
Garnish: freshly grated nutmeg

BRANDY

Alexander Cocktail (Harry MacElhone Recipe)
(aka **Brandy Alexander**)
Harry of Ciro's ABC of Mixing Cocktails, *Harry MacElhone, 1923*
1½ oz (45 ml) Cognac
1 oz (30 ml) Tempus Fugit Crème de Cacao
1 oz (30 ml) house cream (p 506)
Shake with ice and strain into a frozen coupe.
Garnish: freshly grated nutmeg

Babbie's Special Cocktail
The Savoy Cocktail Book, *Harry Craddock, 1930*
1½ oz (45 ml) apricot brandy
1 oz (30 ml) gin
1 oz (30 ml) house cream (p 506)
Shake with ice and strain into a frozen coupe.

Coffee Alexander
(See p 466)

Delta Kream
Jason Crawley, Sydney, 2018
1½ oz (45 ml) Cognac
1 oz (30 ml) house cream (p 506)
½ oz (15 ml) ginger syrup (p 496)
3 dashes absinthe
2 dashes Peychaud's Aromatic Cocktail Bitters
2 dashes Angostura Bitters
Shake with ice and strain into a frozen coupe.
Garnish: freshly grated nutmeg and pinch of ground ginger

Dreamsong
Edwin Rios, Death & Co, Los Angeles, 2024
¾ oz (22 ml) Cognac
½ oz (15 ml) gin
½ oz (15 ml) white crème de cacao
¼ oz (7 ml) hazelnut liqueur
¾ oz (22 ml) house cream (p 506)
¼ oz (7 ml) cane syrup (p 494)
½ teaspoon (2.5 ml) overproof Jamaican dark rum
½ strawberry
Muddle strawberry with cane syrup, add remaining ingredients, then shake with ice and strain into a frozen coupe.
Garnish: half a strawberry

Fifth Avenue Cocktail
The Savoy Cocktail Book, *Harry Craddock, 1930*
1¼ oz (37 ml) apricot brandy
1¼ oz (37 ml) white crème de cacao
1 oz (30 ml) house cream (p 506)
Shake with ice and strain into a frozen double rocks glass with ice.

Hedgehog
Sene Hui, Caretaker, Auckland, 2021
1½ oz (45 ml) Cognac
¾ oz (22 ml) house cream (p 506)
½ oz (15 ml) ginger syrup (p 496)
½ oz (15 ml) maple syrup
Shake with ice and strain into a frozen coupe.
Garnish: candied ginger

Keoke Coffee (Jeffrey Morgenthaler Recipe)
(See p 466)

Moonlight Sonata
Erick Castro, 2017
1½ oz (45 ml) Cognac
½ oz (15 ml) Becherovka
½ oz (15 ml) cinnamon syrup (p 495)
House cream, to float (p 506)
Stir with ice and strain into a frozen coupe, then float cream.
Garnish: freshly grated cinnamon

Vanilla Cobbler
(See p 272)

Yankee Clipper
(See p 148)

AMERICAN WHISKEY

Haberdasher (Pouring Ribbons Recipe)
Pouring Ribbons, NYC
1½ oz (45 ml) bourbon
1 oz (30 ml) Tempus Fugit Crème de Cacao
¼ oz (7 ml) Fernet-Branca
1 oz (30 ml) hand-whipped house cream (p 506), to float
½ oz (15 ml) Green Chartreuse, to float
Add the cream and Green Chartreuse to a shaker and whip to combine. Stir remaining ingredients with ice, then strain into a frozen coupe and float cream mixture.

Milk Punch (New Orleans Style)
1700s
1½ oz (45 ml) bourbon
½ oz (15 ml) Goslings Black Seal Rum
½ oz (15 ml) vanilla syrup (p 502)
¼ oz (7 ml) simple syrup
1½ oz (45 ml) house cream (p 506)
1 oz (30 ml) milk
Shake with ice and strain into a frozen double rocks glass with ice.
Garnish: freshly grated nutmeg

Molly's Medicine
Michael Madrusan, The Everleigh, Melbourne, 2021
1½ oz (45 ml) bourbon
¾ oz (22 ml) Tempus Fugit Crème de Banane
1 oz (30 ml) house cream (p 506)
3 blueberries
Muddle blueberries with house cream, add remaining ingredients, then shake with ice and strain into a frozen coupe.
Garnish: blueberry
▾ "She was eating blueberries, I was sipping the banana liqueur."

Olson Cocktail
(Whiskey Zoom with nutmeg)
The How and When, *Hyman Gale and Gerald F. Marco, 1937*
2 oz (60 ml) bourbon
¾ oz (22 ml) honey syrup (p 496)
¾ oz (22 ml) house cream (p 506)
Shake with ice and strain into a frozen coupe.
Garnish: freshly grated nutmeg

Third Date
Zachary Gelnaw-Rubin, Lion Lion, NYC, 2018
1½ oz (45 ml) bourbon
¾ oz (22 ml) Giffard Crème de Pêche de Vigne
½ oz (15 ml) white crème de cacao
1 teaspoon (3 ml) honey syrup (p 496)
House cream, to float (p 506)
Stir with ice and strain into a frozen coupe, then float cream.

SCOTCH

Athol Brose No. III
(Scotch Zoom with a cream float)
The Gentleman's Companion, *Charles H. Baker Jr., 1939*
2 oz (60 ml) Scotch
¾ oz (22 ml) honey syrup (p 496)
House cream, to float (p 506)
Stir with ice and strain into a frozen coupe, then float cream.
▾ This is our house Athol Brose.

Scottish Breakfast
Erick Castro, Rickhouse, San Francisco, 2009
1½ oz (45 ml) Scotch
½ oz (15 ml) bonded apple brandy
½ oz (15 ml) maple syrup
1 oz (30 ml) house cream (p 506)
1 teaspoon (5 ml) simple syrup
Shake with ice and strain into a frozen double rocks glass with ice.
Garnish: freshly grated cinnamon

The Barbary Coast Cocktail
The Savoy Cocktail Book, *Harry Craddock, 1930*
¾ oz (22 ml) Scotch
¾ oz (22 ml) gin
¾ oz (22 ml) white crème de cacao
¾ oz (22 ml) house cream (p 506)
Shake with ice and strain into a frozen double rocks glass with ice.

The Black Eye
(Alexander with Scotch)
Here's How Again!, *Judge Jr., 1929*
1½ oz (45 ml) Scotch
1 oz (30 ml) white crème de cacao
1 oz (30 ml) house cream (p 506)
Shake with ice and strain into a frozen coupe.
Garnish: freshly grated nutmeg
▾ *"The gent who invented this said that he had a very good reason for naming it thusly."*

WORLD WHISK(E)Y

Irish Coffee
(See p 467)

Irish Coffee (Madrusan Recipe)
(See p 467)

Irish Cream
Toby Maloney, 2008
1 oz (30 ml) Irish whiskey
1 oz (30 ml) spiced rum
½ oz (15 ml) Licor 43
½ oz (15 ml) Demerara syrup (p 495)
1 oz (30 ml) house cream (p 506)
1 dash Angostura Bitters
Shake with ice and strain into a frozen double rocks glass with ice.
Garnish: flamed orange twist (discard)

FORTIFIED & LIQUEUR

Banshee
Bryant's Cocktail Lounge, Milwaukee, 1970s
1¼ oz (37 ml) white crème de cacao
1¼ oz (37 ml) Giffard Banane du Brésil et des Caraïbes
1 oz (30 ml) house cream (p 506)
Shake with ice and strain into a frozen coupe.
Garnish: banana chip and freshly grated nutmeg

Chapuline
Toby Maloney, 2007
1 oz (30 ml) Tempus Fugit Crème de Cacao
1 oz (30 ml) green crème de menthe
¾ oz (22 ml) pisco (preferably acholado)
1 oz (30 ml) house cream (p 506)
Shake with ice and strain into a frozen coupe.
Garnish: mint leaf

Chartreuse Alexander

Jon Armstrong, Death & Co, Los Angeles, 2015

¾ oz (22 ml) Green Chartreuse
¾ oz (22 ml) Cognac
½ oz (15 ml) white crème de cacao
½ oz (15 ml) house cream (p 506)
1 dash Bittermens Xocolatl Mole Bitters
Shake with ice and strain into a frozen coupe.
Garnish: freshly grated nutmeg

Flying Grasshopper

Jones' Complete Barguide, *Stan Jones, 1977*

¾ oz (22 ml) white crème de menthe
¾ oz (22 ml) white crème de cacao
¾ oz (22 ml) vodka
1 oz (30 ml) house cream (p 506)
Shake with ice and strain into a frozen coupe.
Garnish: mint leaf

Golden Cadillac (Madrusan Recipe)

(aka **Gold Cadillac**)

Frank Klein, Poor Red's Bar-B-Q, El Dorado, 1952
Michael Madrusan, The Everleigh, Melbourne, 2011

1 oz (30 ml) dark crème de cacao
½ oz (15 ml) Galliano Vanilla
1¼ oz (37 ml) orange juice
1 oz (30 ml) house cream (p 506)
Shake with ice and strain into a frozen double rocks glass with ice.
Garnish: orange wedge
▼ Originally made with white crème de cacao and without orange juice.

Golden Dream

Jones' Complete Barguide, *Stan Jones, 1977*

1 oz (30 ml) triple sec
¼ oz (7 ml) Galliano Vanilla
1½ oz (45 ml) orange juice
¾ oz (22 ml) house cream (p 506)
Shake with ice and strain into a frozen coupe.

Grasshopper

Harry O'Brien, Palace Hotel, San Francisco
The World's Drinks and How to Mix Them, *Wm. T. Boothby, 1908*

1¼ oz (37 ml) white crème de cacao
1¼ oz (37 ml) white crème de menthe
1 oz (30 ml) house cream (p 506)
10–12 mint leaves
Shake with ice and strain into a frozen coupe.
Garnish: mint leaf

Grasshopper No. 2

Naren Young, Sweet Liberty, Miami, 2021

¾ oz (22 ml) white crème de menthe
¾ oz (22 ml) white crème de cacao
½ oz (15 ml) mezcal
¼ oz (7 ml) Branca Menta
1¼ oz (37 ml) house cream (p 506)
1 teaspoon (5 ml) absinthe
Toss and strain into a frozen double rocks glass with crushed ice.
Garnish: mint sprig and freshly grated milk chocolate

Pelican

(See p 468)

Pink Squirrel

Bryant Sharp, Bryant's Cocktail Lounge, Milwaukee, 1940s

1¼ oz (37 ml) white crème de cacao
1¼ oz (37 ml) crème de noyaux (preferably Tempus Fugit Crème de Noyaux)
1 oz (30 ml) house cream (p 506)
Shake with ice and strain into a frozen coupe.
Garnish: freshly grated nutmeg

From *Irish and English bar toasts of the early 1900s*:

Here's to good health, bad habits, and great stories!

NON-ALCOHOLIC

La Piña p 486 (left), Designated Diver p 484 (right)

Non-alcoholic

Non-alcoholic cocktails are now as remarkable and relevant as ever, finally getting the respect that they deserve as more and more people seek mindful drinking options that don't sacrifice flavour, intrigue or sophistication.

Indeed, today's 'zero-proof' cocktails have succeeded largely because they've looked beyond sugar and found balance, refinement and depth in combinations of high-quality ingredients put together with precise technique. As a result, those who choose to abstain are no longer made to feel second tier and face an abundance of choices far beyond a lemon, lime and bitters or bottled fruit juice.

While bartenders have picked up their game substantially, so, too, have producers large and small, who've worked tirelessly to mimic the look and feel of alcoholic spirits and liqueurs. The marketplace is now chock-full of exceptional non-alcoholic alternatives and innovation is a constant. That said, age-old ingredients and methods have also found their way back into the fold, and the category is alive and well with cocktails that feature aromatic shrubs, teas, kombucha, verjus, herbs and spices.

The drinks we've showcased in this chapter only scratch the surface of what's possible with non-alcoholic cocktails, and its popularity as a category shows no signs of slowing down.

Non-alcoholic

Aguafresca de Pimiento Rojo

Side Hustle, London

1 oz (30 ml) pink grapefruit juice
1 oz (30 ml) coconut water
¾ oz (22 ml) red capsicum (red pepper) juice
½ oz (15 ml) lemon juice
½ oz (15 ml) honey syrup (p 496)
¼ oz (7 ml) passionfruit syrup (p 499)
¼ oz (7 ml) morita water (p 507)
1 cucumber wheel
5 mint leaves

Press cucumber with honey syrup, add remaining ingredients, then shake with ice. Strain into a frozen double rocks glass with ice.

Garnish: cucumber wheel

Americano N/A

Sam Ross and Haley Traub, Attaboy, NYC, 2024

1½ oz (45 ml) Martini Vibrante
1½ oz (45 ml) Ritual Zero Proof Aperitif Alternative
Soda, to top

Build in a frozen Highball glass with ice and top with soda.

Garnish: grapefruit twist

Bengal Fizz

David Molyneux, The Everleigh, Melbourne, 2019

1 oz (30 ml) lime juice
1 oz (30 ml) passionfruit syrup (p 499)
½ oz (14 g) Greek yoghurt
1 egg white
Soda, to top

Dry shake, then add ice and shake again. Strain into a frozen footed Delmonico glass and top with soda.

Garnish: mint sprig

Cease and Desist

The NoMad Bar, NYC

3 oz (90 ml) orange juice
1 oz (30 ml) house cream (p 506)
1 oz (30 ml) simple syrup
5 drops orange blossom water
Soda, to top

Pour ¼ oz (7 ml) soda into a frozen footed Delmonico glass. Add remaining ingredients to a shaker, dry shake, add ice and shake again, then strain into the footed Delmonico glass and top with soda.

Champaxne Cocktail

Stacey Swenson, Swan Room, NYC

4⅓ oz (130 ml) non-alcoholic sparkling wine
1 white sugar cube
10 drops All the Bitter New Orleans Bitters
4 dashes orange blossom water

Soften sugar cube with bitters and orange blossom water in a small dish, then gently drop the cube into a chilled flute of non-alcoholic sparkling wine.

Garnish: orange twist

Chill Out

The Connaught Bar, *Agostino Perrone, Giorgio Bargiani & Maura Milia, 2024*

1¼ oz (37 ml) orange juice
¾ oz (22 ml) lemon juice
¾ oz (22ml) fresh passionfruit pulp
¾ oz (22 ml) chilli syrup (p 494)
½ oz (15 ml) passionfruit syrup (p 499)

Shake with ice and strain into a small chilled wine glass with ice.

Garnish: passionfruit half-shell and pinch dried chilli powder

Coffee Time Cocktail

Sam Ross and Haley Traub, Attaboy, NYC, 2024

1½ oz (45 ml) Lyre's Coffee Originale
½ oz (15 ml) Dr. Zero Zero AmarNo
½ oz (15 ml) cane syrup (p 494)
½ oz (15 ml) house cream (p 506)
1 egg yolk

Dry shake, then add ice, shake again and strain into a frozen coupe.

Garnish: freshly grated nutmeg

Damascus Fizz

Oscar Shaw, The Everleigh, Melbourne, 2021

2 oz (60 ml) orange juice
1 oz (30 ml) salted apricot purée (p 507)
½ oz (15 ml) house cream (p 506)
¼ oz (7 ml) lemon juice
¼ oz (7 ml) Coco López
Soda, to top

Shake with ice and strain into a frozen footed Delmonico glass, then top with soda.

Decaf Colada

Sam Ross and Haley Traub, Attaboy, NYC, 2024

1½ oz (45 ml) Lyre's Coffee Originale
1½ oz (45 ml) pineapple juice
¾ oz (22 ml) lime juice
¾ oz (22 ml) Coco López

Toss and strain into a frozen tiki mug with crushed ice, then swizzle and top with more crushed ice.

Garnish: mint bouquet and freshly grated nutmeg

Designated Diver

Jeff "Beachbum" Berry, 2008

1½ oz (45 ml) orange juice
¾ oz (22 ml) lemon juice
¾ oz (22 ml) passionfruit syrup (p 499)
¾ oz (22 ml) vanilla syrup (p 502)
Soda, to top

Toss and strain into a frozen tiki mug with ice, then top with soda.

Garnish: orange half-wheel, lemon half-wheel and cherry

Eden's Fix

Nat Yao, Bar Margaux, Melbourne, 2022

1½ oz (45 ml) English breakfast tea (1 bag in 3½ oz or 100 ml cold water for 1 hour)
½ oz (15 ml) lemon juice
½ oz (15 ml) maple syrup
½ oz (15 ml) ginger syrup (p 496)
1 teaspoon (5 ml) apple purée
1 teaspoon (5 ml) apple-cider vinegar

Toss and strain into a frozen double rocks glass with ice.

Garnish: apple fan

El Diablito

Side Hustle, London

1 oz (30 ml) ginger syrup (p 496)
¾ oz (22 ml) lime juice
½ oz (15 ml) hibiscus syrup (p 496)
Soda, to top

Cube whip and pour into a frozen Collins glass with ice, then top with soda.

Garnish: lime wheel and candied ginger

Forbidden Passion

The Connaught Bar, *Agostino Perrone, Giorgio Bargiani & Maura Milia, 2024*

1½ oz (45 ml) cranberry juice
¾ oz (22 ml) lemon juice
¾ oz (22 ml) grenadine (p 496)
½ oz (15 ml) ginger syrup (p 496)
2 raspberries
2 blueberries
2 blackberries
1 oz (30 ml) soda, to top

Muddle berries with ginger syrup, add remaining ingredients, then toss and strain into a frozen Collins glass with crushed ice. Shimmy and top with more crushed ice and soda.

Garnish: raspberry, blackberry and blueberry

Fresco

Felix Woods, The Everleigh, Melbourne

¾ oz (22 ml) lime juice
¾ oz (22 ml) simple syrup
4 watermelon chunks
2 slices red cayenne chilli, deseeded
6–8 mint leaves
Soda, to top

Muddle all ingredients, then shake and strain into a frozen Collins glass with ice and top with soda.

Garnish: lime wedge and pinch of salt flakes

Gari's Toupée

Michael Madrusan, The Everleigh, Melbourne, 2021

1½ oz (45 ml) Lyre's Italian Spritz
2 oz (60 ml) pink grapefruit juice
1 oz (30 ml) bitter lemon soda, to top
½ oz (15 ml) soda, to top

Toss and strain into a frozen double rocks glass with ice, then top with bitter lemon soda and soda.

Garnish: grapefruit half-wheel

Gunner

(House ginger beer)

Ewen Fergusson & Robert Renton, Singapore Golf Club, mid-1800s

1 oz (30 ml) ginger syrup (p 496)
1 oz (30 ml) lemon juice
2 dashes Angostura Bitters
2 drops saline solution (p 493)
Soda, to top

Cube whip and pour into a frozen Collins glass with ice, then top with soda.

Garnish: candied ginger

High Noon

Nat Yao, Bar Margaux, Melbourne, 2023

2 oz (60 ml) non-alcoholic sauvignon blanc
1 oz (30 ml) Seedlip Spice 94
½ oz (15 ml) elderflower cordial

Stir with ice and strain into a frozen coupe.

Garnish: lemon twist

From *The Gentleman's Companion* (1939):

Here's to the men of old: If they were half as brave as their drinks were strong, the world was in good hands.

Horchata

Side Hustle, London

1 cup (125 g) sliced almonds
13 oz (375 g) white long-grain rice
½ oz (15 g) whole cinnamon stick
52 oz (1.5 litres) boiling filtered water
34 oz (1 litre) cold filtered water
1½ oz (40 g) caster (superfine) sugar

Spread the almonds out on a baking tray and toast at 200°C (400°F) for 5 minutes. Combine the rice, almonds, cinnamon and boiling water in a heatproof bowl, cover and leave to cool completely overnight. The next day, add the cold water and blend in a Vitamix until very smooth. Strain through a chinois. Add the sugar and blend again. Store in an airtight container in the fridge for up to 3 days. To serve, shake the bottle then pour into a frozen double rocks glass with ice.

Garnish: orange half-wheel

Horse Before the Cart

Michael McIlroy, Attaboy, NYC, 2024

1½ oz (45 ml) Martini Vibrante
1 oz (30 ml) pink grapefruit juice
¾ oz (22 ml) ginger syrup (p 496)
½ oz (15 ml) lime juice
Soda, to top

Cube whip and pour into a frozen Collins glass with ice, then top with soda.

Garnish: candied ginger

Jungle Bird N/A

Sam Ross and Haley Traub, Attaboy, NYC, 2024

1¼ oz (37 ml) Dr. Zero Zero AmarNo
¾ oz (22 ml) Martini Vibrante
1½ oz (45 ml) pineapple juice
½ oz (15 ml) lime juice
½ oz (15 ml) simple syrup

Shake with ice and strain into a frozen double rocks glass with ice.

Garnish: 2 orange half-wheels on a cocktail skewer

Kama's Arrow
Tyson Buhler, Death & Co, NYC, 2018
1 oz (30 ml) mango purée
1 oz (30 ml) vanilla syrup (p 502)
½ oz (15 ml) lemon juice
½ oz (15 ml) Coco López
1 dash Scrappy's Bitters Cardamom Bitters
Soda, to top
Shake with ice, then strain into a frozen Collins glass with ice and top with soda.
Garnish: pinch of crushed pistachios

Ladybug Spritz
Nat Yao, Bar Margaux, Melbourne, 2023
1 oz (30 ml) Lyre's Italian Orange
1 oz (30 ml) pink grapefruit juice
1 oz (30 ml) strawberry purée
½ oz (15 ml) lemon juice
Soda, to top
Toss and strain into a frozen Collins glass with ice, then top with soda.
Garnish: half a strawberry

La Lambada
The Connaught Bar, *Agostino Perrone, Giorgio Bargiani & Maura Milia, 2024*
1 oz (30 ml) pineapple juice
1 oz (30 ml) Coco López
½ oz (15 ml) lime juice
1 lemongrass stalk, halved
Bitter lemon soda, to top
Muddle lemongrass with all ingredients, then shake with ice, then strain into a frozen Collins glass with crushed ice and top with bitter lemon soda.
Garnish: mint sprig and half a lemongrass stalk

La Piña
Jessica Gonzalez, The NoMad Bar, NYC
2 oz (60 ml) pineapple juice
¾ oz (22 ml) lime juice
¾ oz (22 ml) agave syrup (p 494)
1 slice fresh jalapeño
Soda, to top
Shake with ice and strain into a frozen footed Delmonico glass with ice, then top with soda.
Garnish: 2 pineapple fronds

Lake House Fix
Felix Woods, The Everleigh, Melbourne
1 oz (30 ml) Seedlip Spice 94
½ oz (15 ml) lemon juice
½ oz (15 ml) simple syrup
¼ oz (7 ml) ginger syrup (p 496)
3 cucumber wheels
Soda, to top
Press cucumber, add remaining ingredients, toss and strain into a frozen double rocks glass with crushed ice, then top with soda.
Garnish: mint sprig, cucumber fan and freshly cracked pepper

Lychee Daiquiri
Mike Capoferri, Thunderbolt, Los Angeles
2 oz (60 ml) lychee daiquiri base (p 498)
¾ oz (22 ml) lime juice
2 drops saline solution (p 493)
Shake with ice and strain into a frozen coupe.
Garnish: lime wedge

Manhattan N/A
Liana Oster, NoMad London, London, 2023
1 oz (30 ml) Seedlip Spice 94
½ oz (15 ml) Three Spirit Nightcap
½ oz (15 ml) verjus
¼ oz (7 ml) Amarena cherry syrup
¼ oz (7 ml) mulled maple syrup (p 498)
1 teaspoon (5 ml) cold-brew coffee
Stir with ice and strain into a frozen coupe.
Garnish: cherry

Midday Stinger
Sam Ross and Haley Traub, Attaboy, NYC, 2024
2 oz (60 ml) Dr. Zero Zero AmarNo
¾ oz (22 ml) lemon juice
¾ oz (22 ml) simple syrup
6 dashes El Guapo Spiced Cocoa Bitters
8–10 mint leaves
Soda, to top
Add bitters, lemon, sugar and mint to a small shaker tin and press. Add the AmarNo and stir to combine. Strain into a frozen double rocks glass and top with soda and crushed ice. Shimmy and top with more crushed ice.
Garnish: mint bouquet

MokEnzo
Vincenzo Errico, L'Artefatto, Forio d'Ischia, 2024
1 oz (30 ml) lemon juice
¾ oz (22 ml) simple syrup
6 red grapes
Sanpellegrino Aranciata Rossa, to top
Press grapes with simple syrup, add remaining ingredients, then shake with ice, strain into a frozen double rocks glass with ice and top with Aranciata Rossa.
Garnish: red grape on a cocktail skewer

Mr. Paradise
The NoMad Bar, NYC
1 oz (30 ml) pineapple juice
1 oz (30 ml) pink grapefruit juice
½ oz (15 ml) lemon juice
½ oz (15 ml) cold-brew coffee
½ oz (15 ml) vanilla syrup (p 502)
¼ oz (7 ml) cane syrup (p 494)
1 strawberry, halved
Tonic water, to top
Muddle strawberry with cane syrup, add remaining ingredients, then shake with ice, strain into a frozen Collins glass with ice and top with tonic water.
Garnish: strawberry half

Nah'liato
Nick Amano-Dolan, Chezchez, San Francisco
1 oz (30 ml) Giffard Aperitif Bitter
2 drops saline solution (p 493)
3 oz (90 ml) bitter lemon tonic water (preferably Fever-Tree Lemon Tonic Water), to top
2 oz (60 ml) non-alcoholic sparkling wine
Build in a chilled Spritz glass with ice.
Garnish: orange half-wheel

Non-Violent Crimes
Sam Ross and Haley Traub, Attaboy, NYC, 2024
1½ oz (45 ml) Ghia Original Apéritif
¾ oz (22 ml) passionfruit syrup (p 499)
¾ oz (22 ml) lime juice
¼ oz (7 ml) honey syrup (p 496)
1 egg white
Dry shake, then add ice, shake again and strain into a frozen Sour glass.
Garnish: dusting of cayenne pepper

Nor'easter
Sam Ross and Haley Traub, Attaboy, NYC, 2024
1½ oz (45 ml) The Pathfinder Spirit
1 oz (30 ml) lime juice
½ oz (15 ml) simple syrup
2 cucumber wheels
6–8 mint leaves
Tonic water, to top
Press cucumber with simple syrup, add remaining ingredients then toss and strain into a frozen Collins glass with ice, then top with tonic water.
Garnish: cucumber fan and mint sprig

Paradise City
The NoMad Bar, NYC
1½ oz (45 ml) pink grapefruit juice
1 oz (30 ml) house cream (p 506)
¾ oz (22 ml) passionfruit syrup (p 499)
½ oz (15 ml) vanilla syrup (p 502)
Soda, to top
Pour ¼ oz (7 ml) soda into a frozen footed Delmonico glass. Add remaining ingredients to a shaker, dry shake, add ice and shake again, then strain into the footed Delmonico glass and top with soda.

Queen Garden Swizzle
Lydia McLuen, Takibi, Portland
2 oz (60 ml) Seedlip Garden 108
¾ oz (22 ml) cold mint tea
½ oz (15 ml) pineapple syrup (p 499)
½ oz (15 ml) lemon juice
¼ oz (7 ml) simple syrup
1 teaspoon (5 ml) umeboshi vinegar
Dry shake, then pour into a frozen Collins glass with crushed ice, swizzle and top with more crushed ice.
Garnish: mint bouquet

Quiet American
Oscar Shaw, The Everleigh, Melbourne, 2021
1 oz (30 ml) Lyre's Apéritif Rosso
1 oz (30 ml) orange juice
¾ oz (22 ml) lemon juice
½ oz (15 ml) honey syrup (p 496)
2 dashes Peychaud's Aromatic Cocktail Bitters
Tonic water, to top
Shake with ice and strain into a frozen double rocks glass with ice.
Garnish: orange half-wheel

Rhubarb & Chamomile
Side Hustle, London
1½ oz (45 ml) rhubarb juice
1 oz (30 ml) chamomile tea, cooled
¾ oz (22 ml) honey syrup (p 496)
1 teaspoon acid water solution (p 504)
Soda, to top
½ oz (15 ml) hibiscus tea, to float
Cube whip and pour into a frozen Collins glass with ice, then top with soda and float hibiscus tea.
Garnish: rhubarb ribbon

Shandy Gaff N/A
Michael McIlroy, Attaboy, NYC, 2024
½ oz (15 ml) lemon juice
½ oz (15 ml) ginger syrup (p 496)
¼ oz (7 ml) honey syrup (p 496)
Non-alcoholic IPA, to top
Cube whip and pour into a frozen Collins glass with ice, then top with IPA.
Garnish: lemon twist (discard) and candied ginger

Sidewalker
Sam Ross, Attaboy, NYC, 2024
2 oz (60 ml) The Pathfinder Spirit
1½ oz (45 ml) pink grapefruit juice
½ oz (15 ml) lime juice
½ oz (15 ml) orgeat
Pebble whip and pour into a frozen Collins glass with crushed ice, then swizzle and top with more crushed ice.
Garnish: mint bouquet

Soft Core Soda
The NoMad Bar, NYC
2 oz (60 ml) Granny Smith apple juice
2 oz (60 ml) brewed chamomile tea, cooled
¾ oz (22 ml) verjus
½ oz (15 ml) agave syrup (p 494)
1 oz (30 ml) soda, to top
Cube whip and pour into a frozen Collins glass with ice, then top with soda.
▼ Originally uncarbonated.

Strawberries & Cream
Andy Chu, The Everleigh, Melbourne, 2016
2 oz (60 ml) orange juice
1 oz (30 ml) honey syrup (p 496)
½ oz (15 ml) lemon juice
½ oz (15 ml) house cream (p 506)
2 strawberries, halved
Soda, to top
Muddle strawberries with honey syrup, add remaining ingredients, then shake with ice and strain into a frozen footed Delmonico glass and top with soda.
Garnish: strawberry and a spritz of rosewater

Tail Feathers
The Fine Art of Mixing Drinks, *David A. Embury, 1948*
2 oz (60 ml) orange juice
¾ oz (22 ml) ginger syrup (p 496)
½ oz (15 ml) lime juice
Soda, to top
Cube whip and pour into a frozen Collins glass with ice, then top with soda.
Garnish: orange half-wheel and candied ginger
▼ *"An excellent Prohibition Highball."*

Talk to Her
Lynnette Marrero, NYC
1½ oz (45 ml) Seedlip Spice 94
2 oz (60 ml) red verjus
¾ oz (22 ml) pineapple juice
½ oz (15 ml) cinnamon syrup (p 495)
Shake with ice and strain into a frozen double rocks glass with ice.
Garnish: 2 pineapple fronds and red grape

Tarzan N/A
Sam Ross and Haley Traub, Attaboy, NYC, 2024
1½ oz (45 ml) Ghia Apéritif
1½ oz (45 ml) pineapple juice
½ oz (15 ml) lemon juice
½ oz (15 ml) simple syrup
Soda, to top
Cube whip and pour into a frozen Collins glass with ice, then top with soda.
Garnish: orange half-wheel

Tea Rinfresco
The Connaught Bar, *Agostino Perrone, Giorgio Bargiani & Maura Milia, 2024*
1½ oz (45 ml) pear juice
1 oz (30 ml) brewed jasmine tea, cooled
¾ oz (22 ml) lemon juice
¾ oz (22 ml) ginger syrup (p 496)
Soda, to top
Cube whip and pour into a frozen Collins glass with ice, then top with soda.
Garnish: mint sprig and dried pear slice

The Silky Way
The Connaught Bar, *Agostino Perrone, Giorgio Bargiani & Maura Milia, 2024*
1¾ oz (52 ml) brewed oolong tea, cooled
1¾ oz (52 ml) pear juice
¾ oz (22 ml) salted date syrup (p 500)
¾ oz (22 ml) lime juice
Shake with ice and strain into a frozen pilsner glass with ice.
Garnish: 2 dried pear slices

Tuileries
Franck Audoux, Cravan, Paris, 2023
2½ oz (75 ml) nettle syrup (p 498)
3½ oz (105 ml) lemon balm soda (p 497)
Build in a frozen Highball glass with ice and stir to combine.

Unrisky Business
Sam Ross and Haley Traub, Attaboy, NYC, 2024
1½ oz (45 ml) Ritual Zero Proof Whiskey Alternative
1½ oz (45 ml) pineapple juice
¾ oz (22 ml) lime juice
¾ oz (22 ml) honey syrup (p 496)
3 dashes El Guapo Fuego Bitters
Shake with ice and strain into a frozen double rocks glass with ice.
Garnish: dusting of cayenne pepper

Vegetarian Bramble
Michael Madrusan, The Everleigh, Melbourne, 2011
¾ oz (22 ml) lemon juice
¾ oz (22 ml) simple syrup
2 oz (60 ml) soda
4 blackberries
Swirl the liquids together in a shaker, then muddle blackberries with a splash of the swirled liquids in a separate shaker. Pour the muddled mixture into a frozen double rocks glass, add crushed ice, then pour in the remaining liquids and top with more crushed ice.
Garnish: blackberry

Virgin Mary (Jeffrey Morgenthaler 'All-Day' Recipe)
Jeffrey Morgenthaler
3 oz (90 ml) Bloody Mary mix (p 494)
3 oz (90 ml) tomato juice
Add ingredients to a shaker with ice, roll back and forth to chill but not aerate, then strain into a frozen 16 oz (455 ml) pint glass with ice.
Garnish: salt-and-pepper rim, lemon wedge and dill pickle spear

Watermelon Agua Fresca
Side Hustle, London
1 oz (30 ml) watermelon juice
1 oz (30 ml) coconut water
½ oz (15 ml) lime juice
½ oz (15 ml) agave syrup (p 494)
¼ oz (7 ml) pickling liquid (p 507)
5 basil leaves
Shake with ice and strain into a frozen double rocks glass with ice.

Woodsman
The NoMad Bar, NYC
1 oz (30 ml) pink grapefruit juice
¾ oz (22 ml) elderflower cordial
¼ oz (7 ml) lemon juice
¼ oz (7 ml) honey syrup (p 496)
2 oz (60 ml) Medahuman Glow (or soda), to top
2 oz (60 ml) The London Essence Co Grapefruit & Rosemary Tonic Water, to top
Cube whip and pour into a frozen Collins glass with ice, then top with Medahuman Glow and tonic.
Garnish: thinly sliced grapefruit wheels inside the glass

Yuzu Lemonade
David Molyneux, The Everleigh, Melbourne, 2019
1 oz (30 ml) pineapple juice
¾ oz (22 ml) simple syrup
½ oz (15 ml) yuzu juice
¼ oz (7 ml) lemon juice
Soda, to top
Pebble whip and pour into a frozen footed Delmonico glass with ice, then top with soda.
Garnish: mint sprig

SYRUPS, INFUSIONS, TINCTURES & MORE

Syrups, Infusions, Tinctures & More

A NOTE ON METHODS

The vast majority of the recipes in this section can be easily made at home, but there have been some great advancements in the industry and the technology we use behind the bar to prep our ingredients, so if you want to take it up a notch, there are several recipes here that use professional equipment.

KEY RECIPES

SIMPLE SYRUP

1 part caster (superfine) sugar + 1 part hot water

Mix by weight and store in an airtight container in the fridge for up to 4 weeks.

SALINE SOLUTION

4 parts hot water + 1 part salt

Combine the water and salt and store in an airtight container in the fridge for up to 4 weeks.

Syrups

Agave Syrup

2:1 light agave nectar and hot water

Combine the agave nectar and hot water by weight and store in an airtight container at room temperature for up to 1 year.

All-Day Bloody Mary Mix (Jeffrey Morgenthaler Recipe)

Makes approx. 17 oz (500 ml)

5 oz (150 ml) water
5 oz (150 ml) fresh lemon juice, strained
5 oz (150 ml) Worcestershire sauce
6 g (⅛ oz; approx. 1 rounded teaspoon) citric acid
4 g (⅛ oz) Tabasco
2 g celery salt
2 g finely ground black pepper
1.5 g MSG

Combine all the ingredients in an airtight container and mix well. Seal and store in the fridge for at least 1 hour but up to 2 days. Strain through a fine-mesh sieve or muslin into a clean container and store at room temperature for up to 6 months.

Used in: Bloody Mary (Jeffrey Morgenthaler 'All-Day' Recipe; p 116)

Apple Cordial

Makes approx. 34 oz (1 litre)

2 g ascorbic acid
34 oz (1 litre) Pink Lady apple juice (juiced with a centrifugal juicer)
caster (superfine) sugar
2% malic acid

Place the ascorbic acid in a jug. Add the apple juice and stir to dissolve the acid. Leave to settle and separate, then strain through a fine-mesh sieve lined with muslin, discarding the solids. Weigh the liquid, then add 15 g (½ oz) sugar per 3½ oz (100 ml) liquid, along with 2% of the total weight of malic acid. Store in an airtight container or bottle in the fridge for up to 1 week.

Used in: Crimson Chin (p 381)

Bloody Mary Mix (Maison Premiere Recipe)

The Maison Premiere Almanac, *Joshua Boissy, et al., 2023*

Makes approx. 34 oz (1 litre)

3 celery stalks
1 onion, peeled
1 carrot, peeled
3 garlic cloves, peeled
34 oz (1 litre) tomato juice
6 tinned chipotle peppers, drained
1 cup (88 g) grated fresh horseradish
1 cup (250 g) Dijon mustard
1 tablespoon Worcestershire sauce
1 tablespoon salt
½ tablespoon ground black pepper
3 oz (90 ml) Tabasco

Juice the celery, onion, carrot and garlic and combine this liquid with the tomato juice in a large container. Blend the chipotle peppers with the horseradish, mustard and a little of the tomato juice mixture. Add the blended chipotle mixture, Worcestershire sauce, salt, pepper and Tabasco and stir well. Store in an airtight container for up to 3 days.

Used in: Bloody Mary (Maison Premiere Recipe; p 116)

Cane Syrup

Makes approx. 5 oz (150 ml)

300 g (10½ oz) unbleached cane sugar
5 oz (150 ml) water

Combine the sugar and water in a blender and process until the sugar has dissolved. Store in an airtight container in the fridge for up to 2 weeks.

Cascara Cordial

Makes approx. 3½ oz (100 ml)

14 g (½ oz) Ethiopian coffee cascara
3½ oz (100 ml) mineral water
18.6 g (¾ oz) caster (superfine) sugar (per 100 g/3½ oz)
0.14 g tartaric acid (per 100 g/3½ oz)

Combine the cascara and mineral water in a vacuum bag and seal. Leave to infuse in the fridge for 24 hours. Filter with a Superbag or piece of muslin, then weigh and add caster sugar and tartaric acid per 100 g (3½ oz). Stir until dissolved, then store in an airtight container for up to 1 week.

Used in: Not An Espresso Martini (p 464)

Chamomile Syrup

Jeremy Blackmore, Mucho Group, Sydney

Makes approx. 10½ oz (300 ml)

4 g (⅛ oz) chamomile flowers or 3 chamomile tea bags
8 oz (250 ml) boiling water
1 cup (220 g) white (granulated) sugar

Allow the flowers, or tea bags, to infuse in the boiling water for 6 minutes. Remove or strain out the tea, add the sugar and stir to dissolve. Chill, then bottle and store in the fridge for up to 2 weeks.

Used in: Matador (Mucho Group Recipe; p 218), The Fitzcarraldo (p 145)

Chenin Blanc Cordial

Makes approx. 34 oz (1 litre)

1 × 26 oz (750 ml) bottle chenin blanc
3 oz (90 ml) rishi peach blossom tea
2.5 kg (5 lb 8 oz) caster (superfine) sugar
42 g (1½ oz) malic acid

Combine the chenin blanc and tea in a cambro. Stir thoroughly, cover and steep 15 minutes, then strain. Add the sugar and acid and blend with an immersion blender. Store in an airtight container in the fridge for up to 3 weeks.

Used in: Honey Rider (p 424)

Chilli Syrup

Makes approx. 24 oz (700 ml)

24 oz (700 ml) simple syrup
2 Scotch Bonnet chillies

Add the simple syrup and chillies to a blender and blitz until the chillies are very finely chopped. Leave to infuse for 30 minutes, then strain through a paper coffee filter. Bottle and store in the fridge for up to 1 week.

Used in: Chill Out (p 484)

Cinnamon Syrup

Makes approx. 17 oz (500 ml)

17 oz (500 ml) simple syrup
10 g (⅓ oz) crushed cinnamon sticks
small pinch of Kosher salt

Fill a large basin with water and place an immersion circulator inside. Set the circulator to 63°C (145°F). Put all the ingredients in a bowl and stir to combine. Transfer to a sealable, heatproof plastic bag. Seal the bag almost completely, then remove as much air as possible by dipping the bag (not the unsealed portion) in the basin of water. Finish sealing the bag, then remove it from the water. When the water has reached 63°C (145°F), place the bag in the basin and 'cook' for 2 hours. After 2 hours, remove the bag and place it in an ice bath, then leave to cool to room temperature. Pass the syrup through a fine-mesh sieve. If any particles remain in the syrup, strain it through a coffee filter or piece of muslin. Transfer to an airtight container and store in the fridge for up to 2 weeks.

Coco Mix

Makes approx. 29 oz (825 ml)

1 × 425 g (15 oz) tin Coco López
1 × 14 oz (400 ml) tin Thai coconut milk

Submerge the tin of Coco López in very hot water for 30 minutes. Remove from the water and shake the tin hard. Open and pour into an airtight container with the coconut milk. Stir well with a whisk, then seal and store in the fridge for up to 1 week.

Used in: Piña Colada (Tyler Kitzman Recipe) (p 451)

Coconut and Pandan Syrup

Makes approx. 34 oz (1 litre)

17 oz (500 ml) coconut milk
17 oz (500 ml) coconut water
350 g (12 oz) caster (superfine) sugar
100 g (3½ oz) pandan leaves

Combine the coconut milk and coconut water in a jug. Add the sugar and stir to dissolve. Transfer to a vacuum bag with the pandan leaves, seal and sous vide at 55°C (131°F) for 1 hour. Strain loosely, then strain through a fine-mesh sieve or piece of muslin. Store in an airtight container in the fridge for up to 1 week.

Used in: Sweet Escape (p 452)

Coconut Cream

Makes approx. 2½ oz (75 ml)

2 oz (60 ml) house cream (page 506)
½ oz (15 ml) Coco López

Mix the house cream and Coco López together then store in an airtight container in the fridge for 3–4 days.

Used in: Coconut Dominicana (p 465)

Condensed Syrup

2:1 condensed milk to rich simple syrup (page 500)

Combine the condensed milk and simple syrup by weight. Store in an airtight container in the fridge for up to 1 week.

Used in: The Chunky Dunk (p 235)

Cranberry Cordial

Makes approx. 52 oz (1.5 litres)

17 oz (500 ml) tart, 100% cranberry juice
650 g (1 lb 7 oz) caster (superfine) sugar
½ cup (200 g) allspice berries

Combine the cranberry juice and sugar in a saucepan. Add the allspice and bring to a rolling boil. Remove from the heat and leave to cool. Store in an airtight container or bottle at room temperature for up to 2 weeks.

Used in: Cosmo #2 (p 194)

Cucumber Syrup

Makes approx. 52 oz (1.5 litres)

16 oz (455 ml) fresh cucumber juice
450 g (1 lb) caster (superfine) sugar
½ oz (15 ml) vodka

Combine the cucumber juice and sugar, then whisk to dissolve. Add the vodka and store in an airtight container in the fridge for up to 1 week.

Used in: Escape Plan (p 198)

Demerara Syrup

Makes approx. 17 oz (500 ml)

2 cups (410 g) Demerara sugar
8 oz (250 ml) water

Combine the sugar and water in a saucepan and simmer over medium heat, without boiling, until the sugar has dissolved. Store in an airtight container in the fridge for up to 3–4 weeks.

Dr Pepper Syrup

Makes approx. 26 oz (750 ml)

68 oz (2 litres) Dr Pepper

Pour the Dr Pepper into a saucepan and reduce over medium heat to 26 oz (750 ml). Store in an airtight container in the fridge for up to 2 weeks.

Used in: Dr Pepper Negroni (p 300)

Dulce De Leche Syrup

Makes approx. 26 oz (750 ml)

500 g (1 lb 2 oz) Dulce De Leche (store bought, Messina is good)
1 cup (250 ml) nut milk (preferably macadamia)

Combine the dulce de leche and nut milk in a jug then pour into a squeeze bottle and store in the fridge for up to 3–4 days.

Used in: Frozen Irish (p 467)

Enhanced Grapefruit Juice

Makes approx. 21 oz (600 ml)

21 oz (600 ml) fresh grapefruit juice (fine strained)
2 g citric acid
0.25 g phosphoric acid

Combine all the ingredients in a blender and blitz together. Store in an airtight container in the fridge for up to 1 week.

Used in: Rio Star Paloma (p 88)

Fruit Cup

gin
sweet vermouth
Grand Marnier
Heering Cherry Liqueur

Fruit Cup is a combination of gin, sweet vermouth, Grand Marnier and Cherry Liqueur.

To make a bottle, combine 6 oz (180 ml) gin, 6 oz (180 ml) sweet vermouth, 3 oz (90 ml) Grand Marnier and 2 oz (60 ml) Cherry Liqueur.

To make a single serve, combine 1 oz (30 ml) gin, 1 oz (30 ml) sweet vermouth, ½ oz (15 ml) Grand Marnier and ¼ oz (7 ml) Cherry Liqueur.

Store in an airtight bottle in the fridge for up to 1 month.

Fruit Cup Syrup

Makes approx. 34 oz (1 litre)

1 kg (2 lb 4 oz) simple syrup
140 g (5 oz) orange half-wheels
100 g (3½ oz) maraschino cherries
1¾ oz (52 ml) cherry syrup
120 g (4¼ oz) orange peel
165 g (5¾ oz) pineapple slices
4 g malic acid
8 g (⅓ oz) citric acid
20 g (¾ oz) Giffard Crème de Pêche de Vigne

Combine the simple syrup and fruit in a vacuum bag and sous vide at 63°C (145°F) for 2 hours. Add the acids and Giffard pêche and blend with a hand-held blender on low speed until well combined. Strain through a Superbag and store in an airtight container in the fridge for up to 1 week.

Used in: New Wave (p 71)

Ginger Syrup

2 parts raw ginger juice
1½ parts caster (superfine) sugar

Mix the ginger juice and caster sugar by weight, adding the sugar to the ginger juice slowly, and stirring until the sugar has completely dissolved. Store in an airtight container in the fridge for up to 1 week.

Grapefruit Oleo-saccharum

Makes approx. 17 oz (500 ml)

5 grapefruits, washed
400 g (14 oz) caster (superfine) sugar
7 oz (200 ml) hot water

Peel the grapefruit skin in large strips, being careful not to get any pith. Place in a bowl and top with the sugar. Stir to fully coat the peels. Cover the bowl with plastic wrap (or, ideally, seal in a vacuum-sealed bag) and leave to sit for 20–24 hours at room temperature. Uncover the bowl, pour the hot water over the peels and stir until the sugar has dissolved. Strain out the peels, leaving the oleo-saccharum to cool, and store in an airtight container in the fridge for up to 1 month.

Used in: Rio Star Paloma (p 88)

Grapefruit Piña Syrup

Makes approx. 52 oz (1.5 litres)

17 oz (500 ml) pineapple juice
8 oz (250 ml) grapefruit juice
17 oz (500 ml) water
1 kg (2 lb 4 oz) caster (superfine) sugar
50 g (1¾ oz) grapefruit peel
8 g (⅓ oz) malic acid
15 g (½ oz) citric acid

Combine the juices, water, sugar and peel in a deep bowl and blend with a hand-held blender. Strain through a paper coffee filter, add the acids and blend again on low speed. Store in an airtight container in the fridge for up to 1 week.

Used in: Honey Rider (p 424)

Grenadine

Makes approx. 34 oz (1 litre)

17 oz (500 ml) pomegranate molasses
17 oz (500 ml) simple syrup
½ teaspoon vanilla essence
¾ teaspoon rosewater
5 dashes orange bitters
3 drops clementine oil

Combine equal parts pomegranate molasses and simple syrup. Per 34 oz (1 litre) of grenadine, add the vanilla essence, rosewater, orange bitters and clementine oil. Store in an airtight container or bottle in the fridge for up to 1 month.

Hibiscus Syrup

Makes approx. 17 oz (500 ml)

17 oz (500 ml) simple syrup
30 g (1 oz) dried hibiscus flowers

Fill a large basin with water and place an immersion circulator inside. Set the circulator to 57°C (135°F). Add the simple syrup and hibiscus to a sealable, heatproof plastic bag. Seal the bag almost completely, then press out as much air as possible by dipping the bag (except the unsealed portion) in the water. Finish sealing the bag, then remove it from the water. When the water has reached 57°C (135°F), place the bag in the basin and cook for 2 hours. Transfer the bag to an ice bath and leave to cool to room temperature. Pass the syrup through a fine-mesh sieve lined with a paper coffee filter. If any particles remain in the syrup, strain it again. Store in an airtight container in the fridge for up to 1 month.

Used in: Empire Fizz (p 146), El Diablito (p 485)

Honey Syrup

3 parts honey
1 part hot water

Combine the honey and water by weight in a jug and stir until completely mixed. Store in a glass jar at room temperature for up to 1 month. Set the jar in a bowl of hot water to soften it, as needed.

Jasmine-infused Agave Syrup

Makes approx. 8 oz (250 ml)

8 oz (250 ml) jasmine tea (made with 4 g/⅛ oz jasmine pearls and 8 oz/250 ml boiling water)
agave nectar

Strain the tea and weigh it. Add 8 oz (250 g) agave nectar for every 4 oz (120 ml) jasmine tea, stirring to dissolve. Store in an airtight container in the fridge for up to 3 months.

Used in: Cantaloupe Paloma (p 87)

Lacto-fermented Mango Honey

Makes approx. 700 g (1 lb 9 oz)
1 tablespoon salt
250 g (9 oz) diced mango, skins reserved
375 g (13 oz) honey
13 oz (375 ml) filtered water
Combine the salt and mango in a bowl and mix well with a gloved hand. Add the honey and water and transfer to a vacuum-sealed bag. Leave at room temperature for 5–7 days to ferment. Strain through a chinois, reserving the mango pieces for garnish (up to 3 days). Store the honey in an airtight container in the fridge for up to 1 week.
Used in: Rusty Nail (Leo Robitschek Recipe; p 383)

Lacto-fermented Peach and Lemon Verbena Syrup

Makes approx. 101 oz (3 litres)
1.5 kg (3 lb 5 oz) peach, diced
140 g (5 oz) Aji Amarillo Paste
30 g (1 oz) lemon verbena leaves
15 g (½ oz) salt
water
unrefined cane sugar
Add all the ingredients except water and sugar to a vacuum bag and seal. Leave to ferment overnight. Weigh the contents and combine 2 parts laco-ferment with 1 part water in a jug. Blend with a hand-held blender.

Weigh the ferment again and add 50 g (1¾ oz) unrefined cane sugar for every 3½ oz (100 ml) liquid. Mix well, then store in an airtight container in the fridge for up to 1 week.
Used in: Peach (p 219)

Lapsang Souchong Vinegar

Makes approx. 34 oz (1 litre)
34 oz (1 litre) lapsang souchong tea
scoby plus mother base
100 g (3½ oz) caster (superfine) sugar
Add the scoby and mother base to the lapsang souchong, cover and rest for about 30 days. Test the pH and store when it reaches 3. Store in an airtight container or bottle in the fridge for up to 2 weeks.
Used in: Ruby Cane (p 232)

Lavender Honey Syrup

3 parts honey
1 part freshly brewed lavender tea
Mix the honey and tea by weight in a heatproof bowl and stir until well combined. Leave to cool, then store in an airtight container at room temperature for up to 1 week.
Used in: Hummingbird (p 171)

Lemon Balm Soda

Makes approx. 34 oz (1 litre)
25 g (1 oz) dry lemon balm leaves
34 oz (1 litre) mineral water
Put the lemon balm leaves in a heatproof jug. Boil the mineral water and pour on top of the leaves. Stir, cover the jug and leave to infuse for 5 minutes. Filter through a Superbag and chill. Pour the infusion into a siphon, add two gas cartridges and store in the fridge for up to 1 week.
Used in: Tuileries (p 488)

Lemon Sherbet

Makes approx. 24 oz (700 ml)
1½ cups (330 g) white (granulated) sugar
peel of 4 lemons
12 oz (350 ml) fresh lemon juice
Combine the sugar and lemon peels in an airtight container, seal and leave to sit overnight to create an oleo-saccharum. The next day, strain the peels and place the liquid in a saucepan with the lemon juice. Set over medium heat and stir slowly to dissolve the sugar, but do not allow to boil. When the syrup has thickened, remove the pan from the heat and strain the sherbet through a chinois. Store in an airtight container in the fridge for up to 3 weeks.
Used in: Golden Hour (p 437)

Lime Cordial

Makes approx. 24 oz (700 ml)
12 large ripe limes, washed and dried
2.5–3 cups (550–660 g) white (granulated) sugar, plus extra if needed
Allow 3 days to make this cordial. Peel the outermost layer of skin from the limes; you want the merest zest. Set aside the peeled fruit to be juiced the following day. Place the zests in a non-reactive container and cover completely with the sugar. Mix to thoroughly coat the peels. Seal and set aside for at least 12 hours, or overnight, to make an oleo-saccharum. The next day, mix the peels, sugar and leached citrus oil together to form a slurry. Juice the reserved limes and add the juice to the oleo-saccharum. Mix well, until homogenous. Cover and leave at room temperature for another 12 hours. The following day, mix it all well again, then strain through a chinois to remove the peels. It should be a thick, very sweet mixture. If it's too thin, add more sugar. Funnel into a clean, airtight bottle and seal. Use immediately or leave it for another day to allow the ingredients to cure. Store in the fridge for up to 1 week.
Used in: Hong Kong (p 318), La Bandera (p 329), Leg Before Wicket (p 300), Mezcaletti Gimlet (p 300), Taxi Cocktail (p 272), The Long Island Bar Gimlet (p 210)

Lime Oleo-saccharum

Makes approx. 28 oz (800 ml)
8–10 limes
330 g (11½ oz) caster (superfine) sugar
8 oz (250 ml) water
Peel the limes and put the rinds in a bowl. Cover with the sugar and leave at room temperature overnight. Remove the rinds and discard. Bring sugar and water to the boil in a saucepan over medium heat, stirring until the sugar has dissolved. Leave to cool, then store in an airtight container in the fridge for up to 1 month.
Used in: Ranch Water (Eight Row Flint Recipe) (p 118)

Lychee Daiquiri Base

Makes approx. 21 oz (600 ml)

1 × 560 g (1 lb 4 oz) tin peeled, pitted lychees
rum emulsion

Blend the lychees and syrup from the tin until completely smooth, then weigh. Add 1%, by weight, of rum emulsion. For example, if the purée weighs 15 oz (425 g), add ⅛ oz (4.25 g) of rum emulsion. Store in an airtight container in the fridge for up to 1 week.

Used in: Lychee Daiquiri (p 486)

Mango Syrup

1 part rich simple syrup (p 500)
2 parts mango purée

Combine the syrup and mango purée by weight and whisk until well incorporated. Store in an airtight container in the fridge for up to 1 week.

Used in: Vernita Green (p 255)

Mineral Syrup

1 part caster (superfine) sugar
1 part high-trace mineral water

Combine the sugar and mineral water by weight and store in an airtight container for up to 1 week.

Used in: Improved Sherry Cocktail (p 332)

Mint Sugar Syrup (Morgenthaler Recipe)

Makes approx. 12 oz (350 ml)

7 fresh mint sprigs
12 oz (350 ml) rich simple syrup (p 500)

Blanch the mint leaves in a saucepan of boiling water for 15 seconds by holding the stems. Remove and immediately submerge in an ice bath. Pat dry with paper towel, then pick the leaves and add to a blender with the simple syrup. Blend for 1 minute, then pass through a fine-mesh sieve into a squeeze bottle. Store in the fridge for up to 4 days.

Used in: Mint Punch (p 132)

Mulled Maple Syrup

Makes approx. 8 oz (250 ml)

4 oz (120 ml) maple syrup
4 oz (120 ml) filtered water
1 cinnamon stick
1 long orange peel
3 whole cloves

Add maple syrup and water to a saucepan and bring to a low simmer. Turn off heat, add remaining ingredients, cover and leave to infuse for 15 minutes. Leave to cool, then bottle and store in the fridge for up to 1 month.

Used in: Manhattan N/A (p 486)

Muscovado Syrup

Makes approx. 30 oz (875 ml)

450 g (1 lb) dark muscovado sugar
15 g (½ oz) granulated sugar
16 oz (455 ml) water

Add all the ingredients to a small saucepan and simmer over medium heat until the sugars have dissolved, but do not boil. Store in an airtight container in the fridge for up to 1 month

Used in: Coffee Cocktail (p 395)

Nautilus Pickle Brine

Makes approx. ⅓ oz (10 ml)

⅓ oz (10 ml) gherkin brine
1 teaspoon (5 ml) jalapeño brine

Combine the brines and store in an airtight container in the fridge for up to 2 weeks.

Used in: Pickle Martini (p 320)

Nettle Syrup

Makes approx. 21 oz (600 ml)

10 g (⅓ oz) dry nettle leaves
20 oz (570 ml) mineral water
180 g (6½ oz) caster (superfine) sugar
2.7 g tartaric acid

Put the nettle leaves in a heatproof jug. Boil the mineral water and pour it on top of the leaves. Add the sugar, stir, cover and leave to infuse for 10 minutes. Filter through a Superbag, then add the acid and stir to dissolve, then chill. Store in an airtight container in the fridge for up to 1 week.

Used in: Tuileries (p 488)

Normandie Club Bloody Mary Mix

Makes approx. 16 oz (455 ml)

6 oz (180 ml) fresh tomato juice
2 oz (60 ml) bottled tomato juice
2 oz (60 ml) fresh celery juice
1½ oz (45 ml) fresh red capsicum (red pepper) juice
1 oz (30 ml) Tomato bouillon concentrate (see below)
½ oz (15 ml) fresh lemon juice
½ oz (15 ml) fresh lime juice
½ oz (15 ml) dill pickle juice
1 tablespoon Worcestershire sauce
2 teaspoons (10 ml) soy-based liquid aminos (preferably Bragg Liquid Aminos)
2 teaspoons (10 ml) Sriracha
2 teaspoons prepared horseradish

Place all the ingredients in a bowl and stir to combine. Store in an airtight container in the fridge for up to 1 week.

Tomato bouillon concentrate

2½ oz (80 ml) tomato and chicken granulated bouillon (preferably Knorr)
1 oz (30 ml) boiling water

Combine the bouillon and water in an airtight container and stir vigorously until the bouillon has dissolved. Store in an airtight container for up to 6 months.

Used in: Normandie Club Bloody Mary (p 120)

Orange Curaçao

1 part Grand Marnier
1 part simple syrup

Combine the Grand Marnier and simple syrup by weight and store in an airtight container at room temperature for up to 1 month.

Orange Marmalade Syrup

Makes approx. 8 oz (250 ml)

115 g (4 oz) marmalade
4 oz (120 ml) simple syrup
5 dashes Regan's Orange Bitters
2 dashes Angostura Bitters (optional)

Combine all the ingredients in an airtight container or shaker and shake to combine. Strain through a fine-mesh sieve and store in a clean airtight container at room temperature for up to 1 month.

Used in: Breakfast Julep (p 284), Dundee (p 316)

Orgeat

Makes approx. 34 oz (1 litre)

14 oz (400 ml) almond milk (see below)
600 g (1 lb 5 oz) caster (superfine) sugar
⅓ oz (10 ml) Cognac
⅓ oz (10 ml) amaretto
1 dash rosewater

Combine the almond milk and sugar in a saucepan over medium-low heat, stirring occasionally, until the sugar has dissolved. Remove from the heat and stir in the Cognac, amaretto and rosewater. Leave to cool to room temperature, then transfer to an airtight container and store in the fridge for up to 2 weeks.

Almond milk

Makes approx. 59 oz (1.7 litres)

600 g (1 lb 5 oz) sliced blanched almonds
59 oz (1.7 litres) filtered water

Combine the almonds and water in a blender and blend until very smooth. Strain through a fine-mesh sieve lined with several layers of muslin and suspended over a bowl. Allow the liquid to drain slowly for up to 2 hours. Press gently on the solids at the end to remove as much liquid as possible, then store in an airtight container in the fridge for up to 1 week.

Pandan Syrup

Makes approx. 34 oz (1 litre)

10 pandan leaves
34 oz (1 litre) simple syrup
2 drops pandan extract
2 g salt

Blend the pandan leaves with the simple syrup. Add the pandan extract and salt and mix well. Pass through a fine-mesh sieve and store in an airtight container in the fridge for up to 2 weeks.

Used in: Buko Gimlet (p 214), L'Alligator C'est Vert (p 399), Leeward Negroni (p 303), Pandan-quiri (p 232)

Passionfruit Syrup

Makes approx. 13 oz (375 ml)

8 oz (250 ml) passionfruit purée
4 oz (120 ml) simple syrup

Combine the purée and syrup in a blender and process until the sugar has fully dissolved. Store in an airtight container in the fridge for up to 1 week.

Pickle Water

Makes approx. 22½ oz (650 ml)

10½ oz (300 ml) apple-cider vinegar
10½ oz (300 ml) onion water
1¾ oz (52 ml) rich simple syrup (p 500)

Combine all the ingredients and store in an airtight container in the fridge for up to 1 week.

Used in: Pickle Martini (Antonello Arzedi Recipe; p 321)

Pineapple Dill Syrup

Makes approx. 17 oz (500 ml)

250 g (9 oz) pineapple flesh, diced
500 g (1 lb 2 oz) caster (superfine) sugar
100 g (3½ oz) fresh dill

Vacuum seal all the ingredients for 24 hours. Pass through a fine-mesh sieve lined with a piece of muslin, pressing down to crush the ingredients. Transfer to a bottle and store in an airtight container in the fridge for up to 1 week.

Used in: Clarabell (p 215)

Pineapple Syrup

Makes approx. 26 oz (750 ml)

250 g (9 oz) unbleached cane sugar
15 g (½ oz) gum arabic
1.5 g citric acid
8 oz (250 ml) fresh pineapple juice

Fill a large basin with water and place an immersion circulator inside. Set the circulator to 63°C (145°F). Combine the sugar, gum arabic and citric acid in a blender and process for 30 seconds. With the blender running, slowly add the pineapple juice and continue to process until all of the dry ingredients have dissolved, about 2 minutes. Pour the mixture into a sealable, heatproof plastic bag. Seal the bag almost completely, then remove as much air as possible by dipping the bag (except the unsealed portion) in the basin of water. Finish sealing the bag, then remove it from the water. When the water has reached 63°C (145°F), place the bag in the basin and cook for 2 hours. Place the bag in an ice bath and leave to cool to room temperature. Strain through a Superbag, then transfer to an airtight container and store in the fridge for up to 1 week.

Pink Cocktail Onion Brine

Makes approx. 21 oz (600 ml)

250 g (9 oz) caster (superfine) sugar
10 g (⅓ oz) salt
17 oz (500 ml) rice-wine vinegar
1 red onion, diced
5 g dried hibiscus

Add the sugar and salt to the vinegar in a saucepan and place over medium heat. When hot, but not boiling, add the diced onion and hibiscus. Remove from the heat and leave to infuse for 1 hour, then strain and allow to cool. Store in an airtight container in the fridge for up to 1 week. You can store your cocktail garnish onions in this brine until you're ready to serve.

Used in: Pink Gibson (p 321)

Pink Peppercorn Shrub

Makes approx. 52 oz (1.5 litres)

44 oz (1.25 litres) simple syrup
7 oz (200 ml) rice-wine vinegar
40 g (1½ oz) whole pink peppercorns

Add all ingredients to a jug and blend using a hand-held blender. Pass through a chinois lined with muslin or a paper coffee filter. Store in an airtight container in the fridge for up to 2 weeks.

Used in: Rhubarb (p 181)

Pink Peppercorn-infused Agave Syrup

Makes approx. 68 oz (2 litres)

100 g (3½ oz) whole pink peppercorns
34 oz (1 litre) agave nectar
34 oz (1 litre) water

Heat a dry frying pan over medium-low heat and toast the peppercorns for a few minutes, being careful not to burn them. Crush them lightly in the pan with the back of a wooden spoon to open them. Add the peppercorns to a large saucepan with the agave nectar and water and bring to a gentle boil. Remove from the heat and leave to cool. Pass through a fine-mesh sieve and store in an airtight container in the fridge for up to 2 weeks.

Used in: Cantaloupe Paloma (p 87), Fancy Paloma (p 87)

Raspberry Syrup

Makes approx. 17 oz (500 ml)

17 oz (500 ml) simple syrup
150 g (5½ oz) fresh raspberries
2.5 g citric acid

Fill a large basin with water and place an immersion circulator inside. Set the circulator to 57°C (135°F). Put all the ingredients in a bowl and stir to combine. Transfer to a sealable, heatproof plastic bag. Seal the bag almost completely, then press out as much air as possible by dipping the bag (other than the unsealed portion) in the water. Finish sealing the bag, then remove it from the water. When the water has reached 57°C (135°F), place the bag in the basin and cook for 2 hours. Place the bag in an ice bath and let cool to room temperature. Pass the syrup through a fine-mesh sieve. If any particles remain in the syrup, strain it through a paper coffee filter or Superbag. Store in an airtight container in the fridge for up to 2 weeks.

Rich Demerara Syrup

2 parts Demerara sugar
1 part water

Combine the sugar and water by weight in a saucepan over medium-low heat, stirring until the sugar has dissolved. Store in an airtight container in the fridge for up to 1 month.

Used in: Motomami (p 231)

Rich Simple Syrup

2 parts caster (superfine) sugar
1 part water

Combine the sugar and water by weight in a saucepan over medium-low heat, stirring until the sugar has dissolved. Store in an airtight container in the fridge for up to 1 month.

Salted Date Syrup

Makes approx. 28 oz (800 ml)

1¼ oz (40 ml) still mineral water
10 g (¼ oz) salt
26 oz (750 ml) date syrup

Make a saline solution by combining the mineral water and salt. Stir until dissolved, then pour into a sterilised 24 oz (700 ml) bottle. Add the date syrup, seal and shake to blend. Store in the fridge for up to 1 week.

Used in: The Silky Way (p 488)

Shiso-Quinine Cordial

Makes approx. 17 oz (500 ml)

peeled zest of 3 limes
1½ cups (330 g) caster (superfine) sugar
20 fresh green shiso leaves
13 oz (375 ml) cold water
1 teaspoon (5 ml) liquid quinine concentrate (available online)
¼ teaspoon malic acid

Muddle the lime zest and sugar, cover and leave to stand for 30 minutes. Add the shiso leaves and muddle, then cover and leave to stand for another 30 minutes. Add the water, quinine and malic acid and stir until the sugar has dissolved. Strain through a fine-mesh sieve lined with a piece of muslin, then store in a sealed container in the fridge for up to 1 week.

Used in: Shiso Gin & Tonic (p 117)

Spiced Pineapple Syrup

Makes approx. 68 oz (2 litres)

3 cinnamon sticks, broken
9 cloves
9 juniper berries
9 whole black peppercorns
6 star anise
9 cardamom pods, bruised
1 tablespoon coriander seeds
1 tablespoon fennel seeds
1 vanilla bean, split lengthways and seeds scraped
freshly grated nutmeg
1 kg (2 lb 4 oz) white (granulated) sugar
34 oz (1 litre) hot water
1 pineapple, finely chopped (skin on)
2 oz (60 ml) Wray & Nephew rum
½ tablespoon sea salt (preferably Maldon)

Heat a dry frying pan over medium heat and toast all the spices for 2–3 minutes until fragrant. Combine the sugar and hot water in a large pot and add the spices and chopped pineapple. Bring to a gentle boil over medium-low heat, then remove from the heat and leave to cool before straining off the spices and pineapple. Add the rum and sea salt to help fortify and preserve the syrup, then store in an airtight container in the fridge for up to 2 weeks.

Used in: Spiced Pineapple Daiquiri (p 235)

Spiced Squash (Pumpkin) Syrup

Makes approx. 74 oz (2.2 litres)

800 g (1 lb 12 oz) Kabocha squash (pumpkin)
10 whole black peppercorns
10 coriander seeds
3 g caraway seeds
4 g fresh sage
10 g (⅓ oz) dried ginger
74 oz (2.2 litres) simple syrup

Preheat the oven to 180°C (350°F). Cut the skin off the squash and cut into 2.5 cm (1 in) dice. Place on a baking tray and roast for 20 minutes. Place the roasted squash in a vacuum-sealed bag with the remaining ingredients, seal and sous vide at 60°C (140°F) for 1 hour. Strain through a chinois lined with a piece of muslin. Store in an airtight container in the fridge for up to 1 week.

Used in: Squash (p 220)

Spicy Agave Syrup

Makes approx. 68 oz (2 litres)

52 oz (1.5 litres) agave nectar
17 oz (500 ml) water
8 jalapeños, sliced
2 Thai bird's eye chillies, sliced lengthways

Add the jalapeños and chillies to the agave nectar and water and leave to infuse at room temperature for 15–20 minutes. Store in an airtight container in the fridge for up to 1 week.

Used in: Joy Ride (p 438)

Strawberry Basil Syrup

Makes approx. 26 oz (750 ml)

450 g (1 lb) strawberries, hulled
26 oz (750 ml) filtered water
Pectinex Ultra SP-L
12 basil leaves
caster (superfine) sugar

Weigh the strawberries and water. Calculate 0.2% of the weight (multiply by 0.002) to get a gram measurement. This is the amount of Pectinex that will need to be added. Place the strawberries, water and Pectinex in a blender and blend for 5 minutes. Transfer to a saucepan and bring to the boil over medium heat. Boil for 5 minutes, then add the basil and boil for another 5 minutes, then remove from the heat. Leave to cool for 10 minutes, then strain the liquid through a fine-mesh sieve. Weigh the liquid and add an equal amount of sugar. Transfer to a blender and process until the sugar has dissolved. Skim any foam from the surface, then transfer to an airtight container and refrigerate for up to 2 weeks.

Used in: Trampoline (p 216)

Strawberry Syrup

Makes approx. 12 oz (350 ml)

250 g (9 oz) strawberries, hulled
250 g (9 oz) unbleached cane sugar
0.5 g Pectinex Ultra SP-L

Combine the strawberries and sugar in a blender and process until very smooth. Once the sugar has dissolved, add the Pectinex and process for another 10 seconds. Transfer to a centrifuge container. Weigh the filled container and fill each of the other containers with an equal weight of water. Run the centrifuge at 4500 pm for 12 minutes. Remove the containers and strain the syrup through a paper coffee filter or Superbag, being careful not to disturb the solids that have collected at the bottom of the container. Transfer to an airtight container and store in the fridge for up to 1 week.

Used in: Boston Club Punch (p 430)

Vanilla Syrup

Makes approx. 17 oz (500 ml)

17 oz (500 ml) simple syrup
2 g vanilla extract

Combine the simple syrup and vanilla extract in an airtight container, seal and shake to combine. Store in an airtight container in the fridge for up to 2 weeks.

Used in: Aces and Eights (p 373), Designated Diver (p 484), Dry Pornstar Daiquiri (p 231), Espresso + Prosecco (p 467), Hot Lips (p 182), Jamaican Milk Punch (p 475), Kama's Arrow (p 486), Milk Punch (p 477), Mr. Brown (p 378), Mr. Paradise (p 486), Only Fans (p 424), Paradise City (p 487), Pemberton Fizz (p 88)

Verjus Syrup

3 parts verjus
2 parts caster (superfine) sugar

Combine the verjus and sugar by weight and stir until the sugar has dissolved. Store in an airtight container at room temperature for up to 2 weeks.

Used in: Suburban Gimlet (p 216)

Yuzu Syrup

Makes approx. 52 oz (1.5 litres)

225 g (8 oz) yuzu peel
2.25 g salt
450 g (1 lb) sugar
17 oz (500 ml) water

Put the yuzu peels in a bowl with the salt and half the sugar, and mix until well coated. Either transfer to a sealed bag or cover the bowl and leave overnight for the sugar and salt to draw out the oils in the fruit. Add the remaining sugar and the water and stir until the sugar has dissolved. Strain through a fine-mesh sieve, discarding the peels. Store in an airtight container in the fridge for up to 2 weeks.

Used in: Doris Diesel (p 230)

Infusions

Almond-infused Gin

Makes approx. 26 oz (750 ml)

¼ cup (40 g) whole almonds
1 × 26 oz (750 ml) bottle gin

Combine the almonds and gin and leave to infuse for 24 hours at room temperature. Strain through a fine-mesh sieve, discarding the almonds, rebottle and store at room temperature for up to 1 month.

Used in: Dr Pepper Negroni (p 300)

Ancho-chilli-infused Lustau East India Solera Sherry

Makes approx. 26 oz (750 ml)

1 × 26 oz (750 ml) bottle Lustau East India Sherry
45 g (1½ oz) ancho chillies, destemmed, deseeded and roughly chopped

Combine the sherry and chilli in a non-reactive container. Cover and leave to infuse at room temperature for 24 hours. Strain through a fine-mesh sieve, then rebottle and store in the fridge for up to 2 weeks.

Used in: Hocus Pocus (Christy Pope and Chad Solomon Recipe; p 329)

Cacao Nib Rum

Makes approx. 24 oz (700 ml)

140 g (5 oz) cacao nibs
24 oz (700 ml) dark rum (preferably Plantation Original Dark Double Aged Rum)

Combine the cacao nibs and rum in a vacuum bag, seal and sous vide at 52°C (125°F) for 30 minutes, then remove and chill. Strain through a chinois and store in a bottle at room temperature for up to 1 month.

Used in: Tiramisù Milk Punch (p 132)

Caramelised Leek-infused Dry Vermouth

Makes approx. 26 oz (750 ml)

50 g (1¾ oz) leeks, sliced in half lengthways and again crossways into 1 cm (½ in) pieces
2 g sugar
1 × 26 oz (750 ml) bottle dry vermouth
2 g black peppercorns
5 g lemon thyme (approx. 2 sprigs)

Heat a frying pan over medium heat with a drop of oil and gently fry the leeks for 1–2 minutes. Add the sugar and cook, stirring occasionally, until the leeks are soft and golden brown, about 10 minutes. Allow to cool then add the leeks to a container with the vermouth, peppercorns and thyme. Cover and leave to infuse for 12 hours, then strain through a paper coffee filter, rebottle and store in the fridge for up to 2 weeks.

Used in: Leek (p 318)

Chamomile-infused Calvados

Makes approx. 26 oz (750 ml)

1 × 26 oz (750 ml) bottle Calvados
5 g dried chamomile flowers

Combine the Calvados and chamomile in a bowl and stir to combine. Leave to stand at room temperature for 1 hour, stirring occasionally. Strain through a fine-mesh sieve lined with several layers of muslin, then funnel back into the bottle. Store in the fridge for up to 3 months.

Used in: Gun Club Toddy (p 406)

Coconut Fat-washed Calvados

Makes approx. 26 oz (750 ml)

100 g (3½ oz) unrefined coconut oil
1 × 26 oz (750 ml) bottle Calvados Manoir de Grandouet 2yr Fine

Combine the coconut oil and Calvados in an airtight container, stir and leave to sit at room temperature for 20 minutes before transferring to a freezer-proof container and freezing overnight. Remove the solidified cap and strain the infusion through a paper coffee filter. Rebottle and store in the fridge for up to 1 month.

Coconut-washed Tequila

Makes approx. 26 oz (750 ml)

¼ cup (50 g) unrefined coconut oil, melted

26 oz (750 ml) tequila

Add oil and tequila to a large container and stir to incorporate, then seal and refrigerate for 24 hours. The oil will rise to the top of the container. Strain the tequila through a paper coffee filter to remove the coconut oil, then funnel the infusion back into the tequila bottle and store at room temperature for up to 1 month.

Coffee-brewed Sweet Vermouth

Cicala, Philadelphia

Makes approx. 1 cup (250 ml)

25 g (1 oz) freshly ground espresso coffee

8 oz (240 ml) sweet vermouth

Combine the coffee and sweet vermouth and brew. Allow to cool, then store in an airtight container in the fridge for up to 3 days.

Used in: Negroni Svegliato (p 298)

Coffee-infused Pedro Ximénez

Makes approx. 26 oz (750 ml)

1 × 26 oz (750 ml) bottle Pedro Ximénez

100 g (3½ oz) coffee beans, cracked (in a blender)

Combine the sherry and coffee in a vacuum bag, seal and leave to infuse overnight in the fridge. Strain through a paper coffee filter and store in the fridge for up to 1 month.

Used in: Chrissy Pud (p 261)

Coffee-leaf-infused Vodka

Makes approx. 24 oz (700 ml)

15 g (½ oz) black coffee leaves, roasted

¾ oz (22 ml) VS Cognac

23 oz (670 ml) vodka

Combine all the ingredients in a vacuum bag and seal, then sous vide at 52°C (126°F) for 20 minutes. Remove and chill, then filter through a Superbag, bottle and store at room temperature for up to 1 month.

Used in: Not An Espresso Martini (p 464)

Coffee-washed Gin

Makes approx. 10½ oz (300 ml)

10½ oz (300 ml) gin

1¾ oz (50 ml) coffee oil

Combine gin and coffee oil in a sous-vide bag, seal and sous vide at 135°C (275°F) for 1 hour. Pour into a freezer-proof container and stir well. Cover and freeze for at least 12 but up to 24 hours. Carefully remove the solidified cap of oil, strain through a chinois and store in an airtight container in the fridge for up to 1 week.

Used in: New Drop (p 464)

Jalapeño-infused Blanco Tequila

Makes approx. 26 oz (750 ml)

4 jalapeños, membranes and seeds separated

1 × 26 oz (750 ml) bottle blanco tequila

Combine the membranes and seeds of 3½ chillies and the chopped flesh of the remaining ½ chilli with the tequila and stir well. Leave to stand at room temperature for 20 minutes, tasting frequently until it has reached the desired level of heat. Strain through a fine-mesh sieve, rebottle and store in the fridge for up to 1 month.

Used in: Hot Lips (p 182), Loisaida Avenue (p 182), Spicy Martini (p 330), Up All Night Swizzle (p 261), Quick Step (p 330)

Jalapeño-infused Vodka

Makes 34 oz (1 litre)

4 jalapeños, halved lengthways, membranes and seeds separated

34 oz (1 litre) Grey Goose vodka

Put all the chilli seeds and membranes in a container with the flesh of two of the chillies (reserve the other two for another use). Add the vodka and stir to combine, then leave to stand at room temperature for 20 minutes, tasting frequently until is has reached your desired level of heat. Strain through a fine-meshed sieve lined with several layers of muslin, then rebottle and store in the fridge for up to 1 month.

Used in: Bloody Mary Verde (p 116)

Jasmine-infused Pisco

Makes approx. 8 oz (250 ml)

5 g (⅛ oz) jasmine pearls

8 oz (250 ml) pisco (preferably La Caravedo Torontel)

Combine the pearls and pisco in a bowl and leave to steep for 2 hours. Strain the pearls and store in an airtight container in the fridge for up to 1 month.

Kombu-infused Japanese Whisky

Makes approx. 24 oz (700 ml)

24 oz (700 ml) blended Japanese whisky

15 g (½ oz) dried kombu sheet

Combine the whisky and kombu, cover and leave to sit at room temperature for 4–5 hours. Strain, rebottle and store in the fridge for up to 1 month.

Used in: Kombu Old Fashioned (p 383)

Lemon Verbena-infused Gin

Makes approx. 26 oz (750 ml)

1 oz (30 ml) lemon verbena tea

1 × 26 oz (750 ml) London Dry gin

Combine the tea and gin, cover and leave to sit at room temperature for 1 hour. Strain through a chinois lined with a paper coffee filter, rebottle and store at room temperature for up to 1 month.

Used in: Rhubarb (p 181)

Lemon Verbena-infused Vodka

Makes approx. 26 oz (750 ml)

1 bunch lemon verbena

1 teaspoon honey

1 long lemon twist

1 × 26 oz (750 ml) bottle vodka

Combine all the ingredients in an airtight container, seal and leave to sit at room temperature for 5 days. Rebottle, then store in the fridge for up to 1 month.

Used in: Sfusato Martini (p 328)

Mandarin Skin Port

Makes approx. 26 oz (750 ml)

1 × 26 oz (750 ml) bottle tawny Port
200 g (7 oz) mandarin skin

Combine 1¾ oz (52 ml) of the Port and the mandarin skin in a vacuum bag. Muddle, allowing the Port to draw out the fruit oils, then add the remaining Port, seal and leave to infuse overnight in the fridge. Strain through a paper coffee filter, rebottle and store in the fridge for up to 1 month.

Used in: Country Livin' (p 376)

Nutmeg-infused Havana Club Añejo 7 Anos Rum

Makes approx. 24 oz (700 ml)

24 oz (700 ml) Havana Club Añejo 7 Anos Rum
5 g (⅛ oz) fresh grated nutmeg

Combine the rum and grated nutmeg, cover and leave to sit overnight. Strain through a fine-mesh sieve lined with a paper coffee filter, then rebottle and store at room temperature for up to 1 month.

Used in: Yuzu Painkiller (p 454)

Olive Oil-infused Gin

Makes approx. 34 oz (1 litre)

2 oz (60 ml) olive oil
34 oz (1 litre) gin

Combine the oil and gin in a freezer-proof container, seal and freeze overnight. Remove any solidified solids, then strain through a fine-mesh sieve lined with a paper coffee filter. Rebottle and store at room temperature for up to 1 month.

Used in: Dirty Negroni (p 300)

Pandan-infused Reposado Tequila

Makes approx. 17 oz (500 ml)

1 pandan leaf
17 oz (500 ml) Tapatio Reposado tequila

Put the pandan leaf in the bottle of tequila, seal and place in a saucepan of water set over low heat. Infuse for 2 hours, then leave to cool. At room temperature, infuse for at least 24 hours. Store in the fridge for up to 1 month.

Used in: Pandan Negroni (p 302)

Pandan-infused The Macallan 12yr Sherry Oak Cask Highland Single Malt Scotch Whisky

Makes approx. 26 oz (750 ml)

3 pandan leaves
1 × 26 oz (750 ml) bottle The Macallan 12yr Sherry Oak Cask Highland Single Malt Scotch Whisky

Combine the pandan leaves and Scotch in a vacuum bag, seal and sous vide at 60°C (140°F) for 30 minutes. Strain through a chinois lined with a paper coffee filter, then rebottle and store at room temperature for up to 1 month.

Used in: Raspberry (p 382)

Pineapple-infused Mezcal

Makes approx. 26 oz (750 ml)

1 × 26 oz (750 ml) bottle mezcal
350 g (12 oz) cubed fresh pineapple

Combine the mezcal and pineapple in a bowl, stir, then leave to stand for 4 hours at room temperature, stirring occasionally. Strain through a fine-mesh sieve, then strain again through a chinois or paper coffee filter to remove any fine particles. Funnel back into the mezcal bottle and store in the fridge for up to 3 months.

Used in: Motomami (p 231)

Raspberry-infused Campari

Makes approx. 34 oz (1 litre)

100 g (3½ oz) raspberries
34 oz (1 litre) Campari

Combine the raspberries and Campari in a vacuum bag, seal and sous vide at 60°C (140°F) for 2 hours. Remove and transfer the bag to an ice bath for 10 minutes. Strain through a chinois, rebottle and store in the fridge for up to 1 month.

Used in: Raspberry (p 382)

Squash (pumpkin)-infused Reposado Tequila

Makes approx. 34 oz (1 litre)

140 g (5 oz) Kabocha squash (pumpkin)
34 oz (1 litre) Don Fulano Reposado tequila

Cut the skin off the squash and dice the flesh into 2.5 cm (1 in) cubes. Roast at 150°C (300°F) for 20 minutes. Place in a large vacuum bag with the tequila, seal and sous vide at 60°C (140°F) for 1 hour. Strain through a chinois lined with a piece of muslin, bottle and store in the fridge for up to 1 month

Used in: Squash (p 220)

Strawberry-infused Campari

Makes approx. 26 oz (750 ml)

900 g (2 lb) strawberries, hulled and sliced
1 × 26 oz (750 ml) bottle Campari

Combine the strawberries and Campari in a non-reactive container, cover and leave to sit at room temperature for 3–4 days. Strain through a fine-mesh sieve lined with a piece of muslin, then rebottle and store in the fridge for up to 1 month.

Used in: Kula Negroni (p 300)

Solutions & Tinctures

Acid Water Solution

Makes approx. 3½ oz (100 ml)

3 g citric acid
2 g malic acid
1 g lactic acid
3¼ oz (95 ml) hot filtered water

Combine all the ingredients and stir. Store in an airtight container in the fridge for up to 2 weeks.

Used in: Rhubarb & Chamomile (p 487)

Champagne Acid

Makes approx. 3½ oz (100 ml)

3¼ oz (95 ml) unfiltered water
3 g tartaric acid powder
3 g lactic acid powder

Combine all the ingredients in a glass bowl and stir until the powders have dissolved. Transfer to a glass dropper bottle or other glass container and store in the fridge for up to 6 months.

Used in: Alpine Negroni (p 299)

Coconut-washed Scotch

Makes approx. 26 oz (750 ml)

1 × 26 oz (750 ml) bottle Scotch (preferably Aberfeldy Single Malt Scotch Whisky 12yr)
100 g (3½ oz) coconut oil

Combine the Scotch and coconut oil in a shaker and shake together, then transfer to a freezer-proof container and freeze for 6 hours. Remove the solidified cap, then strain the Scotch through a paper coffee filter, rebottle and store at room temperature for up to 1 month.

Used in: Porridge Colada (p 457)

Coffee Tincture

Makes approx. ⅓ oz (10 ml)

4.3 g (⅛ oz) coffee beans
⅓ oz (10 g) 96% ABV pure alcohol

Finely grind the coffee beans. Put in a vacuum bag with the alcohol, seal the bag and sous vide at 60°C (140°F) for 1 hour, then remove from the bag and chill. Pass the chilled mixture through a paper coffee filter, then store in a pipette in the fridge for up to 2 weeks.

Used in: Not An Espresso Martini (p 464)

House Orange Bitters

equal parts Regan's Orange Bitters and Fee Brothers West Indian Orange Bitters
2 drops clementine oil per 3½ oz (100 ml)

Combine the bitters by weight in an airtight container or bottle. Weigh, then add the clementine oil and store at room temperature for up to 1 year.

Lactic acid solution

Makes approx. 3½ oz (100 ml)

3½ oz (100 ml) filtered water
⅓ oz (10 g) lactic acid powder

Combine the water and lactic acid in a glass bowl and stir until the powder has dissolved. Transfer to a glass dropper bottle or other glass container and store in the fridge for up to 6 months.

Used in: Tiramisù Milk Punch (p 132)

MFG Spicy Bitters

Makes approx. 17 oz (500 ml)

17 oz (500 ml) tequila
500 g (1 lb 2 oz) jalapeños
125 g (4½ oz) green serrano chilli
10 g (⅓ oz) Scotch Bonnet chilli (approx. 1)
5 g (⅛ oz) Thai red chilli
2 g Szechuan peppercorn

Combine all the ingredients in a container, cover and leave to sit at room temperature for 24 hours. Strain through a paper coffee filter and store in an airtight container in the fridge for up to 1 week.

Used in: Spicy Margarita (Nathan McCarley-O'Neill Recipe; p 199), Yuzu Serrano Margarita (p 199)

Oaxacan Bitters

Makes approx. 26 oz (750 ml)

10 g (⅓ oz) pasilla chilli, sliced
10 g (⅓ oz) ancho chilli, sliced
10 g (⅓ oz) morita chipotle, sliced
8 oz (250 ml) Everclear
17 oz (500 ml) tequila

Combine the chilli, Everclear and tequila in a container, cover and leave to infuse at room temperature for 24 hours, then strain through a paper coffee filter, bottle and store in the fridge for up to 1 month.

Used in: Spicy Margarita (Nathan McCarley-O'Neill Recipe; p 199)

Thai Chilli Firewater Tincture

1 part Thai chillies, destemmed and split in half lengthways
5 parts Everclear (or other food-grade ethanol)
water

It's a good idea to wear nitrile gloves and protective eyewear when handling Thai chillies. Combine the chillies and Everclear by weight in a vacuum bag, seal and sous vide at 70°C (158°F) for 2 hours. Strain and discard the chillies. Weigh the infused Everclear and add the same quantity of plain water, then transfer to a dasher bottle. Store in the fridge for up to 2 weeks. One dash should be used for a very spicy drink, two-thirds of a dash for a regular spicy drink, and one-third of a dash for a slightly spicy drink.

Used in: Fire Lily (p 317)

Thai Chilli Tincture

Makes approx. 10½ oz (300 ml)

10½ oz (300 ml) vodka
100 g (3½ oz) Thai chilli, destemmed and split in half lengthways

It's a good idea to wear nitrile gloves and protective eyewear when handling Thai chillies. Combine the vodka and chilli in a container, cover and leave to infuse in the fridge for 2 weeks. Strain and discard the chilli then store in a dropper bottle in the fridge for up to 2 weeks.

White Chocolate-washed Aged Cachaça

Makes approx. 26 oz (750 ml)

300 g (10½ oz) white chocolate, chopped
1 × 26 oz (750 ml) bottle Avuá Amburana Cachaça

Combine the white chocolate and cachaça in a vacuum bag, seal and sous vide at 60°C (140°F) for 2 hours. Transfer the bag to the freezer and freeze to solidify. Strain through a chinois then rebottle and store in the fridge for up to 2 weeks.

Used in: Raspberry (p 382), Rhubarb (p 181)

More

Butter Gardenia

The Lafayette Hotel
Makes approx. 600 g (1 lb 5 oz)
100 g (3½ oz) unsalted butter
7 oz (200 ml) Giffard Vanille de Madagascar
200 g (7 oz) clover honey
200 g (7 oz) cinnamon syrup (p 495)
4 g Hamilton Pimento Dram
Ticaloid

Melt butter in a saucepan over medium heat, then add the vanilla, honey, cinnamon syrup and Hamilton Pimento Dram. Continue to heat over a medium heat until hot. Weigh the butter mixture and add 3 teaspoons Ticaloid for every 34 oz (1 litre) butter mixture. Stir well. Blend with a hand-held blender on high speed until smooth. Strain through a chinois and store in an airtight container for up 1 week.

Used in: Motomami (p 231)

Cacao Cream

Makes approx. 4½ oz (135 ml)
½ cup (125 ml) thick (double/heavy) cream
¼–½ oz (10–20 ml) crème de cacao
pinch of sea salt

Combine cream, crème de cacao and salt in a shake. Shake until the cream can hold its shape, then store in an airtight container in the fridge for up to 3 days.

Used in: Irish Breakfast Stout (p 440)

Cacao Nib Dolin Blanc

Makes 17 oz (500 ml)
50 g (1¾ oz) cacao nibs, toasted
17 oz (500 ml) Dolin Blanc

Combine the cacao nibs and vermouth in a vacuum bag and sous vide at 57°C (135°F) for 30 minutes. Allow to cool, then strain through a paper coffee filter and store in an airtight container in the fridge for up to 2 weeks.

Used in: New Drop (p 464)

Cocktail Onions

Makes approx. 1 kg (2 lb 4 oz)
36 juniper berries
10 g (⅓ oz) mustard seeds
48 black peppercorns
5 g (⅛ oz) coriander seeds
6 star anise
6 cloves
2 cinnamon sticks
5 g (⅛ oz) chilli flakes
700 g (1 lb 9 oz) cane sugar
185 g (6½ oz) light brown sugar
500 g (1 lb 2 oz) Kosher salt
34 oz (1 litre) filtered water
24 oz (700 ml) sherry vinegar
8 oz (250 ml) white balsamic vinegar
1 kg (2 lb 4 oz) pearl onions
1 head garlic, broken into cloves
70 g (2½ oz) rosemary
70 g (2½ oz) fennel fronds
10½ oz (300 ml) Dolin Dry vermouth

Place all the spices, except the chilli flakes, in a frying pan set over medium heat and toast for 1–2 minutes. Add the chilli flakes, stir briefly, then add the sugars, salt, water and vinegars. Bring to a simmer then turn off the heat. Put the pearl onions in a large piece of muslin and tie into a bundle. Place the bag in a large glass jar and place baking weights on top to weigh down the bundle. Pour the brine over the onions, ensuring that the onions are fully submerged in the liquid. Add the garlic, rosemary and fennel fronds and allow the brine to cool. Once cool, add the vermouth. Seal and leave to pickle for 2 weeks before using. Store in a sealed jar in the fridge for up to 6 months.

Coconut Demerara

1 part coconut milk
1 part Demerara sugar

Combine the coconut milk and sugar by weight in a high-speed blender and blitz until the sugar is fully dissolved. Store in an airtight container in the fridge for up to 1 week.

Used in: Vespa (p 261)

Irish Cream

Makes approx. 26 oz (750 ml)
13 oz (375 ml) Irish whiskey
14 oz (400 ml) sweetened condensed milk
2 oz (60 ml) thick (double/heavy) cream
¾ oz (20 g) honey
¾ oz (22 ml) vanilla extract
2 g instant coffee
6 g unsweetened cacao powder

Blend all ingredients until smooth, bottle and store in the fridge for up to 2 months. Shake before use.

House Cream

4 parts excellent-quality thick (double) cream
1 part full-cream (whole) milk
2 white sugar cubes, for whipping

Add the cream and milk to a clean squeeze bottle with the sugar cubes. Seal and shake the bottle one hundred times (be sure to put your finger over the nozzle opening first). You will know when the cream has been sufficiently whipped when you can rest a bead of cream on your finger. Store in the fridge for up to 3 days. Shake again before each use. To float cream on a drink, shake the cream first to aerate the mixture, but not too much or it will thicken. Aim the nozzle just above the drink and squeeze slowly. Aim to cover the surface of the drink with a thin, even layer of cream. For a faster flow, trim 1 cm (½ in) off the top of the nozzle to create a larger opening.

▼ For **Hand-whipped House Cream**, give the cream a good shake in the bottle to aerate it before floating on top of the drink.

Lemon Pepper Salt

Makes approx. 80 g (2¾ oz)

20 g (¾ oz) dehydrated lemon slices
10 g (⅓ oz) freshly ground black pepper
50 g (1¾ oz) Kosher salt

Put the lemon slices in a spice grinder or blender with the pepper and half of the salt and process to a powder. Transfer to an airtight container, add the remaining salt, seal and shake to combine. Store in a dry place. It will keep indefinitely.

Used in: Normandie Club Bloody Mary (p 120)

Morita Water

Makes approx. 17 oz (500 ml)

15 g (½ oz) dried morita chilli
17 oz (500 ml) filtered water

Heat a dry frying pan over medium heat and toast the dried chilli for 1 minute. Combine the chilli and water in a vacuum bag, seal and place on a sheet tray. Steam in a combi oven at 60°C (140°F), 100% humidity, for 20 minutes. Alternatively, combine the chilli and water in a saucepan and heat over low-medium heat, tasting regularly, until the infusion reaches your desired heat level. Strain through a Superbag or paper coffee filter and store in an airtight container in the fridge for up to 2 weeks.

Used in: Aguafresca de Pimiento Rojo (p 484)

Peach Salt

Makes approx. 1.3 kg (3 lb)

1 kg (2 lb 4 oz) Kosher salt
10½ oz (300 ml) peach nectar

Combine the salt and peach nectar on a sheet tray and mix well. Spread out into a thin layer and dry in a food dehydrator for 48 hours. Store in an airtight container for up to 2 weeks.

Used in: Peach (p 219)

Pickling Liquid

Makes approx. 52 oz (1.5 litres)

14 oz (400 ml) filtered water
34 oz (1 litre) white balsamic vinegar
100 g (3½ oz) Kosher salt
100 g (3½ oz) caster (superfine) sugar

Combine all the ingredients in a saucepan and simmer over medium heat for 5 minutes. Pass through a chinois, then chill and store in an airtight container in the fridge for up to 2 weeks.

Used in: Watermelon Agua Fresca (p 488)

Riviera Mix

Makes approx. 34 oz (1 litre)

17 oz (500 ml) gin
8 oz (250 ml) Campari
4 oz (120 ml) maraschino liqueur
1 oz (30 ml) orange bitters
160 g (5¾ oz) chopped pineapple

Purée all ingredients in a blender, cover and refrigerate overnight, stirring occasionally. Strain through a chinois then store in an airtight bottle in the fridge for up to 1 month.

Used in: The Riviera (p 163)

Salted Apricot Purée

Makes approx. 24 oz (700 ml)

700 g (1 lb 9 oz) peaches in juice
350 g (12 oz) caster (superfine) sugar
saline solution (p 493)

Purée peaches and juice and mix with the sugar. Weigh, and add saline solution at a ratio of 3:1 apricot purée to saline solution. Store in an airtight container in the fridge for up to 3 days.

Used in: Damascus Fizz (p 484)

Savoiardi Milk

Makes approx. 26 oz (750 ml)

150 g (5½ oz) Savoiardi biscuits, snapped in half
26 oz (750 ml) full-cream (whole) milk

Add biscuits to milk in a bowl and stir until you have a loose paste. Infuse for 1 hour, then strain through a chinois. Store in an airtight container in the fridge for up to 4 days.

Used in: Tiramisù Milk Punch (p 132)

Tiki Juice

2 parts fresh pressed orange and pink grapefruit juice
1 part fresh pressed lemon and lime juice

Combine the juices by weight and store in an airtight container in the fridge for up to 1 week.

Used in: Yuzu Painkiller (p 507)

Vanilla Olive Oil

Makes approx. 8 oz (250 ml)

2 vanilla beans, split lengthways and seeds scraped
8 oz (250 ml) olive oil

Combine vanilla seeds and oil in a jar, seal and shake. Store at room temperature for up to 1 month.

Used in: Teal (p 220)

Verde Mix

Makes approx. 68 oz (2 litres)

625 kg (1 lb 6 oz) cucumber, peeled and chopped
17 oz (500 ml) tomatillo juice
11 oz (325 ml) green capsicum (bell pepper) juice
8 oz (250 ml) fresh pineapple juice
8 oz (120 ml) fresh lime juice
2½ oz (80 ml) saline solution (p 493)
10 g (⅓ oz) serrano chilli, deseeded
7 g (⅓ oz) garlic, peeled

Purée cucumber in a blender. Combine purée with juices, saline solution, chilli and garlic in a blender and blend until smooth. Store in an airtight container in the fridge for up to 1 week.

Used in: Bloody Mary Verde (p 116)

Verdita

Makes approx. 34 oz (1 litre)

34 oz (1 litre) pineapple juice
1 oz (30 ml) lime juice
8–10 mint leaves
20–25 coriander (cilantro) leaves
1 jalapeño, partially deseeded and chopped

Combine all the ingredients in a high-speed blender until smooth. Strain through a paper coffee filter and store in an airtight container in the fridge for up to 1 week.

Used in: Vernita Green (p 255)

WORKS CITED

100 Cocktails: How to Mix Them, "Bernard", 1958
1700 Cocktails for the Man Behind the Bar, R. de Fleury, 1934
ABC of Mixing Cocktails, Harry MacElhone, 1923
A Book of Appetizers, Helen Evans Brown, 1958
A Life-Time Collection of 688 Recipes for Drinks, 1934
A Quick Drink, Lynette Marrero and Ivy Mix with Megan Krigbaum, 2024
About Town Cocktail Book, Joe Fitchett, 1925
All Day Cocktails, Shaun Byrne and Nick Tesar, 2019
American & Other Drinks, Leo Engel, 1875
American and Other Drinks, Charlie Paul, 1884
American and Other Iced Drinks, Charlie Paul, 1902
American Bar, Frank P. Newman, 1900
An Anthology of Cocktails, 1930s
An Universal Etymological English Dictionary, Nathan Bailey, 1721
Angostura Recipes, Charles Scotto, 1934
Applegreen's Barkeeper's Guide, John Applegreen, 1904
Approved Cocktails, United Kingdom Bartenders' Guild, 1937
Bacardí y sus muchos usos, 1930
Bar La Florida Cocktails, 1935
Barflies and Cocktails, Harry MacElhone, 1927
Bariana, Louis Fouquet, 1896
Bartender's Sixth Sense, Jose Maria Vazquez, 1940s
Batched & Bottled, Max and Noel Venning, 2018
Beachbum Berry Remixed, Jeff Berry, 2010
Beachbum Berry's Sippin' Safari, Jeff Berry, 2007
Beverages de Luxe, George R. Washburne, 1914
Brian's Booze Guide, Brian F. Rea, 1976
Burke's Complete Cocktail & Drinking Recipes, Harman Burney Burke, 1934
Café Royal Cocktail Book, W.J. Tarling, 1937
Cheerio!, Charles formerly of Delmonico's, 1928
Classic Cocktails: A Modern Shake, Mark Kingwell, 2007
Cocktail Bill Boothby's World Drinks and How to Mix Them, Wm. T. Boothby, 1934
Cocktail and Wine Digest, Oscar Haimo, 1943
Cocktail Parade, 1933
Cocktail: The Drinks Bible for the 21st Century, Paul Harrington and Laura Moorhead, 1998
Cocktails by "Jimmy" Late of Ciro's London, 1930
Cocktails de Paris, Georges Gabriel Thenon, 1929
Cocktails for Two, Helen Spence, 1982
Cocktails Portfolio, Amedeo Gandiglio, 1947
Cocktails: How to Mix Them, Robert Vermeire, 1922
Crosby Gaige's Cocktail Guide and Ladies' Companion, Crosby Gaige, 1941
Cure: New Orleans Drinks and How to Mix 'Em, Neal Bodenheimer and Emily Timberlake, 2022
Daly's Bartenders' Encyclopedia, Tim Daly, 1903
Death & Co Welcome Home, Alex Day, Nick Fauchald and David Kaplan, 2021
Difford's Guide, 1997
DrinkBoy, Robert Hess, 2003
Drinks - Long & Short, Nina Toye and A. H. Adair, 1925
Drinks, Jacques Straub, 1914
El Arte del Cantinero, Hilario Alonso Sanchez, 1948
Esquire, 1933
Esquire Drink Book, Frederic A. Birmingham, 1956
Famous New Orleans Drinks and How to Mix 'Em, Stanley Clisby Arthur, 1937
Fancy Drinks: How They Are Mixed, 1902
Floridita Cock-tails, Constante Ribalaigua Vert, 1939
Good Things to Drink with Mr Lyan & Friends, Ryan Chetiyawardana, 2015
Harper's New Monthly Magazine, 1857
"Harry" of Ciro's ABC of Mixing Cocktails, Harry MacElhone, 1923
Here's How Again!, Judge Jr., 1929
Here's How: Mixed Drinks, W.C. Whitfield, 1941
Here's How! New and Revised Edition, Judge Jr., 1928
Here's How!, Judge Jr., 1927
Hoffman House Bartender's Guide, Charles S. Mahoney, 1905
How to Mix Drinks, James C. Maloney, 1903
How to Properly Mix Drinks, 1930s
I'm Just Here for the Drinks, Sother Teague, 2018
Imbibe!, David Wondrich, 2007
Irvin S. Cobb's Own Recipe Book, Irvin S. Cobb, 1936
Jack's Manual, J.A. Grohusko, 1908
Jayne's Bartender's Guide, 1934
Jones' Complete Barguide, Stan Jones, 1977
Just Cocktails, W.C. Whitfield, 1939
Libro de Cocktail, Juan A. Lasa, 1929
Louis' Mixed Drinks, Louis Muckensturm, 1906
Manual del Cantinero, John B. Escalante, 1915
Modern American Drinks, George J. Kappeler, 1895
My New Cocktail Book, G.F. Steele, 1934
New and Improved Bartender's Manual, Harry Johnson, 1882
New and Improved Illustrated Bartender's Manual, Harry Johnson, 1888
Nuevo Manual de Cocina a la Criolla, S.E. Ledesma, 1903
Old Mr. Boston Deluxe Official Bartender's Guide, Leo Cotton, 1935
Old Waldorf Bar Days, Albert Stevens Crockett, 1931
Pioneers of Mixing at Elite Bars: 1903–1933, Charles Christopher Mueller, 1936
Punch Magazine, 1841–2002
Recipes for Mixed Drinks, Hugo R. Ensslin, 1916
Sardi's Bar Guide, Vincent Sardi and George Shea, 1988
Session Cocktails, Drew Lazor, 2018
Shake 'Em Up!, Virginia Elliott and Phil D. Strong, 1930
Sloppy Joe's Cocktails Manual, José Abeal, 1932
Smuggler's Cove: Exotic Cocktails, Rum and the Cult of Tiki, Martin and Rebecca Cate, 2016
Spirits of Latin America, Ivy Mix, 2020
Straub's Manual of Mixed Drinks, Jacques Straub, 1913
Stuart's Fancy Drinks and How to Mix Them, Thomas Stuart, 1904

Ted Saucier's Bottoms Up, Ted Saucier, 1951
The Art of Mixing, James A. Wiley and Helene M. Griffith, 1932
The Artistry of Mixing Drinks, Frank Meier, 1936
The Bar Book: Elements of Cocktail Technique, Jeffrey Morgenthaler, 2014
The Bar-Tender's Guide, Jerry Thomas, multiple eds., 1862, 1876, 1887
The Bartender's Pantry, Jim Meehan and Bart Sasso with Emma Janzen, 2024
The Book of Cocktail Ratios: The Surprising Simplicity of Classic Cocktails, Michael Ruhlman, 2023
The Canon Cocktail Book, Jamie Boudreau and James O. Fraioli, 2016
The Cocktail Book: A Sideboard Manual for Gentlemen, Frederic Lawrence Knowles, 1900
The Cocktail Book: A Sideboard Manual for Gentlemen, Repeal Edition, 1933
The Cocktail Hour, Louis P. De Gouy, 1951
The Connaught Bar, Agostino Perrone and Giorgio Bargiani with Maura Milia, 2024
The Fine Art of Mixing Drinks, David A. Embury, 1948
The Flowing Bowl: What and Where to Drink, William Schmidt, 1891
The Gentleman's Companion, Charles H. Baker Jr., 1939
The Gentleman's Table Guide, E. Ricket and C. Thomas, 1871
The Home Bartender's Guide and Song Book, Charlie Roe and Jim Schwenck, 1930
The How and When, Hyman Gale and Gerald F. Marco, 1937
The Ideal Bartender, Tom Bullock, 1917
The Joy of Mixology, Gary Regan, 2003
The Mixicologist, C.F. Lawlor, 1895
The Modern Bartenders' Guide, O.H. Byron, 1884
The Negroni: Drinking to La Dolce Vita, with Recipes & Lore, Gary Regan, 2015
The New American Bartender's Guide, John J. Poister, 1989
The New and Improved Illustrated Bartenders' Manual, Harry Johnson, 1900
The New Craft of the Cocktail, Dale DeGroff, 2020
The Official Mixer's Manual, Patrick Gavin Duffy and Robert Jay Misch, 1956 [1934]
The Old Waldorf-Astoria Bar Book, Albert Stevens Crockett, 1935
The One-Bottle Cocktail, Maggie Hoffman, 2018
The Reminder, J.A. Didier, 1909
The Saloon in the Home or a Garland of Rumblossoms, Ridgley Hunt and George S. Chappell, 1930
The Savoy Cocktail Book, Harry Craddock, 1930
The South American Gentleman's Companion, Charles H. Baker Jr., 1951
The Stork Club Bar Book, Lucius Beebe, 1946
The Way of the Cocktail, Julia Momosé, 2021
The World's Drinks and How to Mix Them, Wm. T. Boothby, 1908
Tiki Drinks: Tropical Cocktails for the Modern Bar, Nicole Weston and Robert Sharp, 2015
To Have and Have Another: A Hemingway Cocktail Companion, Philip Greene, 2012
Trader Vic's Bartender's Guide, Revised, Trader Vic, 1972
Trader Vic's Bartender's Guide, Trader Vic, 1947
Trader Vic's Book of Food and Drink, Trader Vic, 1946
Two Years in the French West Indies, Lafcadio Hearn, 1890
Vintage Spirits and Forgotten Cocktails, Ted Haigh, 2004
What Shall We Drink?, Magnus Bredenbek, 1934
What'll You Have?, Julien J. Proskauer, 1933
Winter Drinks, Editors of Punch, 2018

CONTRIBUTORS

ABOUT THE AUTHORS

Michael Madrusan

Michael Madrusan is an Australian drinks educator and creative consultant, and one half of Bartender's Choice Consultancy. Michael built his reputation as the founder of world-renowned, Melbourne-based venues including The Everleigh, Heartbreaker, Connie's Pizza and Bar Margaux, and pioneered both the packaged cocktail and clear ice movements back in 2015 with The Everleigh Bottling Co. and Navy Strength Ice Co.

Over more than two decades, Michael has worked in some of the most revered bars in the world, including as a protégé of the late Sasha Petraske at New York's Milk & Honey, Little Branch and PDT. Michael has been named #1 Most Influential Person by *Australian Bartender Magazine* and is an internationally respected industry leader and resource, regularly appearing at industry conferences and on spirits and cocktail judging panels. Michael owns one of the largest collections of classic cocktail books globally and is passionate about classic cocktails and their influence on the way we drink today.

Zara Madrusan

Zara Madrusan is a writer and creative consultant, and one half of Bartender's Choice Consultancy. Born in the UK, and with a performing arts and production background, Zara has spearheaded the brand development and marketing of the duo's world-renowned venues, The Everleigh, Heartbreaker, Connie's Pizza and Bar Margaux. Zara also co-founded premium packaged cocktail company, The Everleigh Bottling Co. and Australia's first hand-cut cocktail ice company, Navy Strength Ice Co.

Together with Michael, Zara co-authored the couple's first book, *A Spot at the Bar*, in 2016 which continues to be a go-to resource for drinks enthusiasts and bar professionals almost a decade on. The pair are also responsible for multiple world-class venue openings, events and educational bar programs under Bartender's Choice Consultancy. Zara is passionate about creating site-specific, multi-sensory hospitality experiences that appeal to the ever-evolving appetite of the modern drinker.

ACKNOWLEDGEMENTS

We dedicate this book to Jane Willson. Without you there would have been no book. Your unwavering belief in us to tackle something so monumental has filled us with strength and persistence. You knew we could do it in the moments we didn't, and in turn we pushed ourselves to our limits and perfected this thing to make you proud. Your passion for pushing the boundaries to support the production of brilliant, unique books is utterly inspirational.

For our girls, Molly and Indy. We hope that when you hold this big book in your little hands you are reminded of the incredible things that can be achieved with passion and dedication. Getting to know a subject so fully begins with establishing that you know nothing at all. May a thirsty and humble sense of curiosity steer you both towards your own unique worlds of wonder.

To all the contributors over the years, and especially this last year, thank you for your generosity, creativity and excitement for this book. Knowing you were all invested in this ambitious work being brought to life, and hearing your gratitude and enthusiasm helped us stay steadfast and focused on our mission. This book started out as an industry resource, and though it has evolved to something far greater, it is still intended to serve as a loyal and generous companion to you all, behind the bar. It is your influence and leadership that makes this industry so exciting to be a part of, and we are grateful to have the opportunity to learn from you all.

To the Murdoch team – Justin, Matty, Sarah O, Murray, Andrea, Jess, Sarah H and Mark Roper, thanks so much for your patience, brilliance and support.

Matty and Justin, especially. This must have felt like the longest edit in history! Thank you for your support, your dedication to this book and, most of all, your patience. Matty, you're too good. We will not miss your edits!! Thank you.

There are so many people to thank for their help and contributions to this book. This list is for those that gave a lot of their time to us and who we slightly annoyed when they saw our names in their inbox, including Liana Oster, Leo Robitschek, Sebastian Tollius, Toby Cecchini, Alex Day, Jim Meehan, Michael McIlroy, Sam Ross, Anthony Schmidt, Enzo Errico, Chad Soloman and Christy Pope, Nathan McCarley-O'Neil, Patrick Dooley, Eric Alperin, Toby Maloney, Jeffrey Morgenthaler and Erick Castro.

These researchers have dedicated their lives to cocktails and their history, and we're grateful to have been able to call on their work to help assemble ours. Special acknowledgement to Julie Reiner, Audrey Saunders, Dale DeGroff, Simon Difford, Jared Brown, Anistatia Miller and Dave Wondrich, whose research has opened so many doors we didn't know we had, to euvslibrary.com whose library is out of this world, and Difford's Guide and Punch Drink for bridging the gap between classic and modern. Thanks also to Cocktail Kingdom, Imbibe and Ten Speed Press for releasing such great bar books.

To our family and friends for their support and patience whilst we rode the emotional waves that arose producing this beast.

To our bar teams past and present who shunned trends and didn't cut corners. Those who strove to push themselves each and every night to make better drinks than the night before.

Sasha – for the gift you gave us all.

Cheers to you, Chief.

Michael & Zara

INDEX

NUMBERS

A

B

C

E

F

I

J

K

L

Q

R

X

Y

Z

Jones complete
THE OFFICIAL MIXER'S MANUAL
BARTENDER'S GUIDE
South American Gentleman's Companion
HERE'S HOW
Bartender's Guide by Trader Vic
THE ARTISTRY OF MIXING DRINKS
BAR-TENDER'S GUIDE HOW TO MIX DRINKS

Published in 2025 by Murdoch Books, an imprint of Allen & Unwin

Murdoch Books Australia
Cammeraygal Country
83 Alexander Street
Crows Nest NSW 2065
Phone: +61 (0)2 8425 0100
murdochbooks.com.au
info@murdochbooks.com.au

Murdoch Books UK
Ormond House
26–27 Boswell Street
London WC1N 3JZ
Phone: +44 (0) 20 8785 5995
murdochbooks.co.uk
info@murdochbooks.co.uk

For corporate orders and custom publishing, contact our business development team at salesenquiries@murdochbooks.com.au

Publishers: Jane Willson and Justin Wolfers
Editorial managers: Justin Wolfers and Andrea O'Connor
Design manager: Sarah Odgers
Designer: Murray Batten
Typesetter: Megan Ellis
Editors: Matty Hirsch and Andrea O'Connor
Photographer: Mark Roper
Stylist: Lee Blaylock
Production manager: Natalie Crouch

Garments for photoshoot: Sam Rush of Handsom Store, Gertrude Street, Melbourne.

Murdoch Books acknowledges the Traditional Owners of the Country on which we live and work. We pay our respects to all Aboriginal and Torres Strait Islander Elders, past and present.

EU Authorised Representative: Easy Access System Europe, Mustamäe tee 50, 10621 Tallinn, Estonia, gpsr.requests@easproject.com

ISBN 978 1 76150 044 2

A catalogue record for this book is available from the National Library of Australia

A catalogue record for this book is available from the British Library

Colour reproduction by Megan Ellis
Printed in China by C&C Offset Printing Co., Ltd.

TABLESPOON MEASURES: We have used 15 ml (3 teaspoon) tablespoon measures.

IMPORTANT: Those who might be at risk from the effects of salmonella poisoning (the elderly, pregnant women, young children and those suffering from immune deficiency diseases) should consult their doctor with any concerns about eating raw eggs.

10 9 8 7 6 5 4 3

MIX
Paper | Supporting responsible forestry
FSC® C008047